AF899950

Communications in Computer and Information Science 799

Commenced Publication in 2007
Founding and Former Series Editors:
Alfredo Cuzzocrea, Xiaoyong Du, Orhun Kara, Ting Liu, Dominik Ślęzak, and Xiaokang Yang

More information about this series at http://www.springer.com/series/7899

Brajendra Panda · Sudeep Sharma
Nihar Ranjan Roy (Eds.)

Data Science and Analytics

4th International Conference on Recent Developments
in Science, Engineering and Technology, REDSET 2017
Gurgaon, India, October 13–14, 2017
Revised Selected Papers

Springer

Editors
Brajendra Panda
University of Arkansas
Fayetteville, AR
USA

Nihar Ranjan Roy
GD Goenka University
Gurugram, Haryana
India

Sudeep Sharma
GD Goenka University
Gurugram, Haryana
India

ISSN 1865-0929 ISSN 1865-0937 (electronic)
Communications in Computer and Information Science
ISBN 978-981-10-8526-0 ISBN 978-981-10-8527-7 (eBook)
https://doi.org/10.1007/978-981-10-8527-7

Library of Congress Control Number: 2018934352

Printed on acid-free paper

This Springer imprint is published by the registered company Springer Nature Singapore Pte Ltd.
part of Springer Nature
The registered company address is: 152 Beach Road, #21-01/04 Gateway East, Singapore 189721, Singapore

Preface

Data science employs techniques and theories drawn from many fields within the broad areas of mathematics, statistics, information science, and computer science, in particular from the subdomains of machine learning, classification, cluster analysis, data mining, databases, and visualization. Data analytics seeks to provide operational observations into issues that we either know or do not know. Analysis is a part of any scientific research and it is the first step in building a theory. The second step is synthesis, which actually builds or creates a theory. It is also important to remember that science is not about results, but about a methodology to get them. The focus is on big data applications to tackle the problem of decision-making under uncertainty by using machine learning methods and graph theory to analyze complex structures in big data to build recommender systems and predictive models.

The 4th International Conference on Recent Developments in Science, Engineering and Technology (REDSET), which was held at the GD Goenka University, Sohna, Gurgaon, India, during October 13–14, 2017 in association with Springer, is our humble effort in this direction. Promotion of inquiry-based education has been the core competence of the School of Engineering at GD Goenka University since its inception and the present conference was yet another step forward. We aim to promote the interdisciplinary nature of scientific enquiry, which leads to engineering efforts to develop scientific and technologically innovative solutions so as to benefit society as a whole.

We received 329 papers and participation from 18 different countries including India, Australia, Canada, Egypt, France, Germany, Kuwait, Lithuania, Namibia, Nigeria, Saudi Arabia, Singapore, South Africa, South Korea, Sweden, Turkey, UK, and USA. After undergoing a rigorous peer-review process following international standards, the acceptance rate was ca. 20%. Selection was based on originality of the idea, innovation, and relevance to the conference theme and relation to the latest trends in the respective domains. We hope that the ideas and subsequent discussions presented at the conference will help the global scientific community to aim toward a nationally and globally responsible society. We also hope that young minds will derive inspiration from their elders and contribute toward developing sustainable solutions for the nation and the world as a whole.

This conference proceedings volume contains the contributions presented during REDSET 2017. We wish to express our sincere appreciation to the members of the Technical Program Committee and the reviewers who helped in the paper selection process. We also thank the authors for their contributions that made us assemble such an exceptional technical set of papers. We thank Springer for being our publication partner for this conference. Our special thanks go to the editorial staff at Springer especially Ms. Suvira and Ms. Nidhi for their outstanding service and support.

January 2018

Brajendra Panda
Sudeep Sharma
Nihar Ranjan Roy

Organization

Patron

Nipun Goenka	GD Goenka Group, India

Co-patron

Shrihari	GD Goenka University, India

Conference Program Chair

Brajendra Panda	University of Arkansas, USA

Steering Committee

Lalit Borana	Hong Kong Polytechnic University, Hong Kong, SAR China
Lalit Goel	Nanyang Technological University, Singapore
Raul Klauss	Technological University of Clausthal, Germany
Shayon Mitra	Manitoba Public Insurance, Canada
Ardyono Priyadi	ITS (Institut Teknologi Sepuluh), Surabaya, Indonesia
S. P. Rauniyar	BMRD, Australia
Atma Sahu (Chair)	Coppin State University, USA
Anurag K. Srivastava	Washington State University, USA
Sham Tickoo	Purdue University, USA

Organizing Committee

Conference Chair

Sudeep Sharma

Organizing Secretary

Usha Batra

Members

Saurav Ambastha
Leesha Aneja
Nidhi Arora
Sameer Arora
Sakshi Babbar
Alina Banerjee
Shivani Batra
Arinjoy Biswas
Anindita Roy Chowdhury
Prashant G. K.
Deepika Garg
Ashu Gautam

International Advisory Committee

Victor Manuel Diez V.	Interconexion Electrica, Colombia
Roshan Dharshana Yapa	University of Peradeniya, Sri Lanka
Naoto Yorino	Hiroshima University, Japan

Technical Committee

Sadiqa Abbas	MRIC, Faridabad, India
Nikhil Agrawal	Career Point University, Kota, India
Prashant Agrawal	Galgotias University, Greater Noida, India
R. K. Aggarwal	JNU, India
Sheetal Agarwal	KITE Jaipur, Rajasthan, India
Swati Aggarwal	NSIT, India
Kamal Uddin Ahamad	Tezpur University, Assam, India
Anis Ahmad	Galgotias University, UP, India
Mansaf Alam	IQAC, Jamia Milia Islamia, India
Mehtab Alam	Jamia Milia Islamia, Delhi, India
Shamshad Alam	Jamia Milia Islamia, Delhi, India
P. Albino Kumar	NIT Manipur, Manipur, India
Ghazi Al-Naymat	Princess Sumaya University for Technology, Jordan
Adnan Al-Rabea	Albalqa' Applied University, Jordan
Anshu	GD Goenka University, India
S. Aravindan	Annamalai University, India
Amarnath Arora	KITE Jaipur, Rajasthan, India
Pawan Arora	Galgotias Institute of Management & Technology, Greater Noida, India
Parma Nand Astya	Galgotias University, India
Sakshi Babbar	GD Goenka University, India
Usha Batra	GD Goenka University, India
Bawa	Punjabi University, India
Ayana Bhaduri	Amity University Haryana, Gurgaon, India
Subhash Bhalla	University of Aizu, Japan
Komal Kumar Bhatia	YMCA, India
Rosy Bhatia	GD Goenka University, India
Amit Bhatt	Dev Bhoomi Group of Institutions, Dehradun, India
Suprakash Biswas	Galgotias University, UP, India
Lalit Borana	Hong Kong Polytechnic University, Hong Kong, SAR China
Poly Buragohain	Mahindra Ecole Centrale, Hyderabad, India
B. P. Chamola	HNB Garwal University, India
Praveen Chandra	GGSIPU, India
Chandrashekhar	Amity University Haryana, Gurgaon, India
Rama Chari	RRCAT, India
Sruti Chattopadhya	CBME, IIT-Delhi, New Delhi, India
Arun Chaturvedi	JIMS, India
Om Chaudhary	Evolphin Software, India
Tanupriya Chaudhary	Amity University, Noida, India

V. K. Chaudhary	Y. S. Parmar University of Horticulture and Forestry, Nauni, India
Alok Chauhan	JIIT, Noida, India
Shailendra Chauhan	Skyline Engineering College, India
Amit Chhabra	Pollard Banknote, Canada
Pooja Choudhary	Defence Institute of Physiology & Allied Science, DRDO, Delhi
Compa Manis Amigui Gcaro Cocotle	Monterry Institute of Technology, Mexico
Bruce Condie	Vancouver Island University, Canada
Anirban Das	Ansyst Consulting, India
B. K. Das	Delhi University, India
Ranadip K. Das	Indian Institute of Technology (ISM), India
Sanjoy Das	Galgotias University, India
Daya	Delhi University, India
Ashoka De	NIT Patna, India
Deepika	GD Goenka University, India
Desai	Pune University, India
Jonathan Dimmock	University of Saskatchewan, Canada
Pinki Dua	Amity University, India
Alok Manas Dubey	IMSEC Ghaziabad, India
Manisha Duseja	DIT university, Dehradun, India
Daniel (Mehdi) Eghbal	Energex, Australia
N. Farahi	Institute of Materials Research, German Aerospace Center, Cologne, Germany
Sunil Gaba	Earnst and Young, Bangalore, India
Pallavi Gahlot	Amity Institute of Biotechnology, Greater Noida, UP, India
Sumeet Gairola	CSIR, Indian Institute of Integrative Medicine, Jammu, India
Swati Gangwar	Madan Mohan Malaviya University of Technology, Gorakhpur, India
Anjali Garg	Northcap University, India
Ashish Garg	Siri, Apple
Bindu Garg	Pune University, India
Deepak Garg	Bennate University, India
Shailender Gaur	RKGEC, Ghaziabad, India
Anujit Ghoshal	JNU, Delhi, India
Emad Girgis	National Research Centre, Egypt
Mania Goyal	Sheffield Hallam University, UK
Manik Goyal C.	Devilal State Institute of Engineering and Technology, Haryana, India
Rahul Goyal	Manipal University, Jaipur, India
Abhinav Gupta	Boston University, USA
Nidhi Gupta	Amity University, Jaipur, Rajasthan, India
Sanjay Gupta	Manav Rachna International University, Haryana, India
Shikhar Gupta	Proctor & Gamble, Singapore

Lukmanul Hakim	Lampung University, Indonesia
Miaoqing Huang	University of Arkansas, USA
Anuj Jain	Northcap University, Gurgaon, India
Jinesh Kumar Jain	Government Engineering College, Ajmer, India
Sapna Jain	University of Petroleum and Energy Studies, Dehradun, India
Vishal Jain	BVICAM, Delhi, India
Dheeraj Joshi	DTU, Delhi, India
Puran Chand Joshi	Birla Institute of Technology, Mesra, India
Nishal Kapoor	IBM Corporation, USA
Nava Raj Karki	Tribhuvan University, Nepal
Jyoti Kataria	Oracle, India
M. Kato	Hiroshima University, Japan
Ajay Kaul	Mata Vaishno Devi University, India
Mulu Sewinet Kerebih	Debren Markos University, India
Mulu Sewinet Kerebih	IIT Delhi, Ethiopia
Iqbal Ahmed Khan	Galgotias University, Greater Noida, India
Shafat Ahmed Khan	Galgotias University, India
Vishal Khandelwal	GLA University
Sourabh Khurana	Guru Jambeshwar University, Hissar, India
Raul Klauss	Technological University of Clausthal, Germany
D. P. Kothari	G P Group of Institutions, India
Rekha Krishnan	Water Energy Food Transitions Research, New Delhi, India
Ajay Kumar	Thapar University, India
Ajay Kumar	KIET, Ghaziabad, India
Ajeet Kumar	Clarkson University, NY, USA
Amit Kumar	INMAS, DRDO, Delhi, India
Anuj Kumar	Yeungnam University, South Korea
Kuldeep Kumar	NIT Kurukshetra, India
Mukesh Kumar	Malaviya National Institute of Technology Jaipur, India
Ram Kumar	Jaypee University, Anoopseher, India
Shiveranjan Kumar	JECRC University, Jaipur, India
Sumit Kumar	KIET, India
T. Kumar	IIT Dhanbad, India
Yugal Kumar	KIET, India
Vikas Kumar	SKIT, Jaipur, India
Anuj Kumar Tyagi	Sarojini Naidu Medical College, Agra, India
Son Kuswadi	Politeknik Elektronika Negeri, Indonesia
Meena Lakhwani	Terrabit Networks, Singapore
Amarsinh Landage	GEC, Karad, India
D. B. Lata	Birla Institute of Technology, Mesra, India
Wei Liu	University of Technology, Sydney, Australia
Vikas Mahto	IIT Dhanbad, India
Siddhartha S. Malu	IIT Indore, India
Lydia Manikonda	Arizona State University, USA

Ilia Manolov	University of Sofia, Bulgaria
M. L. Meena	Malaviya National Institute of Technology Jaipur, India
Rajeev Mehta	Thapar University, Patiala, India
V. A. Mendhe	CSIR-CIMFR, Dhanbad, India
D. K. Mishra	NPL, India
R. S. Mishra	Delhi Technical University, India
Sanjay Mishra	ITS Engineering College, Greater Noida, India
Sudipta K. Mishra	GD Goenka University, India
Shayon Mitra	Manitoba Public Insurance, Canada
Gaurav Mittal	INMAS, DRDO, Delhi, India
Feroz Mohammad	Oracle, USA
Syed Mohammad Abbas	Jamia Milia Islamia, Delhi, India
Sandip Mondal	NIT Durgapur, West Bengal, India
Varun Monga	MVN University, India
Saurabh Mukherjee	Banasthali University, India
Pawan Nain	Galgotia University, Greater Noida, India
Khoa Nguyen	Commonwealth Scientific and Industrial Research Organisation
Jos Nolle	Seneca College, Toronto, Canada
Arman M. Ottagvari	University of Mazandaran, Iran
Özen Özer	Kırklareli University, Turkey
Sameer K. Pachalla	Mahindra Ecole Centrale, Hyderabad, India
G. L. Pahuja	NIT, Kurukshetra, India
Vineet Panday	Banasthali University, India
P. M. Pandey	Indian Institute of Technology Delhi, India
Prateek Pandya	Amity University, Noida, India
Linsey Pang	IBM, California, USA
Jinen Patel	Mastercard, Ireland
Om Shankar Prajapati	Rajasthan Technical University, Kota, India
Ravi Shankar Prashad	RKGIT, Ghaziabad, India
Mohd. Asim Qadri	Galgotias Institute of Management & Technology, Greater Noida, India
Paras Ram	NIT Kurukshetra, India
Kunj Bihari Rana	Rajasthan Technical University, Kota, India
S. P. Rauniyar	BMRD, Australia
Surendra Rauniyar	Bureau of Meteorology Melbourne, Australia
Surendra Roy	PSIT College of Engineering, Kanpur, India
Shelly Sachdeva	Jaypee University, Noida, India
A. Sahu	Coppin State University USA
Sanjib Sahu	GGSIPU, Delhi, India
Ashish Saini	Cognizent, India
V. K. Saini	IMS Engineering College, Ghaziabad, India
Varinder Saini	Delhi University, India
German Salazar Alvare	Stockholm University, Sweden

Luciano Saso	University of Rome, Italy
Pranveer Singh Satvat	Anand International College of Engineering, Jaipur, Rajasthan, India
V. K. Saxena	IIT Dhanbad, India
Dalip Sethi	Reseach & Development, CESCA Therapeutics, USA
A. K. Sharma	MIET Meerut, India
Ajay Sharma	Kurukshetra University, India
Ashwini Sharma	Northcap University Gurgaon, India
D. K. Sharma	Manav Rachna University, India
D. K. Sharma	SKIT Jaipur, Rajasthan, India
Dinesh Kumar Sharma	Manav Rachna University, Faridabad, India
Divya Sharma	Northcap University, India
Durgesh Sharma	RKGEC, Ghaziabad, India
Harshdeep Sharma	Galgotias University, Greater Noida, India
Kapil Sharma	Delhi Technological University, India
Nipun Sharma	Vodafone India Limited, India
Paramanand Sharma	Tohoku University, Japan
Pradeep Sharma	Maulana Azad National Urdu University, India
Priyanka Sharma	GD Goenka University, India
Priyanka Sharma	Defence Institute of Physiology & Allied Science, DRDO, Delhi
Satendra Sharma	Yobe State University Nigeria
Saeed Shirzadian	Iranian Research Institute of Tehran, Iran
Sulabh Shrama	Hero Motocorp Limited
Amit Prakash Singh	IP University, India
Anurag Singh	NIT, Delhi, India
B. K. Singh	Rawal Institute of Technology, Faridabad, India
Dimple Singh	Amity University, Gurgaon, India
Dinesh Singh	MGMCET, Navi Mumbai, India
Harpal Singh	Guru Nanak Dev Engineering College, Ludhiana, India
Harpal Singh	CBME, IIT Delhi, India
Jagbir Singh	Guru Nanak Dev Engineering College, Ludhiana, India
Prabhakar Singh	Mahindra Ecole Centrale, Hyderabad, India
Prabhakar Singh	Galgotias University, UP, India
Pradeep Kumar Singh	Jaypee University, Noida, India
Prahlad Singh	DPGITM Gurgaon, India
S. P. Singh	IMSEC Ghaziabad, India
Shyamli Singh	Indian Institute of Public Administration, Delhi University, India
Sitesh Kr. Singh	Carrer Point University, Kota, Rajasthan, India
Sujit Singh	MVN University Palwal, India
Surya Prakash Singh	IIT Delhi, India
Sushil Kumar Singh	Galgotias University, UP, India
Varinder Singh	Guru Kashi University, Bathinda, India
Piyush Singhal	GLA University, Mathura, India
Jolanta Slowik	George August University of Goettingen, Germany

E. Sourabh	Silvertech Middle East, Dubai, Arab Emirates
Ashish Srivastava	Saint Louis University, USA
Neha Srivastava	SKIT Jaipur, Rajasthan, India
Satyajeet Srivastava	GCET, Greater Noida, India
Andrea Stern	University of Sydney, Australia
Christian Stiewe	Institute of Materials Research, German Aerospace Center, Cologne, Germany
Viqaruddin Surki	IBM, India
Abhishek Swaroop	Galgotias University, India
Jeevan Talegaonkar	Erricson
Kamarul Hasan Talukdar	Kulna University, Bangladesh
Sudeep Tanwar	Nirma University, India
Denish Thomas	Central University of Kerala, Kasargod, India
Sham Tickoo	Purdue University, USA
Arvind Tiwari	Noida Institute of Technology, India
Kushboo Tripathi	Amity University, India
Ankit Kumar Tyagi	Uppsala University, Sweden
Deepak Unune	LNMIIT, Jaipur, India
Ashish Upadhyay	IIT, Patna, India
Victor Manuel Diez V.	Interconexion Electrica, Colombia
Sharda Vashisth	Northcap University, India
Ruchi Verma	University of Rhode Island, Brown University, RI, USA
Seema Verma	Amity University Noida, India
Vikram Verma	Methodica Technologies, USA
Ankush Vij	Amity University Haryana, Gurgaon, India
Hitesh Vohra	Kurukshetra University, India
Mukesh Yadav	GITM, Gurgaon, India
Sanjay Yadav	ITS Engineering College, Greater Noida, India
Surya Prakash Yadav	BML Munjal University Gurgaon, India
Vinod Yadav	Manipal University, Jaipur, India
Lalit Yagnik	IBM, India
Roshan Dharshana Yapa	University of Peradeniya, Sri Lanka
Naoto Yorino	Hiroshima University, Japan
Xiao ZhiGao	Lappeenranta University of Technology, Finland

REDSET
GD GOENKA UNIVERSITY
OCTOBER 13-14, 2017

Contents

Big Data Analytics

Data Centric Programming

Social and Web Analytics

Security in Data Science Analytics

Big Data Analytics

System Behavior Analysis in the Urea Fertilizer Industry

Arun Kumar[1(✉)], Pardeep Goel[2], Deepika Garg[1], and Atma Sahu[3]

[1] G.D. Goenka University, Gurugram, Haryana, India
rnkumar535@gmail.com, deepika.garg@gdgoenka.ac.in
[2] M.M. (P.G.) College, Fatehabad, Haryana, India
pardeepgoel1958@gmail.com
[3] Coppin State University, Baltimore, MD, USA
sahuatma@yahoo.com

Abstract. This paper models and analyses a urea plant having subsystems of different operational nature for system parameters using Regenerative Point Graphical Technique (RPGT). A common cause failure is also considered in modeling. Problem is formulated and solved for constant failure/repair rates for each subsystem. A state diagram of the system depicting the transition rates is drawn and expressions for path probabilities mean sojourn times are derived. Analytical discussion is carried out by tables and graphs. Behavioral inferences have been drawn which may useful to concerned industrial personals.

Keywords: Fuzzy logic · RPGT · System parameters

1 Introduction

In this paper, behavior analysis of a urea fertilizer industry consisting of six sub-units Ammonia Making Section (A), Medium Pressure Section (B), Low Pressure Section (C), Pre-vacuum Section (D), Vacuum Section (E) & Periling Section (F) and three pressure units named low, medium and high pressure units (P_1, P_2 & P_3 respectively) is carried out. Fuzzy logic is used to determine good state of a unit. When low or high pressure units fail, then low and medium pressure steams are obtained from high pressure unit by scientific logic and however when high pressure unit fail then whole system fails. The failed pressure units can be repaired only when the whole system is in failed state. System works in full capacity when all units are good and fails when any one of the six sub-systems fails. A common cause failure which may cause the system to complete failure has also been considered in the study. All the units have sub units in series, whenever any one of the sub unit fails then that unit fails causing the system failure. There is single repair facility which is always available. Taking failure/repair rates constant and independent, a transition diagram of the system is drawn in Fig. 1 to find Primary circuits, Secondary circuits & Tertiary circuits and Base state. System behaviour analysis is discussed for different repair and failure rates of sub-units.

A number of researchers have analyzed availability parameters of various industrial system using different methods. In this research paper sensitivity analysis of Urea Fertilizer Industry has been discussed using regenerative point graphical technique

B. Panda et al. (Eds.): REDSET 2017, CCIS 799, pp. 3–16, 2018.
https://doi.org/10.1007/978-981-10-8527-7_1

(RPGT). Reporting related research in brief, Kumar et al. [1] have discussed the concept of preventive maintenance for a single unit system. Lilu, K. et al. [2] some interconnected studies were also found such as, Nakagawa, T. et al. [3], Goel and Sing [4], Gupta et al. [5], Kumar. S and Goel P. [6], Gupta et al. [7], Nidhi et al. [8], Sharma and Goel [9], Goyal and Goel [10], Gupta et al. [11], Sethi, Rachita and Garg D. [12], Garg and Yadav [13], Kumar and Ritikesh [14] have discussed behavior with perfect and imperfect switch over of system using various techniques.

Assumptions:

1. Repaired unit is as good as new one.
2. When the system is in failed state nothing can fail further.

Notations:

$\left(i \xrightarrow{s_k} j\right)$:	k-th simple path from ith-state to jth-state.
$\left(\xi \xrightarrow{sff} i\right)$:	Simple failure free path from ξth-state to ith-state.
$V_{m,k}$:	probability of mth-state reachable from the terminal state kth-state.
μ_i:	Sojourn mean time in state i, before visiting any other states;
μ_i:	$= \int_0^\infty R_i(t)dt$.
n_i:	$W_i^*(0)$ at zero time.
ξ:	Base state of the system.
f_j:	Fuzziness measure of the j-state.
○:	Full Capacity Working State
□:	Failed State
$\alpha_i, \beta_i (1 \le i \le 6)$:	Constant failure/repair rates of subunit A, B, C, D, E, F respectively.
α_7, α_8, α_9:	Constant failure rate of pressure unit P_1, P_2 and P_3 respectively.
α_0:	Study failure rate of entire system from working state.
h:	Steady repair rate of system on failure of pressure unit P3.
c:	Steady repair rate of system due to common cause failure.
a:	subsystem A is failed, similarly for other units.
S_0:	Initial state when all units are good.
S_{21}:	Failed state due to the failure of pressure unit P_3.
S_{22}:	Failed state due to the common cause failure.
S_i, S_{7+i}, S_{14+i}, S_{23+i}:	Failed states due to the failure of subsystem A, B, C, D, E, F respectively for i = 1, 2, 3, 4, 5 and 6.

2 Research Problem Statement

A urea fertilizer industry consists of six sub-units Ammonia Making Section (A), Medium Pressure Section (B), Low Pressure Section (C), Pre-vacuum Section (D), Vacuum Section (E) & Periling Section (F) and three pressure units low pressure, medium pressure and high pressure units (P_1, P_2 & P_3), whenever low or high pressure units fail, then low and medium pressure steams can be obtained from high pressure unit and whenever high pressure unit fail then high pressure steam cannot be obtained, thus the whole system is failed. The failed pressure units are repaired only when the whole system is in failed state. System works in full capacity when all units are good and fails when any one of the six sub-systems fails. Common cause failures may also lead the system to complete failure. All the units have sub units in series, so any one of the sub unit fails then the unit fails and the system fails when the number of failed units is more than two. In this research the *Fuzzy concept* is used to determine failure/working state of a unit. Taking failure rates/repair rates constant & independent and taking into consideration various probabilities, a transition diagram of the system is drawn in Fig. 1 to find Primary circuits, Secondary circuits & Tertiary circuits and Base state. Problem is solved using RPGT to determine system parameters. System behavior is discussed with the help of graphs and tables. Particular cases are also taken for different repair and failure rates of the system.

The state transition Fig. 1, display that there are maximum number of primary circuits and minimum number of secondary circuits; hence vertex '0' is the base state (Table 1).

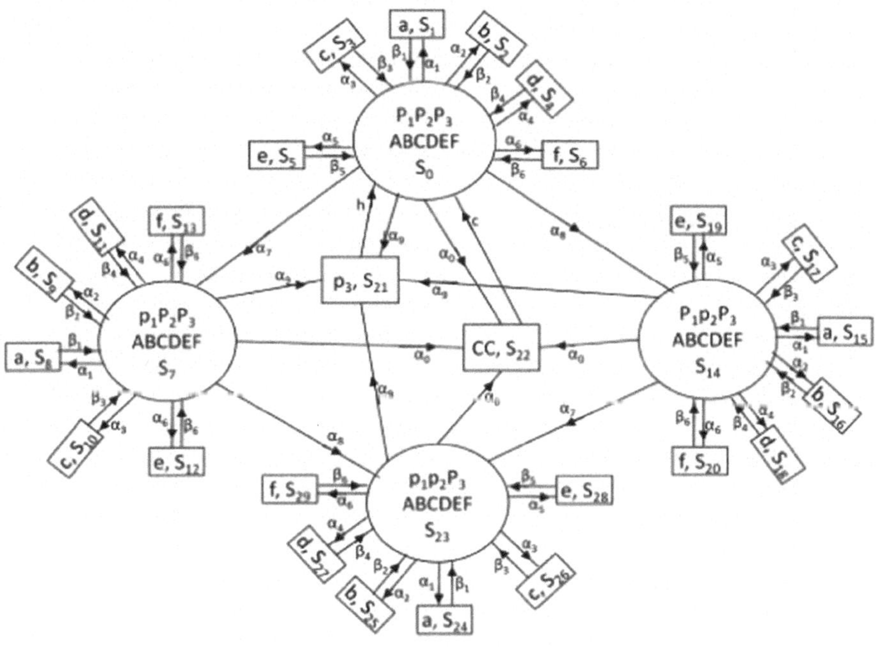

Fig. 1. Transition diagram of the system design

Table 1. Primary, secondary, tertiary circuits w. r. t. the simple paths (Base-State '0')

Vertex j	$\left(0 \xrightarrow{S_r} j\right)$: ($P_0$)	(P_1)
0	$\left(0 \xrightarrow{S_0} 0\right)$: (0,1,0) $\left(0 \xrightarrow{S_1} 0\right)$: (0,2,0) $\left(0 \xrightarrow{S_2} 0\right)$: (0,3,0) $\left(0 \xrightarrow{S_3} 0\right)$: (0,4,0) $\left(0 \xrightarrow{S_4} 0\right)$: (0,5,0) $\left(0 \xrightarrow{S_5} 0\right)$: (0,6,0) $\left(0 \xrightarrow{S_6} 0\right)$: (0,22,0) $\left(0 \xrightarrow{S_7} 0\right)$: (0,21,0) $\left(0 \xrightarrow{S_8} 0\right)$: (0,14,22,0) $\left(0 \xrightarrow{S_9} 0\right)$: (0,23,22,0) $\left(0 \xrightarrow{S_{10}} 0\right)$: (0,7,21,0) $\left(0 \xrightarrow{S_{11}} 0\right)$: (0,7,22,21,0) $\left(0 \xrightarrow{S_{12}} 0\right)$: (0,7,23,22,0) $\left(0 \xrightarrow{S_{13}} 0\right)$: (0,7,22,0) $\left(0 \xrightarrow{S_{14}} 0\right)$: (0,14,21,0)	- - - - - - - - (14,19,14), (14,16,14), (14,17,14), (14,20,14) (14,15,14), (14,18,14) (14,19,14), (14,17,14), (14,15,14), (14,16,14) (14,20,14), (14,18,14), (23,24,23), (23,25,23) (23,26,23), (23,27,23), (23,28,23), (23,29,23) (7,8,7), (7,9,7), (7,10,7), (7,11,7), (7,12,7), (7,13,7) (7,8,7), (7,9,7), (7,10,7), (7,11,7), (7,12,7), (7,13,7) (23,24,23), (23,25,23), (23,26,23), (23,27,23) (23,28,23), (23,29,23) (7,8,7), (7,9,7), (7,10,7), (7,11,7), (7,12,7), (7,13,7) (23,24,23), (23,25,23), (23,26,23), (23,27,23) (23,28,23), (23,29,23) (7,8,7), (7,9,7), (7,10,7), (7,11,7), (7,12,7), (7,13,7) (14,19,14), (14,17,14), (14,15,14), (14,16,14) (14,20,14), (14,18,14)
1	$\left(0 \xrightarrow{S_1} 1\right)$: (0,1)	-
2	$\left(0 \xrightarrow{S_1} 2\right)$: (0,2)	-
3	$\left(0 \xrightarrow{S_1} 3\right)$: (0,3)	-
4	$\left(0 \xrightarrow{S_1} 4\right)$: (0,4)	-
5	$\left(0 \xrightarrow{S_1} 5\right)$: (0,5)	-

(continued)

Table 1. *(continued)*

6	$\left(0 \xrightarrow{S_1} 6\right)$: (0,6)	-
7	$\left(0 \xrightarrow{S_1} 7\right)$: (0,7)	(7,8,7), (7,9,7), (7,10,7), (7,11,7), (7,12,7), (7,13,7)
8	$\left(0 \xrightarrow{S_1} 8\right)$: (0,7,8)	(7,8,7), (7,9,7), (7,10,7), (7,11,7), (7,12,7), (7,13,7) (8,7,8)
9	$\left(0 \xrightarrow{S_1} 9\right)$: (0,7,9)	(7,8,7), (7,9,7), (7,10,7), (7,11,7), (7,12,7), (7,13,7) (9,7,9)
10	$\left(0 \xrightarrow{S_1} 10\right)$: (0,7,10)	(7,8,7), (7,9,7), (7,10,7), (7,11,7), (7,12,7), (7,13,7) (10,7,10)
11	$\left(0 \xrightarrow{S_1} 11\right)$: (0,7,11)	(7,8,7), (7,9,7), (7,10,7), (7,11,7), (7,12,7), (7,13,7) (11,7,11)
12	$\left(0 \xrightarrow{S_1} 12\right)$: (0,7,12)	(7,8,7), (7,9,7), (7,10,7), (7,11,7), (7,12,7), (7,13,7) (12,7,12)
13	$\left(0 \xrightarrow{S_1} 13\right)$: (0,7,13)	(7,8,7), (7,9,7), (7,10,7), (7,11,7), (7,12,7), (7,13,7) (13,7,13)
14	$\left(0 \xrightarrow{S_1} 14\right)$: (0,14)	(14,19,14), (14,17,14), (14,15,14), (14,16,14) (14,20,14), (14,18,14)
15	$\left(0 \xrightarrow{S_1} 15\right)$: (0,14,15)	(14,19,14), (14,17,14), (14,15,14), (14,16,14) (14,20,14), (14,18,14), (15,14,15)
16	$\left(0 \xrightarrow{S_1} 16\right)$: (0,14,16)	(14,19,14), (14,17,14), (14,15,14), (14,16,14) (14,20,14), (14,18,14), (16,14,16)
17	$\left(0 \xrightarrow{S_1} 17\right)$: (0,14,17)	(14,19,14), (14,17,14), (14,15,14), (14,16,14) (14,20,14), (14,18,14), (17,14,17)
18	$\left(0 \xrightarrow{S_1} 18\right)$: (0,14,18)	(14,19,14), (14,17,14), (14,15,14), (14,16,14) (14,20,14), (14,18,14), (18,14,18)
19	$\left(0 \xrightarrow{S_1} 19\right)$: (0,14,19)	(19,14,19), (14,19,14), (14,17,14), (14,15,14) (14,16,14), (14,18,14), (14,20,14)
20	$\left(0 \xrightarrow{S_1} 20\right)$: (0,14,20)	(14,19,14), (14,17,14), (14,15,14), (14,16,14) (14,20,14), (14,18,14), (20,14,20)

(continued)

Table 1. *(continued)*

21	$\left(0 \xrightarrow{S_1} 21\right)$: (0,21)	-
	$\left(0 \xrightarrow{S_2} 21\right)$: (0,14,21)	(14,19,14), (14,17,14), (14,15,14), (14,16,14) (14,20,14), (14,18,14)
	$\left(0 \xrightarrow{S_3} 21\right)$: (0,7,21)	(7,8,7), (7,9,7), (7,10,7), (7,11,7), (7,12,7), (7,13,7)
	$\left(0 \xrightarrow{S_4} 21\right)$: (0,7,23,21)	(7,8,7), (7,9,7), (7,10,7), (7,11,7), (7,12,7), (7,13,7) (23,24,23), (23,25,23), (23,26,23), (23,27,23) (23,28,23), (23,29,23)
	$\left(0 \xrightarrow{S_5} 21\right)$: (0,14,23,21)	(14,19,14), (14,17,14), (14,15,14), (14,16,14) (14,20,14), (14,18,14), (23,24,23), (23,25,23) (23,26,23), (23,27,23), (23,28,23), (23,29,23)
22	$\left(0 \xrightarrow{S_1} 22\right)$: (0,22)	-
	$\left(0 \xrightarrow{S_2} 22\right)$: (0,14,22)	(14,19,14), (14,17,14), (14,15,14), (14,16,14) (14,20,14), (14,18,14)
	$\left(0 \xrightarrow{S_3} 22\right)$: (0,7,22)	(7,8,7), (7,9,7), (7,10,7), (7,11,7), (7,12,7), (7,13,7)
	$\left(0 \xrightarrow{S_4} 22\right)$: (0,7,23,22)	(7,8,7), (7,9,7), (7,10,7), (7,11,7), (7,12,7), (7,13,7) (23,24,23), (23,25,23), (23,26,23), (23,27,23) (23,28,23), (23,29,23)
23	$\left(0 \xrightarrow{S_1} 23\right)$: (0,7,23)	(7,8,7), (7,9,7), (7,10,7), (7,11,7), (7,12,7), (7,13,7) (23,24,23), (23,25,23), (23,26,23), (23,27,23) (23,28,23), (23,29,23)
	$\left(0 \xrightarrow{S_2} 23\right)$: (0,14,23)	(14,15,14), (14,16,14), (14,17,14), (14,18,14) (14,19,14), (14,20,14), (23,24,23), (23,25,23) (23,26,23), (23,27,23), (23,28,23), (23,29,23)
24	$\left(0 \xrightarrow{S_1} 24\right)$: (0,14,23,24)	(14,15,14), (14,16,14), (14,17,14), (14,18,14) (14,19,14), (14,20,14), (23,24,23), (23,25,23) (23,26,23), (23,27,23), (23,28,23), (23,29,23) (24,23,24)
	$\left(0 \xrightarrow{S_2} 24\right)$: (0,7,23,24)	(7,8,7), (7,9,7), (7,10,7), (7,11,7), (7,12,7), (7,13,7) (23,24,23), (23,25,23), (23,26,23), (23,27,23) (23,28,23), (23,29,23), (24,23,24)
25	$\left(0 \xrightarrow{S_1} 25\right)$: (0,14,23,25)	(14,15,14), (14,16,14), (14,17,14), (14,18,14) (14,19,14), (14,20,14), (23,24,23), (23,25,23) (23,26,23), (23,27,23), (23,28,23), (23,29,23) (25,23,25)
	$\left(0 \xrightarrow{S_2} 25\right)$: (0,7,23,25)	(7,8,7), (7,9,7), (7,10,7), (7,11,7), (7,12,7), (7,13,7) (23,24,23), (23,25,23), (23,26,23), (23,27,23) (23,28,23), (23,29,23), (25,23,25)

(continued)

Table 1. *(continued)*

26	$\left(0 \overset{S_1}{\rightarrow} 26\right)$: (0,14,23,26)	(14,15,14), (14,16,14), (14,17,14), (14,18,14) (14,19,14), (14,20,14), (23,24,23), (23,25,23) (23,26,23), (23,27,23), (23,28,23), (23,29,23) (26,23,26)
	$\left(0 \overset{S_2}{\rightarrow} 26\right)$: (0,7,23,26)	(7,8,7), (7,9,7), (7,10,7), (7,11,7), (7,12,7), (7,13,7) (23,24,23), (23,25,23), (23,26,23), (23,27,23) (23,28,23), (23,29,23), (26,23,26)
27	$\left(0 \overset{S_1}{\rightarrow} 27\right)$: (0,14,23,27)	(14,15,14), (14,16,14), (14,17,14), (14,18,14) (14,19,14), (14,20,14), (23,24,23), (23,25,23) (23,26,23), (23,27,23), (23,28,23), (23,29,23) (27,23,27)
	$\left(0 \overset{S_2}{\rightarrow} 27\right)$: (0,7,23,27)	(7,8,7), (7,9,7), (7,10,7), (7,11,7), (7,12,7), (7,13,7) (23,24,23), (23,25,23), (23,26,23), (23,27,23) (23,28,23), (23,29,23), (27,23,27)
28	$\left(0 \overset{S_1}{\rightarrow} 28\right)$: (0,14,23,28)	(14,15,14), (14,16,14), (14,17,14), (14,18,14) (14,19,14), (14,20,14), (23,24,23), (23,25,23) (23,26,23), (23,27,23), (23,28,23), (23,29,23) (28,23,28)
	$\left(0 \overset{S_2}{\rightarrow} 28\right)$: (0,7,23,28)	(7,8,7), (7,9,7), (7,10,7), (7,11,7), (7,12,7), (7,13,7) (23,24,23), (23,25,23), (23,26,23), (23,27,23) (23,28,23), (23,29,23), (28,23,28)
29	$\left(0 \overset{S_1}{\rightarrow} 29\right)$: (0,14,23,29)	(14,15,14), (14,16,14), (14,17,14), (14,18,14) (14,19,14), (14,20,14), (23,24,23), (23,25,23) (23,26,23), (23,27,23),(23,28,23), (23,29,23) (29,23,29)
	$\left(0 \overset{S_2}{\rightarrow} 29\right)$: (0,7,23,29)	(7,8,7), (7,9,7), (7,10,7), (7,11,7), (7,12,7), (7,13,7) (23,24,23), (23,25,23), (23,26,23), (23,27,23) (23,28,23), (23,29,23), (29,23,29)

There are no tertiary circuits for all simple paths.

Transition Probability and the Sojourn Mean times Definitions (Table 2).

$q_{i,j}(t)$: Probability density function from a state 'i' to a state 'j'.

$p_{i,j}$: Transition probability in moving from ith-state to jth-state $p_{i,j} = q^*_{i,j}(0)$;

Sojourn Mean Times (Table 3).

$R_i(t)$: Reliability at time t at state i.

μ_i: Sojourn mean time spent in state i.

Table 2. Transition probabilities

$q_{i,j}(t)$	$P_{ij} = q^*_{i,j}(0)$
$q_{0,i}(t) = \alpha_i e^{-kt}$ $q_{0,14}(t) = \alpha_8 e^{-kt}$ $q_{0,21}(t) = \alpha_9 e^{-kt}$ $q_{0,22}(t) = \alpha_0 e^{-kt}$ Where i = 1 to 7	$p_{0,i} = \alpha_i/k$ $p_{0,14} = \alpha_8/k$ $p_{0,21} = \alpha_9/k$ $p_{0,22} = \alpha_0/k$ $k = \alpha_1 + \alpha_2 + \alpha_3 + \alpha_4 + \alpha_5 + \alpha_6 + \alpha_7 + \alpha_9 + \alpha_8 + \alpha_0$
$q_{i,0}(t) = \beta_i e^{-\beta_i t}, q_{7+i}(t) = \beta_{7+i} e^{-\beta_i t}$ $q_{14+i}(t) = \beta_{14+i} e^{-\beta_i t}, q_{21+i}(t) = \beta_{21+i} e^{-\beta_i t}$	$p_{7+i} = 1, p_{14+i} = 1, p_{21+i} = 1$ $p_{i,0} = 1$, where $1 \le i \le 6$
$q_{7,7+i}(t) = \alpha_i e^{-(k-\alpha_7)t}$ $q_{7,23}(t) = \alpha_8 e^{-(k-\alpha_7)t}$ $q_{7,21}(t) = \alpha_9 e^{-(k-\alpha_7)t}$ $q_{7,22}(t) = \alpha_0 e^{-(k-\alpha_7)t}$	$p_{7,7+i} = \alpha_i/(k-\alpha_7)$ $p_{7,23} = \alpha_8/(k-\alpha_7)$ $p_{7,21} = \alpha_9/(k-\alpha_7)$ $p_{7,22} = \alpha_0/(k-\alpha_7)$
$q_{7+i,7}(t) = \beta_1 e^{-\beta_1 t}$	$p_{7+i,7} = 1$, where $1 \le i \le 6$
$q_{14,14+i}(t) = \alpha_i e^{-(k-\alpha_8)t}$ $q_{14,22}(t) = \alpha_0 e^{-(k-\alpha_8)t}$ $q_{14,23}(t) = \alpha_7 e^{-(k-\alpha_8)t}$ $q_{14,21}(t) = \alpha_9 e^{-(k-\alpha_8)t}$	$p_{14,14+i} = \alpha_i/(k-\alpha_8)$ $p_{14,22} = \alpha_0/(k-\alpha_8)$ $p_{14,23} = \alpha_7/(k-\alpha_8)$ $p_{14,21} = \alpha_9/(k-\alpha_8)$
$q_{14+i,14}(t) = \beta_1 e^{-\beta_1 t}, q_{23+i,23}(t) = \beta_i e^{-\beta_i t}$	$p_{14+i,14} = 1, p_{23+i,23} = 1$, where $1 \le i \le 6$
$q_{21,0}(t) = \text{h}e^{-ht}, q_{22,0}(t) = \text{c}e^{-ct}$	$p_{21,0} = 1, p_{22,0} = 1$
$q_{23,22}(t) = \alpha_0 e^{-(k-\alpha_7-\alpha_8)t}$ $q_{23,23+i}(t) = \alpha_i e^{-(k-\alpha_7-\alpha_8)t}$ $q_{23,21}(t) = \alpha_9 e^{-(k-\alpha_7-\alpha_8)t}$	$p_{23,22} = \alpha_0/(k-\alpha_7-\alpha_8)$ $p_{23,23+i} = \alpha_i/(k-\alpha_7-\alpha_8)$ $p_{23,21} = \alpha_9/(k-\alpha_7-\alpha_8)$

Table 3. Sojourn mean times

$R_i(t)$	$\mu_i = R_i^*(0)$
$R_0(t) = e^{-kt}$	$\mu_0 = 1/k$
$R_{n+i}(t) = e^{-\beta_i t}$	$\mu_i = 1/\beta_i$, where $1 \le i \le 6$, n = 0, 7, 14, 23
$R_j(t) = e^{-(k-\alpha_7)t}$, where j = 7, 14, 23	$\mu_j = 1/(k-\alpha_7)$
$R_{21}(t) = e^{-ht}, R_{22}(t) = e^{-ct}$	$\mu_{21} = 1/h$, $\mu_{22} = 1/c$

The following paragraphs outline definitions of the parameters evaluation, MTSF (T_0), Availability of the system (A_0), Busy period of the server, and Expected Fractional Number of Inspection by the repair man. With some modifications, the notations are adapted from Kumar and Ritikesh [11].

Parameters Evaluation: The transition probability of states from the base state 'ξ' = '0' are:

Probabilities from state '0' to different vertices are given as

$V_{0,0} = 1, V_{0,1} = (0,1) = p_{0,1}, V_{0,2} = (0,2) = p_{0,2}, V_{0,3} = (0,3) = p_{0,3}, V_{0,4} = (0,4) = p_{0,4}$
$V_{0,5} = (0,5) = p_{0,5}, V_{0,6} = (0,6) = p_{0,6}, V_{0,7} = (0,7)/L$
$V_{0,8} = (0,7,8)/L(1 - L_7)$

Where $L = (1-L_1)(1-L_2)(1-L_3)(1-L_4)(1-L_5)(1-L_6)$, here L_i are cycles. Similarly other path probabilities are evaluated.

MTSF (T_0): The system is in working states (from initial state) before failure states are 0, 7, 14, 23, hence MTSF is given by

$$\text{MTSF } (T_0) = \left[\sum\nolimits_{i,sr}\left\{\frac{\left\{pr\left(\xi \xrightarrow{sr(sff)} i\right)\right\}\mu i}{\Pi_{m_1 \neq \xi}\{1 - V_{\overline{m_1 m_1}}\}}\right\}\right] \div \left[1 - \sum\nolimits_{sr}\left\{\frac{\left\{pr\left(\xi \xrightarrow{sr(sff)} \xi\right)\right\}}{\Pi_{m_2 \neq \xi}\{1 - V_{\overline{m_2 m_2}}\}}\right\}\right]$$

$$\begin{aligned} T_0 = &(V_{0,0}\mu_0 + V_{0,7}\mu_7 + V_{0,14}\mu_{14} + V_{0,23}\mu_{23})/[\{1 - (0,7,21,0) - (0,7,23,21,0) \\ &-(0,7,23,22,0) - (0,14,21,0) - (0,14,22,0) - (0,14,23,21,0) - (0,14,23,22,0)\}] \\ = &(V_{0,0}\mu_0 + V_{0,7}\mu_7 + V_{0,14}\mu_{14} + V_{0,23}\mu_{23})/(1 - p_{0,7}p_{7,21}p_{21,0} - p_{0,7}p_{7,23}p_{23,21}p_{21,0} \\ &- p_{0,7}p_{7,23}p_{23,22}p_{22,0} - p_{0,14}p_{14,21}p_{21,0} - p_{0,14}p_{14,22}p_{22,0} - p_{0,14}p_{14,23}p_{23,21}p_{21,0} \\ &- p_{0,14}p_{14,23}p_{23,22}p_{22,0}) \end{aligned}$$

Availability of the System (A_0): The states at which the system is available are 'j' = 0, 7, 14, 23 taking 'ξ' = '0' the total fraction of time for which the system is available is given by

$$A_0 = \left[\sum\nolimits_{j,sr}\left\{\frac{\{pr(\xi^{sr\rightarrow} j)\}fj, \mu j}{\Pi_{m_{1} \neq \xi}\{1 - V_{\overline{m_1 m_1}}\}}\right\}\right] \div \left[\sum\nolimits_{i,s_r}\left\{\frac{\{pr(\xi^{sr\rightarrow} i)\}\mu_i^1}{\Pi_{m_2 \neq \xi}\{1 - V_{\overline{m_2 m_2}}\}}\right\}\right]$$

$$\begin{aligned} A_0 &= \left[\sum\nolimits_j V_{\xi,j}, f_j, \mu_j\right] \div \left[\sum\nolimits_i V_{\xi,i}, f_j, \mu_i^1\right] \\ &= (V_{0,0}\mu_0 + V_{0,7}\mu_7 + V_{0,14}\mu_{14} + V_{0,23}\mu_{23})/D \end{aligned}$$

Where

$$\begin{aligned} D = (&V_{0,0}\mu_0 + V_{0,1}\mu_1 + V_{0,2}\mu_2 + V_{0,3}\mu_3 + V_{0,4}\mu_4 + V_{0,5}\mu_5 + V_{0,6}\mu_6 + V_{0,7}\mu_7 + V_{0,8}\mu_8 \\ &+ V_{0,9}\mu_9 + V_{0,10}\mu_{10} + V_{0,11}\mu_{11} + V_{0,12}\mu_{12} + V_{0,13}\mu_{13} + V_{0,14}\mu_{14} + V_{0,15}\mu_{15} + V_{0,16}\mu_{16} \\ &+ V_{0,17}\mu_{17} + V_{0,18}\mu_{18} + V_{0,19}\mu_{19} + V_{0,20}\mu_{20} + V_{0,21}\mu_{21} + V_{0,22}\mu_{22} + V_{0,23}\mu_{23} + V_{0,24}\mu_{24} \\ &+ V_{0,25}\mu_{25} + V_{0,26}\mu_{26} + V_{0,27}\mu_{27} + V_{0,28}\mu_{28} + V_{0,29}\mu_{29}) \end{aligned}$$

Busy Period of the Server: The states where the server is busy are S_i, S_{7+i}, S_{14+i}, S_{23+i}, where $1 \leq i \leq 6$, S_{21}, S_{22} taking ξ = '0', the total fraction of time for which the server remains busy is

$$B_0 = \left[\sum\nolimits_{j,sr}\left\{\frac{\{pr(\xi^{sr\to}j)\}, nj}{\Pi_{m_1\neq\xi}\{1 - V_{\overline{m_1m_1}}\}}\right\}\right] \div \left[\sum\nolimits_{i,s_r}\left\{\frac{\{pr(\xi^{sr\to}i)\}\mu_i^1}{\Pi_{m_2\neq\xi}\{1 - V_{\overline{m_2m_2}}\}}\right\}\right]$$

$$B_0 = \left[\sum\nolimits_j V_{\xi,j}, n_j\right] \div \left[\sum\nolimits_i V_{\xi,i}, \mu_i^1\right]$$

$$\begin{aligned} B_0 = (&V_{0,1}\mu_1 + V_{0,2}\mu_2 + V_{0,3}\mu_3 + V_{0,4}\mu_4 + V_{0,5}\mu_5 + V_{0,6}\mu_6 + V_{0,8}\mu_8 + V_{0,9}\mu_9 \\ &+ V_{0,10}\mu_{10} + V_{0,11}\mu_{11} + V_{0,12}\mu_{12} + V_{0,13}\mu_{13} + V_{0,15}\mu_{15} + V_{0,16}\mu_{16} + V_{0,17}\mu_{17} \\ &+ V_{0,18}\mu_{18} + V_{0,19}\mu_{19} + V_{0,20}\mu_{20} + V_{0,21}\mu_{21} + V_{0,22}\mu_{22} + V_{0,24}\mu_{24} + V_{0,25}\mu_{25} \\ &+ V_{0,26}\mu_{26} + V_{0,27}\mu_{27} + V_{0,28}\mu_{28} + V_{0,29}\mu_{29})/D \end{aligned}$$

Expected Fractional Number of Inspections by the Repair Man: The states where the repairman do visit's a fresh are S_i, S_{7+i}, S_{14+i}, S_{23+i}, where $1 \leq i \leq 6$, S_{21}, S_{23}taking 'ξ' = '0', the number of visit by the repair man is given by

$$V_0 = \left[\sum\nolimits_{j,sr}\left\{\frac{\{pr(\xi^{sr\to}j)\}}{\Pi_{k_1\neq\xi}\{1 - V_{\overline{k_1k_1}}\}}\right\}\right] \div \left[\sum\nolimits_{i,s_r}\left\{\frac{\{pr(\xi^{sr\to}i)\}\mu_i^1}{\Pi_{k_2\neq\xi}\{1 - V_{\overline{k_2k_2}}\}}\right\}\right]$$

$$V_0 = \left[\sum\nolimits_j V_{\xi,j}\right] \div \left[\sum\nolimits_i V_{\xi,i}, \mu_i^1\right]$$

Analytical Example with Particular Cases: Data Analysis and Regenerative Point Graphical Results

$$\alpha_i = \alpha,\ (0 \leq i \leq 9), \quad \beta_i = \beta,\ (1 \leq i \leq 6), \quad h = 1, \quad c = 1$$

Mean Time to System Failure (T_0) are (Table 4):

Table 4. Mean time to system failure (T_0)

T_0	β = 0.5	β = 0.6	β = 0.7	β = 0.8
α = 0.1	40.5644	40.5644	40.5644	40.5644
α = 0.2	20.2821	20.2821	20.2821	20.2821
α = 0.3	13.5212	13.5212	13.5212	13.5212
α = 0.4	10.1410	10.1410	10.1410	10.1410

Mean Time to System Failure Graph is (Fig. 2):

From the above table and graph we analyze that MTSF is constant with the increase in repair rates (Horizontal) i.e. MTSF is independent of repair rates and decreases with increases in failure rates (Vertical) which is the practical trend. Given below in figure

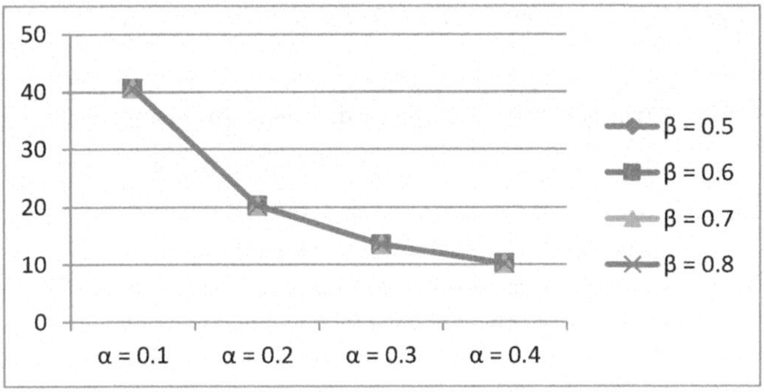

Fig. 2. Mean time to system failure graph

Availability of the System (A_0) (Table 5):

Table 5. Availability of the system (A_0) table

A_0	β = 0.5	β = 0.6	β = 0.7	β = 0.8
α = 0.1	0.40790	0.44597	0.47782	0.50487
α = 0.2	0.25620	0.28697	0.31391	0.33767
α = 0.3	0.18674	0.2155	0.23372	0.25366
α = 0.4	0.14692	0.16752	0.18617	0.20313

The Availability of the System (A_0) Graph shown below (Fig. 3):

From the above table and graph while looking horizontally it is seen that with the increase of repair rate availability and with the increase in failure rate, while observing vertically availability decreases which is the practical trend, so for optimum value of availability the repair rates of units should be kept maximums far as possible and failure rates of units should be minimum.

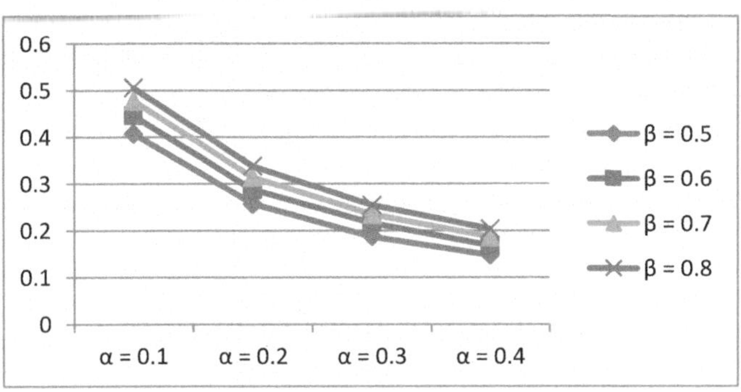

Fig. 3. Availability of the system (A_0) graph

The Busy Period of the Server (B_0) tabulated below (Table 6):

Table 6. Busy period of the server (B_0) table

B_0	$\beta = 0.5$	$\beta = 0.6$	$\beta = 0.7$	$\beta = 0.8$
$\alpha = 0.1$	0.74116	0.71701	0.69679	0.67963
$\alpha = 0.2$	0.83742	0.81789	0.80080	0.78572
$\alpha = 0.3$	0.88149	0.86575	0.85168	0.83903
$\alpha = 0.4$	0.90677	0.89369	0.88186	0.87110

The Busy Period of the Server Graph shown below (Fig. 4):

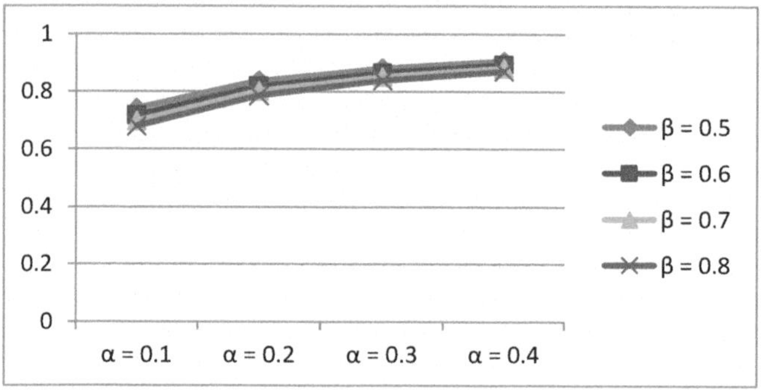

Fig. 4. Busy period of the server graph

From the above table (Horizontally) we see that busy period of the server decreases with the increase in the repair rate, but having a look vertically it increases with the increase in failure rate which match the practical situations.

The Expected Fractional Number of Inspections by the Repairman (V_0) are:

The Expected Fractional Number of Inspections by the Repairman Graph are:

From the Table 7 and Fig. 5 we see that expected fractional value of server increases significantly with the increase in failure rates in comparison to increase in repair rates.

Table 7. Expected fractional number of inspection by the repairman (V_0) table

V_0	$\beta = 0.5$	$\beta = 0.6$	$\beta = 0.7$	$\beta = 0.8$
$\alpha = 0.1$	0.13091	0.14313	0.15336	0.16204
$\alpha = 0.2$	0.16445	0.18421	0.20150	0.21675
$\alpha = 0.3$	0.17981	0.22500	0.22505	0.24425
$\alpha = 0.4$	0.21005	0.22607	0.23901	0.24847

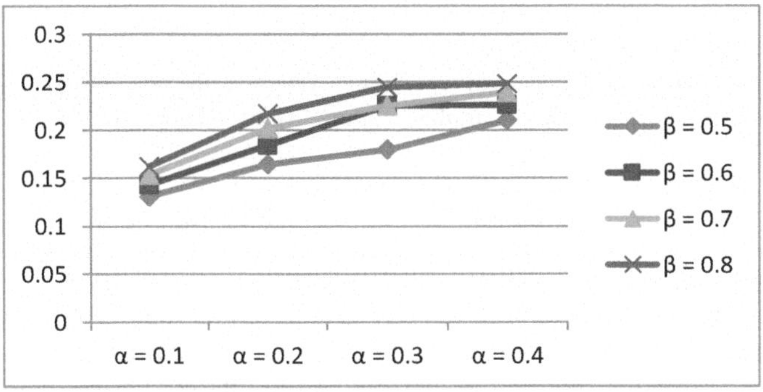

Fig. 5. Expected fractional number of inspection by the repairman graph

3 Resulting Conclusion

In order for the urea fertilizer factory system, to have optimum value of system parameters management can control the failure and repair rates of units depending upon the availability of finances and market circumstances. In particular, the optimum value of availability repair rates of units should be kept maximum as far as possible and failure rates of units should be minimum. Also, the expected fractional value of server increases significantly with the increase in failure rates in comparison to increase in repair rates.

References

1. Kumar, J., Kadyan, M.S., Malik, S.C., Jindal, C.: Reliability measures of a single-unit system under preventive maintenance and degradation with arbitrary distributions of random variables. J. Reliab. Stat. Stud. **7**, 77–88 (2014). ISSN 0974-8024
2. Liu, R., Liu, Z.: Reliability analysis of a one-unit system with finite vacations. In: International Conference on Management Science Industrial Engineering (MSIE), pp. 248–252 (2011)
3. Nakagawa, T., Osaki, S.: Reliability analysis of a one-unit system with un-repairable spare units and its optimization application. Q. Oper. Res. **27**(1), 101–110 (1976)
4. Goel, P., Singh, J.: Availability analysis of a thermal power plant having two imperfect switches. In: Proceedings (Reviewed) of 2nd Annual Conference of ISITA (1997)
5. Gupta, P., Singh, J., Singh, I.P.: Availability analysis of soap cakes production system – a case study. In: Proceedings of National Conference on Emerging Trends in Manufacturing System, SLIET, Longowal (Punjab) Pb, pp. 283–295 (2004)
6. Kumar, S., Goel, P.: Availability analysis of two different units system with a standby having imperfect switch over device in banking industry. Aryabhatta J. Math. Inf. **6**(2), 299–304 (2014). ISSN 0975-7139
7. Gupta, V.K.: Analysis of a single unit system using a base state. Aryabhatta J. Maths Inf. **3** (1), 59–66 (2011)
8. Nidhi, C., Goel, P., Surender, K.: Developing the reliability model for availability and behavior analysis of a distillery using Regenerative Point Graphical Technique. IJIFR, **1**(4), 26–40 (2013). ISSN (Online) 2347-1697

9. Sharma Sandeep, P.: Behavioral analysis of whole grain flour mill using RPGT. IJETMAS, **3** (2015). ISSN (Online) 2349-4476
10. Goyal, G.: Behavioral analysis of two unit system with preventive maintenance and degradation in one unit after complete failure using RPGT. IJCMS, **4** (2015). ISSN 2347-8527
11. Gupta, R., Sharma, S., Bhardwaj, P.: Cost benefit analysis of a urea fertilizer manufacturing system model. J. Stat. Appl. Probab. Lett. **3**, 119–132 (2016)
12. Sethi, R., Garg, D.: Transient analysis of markovian queue model with multi stage service. In: REDSET 2016, pp. 264–272, 21–22 October 2016
13. Garg, D., Yadav, R.: Systems modeling and analysis: a case study of EAEP manufacturing plant. In: INDIACom-2017, IEEE ID-40353 (accepted for publication)
14. Kumar, R.: Availability modeling of two unit system subject to degradation perfect repair post failure is feasible using RPGT. In: International Conference on Emanations in Modern Technology and Engineering (ICEMTE-2017), vol. 5, no. 3, pp. 31–36 (2017). http://www.ijritcc.org/download/conferences/ICEMTE_2017/Track_6_(Others)/1487915588_23-02-2017.pdf. ISSN 2321-8169

Performance Analysis of Machine Learning Techniques on Big Data Using Apache Spark

Garima Mogha, Khyati Ahlawat(✉), and Amit Prakash Singh(✉)

University School of Information Communication and Technology, Guru Gobind Singh Indraprastha University, New Delhi, India
{garima.usict.008164,khyatiahlawat,amit}@ipu.ac.in

Abstract. Applying Intelligence to the machines is a need in today's world and this need leads to the evolution of machine learning. The analysis of data using machine learning algorithms is a trending research area and this analysis lead to some problems when the data comes out to be big data. This paper compares various classification based machine learning algorithms namely, Decision Tree Learning, Naïve Bayes, Random Forest and Support Vector Machines on big data using Apache Spark. The accuracy is evaluated to find out which classification based algorithm gives fast and better result.

Keywords: Big data · Apache spark · Machine learning · Apache hadoop

1 Introduction

Machines now-a-days are replacing humans gradually as the intelligence that is the main asset of human beings can be incorporated by machines. The evolution of machine learning in this ever trending big data era is an amiable area of research concern, leading to a quest for incorporating intelligence in machine to exploit the data it to full potential. The new emerging technologies are changing the practical usage of the current work accordingly. Apache Hadoop is a framework used for batch file processing that focuses on the analysis of static data. It works well when periodic batch processing is done but it gives inappropriate results when it comes to dynamic datasets. This drawback leads to the development of more flexible and scalable framework that is Apache Spark [2, 13]. The main advantage of Apache Spark is that it can be used for batch file processing as well as real time data processing in a very efficient manner. It can handle iterative and streaming processes with speed and accuracy [2]. Humans are capable enough to design a field in which machines deal with the various real time scenarios by learning from their past experiences in an effective and efficient manner. The more possibility of learning within a machine incorporates more its ability to intelligently handle the various applicable scenarios on its own [8]. If the performance of the machines improves with the tasks assigned to it using experiences then it can be stated that which algorithms leads to the best possible results.

B. Panda et al. (Eds.): REDSET 2017, CCIS 799, pp. 17–26, 2018.
https://doi.org/10.1007/978-981-10-8527-7_2

Knowledge Discovery in Database

The filtering of relevant information from voluminous, heterogeneous data sources by applying various theories, methodologies and techniques to attain some sense out of the extracted data and information. Knowledge Database Discovery (KDD) has various phases that includes (a) Selection of the relevant data, (b) applying pre-processing (c) transforming it to required data, (d) applying data mining techniques to the transformed data to get various patterns and (e) lastly, evaluating the patterns giving emergent knowledge [3]. This paper comprises of four sections which are organized as follows: Sect. 2 discusses various categories of machine learning for Big Data and various algorithms for machine learning, Sect. 3 presents a framework for the experiment, description of the dataset used in the experiment, description of the tool Apache Spark used for experimentation and the results, Sect. 4 is the conclusion followed by section "References".

2 Machine Learning for Big Data

Machine Learning is a science in which the machines are led to learn the predictions that are possible for the given input afterwards they are intended to take their own decisions based on those predictions [10].

Machine Learning enables the intelligence in the machines by recognizing the past patterns and applying some data mining methods. These widely used data mining methods [2] are:

Pattern Matching: The intelligence is embedded after examining the frequent running trends in the data that defines the rules for further decisions.

Classification: In this method data is classified into training and testing sets after which a classifier model is competent using training to predict class labels.

Clustering: It divides the dataset into number of groups also called clusters for the data analysis [14].

Regression: It recognizes the relationship between the dependent and independent variables using a continuous set of data [2].

2.1 Categories of Machine Learning

2.1.1 Supervised Learning

Supervised learning whose main theme is Class learning in which the description of the data has been given, on anatomizing which, one can predict to which class a new entity can be appended [3, 8]. For example a variety of cars are analyzed and the different classes to different categories of cars are assigned. If the racing cars form a class, then the description given to all the cars that come under racing cars should be similar. Thus if the description of a new car is provided, will lead to learning from that description and extracting knowledge to predict whether the given car can be categorized as racing car or not [8] (Fig. 1).

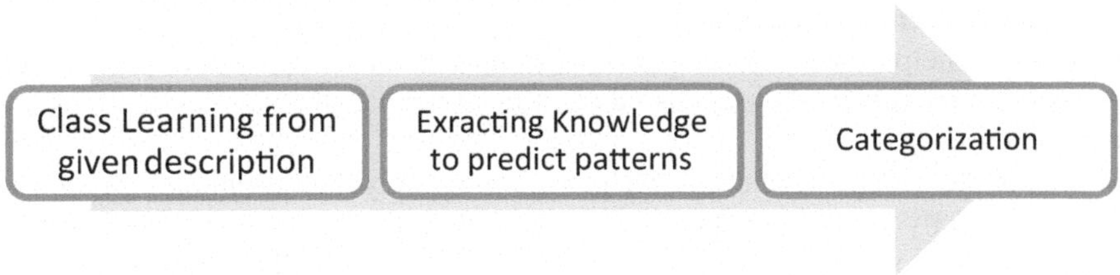

Fig. 1. Supervised learning

2.1.1.1 Classification

The classification is a method which predicts the class of the new entity based on the previous history of classification model [8, 11].

For example: A customer wants a loan from a bank. The bank has two classes of high risk customers and low risk customers. Based on the financial history if the customer comes under the class of low risk customers the bank will grant loan to the customers but if it comes under the class of high risk customers that means either the income of the customer, savings of the customer or both are less than the required amount needed by the bank to grant the loan. Therefore, it is easier for the bank to classify and make a decision if the information about its past financial history is provided [8].

2.1.2 Unsupervised Learning

The supervised learning intends to map the inputs to the output whose actual values are stipulated by some entity. But, in unsupervised learning this external entity is missing. By providing only input data, the pretention is to find out the regularities in the input. The common data patterns have a particular structure that separates the pattern from others. Afterwards, we try to examine what can happen or what not [3, 8].

2.1.2.1 Clustering

The clustering is a method in which the input dataset is assorted in such a way that they form informative patterns called clusters. Each cluster gathers similar instances out of whole dataset [3].

For example: A company having dataset related to airlines in which the past information of the booked airlines, distance, origin of the journey, destination of journey, delay (if any) as well as customer's personal details are stored. Also it stores all the past booking and transaction of all the airlines. The bourne is to distribute the profile of the airlines which are chiefly used to travel and to discover the reason behind the using the services of a particular airline, whether it's the cheap fares, the services provided, flight delay, traveling time of the number of halts in the journey. Here the clustering groups the airlines with similar instances (ar attributes) to same cluster. Once the clusters are recognized, the further strategies are applied by considering the most suitable instance for flight booking. Also, It helps the other aspiring airlines to improve their lacking field by dissecting the past data.

The applications of clustering includes Image Compression, Document Clustering, and Bio-Informatics [8].

2.1.3 Reinforcement Learning

This algorithm helps to consider the series of actions taken to implement a policy, which assesses the goodness of the actions taken at the intermediate stage by learning from past experiences [3].

For example: in a game of chess, the game is good only if all the moves for the game are taken correctly at the right time. Here it is well considered that the game is won if all intermediate moves are skilfully taken. Thus to win a game like chess having many possible series of moves with limited number of moves, requires a good learning algorithm to carry out the task of winning the game. Reinforcement learning is popularly used in applications like robotics and strategic games [3].

2.2 Classification Based Algorithms

2.2.1 Decision Tree Learning

Decision Tree is the widely used machine learning algorithm that helps in approximately discreate valued functions. It is a tree like structure having root node, internal node and leaf nodes [11, 18]. At each interval node a condition is applied to test some attribute of the instances based on which the node is splitted further to get the possible values of the attribute. Whenever a new node comes starting from the root moving down the tree, the attribute is tested specified by the node to classify in the required class. The Attribute Selection is a parameter to select the best splitting criterion for dividing the data D from class labeled training records to individual classes [5, 11, 21].

Gini Impurity Index

The Gini Index is a parameter used to check node impurity that searches for the homogeneity of the labels at the nodes [5, 11]. It is given by:

$$Gini(d) = 1 - \sum_{n=1}^{m} P_n^2$$

Where ‘m’ is the number of distinct classes and P_n is the probability that a tuple in dataset ‘d’ belongs to class C_n which can be evaluated by $(C_{n,d})|d$ over m classes [11].

2.2.2 Naïve Bayes

The Bayesian learning methods uses a probabilistic approach to inference. It calculates the explicit probabilities and delivers important perspective for explaining many learning algorithms that do not calculates probabilities [12, 17].

Naïve Bayes is a classification algorithm which considers that all features are independent and if a feature is present in a class then some other feature in the same class has no relation with the above mentioned feature as all are independent [12].

The prior probability is the initial probability that supposition holds, where s is the hypothesis and d is the training data. Here, P(s/d) is the posterior probability of s given by:

$$P\left(\frac{s}{d}\right) = \frac{\left(P(s)P\left(\frac{d}{s}\right)\right)}{P(d)}$$

Also, P(s) is the prior probability that s holds, P(d) is the prior probability that training data will conformed, P(d/s) is the probability of conforming data given that hypothesis s holds is true and P(s/d) is the probability of s holds given the data d is true [1, 17].

2.2.3 Random Forest

The Random Forest algorithm is an ensemble of decision trees that reduces the overfitting risk of decision trees [1]. It trains more than one decision trees each on random training dataset or random subset of input patterns and find outs the overall accuracy by combining the prediction [8]. For predicting a point in random forest that uses multiple tree classification for a particular class in which tree votes for, is done and the class with maximum votes is selected by the model. Each decision tree is different from another as random forest intercalates some randomness in the training procedures. The aggregated prediction of each decision tree and the accuracy are calculated that improves the overall performance on the test data [8, 16].

2.2.4 Support Vector Machine

The Support Vector Machine algorithm classifies linear and non-linear data in such a way that a non-linear mapping is used to obtain a higher dimensional dataset by transforming the training dataset. Support Vector Machine creates a maximum margin hyperplane which is a decision boundary that separates the essential tuples (also called support vectors) belong to a class within the new transformed dimension. The data belong to different classes are separated by a hyperplane that can be distinguish using support vectors and margins that are defined by support vectors [11]. It can solve the scientific problems as well as problems related to complex datasets.

3 Experiment and Simulation

3.1 A Framework Used for Classification Based Model

In this section, a framework is provided that delineates the procedure that is applied to do a comparative study of various classification based algorithms. Also, it outlines the components included that compare which algorithm gives the best accuracy for this work (Fig. 2).

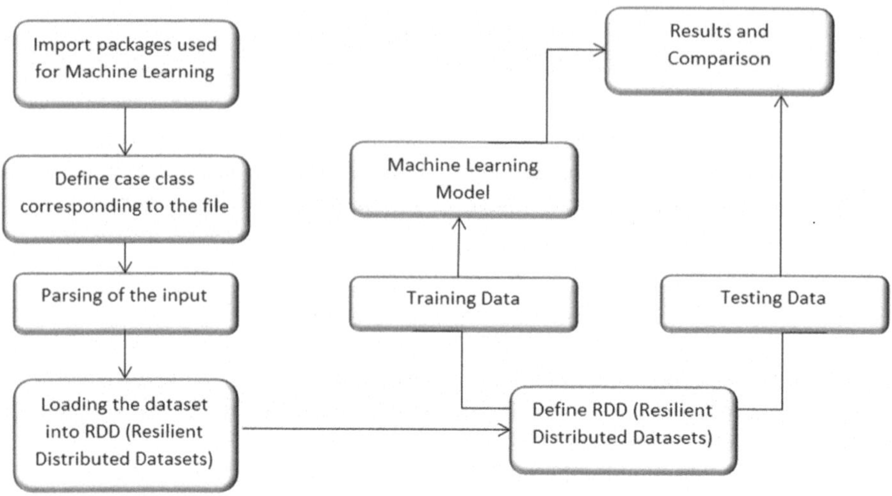

Fig. 2. Framework for classification model

3.2 Dataset Description

In order to find the accuracy of the model efficiently, the Airlines Dataset was procreated and downloaded from [20] which consists of 17 attributes and approximately half a

Table 1. Dataset description

S. No.	Attribute name	Data type	Range
1.	Day of month	String	1–31
2.	Day of week	String	1–7
3.	Carrier code	String	-
4.	Unique identifier [tail number]	String	-
5.	Flight number	Integer	1–8404
6.	Airport ID of origin	String	-
7.	Airport code of origin	String	-
8.	Airport ID of destination	String	-
9.	Airport code of destination	String	-
10.	Scheduled departure time	Double	0–1440 min
11.	Actual departure time	Double	0–1440 min
12.	Departure delay	Double	0–1440 min
13.	Scheduled arrival time	Double	0–1440 min
14.	Actual arrival time	Double	0–1440 min
15.	Actual delay	Double	0–1440 min
16.	Elapsed time	Double	0–1440 min
17.	Distance	Integer	31–4983 miles

million instances. On the dataset, various machine learning algorithms are applied and a comparative study has been done (Table 1).

3.3 Big Data Processing Tool: Apache Spark

For computing the machine learning algorithms on big data, Apache Spark is used which an open source cluster computing framework provides in-memory processing of data. Apache Spark is a distributed data processing engine which is 10 times better than Apache Hadoop as it can perform online and streaming data analysis which was lacking in Hadoop [2, 13].

Apache Spark not only meets the challenges of big data but also supports an efficacious set of machine learning algorithms [2]. This general purpose platform can operate real time data analysis on dynamic dataset whereas Apache Hadoop was limited to batch processing on static data [2, 19].

Also, Apache Spark is a fast, scalable and flexible platform for big data analysis. Apache Spark reinforces multiple programming languages like Scala, Java and python [1]. The Resilient Distributed Dataset (RDD) is the batch of data which is distributed for parallel processing that makes Apache Spark highly scalable and fast than other frameworks [1, 15].

The architecture of Apache Spark explains the distributed in-memory execution of code which is broadly classified into three components that is Driver Program, Cluster Manager and Worker Node. The Driver Program is a client program that defines SparkContext. Also, it requests the Cluster Manager for the resources and submits the Jar files along with configured dependencies to the Worker Nodes.

The Worker Nodes are processes that execute jobs, return respective results and secure the data. Whereas Cluster Manager manages, allocates the resource and keep track of the status of the submitted jobs [22, 23] (Fig. 3).

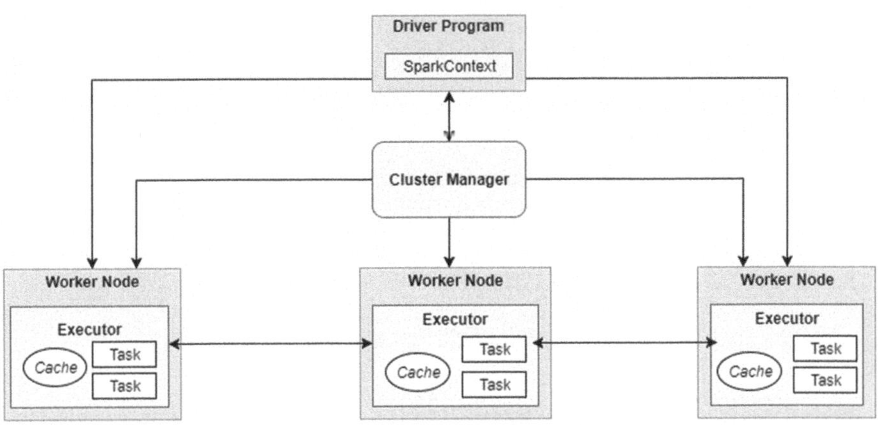

Fig. 3. Architecture of apache spark

3.4 Result Analysis

In this section, the result of various classification algorithms is shown that compares the accuracy of the algorithms (Table 2 and Figs. 4, 5, 6, 7 and 8).

Table 2. Performance evaluation of classification algorithms

S. No.	Experiment technique	Accuracy
1.	Decision tree learning	0.6970503
2.	Naïve Bayes	0.5770275
3.	Random forest	0.6946061
4.	Support vector machines	0.6128629

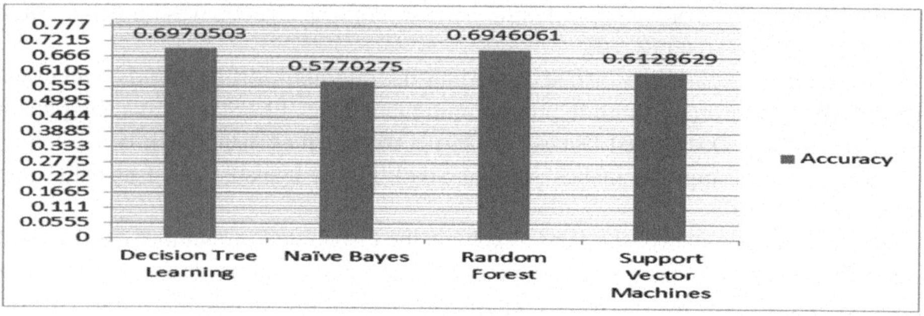

Fig. 4. Performance comparison of classification algorithms

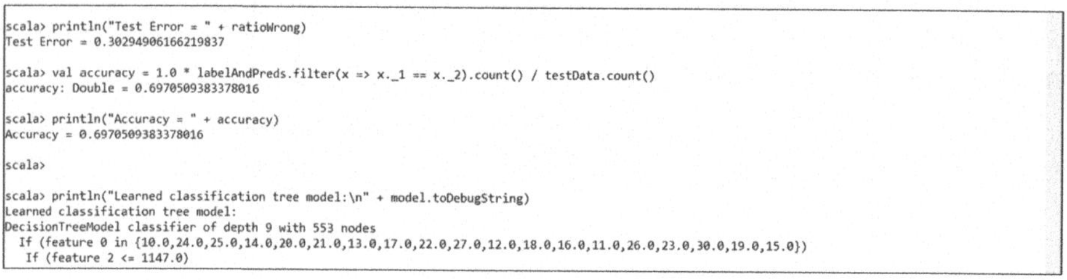

```
scala> println("Test Error = " + ratioWrong)
Test Error = 0.30294906166219837

scala> val accuracy = 1.0 * labelAndPreds.filter(x => x._1 == x._2).count() / testData.count()
accuracy: Double = 0.6970509383378016

scala> println("Accuracy = " + accuracy)
Accuracy = 0.6970509383378016

scala>

scala> println("Learned classification tree model:\n" + model.toDebugString)
Learned classification tree model:
DecisionTreeModel classifier of depth 9 with 553 nodes
  If (feature 0 in {10.0,24.0,25.0,14.0,20.0,21.0,13.0,17.0,22.0,27.0,12.0,18.0,16.0,11.0,26.0,23.0,30.0,19.0,15.0})
   If (feature 2 <= 1147.0)
```

Fig. 5. Result of decision tree learning

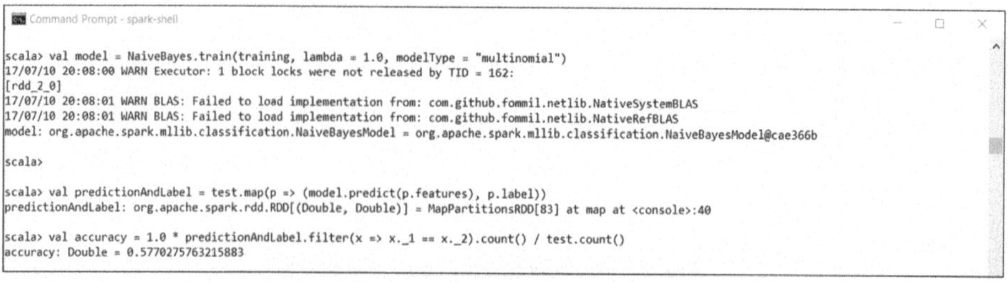

```
Command Prompt - spark-shell

scala> val model = NaiveBayes.train(training, lambda = 1.0, modelType = "multinomial")
17/07/10 20:08:00 WARN Executor: 1 block locks were not released by TID = 162:
[rdd_2_0]
17/07/10 20:08:01 WARN BLAS: Failed to load implementation from: com.github.fommil.netlib.NativeSystemBLAS
17/07/10 20:08:01 WARN BLAS: Failed to load implementation from: com.github.fommil.netlib.NativeRefBLAS
model: org.apache.spark.mllib.classification.NaiveBayesModel = org.apache.spark.mllib.classification.NaiveBayesModel@cae366b

scala>

scala> val predictionAndLabel = test.map(p => (model.predict(p.features), p.label))
predictionAndLabel: org.apache.spark.rdd.RDD[(Double, Double)] = MapPartitionsRDD[83] at map at <console>:40

scala> val accuracy = 1.0 * predictionAndLabel.filter(x => x._1 == x._2).count() / test.count()
accuracy: Double = 0.5770275763215883
```

Fig. 6. Result of Naïve Bayes algorithm

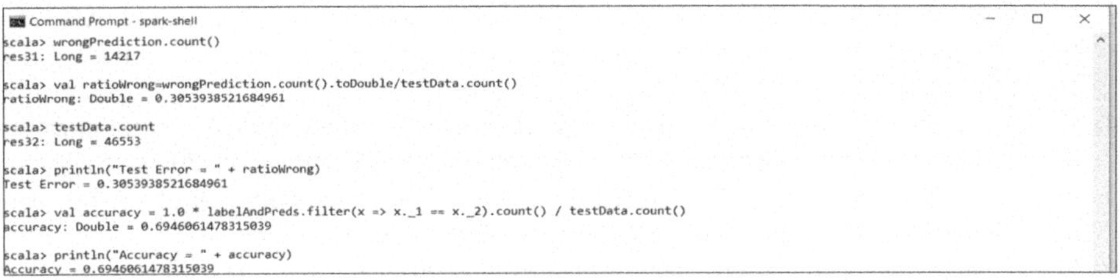

Fig. 7. Result of random forest algorithm

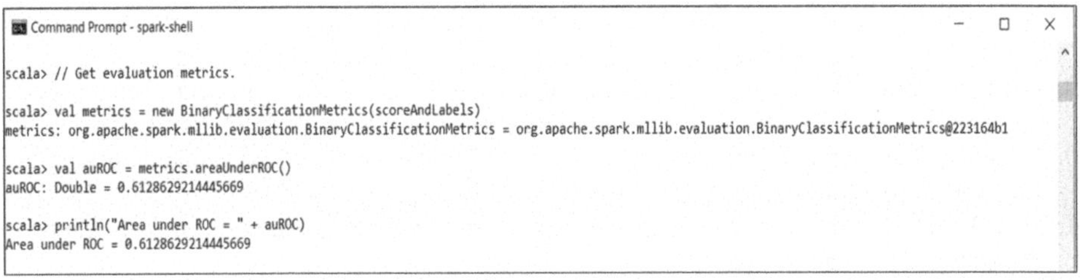

Fig. 8. Result of support vector machine

4 Conclusion

This paper discussed a framework in which a comparative study has been done which evaluates the performance of various classification based algorithms on Big Data using Apache Spark. The dataset used in the paper is a Big Data having approximately half a million rows, therefore Apache Spark is the most efficient Big Data tool to rely on which does fast, scalable and flexible data processing. Here, the accuracy provided by Decision Tree Learning is the highest so it is better among the other algorithms followed by Random Forest, Support Vector Machine and then Naïve Bayes. However, these results can be data specific as we have used only one dataset. The Data Science is an emergent field which is enthralled by other areas by indirectly digging the depths of artificial intelligence and machine learning. As per the future scope, same analysis can be done on multiple datasets so that influence of specific dataset on performance of algorithms can be predicted. Also, real time data analysis can be used on Apache Spark for dynamic dataset.

References

1. Gupta, G.P., Kulariya, M.: A framework for fast and efficient cyber security network intrusion detection using apache spark. Procedia Comput. Sci. **93**, 824–831 (2016)
2. Shyam, R., Bharathi Ganesh, H.B., Kumar, S., Poornachandran, P., Soman, K.P.: Apache spark a big data analytics platform for smart grid. Procedia Technol. **21**, 171–178 (2015)

3. Kavakiotis, I., Tsave, O., Salifoglou, A., Maglaveras, N., Vlahavas, I., Chouvarda, I.: Machine learning and data mining methods in diabetes research. Comput. Struct. Biotechnol. J. **15**, 104–116 (2017)
4. Kumar, D., Singh, R., Kumar, A., Sharma, N.: An adaptive method of PCA for minimization of classification error using Naïve Bayes classifier. Procedia Comput. Sci. **70**, 9–15 (2015)
5. Zhang, P., Wu, X., Wang, X., Bi, S.: Short-term load forecasting based on big data technologies. CSEE J. Power Energy Syst. **1**(3), 59–67 (2015)
6. Liu, S., Wang, X., Liu, M., Zhu, J.: Towards better analysis of machine learning models: a visual analytics perspective. Vis. Inf. **1**(1), 48–56 (2017)
7. Panigrahi, S., Lenka, R.K., Stitipragyan, A.: A hybrid distributed collaborative filtering recommender engine using apache spark. Procedia Comput. Sci. **83**, 1000–1006 (2016)
8. Alpaydin, E.: Introduction to Machine Learning, 3rd edn. The MIT Press, Cambridge, London (2014)
9. Berthold, M.R., Borgelt, C., Höppner, F., Klawonn, F.: Guide to Intelligent Data Analysis, 2nd edn. Springer, London (2010). https://doi.org/10.1007/978-1-84882-260-3
10. Kelleher, J.D., Mac Namee, B., D'Arcy, A.: Fundamentals of Machine Learning for Predictive Data Analytics. The MIT Press, Cambridge, London (2015)
11. Han, J., Kamber, M.: Data Mining: Concepts and Techniques, 2nd edn. Morgan Kaufman Publishers, Burlington (2011)
12. Mitchell, T.M.: Machine Learning. Mcgraw Hill Education Private Limited, New York (1997)
13. Scott, J.A.: Getting Started with Apache Spark: Inception to Production, 1st edn. MapR Technologies, San Jose (2015)
14. Sivarajah, U., Kamal, M.M., Irani, Z., Weerakkody, V.: Critical analysis of big data challenges and analytical methods. J. Bus. Res. **70**, 263–286 (2017)
15. Reyes-Ortiz, J.L., Oneto, L., Anguita, D.: Big data analytics in the cloud: spark on Hadoop vs MPI/OpenMP on Beowulf. Procedia Comput. Sci. **53**, 121–130 (2015)
16. Shafique, M.A., Hato, E.: Classification of travel data with multiple sensor information using random forest. Transp. Res. Procedia **22**, 144–153 (2017)
17. Swetapadma, A., Yadav, A.: Protection of parallel transmission lines including inter-circuit faults using Naïve Bayes classifier. Alexandria Eng. J. **55**(2), 1411–1419 (2016)
18. Jayasree, V., Balan, R.S.: Money laundering regulatory risk evaluation using bitmap index-based decision tree. J. Assoc. Arab Univ. Basic Appl. Sci. **23**, 96–102 (2017)
19. Götz, M., Richerzhagen, M., Bodenstein, C., Cavallaro, G., Glock, P., Riedel, M., Benediktsson, J.A.: On scalable data mining techniques for earth science. Procedia Comput. Sci. **51**, 2188–2197 (2015)
20. Github. https://github.com/caroljmcdonald/sparkmldecisiontree/blob/master/data/rita2014jan.csv. Accessed 10 July 2017
21. Apache Spark. https://spark.apache.org/docs/2.1.0/mllib-decision-tree.html#basic-algorithm. Accessed 10 July 2017
22. Packt Pub. https://www.packtpub.com/books/content/spark-%E2%80%93-architecture-and-first-program. Accessed 23 Sept 2017
23. Apache Spark. https://spark.apache.org/docs/latest/cluster-overview.html. Accessed 23 Sept 2017

A Comparative Study of Consumption Behavior of Pharmaceutical Drugs

Keerti Jain(✉), Priyanka Sharma, and Medathati Jayalakshmi

School of Engineering, GD Goenka University, Sohna, Gurgaon, India
keerti2401@gmail.com, sharmapriyanka.11@gmail.com, medathatijayalakshmi@gmail.com

Abstract. The research is done to identify the significance of gender, profession, income and age on the consumption behavior of various classes of drugs. In this research paper a comparative study is carried out to understand about the consumption behavior of pharmaceutical drugs using primary data collected from NCR area, India through questionnaire and analyzed using R-programming. On analysis we found that antibiotics and analgesic classes of drug are most frequently used by consumers whereas consumption of significantly depends on age group. It was also found that there is no significant difference in consumption behaviour due to gender and profession. However income of the respondent is affecting consumption of newly launched drugs of same salt. These results will be helpful for pharmacy market to understand consumption behaviour of common people.

Keywords: Pharmaceutical drugs · Consumption behavior · Classes of drug Consumption behavior · Consumer behavior

1 Introduction

A pharmaceutical drugs or medications are used in diagnosis, cure, and treatment or prevention of diseases. Medications are classified as prescription drug which is prescribed by physician and over-the-counter drugs which consumers themselves can order. Another way to classify medications are by mode of action i.e. route of administration, biological system affected, or therapeutic effects. Drug therapy is an important part of medical field and relies on pharmacology for continual advancement and on pharmacy for appropriate management. Drug development & discovery is undertaken by pharmaceutical companies, scientists, academicians and governments. Governments generally regulate what type and how drugs can be marketed. A number of classes of drugs are available in the market like antipyretic, analgesic, antimalarial, anti-biotic, antiseptics, hormone replacement, tranquilizer, anti-inflammatory, cardiovascular, anti-convulsant, anti-allergic, antihistamine, gastrointestinal, antidiabetic, antineoplastic, antiviral, fertility, HIV drugs, endocrine disorder drug, metabolic drugs, ophthalmic etc. from more than one pharmaceutical company.

The structure of pharmaceutical industry is very interesting, since the prices of medicines of various pharmaceutical companies are almost similar. There is least

B. Panda et al. (Eds.): REDSET 2017, CCIS 799, pp. 27–33, 2018.
https://doi.org/10.1007/978-981-10-8527-7_3

competition in price as compared to other daily consumer goods trade. Also, due to advancement in research and technology in Pharmaceutical industries, nowadays more product options are available as more generic medicines are in the market which can challenge original products with their lower price. Hence, the focus of the research is on customers who are paying large for common pharmaceutical drugs and their consumer behaviour in regards to pharmacies and similarly priced over-the-counter (OTC) medicines, thus medicines which are not on prescription but are available to all consumers and that are advertised publicly [1, 2].

Consumer behaviour is a very interesting topic for marketing professionals because command on this field can be vital and game changer in terms of choosing precise marketing strategy, and if they get it right, it make business prosperous.

The understanding of the process that an individual or a group go through to satisfy the requirements by selecting and buying as well as using and disposing products is said to be consumer behaviour. This process is not only related to products as it can likewise be ideas and experiences that satisfy the need. If an organization understand the behavior and consumption pattern of the consumers, then they can adapt such strategies that will give them the preferred outcome in terms of consumer response.

The 4P's people, product, place and promotion are the important concept of marketing. The acquaintance of consumer behaviour helps companies to determine their this marketing mix [3, 4]. The exposure of a consumers to and which will affect their behavior, this can be stimuli using the above mentioned 4P's of marketing. The ultimate purpose of an organization is to exist and to satisfy the needs of their consumers. A company could be successful only if they know what is the needs and requirements of their consumers. A knowledge of consumer behaviour helps to explore and understand these needs and requirements.

The way that consumer behave and how they purchase goods and services is influenced by different factors like cultural, social, personal, psychographic and psychological with these many factors, media also contributed a lot for changing consumer trends [5–7].

Culture creates the foundation of the individual's values, opinions and behaviour. These traits create what the consumer wants and therefore do affect the way the consumer acts. Consumers buying behaviour also affected by group of people with whom they surrounded. This social group include family, friends and colleagues as well as on social status & role. The consumers are usually classified or segmented according to their individualities, personality type, age & stage in life cycle, profession & economic statuses, life style as well as self-concept that shape their consumer behaviour. The consumer's pattern of consumption, allocation of money and choice of products is based on the lifestyle also. Lifestyle is unique which is characterized by the consumer's life interests. Lifestyle differences resulted into differentiation of behavior even if consumers share many similar factors like social class, leisure time activities and cultural interests. These contrasts make up the consumer's own unique lifestyle that influences the consumer's consumption pattern. Psychological factors like motivation, perception, learning, beliefs and attitudes also affects consumption behaviour. The process of choosing, organizing and interpreting stimuli, consumers create their own perception about any product, this perception of a person differs to one another, the buying behaviour does as well. Similarly learning, beliefs and attitude will also influence purchasing of pharmaceutical drugs by an individual or prescribed by practitioners. Psychographic factor which includes values, attitudes & lifestyle survey, is also equally important for marketers so as to understand consumer behaviour.

The aim of the research is to find out about factors influencing the customer's choice of pharmacy as well as OTC medicines. The aim is to understand and explore consumer behavior and to relate it to pharmacy clientele.

The results aid to understand the pharmaceutical market a little better and to gain knowledge on pharmacy customers in the National Capital Region, India.

2 Methodology

The research work is based on literature of marketing and consumer behaviour towards the various products. Relevant information is obtained from online publications and websites of the pharmaceutical industry and theories and former discoveries. To know consumption behaviour of pharmaceutical drugs the quantitative research is conducted as a survey in the National Capital Region (NCR), India. The survey has been conducted with a questionnaire form in paper as well as Google form. The questionnaire contains twenty two research questions, out of which four questions are used to collect personal information about the respondent. However, the information, cannot identify the respondent later on. Additionally the survey contains information about the purpose of the study and points out that participation is voluntary. The questionnaire contains closed-ended, multiple-choice questions, as well as questions asking the respondent to rank a few options depending on their importance to the respondent. The questions are designed to be clear so that respondents are able to answer quickly and independently, also elderly people.

Table 1. Consumption of various class of medicines

Class of medicine	Consumption
Antipyretics	41.9%
Analgesic	50%
Antibotics	51.6%
Antiseptics	14.5%
Anti-depressant	19.8%
Anti-inflammatory	19.4%
Anti-allergic	22.6%

A questionnaire in the research is always a suitable way of collecting relevant information, since it is useful in collecting information from a large amount of individuals. A questionnaire also serves the purpose well since it facilitates to gather information more quickly and about a vast set of questions. In order to best reach customers of all ages the research was conducted online as well as through a paper form.

For the comparative study seven classes of medicines are considered namely Anti-pyretics (used in fever), Analgesics (Pain reliever), Anti-biotic, Antiseptics, Anti-depressant (tranquilizers), Anti-inflammatory and Anti-allergic as shown in Table 1. Also four to five medicines of each class of drugs are considered for study as shown in Table 2.

Table 2. List of medicine of all the categories along with percentage of their usage by the respondents.

Class of medicine	Brand of medicine (Consumption)					
Antipyretics	Combiflame (47%)	Crocin (12%)	Ibuprofen (11%)	Paracetamol (53%)	Sumo (12%)	Other (3%)
Analgesic	Vovran (10%)	Aspirin (18%)	Crocin (44%)	Combiflame (44%)	Saridon (2%)	Other (4%)
Anti-botics	Ciplox (40%)	Betrium DS (6%)	Azethromycin (28%)	Roxid (6%)	Amoxcylin (38%)	Other (3%)
Antiseptics	Betadin (39%)	Sofrmycin (32%)	Savlon (37%)	Dettol (65%)	Borolin/ BoroPlus (20%)	Other (0%)
Anti-depressant	Dixad (13%)	Alpraquil (13%)	Metrozol (42%)	Clobazam (0%)	Stilnox (25%)	Other (25%)
Anti-inflammatory	Moov/Volini (76%)	Zandu Baam / TigerBaam (20%)	Iodex (27%)	Vicks (39%)	Other (2%)	
Anti-allergic	Avil (35%)	Cetrizin (56%)	Allegra (15%)	Montaire-Fx (8%)	Levocet (6%)	Other (6%)

Apart from this, four other parameters are considered i.e. sources of information about the medicines, consumption of newly launched drugs of same salts, influence of brand ambassador of particular medicines and whether respondents take drug as prescribed by doctors.

R–programming is used to identify, is there any significant difference on gender, profession, income and age groups over source of information of medicine, influence of brand ambassadors of the drugs, preference of newly launched drugs of same salt, also which class of medicines are preferred and whether respondents take drug as prescribed by doctors. For this analysis chi-square test is applied on various combinations.

Apart from this chi-square test is also applied to explore is there any significant difference on the gender, profession, income and age groups over frequency of consumption of all the seven categories of drugs which are considered for the present study.

Chi-square test is also applied to identify, is there any significant difference on gender, profession, income and age group over different medicines of various classes of drugs consumed by the respondents.

3 Result and Discussion

The research has been conducted with 243 respondents practicing different professions. 18% of the respondents are of age group between 15 years to 25 years, Majority of respondent are between ages 25 years to 45 years 38% of the respondents belong to age group 25 years to 35 years, 27% are of age group 35 years to 45 years. Very few of them only 5% respondents belongs to age group 45 years to 55 years and rest 12% are above 55 years. There are 53% respondents are male and rest 47% are females.

Majority of the respondents around 70% of them belongs to service class, 18% are students, 10% are self-employed only and 2% belongs to business class. 17% of the respondents are either housewives or students who are unemployed. 11% have annual income less than 2.5 lakhs. 33% of respondents has annual income between 2.5 lakhs to 5 lakhs. 23% have 5 lakhs to 10 lakhs and rest of them have annual income more than 10 lakhs. 47% of the respondents take medicines mostly as prescribed by the doctors, 29% take medicines always which are prescribed by the doctors. 24% of them follows doctor's prescription sometimes.

Around 50% of the respondents believe in the consumption of newly launched drug of the same salt sometimes. 20% never try newly launched drugs of same salt. 27% of them often try new drugs of same salt. Only 3% of the respondent always try newly launched drugs of same salt. 68% of the respondents never influenced by brand ambassador of a particular drug. 18% influenced sometimes while 11% influenced often. Only 3% of the respondents influence by the brand ambassadors always.

From the data it is clear that 90% of the respondents consult doctors. Sometimes 35% of the respondents take medicine as prescribed by Chemists. Even 27% of the respondents take medicines as suggested by their relatives or friends. Internet/Print media or Television/Radio are rarely source of information about medicines to the respondents.

Table 1 shows that Antibiotics and Analgesic are commonly consumed by the respondents, almost 50% of the respondents use these medicines. 42% respondent use to take Antipyretics. Around 20% respondent consume Anti-inflammatory, Anti-depressant and Anti-allergic. Only around 15% respondent use Antiseptics. Among antipyretics Paracetamol is most popular followed by Combiflame and Crocin, though Corcin and Combiflame are most popular in analgesic category, Asprin and Vovran are also used in this category but are rarely used. Ciplox, Amoxcylic and Azethromycin are popular anti-biotic others are rarely used. Dettol is the most popular antibiotic, Betadin, Sofromycin and Savlon are also used by people as anti-biotic but Borolin or Boroplus are rarely used in this category.

Metrozol is popularly used as anti-depressant, 25% of the respondents of the category are also stilnox as anti-depressant. 25% of the respondents of is this category also consuming some other medicines. Moov and Volini are most popular Anti-inflammatory followed by Vicks, Indox, Zandu baam or Tiger baam are rarely used for this purpose. The most popular anti allergic is cetrizin, 55% of respondents of this category are consuming it as anti-allergic, some of the respondents also consuming Avail as anti-allergic, and others medicines of this category are rarely used. Table 2 shows the list of medicine of all the categories with are considered for the present study, along with percentage of their usage by the respondent.

From the Table 3, it is clear that most of the respondents take medicines rarely. Still Analgesic are commonly used by respondents, 23% of respondent take Analgesic at least once in a month. 13% of respondents are taking Antipyretics once in a month. 11% of respondents take Anti-inflammatory once in a month. Very few respondents use to take Anti-depressant. Those who take it, most of the time they have to take it on daily basis.

Table 3. Consumption pattern of various class of medicines

Frequency of consumption	Class of medicine						
	Anti-pyretics	Analgesic	Anti-biotics	Anti-septics	Anti-depressant	Anti-inflammatory	Anti-allergic
Daily	5%	2%	0%	4%	6%	2%	2%
Once/twice a week	5%	5%	7%	2%	0%	4%	5%
Once in 15 days	2%	12%	0%	2%	2%	4%	5%
Once in a month	13%	23%	14%	8%	2%	11%	7%
Rarely	76%	59%	80%	85%	90%	80%	80%

Chi-square test at 5% level of significance shows that there is no significant difference due to gender and profession, on various parameters included in the present research. However it is found that there is significant difference due to income on consumption of newly launched drugs of same salts. The respondents having income 2.5–5 lakhs they are quite liberal in taking newly launched drugs of same salt. If the found drugs of same salt at cheaper rate they prefer to take them. While respondents of income group less than 2.5 lakhs rarely purchase newly launched drugs of same salts. May be due to lack of knowledge and awareness. Respondents having income greater than 10 lakhs are also not too interested in newly launched drugs of same salt.

Also, it is found from the study that there is significant difference due to age on the consumption of anti-biotic and anti-inflammatories. Anti-biotic are highly consumed by the respondents of age group 15 years to 25 years and age group 45 years to 55 years.

4 Conclusion

On analysis we found that antibiotics and analgesic classes of drug are most frequently used by consumers whereas consumption of these drugs are significantly depend on age group. Gender and profession are not effecting the consumption behaviour of the various classes of drugs. It is also found from the study that income of the respondents is affecting consumption of newly launched drugs, may be due to lots of variation in the cost of medicines of same salt. The present study is useful for pharmacy industry and market to explore consumption behaviour of common people.

References

1. Pujari, N.M., Sachan, A.K., Kumari, P., Dubey, P.: Study of consumer's pharmaceutical buying behavior towards prescription and non-prescription drugs. J. Med. Health Res. **1**(3), 10–18 (2016)
2. Kamath, K.: Consumer behavior towards consuming medicines without prescription in Pune City – an empirical analysis. Int. J. Manag. Soc. Sci. **3**(2), 930–946 (2015)
3. Kotler, P.: Marketing Management, 11th edn., 706 p. Prentice Hall, Upper Saddle River (2003)
4. Kotler, P., Wong, V., Saunders, J., Armstrong, G.: Principles of Marketing, 4th edn., 954 p. Pearson Education Limited, London (2005)

5. Solomon, M.R.: Consumer Behaviour: Buying, Having and Being, 7th edn. Prentice Hall, Upper Saddle River (2006). 654 p. ISBN 0-13-218694-2
6. Solomon, M., Bamossy, G., Askegaard, S.: Consumer Behavior: A European Perspective. Prentice Hall, Upper Saddle River (1999). 589 p. ISBN 0-13-751983-4
7. Kumar, A.H., John, S.F., Senith, S.: A study on factors influencing consumer buying behavior in cosmetic products. Int. J. Sci. Res. Publ. **4**(9), 1–6 (2014). ISSN 2250-3153

Trend Analysis of Machine Learning Research Using Topic Network Analysis

Deepak Sharma[1(✉)], Bijendra Kumar[1], and Satish Chand[2]

[1] Department of Computer Engineering, Netaji Subash Institute of Technology, New Delhi, India
deepak.btg@gmail.com, bizender@gmail.com

[2] School of Computer and Systems Sciences, Jawaharlal Nehru University, New Delhi, India
schand20@gmail.com

Abstract. In this paper, a topic network analysis approach is proposed which integrates topic modeling and social network analysis. We collected 16,855 scientific papers from six top journals in the field of machine learning published from 1997 to 2016 and analyzed them with the topic network. The dataset is break down into 4 intervals to identify topic trends and performed the time-series analysis of topic network. Our experimental results show centralization of the topic network has the highest score from 2002 to 2006, and decreases for next 5 years and increases again. For last 5 years, centralization of the degree centrality and closeness centrality increases, while centralization of the betweenness centrality decreases again. Also, data analytic and computer vision are identified as the most interrelated topic among other topics. Topics with the highest degree centrality evolve component analysis, text mining, biometric and computer vision according to time. Our approach extracts the interrelationships of topics, which cannot be detected with conventional topic modeling approaches, and provides topical trends of machine learning research.

Keywords: Topic network analysis · Social network analysis · Topic modeling Latent Dirichlet Allocation · Research trend analysis

1 Introduction

As the Big Data interest has exploded recently, machine learning techniques, which are key technologies for big data analysis, are getting attention by data scientist. Machine learning is an interdisciplinary area of research in various disciplines such as statistics, artificial intelligence, and databases, has been studied steadily since the word 'machine learning' coined by Arthur Samuel. In particular, since last two decades, existing machine learning techniques have been applied to large-scale data processing environments or have been extended to various application areas such as fraud detection, stock market, weather forecasting etc. Also, the algorithm is changed according to newly emerged technology. So understanding the machine learning research themes of the past two decades will help, studying current machine learning trends and applies it to practical applications.

B. Panda et al. (Eds.): REDSET 2017, CCIS 799, pp. 34–47, 2018.
https://doi.org/10.1007/978-981-10-8527-7_4

Text mining techniques have been commonly used to automatically classify documents [1, 2]. In particular, topic modeling [3] used to understand trend analysis in research from research papers and its many subjects of interest by applying the transform algorithm i.e. hot topic and less interested subject i.e. cold topic in finding research trends. In [4], a study of trends in the field of library and information science literature has performed using Latent Dirichlet Allocation (LDA) in order to analyze literature of information management. In [5], again LDA was applied to discovered topics in the field of law literature about contract law and discrimination.

The topic modeling technique is effective in analyzing research articles and trends according to research topics and time, but there are few studies considering the relationship between them. In particular, in research fields where interdisciplinary interactions such as machine learning are active, other topics may coexist within one topic rather than being independent, and the relationship between topics may be important information. Therefore, it is essential to re-analyze the topic that has a great influence on other topics, such as the relationship between topics, and the topic that coexists in a topic.

Social Network Analysis [6] is a popular technique for analyzing the relationships among interested entities. For text documents, keyword network analysis is used to find relationships between keywords in the document. In [7], a keyword is considered as a node in a research article and the connection established between the concurrent words found in a research article. The weight of each connection has assigned in a keyword network with the number of words appearing in another article. In the keyword network analysis, since each node is a single word, it is difficult to know a topic composed of a plurality of words as in the topic modeling, so there is a limitation in grasping macroscopic research trends.

In this study, a topic network analysis method that applies the network analysis technique to the topics generated as a result of topic modeling to analyze the relationship between topics. In order to construct a topic network, correlation amongst the topics discovered by LDA depending on the terms probability that appeared in common terms instead of the common number of terms between two different topics as weights. By analyzing the constructed topic network, we found the topics with the highest degree, closeness, and betweenness.

Next, to understand the trends of topics over time, we divided the articles published over two decades into four sets for 5 years to analyzed the topic network and analyzed the trends changes of the network structure over time.

In order to analyze the research topic, six prominent journals in the field of machine learning were selected, the subject term was designated as machine learning field and the research papers published in six journals for 20 years from 1997 to 2016. Almost 16,855, research articles were collected and applied to the topic network analysis. Table 1 shows, in particular, the summary of articles collected as 2988 papers published between 1997–2001, 3825 papers published between 2002–2006, 4641 papers published between 2007–2011, and 5401 papers published between 2012–2016 are analyzed.

Table 1. Distribution of number of articles in our corpus

Journals/Year	1997–2001	2002–2006	2007–2011	2012–2016
IEEE-PAMI	656	814	905	973
IEEE-NN	727	729	857	1047
JMLR	25	358	509	740
ScD-PR	821	1132	1507	1596
ScD-NN	547	563	618	742
Springer-ML	212	229	245	303
#ArticlesCount = 16855	2988	3825	4641	5401

In order to identify the trends of the most influential topics, the topics with the highest degree, closeness, and betweenness were analyzed. In the case of degree centrality, the topics are identified as component analysis, text mining, biometric, and computer vision. The topics of betweenness centrality are changed to image or video processing, text mining, biometric, and data analysis. Finally, topics of high closeness centrality are same as degree centrality.

It is noteworthy that the topic trends of text mining and biometric has emerged as an influential topic in several sections and these influential topics in research articles published between 2002–2006 and 2007–2011 respectively. In addition, since the patterns of degree centrality and closeness centrality are similar to each other, as shown in the topic network structure.

The contribution of this paper is as follows. First, we discussed a network analysis technique that combines topic modeling and network analysis to find topics. Then, established the link between topics that have influenced on other topics and topics that are closest to other topics. Secondly, we divide the papers published over the past 20 years into four sets, and then analyzed the topic network to identify changes in network structure over time and trends in influential topics.

This paper is composed as follows. In Sect. 2, the related research is reviewed. In Sect. 3, the topic network analysis technique discussed in this study is explained in detail and experimental results are presented. In Sect. 4, we review the research trends of topics that have been selected as influential topics and how the themes change with time. Finally, in Sect. 5 present conclusions and future research.

2 Related Work

The LDA algorithm [3] used in this study is a based on Bayesian probabilistic topic model. As the document consists of several topics and each topic is made up of the distribution of words, the topic is generated based on the probability of words. In [8], topic modeling by using LDA algorithm has been successfully applied to analyzing research trends. Also in [9], LDA has used in issue tracking systems that became a very popular subject in Twitter. However, since the LDA algorithm does not take into account the relationship between the topics, there is a limitation in that it is impossible to grasp the relationship between the research topics and the relationship between them.

In [10], the limitation of the LDA is overcome by introducing Correlated Topic Models (CTM) that takes into account the correlation between topics. CTM is a more realistic model because it generates a topic considering the case where another topic comes together in one topic. Also, considering the correlation between the topics is similar to the problem of grasping the relationship between the topics covered in this study. The topic network analysis proposed in this study uses the LDA algorithm to find independent topics first, and then builds a topic network by generating the correlation matrix amongst the topics discovered by LDA depending on the number of words that appeared in common between two different topics as weights to find degree centrality, closeness centrality, and betweenness to other topics.

In [11], a social network was constructed based on the authorship of their research articles, and then applied topic modeling to interested nodes to find out topics in the network structure. This study is most similar to the present study in that it integrates social network analysis and topic modeling techniques. The main point of this study is to analyze the social network structure of the formed topics. However, research on forming and analyzing a topic network based on correlation among topics generated as a result of topic modeling has been rarely performed.

The topic generated by topic modeling can consist of several subtopics. In [12], proposed a framework for integrating hierarchical LDA and latent topics to represent the hierarchy of topics. Also, in [13] proposed a non-Markov model for finding topics over time. The most significant difference between these studies and the present study is that the topic network analysis is based on the network structure that these topics can form rather than the topics found through topic modeling. Similar study was also being performed in [14] on trend analysis of data mining research, where only the common words between the topics were considered as weight for topic network graph. In our present study, we are generating the correlation amongst the topics discovered by LDA depending on the terms probability that appeared in common terms instead of the common number of terms between two different topics as weights.

3 Analysis of Topic Network

In this section, we first look at the methodology for analysis of topic network. Then, discussed the algorithm for topic network construction. Finally, we present the time-series analysis of the topic network.

3.1 Methodology for Analysis of Topic Network

Figure 1 shows the method for topic network analysis. We started collecting data with the preparation of a list of appropriate well-known journals for publishing high-quality research in machine learning. We include established journals like Journal of machine learning research (JMLR), Springer machine learning (Sp-ML), Science Direct pattern recognition (ScD-PR), Science Direct neural networks (ScD-NN), IEEE transactions on pattern analysis and machine intelligence (IEEE-PAMI) and IEEE transactions on neural networks (IEEE-NN). Titles and abstracts of research papers are taken from the electronic library of mentioned journal articles. We have considered only journal articles in our study. Table 1 lists the number of articles included in our study.

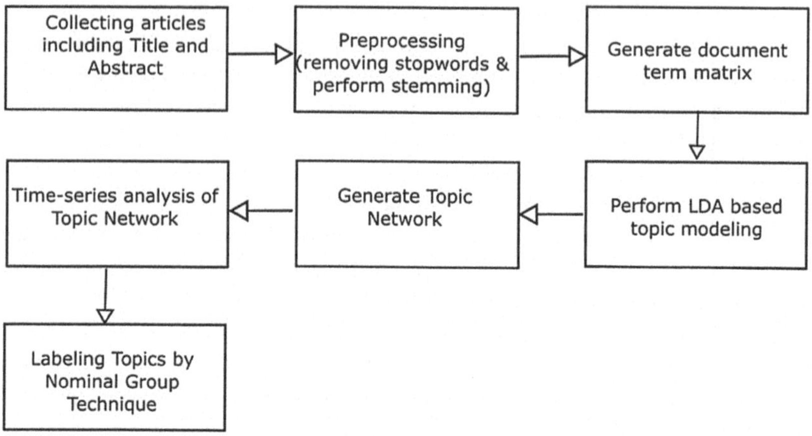

Fig. 1. Topic network analysis method

Next, the statistical analysis software environment R [15] and topicmodels package [16] were used to apply the LDA algorithm to the titles and abstracts of the collected articles. Preprocessing of the articles is done by filtering terms (words) by applying a custom stop word list including "title" and "abstract" along with the original stop words of the SMART system (available for download from ftp://ftp.cs.cornell.edu/pub/smart/english.stop) is a common pre-processing step in text mining. Next, applying stemming [17] to words before generating Document Term Matrix (DTM). Thereafter, perform LDA based topic modeling by using DTM. In order to select the most appropriate number of topics, we investigated with 10, 20, 30, and 40 topics. After this investigation, 30 is the number of topics which mostly suits for our study.

Based on the results of the topic modeling, we construct a topic network and compare the degree centrality, betweenness centrality, and closeness centrality defined in [6] as important measures of the network for the generated topic network. In order to examine the change process of topic network in the field of machine learning research for the past 20 years, we analyzed topic network by dividing it into 4 sets for 5 years from 1997–2001 refers as S1, 2002–2006 refers as S2, 2007–2011 refers as S3, and finally 2012–2016 refer as S4.

Finally, we applied Nominal Group techniques (NGT) [18] for labeling topics which are highly subjective. We have consulted two senior researchers and two peer researchers working in area of machine learning. The results in form of topic name for each topic have been ranked and selected through voting.

3.2 Topic Network Construction

Algorithm 1 is an algorithm for building a topic network. The LDA algorithm used in the experiment was the LDA () function of the topicmodels package that implements the model in [1].

In this paper, we generate a document-term matrix DTM $[f_{ij}]$ by inputting the title and abstract refer as TA, where f_{ij} is the frequency at which the j_{th} word appears in the i_{th} document. Here, considering only the frequency of terms. The most commonly terms found in machine learning field such as model, data, network, learn and algorithm are ranked at the top. Therefore, we selected terms whose frequency is greater than 2 and its word length is greater than 4.

```
Algorithm 1. Algorithm for Topic Network Construction
Input: a set of titles and abstracts TA
Output: Topic Weights Matrix TWM[i,j]
Step1. generate document-term matrix DTM[fi,j]
Step2. extract important terms by filtering out
fi,j>= 3 and len(word) >=4
Step3. create LDA model asldamodel with 30 topics
Step4. generate Topic Weights Matrix TWM based on the
correlation among topics
for each i from 0 to 29
  for each j from 0 to 29
    if i == j then
      TWM[i,j] <- 0
    else
      TWM[i,j] <- cor(ti,tj)
    endif
  endfor
endfor
```

The topic modeling was performed by applying the LDA algorithm to the generated document-word matrix. The hyper parameter value of alpha represents document-topic density is calculated as $50/k$ when k is the number of topics, and is set to 30. The beta represents topic-word density and its values for the word distribution for the topic can be estimated by fixing the topic distribution. In this study, we are filtered out the correlation coefficient among topics having value less than or equal to 0.02.

Table 2 shows the results of topic modeling by applying the LDA algorithm to the top ten keywords for 30 topics.

Table 2. Top 10 keywords in 30 topics from latent Dirichlet Allocation (1997–2016)

Topic0		Topic1		Topic2		Topic3		Topic4	
data,	number,	error,	show,	measur,	evalu,	recognit,	text,	approach,	improv,
cluster,	propos,	general,	loss,	differ,	rank,	face,	rate,	techniqu,	combin,
fuzzi,	real,	bound,	case,	similar,	metric,	databas,	facial,	result,	present,
group,	base,	regress,	result,	distanc,	compar,	document,	word,	perform,	strategi,
partit,	unsupervis	regular,	squar	perform,	correl	charact,	system	search,	compar
Topic5		**Topic6**		**Topic7**		**Topic8**		**Topic9**	
problem,	convex,	function,	general,	structur,	represent,	implement,	applic,	match,	invari,
optim,	formul,	approxim,	continu,	rule,	repres,	process,	provid,	transform,	code,
graph,	constraint,	paramet,	deriv,	tree,	concept,	oper,	present,	pattern,	base,
solut,	minim,	valu,	properti,	relat,	describ,	comput,	system,	scheme,	fingerprint,
solv,	program	basi,	discret	hierarch,	present	design,	power	propos,	paper
Topic 10		**Topic11**		**Topic12**		**Topic13**		**Topic14**	
featur,	base,	object,	human,	method,	result,	local,	global,	analysi,	research,
select,	relev,	detect,	target,	propos,	novel,	robust,	effect,	applic,	work,
inform,	subset,	visual,	motion,	base,	effect,	nois,	scale,	studi,	provid,
extract,	import,	track,	appear,	paper,	exist,	propos,	enhanc,	develop,	recent,
propos,	effect	video,	multipl	compar,	experiment	filter,	show	import,	mani
Topic15		**Topic16**		**Topic17**		**Topic18**		**Topic19**	
kernel,	matrix,	point,	contour,	imag,	retriev,	view,	estim,	model,	probabilist,
space,	data,	shape,	boundari,	segment,	pixel,	imag,	motion,	variabl,	process,
analysi,	spars,	curv,	comput,	region,	spatial,	surfac,	scene,	bayesian,	markov,
linear,	dimension,	object,	geometr,	color,	base,	reconstruct,	correspond,	infer,	paramet,
discrimin,	represent	line,	correspond	textur,	level	camera,	illumin	prior,	framework
Topic20		**Topic21**		**Topic22**		**Topic23**		**Topic24**	
network,	output,	estim,	gaussian,	network,	delay,	learn,	problem,	vector,	complex,
neural,	layer,	distribut,	compon,	neural,	global,	task,	knowledg,	comput,	larg,
train,	architectur,	probabl,	densiti,	condit,	numer,	domain,	supervis,	machin,	reduc,
input,	unit,	statist,	random,	stabil,	paper,	framework,	exampl,	number,	size,
weight,	recurr	independ,	sourc	result,	exampl	multipl,	reinforc	support,	effici
Topic25		**Topic26**		**Topic27**		**Topic28**		**Topic29**	
time,	seri,	algorithm,	gradient,	neuron,	cell,	classif,	perform,	system,	design,
predict,	show,	converg,	present,	activ,	behavior,	classifi,	sampl,	control,	robot,
sequenc,	differ,	iter,	base,	model,	spike,	class,	accuraci,	adapt,	propos,
chang,	result,	onlin,	updat,	memori,	respons,	label,	ensembl,	dynam,	simul,
state,	process	effici,	step	mechan,	associ	train,	instanc	nonlinear,	develop

The topic network was constructed based on the correlation between the terms among the topics. The nodes of the network are topic, and the edge connecting the node uses the correlation coefficient between the two topics as the weight. The number of words considered per topic is the top 10 terms in topic. In order to calculate the weight value, the correlation of the i_{th} topic and the j_{th} topic is obtained, and the result of this correlation as its correlation coefficient is determined as the weight. In this way, a topic weighting matrix $TWM\left[cor\left(t_i, t_j\right)\right]$ is generated that takes into consideration the relationship that 30 topics share the terms.

Figure 2 is a topical network graph generated by applying Algorithm 1 to the titles and abstracts of research articles published over the 20 years from 1997 to 2016. The size of each node is expressed as a degree centrality of the topic so that the node with high degree centrality can be seen at a glance.

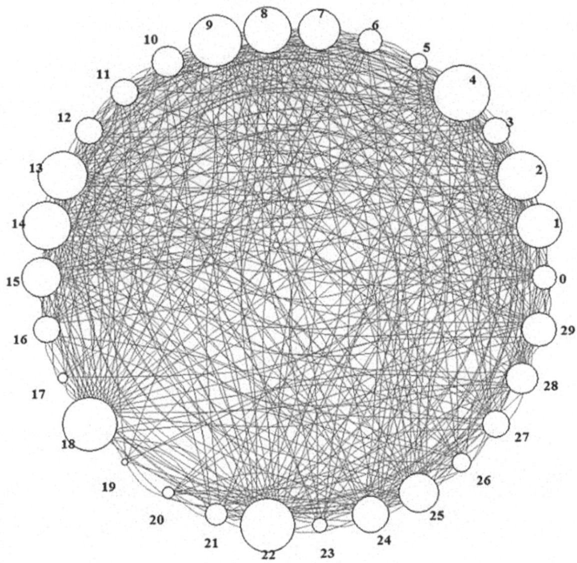

Fig. 2. Topic network graph (1997–2016)

3.3 Time-Series Analysis of Topic Network

To analyze the generated topic network, the centralization measures like centrality of the degree, the betweenness, and the closeness are commonly [19] used in social network analysis. Particularly, in order to investigate the change of topic networks generated over the past twenty years, we divided the topic network into five years to rebuild the topic network.

Connectivity between nodes is measured by degree centrality, as the number of nodes connecting to each node. Even if the number of connection edges is not small, this node also plays an important role if one node is at the shortest distance connecting the other two nodes. This node can be determined by measuring the closeness centrality. Finally, the node with the shortest neighbor distance to all nodes can also be regarded as an important node, which can be determined by measuring the betweenness centrality.

Figure 3(a) is a topic network analyzing the titles and abstracts of research articles from 1997–2001, in the same way, Fig. 3(b) from 2002–2006, Fig. 3(c) from 2007–2011, and Fig. 3(d) from 2012–2016.

In order to grasp the structural characteristics of the four topic networks, we have grasped the centrality of each network. Centrality is a concept of identifying the most important vertex in the whole network and is used to hold the overall characteristics of the network. The centrality of each measure of centrality can be determined by Freeman [19] and defined as Eq. (1).

$$C_A = \frac{\sum_{i=1}^{g}[C_A(n^*) - C_A(n_j)]}{\max \sum_{i=1}^{g}[C_A(n^*) - C_A(n_j)]} \quad (1)$$

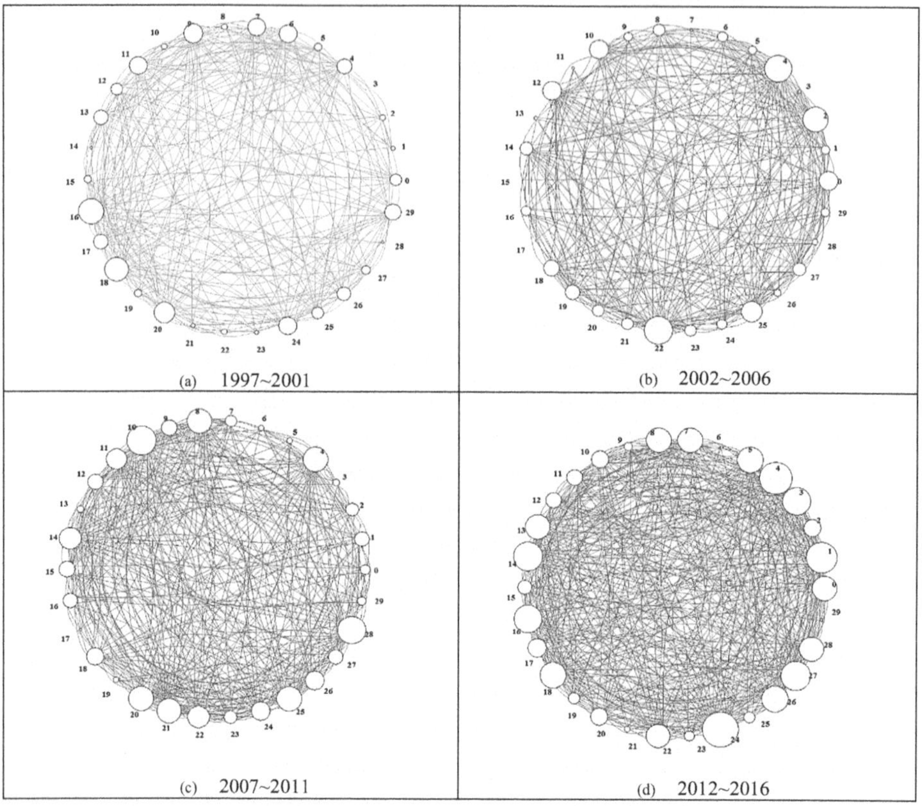

Fig. 3. (a) Topic network of 1997–2001, (b) Topic network of 2002–2006, (c) Topic network of 2007–2011, (d) Topic network of 2012–2016

whereas, $C_A(n_j)$ is called the center of a node, and $C_A(n^*)$ is the maximum value of the centroid of all the nodes belonging to the network. $\sum_{i=1}^{g} [C_A(n^*) - C_A(n_j)]$ is the sum of the differences between the maximum centroid value and the centroid of all nodes and finally, max $\sum_{i=1}^{g} \left[C_A(n^*) - C_A\left(n_j\right)\right]$ is logically the maximum difference. The central value is the sum of the differences between the maximum centrality value and the centrality of all nodes logically divided by the sum of the largest differences.

Figure 4 shows the result of analyzing the centrality of the topic network over time. The values of degree centrality, closeness centrality, and betweenness centrality are expressed as normalization values. First, in the case of the degree centrality is the highest value in 2002–2006, which was the time rise of machine learning research, decreased in the next five years because of the transition in the research of machine learning, this is the era when deep learning and computer vision just emerging area of research. Then, the trend is gradually increasing over the next five years. Also, the closeness centrality shows the same pattern as degree centrality. However, the betweenness centrality is the highest value in 2002–2006 and then its shows gradually decreasing trend since then.

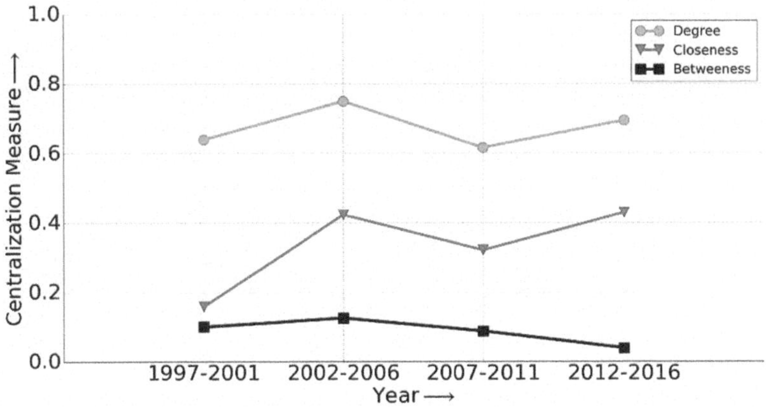

Fig. 4. Time series analysis of centralization

4 Trend Analysis of Machine Learning Research

In this section, we will look specifically at topics that are selected as important topics by topic network analysis. Table 3 shows the top ten keywords of the topic with the highest degree centrality. In all tables, S1 refer as time period of 1997–2001, S2 refer as time period of 2002–2006, S3 refer as time period of 2007–2011, and S4 refer as time period of 2012–2016.

Table 3. Top 10 keywords in topics with highest degree centrality

Year	Topic	Keywords
S1: 1997–2001	Component analysis	analysi, compon, paper, applic, result, provid, independ, theoret, mani, present
S2: 2002–2006	Text mining	robust, nois, filter, result, show, document, text, effect, paper, threshold
S3: 2007–2011	Biometric	propos, perform, system, paper, match, fingerprint, identif, scheme, level, fusion
S4: 2012–2016	Computer Vision	recognit, face, propos, databas, express, facial, differ, result, variat, base

Figure 5 shows the degree centrality of 30 topics. The following topics with highest degree centrality are Topic16, Topic22, Topic10, Topic24, and Topic4 in time period 1997–2001, 2002–2006, 2007–2011, 2012–2016 and 1997–2016 respectively.

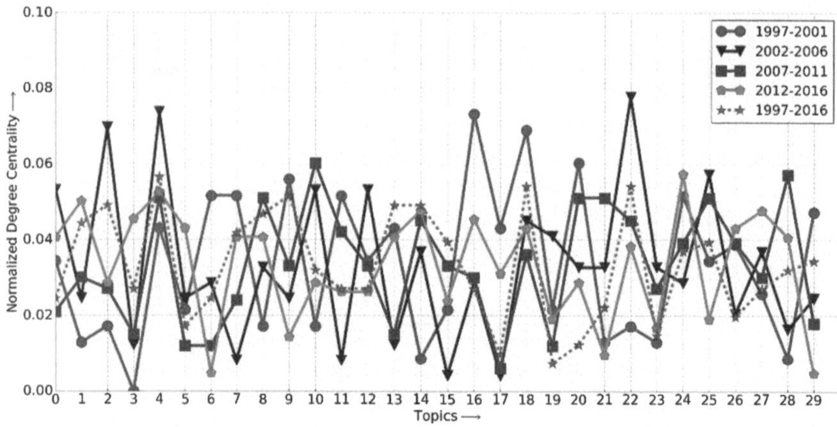

Fig. 5. Normalized degree centrality of 30 topics

Table 4 shows the top ten keywords of the topic with highest betweenness centrality. First of all, the topic with highest betweenness centrality during time period S1 is *Image or Video Processing*, which includes the words like *motion, camera, image, and track.* The *text* and *documents* words along with *filter* and *threshold* words appeared during time period S2 which gave intuition of *Text Mining* topic. Similarly, the topics identified during the time period of S3 and S4 are *Biometric* and *Data Analysis* respectively.

Table 4. Top 10 keywords in topics with highest betweenness centrality

Year	Topic	Keywords
S1: 1997–2001	Image or video processing	motion, sequenc, camera, project, track, imag, estim, correspond, constraint, paramet
S2: 2002–2006	Text mining	robust, nois, filter, result, show, document, text, effect, paper, threshold
S3: 2007–2011	Biometric	propos, perform, system, paper, match, fingerprint, identif, scheme, level, fusion
S4: 2012–2016	Data analysis	discrimin, analysi, data, space, compon, project, dimension, subspac, manifold, linear

Figure 6 shows the betweenness centrality of 30 topics. The following topics with highest betweenness centrality are Topic18, Topic4, Topic10, Topic24, and Topic4 in time period 1997–2001, 2002–2006, 2007–2011, 2012–2016 and 1997–2016 respectively.

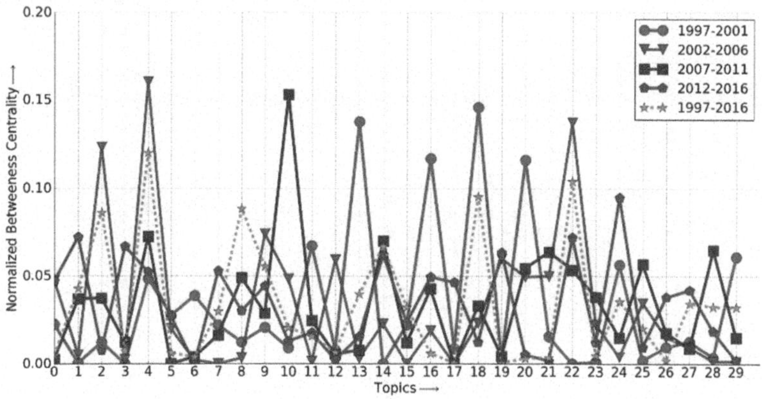

Fig. 6. Normalized betweenness centrality of 30 topics

Table 5 shows the top ten keywords of the topic with highest closeness centrality. A closeness centered topic is a topic that connects two independent topics. The topics identified with closeness centrality are same topics as with degree centrality. In the time period of S1, the *Component Analysis* topic is most relevant due to following words like component, analysis, and independent. In the time period of S2, the *Text Mining* topic comes out to be related due to words like *document, text, threshold, and filter*.

Table 5. Top 10 keywords in topics with highest closeness centrality

Year	Topic	Keywords
S1: 1997–2001	Component analysis	analysi, compon, paper, applic, result, provid, independ, theoret, mani, present
S2: 2002–2006	Text mining	robust, nois, filter, result, show, document, text, effect, paper, threshold
S3: 2007–2011	Biometric	propos, perform, system, paper, match, fingerprint, identif, scheme, level, fusion
S4: 2012–2016	Computer vision	recognit, face, propos, databas, express, facial, differ, result, variat, base

Similarly, the topics in the time period of S3 and S4 are come out as *Biometric and Computer Vision* respectively.

Figure 7 shows the closeness centrality of 30 topics. The following topics with highest degree centrality are Topic16, Topic22, Topic10, Topic24, and Topic4 in time period of 1997–2001, 2002–2006, 2007–2011, 2012–2016 and 1997–2016 respectively.

It is noteworthy that computer vision and text mining topics are emerged as a topic with a high degree of degree centrality, closeness centrality, and betweenness centrality in the research articles published in period S2 and S4 respectively. *Component analysis and Image or video processing* is also included in high centrality topics during the S1 time period of machine learning research.

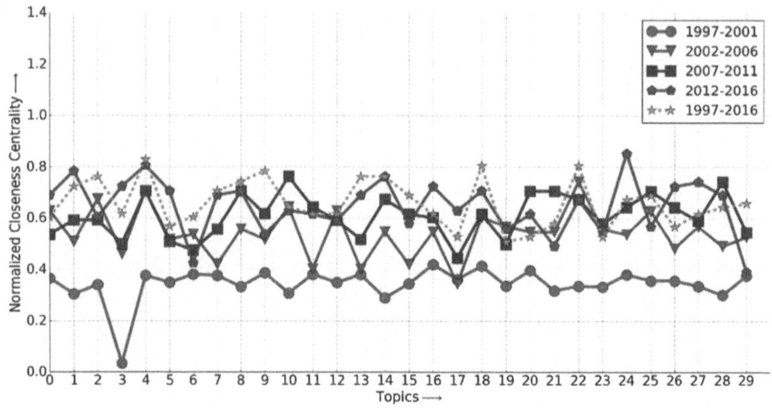

Fig. 7. Normalized closeness centrality of 30 topics

In the most recent 5-year interval computer vision and data analytics are high centrality topics.

5 Conclusions and Future Work

In this study, we performed the trend analysis of the last two decades of machine learning research articles published in six well-known journals for the period of 1997–2016. In order to understand the trends of the research topic for 20 years, we divided topic network into 4 sets and conducted topic network analysis. Topic modeling was performed to select 30 topics and related words corresponding to topics, and a topic network was constructed using the correlation amongst the topics discovered by LDA depending on the terms probability that appeared in common terms instead of the common number of terms between two different topics as weights. By applying social network analysis techniques to established topic networks, we found topics with high degree, closeness, and betweenness.

The contribution of this study was to construct a topic network and analyze it to find out the correlation between topics and identify the influential topics. Also, in order to overcome the limitation of LDA topic model, that cannot consider relation between topics. In addition, by analyzing the topic network analysis in a time series, we have found out what trends the most influential topics show over time.

Future research will build a web application where the interested researcher who is newly venturing into this field can run the model to understand the effectiveness of the proposed topic network analysis results and have directed the latest trending topics pertaining to research area. We collect titles and abstracts of machine learning research articles. Similar study can also be performed on other newly emerging areas such as 'Internet of Things' as well as 'cloud computing' and use them as test cases.

References

1. Kim, C., Hong, Y.-S.: Classification techniques for XML document using text mining. J. Korea Soc. Comput. Inf. **11**(2), 15–23 (2006)
2. Moon, J.-P., Lee, W.-S., Chang, J.-H.: A proper folder recommendation technique using frequent item sets for efficient e-mail classification. J. Korea Soc. Comput. Inf. **16**(2), 33–46 (2011)
3. Blei, D.M., Andrew, Y.N., Jordan, M.I.: Latent dirichlet allocation. J. Mach. Learn. Res. **3**, 993–1022 (2003)
4. Park, J.H., Song, M.: A study on the research trends in library & information science in Korea using topic modeling. J. Korean Soc. Inf. Manag. **30**(1), 7–32 (2013)
5. Blei, D.M.: Probabilistic topic models. Commun. ACM **55**(4), 77–84 (2012)
6. Wasserman, S., Faust, K.: Social Network Analysis: Methods and Applications. Cambridge University Press, Cambridge (1994)
7. Duvvuru, A., Kamarthi, S., Sultornsanee, S.: Undercovering research trends: network analysis of keywords in scholarly articles. In: Proceedings of the 9th International Joint Conference on Computer Science and Software Engineering, pp. 265–270 (2012)
8. Griffiths, T.L., Steyvers, M.: Finding scientific topics. In: Proceedings of the National Academy of Sciences of the USA, vol. 101, no. 1, pp. 5228–5235, April 2004
9. Bae, J., Han, N., Song, M.: Twitter issue tracking system by topic modeling techniques. J. Intell. Inf. Syst. **20**(2), 109–122 (2014)
10. Blei, D.M., Lafferty, J.D.: Correlated topic models. In: Proceedings of Neural Information Processing Systems, pp. 147–154 (2005)
11. Mei, Q., et al.: Topic modeling with network regularization. In: Proceedings of International Conference on World Wide Web, pp. 101–110 (2008)
12. Mao, X.-L., et al.: SSHLDA: a semi-supervised hierarchical topic model. In: Proceedings of the 2012 Joint Conference on Empirical Methods in Natural Language Processing and Computational Natural Language Learning, pp. 800–809 (2012)
13. Wang, X., McCallum, A.: Topics over time: a non-Markov continuous-time model of topical trends. In: Proceedings of the 12th International Conference on Knowledge Discovery and Data Mining, pp. 424–433 (2006)
14. Kim, C., Hong, Y.-S.: Trend analysis of data mining research using topic network analysis. J. Korea Soc. Comput. Inf. **11**(5), 141–148 (2016)
15. R: The R Project for Statistical Computing. https://www.r-project.org/
16. Gruen, B., Hornik, K.: topicmodels: an R package for fitting topic models. J. Stat. Softw. **40**(13), 1–29 (2011)
17. Porter, M.: An algorithm for suffix stripping. Program **14**(3), 130–137 (1980)
18. Delp, P., Thesen, A., Motiwalla, J., Seshardi, N. (eds.) System Tools for Project Planning. International Development Institute, Bloomington (1977)
19. Freeman, L.C.: Centrality in social networks: conceptual clarification. Soc. Netw. **1**, 215–239 (1979)

Impact of Ontology on Databases

Mohini Goyal[1(✉)] and Geeta Rani[2]

[1] TCS, Gurugram, India
mohinigoyal081290@gmail.com
[2] GDGU, Sohna, India
geetachhikara@gmail.com

Abstract. There is a boom in research works in the arena of devising new methodologies for indexing and accessing hidden web data available in databases. To exploit this hidden web data, users need to fill various search forms available on World Wide Web with appropriate values. For a common user with non technical background, this is quite difficult to find suitable values. Ontology provides a way to find these values. Ontology is useful in constructing, a semantic database that provides values for various fields of search form interfaces. Ontology based data extraction is efficient in dealing with large amount of information available on the World Wide Web. This information may be available in different formats such as Hypertext Mark UP Language, HTML, Web Ontology Language, OWL, Recognition Form Designer, RDF and Extensible Markup Language, XML files. This paper creates an ontology database which provides us relevant information about book domain. It presents relevant data before the user rather than giving vague and irrelevant results as traditional databases generate.

Keywords: Ontology · Database · Data extraction · Information retrieval

1 Introduction

In the present era, World Wide Web is the largest and round the clock accessible source of information. This has increased the database size tremendously. Therefore it becomes challenging to access the relevant information from web. Moreover, the sequence of web pages on a website is dependent upon the structure of a website. The web pages such as home page of a website or other pages for which links are available on home page are easier to access in comparison to pages available at deeper level of a website. Therefore authors in [1] categorize web into two categories namely surface web and hidden web. The format of web pages varies in both the categories. The surface web is a collection of web pages designed using Hypertext Markup Language, HTML. These pages are well connected to each other. These are accessible publicly without going through registration and login phase. Each page is uniquely identified by a static logical address called Unique Resource Location, URL. The URL provides an easy path to navigate among different pages.

The contents available at deep web are hidden behind query interfaces of search engines. These pages are accessible only by submitting queries to query interfaces of search systems. Web pages available in deep web contain structured data such as records

B. Panda et al. (Eds.): REDSET 2017, CCIS 799, pp. 48–60, 2018.
https://doi.org/10.1007/978-981-10-8527-7_5

stored in a database system. These pages are presented to users in the form of dynamically generated web pages. These are not accessible via hyperlinks. Therefore, traditional search engines are inefficient in retrieving information from deep web. Let a query interface for a book database allows users to give search conditions on field names such as author name, title, International Standard Book Number (ISBN) etc. This scenario demands a new crawler where hidden web crawler can download the search interfaces, fill the content automatically and submit the information to a hidden web page. But retrieving information from hidden web needs to address the following four issues [2].

(i) Generating ontology for a particular domain.
(ii) Creating database of ontology.
(iii) Mapping of interface.
(iv) Creating common interface for users.

This is quite challenging to resolve all the above said issues simultaneously. This paper focuses on resolving an issue namely "creation of database of ontologies". The survey of existing literature in the arena of ontology storage reveals that a lot of work has already been done in direction of filling forms [3]. But the works in [4–6] use relational databases for filling the search forms. The schemes presented in [4–6] make a comparison between labels of form's interfaces and columns of databases. This is useful in finding relevant search results. The works in [4–7] use keyword based searching techniques for retrieving the desired data. This makes it difficult to obtain precise results. Therefore, a semantic database is required for finding appropriate values required to fill the forms' interfaces.

The information extraction component of a semantic database extracts the structure of a document [8]. It also exploits the relevant metadata from semantic web. This metadata is available in the form of a Resource Description Framework (RDF), Extensible Markup Language XML or Ontology Web Language (OWL) files. These files are recorded in the form of ontology graphs named as RDF triples. RDF is a directed graph which is used as a standard for representing metadata. It can be easily identified using a Universal Resource Identifier. Moreover, RDF is the primary representation language for creating classes and objects of ontology. For creation of more detailed ontologies we use of OWL. OWL adds semantics to values that are submitted to multi-attribute search interfaces. Ontology is more preferable than relational database as it avoids data redundancy, allows sharing and reuse of information. It also gives a common understanding of domain structure. It creates an easy reasoning in terms of Subject Predicate Object (<S P O>) triples. This kind of reasoning is unavailable in relational databases. Ontology is also useful in dealing with questions such as which entities exist?, how many entities can be grouped within a hierarchy?

Ontology provides a data model that defines a set of concepts within a domain and represents an area of knowledge and relationships among those concepts. Ontology for a domain comprises of two components:

(i) an ontology attribute model, for describing the organization of attributes such as Title, Price, Author and ISBN of an entity within a domain.
(ii) an attribute description list that contains the value for each attribute field in ontology.

2 Prior Work

Study of existing literature shows that there is a boom in the content availability at the hidden web. A crawler needs a mechanism that can establish an interaction with the search interface for downloading the content from hidden web. Hidden web is accessible via a query interface. Query interface receives values into its different fields. It enables a comparison between values at various fields and values recorded in a pre-designed database.

Researchers in [1] proposed various schemes to address the problem of crawling and retrieving the hidden web content. These schemes are discussed below.

(2.1) **Hidden Web Exposer, HiWE:** The authors in [2] introduces a task-specific and human-assisted approach to crawl the hidden web. They designed a model HiWE that automatically processes, analyzes, and submit forms. This model is incapable in recognizing and responding to dependencies between various form elements. This can be exemplified as: Let us consider two form elements "state" and "city". The name of city assigned to a 'city' element must be present in the list of cities in a state written in the 'state' element. HiWE is unable to find such relationship among data elements. Moreover, HiWE is not suitable for partially filled forms.

(2.2) **Exploiting ontology for retrieving hidden web behind searchable forms**: Authors in [3] classify each searchable form to its relevant domain. Their system finds a suitable ontology that automatically fills the forms. The system retrieves and analyzes the result pages for further indexing.

(2.3) **Framework for information retrieval using wrapper induction technique**: It is quite challenging and time consuming to retrieve information in case one needs to refer too many Hypertext Mark UP Language, HTML pages for collecting data. Authors in [4] proposed a model for extraction of content from HTML pages. It stores HTML pages into RDF format. However their system applies extraction rules and wrapper induction technique for easy extraction of information. But it does not support creation of semantic relationships between extracted data.

(2.4) **Storing OWL ontologies in relational databases**: The system proposed in [5] stores knowledge contained in the ontology in relational databases. It uses a query mechanisms improves usability of semantic web. This storage model is an optimized memory model which is scalable and efficient.

(2.5) **Framework for generating Domain specific ontology:** Authors in [6] developed a framework to organize domain specific information in the form of ontology database. Moreover, a user can submit query to it in order to receive results of queries from knowledge base stored in <SPO> triples in terms of ontology. This is challenging to store the SPO triples in the form of semantic database from where a large amount of domain information can be queried and processed.

(2.6) **A novel architecture of ontology based adaptive crawler for hidden web:** The work proposed in [7] differs from previous studies. They proposed an architecture for analyzing the process of query generation. This work reveals a conclusion that submitting a query provides an entry to hidden web pages. Furthermore, there are two core challenges in implementing an effective Hidden web crawler:

(i) The crawler need to understand as well as frame a model of a query interface.
(ii) The crawler needs to identify meaning of a query before submitting to query interface.

Raghavan and Garcia-Molina in [5] presents solutions for the above said challenges. Table 1 shows a comparison among three web languages of ontology.

Table 1. Comparison among three ontology web languages

Characteristics	Resource description framework, RDF	Resource description framework schema RDFS	Ontology web language, OWL
Level of expression	Lowest level to build ontologies Unable to express more complex relations	Capability to express more relation properties than RDF but less than OWL	It is the highest level to build ontologies or schema on the top of RDF dataset
Degree of inferencing	RDF cannot define special meaning to vocabulary such as type, subclass, sub property, no equivalence, no disjointness etc.	RDF Schema defines vocabulary terms and the relations between those terms It gives "extra meaning" to a particular RDF predicates and resources. This "extra meaning" specifies how a term should be interpreted	OWL adds more semantics to the schema. It specifies more about the properties and classes. It joins data of two different schemas if keywords are synonyms
Richness in tag property	RDF provides few predicates to define class and relations i.e. rdf:type, rdf:class	RDFS provides a new predicate rdfs:sub class of, rdfs: sub property of, rdfs: domain and rdfs: range	OWL provides a predicate such as owl: disjoint with, owl: functional property, owl: inverse functional property, owl: inverse of, owl: symmetric property
Validity of ontology	RDF defines a way how to write stuff. It may be wrong and not a valid ontology in few cases		OWL defines a way to write stuff and its specification defines what exactly can be written with RDF in order to have valid ontology

3 Motivation

Study of prior works available in literature uncovers the following issues in automatic filling of search interfaces.

- Traditional web crawlers use pre-designed relational databases for writing details in online available forms. These crawlers do not consider semantic relationships between different fields of a form.
- HiWE provides only a few values for filling the form. It lacks the support for partially filled forms.
- Hidden web crawlers use attributes based matching processes for filling search interface. This work can be done more precisely using specified ontologies.

In order to solve the identified problems, there is a need to design a database that stores semantic information about various objects and their relations. We use the concept of ontology to define the database. The database stores all the information as a knowledge base in form of RDF triples <Subject Predicate Object>. This knowledge base is useful for extraction of hidden web pages. The system applies reasoning rules over semantic database. This generates high quality data that is recorded in hidden web pages.

4 Proposed Work

In this paper, we propose the ontology based semantic database system which is useful in accessing hidden web pages. WWW is a collection of large number of web pages. These web pages vary in their formats such as RDF, HTML, OWL and XML. This work creates a generic and well populated database. This takes the assistance of a traditional crawler that downloads web pages available in the domain name, Book.

The system classifies web pages into different categories on the basis of type of contents it contains. These web pages are submitted to different parsing modules. Each module extracts the complete information in form of RDF triples. The system forwards these triples into an ontology based semantic database. Figure 1 shows the architecture of our proposed system.

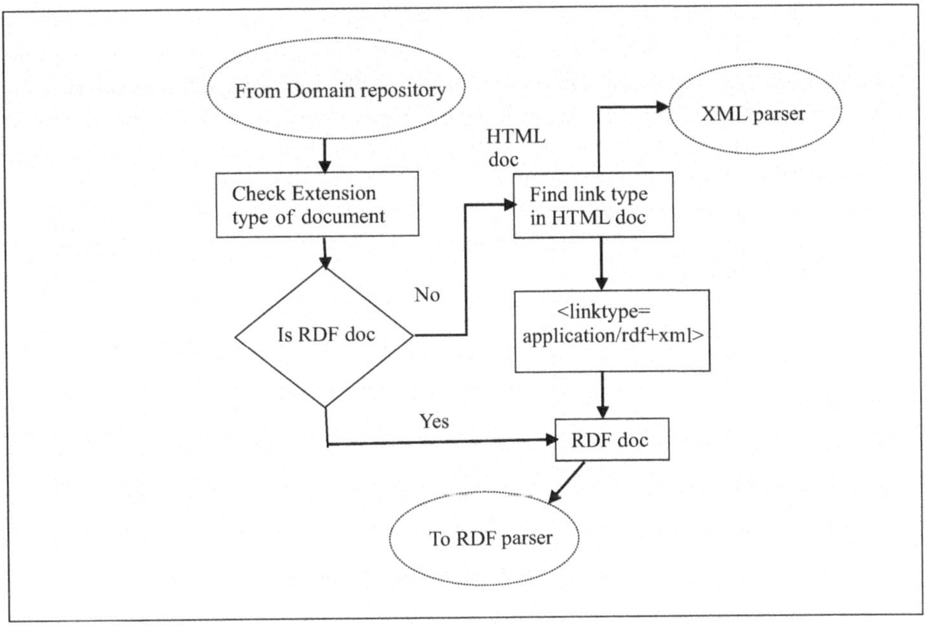

Fig. 1. Architecture of proposed system

Components of the proposed system: This system comprises of the following components.

(a) **Crawler:** This component takes input in the form of a URL from a seed set of URLs. It downloads web pages available at the fed URL. The system stores the downloaded pages into a repository. The system categorizes these web pages on the basis of their domain.
(b) **Domain specific Repository**: The system maintains a separate repository for each domain. Each repository stores web pages of a particular domain.
(c) **Classifier:** This component receives web pages from a domain specific repository. It classifies these pages on the basis of their formats such as RDF, XML, HTML and OWL. The system submits the segregated pages to a specific parser module. A web page in RDF format is submitted to a RDF parser module. A web page in HTML or XML format is forwarded to HTML or XML parser module. A parser extracts text from a web page.
(d) **RDF file discovery**: The system searches a <link> element for RDF file in the <Head> element of a HTML page. It does so to point additional RDF documents available in a repository without showing their direct link. Such links exist if RDF or XML content is not embedded in a web page but its' reference is saved in a web page. The href element refers to a Uniform Resource Identifier, URI of RDF or XML content.
(e) **HTML/XML parser module:** RDF file discovery module operates on output web pages given by a classifier. It accepts XML or HTML web pages in the form of

tags. It gives <SPO> triples as an output which retrieves relevant information from a XML file. This module forwards its output in the form of <SPO> triples to the domain specific database. The system invokes the domain specific database only for parsing of XML or HTML web pages. The system chooses Document Object Model, DOM parser for parsing XML documents. It loads the parsed document into memory. It records the content of a XML document at different nodes of a tree. An element node represents a XML element and an attribute node represents an attribute. Figure 2 shows the components of XML parser and Fig. 3 shows the workflow of XML parser.

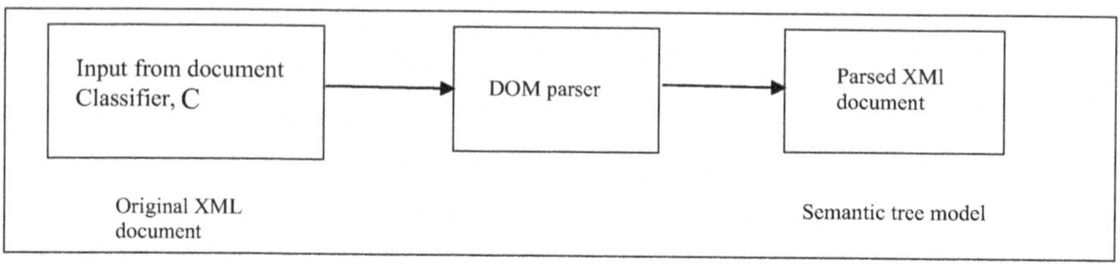

Fig. 2. XML parser components

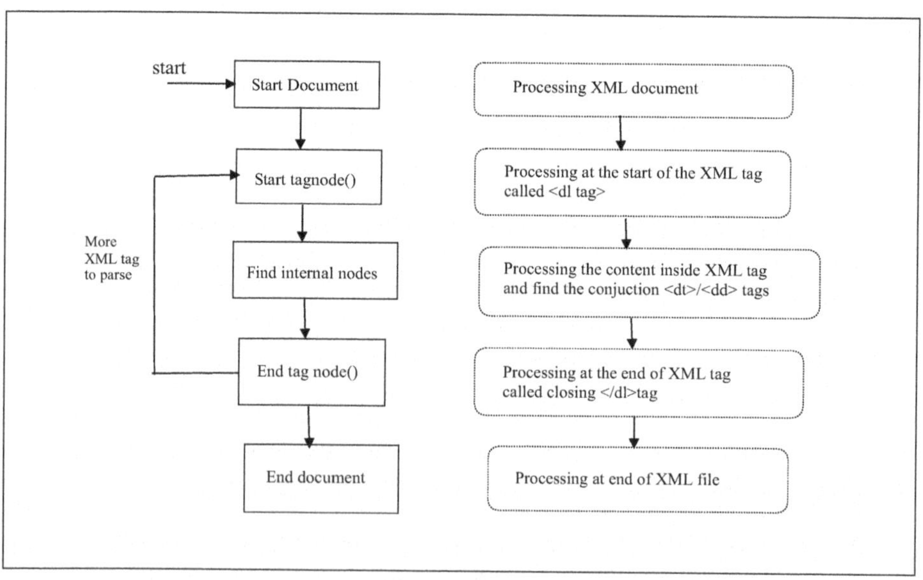

Fig. 3. XML parser workflow

The workflow can be explained in a better way by taking an example. Let <BOOK> is a root node in XML file. **getnodename()** is the function to retrieve all other nodes in a document. A root node <BOOK> has children nodes that are counted as number of <dl> tags. These tags are traversed in a XML file. A variable **nlist** records the number of dl tags. A variable **Nodelist** stores the type of tags. Calling a Nodelist returns all descendent nodes of a node such as its children nodes and grandchildren nodes. Calling a function **Getelementsbytagname()** returns a DOM node list of all the elements with a given tag name in an order in which they would be evaluated in a preorder traversal of a document tree. Giving a call to a method **Getnodename()** retreives the name of a DOM Node its metadata. A method getelementsbytagname (dt) gives the **Label L** of a node. A tag <dt> in <dl> tag extracts the **Label L** of empty nodes. <dd> and <dt> tags together extract the label instances of a tag.

For a domain name Book, Let Book is a root node that acts as a class. Dl tag creates empty nodes which represent a subclass. <dt> tag provides labels to empty nodes such as author, title, price, ISBN and publication. <dd> tag gives instances of these subclasses.

The extraction of <dt> and <dd> tags continues until the count of <dl> tag becomes null and nlist variable becomes empty.

Figure 4 presents the algorithm for showing working of our proposed system.

Algorithm

(1) Find root element by *getnodename*() function.
(2) Create variable ***nlist*** of type nodelist.
(3) Intialise ***nlist*** with count of all ***<dl>*** tags found in XML file by *getelementsbytagname*(*dl*).
(4) Set ***nlist*** value equal to number of children nodes of root node.
(5) Repeat steps 4 to 6 for each children node while ***nlist*** length $\neq$ to null.
(6) Create variable of type ***Node.*** One ***empty node*** created in each iteration of loop.
(7) Extract a node label L by calling getelementsbytagname(dt) by <dt> Tag.
(8) Extract Label value v by calling getelementsbytagname(dd) by <dd> tag.
(9) Call getattribute() to display required attributes and more information related to <dt> tag.
(10) return(L, v).

// ***Label L*** of children node is retrieved with help of ***<dt>*** tag and can be classified as ***subclass***, whereas ***Label value*** v may be found in form of ***<dd>*** tag in conjuction with ***<dt>*** tag and can be classified ***as instances*** of subclasses

Fig. 4. An Algorithm showing impact of ontology on databases

Tree model of XML/HTML file: This is difficult to interpret the XML and HTML files. Therefore, it needs a methodology which reduces the efforts of interpreting the XML or HTML file. Tree model provides a solution for it. Figure 5 represents a tree model for XML/HTML file.

RDF Parser

RDF is a standard for describing resources. It is similar to conceptual model approach such as entity-relationship. It represents the resources in form of subject-predicate-object expressions that are named as triples. In a triple, the subject denotes the resource, predicate denotes the relationships between the subject and object of that resource. For example in a triple "Book on operating system" the '**book**' denotes the **subject**, '**on**' denotes the **predicate**, and '**operating system'** denotes the **object.** The subject of an RDF statement is either a URI or blank node, both denotes the resources. Resources indicated by blank nodes called anonymous resources. The predicate is a URI which also represents a resource relationship. The object is a URI, blank node or string literal.

Here **URI** is a string of characters which is used to identify name of a resource. This identification represents a resource over the network (WWW). Web page address is the most common example of URI. URI gives the following information.

(i) The mechanism used to access the resources.
(ii) Computer that contains the resource.
(iii) A file name of resource on the computer.

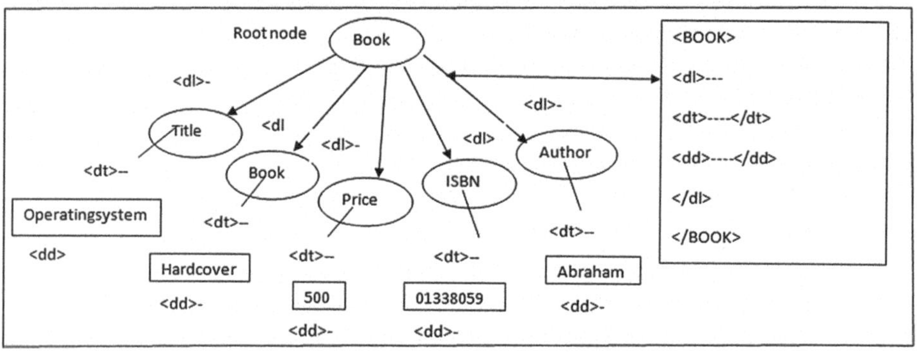

Fig. 5. Tree model of XML/HTML file

5 Implementation

Hardware and Software Requirements

This system is implemented using Protege 4.2. Protégé 4.2 is an open source ontology editor and knowledge base framework. It creates an OWL file that uses Ontolograph utility. This utility supports the display of class-superclass relationships, Domain-Range property and relationship.

The system uses Jena, a Java API to create and manipulate RDF graphs. Jena has object classes to represent graphs, resources, properties and literals. In Jena, a graph is called a RDF model which is represented by the model interface. Each arc in a RDF model is called a statement. Each statement asserts a fact about a resource. A statement includes the following three parts.

(i) *subject*: It is the resource from where an arc leaves.
(ii) *predicate*: It is the property that labels an arc.
(iii) *object*: It is the resource or literal pointed by an arc.

Dataset: The authors in this paper, considers the domain "Book" for evaluation of the proposed system. The dataset has been collected from a website "www.cheapesttestbooks.com". The system extracts various tags and meta tags from the source code of the above written website. It retrieves the values that are to be fed to the search interface. The retrieved values are stored in the form of <SPO> triples. Figure 6 shows the snapshot of the source code of the "www.cheapesttestbooks.com".

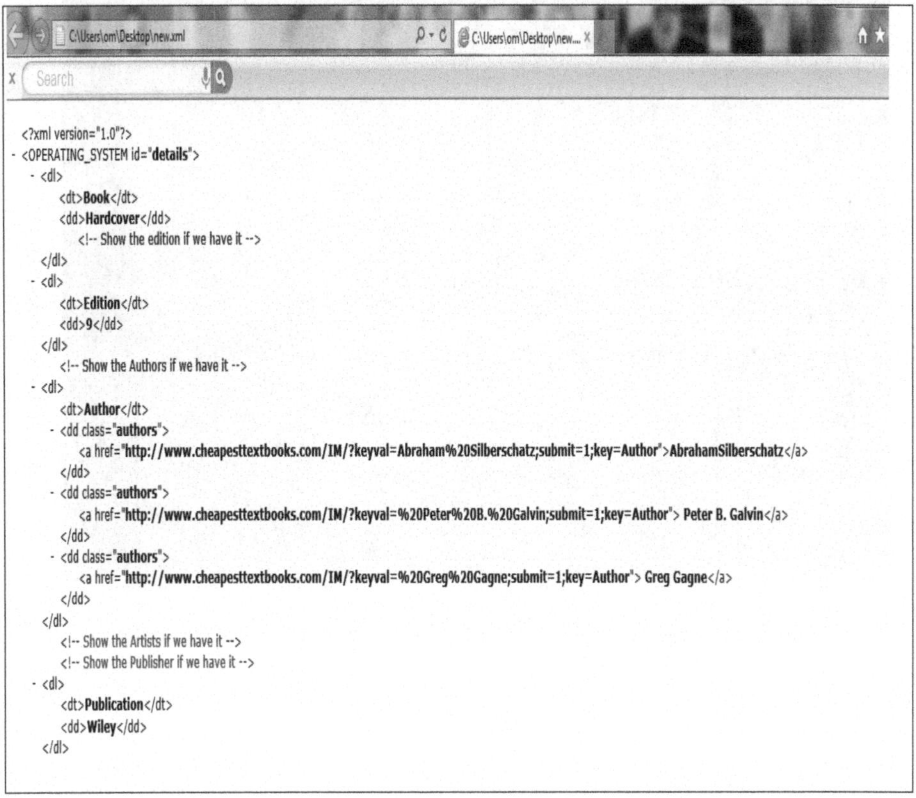


```
<?xml version="1.0"?>
- <OPERATING_SYSTEM id="details">
  - <dl>
      <dt>Book</dt>
      <dd>Hardcover</dd>
        <!-- Show the edition if we have it -->
    </dl>
  - <dl>
      <dt>Edition</dt>
      <dd>9</dd>
    </dl>
      <!-- Show the Authors if we have it -->
  - <dl>
      <dt>Author</dt>
    - <dd class="authors">
        <a href="http://www.cheapesttextbooks.com/IM/?keyval=Abraham%20Silberschatz;submit=1;key=Author">AbrahamSilberschatz</a>
      </dd>
    - <dd class="authors">
        <a href="http://www.cheapesttextbooks.com/IM/?keyval=%20Peter%20B.%20Galvin;submit=1;key=Author"> Peter B. Galvin</a>
      </dd>
    - <dd class="authors">
        <a href="http://www.cheapesttextbooks.com/IM/?keyval=%20Greg%20Gagne;submit=1;key=Author"> Greg Gagne</a>
      </dd>
    </dl>
      <!-- Show the Artists if we have it -->
      <!-- Show the Publisher if we have it -->
  - <dl>
      <dt>Publication</dt>
      <dd>Wiley</dd>
    </dl>
```

Fig. 6. Snapshot of the source code of the "www.cheapesttestbooks.com".

Extraction of <SPO> Triples: The system receives the XML file as an input. It represents this file in the form of a tree. For example <BOOK> is the root node of the tree. Title, Price, ISBN and Publication acts as children nodes. These are the subclasses. Each subclass creates its instances. Figure 7 displays the snapshot of the extraction of <SPO> triples from the source code of the "www.cheapesttestbooks.com". Figure 8 shows <SPO> triple extracted.

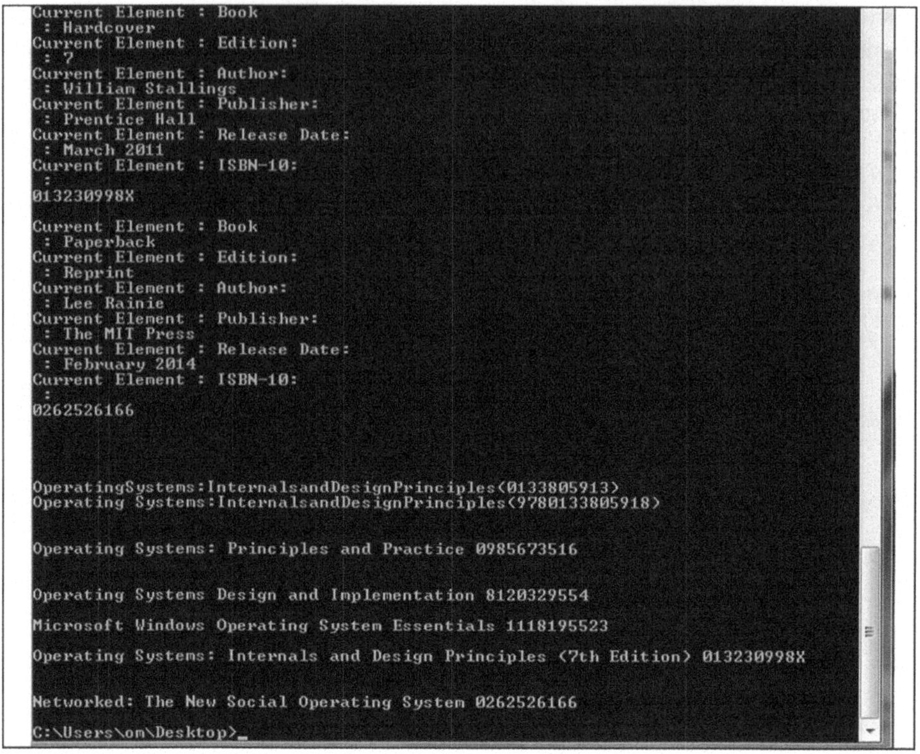

Fig. 7. Snapshot of extraction of <SPO> triples from XML/HTML file.

Query | Count Rows | Insert Row

EDIT	SUB	PRED	OBJ	URL
	OperatingSystems:InternalsandDesignPrinciples(0133805913)	published in	December 2012	http://www.cheapesttextbooks.com/IM/?keyval=Abraham%20Silberschatz;submit=1;key=Author
	OperatingSystems:InternalsandDesignPrinciples(0133805913)	has ISBN	0133805913	http://www.cheapesttextbooks.com/IM/?keyval=Abraham%20Silberschatz;submit=1;key=Author
	OperatingSystems:InternalsandDesignPrinciples(0133805913)	written by	AbrahamSilberschatz	http://www.cheapesttextbooks.com/IM/?keyval=Abraham%20Silberschatz;submit=1;key=Author
	AbrahamSilberschatz	haswritten	OperatingSystems:InternalsandDesignPrinciples(0133805913)	http://www.cheapesttextbooks.com/IM/?keyval=Abraham%20Silberschatz;submit=1;key=Author
	GregGagne	haswritten	OperatingSystems:InternalsandDesignPrinciples(0133805913)	http://www.cheapesttextbooks.com/IM/?keyval=%20Greg%20Gagne;submit=1;key=Author
	Peter Galvin	haswritten	OperatingSystems:InternalsandDesignPrinciples(0133805913)	http://www.cheapesttextbooks.com/IM/?keyval=%20Peter%20B.%20Galvin;submit=1;key=Author
	Thomas Anderson	haswritten	Operating Systems: Principles and Practice 0985673516	http://www.cheapesttextbooks.com/IM/?keyval=Thomas%20Anderson;submit=1;key=Author
	Michael Dahlin	haswritten	Operating Systems: Principles and Practice 0985673516	http://www.cheapesttextbooks.com/IM/?keyval=%20Michael%20Dahlin;submit=1;key=Author
	Andrew S. Tanenbaum	haswritten	Operating Systems Design and Implementation 8120329554	http://www.cheapesttextbooks.com/IM/?keyval=Andrew%20S.%20Tanenbaum;submit=1;key=Autho
	Albert Woodhull	haswritten	Operating Systems Design and Implementation 8120329554	http://www.cheapesttextbooks.com/IM/?keyval=%20Albert%20S.%20Woodhull;submit=1;key=Autho
	Tom Carpenter	haswritten	Microsoft Windows Operating System Essentials 1118195523	http://www.cheapesttextbooks.com/IM/?keyval=Tom%20Carpenter;submit=1;key=Author
	Lee Rainie	haswritten	Networked: The New Social Operating System 0262526166	http://www.cheapesttextbooks.com/IM/?keyval=Lee%20Rainie;submit=1;key=Author
	Wiley	has published	OperatingSystems:InternalsandDesignPrinciples(8thEdition)0133805913	http://www.cheapesttextbooks.com/IM/?keyval=Abraham%20Silberschatz;submit=1;key=Author
	OperatingSystems:InternalsandDesignPrinciples(0133805913)	published in	December 2012	http://www.cheapesttextbooks.com/IM/?keyval=Abraham%20Silberschatz;submit=1;key=Author
	OperatingSystems:InternalsandDesignPrinciples(0133805913)	has ISBN	0133805913	http://www.cheapesttextbooks.com/IM/?keyval=Abraham%20Silberschatz;submit=1;key=Author

Fig. 8. Snapshot of saved <SPO> triples in database for an XML/HTML file

The extracted triples <subject, predicate, object> and their URLs are recorded in the Oracle 10g. Figure 9 presents the snapshot of SPO triples recorded in oracle 10g. The source file is saved in the form of ontology database. Relationship between subject and object varies on the basis of query string written in a search interface. The subjects and objects may be interchangeable. Consider a statement "Abraham has written operating systems and design principles". In the given statement Abraham is subject and operating systems and design principles is the object. But operating systems and design principles become the subject and Abraham becomes the object in case the predicate is 'by'.

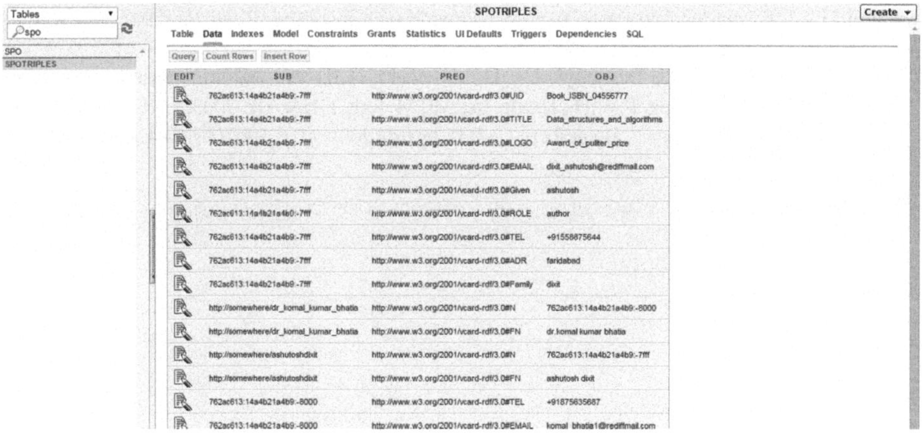

Fig. 9. Output in Oracle 10g database

6 Conclusion and Future Scope

The existing literature in the arena of information management reveals the use of relational tables for storage of domain specific information. But this paper involves the concept of ontology for successful creation of semantic databases. This work focuses on storing the retrieved information in the form of RDF triples. The RDF triples are useful in extracting relevant data from hidden web. Moreover, the system establishes a relevant mapping between entries in the query interface and information available in the oracle 10g database. This work can be extended in the field of designing a module which can filter RDF tags from a given OWL file.

References

1. Manvi, D,A., and Bhatia, K.K.: Design of an ontology based adaptive crawler for hidden web. In: International Conference on Communication Systems and Network Technologies, Gwalior, pp. 659–663 (2013)
2. Bhatia, K.K, Sharma, A.K.: A Framework for domain-specific interface mapper (DSIM). Int. J. Comput. Sci. Netw. Secur. (IJCSNS), **8**(12), 56-65 (2008)

3. Ntoulas, A.: Downloading textual hidden-web content through keyword queries. In: Proceedings of the Joint Conference on Digital Libraries (JCDL), Denver, USA. Computer Science Department, University of California Los Angeles (2005)
4. Chandrasekaran, B., Josephson, J.R.: What are ontologies, and why do we need them? Ohio State University. http://www.w3.org/TR/owl-ref/.Last. Accessed Dec 2016
5. Raghavan, S., Garcia-Molina, H.: Crawling the hidden web. In: VLDB (2001). Stanford Digital Libraries Technical report (2008)
6. Guarino, N.: Formal ontology in information systems. In: Guarino, N. (ed.) Proceedings of Formal Ontology in Information Systems, FOIS 1998, Trento, Italy, 6–8 June 1998, pp. 3–15. IOS Press, Amsterdam (1998)
7. Eikvil, L.: Information extraction from world wide web-a survey. Report no. 945, Norweigan Computing Center, July 1999
8. Varga, P., Mészáros, T., Dezsényi, C., Dobrowiecki, T.P.: An ontology-based information retrieval system. In: Chung, P.W.H., Hinde, C., Ali, M. (eds.) IEA/AIE 2003. LNCS (LNAI), vol. 2718, pp. 359–368. Springer, Heidelberg (2003). https://doi.org/10.1007/3-540-45034-3_36

Design and Implementation of Virtual Hadoop Cluster on Private Cloud

Garima Singh(✉) and Anil Kumar Singh

Motilal Nehru National Institute of Technology, Allahabad, India
singhgarima4688@gmail.com, ak@mnnit.ac.in

Abstract. Virtualization has made it feasible to deploy hadoop in cloud environment. Virtualized hadoop offers unique benefits like setting up a cluster in short time, flexibility to use variety of hardware (SAN, NAS, DAS), high availability and many more. With companies like Google, Microsoft, Rackspace and IBM providing their own infrastructure for cloud service more and more business is assumed to move on cloud in the near future. Apart from public cloud business can make use of private, community or hybrid cloud deployment model. In this paper, the focus is on private cloud deployment which offers its own benefits like security, reduced cost, more control over resources etc. The design and implementation of private cloud using Xen 6.5 bare metal hypervisor is discussed in this paper. Further it also discusses deploying hadoop as service on the cloud with the help of shell script. For experimental purpose 8 physical hosts are connected to 60 Tb SAN with QLogic 20-Port 8 Gb SAN switch module which provides fiber connectivity to the storage. Finally, the performance of hadoop on the cloud is evaluated.

Keywords: Virtualization · SAN · Hadoop · MapReduce
High availability

1 Introduction

Cloud [1] has appeared as a new buzzword in the distributed computing world. It is aimed to reshape the way business will be done in the near future. With companies like Google, Microsoft, Rackspace and IBM providing their own infrastructure for cloud service more and more business will be migrated to cloud. Many formal definition of cloud computing have been proposed. But, one provided by U.S. NIST (National Institute of Standards and Technology) [2] has been most widely and is as follows:

> *"Cloud computing is a model for enabling convenient, on-demand network access to a shared pool of configurable computing resources (e.g., networks, servers, storage, applications, and services) that can be rapidly provisioned and released with minimal management effort or service provider interaction."*

B. Panda et al. (Eds.): REDSET 2017, CCIS 799, pp. 61–71, 2018.
https://doi.org/10.1007/978-981-10-8527-7_6

Cloud computing can make use of existing four deployment models [3,4] which are public, community, private and hybrid cloud. In public cloud, the cloud service provider has the cloud ownership with their own policy and cost model. So, businesses can switch to public cloud platform without worrying for infrastructure. Companies like Google, Rackspace, IBM etc. are among some of the public cloud service providers. They all use different virtualization technologies like Google Cloud uses KVM, Amazon uses Xen and Microsoft Azure uses Hyper-V [5].

This paper mainly focus on private cloud deployment model which is mostly used when infrastructure is available and the user has security concerns to move data to public cloud. Here, the cloud infrastructure is usually maintained by cloud owner or by some third party. It offers benefits like security, easy customization of compute, network and storage resources which is not so easily available with the public cloud. Also, public cloud often incurs significant data transfer cost which can be reduced using private cloud [3].

Cloud computing leverages virtualization to enable sharing and dynamic provisioning of resources. Virtualization makes separation of a service request from the underlying delivery of that service [6,7]. It facilitate to run multiple OS instances on the same physical machine concurrently and offers many features like live migration [8], server consolidation [9], high availability etc. With server consolidation, several VMs can be placed on a single physical machine in order to utilize the resources and save energy as even an idle machine consumes considerable power [10].

Another feature provided by virtualization is high availability which is responsible for managing the pool resources in the event of failure. It ensures that in case a server failed, the services running on that server are not stopped and are automatically restarted at new server in the pool.

Meanwhile, big data has gained considerable attentiveness due to the enormous volume of data generated by various applications which could be one of the most valuable intangible assets in the future. How to process and store such sheer volume of data was a challenging task for traditional architecture and methods. As a result, new tools have emerged to process and store it. MapReduce [11] is one such parallel programming model for large and distributed datasets. It frees user from complicated tasks of parallelization, failure handling and distribution of data.

So, with virtualization and big data it is now possible to use virtual machine for big data computing [12,13]. This paper discusses to setup private cloud using Xen 6.5 [14], an open source hypervisor. It is type-1 hypervisor that uses microkernel design and runs on the top of hardware. On the other hand, type-2 or hosted hypervisor runs on top of an operating system. The private cloud provides high availability that is achieved by adding a shared storage to the pool using Qlogic 20 port 8 Gb SAN switch module which provides fiber connectivity to storage. The paper further discusses the deployment of virtual hadoop cluster with the help of script.

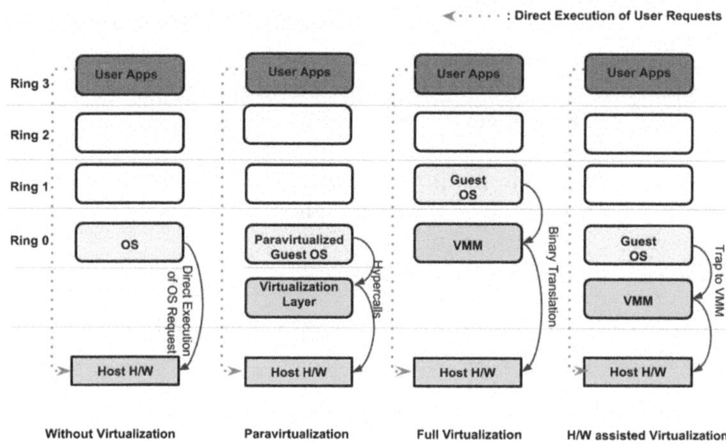

Fig. 1. Different approaches to virtualization

The remaining of the paper is organized as follows. Section 2 describes the related work. Section 3 presents setting up private cloud and deploying hadoop on virtual machine. Section 4 discuss the performance of hadoop on virtual machine. Lastly, Sect. 5 presents conclusion and future work.

2 Related Work

Virtualization Overview: Virtualization has emerged as a core driving technology for cloud computing by providing abstraction of the underlying resources. It provides features like server consolidation [9], live migration [8], load balancing etc. There are three approaches to virtualization [15] as shown in Fig. 1. They are paravirtualization, full virtualization and hardware assisted virtualization.

In paravirtualization, the guest kernel is modified to support virtualization. Guest OS knows that it is running in virtualized environment. The main drawback of this approach is that it does not support to run unmodified guest OS. However, it offers low virtualization overhead and is faster than other approaches. This technique is currently supported by Xen [14] hypervisor.

Second way to achieve virtualization is full virtualization using binary translation that allows to run unmodified OS. As compared to paravirtualization, it is slow and incurs more overhead. This technique is currently supported by VMWare. Lastly, third approach is hardware assisted virtualization where the ISA (Instruction Set Architecture) is modified to support virtualization. Intel virtualization technology (VT-x) and AMD's AMD-V support hardware assisted virtualization.

MapReduce Overview: MapReduce [11] is a parallel programing model for processing large and distributed dataset. It simplifies programming for parallel and distributed applications by requiring user to just specify the map and reduce function only. It exempts user from complex details of parallelization, fault tolerance and concurrency control by handling them itself. The map and reduce functions are as described below:

- Map function is responsible for processing key/value pair. It generates intermediate result which is a set of key/value pair.

  map (key1, value1)$\rightarrow$ *list (key2, value2)*

- Reduce function process this intermediate data generated by map function by merging values associated with same key.

  reduce (key2, list (value2)) $\rightarrow$ *list (value3)*

Hadoop [16] is an open source implementation of MapReduce. It has computational power of MapReduce with HDFS (Hadoop Distributed File System) which can process terabytes of data on multiple cores.

Meanwhile with virtualization it possible to the use cloud infrastructure for running hadoop job. Ibrahim et al. [17] have discussed the challenges and opportunities of hadoop deployment on virtual machine. They have discussed that hadoop being data intensive application suffers due to IO virtualization overhead. They have further proposed a new framework for MapReduce in [18]. This paper aims to reduce the IO overhead while retaining the benefits provided by cloud.

Xu et al. in [19] have discussed the deployment of cloudstack and hadoop on virtual machines. The paper also analyzes the performance of hadoop cluster in a virtualized environment with VMs running on same and different physical machines.

In [20], Wendt has performed a price-based comparison of hadoop cluster on various cloud deployment models. The author has discussed various deployment model and benefit of deploying hadoop on the top of bare metal hypervisor. They have concluded that although virtualization adds overhead but performance tunning and scalability provided by virtualized hadoop is so high that it could be beneficial to invest in deploying hadoop on VM. However, this performance tuning is a time-consuming and complex process.

Conley et al. in [21] has analyzed the performance of MapReduce on Amazon public cloud (AWS). Performance is measured using amazon virtualized storage and network IO provide by AWS. The author have used flash storage that support storage repository IO virtualization. This, high speed fabric enhances the performance of MapReduce on virtual machine.

3 Private Cloud and Hadoop Deployment

This section discusses how to setup private cloud and configure hadoop on VM. This private cloud is based on open source Xen 6.5 hypervisor. It runs directly on

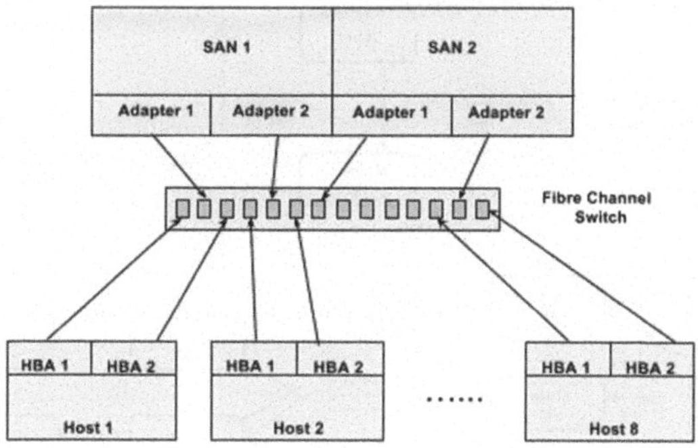

Fig. 2. Cloud setup with eight hosts providing fiber connectivity to the SAN.

the top of the hardware and hosts guest operating systems. A web based interface is provided for easy access to the cloud. In addition to providing hadoop-as-a-service, it also offers infrastructure and storage as service. The virtual hadoop cluster has hadoop 2.7.1 running on Ubuntu 10.04 VM.

To access the cloud service, the user is required to first register using the web interface. Once registered, the user can request for cloud services as per requirement. However, the service is provided only after the administrator approves the request.

3.1 Deploying Our Private Cloud

The private cloud has 8 blade servers. Each blade server has 2×4 core Intel(R) Xeon(R) CPU E5-2665 @ 2.40 GHz processor and 32 Gb of RAM. Each blade has hyper threading enabled with two thread running on each CPU core. All the eight hosts are added to a shared pool which is connected to 60 Tb SAN by QLogic 20-Port 8 Gb SAN switch.

High availability is configured on the pool so that services running on a particular server are not stopped if the server hosting that service fails. They are automatically restarted at new host in the pool. Figure 2 shows our cloud setup with eight blade servers and fiber switch connected to SAN. The steps to configure cloud are given below:

1. Install Xen server 6.5 on each blade server.
2. Configure management interface and ntp server setting for each server.
3. Create a pool and add all the servers to that pool.
4. Login to the Qlogic fabric to create a zoneset.
5. In that zoneset, create a zone with eight initiators (servers) and one target (60 TB SAN).
6. Next activate the zoneset.
7. Once activated, login to SAN module to map the volume to the hosts.
8. After that add shared storage as HBA to the pool. The shared storage can also be added as software iSCSi or NFS.
9. Once shared storage is added turn on high availability.

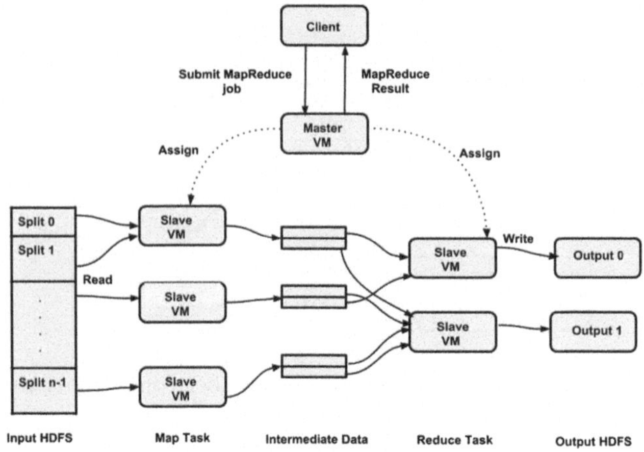

Fig. 3. MapReduce architecture on cloud

Before adding servers to pool it must be ensured that the network configuration is setup correctly (like same nic has to be configured as a primary management interface on each of the server etc.). For detailed networking of Xen server one can refer [22].

To ensure that pool function properly, the clock of each server must be synchronized as they are frequently communicating important information with each other. For experimental purpose a local system is configured as an NTP server and all blade servers are synchronized to this internal NTP server.

Also, it is recommended to have atleast three servers in the pool. This due to the fact that a pool of two server usually faces fencing problem. With more that two hosts, in case heartbeat is lost the high availability (HA) daemon will keep the partition that is larger and fences the smaller one. Next the hosts in the smaller partition are rebooted. However, with two hosts HA daemon cannot choose between the partition of equal size and it reboots the host having higher HOST-UUID.

Fencing could also result due to existing timeout settings for HA daemon. Normally, this value is setup between 30–75 sec. In this case, it was changed 90 sec. To change high availability time out setting use the following command:

xe pool-ha-enable heartbeat-sr-uuids = <SR-UUID>ha-config:timeout = <Ti-meout>.

3.2 Hadoop Deployment

Virtualization facilitates use of virtual machine for deployment of hadoop cluster. In virtualized environment, map and reduce tasks are executed on virtual machines instead of physical machines. Figure 3 shows the MapReduce architecture on cloud.

Request for virtual hadoop cluster is submitted through web portal. User specifies cluster name, cluster size, storage size, RAM requirement etc. Once the request is approved by administrator the script to setup hadoop cluster is executed to create VMs running hadoop.

A pool of IP address is reserved for cloud. The administrator is responsible for maintaining the list free and allocated ip address. The IP address, host name, master & slaves details etc. are passed to each VM as OS boot parameter. The script inside VM uses this OS boot parameter to configure various settings. Figure 4 presents the flowchart for our workflow. To setup virtual hadoop cluster the steps are as given below:

1. Install hadoop on two VMs. Configure one VM as master and other as slave.
2. Create a script inside both to configure VM and hadoop settings.
3. In rc.local add full path to the script so that it is automatically executed after reboot.
4. Convert VM to master and slave template.
5. Ask user to specify the cluster size, cluster name, memory requirement and other parameters.
6. Executes shell script to create master and slave VMs.
7. Set configuration parameter for VMs and pass them as OS boot time parameter to VM.
8. The script inside the VM sets IP, hostname, master & slaves details etc. for each machine.
9. Once cluster is setup, the user can submit a MapReduce job to the master.
10. On job completion, master returns the result to the user.

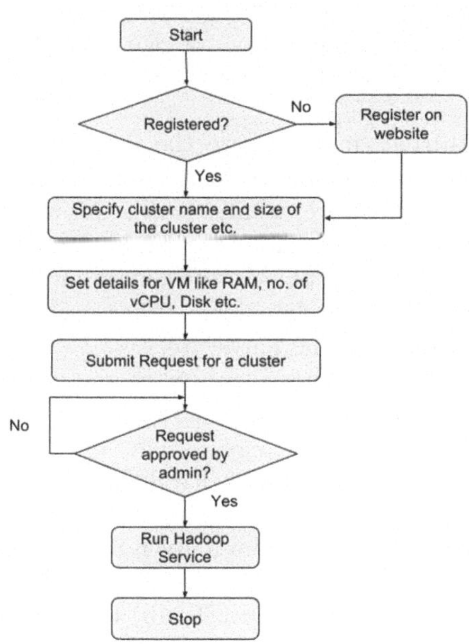

Fig. 4. Flowchart for requesting hadoop as a service

4 Performance and Result Analysis

To analyze the performance of hadoop on VM we first need to understand the split driver mode in Xen. This section will help in understanding how the virtual machine access the real hardware resources and why virtualization adds overhead.

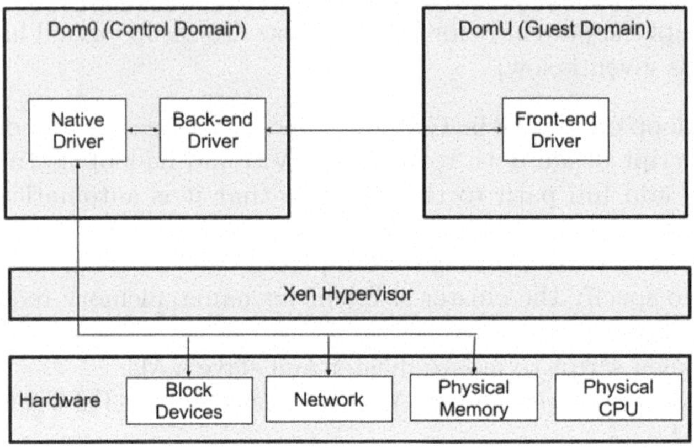

Fig. 5. Xen split-driver mode

In virtualized environment, Xen is unaware of any real hardware. To access the hardware it contains a control or privileged domain known as Dom0 which is a standard Linux system and has native device drivers to communicate with the hardware. For guests (DomU), device drivers are supplied by installing XenServer tool.

Xen supports split-driver mode where the driver is split as shown Fig. 5. The front-end driver is in the DomU (Guest) and back-end driver is in Dom0 (Control). To access the hardware, application sends request to the front-end driver in DomU which in turn communicate with back-end driver on Dom0 using a circular queue. This circular queue is in the shared memory that is maintained by the Xen hypervisor. Next, the back-end driver request native device driver which finally communicate with the hardware.

So, with split-driver mode virtualization of resources adds overhead. As hadoop is an IO intensive application its performance is degraded on VM due to this overhead.

The performance of hadoop on cloud with different cluster size of 2, 4, 6 and 8 nodes is studied in this paper. Experiments are conducted with input file size of 128, 256, 512 and 1024 Mb. Usually, for a given file size as the number of nodes in the cluster is increased the job completion is reduced as shown in Fig. 6.

However, for small file size (128 and 256 Mb) their is small reduction in job completion time with increase in cluster size. This is due to the reason that,

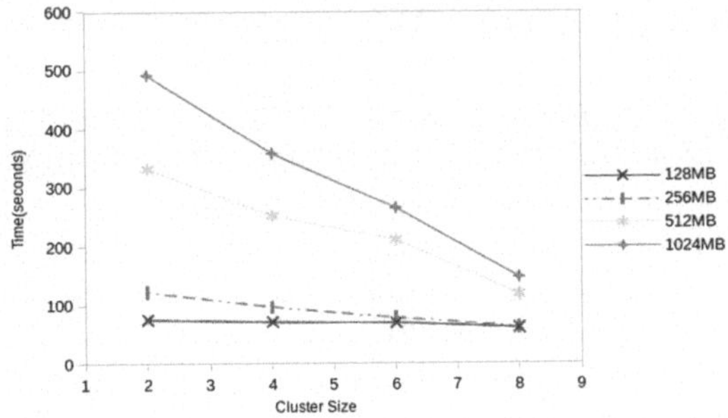

Fig. 6. Time to complete hadoop job

when a file is stored on HDFS it is usually split into chunks depending on split size (usually 64 MB) specified by mapred.max.split.size. The number of map task that process the file in parallel are equal to the number of splits. So, with small input size the number of splits and accordingly the number of map tasks are less.

Thus, increasing the number of VMs in the cluster does not improve the performance as the number of map task are less to fully utilize the VMs computational power. However, with large file size (512 and 1024 Mb) the number of file splits are more and consequently more number of mappers are their. So, with increase in cluster size these map task will be running on different machines and can utilize VM's computational power. Thus, as the cluster size increases, the job completion time will be reduced.

Figure 7, shows the time taken by map and reduce task with different file size. With small file size (128 and 256 Mb) their is a small decrease in time taken by map and reduce task with increase in cluster size. However, with large file size as the cluster size increases, the time taken by map and reduce task decreases and the performance is improved. This is due to the same reason stated above i.e. with small file size (128 and 256 MB) the number of map task are less but with large file they are increased.

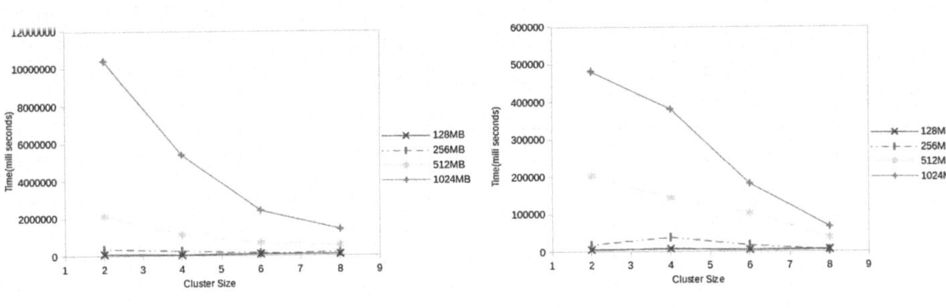

Fig. 7. Performance of map and reduce task on cloud

5 Conclusion and Future Work

This work provides a document to setup private cloud and deploy hadoop on VM with the help of script. The private cloud is based on Xen 6.5 hypervisor which provides hadoop, infrastructure and storage as a service. It has 60 TB of shared storage which is connected to hosts using QLogic 20-Port 8 Gb SAN switch module. To ensure services running on a server are not stopped in case the server hosting that services fails, high availability (HA) is enabled for pool.

Virtual hadoop cluster has its own pros and cons. Although virtualization causes low performance of hadoop but it offers its own benefits like easy management, easy setup, resource consolidation, easy scalability etc. It also benefits from high availability by restarting hadoop service at new host in case the original server hosting the hadoop VM fails. In future, the performance of virtual hadoop cluster with different kind of storage and workloads will be studied.

References

1. Armbrust, M., Fox, A., Griffith, R., Joseph, A.D., Katz, R., Konwinski, A., Lee, G., Patterson, D., Rabkin, A., Stoica, I., et al.: A view of cloud computing. Commun. ACM **53**(4), 50–58 (2010)
2. Mell, P., Grance, T., et al.: The NIST definition of cloud computing. Commun. ACM **53**, 50 (2011)
3. Dillon, T., Wu, C., Chang, E.: Cloud computing: issues and challenges. In: 2010 24th IEEE International Conference on Advanced Information Networking and Applications (AINA), pp. 27–33. IEEE (2010)
4. Savu, L.: Cloud computing: deployment models, delivery models, risks and research challenges. In: 2011 International Conference on Computer and Management (CAMAN), pp. 1–4. IEEE (2011)
5. Li, A., Yang, X., Kandula, S., Zhang, M.: CloudCmp: comparing public cloud providers. In: Proceedings of the 10th ACM SIGCOMM Conference on Internet Measurement, pp. 1–14. ACM (2010)
6. Rimal, B.P., Choi, E., Lumb, I.: A taxonomy and survey of cloud computing systems. In: INC, IMS and IDC, pp. 44–51 (2009)
7. Wang, L., Tao, J., Kunze, M., Castellanos, A.C., Kramer, D., Karl, W.: Scientific cloud computing: early definition and experience. In: 2008 10th IEEE International Conference on High Performance Computing and Communications, HPCC 2008, pp. 825–830. IEEE (2008)
8. Clark, C., Fraser, K., Hand, S., Hansen, J.G., Jul, E., Limpach, C., Pratt, I., Warfield, A.: Live migration of virtual machines. In: Proceedings of the 2nd Conference on Symposium on Networked Systems Design and Implementation, vol. 2, pp. 273–286. USENIX Association (2005)
9. Padala, P., Zhu, X., Wang, Z., Singhal, S., Shin, K.G., et al.: Performance evaluation of virtualization technologies for server consolidation. HP Labs Technical report (2007)
10. Barroso, L.A., Hölzle, U.: The case for energy-proportional computing. Computer **40**(12), 33–37 (2007)
11. Dean, J., Ghemawat, S.: MapReduce: simplified data processing on large clusters. Commun. ACM **51**(1), 107–113 (2008)

12. Zhang, Q., Liu, L., Lee, K., Zhou, Y., Singh, A., Mandagere, N., Gopisetty, S., Alatorre, G.: Improving Hadoop service provisioning in a geographically distributed cloud. In: 2014 IEEE 7th International Conference on Cloud Computing (CLOUD), pp. 432–439. IEEE (2014)
13. Guo, Y., Rao, J., Jiang, C., Zhou, X.: Moving Hadoop into the cloud with flexible slot management and speculative execution. IEEE Trans. Parallel Distrib. Syst. **28**(3), 798–812 (2017)
14. Barham, P., Dragovic, B., Fraser, K., Hand, S., Harris, T., Ho, A., Neugebauer, R., Pratt, I., Warfield, A.: Xen and the art of virtualization. In: ACM SIGOPS Operating Systems Review, vol. 37, pp. 164–177. ACM (2003)
15. Abels, T., Dhawan, P., Chandrasekaran, B.: An overview of xen virtualization. Dell Power Solut. **8**, 109–111 (2005)
16. Borthakur, D.: The Hadoop distributed file system: architecture and design. Hadoop Proj. Website **11**(2007), 21 (2007)
17. Ibrahim, S., Jin, H., Lu, L., Qi, L., Wu, S., Shi, X.: Evaluating MapReduce on virtual machines: the Hadoop case. In: Jaatun, M.G., Zhao, G., Rong, C. (eds.) CloudCom 2009. LNCS, vol. 5931, pp. 519–528. Springer, Heidelberg (2009). https://doi.org/10.1007/978-3-642-10665-1_47
18. Ibrahim, S., Jin, H., Cheng, B., Cao, H., Wu, S., Qi, L.: CLOUDLET: towards mapreduce implementation on virtual machines. In: Proceedings of the 18th ACM International Symposium on High Performance Distributed Computing, pp. 65–66. ACM (2009)
19. Xu, G., Xu, F., Ma, H.: Deploying and researching Hadoop in virtual machines. In: 2012 IEEE International Conference on Automation and Logistics (ICAL), pp. 395–399. IEEE (2012)
20. Wendt, M.E.: Cloud-based Hadoop deployments: benefits and considerations. Technical report (2014)
21. Conley, M., Vahdat, A., Porter, G.: Achieving cost-efficient, data-intensive computing in the cloud. In: Proceedings of the Sixth ACM Symposium on Cloud Computing, pp. 302–314. ACM (2015)
22. Citrix XenServer Design. Designing xenserver network configurations

Healthcare Waste Management and Application Through Big Data Analytics

Poorti Sahni[1], Ginni Arora[1], and Ashwani Kumar Dubey[2](✉)

[1] Amity Institute of Information Technology, Amity University Uttar Pradesh, Noida, UP, India
poortisahni@gmail.com, garora@amity.edu

[2] Amity School of Engineering and Technology, Amity University Uttar Pradesh, Noida, UP, India
dubey1ak@gmail.com

Abstract. Healthcare is one most rapidly growing and largest sector in India. Healthcare comprises hospitals, medical devices, clinical trials, telemedicine, health insurance and medical equipment. Such a large industry generates huge amount of waste such as syringes, needles, disposable scalpels and blades, used cotton and bandages, plastic and glass bottles, chemicals, pharmaceuticals and other infectious waste. Waste is not managed properly due to lack of awareness about the health hazards related to health-care waste, inadequate training in proper waste management, absence of waste management and disposal systems, insufficient financial and human resources, and low priority to the task connected with the health-care wastes. This paper highlights the use of Big Data Analytics to provide application of healthcare waste in agriculture and disaster management sector. The predictions show that if planning is adequate then waste of one sector can be fully utilized in another sector with low cost.

Keywords: Health care waste management · Big data · 3R'S · Data analytics

1 Introduction

Health-care waste is the waste generated at the hospitals, clinical trials, laboratories and during research work. Around 75% to 90% of the waste generated in the healthcare sector is non-hazardous waste which is considered as domestic waste including the plastic bottles, broken glasses, knives, blades, boxes [1]. As the healthcare industry is growing and waste generation rate is high. Waste management and minimization is the need of the hour. Big Data analytics helps to examine the data, develop new insights and define new patterns and correlation. Big data analytics in healthcare sector can help to identify the sources of waste and analyzing how they can be reduced or managed more effectively [2]. There are four V's defined in big data:

Volume – Large amount of data that is generated and is collected to study to gain insights.

Velocity – Data is being generated at a very speed. Faster processing of data is required for timely results and report generation.

B. Panda et al. (Eds.): REDSET 2017, CCIS 799, pp. 72–79, 2018.
https://doi.org/10.1007/978-981-10-8527-7_7

Variety – Huge variety of data is generated and is available in the form of text, videos, documents, reports and audio files.

Veracity – It represents the trustworthiness of the data. Data is available in abundance from various sources. Data which is available is cleaned i.e., noise is being removed and various transformations are performed so that the data is meaningful for analytics.

More V's have been defined for the large amount of data – value, validity, volatility which further describes the attributes for the data. Validity correlates to the correctness of the data for intended use. Volatility is for how long the data is valid and can be used. Value relates to the quality of the analytics provided by the collected data that assist in decision making [3].

Earlier waste intelligence methods have been used, which tackle the waste after being generated. Big data analytics and IOT (internet of things) are providing waste analytics methods – which helps us to analyze how much waste is generated in advance so that it can be minimized and managed properly [4]. Big data analytics can help to find various applications of waste generated. An efficient waste management hierarchy is shown in Fig. 1.

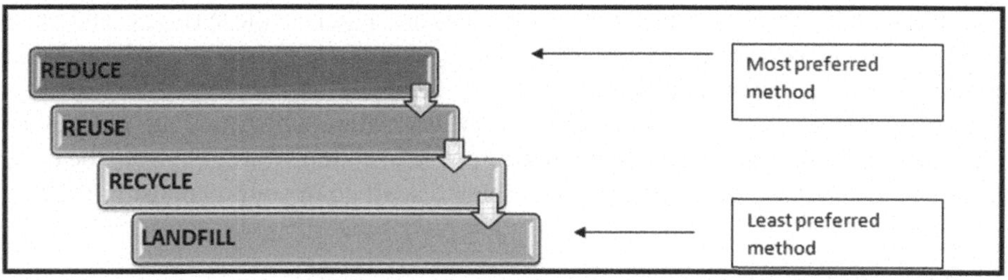

Fig. 1. Waste management hierarchy

Landfill is the least preferred method as the waste disposed off in landfill may take lot of time to decompose and can cause lot of environmental problems such as lowering of ground water levels [5]. Most of the waste generated is subjected to land filling without proper segregation which further deepens the problem. The waste generated contains plastics, heavy metals, papers, glasses therefore should be segregated and proper waste hierarchy should be followed. Land filling should only be opted when the 3R's cannot be followed. Land filling should be done with proper study and analyzing the impact of the waste to the environment.

2 Application of Waste in Agriculture and Disaster Management

Medical industry generates different types of waste which includes infectious waste, sharps, chemicals, radioactive waste [6]. If we want to recycle or reuse the waste generated in healthcare sector- all the materials and things should be properly sanitized before they are used.

Plastic is the general common term for a wide range of synthetic or semi-synthetic materials used in huge, and growing, range of applications. The incorporation of plastic into modern medicine has steadily increased in the last decade. With such wide range of applications using plastic, innovative and divergent methods have to incorporate to recycle the plastic. Plastics can be used to create nursery pots and silage bags [7].

Use of plastic irrigation pipes prevents loss of water and nutrients. Crops can be stored in greenhouses under a plastic film. Other plastic applications include boxes; crates for crop collecting, handling and transport; components for irrigation systems like fittings and spray cones. [8] Plastics can be used to build shelters. In extreme conditions such as in flood prone areas, tsunamis, earthquakes where quick and reliable shelters are required, plastics sheets can be used. Now days; waste plastic is also used in constructing roads in many countries.

Waste glass is not waste it's a new resource. Hospitals generate glass waste in form bottles, test tubes, medicine jars. Glass bottles are mostly recycled without any loss in the quality of the products. Recycled glass can be substituted for up to 95% of raw materials [9]. Glasses can be used in filtration industry as crushed glasses granules can be used as filters which produce extremely clear water [10].

Other waste include syringes (without needles and fixed needle syringes) and vacationers with their needles cut) and gloves. These wastes are treated properly and then recycled and are used for road making [11].

Biodegradable waste from hospitals can be land filled which will act as manure. Cotton is also fodder for the compost bin. Cotton balls, cotton swabs, lint from the dryer and even old shredded cotton and wool clothing can all go in your compost bin [12].

3 Proposed Model

Big data analytics can be used at various levels of waste management hierarchy. At each level we apply analytics to serve the intended purpose. At the first stage- Reduce; predictive analytics is applied because we want to predict how much waste an activity can generate. The second and third stage- Reuse and Recycle; exploratory analytics is applied because at this stage we required to explore materials which can be reused and recycled and application where they can be implemented. At the final stage, Land filling; we are required to perform segregation and treatment of material and define a course of action. Therefore we apply prescriptive analytics.

3.1 Stage-1: Predictive Analytics

At the very first stage, for reducing the waste we are required to imply predictive analytics. It is important to analyze the current data and make use of it to predict a solution for the future. If we are able to identify the sources of the waste then we can develop remedies to reduce the waste. It uses information technology, data mining statistics, modeling, machine learning, and artificial intelligence to analyze current data and make prediction about the future.

Predictive analytics work in steps:

- What happened and why happened? [historical data]
- What is happening now? [present data]
- What will happen in future?

Predictive models are developed to best predict the probability of an outcome. Models are developed using one or more algorithms on the data set. Algorithms imply data mining and statistical analysis in order to unfold trends and patterns in data. [13] Various software solutions for predictive analytics have built in algorithms such as regression, time-series, decision trees, neural networks. The purpose of these models is to analyze the past performance for future predictions.

Predictive modeling is an iterative process- which involves pre-processing the data (removing noise, missing values), applying the data mining techniques, validating the results, then modeling the data, evaluating it and deployment. Monitoring and improvement are done after deployment. Various models are applied on the same data and the one that gets the best results is selected.

3.2 Stage-2: Exploratory Analytics

It will help to gain new insights and uncover applications which can be used to reuse and recycle waste. It is an approach to analyzing data sets to find previously unknown relationships.

- Exploratory models are good for discovering new connections.
- They are also useful for defining future studies/questions [14].

Exploratory data analytics makes most use of graphical techniques. Some of them are box plot, histograms, normal probability plots, scatter plots. Scatter plots represent the series of points to show relation between two variables. Histograms represent data for individual values or range of values as vertical bars. Box plots provide the minimum value, maximum values, and quartiles for the given dataset.

Normal probability plot is used to assess whether the data set is normally distributed. Graphical techniques represent the data in the most understandable form which makes it most suitable for analytics. Determining connections and correlations is much easier when data is represented in terms of graphs. EDA also uses quantitative techniques – internal estimation and hypothesis testing [15].

Exploratory analytics can help to identify the area where waste can be reused within the industry or if it can be used anywhere else in any other industry. Applications presented in this paper deals with the hospital waste being used in the agriculture industry and disaster management.

3.3 Stage-3: Prescriptive Analytics

It typically defines – "what should we do?" It is appropriate at the level of land filling so that proper course of action is determined to dispose of the waste. These analytics are all about providing advice. Mostly the land filling is done without proper segregation and treatment of the waste. Prescriptive analytics at this stage will define the proper method to dispose off the waste. The prescriptive analytics works with a predictive model having additional component-actionable data and feedback system to know the outcome produced by the action taken. Optimization techniques are used in prescriptive analytics so that most optimal decision is taken. Therefore optimization models are been built [16]. Powerful optimization methods and software can coherently solve deterministic optimization problems. Second approach to the prescriptive analytics is simulation. Simulation is the analysis of a large number of alternatives under different realistic scenarios identified by decision-makers. This method requires decision-makers to have wide knowledge of the field to ensure the right selection of a single option from a potential field of thousands, in order to arrive at the best possible outcome. Simulation develops the understanding of the outcome of certain events and behavior of a certain system. It also provides a virtual experience of real world operations and data using a variety of realistic conditions [17] (Fig. 2).

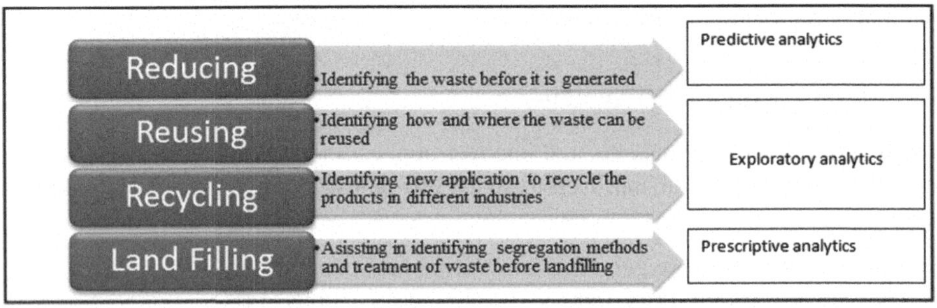

Fig. 2. Mapping waste management hierarchy and data analytics

4 Process Flow Diagram

Waste minimization relates to the techniques which are applied to reduce the generation of waste. Implementation of the practices of the waste minimization technique of reusing and recycling have been promoted a lot but not implemented properly. [18] The flow chart in the Fig. 3 suggests in selecting the best waste minimization solution which involves assessing the technical feasibility, assessing economic viability, evaluate environmental factors. Implementing waste minimization solutions involves the preparation of implementation (selecting teams, making material and energy balance, assigning costs to waste streams), review of process to identify waste causes, monitor and evaluate results. It is important to maintain waste minimization solutions to ensure sustainability and review of processes and activities which can be improved or require changes. [19] Waste management becomes easy if waste minimization techniques are followed properly as it reduces the amount of waste making it easy to handle and segregate [20].

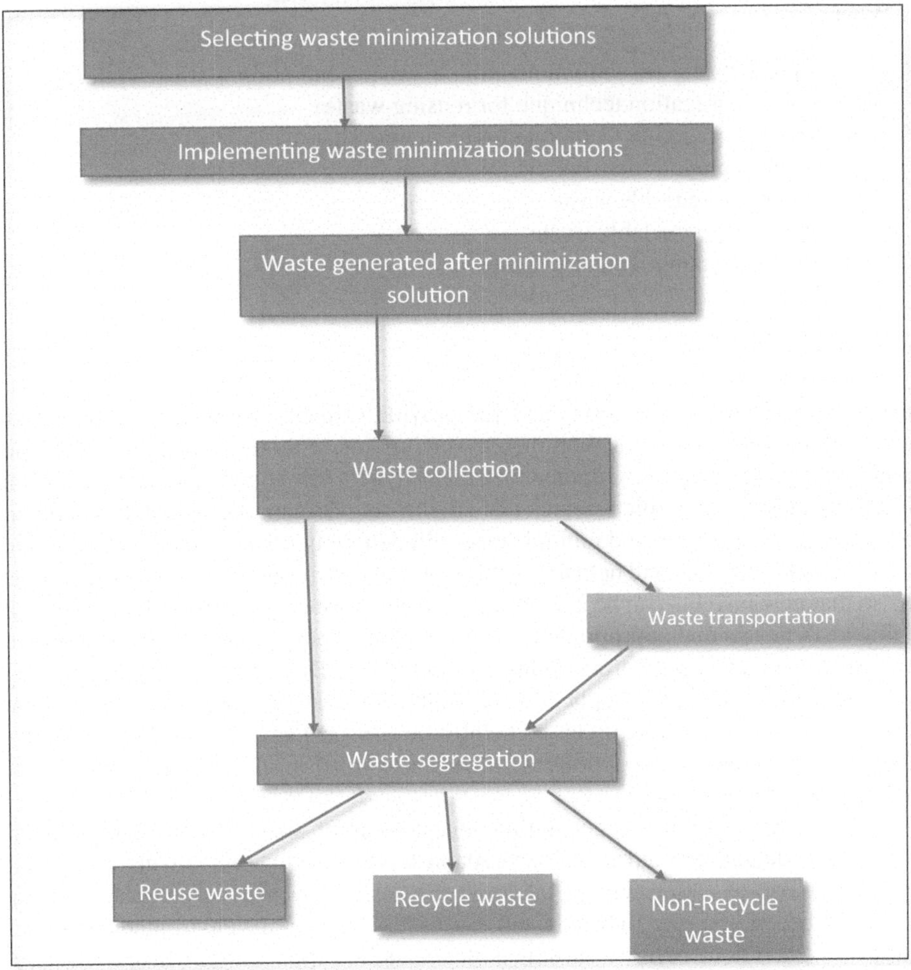

Fig. 3. Process flow diagram

Following are equations which define different segregation techniques.

$$W_{TR} = W_{min} + W_{gen} + W_{col} \quad (1)$$

$$W_{seg1} = W_{TR} + R_w \quad (2)$$

$$W_{seg2} = W_{TR} + R_c \quad (3)$$

$$W_{seg3} = W_{TR} + R_{NC} \quad (4)$$

Where,

W_{TR} = represents the waste minimization + waste generation + waste collection
W_{seg1} = waste segregation technique for reusing waste
W_{seg2} = waste segregation technique for recycling waste
W_{seg3} = waste segregation technique for non-recycling waste (landfilling)
R_w = stands for reusable waste
R_c = stands for recyclable waste
R_{NC} = stands for non-recyclable waste

5 Conclusion

Data is available in various forms and can provide valuable information to minimize waste and maximize the utilization thereby saving lots of money for organization and maintaining sustainable environment. Data analytics has shown eminent results in various businesses, scientific research and engineering domain. Data analytics application in waste management and minimization will definitely reveal some great ideas and practices. Data analytics will help to use this storm of data properly. It will help to model data so that new insights can be gained. Each step of waste management hierarchy will require analytics so that appropriate measures are taken accordingly. Three R's should be considered and utilized before opting for land filling. Different industries can utilize the waste in different ways. Application of healthcare waste in suggested in agriculture industry and as well as how it can be helpful in disaster management. Data analytics will open more avenues and options to utilize waste either in same industry or if can be used in some other industry.

Each industry right now is generating huge amount of waste. Proper segregation of waste into biodegradable and non-biodegradable has begun but is not into much practice. Required course of action will be taken on the basis of what type of waste is being handled. It becomes easier to handle and causes less harm to the environment if segregation of waste is done before disposing it off and finding applications where it can used. The proposed model has tried to incorporate different type of analytics at each stage pertaining to the hierarchy. It will mitigate the problem at each stage and provide solution at each stage. Predictive analytics can help to reduce the amount of waste generation. Exploratory analytics can help to develop new relationships and find new applications to reuse and recycle waste.

Prescriptive analytics will define the proper course of action at the last stage –Land Filling. This will help to bring out the best results in waste management and minimization which is the need of the hour.

References

1. http://www.who.int/mediacentre/factsheets/fs253/en/. Accessed 14 July 2017
2. Raghupathi, W., Raghupathi, V.: Big data analytics in healthcare: promise and potential. Health Inf. Sci. Syst. **2**(3), 1–10 (2014)
3. Williamson, J.: The 4 V's of big data. http://www.dummies.com/careers/find-a-job/the-4-vs-of-big-data/. Accessed 13 July 2017
4. Bilal, M., Oyedele, L.O., Akinade, O.O., Ajayi, O.S., Alaka, H.A., Owolabi, H.A., Qadir, J., Pasha, M., Bello, S.A.: Big data architecture for construction waste analytics (CWA): a conceptual framework. J. Build. Eng. **6**, 144–156 (2016)
5. Thomas, J., Wilson, P.M.: Construction waste management in India. Am. J. Eng. Res. (AJER) **2**, 6–9 (2013)
6. Waste Reduction Tips for Hospitals. http://www.bwaste.com/waste-reduction-tips-for-hospitals/. Accessed 15 July 2017
7. The Ultimate Guide to Plastic Recycling. http://www.conserve-energy-future.com/recyclingplastic.php. Accessed 14 July 2017
8. Grossman, E.: How can agriculture solve its $5.87 billion plastic problem? (2015). https://www.greenbiz.com/article/how-can-agriculture-solve-its-1-billion-plastic-problem. Accessed 15 July 2017
9. Glass Container Recycling Loop. http://www.gpi.org/recycling/glass-recycling-facts. Accessed 14 July 2017
10. Recycled Crushed Glass and Its Many Uses. https://www.slideshare.net/sipepxjyb/the-many-uses-of-recycled-crushed-glass. Accessed 14 July 2017
11. Bio-medical waste and its segregation. http://vikaspedia.in/energy/environment/waste-management/bio-medical-waste-management/what-is-bio-medical-waste. Accessed 14 July 2017
12. Things You Never Thought were Recyclable. http://blog.etoncorp.com/index.php/2011/06/5-things-you-never-thought-were-recyclable/. Accessed 14 July 2017
13. What is Predictive Modeling? https://www.predictiveanalyticstoday.com/predictive-modeling/. Accessed 14 July 2017
14. Exploratory data analytics. ftp://ftp.nist.gov/pub/itl/wguthrie/eda.pdf
15. Anderson, A., Semmelroth, D.: Quantitative Exploratory Data Analysis (EDA) Techniques. http://www.dummies.com/programming/big-%20data/data-science/quantitative-exploratory-data-analysis-eda-techniques/. Accessed 14 July 2017
16. Praseeda, C.K., Shivakumar, B.L.: A review of trends and technologis in business analytics. Int. J. Adv. Res. Comput. Sci. **5**(8), 225–229 (2014)
17. Lee, T.: Optimization vs. Simulation. https://www.kisters.net/NA/fileadmin/KNA/Products/Optimization_vs_Simulation.pdf. Accessed 15 July 2017
18. Senami, A., Ejiga, O.: Waste minimization with architectural design practices in lagos (2017). www.uia2017seoul.org/P/papers/Full_paper/Paper/Oral/PS2-31/O-0379.pd
19. Global waste management conference (2017)
20. Kumar, S., Smith, S.R., Fowler, G., Velis, C., Kumar, S.J., Arya, S., Rena, Kumar, R., Cheeseman, C.: Challenges and opportunities associated with waste management in India. Accessed 22 Mar 2017

Detecting Internet Addiction Disorder Using Bayesian Networks

Anju Singh(✉) and Sakshi Babbar

Department of Computer Science and Engineering, GD Goenka University, Gurugram, India
anjusingh40@gmail.com, sakshi.babbar@gdgoenka.ac.in

Abstract. 21st century being the digital age has produced social, economic and communication revolution. Proliferation of Internet has made a globally connected world. Internet per se is a harmless technology with significant benefits, on contrary its excessive usage and dependence leads to high risk of addiction. It is preordained society need and requirement of continual research to develop efficient tools to identify and predict the potential Internet Addiction Disorder among the internet users. Our aim is to automate task of predicting prevalence of Internet Addiction disorder using Bayesian Network and propose a machine learning graphical framework, namely, Internet Addiction Disorder Bayesian Network. In this work, we exploit the unique features of Bayesian Network to explore the influence of causal symptoms on the probability of occurrence of Internet Addiction Disorder (IAD). The model is constructed with Internet Addiction Test as platform and Internet Addiction Disorder absence or presence is measured through six parameters of Internet Addiction Test (Salience, Excessive use, Neglect work, Anticipation, Lack of control, Neglect Social Life). The six attributes are classified into four groups: normal, mild, moderate and severe on the basis of the item scores obtained by the individuals in the parameters, which are summed to obtain the total score. The total score is utilized to classify the samples into two groups: IAD Present and IAD Absent. To achieve graphical user interface for the model, a high performance Netica software is used for the study. The results obtained are promising and reveals that the model can predict the IAD presence and absence with 100% accuracy. The model also shows that out of six parameters, excessive use of internet plays significant role in increasing the risk of IAD preceded by Salience.

Keywords: Bayesian Network · Internet Addiction · Sensitivity Salience

1 Introduction

In present digital age, addiction to technology is widespread. Technology addiction dates back to early ages, became more and more pronounced in early 30' with radio followed by Television in mid-sixties and is becoming chronic and pervasive with extensive spread of Internet. Though Internet usage improves productivity and efficiency, it actually saves time in tasks like online banking, online shopping, social communication, educational pursuits and entertainment. In-fact it has revolutionized

B. Panda et al. (Eds.): REDSET 2017, CCIS 799, pp. 80–95, 2018.
https://doi.org/10.1007/978-981-10-8527-7_8

the whole world to a great extent. Going online is the latest trend and is on high priority for many and life outside the virtual world suffers. Unfortunately, the excessive use of internet significantly interferes with the personal, social, emotional and professional aspects of life.

Brent Conrad in an article [1] mentioned a general Internet Addiction thumb rule that, if a person continually use internet to stay away from the real world responsibilities or problems and this escaping creates even more trouble in their life, then this may imply the presence of an addiction to the Internet. According to BrandonGaille recent surveys, statistics indicated that in the general population of United States and Europe the internet addiction rate was prevalent as high as 8.2% and it could be higher as 18.5% in some regions. In countries like South Korea and China internet addiction has been classified as a serious health risk, as it interferes with the functional aspects of life and subsequently creates a negative impact on life [2].

Since the craze of Internet is increasing at a fast pace and its pervasiveness in the life of people has escalated the risk of addiction to it, it is necessary to continually study the pros and cons of Internet on the health of its users. Researches have been conducted to detect the Internet addiction disorder (IAD) in the Internet users using traditional statistical methods. The studies show that researchers are exploring the machine learning models for evaluation, prediction and detection of IAD in the online users. Machine learning models provides a complementary platform for psychiatrists, counsellors, clinicians and health care-takers, to support their prognosis and decision making, in identifying the potential IAD cases so that the treatment can be started early. Our study is different from other researches, because in this study we construct an appealing graphical representation of the determinants of IAD, facilitating better understanding of the disorder and which may be used as an efficient tool to detect the occurrence of IAD in order to safeguard health of the internet users.

We develop a machine learning graphical model, namely Internet Addiction Disorder Bayesian Network (IAD-BN) to evaluate, detect and predict IAD probable cases using Bayesian Networks. The reasons for choosing BN model to detect and predict the potential IADs are summarised as follows:

1. BN represents prior data and knowledge, using probabilistic and causal semantics.
2. BN is best suited for learning causal relationships among the variables which helps in better understanding of the problem domain and forecast the consequences of an intervention.
3. BN model grows as new domain knowledge is acquired and can also relearn the enhanced domain knowledge. This adaptable quality of BN renders it useful for future use.
4. Causal relationships among the variables, diagnostic inference, sensitivity analysis and prediction are some important characteristics of BN and we exploit these features to efficiently detect the presence and absence of IAD in the internet users.

However the primary motivation to use BN in this study is to reduce computation time, test time and material cost but the useful properties of probabilistic graphical models and advantages of BN mentioned above cannot be ignored.

In this study the Internet Addiction Bayesian network model (IAD-BN) is constructed on the domain knowledge of Young's Internet Addiction Test (IAT) [3].

According to IAT, internet addiction develops due to six discriminate underlying causes which constitute the 20 items in the test. The six causal symptoms are: Salience, Excessive use, Neglect work, Anticipation, Lack of control, Neglect social life. The proposed IAD-BN graphical model is visually appealing and facilitates basic understanding of the disorder. As a diagnostic tool the model is easy to decipher and can be implemented with efficiency.

The Sect. 2, of the paper highlights the study area of internet addiction disorders. It also explores the role of machine learning models in the detection and prediction of IADs. In Sect. 3, Bayesian network is briefly presented and the formalisation of IAD-BN model is described. Section 4, of the paper covers experimental results and inference ability of the model. The Proposed future work and conclusion is presented in Sect. 5.

1.1 Contributions

Following points are the contributions of this Paper:

1. We show that core features of Bayesian Network are useful in the decision process for psychiatrists to predict the probability of a person suffering from Internet Addiction Disorder based on the evident causes and symptoms.
2. BN causal reasoning representation offers a platform for teachers and counsellors to identify and predict the probability of occurrence of IAD in students showing one or more symptoms.
3. The BN model is adaptable and is useful in medical diagnosis to predict simultaneous presence of mental disorders.
4. The model saves time and enormous computations required in predicting the prevalence of IAD.
5. The graphical representation helps intuitive understanding of the problem domain area and is a motivation to internet users to recognize the pathological online behaviour and therefore model may be adopted as an IAD diagnostic tool.
6. The IAD-BN model is formulated on the data set obtained from the internet addiction test. The model predicts prevalence of IAD with 100% accuracy.
7. The sensitivity test on the IAD-BN model showed that the occurrence of IAD is most sensitive towards excessive use of internet preceded by salience. Thus we propose that, if these two key determinants are controlled then the occurrence of IAD can be minimised to a large extent.

2 Detection of Internet Addiction Disorder

IAD is a major health threat for the well being of the society and it needs to be addressed continually by the researcher and clinicians. Flisher explored concept of interent addiction and presented an overview on its occurrence, diagnostic criteria, treatment and consequences. According to the researcher, the term internet addiction includes various subtypes like: Net compulsion; Internet gaming addiction; Online research addiction; Cyber sexual addiction; Cyber-relational addiction [4].

For almost a decade, the researchers have suggested several diagnostic criteria but still there are no uniform diagnostic criteria to confirm the presence of IAD. Cash et al. researched on internet addiction practices and concluded that, though internet addiction is rapidly advancing yet it has not found a place in the Diagnostic and Statistical Manual of Mental Disorders [5] as a separate behavioural disorder. The study also summarised that, different types of IAD (e.g., cybersex addition, internet gaming, excessive net surfing) fits in one category, due to various common factors like anonymity, virtual interaction, increased online time and also due to common underlying behaviours like avoidance, fear, pleasure and entertainment [6].

According to studies, the physical health symptoms and signs of IAD like insomnia, vision problems, body aches, weight gain or loss, poor nutrition and personal hygiene are easy to diagnose but the emotional manifestations like lying, guilt feeling, nervousness, euphoric feeling while on-line, inability to prioritize personal and professional schedules, loneliness, time mismanagement, defensiveness, laziness, agitation and mood swings are passive and cannot be diagnosed easily. Also the symptoms or intervention for one person may be different for another due to demographic, social and familial factors. Due to these reasons, the process of diagnosis of IAD is complex and challenging, but researchers are attempting to propose improved procedures and factors for the assessment, diagnosis and interventions for the probable addicted internet users. The diagnosis and detection of IAD is studied and researched mainly using questionnaires and statistical tools. Young's Internet Addiction Test (IAT), the Problematic Internet Use Questionnaire (PIUQ), and the Compulsive Internet Use Scale (CIUS) are the most popular and common assessment tools, used to help make a diagnosis of Internet Addiction Disorder [7].

The use of machine learning algorithms to predict and make prognosis of psychiatric diseases due to excessive use of internet is the latest attraction for researchers and psychiatrists. Providing an accurate predictive complementary platform using machine learning frameworks, to supplement the conventional method (statistical methods, questionnaires and interviews) of detection of internet related disorders is a challenging task. Ioannidis et al. evaluated problematic internet use using machine learning predictive models based on logistic regression, random forest and Naive Bayes algorithms. The authors, collected 2006 cases from two sites (Chicago USA, Stellenbosch South Africa) and analyzed the sample using IAT. 181 (9%) were found to have moderate/ severe problematic internet use. The accuracy of the machine learning models was measured by plotting a receiver operating characteristic (ROC) graph. The logistic regression and Naive Bayes algorithm models, predicted ROC area under curve as 0.83 (SD = 0.03) and the model based on random forest algorithm predicted ROC area as 0.84 (SD = 0.03). The study found that the models predicted the result accurately [8]. In another research, Nandhini et al. applied classification algorithms to evaluate and analyze internet addiction and related data. The researcher applied five classification algorithms (Naive Bayes, JRip, ZeroR, J48, RepTree) on a sample of 100 college students and concluded that JRip performance was better as compared to other four algorithms by identifying 70 students as addicted to internet (5 highly and 65 moderately) and remaining 30 as normal [9].

3 IAD Modelling Using Bayesian Network

In this paper, we exploit a machine learning graphical framework (Bayesian Network) for predicting the probability of occurrence of Internet addiction disorder in the internet users, which helps the users to go for a medical intervention before addiction results in adversely affecting their lives.

3.1 Bayesian Network

The probability theory consists of two simple equations corresponding to the sum rule and the product rule [10]:

$$\text{Sum rule}\ \mathrm{p}(X) = \sum\nolimits_{y} p(X, Y) \tag{1}$$

$$\text{Product rule}\ \mathrm{p}(X, Y) = \mathrm{p}(Y|X)p(X) \tag{2}$$

Here X and Y are two events, $\mathrm{p}(X, Y)$ is a joint probability of X and Y. $\mathrm{p}(Y|X)$ is a conditional probability of Y given X, whereas the quantity $\mathrm{p}(X)$ is a marginal probability of X. Eqs. (1) and (2) form the basis for all probabilistic problems and are also used to obtain Baye's theorem, which is fundamental to machine learning and pattern recognition process. The Bayes' theorem is a relationship between the probabilities of X and Y i.e. $\mathrm{p}(X)$ and $\mathrm{p}(Y)$ and the conditional probabilities of X given Y and Y given X. Mathematically it can be expressed as:

$$p(X|Y) = \frac{p(Y|X)p(X)}{p(Y)} \tag{3}$$

where $p(Y) \neq 0$, p(X) and p(Y) are independent probabilities of X and Y, p(X|Y) is conditional probability of event X given Y is true and p(Y|X) is probability of observing Y given X is true.

Probabilities play an important role in classifying input data into objects or classes on key features. The repeated application of the probabilistic equations forms the background for all probabilistic deduction and formulation of learning manipulations. The diagrammatic representation of the probability distribution called Graphical models (GMs) are advantageous and augment the data analysis process. They offer the following useful properties: 1. Due to their simple visualization of the probabilistic structure they enable better understanding of the problem; 2. The inspection of the graph provides insights into the conditional independence properties of the model; 3. Mathematical expressions and complex computations underlying the deduction and learning in models, can be carried implicitly in GMs [10].

Bayesian Networks (BNs), belongs to the family of probabilistic graphical models (GMs). The Bayesian Network is a Directed Acyclic Graphs (DAG) having two parameters as components: Qualitative parameters comprised of nodes that represent random variables and the edges or links between nodes represent direct dependencies among the variables. The nodes from where the edge originates are referred as Parent of the nodes to which the edge points to. Quantitative parameter of DAG constitutes the conditional probability table (CPT) which provides the probability at each node depending on the values for each combination of values of its parents [11]. The joint probability distribution (JPD) can be determined by the CPT of all the random variables. Formally, a Bayesian Network can be defined over variables X as a pair, B = <G, P_r> where:

1. G is a Directed Acyclic Graph (DAG) over variables X. Variables can be discrete or continuous.
2. P_r is a set of conditional probability tables (CPTs) $P_r = P_r\ [P(x \mid \mu_x)]$ for each variable x and its parent μ in G such that $\sum_x P(x \mid \mu) = 1$. The conditional probability is used to measure the causal dependencies and μ_x is the set of parent nodes of x
3. A BN thus specifies a unique joint probability over x as product of conditional probability table of all variables:

$$P(x_1, x_2, \ldots\ldots x_n) = \prod_{i=1}^{n} P(x_i|\mu_i) \tag{4}$$

where n is the number of nodes in Bayesian Network [12].

3.2 Formalisation of BN Model for Detecting IAD (IAD-BN Model)

The BN model for analyzing IAD is constructed with the specific objective of helping psychiatrists, health organizations, teachers and counsellors, to facilitate them in their decision making process of detecting the IAD cases. In this paper, we construct BN model using the Young's Internet Addiction Test as domain knowledge. The model consists of a variable which is target variable (output of the network) and observation variables (evidence variables, inputs to the network). The cause and effect relationships (dependence and independence relationship) among the variables are analysed and the graphical model is constructed.

The Bayesian Network graphical Model of Internet Addiction Disorder is presented in the following Fig. 1

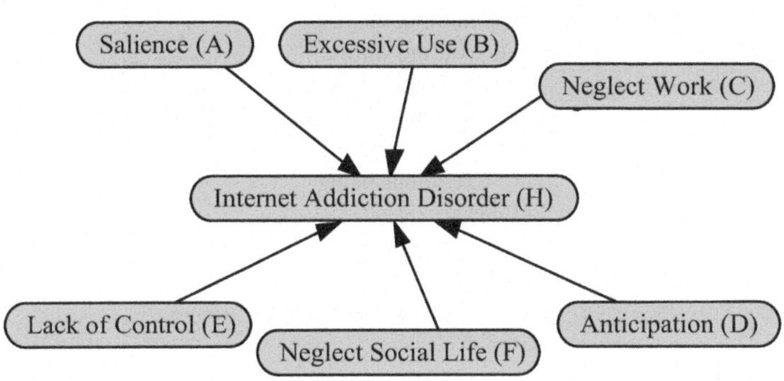

Fig. 1. The Bayesian graphical model of Internet Addiction Disorder

Analysing the model in Fig. 1 we can observe that there are 7 nodes (A, B, C, D, E, F and H) having significant roles and each node establishes an influence on the network. The nodes represent the random variables in our domain and the edges (arrows) represent the influence of one variable on another.

3.2.1 Description of Observation and Target Variables

The studies show that the Internet Addiction Test (IAT) is the most common reliable and validated tool to measure addictive use of the Internet [3]. The IAT is a 20-item questionnaire, encompassing co-morbid symptoms which assist in effective analysis of the data and also measures mild, moderate, and severe levels of internet addiction. The total score of IAT is the sum of the ratings given for the 20 item responses. Each item is rated on a 5-point scale ranging from 0 to 5. The maximum score is 100 points and it provides only an estimate of the overall severity of Internet addiction disorder. The questions of IAT are grouped in six psychometric properties, which constitutes observation variables for the study, described in the following Table 1.

Table 1. Psychometric properties of observation variables

Variables (Observation/ Target)	Variable description	Questions	5 point scale (0 to 5)	Total Score with classification (normal, mild, moderate, severe)
Salience (node A) observation variable	Most reliable factor of IAD, where internet dominates the user's thoughts and behaviour	1.How often do you block out disturbing thoughts about your life with soothing thoughts of the Internet? 2.How often do you fear that life without the Internet would be boring, empty, and joyless? 3.How often do you snap, yell, or act annoyed if someone bothers you while you are online? 4.How often do you feel preoccupied with the Internet when off-line, or fantasize about being online? 5.How often do you choose to spend more time online over going out with?	0: Does not apply 1: Rarely 2: Occasionally 3: Frequently 4: Often 5: Always	Total score - 25 0 to 6 normal; 6 to 12 mild; 12 to 18 moderate; 18 to 25 severe

(*continued*)

Table 1. (*continued*)

Variables (Observation/ Target)	Variable description	Questions	5 point scale (0 to 5)	Total Score with classification (normal, mild, moderate, severe)
Excessive use (node B) observation variable	Factor which shows excessive online engagement and indicate compulsive online behaviour of the internet users	1.How often do you find that you stay online longer than you intended? 2.How often do you neglect household chores to spend more time online? 3.How often do you lose sleep due to late-night log-ins? 4.How often do you try to hide how long you've been online? 5.How often do you feel depressed, moody or nervous when you are off-line, which goes away once you are back online?	0: Does not apply 1: Rarely 2: Occasionally 3: Frequently 4: Often 5: Always	Total score - 25 0 to 6 normal; 6 to 12 mild; 12 to 18 moderate; 18 to 25 severe
Neglect work (node C) observation variable	Major factor which hampers the performance and productivity of the internet users	1.How often do your grades or school work suffers because of the amount of time you spend online? 2.How often does your job performance or productivity suffer because of the Internet? 3.How often do you become defensive or secretive when anyone asks you what you do online?	0: Does not apply 1: Rarely 2: Occasionally 3: Frequently 4: Often 5: Always	Total score - 15 0 to 3 normal; 3 to 7 mild; 7 to 11 moderate; 11 to 15 severe
Anticipation (D node) observation variable	This refers to dreaming about being online and keeps the internet users preoccupied	1.How often do you check your e-mail before something else that you need to do? 2.How often do you find yourself anticipating when you will go online again?	0: Does not apply 1: Rarely 2: Occasionally 3: Frequently 4: Often 5: Always	Total score - 10 0 to 2 normal; 2 to 5 mild; 4 to 8 moderate; 8 to 10 severe

(*continued*)

Table 1. (*continued*)

Variables (Observation/ Target)	Variable description	Questions	5 point scale (0 to 5)	Total Score with classification (normal, mild, moderate, severe)
Lack of control (E node) observation variable	Factor which is identified by staying online longer than intended	1.How often do others in your life complain to you about the amount of time you spend online? 2.How often do you find yourself saying "just a few more minutes" when online? 3.How often do you try to cut down the amount of time you spend online and fail?	0: Does not apply 1: Rarely 2: Occasionally 3: Frequently 4: Often 5: Always	Total score - 15 0 to 3 normal; 3 to 7 mild; 7 to 11 moderate; 11 to 15 severe
Neglect social life (F node) observation variable	Social relationship deficit factor	1.How often do you prefer the excitement of the Internet to intimacy with your partner? 2.How often do you form new relationships with fellow online users?	0: Does not apply 1: Rarely 2: Occasionally 3: Frequently 4: Often 5: Always	Total score - 10 0 to 2 normal; 2 to 5 mild; 4 to 8 moderate; 8 to 10 severe
Internet addiction disorder (H Node) target variable	Unobserved node which represent the absence and presence of IAD in the internet users	—	—	Total score - 100 0 to Below 50 IAD Absent; 50 to 100 IAD Present

4 Experiments and Results

In this section, we explain the quantitative aspect of the IAD-BN model and its prior learning of the model using a training data set and the accuracy of the model.

4.1 Experiment Setup

After the qualitative aspect of IAD-BN model is designed as represented in Fig. 1, we need to indicate the quantitative aspect of the IAD-BN model that is the conditional probability tables (CPT) of the nodes. For this purpose we make use of a high performance Netica Software from Norsys [13]. We chose Netica for Bayesian Network model because of its advanced graphical user interface features in addition to its conceptually simple structure. Netica facilitates the quantitative construction of the model and its graphical interface allows prior learning of the model using statistical data.

In order to achieve the prior learning and conditional probability table (CPT) at each node, the dataset of 500 samples is randomly generated. The scores of the six parameters in the data are added to get the total internet addiction score ranging from 0 to 100. According to IAT addiction criteria [3], scores ranging from 0–30 represent normal user, 31–49 represent mild user, 50–79 as moderate user and 80–100 as severely addicted internet user. This criterion is used to classify the Internet addiction disorder node (node H) into two categories: IAD present (score 50 and above) and IAD absent (score below 50).

The data was split into training set (80% of cases) and test set (20% of cases). The learning capability of Netica was utilized to train the IAD-BN model using the training data set (Fig. 2). The model obtained in Fig. 2, is the outcome of the parameter learning with the training set and it is observed that the probability of absence of IAD in the dataset is 49.1% and the probability of presence of IAD in the dataset is 50.9%.

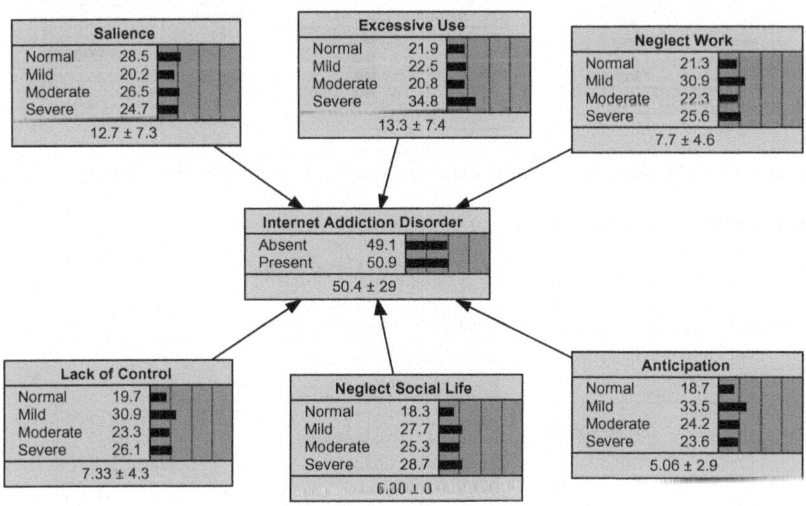

Fig. 2. The IAD-BN model after prior learning

Before the IAD-BN model application in real-life practice, we established its quality by performing probabilistic inference such as causal reasoning (called top-down reasoning) and diagnostic test (called bottom-up reasoning). The result obtained is presented below:

(i) **Causal Reasoning**

The causal reasoning in Bayesian Network greatly simplifies probability assessment as well as probabilistic inference [14]. We seek to explain the influence of varying the values of evidence nodes on the probability of occurrence of IAD. Let us consider an arbitrary query and try to interpret the answer obtained from our IAD-BN model.

P(IAD = "Absent" | Salience = "Severe", Anticipation = "Moderate") = ?

We see in the figure below that IAD absent probability comes down from 49.1% to 44.4%; IAD Present probability goes up from 50.9% to 55.6% (Refer Figs. 2 and 3). So we infer that the user has high probability to be diagnosed as addicted to internet.

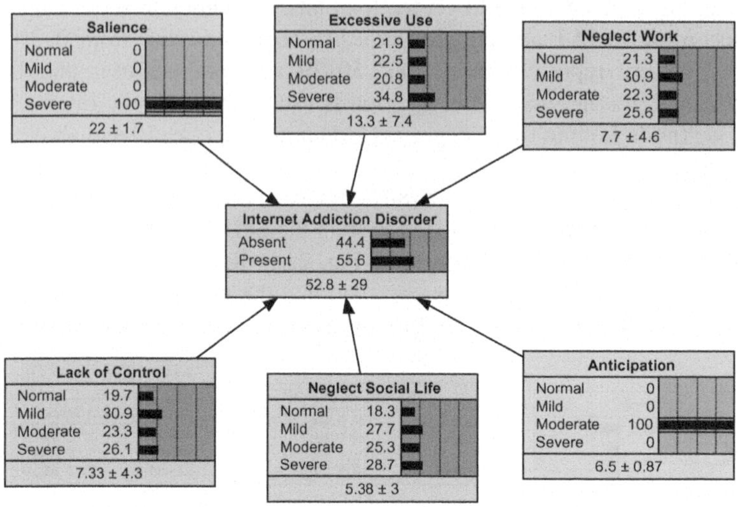

Fig. 3. The IAD-BN model with severe salience and moderate anticipation evidence

Let us consider another query

P(IAD = "Present" | Salience = "Mild", Excessive Use = "Moderate",

Anticipation = "Severe", Neglect Social Life = "Severe") = ?

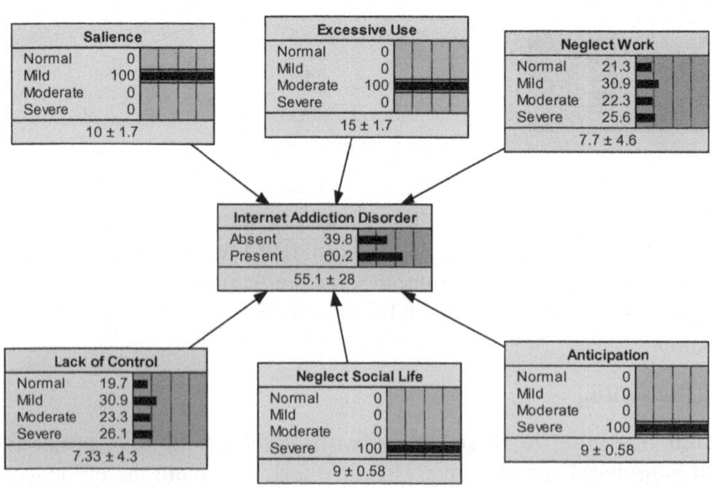

Fig. 4. The IAD-BN model with mild salience, moderate excessive use, severe anticipation and severe neglect social life evidence

We see in the IAD-BN model (Fig. 4) that probability of IAD absent comes down to 39.8% from 49.1% and probability of IAD present jumps up to 60.2% from 50.9% (refer Figs. 2 and 4). Thus we infer that chances of the user to be diagnosed as addicted is very high.

(ii) **Diagnostic Inference**

Let us consider a example of a person who is diagnosed as 100% addicted to the internet, we infer from Fig. 5 that the person may be suffering from moderate level of salience, severe level of excessive use and neglect social life, mild level of neglect work, lack of control and Anticipation.

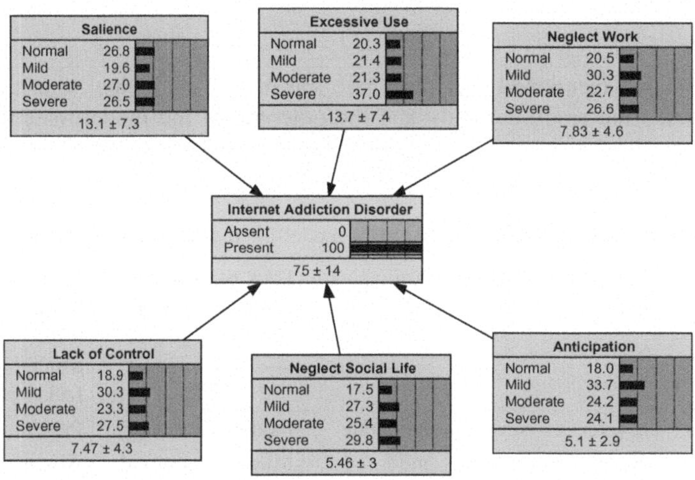

Fig. 5. The IAD BN model showing diagnostic inference

After performing the aforementioned probabilistic inferences, we propose that IAD-BN model may be considered as an efficient tool, to help predict the occurrence of IAD in the internet users. The model supports and guides the internet users to find the probability of occurrence of internet addiction, given one or more evidence. The model also assists in the identification of the levels (normal, mild, moderate and severe) of the underlying factors, playing a vital role in increasing the risk of internet addiction disorder.

4.2 Evaluation

In this section, we discuss the testing and evaluation of IAD-BN model.

4.2.1 IAD-BN Prediction Analysis

The BN model robustness in predicting the probability of presence and absence of internet addiction disorder is evaluated by the prediction and sensitivity analysis.

These tests provide insight into the performance of the BN model and also find out the possibility of inaccuracies underlying the probability distribution (Lucas et al.) [14].

The IAD-BN model in Fig. 1 is tested with real cases to see how well the model outcome matches with the actual cases. Let us consider an example of real test case, shown in Table 2:

Table 2. Example of real test cases

Case	Salience	Excessive use	Neglect work	Anticipation	Lack of control	Neglect social S life	IAD
I	severe	severe	severe	moderate	moderate	moderate	?
II	mild	mild	mild	mild	mild	Normal	?

For the above mentioned real cases, we see in Table 3 below, that the IAD-BN model predicted the result correctly and the outcome of the model matched with the actual result.

Table 3. Outcome of the IAD-BN model for the test cases in Table 1

Case	Salience	Excessive use	Neglect work	Anticipation	Lack of control	Neglect social life	IAD actual result using IAT	IAD prediction using IAD-BN model
I	severe	severe	severe	moderate	moderate	moderate	Present	Present
II	mild	mild	mild	mild	Mild	normal	Absent	Absent

The Netica interface is used to test the sensitivity and the test report shows the error rate as 0.057%. This means that the model predicted wrong value in 5.7% of the cases. Results are listed in Table 4.

The sensitivity in the Table 4, is the ability of the BN model to correctly detect cases which have internet addiction disorder. Specificity is the ability of the IAD BN

Table 4. Results of the evaluation of the test data

Cutoff	Sensitivity	Specificity	Predictive	Predict-Neg
0	100	0	50.57	100
5	100	98.84	98.88	100
98	55.68	100	100	68.8
100	0	100	100	49.43

model to correctly detect cases which do not have internet addiction disorder. Cutoff points are the optimal values to classify the test cases into IAD present and absent categories.

The accuracy of the model establishes how well the model can separate the group into IAD present and IAD absent categories. To ascertain the accuracy of the model, the receiver operating characteristic (ROC) curve is obtained by plotting sensitivity and 1-specifity mentioned in Table 4. The area under the ROC curve determines and establishes the accuracy of the model. A perfect test is represented by an area of 1 and an area of 0.5 represents a worthless test. Since we obtained the area of 0.999 under the curve (AUC) we infer that the overall performance of the model is excellent (Fig. 6).

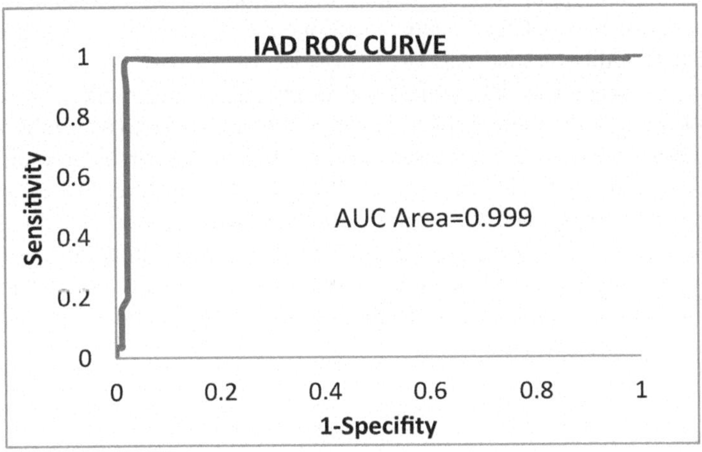

Fig. 6. ROC curve – Result of evaluation using test data

The Netica software is also used to measure the sensitivity of Internet addiction disorder node to a finding at another node. Result is listed in Table 5. Among the six parameters, the most sensitivity of the IAD node is related to the node of Excessive use preceded by the salience parameter.

Table 5. Sensitivity of IAD to a finding at another node

Node	Percent
Internet addiction disorder	100
Excessive use	0.245
Salience	0.194
Lack of control	0.098
Neglect work	0.0675
Neglect social life	0.0655
Anticipation	0.0258

5 Conclusion and Future Scope

In this paper, Bayesian Network features were exploited to predict the prevalence of Internet Addiction Disorder in a nonclinical random sample. The BN model was constructed by using the properties of Internet Addiction Test as domain knowledge. Netica interface was used to define the quantitative aspect of the model. The six parameters of the IAT test were used as evidence nodes to observe their effect on the probability of occurrence of internet addiction disorder in the internet users. The model was evaluated and the area under the receiver operating characteristic curve showed the performance between 0.9 and 1 i.e. an excellent test.

The impact of certain variables on the probability of Internet addiction disorder is also shown through cauasal analysis. The results of the IAD-BN model was promising and the model can be used for health practitioners, teachers and counsellors in diagnosis of internet addiction disorder.

However, the statistical data considered in this study is a random set of data, so general application of the finding to any other population needs to be implemented with caution. In future, dataset can be revised and IAD-BN model can be used efficiently, to predict probable internet addiction cases. We plan to construct Bayesian Network models based on the domain knowledge of other two popular tests to detect IAD (Problematic Internet Use Questionnaire and the Compulsive Internet Use Scale). We also plan to evaluate the result of three models and to find out the best fit Bayesian Network model among the three, to detect and predict the Internet addiction disorder occurrence in the internet users.

References

1. Brent Conrad Techaddiction Internet Addiction – Symptoms, Signs, Treatment, and FAQS. http://www.techaddiction.ca/internet-addiction.html
2. Brandongaille statistics 33 Interesting Internet Addiction Statistics (2017). http://brandongaille.com/32-interesting-internet-addiction-statistics/
3. Young, K.: IAT Manual – Center for Internet Addiction (1998). https://www.netaddiction.com/wp-content/uploads/2015/11/IAT-Manual.doc
4. Flisher, C.: Getting plugged in: an overview of Internet addiction. J. Paediatr. Child Health **46**, 557–559 (2010)
5. American Psychiatric Association: Diagnostic and Statistical Manual of Mental Disorders. (4th edition, Text Review). American Psychiatric Association, Washington D.C. (2000)
6. Cash, H., Rae, C.D., Steel, A.H., Winkler, A.: Internet addiction: A brief summary of research and practice. Current psychiatry reviews **8**(4), 292–298 (2012)
7. Gregory, C.: PSYCOM Internet addiction disorder Signs, Symptoms, and Treatments (2017). https://www.psycom.net/iadcriteria.html
8. Ioannidis, K., Chamberlain, S.R., Treder, M.S., Kiraly, F., Leppink, E.W., Redden, S.A., Stein, D.J., Lochner, C., Grant, J.E.: Problematic internet use(PIU): associations with the impulsive-compulsive spectrum. An application of machine learning in psychiatry. J. Psychiatr. Res. **83**, 94–102 (2016)
9. Nandhini, C., Krishnaveni, K.: Evaluation of internet addiction disorder among students. Indian J. Sci. Technol. **9**(19) (2016). https://doi.org/10.17485/ijst/2016/v9i19/93864

10. Bishop, C.M.: Pattern Recognition and Machine Learning. LLC, pp. 14–15, 359–360 Springer Science+Business Media, Berlin (2006)
11. Ben-Gal, I.: Bayesian networks. In: Ruggeri, F., Faltin, F., Kenett, R. (eds.) Encyclopedia of Statistics in Quality and Reliability. Wiley, Hoboken (2007)
12. Yu, H., Chen, G., Liu, D.: A simplified Bayesian network model applied in crop or animal disease diagnosis. In: Li, D., Zhao, C. (eds.) CCTA 2008. IAICT, vol. 294, pp. 1001–1009. Springer, Boston, MA (2009). https://doi.org/10.1007/978-1-4419-0211-5_25
13. Application for belief networks and influence diagrams. Norsys Software Corporation. http://www.norsys.com
14. Lucas, P.J., Van der Gaag, L.C., Abu-Hanna, A.: Bayesian networks in biomedicine and health-care. Artif. Intelli. Med. **30**(3), 201–214 (2004)

A Semantic Web-Based Framework for Information Retrieval in E-Learning Systems

Olaperi Yeside Sowunmi[1], Sanjay Misra[1(✉)], Nicholas Omoregbe[1], Robertas Damasevicius[2], and Rytis Maskeliūnas[2]

[1] Covenant University, Ota, Ogun State, Nigeria
{olaperi.sowunmi,sanjay.misra}@covenantuniversity.edu.ng
[2] Kaunas Technological University, Kaunas, Lithuania

Abstract. The advent of the internet, the evolution of the World Wide Web (WWW), coupled with the e-learning paradigm has resulted in the availability of a plethora of learning resources on the Web. However, these resources are not being fully utilized to their greatest potential. Learners, educators and researchers seeking educational content usually spend a great deal of time sorting through resources on the web without satisfactory results. Most times, this is not because the information is not available, but because the techniques being applied by major search engines do not handle the semantics and personalization required in this context. In a bid to proffer a solution to the problem of discovering relevant resources online by different categories of users, this work presents an integrated framework for personalized information retrieval of educational content. The framework exploits semantic web technologies. Further work will include the implementation and testing of the framework.

Keywords: Personalized information retrieval · E-learning · Semantic web Ontology

1 Introduction

The web has transitioned gradually from what is called Web 1.0 to Web 2.0 and now Web 3.0. The World Wide Web (WWW) at inception also known as Web 1.0 was a static web where only few publishers could upload content and majority of users were mere readers. Then came Web 2.0, which brought a new dimension to this, rather than 'read-only' which characterized Web 1.0, it became 'read-write'. Majority of users could upload their own content on the web, and this led to so much content being generated on the WWW. Web 2.0 also witnessed the advent of social networks and other forms of collaborative activities on the web. However, the large volume of useful information available on the WWW is not being utilized to its fullest potential, the information is so much that users do not go past the first page of search results returned by search engines. The most efficient utilization of this massive volume of data would be largely dependent on the ability of application programs to autonomously extract and make meaning out of the data despite the dynamic nature of information systems today. This is the problem that the semantic web also known as Web 3.0 has been brought on stage to solve [1, 2].

B. Panda et al. (Eds.): REDSET 2017, CCIS 799, pp. 96–106, 2018.
https://doi.org/10.1007/978-981-10-8527-7_9

The Semantic Web envisions an era when the content available on the WWW will be readable, understandable and used appropriately by machines autonomously. As such, agents would be able to carry out knowledgeable tasks for users unaided, for example, schedule an appointment with a physician based on a doctor's diagnosis, one's location, personal schedule and cost preferences [3]. The semantic web however will only enable machines to interpret the meaning of semantic documents and data, and not human speech and writings.

With the arrival of e-Learning which is defined as "is the use of electronic media for a variety of learning purposes that range from add-on functions in conventional classrooms to full substitution for the face-to-face meetings by online encounters" [4] there are a plethora of resources available for learners on the web. However, learners, educators and researchers seeking educational content usually spend a great deal of time sorting through resources on the different e-learning platforms on the web without satisfactory results most times, this is not always because the information is not available, but because the techniques being applied by major search engines do not properly handle semantics and personalization. Different users seek information on the web for different purposes; however, at the present they all get the same result for their search. It is this problem that we seek to proffer a suitable solution to via the framework discussed. Therefore, the remainder of this work is organized as follows: Sect. 2 gives the background study and literature review, Sect. 3 discusses the proposed framework, it components and provides a dry run simulation of how it would work, while Sect. 4 presents further work and conclusion.

2 Literature Review

This section gives background information on the domain of the application of semantic technologies and e-learning, as well as related works.

2.1 Semantic Web Technologies

In this section, several technologies that enable and encompass the semantic web are discussed. They include: The Semantic Web Stack, Semantic Annotation, Vocabularies (Ontologies), Linked Open Data and Knowledge Graphs, and Semantic Information Retrieval.

The Semantic Web Stack. Several technologies underlie the semantic web, and most of them are properly captured in the layered architecture developed by Tim Berners Lee called the semantic web stack shown in Fig. 1 [1, 5].

They include: **Unicode and Uniform Resource Identifier (URI)** - The Unicode is a character encoding standard that provides a unique number for every character regardless of the platform, program or language. This allows for consistent representation and interpretation of text. The URI on the other hand is a standardized identifier that allows for the unique identification of resources. This layer thus provides a universal way to

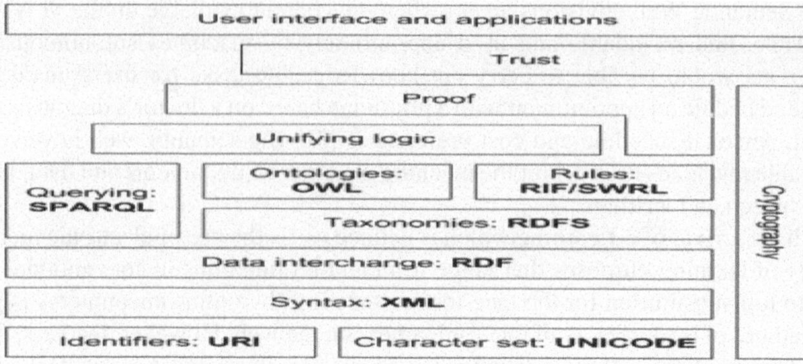

Fig. 1. The semantic web stack [5]

represent and identify resources on the web. **eXtensible Mark-up Language (XML)** - This layer defines syntax. XML which is a general purpose mark-up language together with the namespace and schema allows for a common syntax for representing structured documents and data objects on the web. **Resource Description Framework (RDF)** - RDF is a data description and representation language. It is used to represent metadata, which is a major requirement for the semantic web vision. It is a data model used to describe resources on the web [6]. **The Resource Description Framework Schema (RDFS)** - It is used to write taxonomies (hierarchy) of web objects i.e. their classes and properties, as well as lightweight ontologies. It is quite primitive for writing ontologies therefore, more powerful languages for writing ontologies, which allow for representations of complex properties and relationships of web objects are presented in the subsequent layer. The next layer comprises of the **Web Ontology Language (OWL)** for writing more robust ontologies, as well as **Rule Interchange Format (RIF)** and **Semantic Web Rule Language (SWRL)**, which are rule languages for writing web rules that can be executed. Rule sets as well as ontologies are used to make new discoveries on the semantic web. They differ from ontologies in that they focus on general mechanisms for the discovery and generation of new relations from existing ones while ontologies focus on classification methods. They are collections of IF-THEN statements otherwise known as rules. Another rule language is RuleML - Rule Markup Language. The RIF allows for rule exchange i.e. sharing, exchange and reusability of rules between rule systems, applications and rule engines with the semantics still preserved. The **Simple Protocol and RDF Query Language (SPARQL)** an SQL-like language is used to query the RDF, RDFS and OWL ontologies. It is also a protocol for accessing data in RDF format. The **Proof layer** involves deductive processes, representations and validation of proofs while the **Trust layer** applies cryptographic techniques, such as digital signatures to verify sources of input. The Trust layer is very important because it is when the operations of the semantic web are trusted for quality that its full potential would be realized. Building on all these layers, user applications are then developed.

2.2 Related Works

According to [7], from the year 2000 there has been a continuous increase in researchers' interest towards the development and usage of ontologies generally as shown in the increased volume of publications having the word 'ontology' in its title or list of keywords. More specifically as seen in Fig. 2, there has also been accelerated interest for the use of ontologies in e-learning systems as indicated in searches conducted on four (4) digital libraries: IEEE, ACM, ScienceDirect, and Google Scholar.

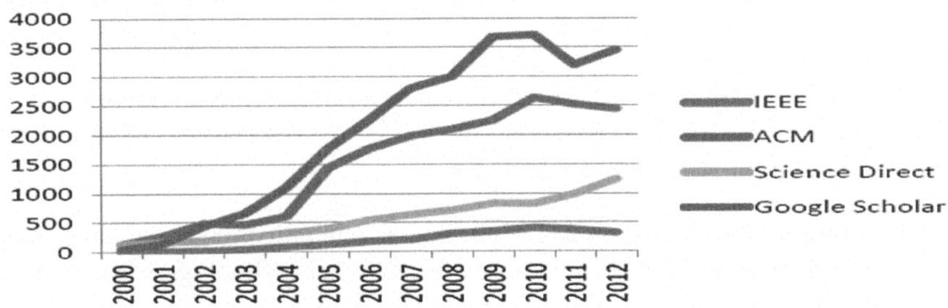

Fig. 2. Population growth for the words 'ontology' and 'e-learning' [7]

Dicheva [8] stated that learning systems using semantic technologies such as ontologies are the third generation of e-learning systems. Ontologies add meaning to the information on the web, they represent knowledge in a way that insights can be inferred and information processed automatically.

Ontologies have been applied to different e-learning tasks. They have been used to augment learning management systems by providing an easier way to manage, distribute and retrieve learning materials. They create a more dynamic learning environment while enhancing personalized learning via the creation of individual learning paths. They have also been proposed to be capable of expediting social learning [9].

According to [10], they provide a common understanding of the structure of information represented both for humans and agents; when built in a robust manner, they are highly reusable while providing thorough analysis of the terms and specifications contained, they also help to distinguish between operational and domain knowledge. Their use also enhances the semantic organization of content online, and can aid in the development of personalized learning [11].

Dicheva et al. [12] in their work, classified the applications of semantic web technologies in e-Learning into five (5) parts: ontologies as enabling technologies, ontologies for authoring instructional systems, instructional support and adaptation, sematic web-based intelligent learning environments and social semantic web applications.

Ontologies as Enabling Technologies. The study in [13] proposed a system to create learning resources by using an agreed vocabulary to collate and annotate learning content. The authors also worked on an algorithm to help learners determine starting points for repository exploration for efficient and faster search.

Ontologies for Authoring Instructional Systems. The study in [14] used an ontology called OMNIBUS to support a theory-aware authoring system called SMARTIES a kind of an expert system that simulates the activities on a human expert during instructional design. The study in [15] focused on the application of ontologies to build a type of Intelligent Tutoring System called constraint-based tutors (where knowledge is represented by constraints).

Instructional Support and Adaptation. Jovanovic et al. [16] applied both ontologies and semantic annotations to build a system that gives contextualized feedback on students' online activities to teachers.

Sematic Web-Based Intelligent Learning Environments and Social Semantic Web Applications. Melis et al. [17] developed the ACTIVE MATH intelligent e-learning platform with different semantic web features.

E-Learning and the Social Semantic Web. Social semantic web is the integration of the semantic web with social web approaches. It combines technologies from the social web popularly known as Web 2.0 and the Semantic Web [18].

On the other hand Al-Yahya opined that ontologies are applicable to four (4) categories of e-learning tasks namely: curriculum modelling and management, description of learning domains, description of learner data and description of e-learning services [7].

Ontologies for Curriculum Management. Modelling of curriculum elements simplifies access to and retrieval of needed information. It also makes it possible to link learning units to their respective outcomes and objectives or to other learning units [7].

CURONTO is an example of an ontology that was developed to model the needed semantics of a curriculum in order to facilitate its review and assessment [19].

Ontologies for Describing the Learning Domain. Ontologies representing the learning domain can either be subject-domain ontologies or task ontologies. Subject-domain ontologies focus on the subject matter and knowledge elements of a domain e.g. a course of study while task ontologies represent structural elements of a learning task such as an activity, assessment, feedback, simulation or search and retrieval [7].

Oele, an ontology based e-assessment system capable of both summative and formative assessment functions was developed [20]. Sameh researched on the application of ontology for effective semantic feedback and support in a e-learning system [21], while [22] built an ontology to represent pedagogical patterns.

Ontology for Describing Learner Data. Ontologies are also used to describe characteristics of the learner such as learner profile, progress and performance.

The study in [23] developed an ontology to represent the student model for an Intelligent Tutoring System, the ontology modelled the student's profile comprising of the student's academic and personal information.

3 Methodology

This section discusses the proposed framework and how provides a solution to the identified problem.

3.1 Components of the Proposed Framework

The diagram shown in Fig. 3 represents the framework of the proposed system. Its components include a learner's profile ontology, learning objects ontology, a semantic web search engine (which will comprise of both a generic web crawler and a RDF crawler), a reasoning engine and inferencing system, a ranking mechanism and a suitable user interface.

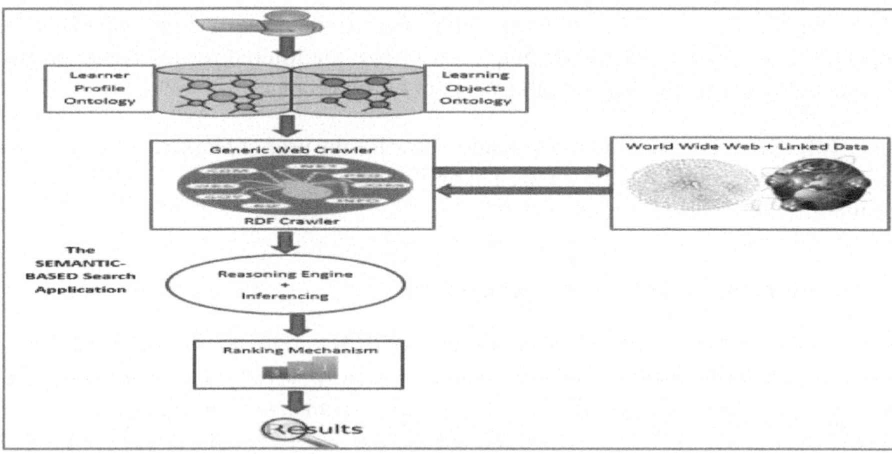

Fig. 3. The Proposed Framework

The Learner's Profile Ontology. This would be a vocabulary to define terms to describe the learner's profile. This would be used to represent the learner's preferences and be able to find a match with available resources.

The Learning Objects/Resources Ontology. This would be a vocabulary that describes various learning resources available on the web. A suitable one to be used is the Learning Resource Metadata Initiative (LRMI). LRMI created a common metadata framework to describe, tag or annotate learning resources published online. The metadata schema that was developed has also being adopted by Schema.org (a schema developed and being used by major search engines), therefore, tagging educational content with the LRMI mark-up ensures their proper recognition by these search engines. It was setup with the aim of making it easier and faster to discover and publish educational content and products online, to facilitate personalized learning, decrease costs through standardization, address demands for standardized description of learning resources and provide parameters that can be used for searching and filtering learning resources online. This makes it very suitable to be adapted to the framework.

A Semantic Web Search Engine. This would be responsible for searching the web of data for available resources. The results being returned to the system are then filtered based on some semantics and the user's preferences. Such search engines already exist such as Swoogle and Watson, they can be adapted and their results further filtered to fit the intended use.

The Reasoning/Inference Engine. This would be responsible for carrying out the matching of the returned resources and the learner's profile based on specified instructions. It would be programmed using the Java language.

A Ranking Algorithm. This component of the system would also be implemented using a programming language; it would help to prioritize the filtered results based on pre-specified preferences and their weights or level of importance.

A User Interface. The user interface would allow for the user or learner to properly and conveniently interact with the system in submitting his queries and giving feedback on the suitability of results returned.

3.2 Operation of the Proposed Framework

The user accesses the system via the user interface on his computer, his preferences and search terms are represented using the standardized terms as represented in the vocabulary. These representations are then used to search, and matches meeting the pre-specified criteria are filtered. They are then ranked and the best-fit results are presented back to the user, together with extra information to guide his decision. Figures 4, 5, 6, 7 and 8 explain the operation in pictorial representations.

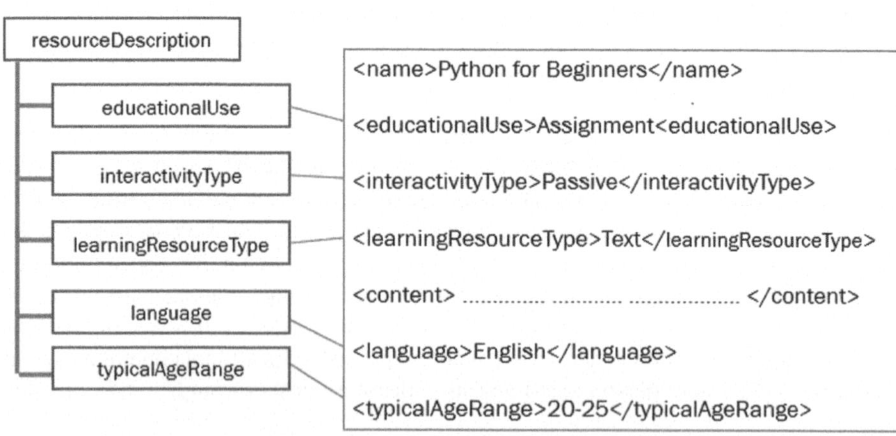

Fig. 4. Some LRMI terms representing the learning object

Figure 4 shows possible terms that will be in the vocabulary to represent the learning objects while Fig. 5 shows that of the learner's profile.

Figure 5 further shows that the learner is searching for Python tutorial materials; he prefers video resources, learns in an active mode, is 12 years old, has no previous knowledge of Python and learns in English.

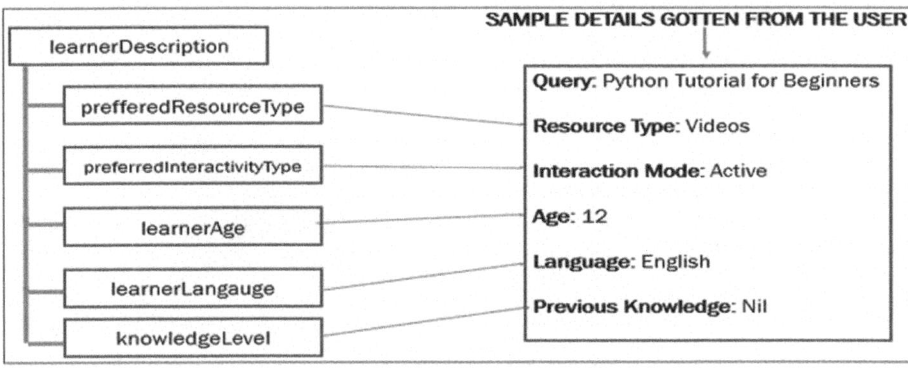

Fig. 5. A representation of the learner's profile

Figure 6 shows the semantic representation of sample web resources, which have been annotated using terms from the vocabulary. The first resource identified by number 1 is an assignment resource (as seen from the '*educationalUse*' tag), it is for learners between 20-25 years (as seen from the '*typicalAgeRange*' tag), it is a text material (as seen from the '*learningResourceType*' tag) and preferable for passive learners (as seen from the '*interactivityType*' tag). The second resource identified by number 2 is a tutorial material for children between 10 and 15, and it is a video. The third resource is also a tutorial for 22-25 years old learners, and it is a video. The fourth resource is a lesson plan for an educator.

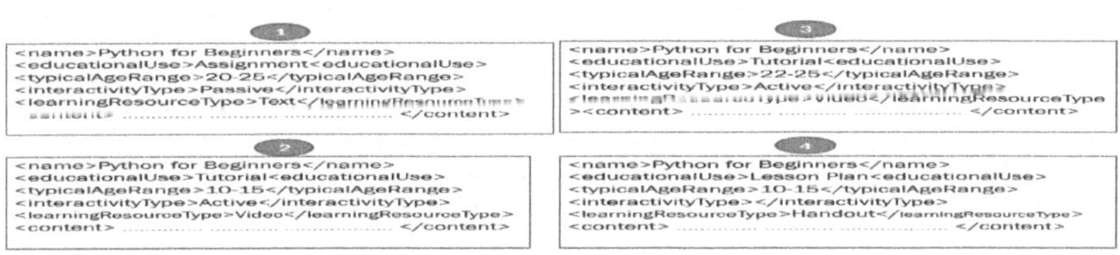

Fig. 6. Sample web resources before filtering

Figure 7 shows the filtering; resources 1 and 4 were dropped because they do not closely match the need of the learner. Resources 2 and 3 were picked since they are video materials, and they are in line with what the learner wants. In Fig. 8, resource 3 ranks lower (75%) because it does not match the learner's age, which is 12 (see Fig. 5) while resource 2 is the best match with 95%.

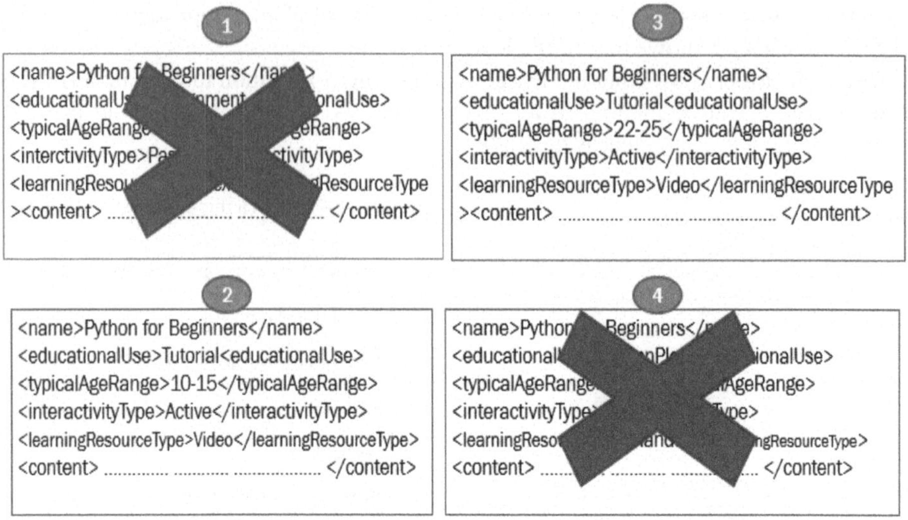

Fig. 7. Filtered web resources

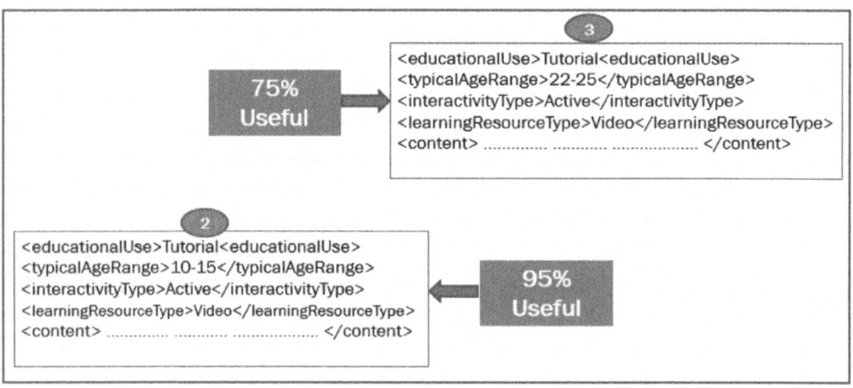

Fig. 8. Ranked result

This scenario shows how the proposed framework can enhance semantic and personalized retrieval, thus improving learner's satisfaction on e-learning systems.

4 Future Works and Conclusion

This proposed integrated framework would be implemented using the various technologies as described in Sect. 3. The framework would then be validated and tested by active users.

This framework when implemented would enhance the personalized information retrieval of educational content and resources. It exploits semantic web technologies including ontologies, standardized metadata annotation schemas, and semantic web search engines to provide users with resources that match their preferences. It also incorporates a ranking algorithm to help prioritize returned relevant results, a social web component to get user ratings of retrieved resources as well as a feedback mechanism to fine tune subsequent results. Instead of having a situation where a learner needs to choose from 571,000 documents returned in 0.35 s or 778,000 videos in 0.37 s from a Google search, using the user's preferences, instead of just retrieval, filtering and personalization will take place as well.

The proposed system is going to help to provide a better approach to use open web content in e-Learning systems. It will also help in the further synergy of the social and semantic web, which would really help to improve learner engagement and collaboration during learning.

Acknowledgements. We acknowledge the support and sponsorship provided by Covenant University through the Centre for Research, Innovation and Discovery (CUCRID).

References

1. Antoniou, G., Groth, P., Van Harmelen, F., Hoekstra, R.: A Semantic Web Primer. The MIT Press, Cambridge (2012)
2. Rubens, N., Kaplan, D., Okamoto, T.: E-learning 3.0: anyone, anywhere, anytime, and *AI*. In: Chiu, D.K.W., Wang, M., Popescu, E., Li, Q., Lau, R. (eds.) ICWL 2012. LNCS, vol. 7697, pp. 171-180. Springer, Heidelberg (2014). https://doi.org/10.1007/978-3-662-43454-3_18
3. Berners-Lee, T., Hendler, J., Lassila, O.: The Semantic Web. Sci. Am. **284**, 28-37 (2001)
4. Guri-Rosenblit, S.: "Distance education" and "e-learning": not the same thing. High. Educ. **49**, 467-493 (2005)
5. Obitko, M.: Semantic web architecture. http://www.obitko.com/tutorials/ontologies-semantic-web/semantic-web-architecture.html#semantic-web-layers
6. Sikos, L.: Mastering Structured Data on the Semantic Web: From HTML5 Microdata to Linked Open Data. Apress, New York (2015)
7. Al-Yahya, M., George, R., Alfaries, A.: Ontologies in E-learning: review of the literature. Int. J. Softw. Eng. Appl. **9**, 67-84 (2015)
8. Dicheva, D.: Ontologies and semantic web for E-learning. In: Adelsberger, H.H., Kinshuk, Pawlowski, J.M., Sampson, D.G. (eds.) Handbook on Information Technologies for Education and Training, pp. 47-65. Springer, Heidelberg (2008). https://doi.org/10.1007/978-3-540-74155-8_3
9. Monachesi, P., Simov, K., Mossel, E., Osenova, P., Lemnitzer, L.: What ontologies can do for eLearning. In: Proceedings of IMCL International Conference on Mobile and Computer Aided Learning, Amman, Jordan (2008)
10. Askar, P., Kalinyazgann, K., Altun, A., Pekince, S.S.: An ontology driven model for E-learning in K-12 education. In: Kidd, T.T., Song, H. (eds.) Handbook of Research on Instructional Systems and Technology, pp. 107-116. IGI Global (2008)
11. Kizilkaya, G., Torun, E.D., Askar, P.: Restructuring e-learning with ontologies. In: Fifth International Conference on Computational Science and Applications, pp. 161-164. IEEE (2007)
12. Dicheva, D., Mizoguchi, R., Greer, J.: Semantic Web Technologies for e-Learning: The Future of Learning, vol. 4. IOS Press, Amsterdam (2009)

13. Dicheva, D., Dichev, C.: Authoring and exploring learning content: share content by sharing concepts. In: Dicheva, D., Mizoguchi, R., Greer, J. (eds.) Semantic Web Technologies for e-Learning: The Future of Learning, vol. 4, pp. 24-43. IOS Press, Amsterdam, The Netherlands (2009)
14. Mizoguchi, R., Hayashi, Y., Bourdeau, J.: Inside a theory-aware authoring system. In: Dicheva, D., Mizoguchi, R., Greer, J. (eds.) Semantic Web Technologies for e-Learning: The Future of Learning, vol. 4, pp. 59-76. IOS Press, Amsterdam (2009)
15. Suraweera, P., Mitrovic, A., Martin, B., Holland, J., Milik, N., Zakharov, K.: Using ontologies to author constraint- based intelligent tutoring systems. In: Dicheva, D., Mizoguchi, R., Greer, J. (eds.) Semantic Web Technologies for e-Learning: The Future of Learning, vol. 4, pp. 77-95. IOS Press, Amsterdam (2009)
16. Jovanovic, J., Gasevic, D., Torniai, C., Devedzic, V.: Using semantic web technologies to provide contextualized feedback to instructors. In: Dicheva, D., Mizoguchi, R., Greer, J. (eds.) Semantic Web Technologies for e-Learning: The Future of Learning, vol. 4, pp. 117-135. IOS Press, Amsterdam (2009)
17. Melis, E., Goguadze, G., Libbrecht, P., Ullrich, C.: ActiveMath - a learning platform with semantic web features. In: Dicheva, D., Mizoguchi, R., Greer, J. (eds.) Semantic Web Technologies for e-Learning: The Future of Learning, vol. 4, pp. 159-177. IOS Press, Amsterdam (2009)
18. Jovanovic, J., Gasevic, D., Devedzic, V.: E-learning and the social semantic web. In: Dicheva, D., Mizoguchi, R., Greer, J. (eds.) Semantic Web Technologies for e-Learning: The Future of Learning, vol. 4, pp. 245-259. IOS Press, Amsterdam (2009)
19. Al-Yahya, M., Al-Faries, A., George, R.: CURONTO: an ontological model for curriculum representation. In: Proceedings of the 18th ACM Conference on Innovation and Technology in Computer Science Education - ITiCSE 2013, p. 358. ACM Press, New York (2013)
20. Litherland, K., Carmichael, P., Martínez-García, A.: Ontology-based e-assessment for accounting: outcomes of a pilot study and future prospects. J. Account. Educ. **31**, 162-176 (2013)
21. Sameh, A.: Ontology-based feedback E-learning system for mobile computing. In: Mastorakis, N., Mladenov, V., Kontargyri, V. (eds.) Proceedings of the European Computing Conference. LNEE, vol 27. Springer, Boston (2009). https://doi.org/10.1007/978-0-387-84814-3_48
22. Cobos, C., Rodriguez, O., Rivera, J., Betancourt, J., Mendoza, M., León, E., Herrera-Viedma, E.: A hybrid system of pedagogical pattern recommendations based on singular value decomposition and variable data attributes. Inf. Process. Manag. **49**, 607-625 (2013)
23. Panagiotopoulos, I., Kalou, A., Pierrakeas, C., Kameas, A.: An ontology-based model for student representation in intelligent tutoring systems for distance learning. In: Iliadis, L., Maglogiannis, I., Papadopoulos, H. (eds.) AIAI 2012. IAICT, vol. 381, pp. 296-305. Springer, Heidelberg (2012). https://doi.org/10.1007/978-3-642-33409-2_31

A Database for Handwritten Yoruba Characters

Samuel Ojumah, Sanjay Misra(✉), and Adewole Adewumi

Covenant University, Ota, Ogun State, Nigeria
{samuel.ojumah, sanjay.misra, wole.adewumi}@covenantuniversity.edu.ng

Abstract. This paper describes a novel publicly available dataset for research on offline Yoruba handwritten character recognition. It contains a total of 6954 characters being made up of several categories from a total number of 183 writers thus making it the largest available dataset for Yoruba handwriting research. It can be used for designing and evaluating handwritten character recognition systems for the Yoruba language as well as provide valuable insights through writer identification. The dataset has been partitioned into training and test sets being shared into 70% and 30% respectively.

Keywords: Database · Character recognition · Yoruba

1 Introduction

Handwriting character recognition has been the interest of machine learning researchers for several decades (Yadav and Yadav 2015). By being able to teach computers handwritings, computers can now be able to understand human interactions in a unique way. Although digitization of services across the globe continues to grow, handwriting is still very much in use today for many important functions such as writing bank cheques. Hence, the need for further research into this area.

The development of character recognition systems hinges on the pace at which databases can be developed and maintained with the best character sets possible required to cover the various languages. Standard handwriting databases have been developed in languages such as English (Marti and Bunke 2002), Chinese (Liu et al. 2011), French, and Arabic (Djeddi et al. 2014) as systems developed have yielded outstanding results. The advent of deep learning in which a feature learning framework for neural networks was developed has led to outstanding successes in image recognition which have been applied to these handwritten datasets with near human-level accuracy (Pascanu et al. 2013).

Handwriting recognition consist of two types: offline and online recognition. In offline recognition, the source of the input is usually a scanner that captures the character to be captured while online refers to inputs from pen or touch based inputs (Graves and Schmidhuber 2009).

The Yoruba language has a worldwide audience of about 18 million speakers with core geographic regions in Nigeria (Oyedotun et al. 2015), Togo and Benin. It is also

B. Panda et al. (Eds.): REDSET 2017, CCIS 799, pp. 107–115, 2018.
https://doi.org/10.1007/978-981-10-8527-7_10

spoken in as far as Brazil, the Caribbean and Cuba. Although, there have been several attempts to develop handwritten character recognition systems, most databases that have been used have been privately held datasets with most not being able to cover the basic character sets of the language. In order to develop character recognition systems that achieve human-level accuracy, the development of standard datasets for the Yoruba language is of paramount importance.

This work introduces a novel Yoruba handwriting dataset for character recognition which integrates features such as writer identification having fields such as the gender and age of the individual. The dataset is publicly available at https://github.com/samuelcesc/yohcrdb. The rest of this paper is as follows: "Related Works" highlights the different databases that have been developed for other languages, "Methodology" describes the processes involved in creating the dataset while "Dataset Statistics" section provides a quantitative analysis of the dataset and the "Conclusion and Future Work" section concludes the paper and gives recommendations for future improvements of this work.

2 Literature Review

This section covers the related works that have been done in the field of handwriting recognition with emphasis on handwriting databases. A review of popular languages in Africa is performed based on the context of this research as well as works done for the Yoruba language.

A major script used on the continent is the Arabic script, which is used for languages such as Swahili. The Swahili language has over 100 million speakers around Africa and is the official language for Tanzania, Kenya and Uganda. It is also spoken in nations such as Rwanda, Sudan, Ethiopia, Burundi and Comoros Islands. (Mahmoud et al. 2014) introduced an open Arabic offline text database made up of 1000 handwritten forms from 1000 different writers. The novel approach to the writer gathering was the population was from different countries. The forms containing the handwritings were scanned in various resolutions: 200, 300 and 600 dpi. These writers varied by a number of criteria such as age, upbringing country, qualification and left/right-handedness. The entire database consists of 2000 text paragraphs which generated 9000 lines and were randomly grouped into different sets for training, validation and testing. Experiments were also conducted on this data set but results show comparatively low recognition rates.

(Saabni and El-Sana 2013) presented a novel approach for generating large datasets in which prototypes for each word can be automatically generated using multiple appearances of the character. This works also shows that offline databases can be generated from online strokes based using standard dilation techniques. Experiments performed showed that the system can efficiently generated large datasets with quality as good as those involving human writers.

Another major language is Amharic, which is the official language of Ethiopia and is the second most spoken language in the country with over 21 million speakers. (Assabie and Bigun 2011) introduced a database of handwritten Amharic documents containing a total of 10,932 distinct word samples were gathered from 177 writers.

The data was collected using a form where each writer was made to write characters without any constraint. A total of 307 samples were collected and scanned at a resolution of 300dpi. Another set of 152 writers were made to write a total of 120,840 isolated character samples in which 256 characters were written thrice by each individual. This dataset was then used for training by a recognition system using the hidden Markov model.

The French language has about 120 million speakers on the African continent with core countries such as Gabon, Mauritius, Cote d'Ivoire, Senegal, São Tomé and Principe, Tunisia, Guinea, Seychelles, Democratic Republic of Congo, and Equatorial Guinea. (Djeddi et al. 2014) created a database containing 62600 French words, 74700 Arabic words, 21000 digits and 1300 signatures which were retrieved from 1300 forms from 100 writers. These forms were scanned using a scanner at 300dpi as characters were extracted and placed in categories. The writers of the handwritten words were from different ages, gender and backgrounds in terms of education which makes the database a good fit for research into writer identification and writer demographic classification.

Amazigh or Berbers is another dialect with majority of speakers in countries such as Algeria, Egypt, Tunisia, Libya, Mali, and Morocco which amount to approximately 30 million speakers of the language (Bentayebi et al. 2014). (Saady et al. 2011) created a database of handwritten Amazigh characters, which included more than 25000 characters written by 60 different writers. The main aim of this work was to create a dataset to be used for Amazigh recognition research by providing training and testing sets so that models could be developed. The samples were collected through forms and scanned at a resolution of 2400dpi and further processed by extracting the characters, which were isolated texts. These isolated texts make up the database, which is available for academic uses and further research.

(Bencharef et al. 2015) created a dataset of handwritten Tifinagh characters which is the official language of the Amazigh language. This dataset was made up of 1376 image characters written by 30 writers, which were 17 males and 13 females. These pages of the 32 handwritten Tifinagh characters were then scanned and extraction was done. The extraction process was done by using horizontal histogram in order to correct the inclination of every page and then the connected components algorithm was applied so as to detect the center of each character. The next step was then to extract 31 sub-images of 30 × 30px that contained the characters and then lastly these characters were named using Latin character set. This dataset provides a platform for efficiently training character recognition systems for Tifinagh handwriting.

(Marti and Bunke 2002) created an English sentence database for offline handwriting recognition based on the Lancaster/Oslo corpus. It consists of full English sentences produced by 1,066 forms and produced by 400 different writers most of which originate from Switzerland. A total of 9,157 lines of text can be used for text recognition while 128 lines contain information not included in the corpus used. The database contains 82227 word instances out of a vocabulary of 10,841 words and is a standard database used for English handwriting research.

As regards the Yoruba language, (Oyedotun et al. 2015) created a dataset used for experiments for deep learning. The drawback of this work is that the dataset used were based on Yoruba vowels and are not publicly available for research. The dataset used is also limited with just five characters although sub-databases containing the characters were also developed.

(Ajao et al. 2015) created a dataset acquired from indigenous writers in which Yoruba handwritten words were retrieved. These words were then scanned and then processed by conversion of RGB to greyscale, binarization, removing noise, normalizing, and performing skew correction. This dataset was then used to conduct experiments in order to calculate entropy measure so as to improve Yoruba recognition systems. However, the dataset used was limited as it does not cover the basic characters of the language and limited to certain handwritten words.

From the related works above, studies show that many standard databases provide a platform for conducting state-of-the-art research in character recognition in which features such as writer-identification can be integrated. Also, there is no publicly available database for Yoruba language with which recognition systems can be trained. In order to serve the over 30 million speakers of the Yoruba language, the creation of a publicly available dataset is of utmost importance. This work therefore addresses this gap as well as integrates other features found in many standard handwriting databases.

3 Methodology

This section describes the processes taken in order to create the Yoruba handwritten dataset.

3.1 Character Set

The Yoruba Character set used in this paper is made up of 31 characters and 7 words which are the words covering numbers one to seven. The stand-alone characters consist of characters with diacritic marks used in the language. Table 1 shows the character set used in the creation of the dataset.

Table 1. Yoruba Character Set

S/N	Character sets	Amount
1	Á À É È Ẹ Ẹ Ẹ ù Í Ì Ó Ò Ọ Ọ Ú Ù á à é è ẹ ẹ́ ẹ̀ í ì ó ò ọ ọ́ ọ̀ ú	31
2	oókàn eéjì ẹẹ́ta ẹẹ́rin aárùn ẹẹ́fà eéje	7

3.2 Data Collection

The first step in order to create the handwritten database was the use of a form in order to get the handwritings from several writers. To do this, literate Yoruba speakers were engaged in order to design the form to be filled. This form contained characters specific to the Yoruba language with the diacritic marks as those similar to the English language were left out. After design of the form, these forms were given to 200 writers shared across both males and females as well as different age groups. The form consisted of a total of 31 characters having fields that showed the characters and a blank

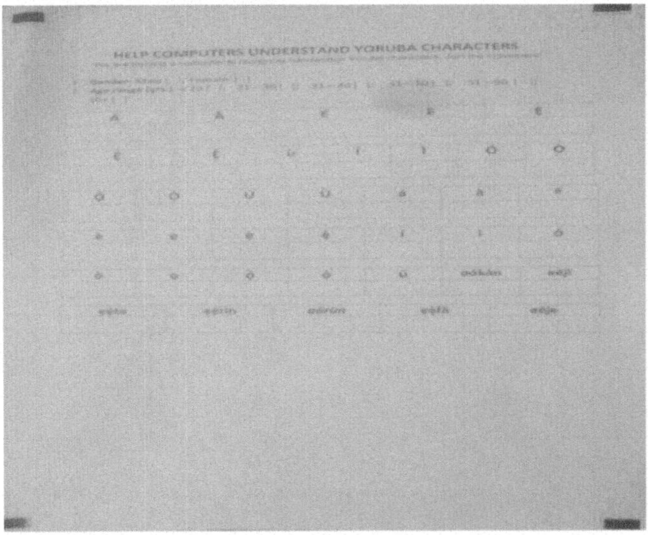

Fig. 1. Blank form consisting of the Yoruba characters

space in a box beneath each character to be filled by the writer. Figure 1 shows a blank form used in data capture of the characters.

3.3 Form Processing

After gathering the forms, the scanning process involved using a high-quality scanner using 300dpi to capture all the forms for further processing. The varying formats such as pdf, jpeg, and bmp were made available but the bmp format was chosen for the characters. The writers captured the characters using pens with black and blue. Figure 2 shows a filled form from one of the writers containing character in each field.

3.4 Character Extraction

In order to extract the characters from the form, each filled form went through the process of cropping where each character block was cropped. This process was manually engineered using the Microsoft Paint software. Table 2. Shows a sample set of cropped characters retrieved from a form.

3.5 Pre-processing

As one of the most important aspects of setting up a database for recognition systems, pre-processing of the images was done in order to improve the quality such that recognition systems could extract features properly.

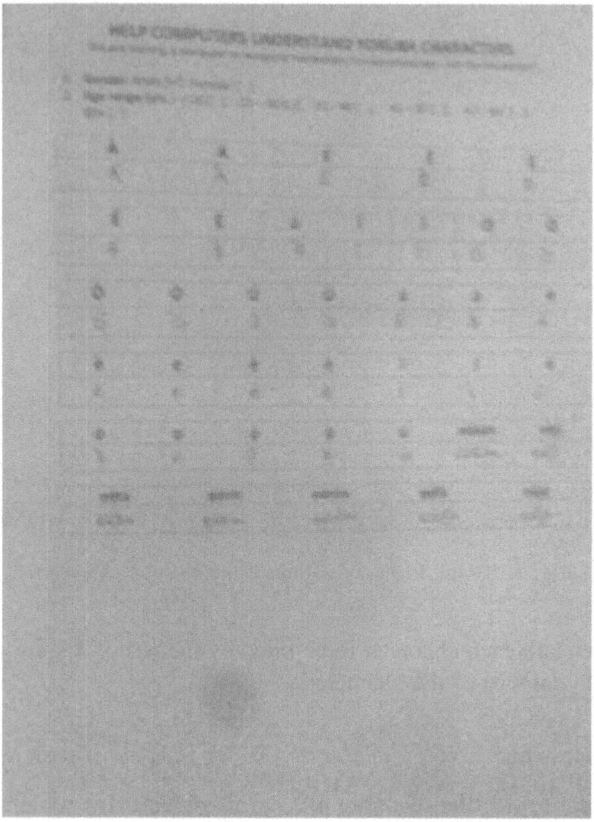

Fig. 2. A filled form showing handwritten characters.

Table 2. Sample of cropped characters

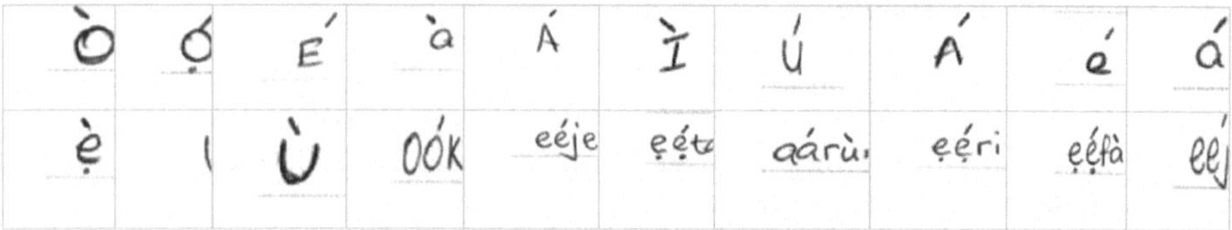

4 Dataset Statistics

From the sample set of 184 persons, a number of 183 were selected after abnormal samples were removed.

4.1 Writers Distribution

All the writers come from Covenant University, Nigeria with most being undergraduate or graduate students. Among the 183 writers, 129 (73%) are male while 54 are female. As regards the ages of the individuals, most of the writers are between the ages 21 and 30. Some writers also refused to disclose their ages. Table 3 gives a more detailed description of the age distribution of the writers. Figure 3 shows a graphic representation of the gender distribution of the writers.

Table 3. Age distribution of writers

Age	#Persons	Percentage
<20	64	34.97%
21–30	68	37.16%
31–40	2	1.09%
>40	1	0.55%
Uncategorized	48	24.59%

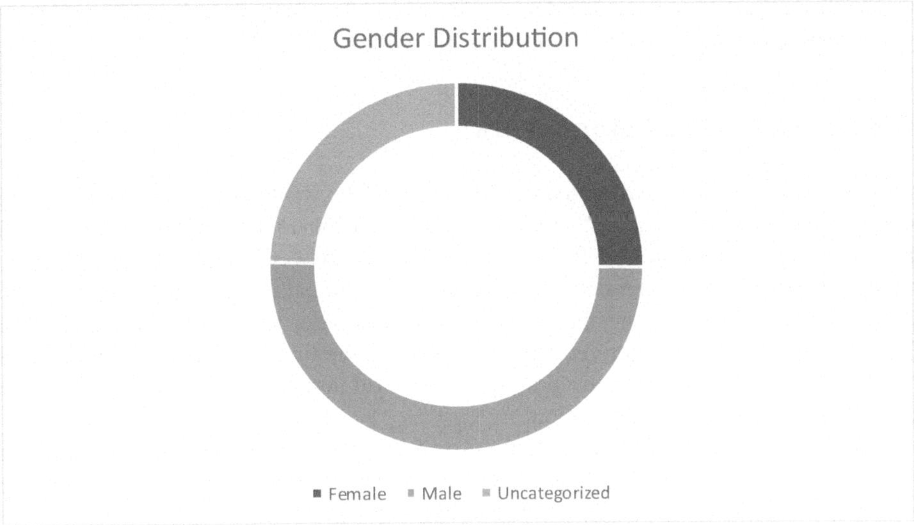

Fig. 3. Gender distribution of writers

Figure 4 shows a graphic representation of the age distribution of the writers.

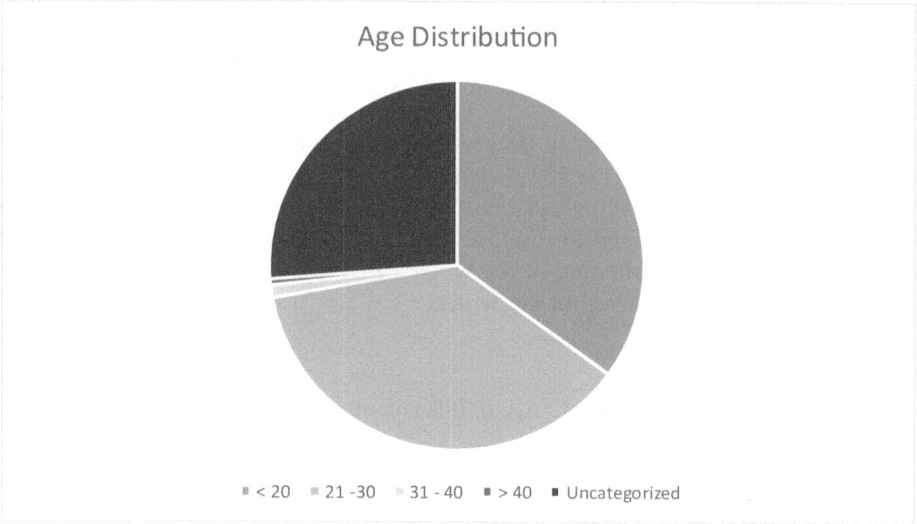

Fig. 4. Age distribution of writers

4.2 Abnormal Samples

Apart from the one sample removed from the sample set, there were no unusual samples from the 183 writers. The sample set removed contained strokes without letters of the language, which renders it, unfit for the dataset.

5 Conclusion and Future Work

A novel Yoruba offline handwritten database (YRHCR) written by several writers with support for writer identification is introduced in this work. A total of 6954 handwritten character images were gotten from 183 writers which were both male and female. Another approach to the creation of the dataset was the gathering of age ranges of the writers. These scanned images had noise removed in order to provide a platform for a clean dataset. The dataset derived from this work is the first publicly available dataset for handwritten research to be used around the world and can be used for handwriting recognition, and writer identification.

However, the database provides a platform for further work to be done as extending the database is of utmost importance in order to create a more comprehensive database that can be used for extensive research into the language in order to create tools that fit in perfectly in various use cases.

Acknowledgements. This generation of this database was done with help from Learnd Technologies, which helped from the design phase to the scanning phase. The authors thank all members of the Learnd team for the collaboration in the creation the dataset. The financial support of Covenant University Centre for Research Innovation and Discovery (CUCRID) is also acknowledged.

References

Ajao, J.F., Olabiyisi, S.O., Omidiora, E.O.: Yoruba handwriting word recognition quality evaluation of preprocessing attributes using information theory approach. Int. J. Appl. Inf. Syst. (IJAIS) **9**(1), 18–23 (2015)

Assabie, Y., Bigun, J.: Offline handwritten Amharic word recognition. Pattern Recogn. Lett. **32** (8), 1089–1099 (2011)

Bencharef, O., Chihab, Y., Mousaid, N., Oujaoura, M.: Data set for Tifinagh handwriting character recognition. Data. Brief **4**, 11–13 (2015)

Bentayebi, K., Abada, F., Ihzmad, H., Amzazi, S.: Genetic ancestry of a Moroccan population as inferred from autosomal STRs. Meta Gene **2**, 427–438 (2014)

Djeddi, C., Gattal, A., Souici-Meslati, L., Siddiqi, I., Chibani, Y., El Abed, H.: LAMIS-MSHD: a multi-script offline handwriting database. In: 2014 14th International Conference on Frontiers in Handwriting Recognition (ICFHR), pp. 93–97. IEEE (2014)

Graves, A., Schmidhuber, J.: Offline handwriting recognition with multidimensional recurrent neural networks. In: Advances in Neural Information Processing Systems, pp. 545–552 (2009)

Liu, C.-L., Yin, F., Wang, D.-H., Wang, Q.-F.: CASIA online and offline Chinese handwriting databases. In: 2011 International Conference on Document Analysis and Recognition (ICDAR), pp. 37–41. IEEE (2011)

Mahmoud, S.A., Ahmad, I., Al-Khatib, W.G., Alshayeb, M., Parvez, M.T., Märgner, V., Fink, G. A.: KHATT: an open Arabic offline handwritten text database. Pattern Recogn. **47**(3), 1096–1112 (2014)

Marti, U.-V., Bunke, H.: The IAM-database: an English sentence database for offline handwriting recognition. Int. J. Doc. Anal. Recogn. **5**(1), 39–46 (2002)

Oyedotun, O.K., Olaniyi, E.O., Khashman, A.: Deep learning in character recognition considering pattern invariance constraints. Int. J. Intell. Syst. Appl. **7**(7), 1 (2015)

Pascanu, R., Mikolov, T., Bengio, Y.: On the difficulty of training recurrent neural networks. ICML **3**(28), 1310–1318 (2013)

Saabni, R.M., El-Sana, J.A.: Comprehensive synthetic Arabic database for on/off-line script recognition research. Int. J. Doc. Anal. Recogn. (IJDAR) **16**(3), 285–294 (2013)

Saady, Y.E., Rachidi, A., Yassa, M., Mammass, D.: AMHCD: a database for amazigh handwritten character recognition research. Int. J. Comput. Appl. **27**(4), 44–48 (2011)

Yadav, P., Yadav, N.: Handwriting recognition system-a review. Analysis, **114**(19), 36–40 (2015)

Facial Expression Recognition for Motor Impaired Users

Krishna Sehgal(✉), Sanchit Goel, and Rachna Jain

Department of Computer Science, Bharati Vidyapeeth's College of Engineering, Delhi, India
krishnasehgal2108@gmail.com, sanch.goel@gmail.com, rachna.jain@bharatividyapeeth.edu

Abstract. In today's world touch screen devices are trending as people are dependent on their smartphones and tablets for much of their work, making it simple and convenient to store and access data anytime and anywhere. In such a bustling framework, some people are not able to access touch screen devices. These users are diseased by motor impairment because of which they find it difficult or nearly impossible to access touch screen devices resulting in a digital divide. This research work revolves around a technology that can be used to aid problems faced by motor impaired users. It provides an alternative solution by using an algorithm that detects emotions and performs action on touch screen devices. Facial expression recognition can support access to touch screen devices with minimal physical interaction. In this proposed work facial expressions of a user are detected.

Keywords: Assistive technology · Emotion analysis · Facial expression Motor impairment · Touch screen

1 Introduction

Touch screen devices are becoming popular and imperative in today's world. People are dependent on mobile driven applications to perform even a trivial task. In this bustling world, people with motor impairment are finding it difficult to access touch screen devices. This results in frustration among such users due to their inability to operate such devices [2]. Facial expression recognition is an emerging user interface that has an inherent future in smartphones. Motor impaired users can deploy emotions such as joy, anger, disgust etc. to communicate with touch screen devices. Facial expressions can exercise different functions on a touchscreen device ranging from swiping to selection of most crowded keys. Moreover, this user interface can render wide range of applications such as when a person is driving car, he/she can make use of facial expressions to accept or reject an incoming call, referred as call control. Furthermore, when a person is cooking food, he/she can use facial expressions to turn pages on an e-reader without any touch interaction. Facial expression recognition technique consists of a program that detects an emotion and returns its corresponding magnitude ranging on a scale of 0–100. Based on values returned by the program, the device will perform functions mapped with different facial expressions. This research will study problems faced by motor

B. Panda et al. (Eds.): REDSET 2017, CCIS 799, pp. 116–125, 2018.
https://doi.org/10.1007/978-981-10-8527-7_11

impaired users and techniques used to overcome such problems. In the second section of this paper we have discussed various studies carried out by research scholars on the same. In third section, we are discussing the background of our research that revolves around certain terminologies used in our research like motor impairment, assistive technology, touch screen, facial expression and emotion analysis. In the fourth section, we will study how facial expressions are recognized and used in smart screen devices followed by the results, conclusion and future work.

2 Literature Survey

In year 2010, Yang li proposed a new method to access touchscreen devices and named it Gesture search [1]. This technology makes use of gestures to access various items in smartphone. He made use of transient and moving nature of gestures. People have to draw gestures on the touch screen device which are then stored in the mobile software programmed to perform a certain task when such gestures are recognized. Currently it is being used by several smartphone companies to make mobile interface more accessible and smart. Moreover, Yang Li and Hao Lu proposed another interaction technique called Gesture Avatar [2]. This technique bridges problem faced in using low precision fingers and high precision screen. Users can now make use of gestures to select small target points that were earlier difficult to access because human fingers could not point to such precision.

In 2014, Benjamin Poppinga studied about activators that trigger the process of gesture recognition. He also studied functionalities often used by users and gestures easily drawable by people [3]. After carrying out research, he proposed that it was easy to draw alphabets when used as gestures to enhance the functionality of a smart screen device.

Zhong along with research scholars Astrid Weber and Casey Burkhardt studied problems faced by motor impaired users [8]. They demonstrated a technique that can be used to access touch screen devices, it was termed as Touch Guard [8]. This technology provided an interface reducing need for precise pointing. He introduced magnification and target list mode. Magnification as the name suggest, magnifies the user interface so that he can easily access points that are difficult to reach. In target list mode, the screen shows a list of potential targets on the entire screen when user accidentally points at an intersection of two or more targets. Ahn along with Kim and Suh developed an alternative mobile-user interaction interface and named it as Octopus Launcher [14]. They proposed an interface that makes use of the joystick of a wheelchair to perform functions on a smart screen device. A switch used to control functioning of mobile as well as the wheel chair. So users with such problems can access touch screen devices without interacting with them physically by making use of the Octopus Launcher.

Barlett along with Littlewort and other scholars demonstrated a technique used to map expressions of user with a percentage [5]. On making different facial expressions, this percentage varies. They used 50 scan points on the face of user. These points represent the entire face and these scan points were stored in a frame. Five such frames were captured in one second. This data set having frames was compared to data points representing facial expressions that were stored in database to recognize which expression has been made.

Yin Kong studied how gaming consoles like Kinect for Xbox are making use of body gestures for controlling the movements of players. Based on that study he researched about the use of hand gestures for interacting with smartphones. He created a real-time hand gesture recognition system [4] with which a user can control their phone without any physical contact.

3 Background Study

(i) **Motor Impairment**
In order to find a solution to the problems faced by motor impaired users, first we need to know what motor impairment is. It is defined as the improper functioning of one or more body parts due to partial or complete loss of limbs. This may result in degradation of stamina, weakness in the body, loss of muscle control and can even result in paralysis. Motor impairment can be of different types depending on the degree to which the user is affected. Tremors are the most common and basic kind of impairment. It is the rhythmic contraction and relaxation of limbs or hands resulting in spontaneous movement of one or more body parts. People suffering from tremors find it difficult to access touch screen devices because they get exhausted while selecting small targets which are crowded and are also unable to perform gestures like sliding, swiping and multi-finger gestures. Another common motor impairment is Quadriplegia [8], which is nothing but the loss of limbs. People suffering from Quadriplegia find it difficult to interact with touch screen devices because they lose control over their limbs resulting in involuntary actions. Such users take a lot of effort in performing the simple task of tapping also [13]. Motor impaired users face another problem called Cerebral Palsy. The body movement of such users is affected due to neurological disorder at a young age. This problem may persist for a long time but does not deteriorate with time. Users can operate a joystick to make selections but find it difficult to perform actions on touch screen devices.

(ii) **Assistive Technology**
Assistive technology is an extensive term that includes assistive, adaptive, and rehabilitative devices for users with disabilities. It also includes the techniques used in locating, selecting and making use of them. These devices are developed to help users who get exhausted while using the conventional ways of accessing their devices. Thus, it provides an alternative method to access devices with ease. People with motor impairment make use of assistive technologies [8] to access touch screen devices because of their inability. Some of the commonly used assistive technologies are joysticks, smart pens, slide boards etc. Users with motor impairment make use of the joystick of their wheelchair to make selections on their smart phone. This technology was first used in Octopus Launcher [8]. Dowell is an assistive technology that allows motor impaired users to connect any human interface device to a smartphone by making use of an USB-OTG cable. This human interface device can be a joystick, smart pen, adaptive mouse or a keyboard. Assistive technologies are becoming popular day by day. Even android and iOS have added this feature to help aid users who are

facing problems while accessing smartphones. Both the operating systems are allowing users to connect their assistive devices to their smartphones also customize these devices as per their choice. On both iOS and Android devices, it halts on the smart phone screen and can be easily accessed by the user whenever he wants to use it. It assists the user in performing tasks like sliding, swiping, multi-finger gestures without physically performing such tasks.

(iii) **Touch Screen**

A touchscreen is an input and output device which is generally layered at the top of electronic devices such as tablets, smartphones and laptops. It was introduced to replace conventional buttons used in mobile phones. Multi-finger gestures or stylus can be used to give input or manage the information processing system. It is an assistive technology with the help of which a user can directly interact with the system without making use of any peripheral device such as keyboard, mouse, touchpad. With the help of a touch-screen users can react to what is displayed and can also control how it is displayed [9]. There are a number of technologies which are used to sense touch such as resistive, surface acoustic wave and capacitive. A resistive touchscreen incorporates a number of layers that are electrically resistive separated by a thin space. Surface acoustic wave makes use of ultrasonic waves where as a capacitive touch screen is based on distortion of electrostatic field. Table 1 shows comparison of methods to access a touch screen device.

(iv) **Facial Expression**

A facial expression is defined as movement of muscles under the skin of an individual's face. These facial expressions may define the voluntary or involuntary emotional state of a person. Various facial expressions that can be recognized are joy, anger, contempt, disgust, fear, sadness and surprise [12]. There are around 50 points that are placed at different positions on the face of a person to recognize these different expressions [5]. These points cover all the major parts and muscles such as the eyebrows, lips, cheeks, eyes and other parts that show drastic changes. Any change in the emotional state of the user can be captured and used to calculate the magnitude of the emotion ranging from 0–100. The position of all these points are stored in a particular frame. Five such frames are captured every second that are then sent to the server for emotion analysis. Face Recognition is often used for security purposes [10], we can extend its application and make use of expressions of the user to select options on smart screen devices without any physical interaction.

(v) **Emotion Analysis**

Human emotions can be classified as positive and negative both of which are easy to detect [12]. Some examples of positive emotions are joy and surprise whereas negative emotions are anger and fear. These expressions can be accomplished by the movement of eyes, eyebrows, cheeks, lips and nose. When we smile our eyes get small, cheeks get raised up, lips become wide. When we are angry, our eyebrows become wide, eyes become small and lines appear on our forehead. When we are amazed or surprised we open our mouth and our eyes bulge out. These movements can be analysed and detected. It has been observed that expressing emotions vary from person to person. Snapchat which is a trending social networking application has made use of facial expressions on the basis of which it applies filters on the user's face. These filters are nothing but different faces that gets chunked upon the user's face making it interesting.

Table 1. Interaction with touch screen device

Techniques	Description	Advantages	Disadvantages	Application example
Touch screen	Using fingers or stylus on touch sensitive display (resistive, capacitive, surface acoustic)	Widespread, mature, cheap, east to use	People with motor impairment find it difficult to access touch screen devices	Touch operating systems (Android OS, iOS, Windows mobile, Windows 8)
Emotion detection	Human emotions can be used to access smartphones. Users identity and state can be drawn out from image [11]	People with disabilities can access touch screen phones without any physical interaction	Different light conditions in different settings remain a challenge	Emotion detection is used in social networking applications like snapchat as filters
Gesture recognition [2]	Various hand gestures can be used to perform actions on touch screen phone	Touch screen devices can be accessed without any physical interaction, making it convenient and fast	Nature of mobility and hardware limitation of smartphone's brings greater difficulty to problem of gesture recognition	Hand gestures are used in operating systems such as android, iOS to perform tasks like selection, sliding and multi-finger gestures

4 Proposed Research Scheme

Interaction of an individual with a touch screen device can take place by (1) Physical Touch (2) Gesture detection (3) Facial expression. In our study, we are concentrating on human interaction by facial expression recognition. As we all know that emotion analysis is a new and emerging area. The more the cameras and the software are becoming powerful, the more efficient this field is becoming. One such boom in the field includes using these analyses and their corresponding values for knowing the feedback of people. For instance, it is being used in theatres and conference halls to analyse their review in a positive or a negative manner. A similar thing is proposed in our paper that uses values calculated by detecting and analysing these emotions for taking responses or inputs from people affected by motor impairment since they find it difficult to interact with their touch screen devices. It would then become easier to use facial expressions to access a touch screen device. After detection of expressions, touch-screen device can perform the intended action. Figure 1 shows a flowchart explaining detection of facial expression and action triggered in a touch-screen device on detection.

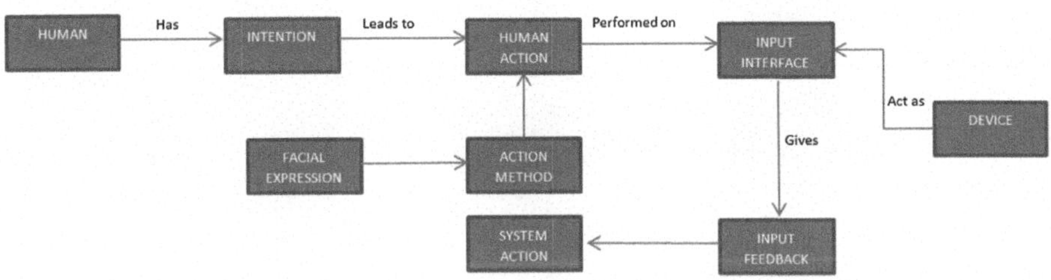

Fig. 1. Flow chart showing detection of facial expression and action triggered on a touch-screen device

The process of facial expression detection is carried out by a program which detects an emotion and returns its corresponding magnitude ranging on a scale of 0–100. Facial expression recognition algorithm detects around fifty points scattered over the face in a particular frame. The algorithm captures five such frames in one second and detects the variation in position of points. The position of these points are compared to positions of similar points representing facial expressions of thousands of people stored in a server, based on this mapping program returns a value that ranges between zero and hundred. This value can carry out a function on a touch screen device. The frames which are sent to the server for analysis every second are compared with various facial expressions of different people already stored on a server [6]. It consists of expressions of thousands of different people in order to give a more accurate result. SDK of Affectiva [7] is used to perform emotion analysis. It provides a function that takes as input only one face in a particular frame and its corresponding time i.e. the time at which the frame was taken as input. This function returns a value after detecting the type of expression and then calculating its magnitude. Figure 2 shows how facial expressions are detected. This program is only suitable for detecting a single person at a time. If the number of faces in front of camera are null or more than 1, it will show an image of the camera. If only one

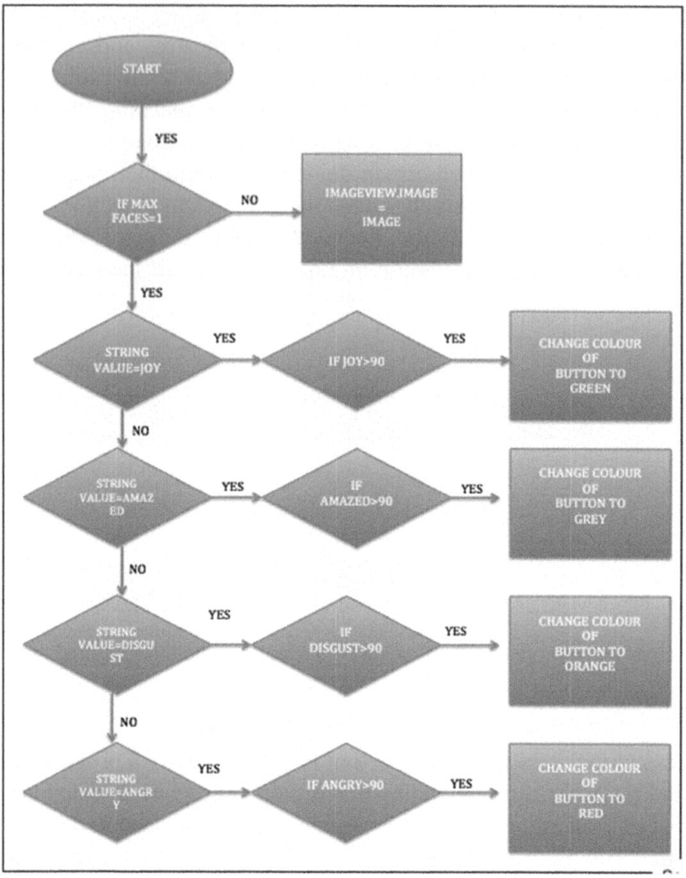

Fig. 2. Flowchart showing change in color of button with different facial expressions

user is present in front of the screen, the program will start calculating deviation from normal. If the user is angry, the colour of the button changes to red. In the same way if the user is joyful, the colour of the button turns to green. In the same way on showing disgust, the colour changes to orange and turns to grey on showing amazement.

Figure 3 shows various facial expressions and values returned. These values switch colour of label from yellow to green, orange, red and grey when user becomes joyful, disgust, angry and amazed respectively. This switching of colour can be mapped with different actions on a touch-screen device.

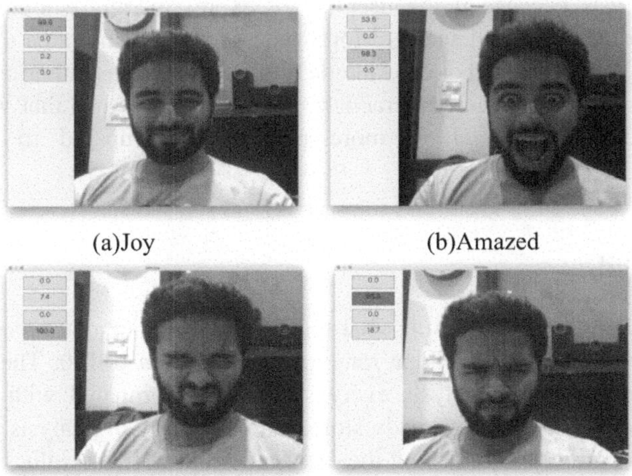

(a)Joy (b)Amazed

(c) Disgust (d) Angry

Fig. 3. Switching colour of label for different facial expressions (Color figure online)

5 Result

We have investigated various facial expressions such as joy, amazement, anger and disgust. In one instance, a user when happy has returned a value of 99.6 which therefore switches the label colour to green. When he is angry a value of 93.3 is returned and the colour of the label switches to red. On showing disgust a value of 100 is returned and the label colour switches to orange and when the user is amazed then a value of 98.3 is returned and the label colour switches to grey. These returned values resulting in switching of label colour can be used to perform tasks on a touch screen device. The tasks that could be performed when a user is happy then a value is returned which results in switching of a colour, this switching of colour could be used to accept or reject a call or turn pages of an e-reader without any physical interaction.

6 Future Work

In this research we have calculated values that are mapped to different facial expressions and are compared with expressions of different people stored on a server. When a value is returned the label colour is switched to some other colour. This switching of colour could be used as a control signal to perform a specified task on a touch screen device. In future we can assign a task on a touch screen device based on varying expressions made by user returning a value. These methods can be combined with motion detection techniques such as detection of hand gestures, head movements etc. Some people express emotions that are clearly visible, on the other hand some appear as transient micro expressions and some are internalized which means they are externally hidden and cannot be recognized. This results in one of the drawbacks of expression analysis because if the user is not expressing his emotions clearly, the machine will not be able to detect it. Moreover, there is another area that needs to be considered while detecting emotions- interaction, which means either a human-human interaction or a human-machine interaction. Research has shown that when there is a human-machine interaction, it is more precise as compared to human-human interaction.

7 Conclusion

We conclude from the above results that touch screen device detects an emotion and returns the corresponding magnitude ranging on a scale of 0–100. The frames which are sent to the server for analysis every second are compared with various facial expressions of different people already stored on a server. Our analysis turns out to be correct as the program was returning the expected values. These values could be used to perform tasks on a touch screen device. This technique may lead to failure when the image is not captured properly due to conditions like low light or poor camera quality.

References

1. Li, Y.: Gesture search: a tool for fast mobile data access. In: Proceedings of UIST, pp. 87–96. ACM (2010)
2. Lü, H., Li, Y.: Gesture avatar: a technique for operating mobile user interfaces using gestures. In: Proceedings of CHI, pp. 207–216. ACM (2011)
3. Poppinga, B., Sahami Shirazi, A., Henze, N., Heuten, W., Boll, S.: Understanding shortcut gestures on mobile touch devices
4. Kong, L.Y.: Gesture recognition on smartphone devices
5. Bartlett, M.S., Littlewort, G., Fasel, I., Chenu, J., Kanda, T., Ishiguro, H., Movellan J.R.: Towards social robots: automatic evaluation of human-robot interaction by face detection and expression classification
6. Sobecki, J., Szymański, J.M., Cichoń, K.: Gesture tracking and recognition in touchscreens usability testing
7. Facial Expression Analysis. https://imotions.com/wpcontent/uploads/Guides/iMotions_Guide_FacialExpressions_2016.pdf
8. Zhong, Y., Weber, A., Burkhardt, C., Weaver, P., Bigham, J.P.: Enhancing android accessibility for users with hand tremor by reducing fine pointing and steady tapping. In: Proceedings of 12th Web for All Conference, p. 29. ACM (2015)
9. Anthony, L., Brown, Q., Nias, J., Tate, B.: Examining the need for visual feedback during gesture interaction on mobile touchscreen devices for kids. In: Proceedings of 12th International Conference on Interaction Design and Children, IDC 2013, pp. 157–164. ACM (2013)
10. Samal, A., Iyengar, P.A.: Automatic recognition and analysis of human faces and facial expressions: a survey. Pattern Recogn. **25**(1), 65–77 (1992)
11. Yang, M.H., Kriegman, D.J., Ahuja, N.: Detecting faces in images: a survey. IEEE Trans. Pattern Anal. Mach. Intell. **24**(1), 34–58 (2002)
12. Bourbakis, N.: A face detection and facial expression recognition method

13. Duff, S.N., Irwin, C.B. Skye, J.L., Sesto, M.E., Wiegmann, D. A.: The effect of disability and approach on touch screen performance during a number entry task. In: Proceedings of Human Factors and Ergonomics Society Annual Meeting (2010)
14. Adolphs, R.: Neural systems for recognizing emotion. Curr. Opin. Neurobiol. **12**(2), 169–177 (2002)

Check for updates

Document Oriented NoSQL Databases: An Empirical Study

Omji Mishra(✉), Pooja Lodhi, and Shikha Mehta

Department of Computer Science, Jaypee Institute of Information Technology, Noida, India
omji.mishra@yahoo.com, poolodhi@gmail.com,
shikha.mehta@jiit.ac.in

Abstract. In today's era, organizations are developing applications which continuously and rapidly generates large amount of data. In this world of big data, NoSQL databases are rapidly becoming popular for storing information among organizations. Therefore, it is essential for an organization to choose a database which is compatible and efficient for their applications. To choose a correct database, it is essential to examine the performance of various databases under diverse workload conditions. In this paper, we are examining different document oriented databases on various workloads, so that we can categorize them according to application need. The evaluation has been performed on four NoSQL document oriented databases: MongoDB, ArangoDB, Elastic search and OrientDB with the help of Yahoo Cloud Service Benchmark (YCSB), which is a popular benchmark tool. Comparison is done in two parts: In the first part, all the databases are compared for single thread on the basis of throughput and runtime. Here, Mongo DB shows better results with highest throughput and lowest runtime among all the databases. In the second part, a thorough analysis is done in which MongoDB and ArangoDB are compared for some threads on different workloads. Here also, Mongo DB outperforms ArangoDB with a high percentage.

Keywords: Big data · MongoDB · ArangoDB · OrientDB · Elastic search
Document oriented databases · YCSB

1 Introduction

1.1 A Subsection Sample

Big data is a term used for large and complex datasets that cannot be processed with the traditional data processing software. Analysis of these large datasets is relevant in finding patterns, spotting trends, preventing crime and enhancing user experience. To manage this big data NoSQL databases are designed. NoSQL databases are those databases which provides the mechanism of storing data in key-value, wide column, graph, document rather than storing data in tabular form as in relational databases. It is also called "Not only SQL". It uses data structures that are faster in terms of relational databases. Examples of NoSQL databases are: Riak, Couchbase, MongoDB, Cassandra, HBase, Neo4j, OrientDB, etc.

B. Panda et al. (Eds.): REDSET 2017, CCIS 799, pp. 126–136, 2018.
https://doi.org/10.1007/978-981-10-8527-7_12

Document databases are subset of NoSQL databases. It is used for storing and managing semi-structured data. In document databases, the term "document" refers to a block of XML or JSON. Collections of documents are used to store data [6]. These databases rely on the internal architecture in the document in order to extract metadata for further optimization.

The Yahoo! Cloud Serving Benchmark (YCSB) is open source software used for evaluating the capabilities of computer program. The goal of YCSB is to provide a platform for performance comparison of NoSQL databases. YCSB framework consists of a workload generating client and a collection of standard workloads that cover interesting aspects of performance space [1, 8]. An important feature of YCSB is its ability to define new workload types.

Today there are various types of NoSQL databases based on different architecture. Databases under different categories preform differently. But it must be understood that various database under same category also perform differently. In this research work, we are doing performance comparison of different NoSQL document-oriented databases like MongoDB, OrientDB, ArangoDB and Elastic Search. Yahoo! Cloud Serving Benchmark framework is used for comparisons of these databases. We have selected workload a, b, c, d and f to compare databases. The workload 'a' contains large number of update operation therefore it is also called update heavy workload whereas; workload 'b' is read heavy. Workload c is only contains read operation while workload 'd' is read latest. Workload 'f' can be used to simulate read modify and updates operation in a group. The detailed explanation of different workloads is provided in Table 1. We have done deep analysis of MongoDB and ArangoDB by comparing their throughput and runtime for different workloads for 1 million records. We have also performed comparison between other databases on different workloads for 1 thousand records.

The paper consists of different sections. In Sect. 1, introduction is provided which gives an overview of main tools and databases used in paper. Section 2, consist of the literature survey. In Sect. 3, we have done background study related to the research work. Section 4 contains experimental setup and the results of all databases with comparison and analysis. In Sect. 5, we have concluded our research work. In our last section that is Sect. 6 we have discussed some of the limitation that we found during the experiment.

2 Literature Survey

Various Studies are conducted to understand how different databases behave under different conditions [2–5, 7, 9–11]. A study to assess the performance difference between RDBMS and NoSQL databases systems was performed in [3]. It also discussed about the optimal design for enhanced functionality when NoSQL databases are used. They created their own dataset and used CRUD operation to perform comparison between NoSQL and RDBMS databases. To perform all these operations, they developed their own program.

In [5], three open source NoSQL databases: MongoDB, Cassandra and HBase, were analyzed in detail. An analysis on the performance compares the NoSQL databases on their ability to scale under different workload conditions and with different dataset sizes.

In order to do the analysis, they generated records of 10 and 20 fields. They also used zipfian strategy to distribute the data. At the end, they provided a benchmark report about which database should be used in what condition.

Literature [4], briefly explained some of the NoSQL unstructured databases and presented performance analysis of MongoDB. It compared the time required for insertion into different databases as well as searching for different number of threads in database with different number of entries. The paper also presented the importance of Sharding and Configuration of the cluster for MongoDB.

The author developed near real-time Twitter data warehouse by NoSQL database, Cassandra, and compare its storing and querying performance [11]. The results show that Cassandra performs better in storing data, whereas it is slower in querying.

From the above research papers, we observe that although abundance of work has been done to compare Relational and NoSQL databases, different types of NoSQL databases and to measure performance of a particular database. But, there has been limited attempt to measure the performance of similar databases. Performance evaluation of similar databases needed attention because it is essential to choose a correct database from a set of similar databases. So, we have evaluated different document-oriented NoSQL databases. In order to do so we have analyzed MongoDB, ArangoDB, OrientDB and Elastic Search.

3 Background

3.1 NoSQL Databases

The databases which provide the different mechanism of storing data other than tabular form are called NoSQL databases. It uses data structures that are faster in terms of relational databases. There are majorly four different types of NoSQL databases.

Key-Value Store is based on the concept of key-value pair and is implemented using big hash tables. This database is well-suited for applications in which small reads and writes are performed frequently.

Document-Based Store uses the central concept of document. This database has the property of being flexible. Therefore they are appropriate solution for application in which data keep varying in terms of attributes.

Column-Based Store data is stored in cells and these cells are grouped in columns. It is different from the traditional way of storing data as rows. Columns are further combined to form column families. These databases are well-suited for data which is distributed to various sites.

Graph-Based Database data is represented in graphical from. The problems that are well represented with networks of connected entities for such scenarios graph databases are most suitable.

3.2 Document Oriented Databases

Document oriented database uses the central concept of document. While every document oriented database implements document in different forms, they all assume document encapsulation and data encoding in some standard formats. Documents can be compared to object concept of programming language. Different encoding used in document oriented databases are XML, YAML, JSON, BSON, etc. The core operations of document-oriented databases are Creation (Insertion), Retrieval (Search or Query), Update (or Edit) and Delete.

Mongo dB is a free open source document oriented database. It uses JSON-like document format.
Arango dB is a NoSQL multi-model open source database. It has been designed specifically to allow key/value, document and graph data to be stored together and queried with a common language. It also uses JSON as a default storage format.
Elastic Search It is an open source search engine based on Lucene. It is developed in JAVA.
Orient dB is a NoSQL database written in JAVA. It is a multi-model database so it is sometimes also considered as a graph database instead of document-oriented database.

3.3 YCSB Workload

Workloads in the benchmark tool are defined by assigning different distributions to two main parameters: which operation we perform and which record is read or write. While doing analysis, loading a database takes longer time than running a database. All the YCSB core package workloads uses the same dataset so that it is possible to load the database only once and then run all the required workloads. Since workload d and e insert records so if database writes are likely to impact the operations of other

Table 1. YCSB workloads [1].

Workload	Operations	Application example
A-update heavy	Read: 50% Update: 50%	Session store where recent actions are recorded in a session
B-read heavy	Read: 95% Update: 5%	Photo tagging
C-read only	Read: 100%	User profile cache, where profiles are constructed elsewhere
D-read latest	Read: 95% Insert: 5%	User status updates; people always want to read the latest statuses of other people
E-short ranges	Scan: 95% Insert: 5%	Threaded conversations
F-read-modify-write	100% Read Modify Write	User database or user profile updates where records are read and modified or to record activity performed by user

workloads then it may be necessary to re-load the database [1]. YCSB has two phases, load and run. In load phase, data is inserted into the source database, which represents the initial state of the database. Then, in the run phase, different workload performs different operation like modify previously uploaded data, insert new data or read the data [10].

4 Experiments and Results

4.1 System Configuration

The experiment was performed on a single machine consisting of Dual core AMD A4-3330MX APU CPU at 2.2 GHz. The RAM of the system was 6 GB and the main memory size was 500 GB. OS of system was Ubuntu 12.04 LTS.

4.2 Testing Process

For the testing process, YCSB tool, Mongo dB, Arango dB, Orient dB and Elastic Search databases were installed on the system. The testing process was divided into two parts. Firstly, we have run the YCSB tool on different databases for different workloads with record count of thousand. We have taken workloads a, b, c, d and f (see Table 1) for evaluation as we want to analyze how large amount of read and write operation affect the databases. Workload e was a short ranges workload which was not much compatible for our analysis as it requires deleting database each time before executing the run command. Secondly, we have conducted the deep analysis of MongoDB and ArangoDB with a dataset having record count of 1 million. Steps for testing are as follows:

1. For each experiment, workload was loaded into the database through terminal.
2. Then the corresponding workload was run for different number of client threads (1, 3, 6, 10, 20, 32, 50, 64 and 128).

Afterwards, the results were interpreted with the help of graphs.

4.3 Results

In this section we evaluate the results of the benchmark testing of different NoSQL databases. First we evaluated various above mentioned document oriented databases on different workloads, for a single thread. Then we compared performance of MongoDB with ArangoDB on different workloads, by varying the thread count.

Performance of Document Oriented Databases. MongoDB, ArangoDB, Elastic search and OrientDB are compared on parameter of runtime and throughput to understand their behavior when different types of operation are performed on them.

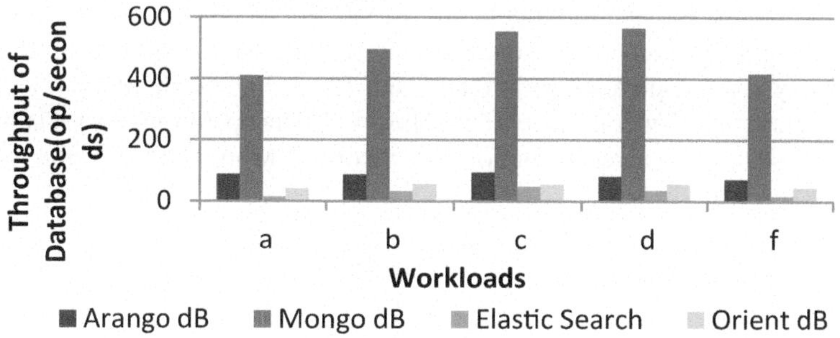

Fig. 1. Workload vs throughput for various databases.

Figure 1 shows that among all the document oriented databases, Mongo dB has highest throughput value for each workload. Elastic Search, ArangoDB and OrientDB has very low throughput compared to MongoDB which show that they cannot handle large number operation of any kind per second.

Figure 2 clearly shows that, Elastic search has highest runtime for all workloads. This implies that Elastic search is not an appropriate solution for any application where time is an important factor. This also shows that more time is required to perform update operation in Elastic search. OrientDB and ArangoDB show similar behavior for all the workloads, while MongoDB perform best with least runtime.

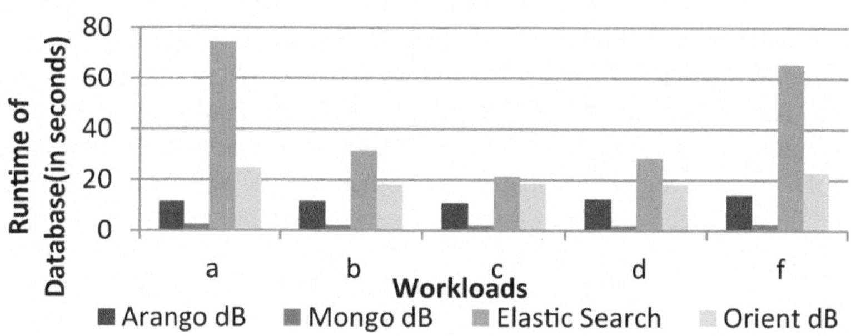

Fig. 2. Workload vs runtime for various databases.

MongoDB vs ArangoDB. Here we analyze how MongoDB and ArangoDB perform when the thread are increased for different type of workloads.

Update heavy workload. The graphs for the execution time of 50% Read and 50% write are given in the above Fig. 3(a). From fig. we observe that MongoDB has low runtime value for every thread as compared to ArangoDB. Low runtime implies that MongoDB is a suitable database to use where there is need of heavy update operation. Graph also shows that thread 1 runtime value for ArangoDB is quite high as compared to its other threads, which means that for heavy update operation for single thread ArangoDB is not a good option.

Figure 3(b) depicts that throughput value of MongoDB is better enough as compared to that of ArangoDB which implies that for heavy update operation MongoDB is a better choice. Heavy update operation for thread 6 and 10 has highest throughput value i.e., it performs highest no. of operation per sec for heavy update operation. So, for applications like session store where recent action are recorded MongoDB is better document oriented database to use.

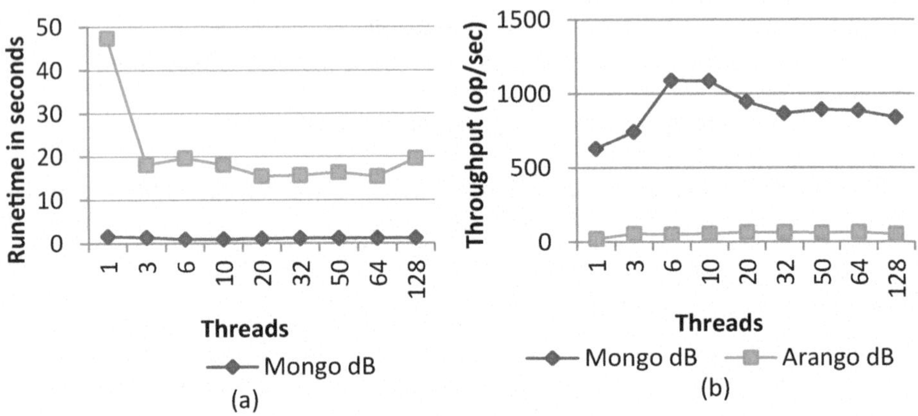

Fig. 3. (a) Threads vs runtime for workload A. (b) Threads vs throughput for workload A

Read mostly workload. Figure 4(a) shows graph of runtime v/s threads for workload b. It is observed that MongoDB has low runtime value for every thread as compared to ArangoDB. This means that MongoDB is more efficient than ArangoDB where read operation happens more frequently. We can also observe that thread 128 runtime value for ArangoDB is quite high as compared to its other threads, which means that for heavy read operation for large number of threads, ArangoDB is not a good match.

From Fig. 4(b), we see that the throughput value of MongoDB is better enough as compared to that of ArangoDB implying that for heavy read operation MongoDB is a good choice. On the other hand when number of threads increases, value of throughput starts decreasing after reaching peak value. Thus MongoDB can be used for photo tagging application like Facebook or investment forecasting where large amount of data is read and analyzed to extract some knowledge.

Read only workload. Given the situation where database execute only read operations like user profile cache, MongoDB has lowest value (see Fig. 5(a)) implying that MongoDB is an efficient database for an application where there is need of only read operation. Thread 1 runtime is quite high for ArangoDB as compared to its other threads, which means that for read only operations on single thread it is not a good database. Figure 5(b) depicts that throughput value of MongoDB is better as to that of ArangoDB.

Read latest workload. From Fig. 6(a) we can see that as usual MongoDB has low runtime value for every thread as compared to ArangoDB. Thus MongoDB is a suitable database to use where there is need of read latest operation. On the other hand, runtime value for ArangoDB is quite high making it not desirable a database for reading latest record. Figure 6(b) depicts that operation performed per second in MongoDB is more, so it is better choice for application where reading latest data is done like, inbox messages in a mailbox or latest posts on Facebook or latest tweets on twitter.

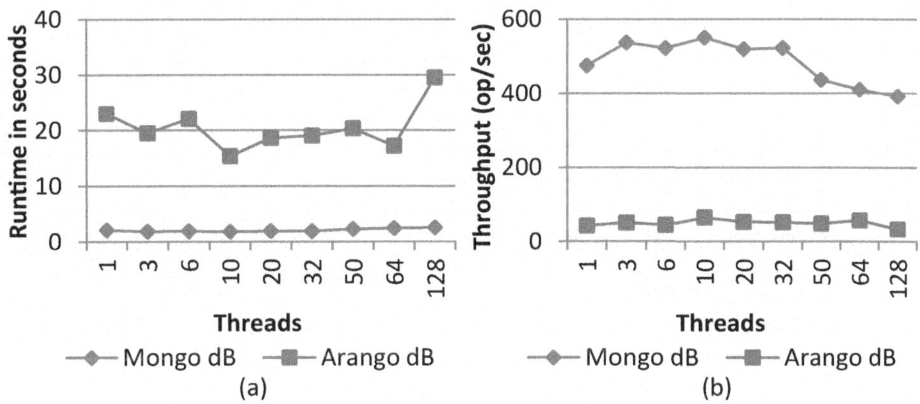

Fig. 4. (a) Threads vs runtime for workload B. (b) Threads vs throughput for workload B

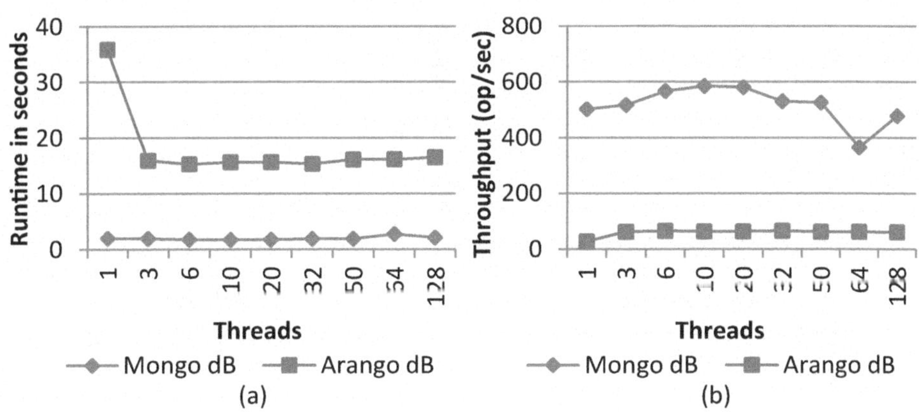

Fig. 5. (a) Threads vs runtime for workload C. (b) Threads vs throughput for workload C.

Read modify write workload. Figure 7(a) clearly shows that ArangoDB has highest runtime for all threads. Therefore it is not an appropriate solution for any application where low running time is preferred. It also shows that more time is required to perform read, modify and write operation in ArangoDB for all threads, while MongoDB requires less running time.

The performance behavior exhibited by workload ‘f’ is given in Fig. 7(b). It shows that among MongoDB and ArangoDB, MongoDB has highest throughput value. ArangoDB has very low throughput as compared to MongoDB which shows that it cannot handle large number operation of read, modify and write per second. Thus, MongoDB is good option to use in scenario such as money transaction where balance in a bank account is read then modified and then finally gets updated in the databases.

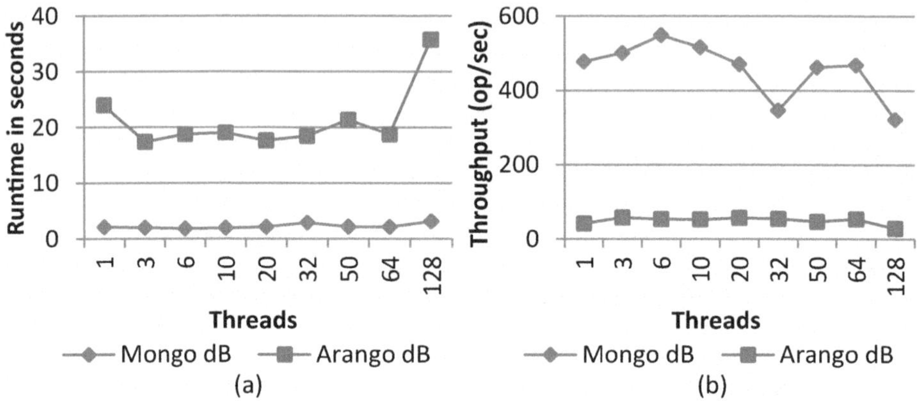

Fig. 6. (a) Threads vs runtime for workload D. (b) Threads vs throughput for workload D.

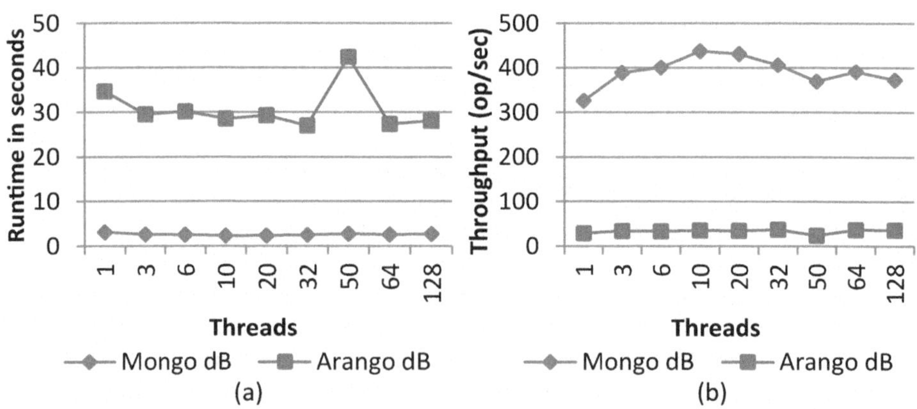

Fig. 7. (a) Threads vs runtime for workload F. (b) Threads vs throughput for workload F

Overall experimental analysis and research concluded that MongoDB outperform other databases because it’s a single model database which is a specialized solution for documents. Its performance increases for single reads and writes. This is because of document model due to which data get more localized and this in turn reduces the need to join separate results. The feature of automatic sharding and replication leads to strong consistency and availability which result in higher performance and scalability of the database.

5 Conclusion

Today large number of NoSQL databases exist which are beneficial to certain types of operations only. So it is necessary to evaluate the behavior of different databases before using them for required operations. In this era large amount of information is generated over web and most of it is in form of documents. So in this research work, different document oriented NoSQL databases like: MongoDB, ArangoDB, Elastic Search and OrientDB were analyzed in detail. An analysis was done on the basis of throughput and runtime of the databases on different number of threads. MongoDB and ArangoDB were deeply analyzed by running them on 1 million records for every thread. The analysis helped us to realize that MongoDB is the best suited document oriented database for every type of workload. This is because of the fact that its runtime is low and operation performed per seconds is high when run for different number of threads.

6 Limitation

Some of the limitations were found while performing the experiment in the tools and the databases. Firstly, MongoDB and ArangoDB run perfectly for 1 million records for any number of thread in given system specification, while Elastic Search and OrientDB were limited to single thread only. Secondly, OrientDB and Elastic search cannot load a large amount of data while being used with YCSB tool. It throws Direct Memory Buffer Error implying that the system memory is not enough to run large number of records. Thirdly, when MongoDB was run for workload f, it was required to load the database for each thread. This was because of the existence of duplicate key while insertion operation performed by workload.

References

1. Cooper, B.F., Silberstein, A., Tam, E., Ramakrishnan, R., Sears, R.: Benchmarking cloud serving systems with YCSB. In: Proceedings of 1st ACM Symposium on Cloud Computing (SoCC 2010), pp. 143–154. ACM, New York (2010)
2. Comparing NoSQL Databases with YCSB Standard Benchmark report by AVALON (2016)
3. Jung, M.G., Youn, S.A., Bae, J., Choi, Y.L.: A study on data input and output performance comparison of MongoDB and PostgreSQL in the big data environment. In: 2015 8th International Conference on Database Theory and Application (DTA), pp. 14–17 (2015)
4. Truică, C.O., Boicea, A., Rădulescu, F., Bucur, I.: Performance evaluation for CRUD operations in asynchronously replicated document oriented database. In: International Conference on Control Systems and Computer Science, pp. 191–196 (2015)
5. Swaminathan S.N., Elmasri R.,: Quantitative analysis of scalable NoSQL databases. In: IEEE International Congress on Big Data, pp. 323–326 (2016)
6. Scofield, B.: NoSQL, death to relational databases. In: Presentation at CodeMash Conference, Sandusky, Ohio (2010)
7. Klein, J., et al.: Performance evaluation of NoSQL databases: a case study. Paper presented at 1st Workshop on Performance Analysis of Big Data Systems, Austin, Texas, USA (2015)

8. Barata, M., Bernardino, J., Furtado, P.: YCSB and TPC-H: big data and decision support benchmarks. In: IEEE BigData Congress, pp. 800–801 (2014)
9. Nyati, S.S., Pawar, S., Ingle, R.: Performance evaluation of unstructured NoSQL data over distributed framework. In: International Conference on Advances in Computing, Communications and Informatics, pp. 1623–1627 (2014)
10. Schmidt, F.M., Geyer, C., Schaeffer-Filho, A., et al.: Change data capture in NoSQL databases: a functional and performance comparison. In: IEEE Symposium on Computers and Communication (2015)
11. Murazza, M.R., Nurwidyantoro, A.: Cassandra and SQL database comparison for near real-time Twitter data warehouse. In: International Seminar on Intelligent Technology and Its Applications (2016)

Data Centric Programming

A Survey of Techniques Used in Processing and Mining of Medical Images

Sudhriti Sengupta[1(✉)], Neetu Mittal[1], and Megha Modi[2]

[1] Amity Institution of Information Technology, Amity University, Noida, Uttar Pradesh, India
ssgupta@amity.edu

[2] Yashoda Super Specialty Hospital, Vaishali, Uttar Pradesh, India

Abstract. Medical image processing is the method to enhance and derive meaningful information from digital medical images. Large collection of medical images has led to the rise in some medical information retrieval system whose aim is storing images, retrieval of images, pattern reorganization etc. All of these are done so that some useful knowledge and information might be derived from them. If proper information can be retrieved from the images, it will help in diagnosis, research and education. This paper studies the various image processing and image mining techniques applied on medical images and their utility. This paper helps to understand the different techniques used in different phases of medical image processing and mining like pre-processing, feature extraction, segmentation, classification, indexing, storing and retrieval. This paper concludes by providing possible directions in future work.

Keywords: Medical images · Pre-processing · Feature extraction
Image indexing · Image retrieval · Image mining · Classification
Image processing

1 Introduction

There are various types of image data available from different domain like remote sensing, robotics vision, satellite image, computer aided visualization etc. Among all the categories of image data, medical image data is of utmost important and very sensitive. Proper methodologies should be developed for medical images processing so that it will help the healthcare stakeholders to provide better treatments and practice improved procedure in diagnosis, treatment and prevention of diseases. Medical Images are the visual representation of the organs, bones and other structure within the body for analysis relating to the observation and treatment of patients. It helps to find internal structure of the body by applying different techniques like CT images, MRI, mammography, nuclear medicines to diagnose disease and provide proper treatment. Due to advancement of technology there has been a substantial increase in the numbers of medical images of different categories. Large amount of data is now available from multiple sources. This has become a challenge for researchers for effective data acquisition, filtering, analysis and deriving meaning information. Deriving useful and timely information from the large repository of medical image data is a challenge for

B. Panda et al. (Eds.): REDSET 2017, CCIS 799, pp. 139–155, 2018.
https://doi.org/10.1007/978-981-10-8527-7_13

the researchers. Another challenge in processing and mining of medical image is the variety of medical image as medical images are of different types. Some of the widely used medical images are X-ray imaging, Computed Tomography (CT), Ultra-Sound Imaging (US), Magnetic Resonance Imaging (MRI), Scintigraphy (Anger camera) etc. These images are used by health practitioners throughout the world for analysis, diagnosis and providing treatment to the patient. These varieties of images provides challenges to the researcher in deriving some method for medical image mining and processing. This study is conducted to find about the various image mining and processing techniques used in medical images for knowledge discovery, prediction and proper treatment of patients. In this paper, Sect. 2 describes the processing phases of medical image data including data acquisition and storage, pre-processing, feature extraction, classification, image indexing and image retrieval. It also describes the different techniques used in medical images processing such as rough set, neural network, association rule mining [2, 3], classification [3], the k-nearest neighbour (kNN) and classification algorithm [4]. Section 2.6 describes the possible direction for future work. In the last section the conclusion of the paper is provided.

2 Medical Image Processing

Medical imaging method is a process to picture different parts of a living being. Some of the images are about the tissue, tissue composition or characteristics of bones, blood or other bodily fluids. Sometimes special substances called traces are injected into the body to image the physiological characteristics. There are various types of medical images which are applicable to many areas of healthcare domain like evaluation of MRI images, Interpretation of CT/X-Ray image etc. The main issue in image processing is to process pixel information present in an image into meaning information. Image processing is the technique of deriving a specific feature or enhancing a particular image. In image processing the main aim is to convert an image in digital form or acquire a digital image and enhance the image to identify specific feature for better analysis and interpretation. Spotting pattern, image compression, image enhancement, image restoration etc. are some techniques used for manipulating the image in image processing. Results obtained after image processing is a modified image or a report based on image analysis. The objective of image processing is extracting information from digital images. Medical image processing is supported by many medical imaging techniques like MRI, mammography, ultrasound, CT etc. These techniques are used for visualizing the internal structure of body which provides the required information to health practitioner and facilities them to provide better patient health care. The availability of huge amount of image data available from multiple sources possesses a challenge for researchers for effective data acquisition, filtering, analysis and deriving meaning information. Image processing is a combination of many different field of studies like data mining, machine learning, computer graphics, database system and artificial intelligent. There are two significant techniques in processing of image data. One of them is to process of image data only and other is to process from a combination of images and related alphanumeric characters. Medical Image processing can be divided into the following categories [5, 6]. It is depicted by the following Fig. 1.

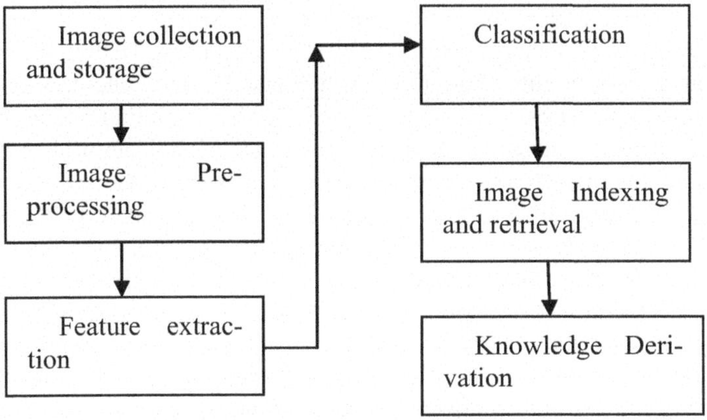

Fig. 1. Image processing stages.

2.1 Image Collection and Storage

There are several ways to store huge volume of image data. Searching for information and knowledge derivation in image database is different from traditional database because spatial information is required in image database whereas no such information is required in traditional database. Semantic values are depicted by the traditional database but in image database values are to be supported by some context. So, applying the methodology of data processing directly in images is not acceptable. This led to the rise of data management in image mining. The data management in image mining and processing is divided in two subdivisions [7]. One of category is to store images and the other one is to index and retrieve images. Storing image data cannot be done by following the rules of database because of difference in image database and traditional database as mentioned above. Many formats have been proposed for storing image data. Some of the format stores the metadata of the image in one file with the image but these have the disadvantage of using more memory and time. Another format proposes storing image metadata into separate relational database for faster and efficient image management. Object Oriented Databases are also proposed as a way for standardizing the image storage [7].

2.2 Image Pre-processing

This is an essential step required for enhancing the quality of image before proceeding to next phase [8]. Its importance ensures the quality of image data and subsequently the overall result. The main objective of analysis is to improving the image quality before applying any techniques for object detection or classification. Some of the techniques applied in image pre-processing are wavelet function, histogram equalization method, median filtering, high pass filter etc. Removal of noise or de-noising is one of the most important steps this state. It can be done by many techniques such as median filtering, wiener filtering and DWT (Discrete Wavelet Transform). Filtering of noise from images can also be done using different techniques such as Gaussian filter, high pass filter, adaptive median filter etc. After removal of noise the focus in pre-processing shifts to recognition or enhancement of object in an image. Histogram equalization techniques, grey scale modification, thresholding and Markov random model are used to enhance different types of images so that further techniques can be applied. Enhancement of biopsy images is done by Grey Scale Modification, thresholding and interpolation. Color Image enhancement is achieved by statistical mixture model like Dirichlet and Gaussian mixture, vector direction filter and markov random model. Contrast enhancement of image can be achieved by using hybrid filter containing simple mean and fuzzy switching median. To improve the segmentation median filter, histogram equalization and normalization are used. To compress images without any loss Haar wavelet functions can be applied. CT scan brain images are pre-processed by Shape priori technique. Alteration of images for presenting them in a format which is suitable for transformation techniques can be achieved by applying wavelet functions.

The different techniques of pre-processing used in medical images are mentioned in the Table 1 given below:

2.3 Feature Extraction

This stage refers to the methods used in analyzing objects or images to extract significant information that are representative of various classes of objects. Feature Extraction basically focuses on changing the identified objects into some sets of attributes. Features are generally mathematical representation of an image which describes the object in term of shape, texture or color. Various transformation and feature extractions techniques are applied to recognize pattern. Inferring knowledge can be done by pattern interpretation which can then be used in an application. 2D Gabor feature, association rule mining, sobel edge detector, grey tone spatial dependencies, fuzzy C mean algorithm, expectation maximization (EM) algorithm are some of the methods used for extraction of useful features from medical images. To find feature which are independent of each other decision tree, naive Bayes classifier, normalized cut algorithm, PCA (Principal Component Analysis), DWT (Discrete Wavelet Transformation), nonlinear anistropic diffusion and automatic thresholding are used. Entropy based discretization; Fuzzy clustering technique and fuzzy connectedness framework are used to group objects of same type. To improve visualization of MRI data and extract feature boundary expectation maximization (EM) algorithm is used. Fuzzy connectedness framework is used to find connectedness between image elements and grouping objects of same type. To incorporate contextual information and segmentation of single and multispectral MR image Markov random field are used. A combination of texture, color and edge extraction techniques is used to improve detection process. Identifying natural cluster of patient population is done by unsupervised neural networks. Support vector machine is used to derive nuclear features from segmented nuclei. Some texture feature extraction techniques are Haralick's statistical measure, GLCM and 2D wavelet transform function. Extraction of feature set essential for classification is done by Texture Features based on gray-tone spatial dependencies, Gabor Feature, Sobel edge detector and Gabor transforms and Histogram Equalization Method.

Table 1. Techniques used in pre-processing of medical images.

References	Techniques	Utility
Sikka et al. [9]	Haar wavelet	Image compression without losses
Nikolic and Tuba [10]	Median filtering process	Detection of edge features
Zäıane et al. [11]	Histogram Equalization Method	Image Enhancement
Rajendran et al. [12]	Shape priori technique	CT-Scan brain image pre-processing
Reni et al. [13]	Contrast enhanced gray-scale conversion algorithm	Morphological filtering of the blood images to remove unwanted components
Diwakar and Kumar [14]	Weiner filtering	Removal of noises in CT images
Wang et al. [15]	Wavelet transform	Alteration of images for presenting them in a format which is suitable for transformation techniques
Trzupek and Ogiela [16]	Aggregation based on the Ferret diameter and centre of gravity	Detection of pathological changes in structure of coronary arteries automatically
Subudhi et al. [17]	Histogram partition combined with maximum entropy divergence	Extracting images of brain in MRI images
Rana et al. [18]	Statistical mixture models like Dirichlet and Gaussian	Colour image enhancement
Aina et al. [19]	First add Gaussian noise in the brain MR images and then noise is removed by Fast discrete Curvelet transform (FDCT)	Removal of noise in MRI images
Jamil et al. [20]	Hair artifact removal of dermatoscope images	Morphological and Gabor wavelet functions
Vijaya and Suhasini [21]	Different filters like-High Pass, Adaptive Medians, Alpha-Trimmed Filter, Laplacian and Gaussian	Undifferentiated noisy and fine detail pixels
Patil and Udupi [22]	Median filter and an algorithm that uses morphological operations	Reduce the over segmentation problem
Kaur and Kaur [23]	Hybrid filter containing simple mean and the fuzzy switching median	Contrast enhancement of image

Table 2 depicts the various techniques used for feature extraction with emphasis on medical images.

2.4 Image Classification

Classification means categorization of objects present in an image. Supervised classification groups the detected objects into some predefined categories. Some methods of supervised classification are support vector machine, rule based classification, decision tree, neural networks etc. Unsupervised classification or image clustering means grouping of objects based on some common factors. Hierarchical clustering, fuzzy clustering and nearest neighbor clustering are some types of unsupervised clustering.

Table 2. Feature extraction techniques used in medical images

Reference	Techniques	Utility
Sikka and Ogiela [9]	Sobel edge detector and Gabor transforms	Edge and texture features extraction
Noorazlan et al. [24]	2D Gabor Filter	Feature extraction from medical images
Zäıane et al. [11]	Histogram Equalization Method	Extracting features so that it can be organized in a database
Wang et al. [15]	Entropy-based Discretization	The majority of the values in a bin correspond to having the same class label
Trzupek and Ogiela [16]	Decision tree or Naive Bayes Classifiers	To find features which are independent of each other
Smitha et al. [25], Kaur and Wasan [26]	Association rule mining	Extraction of hidden information from medical image data sets
Kovacevic and Loncarec [27]	A receptive field (RF)	Feature extraction and normalization
Elsayed et al. [28]	Normalized Cuts algorithm, Spectral Segmentation with multiscale graph decomposition, Modified Spectral Segmentation	Application in brain MR images to extract the Corpus Callosum segment from these image
Rajani et al. [29]	PCA (Principal component analysis), DWT (Discrete wavelet transformation)	Extraction of frequency space information from non-stationary signals
Haralick et al. [30]	Texture Features based on gray-tone spatial dependencies	Extracting feature set which are essential for classification
Liu and Wechsler [31]	Gabor Feature	Extracting features of the image useful for classification purpose
Kociolek et al. [32]	Transformation by Discrete Wavelet	Texture Analysis of Digital Image
Haralick et al. [33]	Decision boundary feature extraction principal component analysis, non-parametric weighted feature extrasion, minimum noise fraction transform, discriminant analysis, analysis of spectra and transformation of wavelet	Reduce the data redundancy by feature extraction
Atkins and Mackiewich [34]	Histogram analysis, nonlinear anisotropic diffusion and automatic thresholding	(1) Removing background noises so that a head mask is left (2) Detecting irregular border of the brain image (3) Refining of the irregular brain border to a final mask
Bezdek [35]	Fuzzy C-Means (FCM) algorithm	Brain tumour extraction from brain MRI images
Boskovitz and Guterman [36]	Fuzzy clustering technique	Image segmentation by using adaptive threshold method in the input images using labels automatically
Whitey and Koles [37]	Thresholds, region growing, edge tracing	To distinguish regions with contrasting intensity levels
Anbeek et al. [38]	K-Nearest Neighbor	Generation of brain structure image for each types of tissue in cranial MR imaging

(continued)

Table 2. (*continued*)

Reference	Techniques	Utility
Zhang et al. [39]	EM (expectation–maximization) algorithm and HMRF (hidden markov random field) model	MR images segmentation
Udupa and Sekera [40]	Fuzzy connectedness framework	Strength of connectedness between image elements is determined connecting paths between the pairs This results in grouping of objects of same type
Wells et al. [41]	Expectation-maximization (EM) algorithm	(1) Improved visualization of MRI (magnetic resonance imaging) data (2) decision boundary feature extraction
Niessen et al. [42]	Segmentation based on edge and region	Minimum user interaction is required for segmentation of, cerebrospinal fluid, grey matter and white
Leemput et al. [43]	Markov random Fields (MRF's)	Segmentation of single- and multi-spectral MR images and incorporation of contextual information
Foschi et al. [44]	Color Feature Extraction, Texture Feature Extraction and Edge Feature Extraction	A combination of this three process to improve the detection process
Zubi and Saad [45]	Pattern recognition	A combination of a feature extraction process
Shalvi and De-Claris [46]	Unsupervised neural networks	Identification of natural clusters formation from patient populations
Tohka et al. [47]	Support Vector Machine	Extraction of nuclear features from segmented nuclei
Fayez et al. [48]	Haralick's statistical measures, GLCM and 2D wavelet transform	Texture features extraction

Supervised classification is also called as parametric or hard classification whereas unsupervised classification is also called as non-parametric or soft classification [20]. There are many different techniques used in image classification. Classification of digital mammography into two sections can be done by using association rule mining. This technique can also be used to divide CT images of brain into three groups namely benign, malign and normal. This is also used to detach corpus callosum region from the rest of brain image. Decision tree algorithms are used for mammography classification and pre-processing of CT brain images and creation of a model to segment brain images. Retrieving and classification of different medical images can be done by text based indexing and classification system, Texture correlogram, support vector machine, self-organizing map and wavelet transformation. Classification is also done by neural network or support vector machine, example is given of classification of digital image of chest X-ray into two groups: abnormal and normal. Classification of medical images based on energy, homogeneity, entropy and contrast is done by test based image classification. To reduce searching time of an image by grouping images into cluster fuzzy C-mean (FCM) may be used. Multilayer perception model are used to classify images on different criteria. Classification of breast mammography and detection of cancerous tissue is done by genetic algorithm, branch - bound algorithm and Grey Level Concurrence matrix, Decision tree c4.5 is used to classify image samples into healthy and unhealthy. K-nearest neighbour (KNN) combined with genetic algorithm improves classification in image database. Categorization of medical images can be done by self-organising map and wavelet transformation.

Table 3 shows the different techniques of image classification with emphasis of medical images in Table 3.

Table 3. Image classification techniques in medical images

Reference	Technique	Utilities
Antonie et al. [3]	Association rule mining and neural networks	Detection of anomaly and classification
Sikka et al. [9]	Naïve Bayes and Support Vector Machine	Classification accuracy of retrieval
Zäıane et al. [11]	Association Rule based classification	Classification of digital mammography into two sections: normal and diseased
Farrugia et al. [49]	A text based indexing system	Retrieving and classification of Mammographic images
Yi et al. [50]	Texture correlogram (a new texture feature) and SVM (support Vector Machine)	High-level image classification
Zäıane et al. [11]	Association Rule based classification	Classification of digital mammography into two sections: normal and diseased
Reni et al. [13]	Nearest neighbour	Image classification
Trzupek and Ogiela [16]	Weighted Association Rule Mining (WARM)	Comparing the symptoms of patients with the existing Database
Subudhi et al. [17]	SVM. Naïve Bayes classification, Decision trees and Neural Network	To create a proto type for segmentation of brain images
Kovacevic and Loncarec [27]	Artificial neural network, radial basis function (RBF)	Classification of image regions and their labelling
Elsayed et al. [28]	Decision Trees, Support Vector Machines, Association Rule based classification	Build classifiers which will detach the Corpus Callosum region from the rest of the Brain image
Tohka et al. [47]	Classification scheme	Analyses of nuclear feature of brain into high, medium and low grade tumours
Fayez et al. [48]	K-Means clustering	Cluster images based on some feature
Kaur and Kaur [51]	Neural network and SVMs.	Classification digital X ray images of chest into two class i.e. abnormal and normal
Beevi et al. [52]	Fuzzy C-Means	Segmentation—of medical images by clustering
Abdul et al. [53]	Text based image classification	Categorization of different types medical images on the basis of energy, homogeneity, entropy and contrast
Zhou et al. [54]	Support Vector Machine	Automatic detection of brain tumour from MRI images
Matthew and Nachamai [56]	K-Means algorithm	Clustering brain MRI images

(*continued*)

Table 3. (*continued*)

Reference	Technique	Utilities
Deepa and Devi [57]	Fuzzy C-Means, Artificial Neural Networks, Support Vector Machine and Multilayer Perceptron model	Classify images based on different criteria
Devasena et al. [58], Purnami et al. [59]	Genetic Algorithm, GLCM (Grey Level co-occurrence Matrix) and fast branch - bound algorithm	Detection of cancerous tissue from mammography images of breast
Purnami et al. [59], Sathees Kumar and Anbu Selvi [60]	MKS (Multiple Knot Spline) with SVM (support vector machine)	Heart disease and diabetes diagnosis
Tu et al. [61]	Decision tree C4.5	Performance of the given method is tested to classify image samples into healthy and unhealthy
Kalaivani and Shunmuganathan [62]	K-nearest neighbour (KNN) combined with genetic algorithm	Improve classification performance in image dataset
Soliz et al. [63]	Neural network-based system	Reduction of both inter- reader variability and intra-reader variability for diagnosing chest radiographs
Thangaraju and Barkavi [64]	Neural Networks, Association Rule Mining, Apriori algorithm	Extraction of features from the database having x-ray of chest and categorizing each x-ray chest film
da Silva and Moreno [65]	Self-organizing map and wavelet transformation	Categorization of medical images
Wang et al. [66]	Combination of local binary pattern and SVMs, combination of wavelet transformation and SVMs	Compares and reveals the general characteristics for identifying of ophthalmic images

2.5 Image Indexing and Retrieval

A suitable indexing scheme is required for efficient retrieval of information from any database. In relational database, the concepts of primary and foreign key are used. This concept is not suitable for image database in image mining because image database is vastly different from relational databases. Hence several indexing techniques are developed for mining in image database. Some common techniques used in image indexing are Non Euclidean similarity measure and signature file access method for multidimensional database. X tree is used to minimizing overlap in image indexing. X tree is also used to create index structure necessary in high dimensional database. Multidimensional indexing method can be created by TV index tree, i-minmax and R* tree. An indexing scheme used for dealing with queries in high-dimensional nearest neighbour is created by using SR tree. Dynamic index structure necessary for spatial searching is created by using R tree.

Table 4 depicts the various techniques used for Image indexing.

Image retrieval system is used to browse, search and retrieve images from a digital images repository. Image retrieval methods can be divided into three categories.

Table 4. Study of image indexing techniques in medical images

Reference	Technique	Utilities
Berchtold et al. [67]	X tree	Split algorithm minimizing overlap in image indexing
Robinson [68]	The K-D-B Tree	Searching in huge multi-dimensional indexes
Gutnum [69]	R Tree	Dynamic index structure used in spatial searching.
Berchtod et al. [70]	X Tree	Index structuring used in high dimensional data
Katayama and Satoh [71]	SR-tree	An index system necessary in high-dimensional nearest neighbour queries
Dahabiah et al. [72]	TV index tree, i-minmax, R* tree, R+ tree	Multidimensional indexing method

(a) Query by Associative attribute is based on retrieval of images where attributes are stored as metadata.
(b) Query by Description is based on context associated with images.
(c) Query by Content is based on visual content such as texture, shape, color etc.

Some applications also apply a hybrid of above techniques for image. A hybrid image retrieval algorithm has been developed which include both two text model and visual features [73]. Deep learning architecture can also be used in image retrieval [74]. Fuzzy production rules are used for high level semantic image retrieval. Clustering techniques based on CBIR is used for retrieving of prominent feature of image. Retrieval of perceivable and textual information from images can be done by clustering and association rule mining. Image retrieval based on texture is done by color histogram. Weighted Euclidean distance is used to retrieve color feature. Pyramid structure wavelet functions are used for retrieval of image based on shape, color and texture. Retrieval of MRI image can be done by edge histogram and texture spectrum histogram. Unsupervised image segmentation technique based on cellular automata is used for image retrieval. Retrieving images having common pattern in medical database is done by image sequence similarity pattern (ISSP) and fuzzy retrieval techniques. Retrieving diagnostic cases similar to medical images is done by Support Vector machine.

Table 5 shows the different image retrieval techniques and their utilities

2.6 Future Directions and Discussion

The main aim of image mining and image processing is to remove loss of data and extract meaningful information as and when required by patients, healthcare providers and other stakeholder in medicine domain. The size and variety of medical image data is increasing in a very fast pace. Development in different energy source like magnetic, radio-frequency, optical and nuclear have added many forms or properties in the variety of medical images. This provides challenges to the researchers in medical images to

Table 5. Image retrieval techniques in medical images.

Reference	Technique	Utilities
Stanhev [75]	High level semantic features image retrieval	Fuzzy production rules
Kannan et al. [76]	Image retrieval on basis of prominent feature of the image	Clustering techniques based on CBIR (Content Based Image Retrieval)
Kannan et al. [77]	Optimum clusters based image retrieval	Improved CBIR with user interaction
Neethu and Wilson [78]	Clustering and association rule mining	Retrieval of visual and textual information from images
Sreelaksmi and Anil [79]	Colour Histogram	Image retrieval based on texture
Jyothi et al. [80]	Clustering technique using steerable filter and pseudo-zernike movements	Shape and feature extraction
Song and He [81]	Improving Precision Priority (IPP) algorithm	Increased precision in Content based Image Retrieval
Dong [82]	Multi-feature based retrieval	Improved retrieval in CT images of chest scan
Zhang et al. [83]	Modal shape description based search engine	Retrieve clinically similar medical images
Youssif et al. [84]	Pyramid structure wavelet	Retrieval of image based on shape, color and texture
Somnugpong and Khiewwan [85]	Color correlograms and edge direction histogram (EDH)	Improved Graphical image retrieval system by combing more than one feature
Huang et al. [86]	Ranking and multi-view learning	Retrieving image on basis of region
Kumuran et al. [87]	Edge histogram and Texture spectrum histogram	Retrieval of MRI images
Rahman et al. [88]	Classification-drive similarity matching	Biomedical image retrieval
Ghosh et al. [89]	Unsupervised image segmentation technique based on cellular automata	Image retrieval based on retrieval
Kawade and Bang [90]	Incorporation of genetic algorithm in CBIR	Image retrieval based on some defined ranked.
Enireddy and Reddy [91]	Naïve Bayes, SVM	Retrieve diagnostic cases similar to query medical images
Pan et al. [92]	Image sequence similarity patterns (ISSP)	Retrieving images having common pattern into medical image database

develop new techniques for analysis, storage, mining and retrieval of correct and timely information for helping in welfare of patients. The field of medical image Processing is in infancy and many issues remain unsolved.

- Retrieving information from fusion of unstructured heterogeneous data.
- Indexing compressed images
- Feature extraction from compressed image.
- Classification of classes into detailed higher level class.
- Improved performance in all the phases of mining process starting from image acquisition, storage, preprocessing, feature extraction, classification and knowledge derivation.

2.7 Conclusions

This paper presents the various image processing techniques that have been applied for medical image data. Fast growth in volume of medical images has made image mining techniques necessary for decision support and prediction in the area of healthcare. This paper has discussed about the various image mining technique used in medical images to provide significant outcome. According to this paper median filtering is the most commonly used technique used in image pre-processing followed by wavelet function and histogram equalization. In feature extraction decision tree model and its variation is mostly used. Other techniques used in feature extraction are Gabor feature, fuzzy techniques and GLCM (Gray-Level Co-Occurrence Matrix. For extracting common features in CT images from image transaction database a novel fuzzy association rule can be applied. For classification of images association rule mining, SVM (Support Vector Machine) fuzzy Techniques and neural network are widely used. Proper storage of medical image data can be achieved by Object Oriented database. Image indexing can be done by X tree, R tree, R+ tree and their variations. One of the main techniques used in image retrieval is CBIR (Content based Image Retrieval). This information should be produced in a way which can be used by medical practitioners and stakeholders in predicting trends in diseases. This will lead to better diagnosis and research which will improves patient care.

References

1. Goel, N., Yadav, A., Mohan Singh, B.: Medical image processing: a review. In: International Innovative Applications of Computational Intelligence on Power, Energy and Controls with Their Impact on Humanity, pp. 18–19 (2016)
2. Rathinam, S., Selvarajan, S.: Comparison of image preprocessing techniques on fundus images for early diagnosis of glaucoma. Int. J. Sci. Eng. Res. **4**, 290–297 (2013)
3. Antonie, M.L., Zäıane, O.R., Oman, A.: Application of data mining techniques for medical image classification. In: ACM SIGKDD Conference (2001)
4. Xu, D., Li, F.: Research and application of CT image mining based on rough sets theory and association rules. In: International Conference on Computer Science and Information Technology (2010)
5. Sudhir, R.: A survey on image mining technique theory and applications. Int. Knowl. Shar. Platf. **2**(6), 44–52 (2011)
6. Wu, C., Weng, Y., Jiang, Q., Wang, C., Guo, W.: Applied research on visual mining technology in medical data. In: International Conference on Cloud Computing and Intelligence Systems (CCIS) (2016)
7. Zahradnikova, B., Schreiber, P., Duchovicova, S.: Image mining: review and new challenges. Int. J. Adv. Comput. Sci. Appl. **6**, 242–246 (2015)
8. Zhang, J., Hsu, W., Lee, M.L.: Image mining in issues, frameworks and techniques. In: Association of Computer Machinery SIG KDD Conference, USA (2001)
9. Sikka, N., Singla, S., Pal Singh, G.: Lossless image compression technique using Haar wavelet and vector transform. IEEE International Conference on Research Advances in Integrated Navigation Systems (RAINS), pp. 1–5 (2016)

10. Nikolic, M., Tuba, E.: Edge detection in medical ultrasound images using adjusted Canny edge detection algorithm. In: IEEE 4th Telecommunications Forum (TELFOR), pp. 22–23, November 2016
11. Zäıane, O.R., Antonie, M., Coman, A.: Mammography classification by an association rule-based classifier. In: International Workshop on Multimedia Data Mining, MMG-SMD (2003)
12. Rajendran, P., Madheswaran, M., Naganandhini, K.: An improved pre-processing technique with image mining approach for the medical image classification. In: IEEE Computing Communication and Networking Technologies, pp. 29–31 (2010)
13. Reni, S.K., Morling, R., Kaleand, I.: Analysis of thin blood images for automated malaria diagnosis. In: IEEE E-Health and Bioengineering Conference (EHB), pp. 19–21, November 2015
14. Diwakar, M., Kumar, M.: Edge preservation based CT image denoising using Wiener filtering and thresholding in wavelet domain. In: IEEE 4th International Conference on Parallel, Distributed and Grid Computing (PDGC), pp. 22–24 (2016)
15. Wang, S., Zhou, M., Geng, G.: Application of fuzzy cluster analysis for medical image. In: International Conference on Mechatronics & Automation (2005)
16. Trzupek, M., Ogiela, M.R.: Supporting the recognition of pathological changes in CT coronary arteries visualizations based on data aggregation approach. In: International Conference on Imaging Systems and Techniques, pp. 22–23 (2013)
17. Subudhi, A., Jena, J., Sabut, S.: Extraction of brain from MRI images by skull stripping using histogram partitioning with maximum entropy divergence. In: International Conference on Communication and Signal Processing, pp. 931–935 (2016)
18. Rana, P.K., Ma, Z., Flier, M., Taghia, J.: Multiple view depth map enhancement by variational Bayes inference estimation of Dirichlet mixture models. In: International Conference on Acoustics and Signal Processing, pp. 1528–1532 (2013)
19. Aina, Q., Jaffar, M.A., Choic, T.: Fuzzy anisotropic diffusion based segmentation and texture based ensemble classification of brain tumor. Elsevier Appl. Soft Comput. **21**, 330–338 (2014)
20. Jamil, U., Khalid, S., Akram, M.U., Digital image pre-processing and hair artifact removal by using Gabor. In: IEEE International SoC Design Conference (ISOCC), pp. 215–216 (2016)
21. Vijaya, G., Suhasini, A.: An adaptive preprocessing of lung CT images with various filters for better enhancement. Acad. J. Cancer Res. **7**, 179–184 (2014)
22. Patil, S., Udupi, V.R.: Preprocessing to be considered for MR and CT images containing tumors. IOSR J. Electr. Electron. Eng. **1**, 54–57 (2012)
23. Kaur, S., Kaur, R.: Comparison of contrast enhancement techniques for medical image. In: Conference on Emerging Device and Smart System, pp. 155–159 (2016)
24. Noorazlan, M., Said, M.M., Ismail, M.: Feature extraction using 2D gabor filer. Appl. Mech. Mater. **52–54**, 2128–2132 (2011)
25. Smita, P., Shaji, L., Mini, M.G.: A review of medical image classification techniques. In: International Conference on VLSI, Communications and Instrumentation (2011)
26. Kaur, H., Wasan, S.: Empirical study on applications of data mining techniques in healthcare. J. Comput. Sci. **2**, 194–200 (2006)
27. Kovacivic, D., Loncarec, S.: Radial basis function-based image segmentation using a receptive field. In: Computer-Based Medical Systems, pp. 11–13 (1997)
28. Elsayed, A., Coenen, F., Fiñana, M., Sluming, V.: Segmentation for medical image mining: a technical report

29. Rajini, N.H., Bhavani R.: Classification of MRI brain images using k-Nearest neighbor and artificial neural network. In: IEEE-International Conference on Recent Trends in Information Technology, pp. 563–568 (2011)
30. Haralick, R.M., Shanmugam, K., Dinstein, I.: Textural features for image classification. IEEE Trans. Syst. Man Cybern. **3**(6), 610–621 (1973)
31. Liu, C., Wechsler, H.: Gabor feature based classification using the enhanced fisher linear discriminant model for face recognition. IEEE Trans. Image Process. **11**, 4 (2002)
32. Kociołek, M., Materka, A., Strzelecki, M., Szczypiński, P.: Discrete wavelet transform – derived features for digital image texture analysis. In: International Conference on Signals and Electronic Systems, pp. 163–168 (2001)
33. Nath, S., Mishra, G., Kar, J.: A survey of image classification methods and techniques. In: International Conference on Control, Instrumentation, Communication and Computational Technologies, pp. 554–557 (2014)
34. Atkins, M., Mackiewich, B.T.: Fully automatic segmentation of the brain in MRI. IEEE Trans. Med. Imaging **17**, 98–107 (1998)
35. Bezdek, J.C.: Pattern Recognition with Fuzzy Objective Function Algorithms. Advanced Applications in Pattern Recognition, pp. 203–209. Springer, New York (1981). https://doi.org/10.1007/978-1-4757-0450-1
36. Boskovitz, V., Guterman, H.: An adaptive neuro-fuzzy system for automatic image segmentation and edge detection. IEEE Trans. Fuzzy Syst. **10**, 247–262 (2002)
37. Withey, D.J., Koles, Z.J.: Medical image segmentation: methods and software. In: International Conference on Functional Biomedical Imaging, pp. 140–143 (2007)
38. Anbeek, P., Vincken, K.L., Der, Van: Grond, J: Probabilistic segmentation of brain tissue in MR imaging. US Nat. Libr. Med. **27**, 795–804 (2005)
39. Zhang, Y., Brady, M., Smith, S.: Segmentation of brain MR images through a hidden Markov random field model and the expectation-maximization algorithm. Trans. Med. Imaging **20**, 45–57 (2001). Institution of Electrical and Electronic Engineers
40. Udupa, J., Sekera, S.S.: Fuzzy connectedness and object definition: theory, algorithms, and applications. Image Segm.: Graph. Model. Image Process. **58**, 246–261 (2001)
41. Wells, W.M., Grimson, W.L., Joseph, F.A.: Adaptive segmentation of MRI data. IEEE Trans. Med. Imaging **15**, 429–434 (1996)
42. Niessen, W.J., Vincken, K.L., Weickert, J., Viergever, M.A.: Three-dimensional MR brain segmentation. In: 6th IEEE International Conference on Computer Vision, pp. 53–58 (1998)
43. Leemput, K., Vandermeulen, D., Maes, F., Suetens, P.: Automated model-based tissue classification of MR images of the brain. IEEE Trans. Med. Imaging **18**, 897–908 (1999)
44. Foschi, P.G., Kolippakkam, D., Liu, H., Mandvikar, A.: Feature extraction for image mining. In: International Conference on Innovations in Information, Embedded and Communication Systems (ICIIECS), pp. 19–20 (2015)
45. Zubi, Z.S., Saad, R.A.: Improves treatment programs of lung cancer using data mining technique. J. Softw. Eng. Appl. **7**, 69–77 (2014)
46. Shalvi, D., De-Claris, N.: An unsupervised neural network approach to medical data mining techniques. In: Proceedings of IEEE International Joint Conference on Neural Networks. IEEE World Congress on Computational Intelligence, pp. 171–176 (1998)
47. Glotsos, D., Tohka, J., Ravazoula, P., Cavouras, D., Nikiforidis, G.: Automated diagnosis of brain tumours astrocytomas using probabilistic neural network clustering and support vector machines. Int. J. Neural Syst. **15**, 1–11 (2005)
48. Fayez, M., Safwat, S., Hassanein, E.: Comparative study of clustering medical images. In: IEEE SAI Computing Conference (SAI), pp. 312–318 (2016)
49. Farruggia, A., Magro, R., Vitabile, S.: A text based indexing system for mammographic image retrieval and classification. Future Gener. Comput. Syst. **37**, 243–251 (2014)

50. Yi, H., Liu, S., Chia, L.T.: Adaptive hierarchical multi-class SVM classifier for texture-based image classification. In: IEEE International Conference on Multimedia, pp. 41–49 (2005)
51. Kaur, A., Kaur, R.: A study of detection of lung cancer using Dat a mining classification techniques. Int. J. Adv. Res. Comput. Sci. Softw. Eng. **3**(3) (2013)
52. Beevi, S.Z., Mohammedthi, S., Yasmin, J.: A robust fuzzy clustering technique with spatial neighborhood information for effective medical image segmentation: an efficient variants of fuzzy clustering technique with spatial information for effective noisy medical image segmentation. In: Institution of Electrical and Electronic Engineer Computing Communication and Networking Technologies, pp. 29–31 (2010)
53. Abdul, S., Radi, M.H., Gaata, T.: Medical image classification approach based on texture information. Int. J. Innov. Res. Comput. Sci. Technol. **4** (2016)
54. Zhou, J., Chong, V.F.H., Chan, K.L., Krishnan, S.M.: Extraction of brain tumor from MR images using one-class support vector machine. In: IEEE Engineering in Medicine and Biology Society, pp. 6411–6414 (2005)
55. Rajendran, P., Madheswaran, M.: An improved image mining technique for brain tumour classification using efficient classifier. Int. J. Comput. Sci. Inf. Secur. **6** (2009)
56. Siji, T.M., Nachamai, M.: Clustering of brain MRI image using data mining algorithm. Int. J. Adv. Comput. Eng. Netw. **3** (2015)
57. Deepa, S.N., Devi, A.: Artificial neural networks design for classification of brain tumour. In: IEEE International Conference on Computer Communication and Informatics, pp. 1–6 (2012)
58. Devasena, C.L., Hemalatha, M., Sumathi, T.: An experiential survey on image mining tools, techniques and applications. Int. J. Comput. Sci. Eng. (IJCSE), **3**(3) (2011)
59. Purnami, S.W., Zain, J.M., Embong, A.: Data mining technique for medical diagnosis using a new smooth support vector machine. In: International Conference on Networked Digital Technologies, pp. 15–27 (2010)
60. Sathees Kumar, B., Anbu Selvi, R.: Feature extraction using image mining techniques to identify brain tumors. In: International Conference on Innovations in Information, Embedded and Communication Systems (ICIIECS), pp. 1–6 (2015)
61. Tu, M.C., Shin, D., Shin, D.: A comparative study of medical data classification methods based on decision tree and bagging algorithms. In: IEEE International Conference on Dependable, Autonomic and Secure Computing, pp. 183–187 (2009)
62. Kalaivani, P., Shunmuganathan, K.L.: An improved K-nearest-neighbor algorithm using genetic algorithm for sentiment classification. In: IEEE Conference on Circuit, Power and Computing Technologies [ICCPCT], pp. 1641–1647 (2014)
63. Soliz, P., Coons, T., Coultas, D., James, D.: Fast-learning neural classifier for chest radiograph. In: IEEE Engineering in Medicine and Biology, vol. 2, pp. 11–40 (1999)
64. Thangaraju, P., Barkavi, G.: Lung cancer early diagnosis using some data mining classification techniques: a survey. Int. J. Adv. Comput. Technol. **3**, 908 (2014)
65. da Silva, L.A., Moreno, R.A., Furuie, S., Hernandez, E.: Medical image categorization based on wavelet transform and self-organizing map. In: IEEE International Conference on Intelligent Systems Design and Applications (ISDA), pp. 353–356 (2007)
66. Wang, L., Zhang, K., Liu, X., Long, E., An, J.Y., Zhang, J., Li, X., Chen, J., Cao, Q., Lee, J., Wu, X., Wang, D., Li, W., Lin, H.: Comparative analysis of image classification methods for automatic diagnosis of ophthalmic images. Natl. Libr. Med. Natl. Inst. Health Sci. Rep. **7**, Article number: 41545 (2017)
67. Berchtold, S., Keim, D., Kriegel, H.: The X-tree: an index structure for high-dimensional data. In: ACM Proceedings of 22nd International Conference on Very Large Data Bases, pp. 28–39 (1996)

68. Robinson, J.T.: The K-D-B-tree: a search structure for large multidimensional dynamic indexes. In: International Conference on Special Interest Group on Management of Data of Association of Computer Machinery, pp. 10–18 (1981)
69. Guttman, A.: R-trees, a dynamic index structure for spatial searching. In: ACM SIGMOD Conference on the Management of Data, pp. 143–147 (1984)
70. Berchtold, S., Keim, D., Kriegel, H.: The X-tree: an index structure for high-dimensional data. In: ACM SIGMOD International Conference on Very Large Data Bases, pp. 28–39 (1996)
71. Katayama, N., Satoh, S.: The SR-tree: an index structure for high-dimensional nearest neighbor queries. In: IACM SIGMOD International Conference on Management of data, pp. 46–53 (1997)
72. Dahabiah, A., Puentes, J., Solaiman, B.: Venous thrombosis supervised image indexing and fuzzy retrieval. In: International Conference of the IEEE Engineering in Medicine and Biology Society, pp. 4528–4531 (2007)
73. Luo, J., Lang, B., Tian, C., Zhang, D.: Image retrieval in the unstructured data management system AUDR. In: IEEE 8th International Conference on E-Science, pp. 1–7 (2010)
74. Liu, S., Liu, S., Cai, W., Che, H., Pujol, S., Kikinis, R., Fulham, M., Feng, D.: High-level feature based PET image retrieval with deep learning architecture. J. Nuclear Med. **1**, 2028 (2014)
75. Stanchev, P.: Using image mining for image retrieval. In: IASTED Conference on Computer Science and Technology, pp. 214–217 (2003)
76. Kannan, A., Mohan, V., Anbazhagan, N.: Image clustering and retrieval using image mining techniques. In: International Conference on Computational Intelligence and Computing Research, pp. 371–376 (2016)
77. Kannan, A., Mohan, V., Anbazhagan, N.: An effective method of image retrieval using image mining techniques. Int. J. Multimed. Appl. (IJMA) **2**(4) (2010)
78. Neethu, J., Wilson, A.: Retrieval of images using data mining techniques. In: IEEE International Conference on Contemporary Computing and Informatics, pp. 204–208 (2014)
79. Sreelekshmi, U., Anil, A.R.: A survey on feature extraction techniques for image retrieval using data mining & image processing techniques. Int. J. Eng. Comput. Sci. **5**(11) (2016)
80. Jyothi, B., Madhavilata, Y., Mohan, P.G.K.: Medical image retrieval using multiple features clustering technique. In: International Conference on Computational Intelligence and Computing Research, pp. 1–4 (2012)
81. Song, J., He, Z.: Content based image retrieval by IPP algorithm. In: International Conference on Computational Intelligence and Virtual Environments for Measurement Systems and Applications (CIVEMSA), pp. 212–214 (2015)
82. Dong, Y.: Multi-feature based medical image retrieval. In: IEEE Symposium on Electrical & Electronics Engineering (EEESYM), pp. 522–524 (2012)
83. Zhang, W., Dickinson, S., Sclaroff, S., Feldman, J., Dunn, S.: Shape-based indexing in a medical image database. In: IEEE Workshop on Biomedical Image Analysis, pp. 221–230 (1998)
84. Aliaa, A., Youssif, A., Darwish, A.A., Mohamed, R.A.: Content based medical image retrieval based on pyramid structure wavelet. IEEE Int. J. Comput. Sci. Netw. Secur. **10**, 79–83 (2010)
85. Somnugpong, S., Khiewwan, K.: Content-based image retrieval using a combination of color correlograms and edge direction histogram. In: IEEE International Joint Conference on Computer Science and Software Engineering (JCSSE), pp. 1–5 (2016)
86. Huang, W., Zeng, S., Chen, G.: Region-based image retrieval based on medical media data using ranking and multi-view learning. In: IEEE International Conference on Affective Computing and Intelligent Interaction (ACII), pp. 845–850 (2015)

87. Kumaran, N., Bhavani, R., Elamathi, E.: MRI image retrieval based on texture spectrum and edge histogram features. In: IEEE International Conference on Communication and Signal Processing, pp. 1059–1063 (2013)
88. Rahman, M.M., Antani, S.K., Thomas, G.: A classification-driven similarity matching framework for retrieval of medical images. In: Association of Computing Machinery Library International Conference on Multimedia Information Retrieval, pp. 147–154 (2010)
89. Ghosh, P., Antani, S.K., Long, L.R., Thoma, G.R.: Unsupervised grow-cut: cellular automata-based medical image segmentation. In: International Conference on Healthcare Informatics, Imaging and Systems Biology, pp. 40–47 (2011)
90. Kawade, V.V., Bang, A.V.: Content based image retrieval using interactive genetic algorithm. In: INDICON (IEEE India Conference), pp. 61–66 (2014)
91. Enireddy, V., Reddy, K.K.: A data mining approach for compressed medical image retrieval. Int. J. Comput. Appl. **52** (2012)
92. Pan, H., Feng, X., Han, Q., Yin, G.: A domain knowledge based approach for medical image retrieval. In: International Conference on Bio-Inspired Computing: Theories and Applications, pp. 1677–1684 (2010)

Weighted Fuzzy KNN Optimized by Simulated Annealing for Classification of Large Data: A New Approach to Skin Detection

Swati Aggarwal, Lehar Bhandari, Karan Kapoor(✉), and Jaswin Kaur

Netaji Subhas Institute of Technology, New Delhi 110078, India
karankapoor.nsit@gmail.com

Abstract. Machine learning is being used in every field. In almost all technical and financial domains, machine learning is being used enormously from predicting new outcomes to classifying a given data into multiple sets. In this research work it has been tried to build and expand upon previously built binary classifiers to develop a unique classifier for skin detection that separates the given input data into two sets – Skin segment and Non-Skin segment. Skin Detection essentially means detecting in an image or video pixels or regions which are of the skin color. The input data given to the classifier has three attributes - value of the red, green and blue channel. The combination of these three values is the color of the object seen. The classifier classifies the input data into the above two classes on the basis of these attributes. In general, this classifier can be extended to any binary class data.

Keywords: Classification · Skin detection · RGB color space · Fuzzy · KNN SA · TPR · FPR

1 Introduction

The classification problem, which is a core concept of Machine Learning aims to classify a test data, as the name itself suggests, to one of the multiple possible classes with the aid of training vectors or samples whose membership is known beforehand. Based on these training samples, and the similarity of attributes of test and training samples, we can predict which classes the test data will belong to. Classification is an example of pattern recognition which can be applied to skin detection [1].

Given a static image or a video, skin detection [2] primarily focuses on locating pixels which are of the skin color. This particularly goes a long way in detecting humans or human body parts in those images. Before that image or video is actually fed to a skin detector, it might have to undergo a change in its color space for better results [3]. The need for skin detection arises from the fact that skin color is something that uniquely identifies humans from other species. Skin detection is finding its use in plethora of fields like biometrics in security systems, medical fields such as in Lasik eye operation, blocking adult images and face detection on social networking sites.

B. Panda et al. (Eds.): REDSET 2017, CCIS 799, pp. 156–163, 2018.
https://doi.org/10.1007/978-981-10-8527-7_14

The research work aims to classify new data sets into skin and non-skin segments using Weighted Fuzzy KNN classifier [4] optimized by Simulated Annealing [5]. The data set being used is the Skin Segmentation Data Set from the UCI repository [6]. The data set has three attributes - Blue, Green and Red values of a segment which may or may not correspond to skin color. The three input attributes are given random weights initially which are then optimized through Simulated Annealing to achieve the best accuracy on the training data through repeated iterations. The input attributes of the test data are then given the final weights eventually obtained and the Fuzzy KNN classifier is one last time run on the test data. The predicted outputs of the classifier are then compared with the actual outputs of the test data to find out the accuracy. Apart from this, the images can also be uploaded via the File Picker Window and skin portion can be detected in those images.

2 A Comparative Evaluation of Previous Models

One of the popular machine learning dataset for skin detection is the Compaq dataset used by Jones and Rehg in 1999. It contains 13640 web images, of which 4675 are composed of skin pixels and remaining 8965 aren't. The results as obtained by them is shown in the below table. It contains true positive and false positive rates for different models proposed by various researchers. Even though the table shows different learning methods used, the true positive and false positive rates obtained give a fair and sufficient idea about the performance of the methods.

Table 1. Performance of different models for skin detection as reported on Compaq dataset [7–9]

Method	TP Rate (TPR)	FP Rate (FPR)
Bayes skin probability map in RGB [10]	93.4%	19.8%
Maximum entropy model in RGB [11]	80%	8%
Self organizing map [12]	78%	32%
Elliptical boundary model in CIE-xy [13]	90%	20.9%
Single Gaussian in CbCr [7]	90%	33.3%
Gaussian mixture in IQ [7]	90%	30.0%
Thresholding of I axis in YIQ [10]	94.7%	30.2%
Gaussian mixture models [14]	90%	15.5%
Batch nearest neighbour model [15]	99.4%	10%

BNN [15] demonstrates the best results in the above table in terms of high TPR and low FPR. The parameter based methods like SOM based detector [12] do not perform as good as the other models do.

While the Bayes SPM model uses the Bayes rule to find the probability ($P_{skin}|c$) of the pixel, given the concrete value of a color c and qualifies it as a skin-colored pixel if its probability value is above a threshold point, the Single Gaussian uses the joint probability density function for the skin pixel detection. Both the models gave a high value for true positives, 93.4% and 90% respectively while the Single Gaussian model gave a greater value for false positives (33.3%) than that obtained in the former (19.8%). As it is observed, Gaussian model results in a high FPR. The Elliptical Boundary Model on the other hand produces great results, i.e. TPR-90% and FPR- 20.9% on the Compaq database. It proves to be a good substitute to the Gaussian model since its training as well as computation is not time consuming. In conclusion, the Bayes SPM and Maximum Entropy Model outshine the other techniques as can be observed from their low FPR for a given correct detection rate, 19.8% and 8% respectively.

3 Proposed Framework

The proposed model is different from the previous work done since different weights have been used for the three input features which are being optimized by Simulated Annealing. The combination of Fuzzy KNN classifier and Simulated Annealing doesn't exist previously. Various classification models and algorithms like Mamdani and Sugeno fuzzy models [16], neural networks [17] and KNN algorithm were tried. Out of these, KNN algorithm gave the best accuracy. However, it has a drawback: it gives equal importance to all the neighbors while classifying a test vector [18]. Fuzzy KNN algorithm overcomes this limitation since it gives more importance to closer neighbors than the farther ones, leading to better classification.

Weights to the 3 input features were then assigned since not all the 3 features might contribute equally in classifying a test sample. These weights then had to be optimized to achieve the best possible classification accuracy, precision and recall. Then Simulated Annealing was used as an optimizing algorithm since it allows worse moves to be accepted in certain cases leading to a desirable property: it doesn't get stuck in local optima [19], leading to good results.

3.1 Preprocessing

The preprocessing step involves random shuffling the data set since the original data set contains all skin segment instances followed by non-skin segment ones. There were no instances with missing values.

3.2 Dividing the Data Set into Training and Test Data

The original data set contains 245057 instances of which 50859 are skin samples and the remaining 194198 are non-skin samples. After random shuffling, 75% of the total sample size was taken as training data and the remaining 25% as the test data. Thus, the training data consists of 183792 instances and the test sample consists of 61265 instances.

3.3 Proposed Model

The proposed model is illustrated below (Fig. 1).

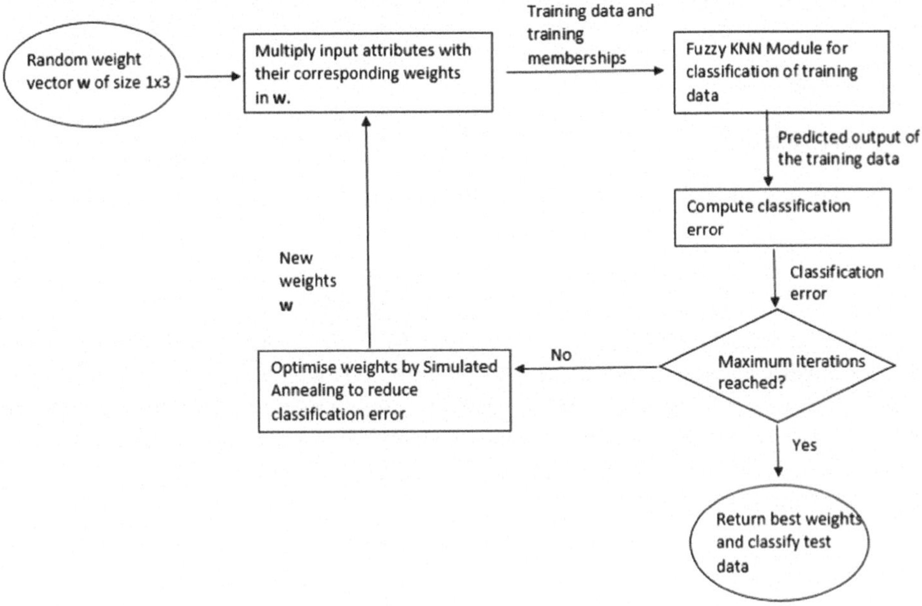

Fig. 1. Flowchart for the proposed work.

In this proposed model, Fuzzy KNN was used to predict the output class (Skin/Non Skin) for a particular set of pixels. The model uses a feature vector of size 1×3 where the three input features were values of the R, G and B color channels in a particular pixel. If the model predicts it to be a skin pixel, it outputs 1, else 0. Since all the input features may not have equal importance in deciding the output class, the weighted features were used. However the weights that need to be assigned to different features were unknown. Hence, initially all of the features were multiplied by random weights. The size of this weight vector was also 1×3. The training data was further divided into two sets of ratio 1:1; training 1 and training 2. Training 1 was given training memberships and training 2 wasn't. Training memberships were assigned on the basis of the class they belonged to. All instances belonging to Skin class were given training membership as [1 0], and those belonging to Non-Skin class were given [0 1]. This set of training memberships was passed to the Fuzzy KNN module. Thus, accuracy was obtained on the training 2 set using training 1 set, their memberships and the set of random weights using Fuzzy KNN algorithm. This set of random weights was optimized by Simulated Annealing to achieve the best possible classification accuracy on the training 2 set.

The training set was quite large. If the model was to run on the entire dataset at once, it would be very time consuming. Hence, during every iteration of Simulated Annealing, the training dataset was randomly shuffled and the first 12000 instances of the shuffled data set were used for training. This ensured that the entire data set was covered for the training purpose.

The model which then contained optimal set of weights was then tested on test data that could predict the output class with high accuracy.

4 Results

4.1 Accuracy

The accuracy used in the classification task was represented as:

$$Accuracy = \frac{tp + tn}{tp + tn + fp + fn} \tag{1}$$

Where tp: True Positives, tn: True Negatives, fp: False Positives, fn: False Negatives

True positives indicate the number of positive files which are rightly classified as positive. Similarly True negatives indicate the number of negative files which are correctly classified as negative. False positives denote the number of negative files which are misclassified as positive. False negatives indicate the number of positive files that are misclassified as negative.

4.2 Precision

Precision, for a positive class is the ratio of two values: the number of samples correctly classified by the classifier as part of the positive class, (True Positives) and the total number of samples classified as part of the positive class (the sum of True Positives and False Positives).

$$Precision = \frac{tp}{tp + fp} \tag{2}$$

4.3 Recall or True Positive Rate (TPR)

Recall, is defined as the ratio of True Positives and the total number of samples that really are members of the positive class (the sum of True Positives and False Negatives). In classification tasks where the data is imbalanced, precision and recall serve as good parameters to judge the system.

$$Recall\ or\ True\ Positive\ Rate = \frac{tp}{tp + fn} \tag{3}$$

4.4 False Positive Rate (FPR)

FPR, also known as the false alarm ratio, is the ratio of the number of negative samples incorrectly classified as positive (false positives) and the total number of actual negative samples, irrespective of what the classifier predicts them to be.

$$False\ Positive\ Rate = \frac{fp}{fp + tn} \tag{4}$$

Result. Simulated Annealing algorithm was allowed to run for about 1400 iterations which took about 11 h and the results are tabulated in the following Tables 2 and 3.

Table 2. Results for simulated annealing (accuracy, precision and recall)

Training data accuracy	Test data accuracy	Test data precision	Test data recall
99.6334	99.8955	0.9951	0.9999

Table 3. Results for Simulated Annealing (TP, TN, FP, FN)

True positive	True negative	False positive	False negative
12828	48373	63	1

Fig. 2. Skin detection using the proposed model on a real image

5 A Comparative Evaluation of the Proposed Model with the Previous Best Model

The following table gives a comparison of the best method in Table 1, i.e. the BN method by Sebe and Huang [15] in terms of True Positive Rate and False Positive Rate in Table 2. It is to be noted, however, that the BN method used the Compaq dataset and the proposed model used the UCI Skin Segmentation dataset (Table 4).

Table 4. Comparison of the proposed model with the previous best model

Skin detection method	True Positive Rate (TPR)	False Positive Rate (FPR)
BN	99.4%	10%
Proposed method	99.99%	0.13%

A good classifier is characterized by a high TPR and a low FPR. The proposed model has a TPR higher than that of the previous best model (99.99 > 99.4) and a FPR lower than that of the previous best model (0.13 < 8), and thus is better than the models till date with significant improvements. The weights assigned to the input attributes of the dataset so that every attribute have an equal say in the classification process and also the optimizing algorithm, that is, Simulated Annealing being used to optimize these weights reduced the classification error on the data, thus resulting in building a promising skin classifier as presented in this paper.

6 Limitations

The model detects undesired skin colored areas too which may not actually be skin. Also, since the dataset is large, it takes time to train and test.

7 Real Life Applications of Skin Detection

The process of skin detection contributes immensely to alarm systems. Detection of skin in a human restricted area can trigger an alarm. Face recognition on social media is another important application. Gaming consoles like Xbox also make use of skin detection. It is also a preliminary step in gesture analysis, tracking and content based image retrieval system [20]. Apart from this, skin detection also has an important part to play in enhancing photographs.

8 Conclusion

The aim of the research project was to create a system to detect skin pixels and generate the accuracy in detecting the skin pixels. The proposed novel approach gave a pretty good accuracy of 99.8955%, a precision value of 0.9951 and a recall of 0.9999. Thus the application can be very easily used to detect skin pixels and be used in other applications that use the concept of skin detection as a preliminary step.

References

1. Alpaydin, E.: Introduction to Machine Learning (2010). [Sl]
2. Elgammal, A., Muang, C., Hu, D.: Skin detection-a short tutorial. Encycl. Biom., 1–10 (2009)
3. Alala, B., Mwangi, W., Okeyo, G.: Image representation using RGB color space. Int. J. Innov. Res. Dev. **3**(8) (2014)
4. Keller, J.M., Gray, M.R., Givens, J.A.: A fuzzy k-nearest neighbor algorithm.IEEE Trans. Syst. Man Cybern. (4), 580–585 (1985)
5. Van Laarhoven, P.J., Aarts, E.H.: Simulated annealing. In: Simulated annealing:Theory and applications, pp. 7–15. Springer, Netherlands (1987)
6. Bhatt, R., Dhall, A.: Skin segmentation dataset. UCI Machine LearningRepository (2010)
7. Vezhnevets, V., Sazonov, V., Andreeva, A.: A survey on pixel-basedskin color detection techniques. In: Proceedings of the Graphicon, vol. 3, pp. 85–92, September 2003
8. Jones, M.J., Rehg, J.M.: Statistical color models with application to skin detection. Int. J. Comput. Vis. **46**(1), 81–96 (2002)
9. Kakumanu, P., Makrogiannis, S., Bourbakis, N.: A survey of skin-colormodeling and detection methods. Pattern Recognit. **40**(3), 1106–1122 (2007)
10. Brand, J., Mason, J.S.: A comparative assessment of three approaches topixel-level human skin-detection. In: Proceedings of the 15th International Conference on Pattern Recognition, vol. 1, pp. 1056–1059. IEEE (2000)
11. Jedynak, B., Zheng, H., Daoudi, M.: Maximum entropy models for skin detection. In: International Workshop on Energy Minimization Methods in Computer Vision and Pattern Recognition, pp. 180–193. Springer, Heidelberg, July 2003
12. Brown, D. A., Craw, I., Lewthwaite, J.: A SOM based approach to skin detection with application in real time systems. In: BMVC, vol. 1, pp. 491–500, July 2001
13. Lee, J.Y., Yoo, S.I.: An elliptical boundary model for skin color detection. In: Proceedings of the 2002 International Conference on Imaging Science, Systems, and Technology, June 2002
14. Joenes, M., Rehg, J.: Statistical color models with application to skin detection. In: IEEE Conference Computer Vision and Pattern Recognition. In: CVPR, vol. 99, pp. 274–280 (1999)
15. Sebe, N., Cohen, I., Huang, T.S., Gevers, T.: Skin detection: a Bayesian network approach. In: Proceedings of the 17th International Conference on Pattern Recognition, ICPR 2004, vol. 2, pp. 903–906. IEEE, August 2004
16. Setnes, M., Roubos, H.: GA-fuzzy modeling and classification: complexity and performance. IEEE Trans. Fuzzy Syst. **8**(5), 509–522 (2000)
17. Saha, P., Mandal, R.: Detection of Dengue Disease Using Artificial Neural Networks (2017)
18. Imandoust, S.B., Bolandraftar, M.: Application of k-nearest neighbor (knn) approach for predicting economic events: Theoretical background. Int. J. Eng. Res. Appl. **3**(5), 605–610 (2013)
19. Goffe, W.L., Ferrier, G.D., Rogers, J.: Global optimization of statistical functions with simulated annealing. J. Econom. **60**(1-2), 65–99 (1994)
20. Liensberger, C., Stöttinger, J., Kampel, M.: Color-based skin detection and its application in video annotation

Comparative Analysis of Edge Detection Techniques for Medical Images of Different Body Parts

Bhawna Dhruv[1(✉)], Neetu Mittal[1], and Megha Modi[2]

[1] Amity University, Noida, UP, India
Bdhruv08@gmail.com, Savini09@gmail.com
[2] Yashoda Super Specialty Hospital, Ghaziabad, UP, India
Dr.meghamodi@gmail.com

Abstract. Medical images are arduous to process since they possess distinct modalities. Therefore, the medical practitioners cannot competently detect and diagnosis the diseases in conventional ways. There should be a system which helps physicians to understand medical images very easily. Image segmentation using edge detection is commonly used for image analysis and better visualization of medical images. Various methods have been used for image segmentation such as Threshold detection, Region detection, Edge detection and Clustering technique. Edge detection is one of the prominently used methods for segmentation. This technique focuses on identifying and analyzing the entire image based upon the detected edges. In this paper, MRI images of human body parts such as abdomen, ankle, elbow, hand, knee, leg, liver and brain are considered for edge detection. Further, filtering has been performed on the segmented images to remove the unwanted noise. This makes the image more clearly for further reference. The effectiveness of the proposed technique has been evaluated quantitatively by using the performance measures like Entropy and Standard Deviation. The proposed technique may be highly beneficial for medical practitioners to carry out the diagnosis for effective treatment.

Keywords: Image segmentation · Medical images · MRI · Edge detection
Entropy · Standard deviation · Noise removal

1 Introduction

With the modern approach in the field of information technology, the revision in the analysis of the medical images has devoted noticeably to the early diagnosis of various diseases. Image segmentation especially edge detection technique give much knowledge that help to explain the medical images and improve the sharpness of detection and further diagnosis of different diseases. Image Segmentation is the process of dividing an image into meaningful structures where each pixel has same attributes [1]. The pixel is similar on the basis of criteria such as texture, color or intensity. Image segmentation aims at improving the pictorial information for interpretation. This process can be achieved by converting a low level image into high level image which may deem to be a challenging task as an image is never partitioned accurately for analysis [2]. One of the

B. Panda et al. (Eds.): REDSET 2017, CCIS 799, pp. 164–176, 2018.
https://doi.org/10.1007/978-981-10-8527-7_15

processes of achieving the same is through Edge detection techniques. The reason behind implementing an edge detector to a set of images is highly suggestive of reduction in amount of data to be processed. This further overlooks insignificant data and captures important properties of an image. Various types of edge detection operators such as Sobel, Roberts, Prewitt, Canny and LoG can applied to study the results on a particular image [3]. The aim of the paper is to study these edge detection techniques and apply them on the MRI images of different body parts to analyze the results. Image Segmentation plays a vital role in medical image processing, particularly for different body parts abnormalities detection in Magnetic Resonance Imaging (MRI) and computed Tomography (CT). The idea behind using MRIs to CT is that the latter doesn't use ionizing radiations, hence giving us a clear picture of the health condition [4]. The results are based upon three parameters i.e. Entropy, Standard Deviation and Execution Time. Entropy, generally defines the amount of information which must be used to compress the image by any compression algorithm [5]. Similarly, the standard deviation explains the variation of the results from the actual value of any parameter in an image.

Moreover, image seized from different sources suffer deterioration which affect the essential features of the image and makes image study difficult. Image restoration attempts to restore the degraded images by removing noise from the image. The process of image restoration completely depends upon accuracy of image analysis and generally removes unwanted pairs [6]. It studies entire degradation process and evaluates the inverse process to assess the original image. It is an objective process and restores the approximation of actual image.

In this paper Edge detection techniques are applied with different operators on MRI images.

A. Magnetic Resonance Imaging:

Magnetic Resonance Imaging (MRI) is a medical imaging technique used to visualize detailed internal structures of respective body part with the help of magnetic radiation. It provides three dimensional real-time views of organs mostly for the soft-tissue. It furnishes good contrast of soft tissue, gives better visualization of soft-tissue structures like brain, spine, muscles, and joints. The MRI machine used to capture in multiple body planes without changing the physical positions of the patient under scanning as it operates in multiple planes. Image segmentation may be widely used in MRI images of brain to detect tumor and other skin lesion or patches like abnormalities. Also Image segmentation on MRI images is also useful after surgery to keep sign the improvement of treatment and to monitor the growth of tumor before surgery.

2 Edge Detection Technique

Edge detection has turned out to be most competent field in image processing which helps in locating sharp discontinuities in an image. These discontinuities are blunt changes in the intensity of pixels which define the edges of image [7]. The edge element is crucial and significant feature of an image. There are several edge detection techniques depending upon the sensitivity of an image which are designed to work upon in vertical, horizontal and diagonal directions [8]. It must be noted that the preferred direction of every convolution mask is weighted with highest coefficients. Apart from edge detection, noise removal also plays an important role in image processing. The goal of removing noise is to discard unwanted pixels.

Different edge detection operators:

A. SOBEL:

The Sobel operator is used to perform spatial gradient measurement on any image. It is used for edge detection of two basic types i.e. Vertical Direction and Horizontal Direction [9]. This operator consists of 3 × 3 convolution mask which is designed in such a way that every edge whether in vertical or horizontal direction is detected relative to the pixel grid [10]. The convolution mask of the image is generally smaller as compared to the actual image. These masks can be applied in any form i.e. Corresponding to G_x or G_y separately or together so as to give an absolute gradient measurement at each point. The intensity of the function at eight distinct points is recognized to sample image point. The G_x mask highlights the horizontal edges in the image while G_y highlights the vertical edges, it further calculate the difference between pixel intensities of the particular direction [11]. As it is visible from the mask, the zeros in the middle row helps to compute the difference between the intensities of the edge [12]. This operator is disrupted by noise easily, therefore cannot detect outermost images easily. The basic advantage of using this operator is that weights can be applied to the coefficients which produce better result.

$$|G| = \sqrt{G_X^2 + G_Y^2}$$
$$G_x = \sum\sum Sobel_{x,i,j} * I_{r+i-2,c+j-2}$$
$$G_y = \sum\sum Sobel_{y,i,j} * I_{r+i-2,c+j-2}$$

B. ROBERTS:

The Roberts operator is used to highlight the high spatial frequency of the corresponding edges of any image. The kernels used for this operator are rotated by 90° therefore the convolution mask is designed to give the maximum results of the edges running at 45°. Similar to Sobel Operator, the edges can be detected separately or absolute gradient can be computed by combining G_X and G_Y [13]. The convolution masks are given below:

$$|G| = \sqrt{G_X^2 + G_Y^2}$$

Robert also proposed the following equation:

$$y_{i,j} = \sqrt{x_{i,j}}$$

$$z_{i,j} = \sqrt{(y_{i,j} - y_{i+1,j+1})^2 + (y_{i+1,j} - y_{i,j+1})^2}$$

x: Initial density of the image.
z: Computed derivate.
i, j: Location of image.

C. PREWITT:

This technique was devised to conquer the problems of Sobel operator i.e. absence of smoothing modules. It detects the edges in both vertical and horizontal direction which is a way of finding the approximations in magnitude and orientation of the edge in an image [14]. It has maximum 8 possibilities of orientation and does not emphasize on central value of the mask. The kernels of this operator are of least values thereby preventing blurring and extra trouble. The convolution mask is given below:

$$|G| = \sqrt{G_X^2 + G_Y^2}$$

$$\text{Also, } G = \sqrt{G^2x + G^2y\theta} = \text{atan2}\,(G_y, G_X)$$

D. CANNY:

This edge detection technique is also known as optimal edge detector as it focuses on improving the results as compared to the other operators [15]. This initially smoothes the image and removes the noise and then gives the output of spatial gradient measurement on any image. This filter helps to smoothen the noise as well detects the edges meticulously. It works to satisfy the conditions like localization of edge, low error rate and single edge detection. The gradient is calculated using the Gaussian filter [16]. The edge identification image is then exhibited to thresholds followed by the process of hysteresis to suppress the non suppressed pixels.

E. LoG:

The laplacian of Gaussian is 2D isotropic measure of 2nd special derivative of the image which focuses on highlighting the region where the intensity of the image changes very rapidly [17]. Therefore this is a highly used edge detection technique. The operation of this detector works in a way that it first smoothes the noise using the Gaussian filter and then gives the output as a gray image only [18]. The laplacian of an image is as given below:

$$L(x, y) = \frac{\partial^2 I}{\partial x^2} + \frac{\partial^2 I}{\partial y^2}$$

As it can be seen that all the three filters deal with second derivate measurement of the image, it becomes necessary to first smoothen the image so as to reduce the noise and then the Gaussian filter is applied [19, 20].

3 Measuring Parameters of Image Analysis

The quality of any image can be determined on two basis i.e. subjective or objective. The subjective as the name suggests consumes more time as compared to the latter. In our work, we have considered two quantity measures as given:

A. Standard Deviation:

The standard deviation is the measure of distribution of the set of data from its mean. It measures the absolute instability of a distribution [21, 22]. Higher instability depicts higher standard deviation. Generally, continuous data is required to calculate standard deviation. It is given by:

$$\sigma = \sqrt{\sum_{i=0}^{L} (i - \bar{i})^2 h_{If}(i), \ldots \bar{i} = \sum_{i=0}^{L} i h_{If}}$$

B. Entropy:

Entropy as defined by the Math works is a statistical measure of randomness that can be used to characterize the texture of input image [23]. Images with low entropy have low contrast whereas high entropy depicts high contrast in an image but are troublesome to compress. It is given by:

$$E = -\sum_{i=0}^{L-1} p_i \, log_2 \, p_i$$

In our work, we have dealt with the MRI images of different body parts. MRI (Magnetic Resonance Imaging) is a medical imaging technique used in radiology to form pictures of the anatomy and the physiological processes of the body in both health and disease. On the images of different body parts, several operators have been applied to study the result.

4 Noise Removal

Digital images play fundamental role in the field of research, medical imaging and information systems using satellites. The images collected from distinct sources are noisy hence de-noising techniques are applied so as to achieve better results for analysis. De-noising still prevails as a challenge in the research therefore techniques like image enhancement are used to improve the image quality. The filtering techniques are treated as first step to obtain images rich in quality.

A. Salt and Pepper:

The pixels in the image get destroyed due to transformation from analog to digital domain. These corrupted images are known as impulse noise which are of two types i.e. fixed value impulse noise and Random value impulse noise. The fixed impulse noise is also referred to as Salt and Pepper which accepts only 2 values, either 0 for pepper or 255 for salt. The random value impulse noise whereas can accept any value ranging from 0 to 255. This noise generally occurs in an image due to defects in camera's sensor cell or synchronization errors (Fig. 1).

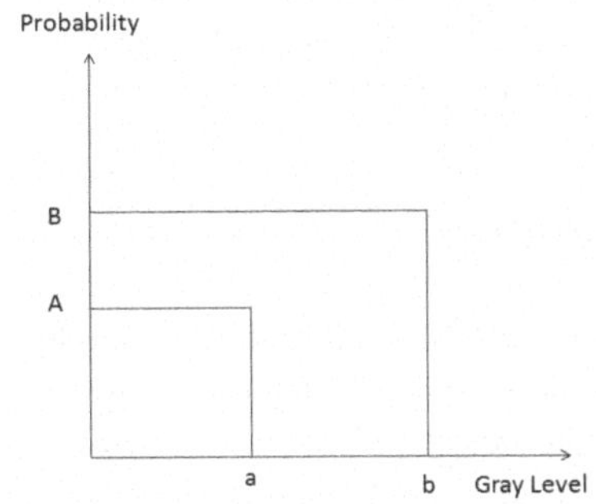

Fig. 1. Probability density functions of salt and pepper noise

B. Wiener:

When an image is blurred using a low pass filter, the original image can be obtained by using the process of inverse filtering, however this process invites additive noise to the image. The wiener filter optimizes inverse filtering and noise smoothing. It not only discards the noise but also performs inverse filtering. Wiener filtering in Fourier domain can be expressed as:

$$W(f_1,f_2) = \frac{H*(f_1,f_2)S_{xx}(f_1f_2)}{(|H(f_1,f_2)|)^2 S_{xx}(f_1f_2) + S_{nn}(f_1,f_2)}$$

While performing image restoration using wiener filter, a low pass filter as shown below is used to blur the image.

$$H = 1/16 \begin{bmatrix} 1 & 1 & 1 & 1 \\ 1 & 1 & 1 & 1 \\ 1 & 1 & 1 & 1 \end{bmatrix}$$

The implementation of this filter requires the calculation of power spectra of both original image as well as additive noise. Power spectrum can be calculated using:

$$S_{yy}^{per} = \frac{1}{N^2}[Y(k,l)Y(k,l)*]$$

Where, Y (k, l) is DFT of observation.

The technique of wiener filter is not highly used but produces best mathematical results.

C. Poisson Noise:

It is an ambiguous association with the measurement of light and independence of photon detection. This noise contributes in varying proportion in an image. This generally occurs when the number of photons is not able to provide exact statistical information. It is also known as photon noise and is signal dependent whose magnitude increases with respect to intensity of light.

5 Simulation and Results

MRI images of different body parts such as abdomen, ankle, elbow, hand, leg, liver and brain have been taken for analysis. Edge detection operators such as Roberts, Sobel, Prewitt, Canny and LoG have been applied to each image. Further Entropy, Standard Deviation and Execution time is evaluated from the resultant images. Table 1 depicts the results obtained from the same highlighting prominent changes in the values of parameters especially in case of Laplace of Gaussian operator.

From the results shown in Table 1, it is clearly indicated that there are noticeable changes in the values of Entropy, Standard Deviation and Time for LoG operator.

For abdomen, entropy of original image is 4.0522. Different filters have been applied for analysis such as Robert, Sobel, Prewitt, Canny, LoG. Entropy of resultant images after applying filters are different from original image such as 4.0522, 0.1539, 4.0522, 4.0522, 4.0522, and 4.0757 are the entropy of different operators respectively.

For ankle, entropy of original image is 7.0966. Entropy of resultant images after applying filters are different from original image such as, 0.1887, 7.0966, 7.0966, 7.0966, 7.0966 and 6.9408 are the entropy of different operators respectively.

For elbow, entropy of original image is 6.2733. Entropy of resultant images after applying filters are different from original image such as, 0.1741, 6.2733, 6.2733, 6.2733 and 6.0439 are the entropy of different operators respectively.

For hand, entropy of original image is 4.9325. Entropy of resultant images after applying filters are different from original image such as 0.1642, 4.9325, 4.9325, 4.9325 and 4.5715 are the entropy of different operators respectively.

For knee, entropy of original image is 4.1647. Entropy of resultant images after applying filters are different from original image such as, 0.1490, 4.1647, 4.1647, 4.1647 and 4.5715 are the entropy of different operators respectively.

For leg, entropy of original image is 5.2013. Entropy of resultant images after applying filters are different from original image such as, 0.1446, 5.2013, 5.2013, 5.2013 and 5.3754 are the entropy of different operators respectively.

Table 1. Analysis of different operators on MRI of different body parts

Image	Original Image	Roberts	Sobel	Prewitt	Canny	LoG
Abdomen	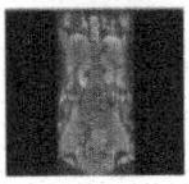	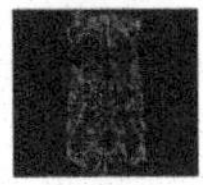				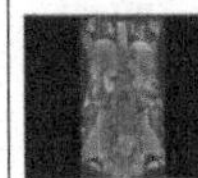
Entropy	4.0522	0.1539	4.0522	4.0522	4.0522	4.0757
Standard Deviation	44.0048	0.1475	44.0049	44.0049	44.0049	43.4800
Execution Time (In Sec)	0.116400	1.849964	0.950286	1.977930	2.329548	0.292388
Ankle	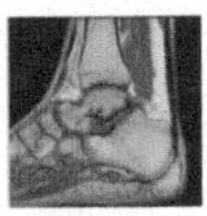	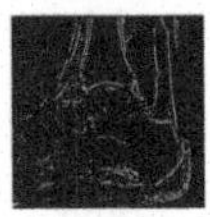	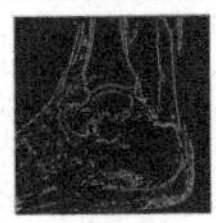	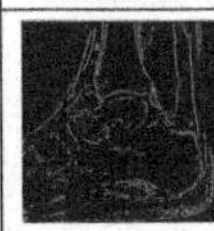		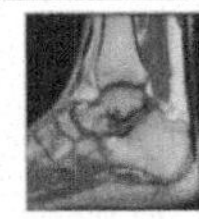
Entropy	7.0966	0.1887	7.0966	7.0966	7.0966	6.9408
Standard Deviation	64.1354	0.1674	64.1356	64.1356	64.1356	62.0044
Execution Time (In Sec)	0.025406	0.364964	0.166824	0.294917	0.320282	0.056844
Elbow	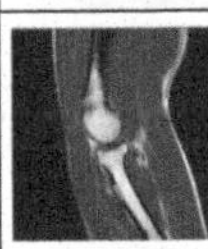	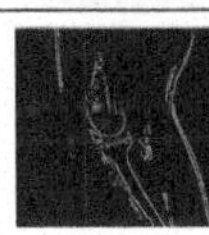		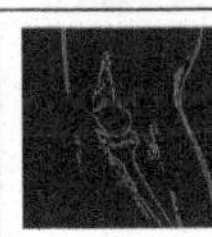	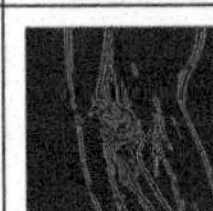	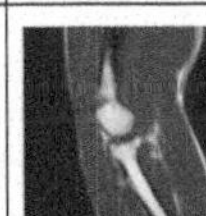
Entropy	6.2733	0.1741	6.2733	6.2733	6.2733	6.0439
Standard Deviation	52.2844	0.1593	52.2846	52.2846	52.2846	49.7832
Execution Time (In Sec)	0.027801	0.291431	0.195056	0.571107	0.373559	0.067847
Hand	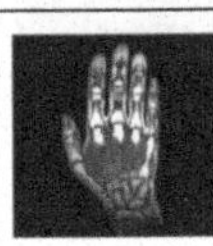	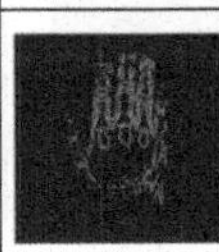		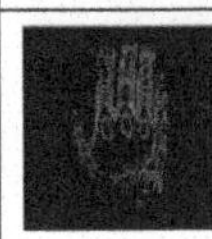	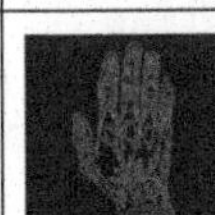	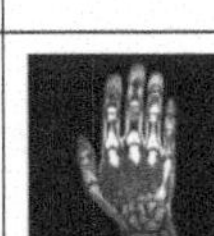
Entropy	4.9325	0.1642	4.9325	4.9325	4.9325	4.5715
Standard Deviation	56.3903	0.1536	56.3903	56.3903	56.3903	54.3642
Execution Time (In Sec)	0.053466	0.866227	0.426349	0.789168	0.898489	0.145112
Knee	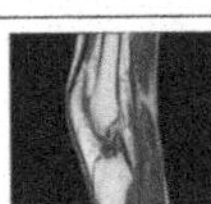	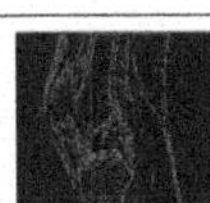		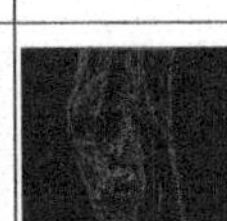	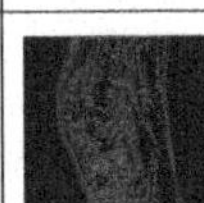	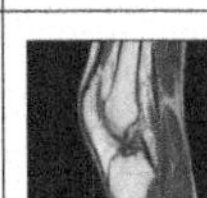

(*continued*)

Table 1. (*continued*)

Image	Original Image	Roberts	Sobel	Prewitt	Canny	LoG
Entropy	4.1647	0.1490	4.1647	4.1647	4.1647	4.1790
Standard Deviation	68.6057	0.1446	68.6057	68.6057	68.6057	68.1572
Execution Time (In Sec)	0.148529	2.613820	1.324256	2.792228	2.453288	0.388934
Leg	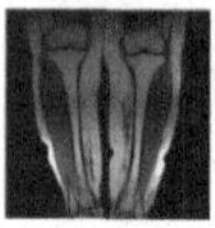				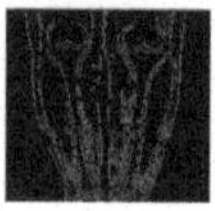	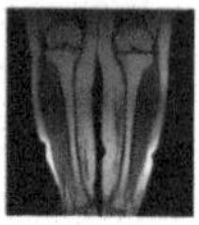
Entropy	5.2013	0.1446	5.2013	5.2013	5.2013	5.3754
Standard Deviation	48.0656	0.1419	48.0659	48.0659	48.0659	46.5672
Execution Time (In Sec)	0.055868	1.365116	0.520580	0.919118	1.057049	0.156223
Liver	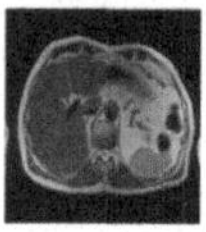	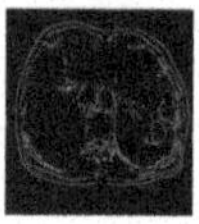	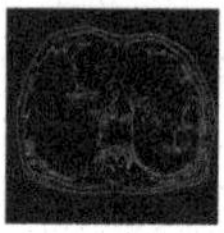		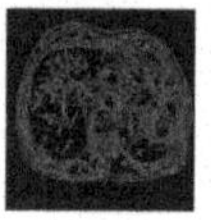	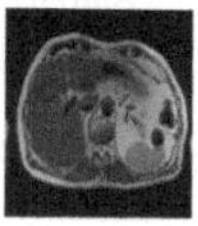
Entropy	5.8791	0.1870	5.8791	5.8791	5.8791	5.9122
Standard Deviation	52.0688	0.1665	52.0688	52.0688	52.0688	50.2168
Execution Time (In Sec)	0.055593	1.286821	0.472204	0.866820	1.024173	0.151872
Brain	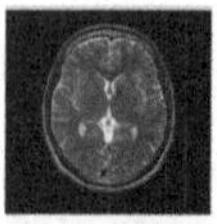	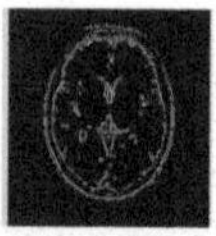	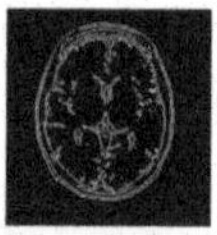		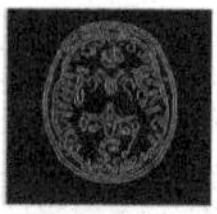	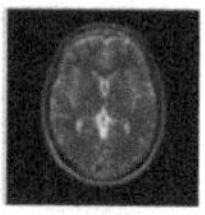
Entropy	5.0652	0.2291	5.0652	5.0652	5.0652	5.1647
Standard Deviation	39.4291	0.1891	39.4293	39.4293	39.4293	34.3848
Execution Time (In Sec)	0.019450	0.209662	0.137743	0.207306	0.186673	0.048438

For liver, entropy of original image is 5.8791. Entropy of resultant images after applying filters are different from original image such as, 0.1870, 5.8791, 5.8791, 5.8791 and 5.9122 are the entropy of different operators respectively.

For brain, entropy of original image is 5.0652. Entropy of resultant images after applying filters are different from original image such as, 0.2291, 5.0652, 5.0652, 5.0652 and 5.1647 are the entropy of different operators respectively.

Further noise removal techniques have been applied to perform image restoration on the above resulting images to perceive and conclude the development of best operator and better image quality. Table 2 explains the noise removal techniques with

Table 2. Noise removal techniques with different operators on resultant images of Table 1

Image	Original Image	Robert	Sobel	Prewitt	Canny	LoG
Abdomen	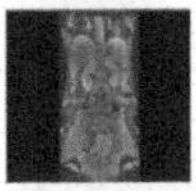			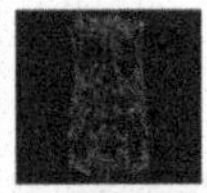	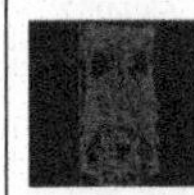	
Entropy	4.0522	0.1539	4.0522	4.0522	4.0522	4.0757
Standard Deviation	44.0048	0.1475	44.0049	44.0049	44.0049	43.4800
Execution Time (In Sec)	0.116400	1.849964	0.950286	1.977930	2.329548	0.292388
Ankle	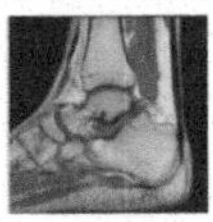	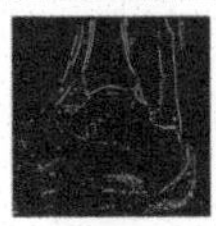	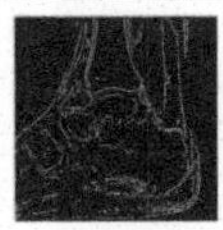	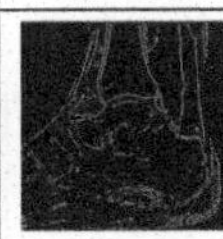	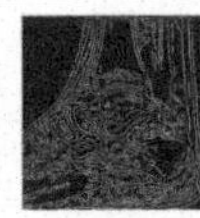	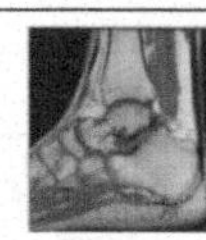
Entropy	7.0966	0.1887	7.0966	7.0966	7.0966	6.9408
Standard Deviation	64.1354	0.1674	64.1356	64.1356	64.1356	62.0044
Execution Time (In Sec)	0.025406	0.364964	0.166824	0.294917	0.320282	0.056844
Elbow	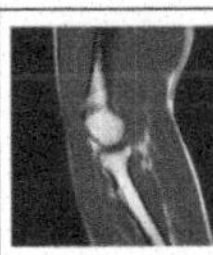	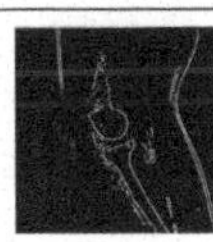	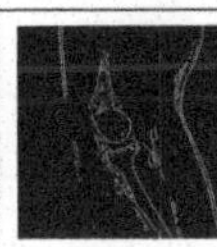	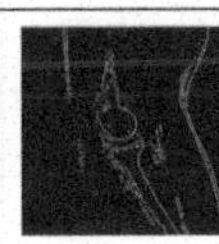	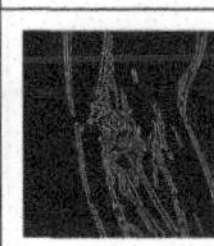	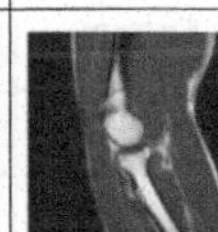
Entropy	6.2733	0.1741	6.2733	6.2733	6.2733	6.0439
Standard Deviation	52.2844	0.1593	52.2846	52.2846	52.2846	49.7832
Execution Time (In Sec)	0.027801	0.291431	0.195056	0.571107	0.373559	0.067847
Hand	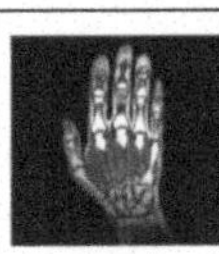		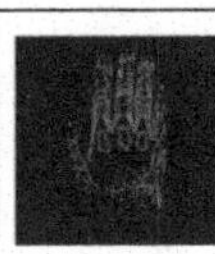		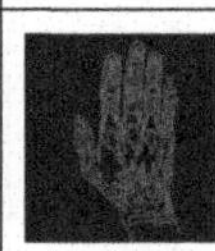	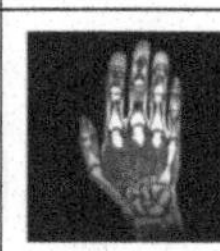
Entropy	4.9325	0.1642	4.9325	4.9325	4.9325	4.5715
Standard Deviation	56.3903	0.1536	56.3903	56.3903	56.3903	54.3642
Execution Time (In Sec)	0.053466	0.866227	0.426349	0.789168	0.898489	0.145112
Knee	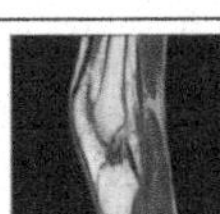	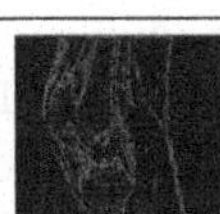		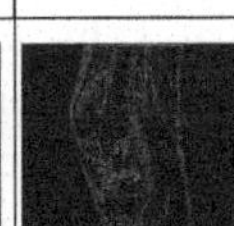	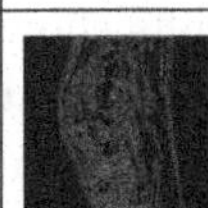	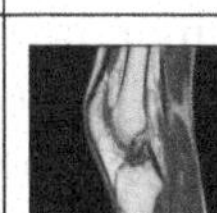

(*continued*)

Table 2. (*continued*)

Entropy	4.1647	0.1490	4.1647	4.1647	4.1647	4.1790
Standard Deviation	68.6057	0.1446	68.6057	68.6057	68.6057	68.1572
Execution Time (In Sec)	0.148529	2.613820	1.324256	2.792228	2.453288	0.388934
Leg	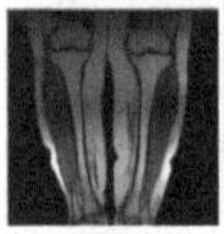			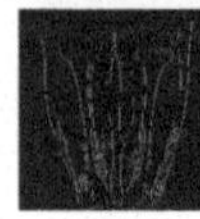	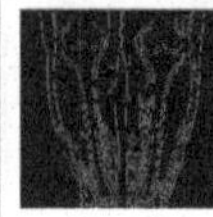	
Entropy	5.2013	0.1446	5.2013	5.2013	5.2013	5.3754
Standard Deviation	48.0656	0.1419	48.0659	48.0659	48.0659	46.5672
Execution Time (In Sec)	0.055868	1.365116	0.520580	0.919118	1.057049	0.156223
Liver	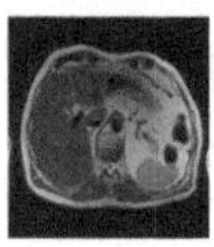	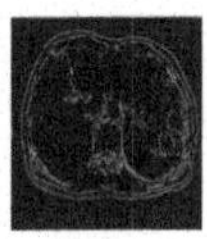	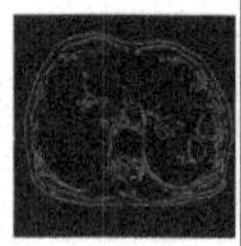	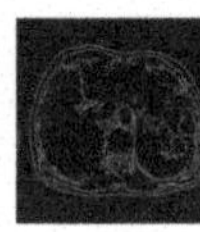	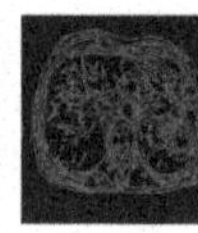	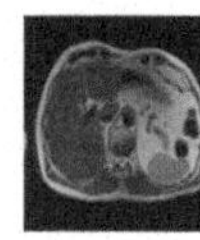
Entropy	5.8791	0.1870	5.8791	5.8791	5.8791	5.9122
Standard Deviation	52.0688	0.1665	52.0688	52.0688	52.0688	50.2168
Execution Time (In Sec)	0.055593	1.286821	0.472204	0.866820	1.024173	0.151872
Brain	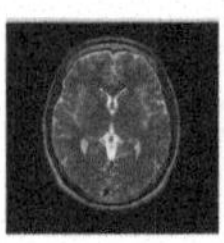	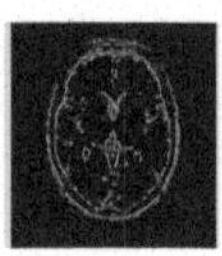	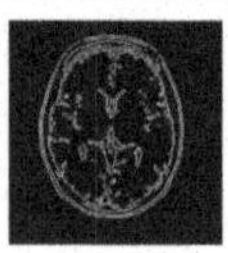	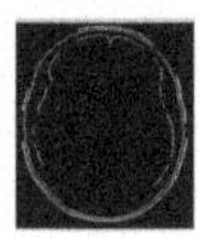		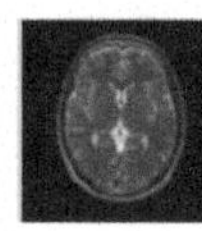
Entropy	5.0652	0.2291	5.0652	5.0652	5.0652	5.1647
Standard Deviation	39.4291	0.1891	39.4293	39.4293	39.4293	34.3848
Execution Time (In Sec)	0.019450	0.209662	0.137743	0.207306	0.186673	0.048438

different operators such as Robert, Sobel, Prewitt, Canny, LoG applied on resultant image from Table 1.

From the results shown in Table 2, it is clearly indicated that there are noticeable changes in the values of Entropy, Standard Deviation and Time for LoG operator.

For abdomen, Entropy of the original image is 4.0522 and 4.0757 for LoG operator. For ankle, the entropy of original image is 7.0966 and 6.9408 for LoG operator. For elbow, the entropy of original image is 6.2733 and 6.0439 for LoG operator. For hand, the entropy of original image is 4.9325 and 4.571 for LoG operator. For knee, the entropy of original image is 4.1647 and 4.1790 for LoG operator. For leg, the entropy of original image is 5.2013 and 5.3754 for LoG operator. For liver, the entropy of original image is 5.8791 and 5.9122 for LoG operator. For brain, the entropy of original image is 5.0652 and 5.1647 for LoG operator.

6 Conclusion

Although edge detection is an initial step in reviewing an image but it becomes crucial to understand different types of edge detection techniques. On the basis of the analysis of different MRI images, it is clear that LoG proves to provide better results as compared to Roberts, Sobel, Prewitt and Canny. The operators can be localized as per the requirement of a user to conform to an environment. Similarly the noise removal techniques also are essential to produce a relevant analysis and study of the images, in support of this, the results of the same give us a clear picture that wiener filter continues to give better results, although there are minute variations but they play very important role in detection algorithms and noise removal techniques.

References

1. Singh, H., Agrawal, D.: A meta analysis on content based image retrieval system. In: Proceedings of the IEEE International Conference on Emerging Technological Trends, pp. 1–6 (2016)
2. Khader, A., Ali, A., Alfaki, A.: Color and texture fusion-base method for content-based image retrieval. In: Proceedings of the IEEE International Conference on Computing for Sustainable Global Development, pp. 3205–3210 (2016)
3. Patel, J.M., Gamit, N.C.: A review on feature extraction techniques in content based image retrieval. In: IEEE International Conference on Wireless Communications, Signal Processing and Networking, pp. 2259–2263 (2016)
4. Manno, A.: Content based image retrieval using salient orientation histograms. In: IEEE International Conference on Image Processing, pp. 2480–2484 (2016)
5. Zaitouna, N.M., Aqelb, M.J.: Survey on image segmentation techniques. Procedia Comput. Sci. **65**, 797–806 (2015). International Conference on Communication, Management and Information Technology
6. Kabai, L., Abdellaoui, M.: Content based image retrieval using local and global feature extractor. In: IEEE International Conference on Advanced Technologies for Signal and Image Processing, pp. 151–154 (2016)
7. Mageswari, S.U., Sridevi, M., Mala, C.: An experimental study and analysis of different image segmentation techniques. Procedia Eng. **64**, 36–45 (2013). International Conference on Design and Manufacturing
8. Abdulrazzaq, M.M., Noah, S.A., Fadhil, M.A.: X-Ray medical image classification based on multi classifiers. In: IEEE International Conference on Advanced Computer Science Applications and Technologies, pp. 218–223 (2015)
9. Zheng, K.: Content based image retrieval for medical image. In: Proceedings of the IEEE International Conference on Computational Intelligence and Security, pp. 219–222 (2015)
10. Lijuan, S., Fengqi, H.: Research on color and texture feature based image retrieval. In: IEEE International Conference on Intelligent, Transportation, Big Data and Smart City, pp. 626–628 (2015)

11. Kumar, T.G.S., Nagarajan, V.: Local smoothness pattern for content based image retrieval. In: IEEE International Conference on Communications and Signal Processing, pp. 1190–1193 (2015)
12. Jyothi, B., Madhavee Latha, Y., Mohan, P.G.K.: An effective multiple visual features of content based medical image retrieval. In: Proceedings of the 9th IEEE International Conference on Intelligent Systems and Control, pp. 1–5 (2015)
13. Rocha, R., Saito, P.T.M., Bugatti, P.H.: Exploiting revolutionary approaches for content based image retrieval. In: International Symposium on Computer Based Medical System, pp. 370–372 (2015)
14. Gupta, N.M.R.: Comparative analysis of medical images fusion using different fusion methods for Daubechies complex wavelet transform. Int. J. Adv. Res. Comput. Sci. Softw. Eng. **3**(6) (2013)
15. Gupta, A., Gangadharppa, M.: Image retrieval based on color, shape and texture. In: 2nd IEEE International Conference on Computing for Sustainable Global Development, pp. 2097–2103 (2015)
16. Bhagyalakshmi, A., Vijayachamundeeswari, V.: A survey on image retrieval using various operators In: IEEE International Conference on Computer Communication and Systems, pp. 18–23 (2014)
17. Wang, Y., Li, Q., Lan, T., Chen, J.: A comparison of image based image retrieval system. In: 17th IEEE International Conference on Computational Science and Engineering, pp. 669–673 (2014)
18. Jenni, K., Mandala, S.: Pre-processing image database for efficient content based image retrieval. In: IEEE International Conference on Advances in Computing, Communications and Informatics, pp. 968–972 (2014)
19. Shriwas, M.K., Raut, V.R.: Content based image retrieval: a past, present and new feature descriptor. In: IEEE International Conference on Circuit, Power and Computing Technologies, pp. 1–7 (2015)
20. Mendoza, O., Melin, P., Licea, G.: A new method for edge detection in image processing using interval type-2 fuzzy logic. In: IEEE International Conference on Granular Computing, pp. 151–155 (2007)
21. Anandakrishnan, N., Santhosh Baboo, S.: An evaluation of popular edge detection techniques in digital image processing. In: IEEE International Conference on Intelligent Computing Applications, pp. 213–217 (2014)
22. Selvakar, P., Hariganesh, S.: The performance analysis of edge detection algorithms for image processing. In: IEEE International Conference on Computing Technologies and Intelligent Data Engineering, pp. 1–5 (2016)
23. Vijaya, A., Sunderesan, M.: Significant image enhancement techniques for removal of noise in LiDar images. In: 3rd International IEEE Conference on Computing for Sustainable Global Development, pp. 3904–3908 (2016)

Classifier Dependent Dimensionality Reduction for Resource Restricted Environments

Divyanshu Kalra, Chaitanya Dwivedi, and Swati Aggarwal(✉)

Netaji Subhas Institue of Technology, Dwarka 110078, New Delhi, India
kalradivyanshu@gmail.com, chaitanyadwivedi96@gmail.com,
swati1178@gmail.com

Abstract. High dimensionality problems have become prevalent in present day machine learning applications. The voluminous datasets acquired from sources like cameras, spectroscopes, and other sensors need to be analysed and modelled in a way that uses the available computational resources most efficiently. The paper proposes a genetic algorithm optimised neural network model that takes care of the issue mentioned above. A comparison is also drawn between the results produced by the proposed model and those produced by other contemporary dimensionality reduction algorithms.

Keywords: Genetic algorithm · Neural networks · t-SNE
Dimensionality reduction

1 Introduction

With the advancement of computer technology, machine learning is now being applied to a wide variety of situations. The applications vary from optical character recognition and object recognition, to biometrics and biomedical classification. Such applications produce a large magnitude of data to be analysed. Data hence produced is often high dimensional in nature. While there are some algorithms like artificial neural network etc., that can handle multidimensional data with relative ease without demanding high amounts of computational resources, other algorithms like fuzzy classification [1], RAFPC [2] and ANFIS [3] tend to be less viable an option in such situations, solely because they require more resources than most small scale labs can offer. Despite the shortcomings that these algorithms suffer from, it is observed in literature [4], that such algorithms perform extremely well on smaller datasets, often outperforming their counterparts.

The proposed model suggests a way to use these algorithms, in conjunction with a GA modified neural net, so that the problem of high dimensionality can

D. Kalra and C. Dwivedi—Co-first authors.

B. Panda et al. (Eds.): REDSET 2017, CCIS 799, pp. 177–186, 2018.
https://doi.org/10.1007/978-981-10-8527-7_16

be addressed to in an effective manner. Therefore, the proposed model permits research to be carried out even with lesser resources.

The aim of this research was not to develop a stand alone model for data classification. Research was rather aimed to develop a mechanism to reduce high dimensional data into a limited number of dimensions such that the reduced data gives an optimum performance in limited resource environment, for the algorithm it is being used on.

It should be brought to the readers notice that this can not be seen analogous to other dimensionality reduction algorithms like t-SNE [5] since these methods rely on statistical measures to extract meaningful information in a given dataset, thereby reducing the dimensions. The proposed model stands apart from other dimensionality reduction algorithms on two aspects:

(1) Statistical methods are independent of the classification algorithms being used. This means that they will produce the same result irrespective of the classification algorithm being used after dimensionality reduction.
(2) In the experiments conducted that are mentioned later in the paper, it was observed that statistical methods such as t-SNE tend to be computationally expensive as well. Therefore in a resource limited environment, it will again be problematic to implement such algorithms.

The discussion that follows makes use of ANFIS classifier in conjunction with the proposed model to depict its usability.

2 Terminology

There are a few frequently used terms that come in handy while evaluating the performance of any model. The following definitions may be important in understanding how the model works.

- True Positive Rate (TPR) or hit-rate: gives information about allowing the correct user in.
$$TPR = \frac{TP}{TP + FN}$$
- False Positive Rate (FPR): informs about the probability of accepting an impostor.
$$FPR = \frac{FP}{FP + TN}$$
- Equal Error Rate (EER): The threshold is varied till FPR and miss rate (1 - TPR) are equal. This common value of miss rate and FPR is known as EER.

3 Literature Review

Fuzzy logic found its application in classification problems long ago. Fuzzy classifiers at their initial stages were characterised by rule sets that were user defined. As the magnitude of data kept increasing, it became progressively difficult to compute the membership function defining parameters manually. This marked the development of hybrid fuzzy systems.

This widely recognized hybridization of fuzzy systems and EAs is known as Evolutionary or Genetic Fuzzy Systems (GFSs) [6]. However, they usually have scalability problems in terms of computational time and convergence in datasets with a high number of variables and with a large amount of data. Anfis, on similar lines, is a fuzzy classifier whose membership functions are optimised by a neural net. In an adaptive network, the nodes and the interconnecting directional links undergo change which is specified by a learning rule so as to minimize error. The architecture of anfis can be studied in detail here [3]. As a result of rise in the quantity of data being analysed, there have been considerable developments in data pre-processing [7] and data information granulation [8]. It must be duly understood that there is a difference between huge and high-dimensional datasets. A dataset consisting of multiple instances, of the order of thousands, may be referred to as a large dataset. On the other hand, a dataset with high number of variables [9] may be referred to as a high-dimensional dataset. There is a difference in the effect these two types of datasets have on the model as well. For example, large size of a dataset may affect the computation related to fitness functions in Genetic fuzzy systems, whereas high dimensionality data increases the search space. The former results in an increase in the computational time, whereas the latter increases the number of rules generated. As a result, the models can be very complex, and may include hundreds of rules [10]. This in turn increases the evaluation computational time and may also lead to overfitting. Thus, even if the objective of the system is to increase accuracy, it should be ensured that the resulting models do not end up being overly complex since this would result in high computational time to evaluate results. It often becomes difficult to find an optimal trade off between accuracy and complexity of the system. In such cases, Multi-Objective Evolutionary Algorithms (MOEAs) [11,12] prove to be useful tools.

In recent years, the need to deal with large or high-dimensional datasets has become more common. It thus remains an open topic for research in fuzzy systems.

4 Related Work

A direct correlation exists between the number of rules and the classification accuracy of the system. Though a vast rule base is preferable, it is limited by the computational capacity of a given machine. For a dataset with large number of parameters, it becomes even more difficult to define a vast rule base and implement such a system. Such an implementation of Fuzzy systems makes for an important branch called Multi-Objective Evolutionary Fuzzy Systems (MOEFSs) [13].

In a research conducted by Obaidat et al. [4] it was shown that fuzzy algorithms outperform several other algorithms on the given dataset.

Here, Users were made to type a phrase 4 character long and keystroke dynamics was performed on the data collected. A comparison of different algorithms were done on the same dataset. It was observed that Fuzzy ARTMAP outperformed its counterparts. A misclassification error of 0% was produced by Fuzzy ARTMAP against 0.05%, produced by back propagation neural network (BPNN).

In an attempt to tackle the problem faced while using fuzzy classification systems Azar et al. [14], developed an approach which gave significant results. The presented model was subdivided into 3 stages: In stage 1, the medical data are classified by LH neuro-fuzzy classifier without feature selection. In stage 2, LH feature selection method is applied to determine the relevant and irrelevant features of the data set. In stage 3, NF classifier with LH is applied for improving the classification accuracy. In stage 4, the performance evaluation of this method is determined using different performance measures described in the next section. A comparison of results produced using feature selection and those without depicts that despite causing a slight reduction in performance, the algorithm proposed speeds up the classification process manifold.

Other algorithms such as KNN suffer from high dimensionality problem as well. Work done by Tomasev et al. [15] tries to overcome hubness in classification using KNN on a high dimensionality dataset subject to label noise.

Parekh et al. [22] made use of neural network to reduce the dimensionality of MRI images of cerebral ischemia, and then classified the combined images. Mansoori et al. [16] made use of a feature selection algorithm to use in conjunction with fuzzy classifiers. Petscharnig et al. [23] used autoencoder neural network to reduce the images from yfcc100m dataset to 256, 128, 64, and 32 dimensional features. The proposed model makes use of distribution of patterns in fuzzy sets that are applied to each feature. The features are selected for each class individually. More relevant features are said to be those which better discriminate the different classes. They have used their approach on multiple datasets and have compared the computational time and accuracies with other algorithms. The datasets are publicly available at UCI machine learning repository [17]. Our research incorporates a few of the datasets used above.

5 Dataset

A short description of the datasets used in the study is mentioned below. Plots of t-SNE reduced data are also provided in Fig. 1 to give insights on the distribution of data. It also helps understand how t-SNE works.

(1) Keystroke Benchmark Dataset [18]
The keystroke dynamic dataset contains the typing timing data for 51 typists each typing a password 400 times, the password was .tie5Roanl. The input contains 31 features, corresponding to time for which one key was pressed, time between two keypresses and time between keydown and keyup. The clock used was accurate upto 200 microseconds.

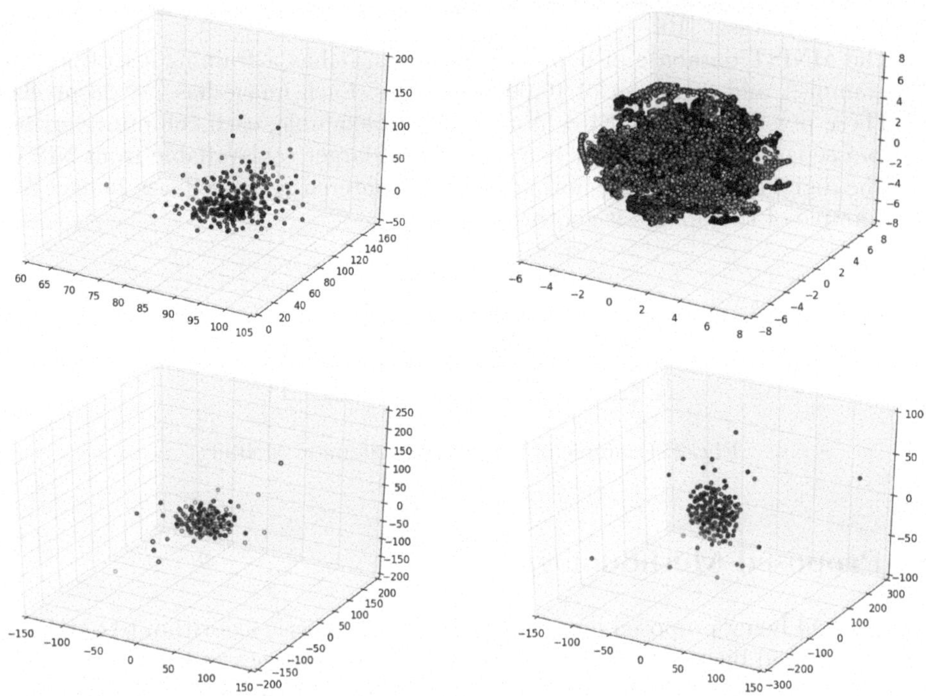

Fig. 1. Clockwise from top left: Bupa dataset, keystrokes benchmark dataset, iris dataset, and sonar dataset reduced to 3 dimensions using t-SNE

(2) Bupa Dataset [17]
Bupa is a liver disorder dataset The first 5 variables are all blood tests which are thought to be sensitive to liver disorders that might arise from excessive alcohol consumption. Each row constitutes the record of a single male individual.

(3) Sonar Dataset [17]
This is the data set used by Gorman and Sejnowski in their study of the classification of sonar signals using a neural network [20]. The task is to train a network to discriminate between sonar signals bounced off a metal cylinder and those bounced off a roughly cylindrical rock.

(4) Iris Dataset
The Iris flower data set is a multivariate data set introduced by Fisher [21]. The data set consists of 50 samples from each of three species of Iris (Iris setosa, Iris virginica and Iris versicolor). Four features were measured from each sample: the length and the width of the sepals and petals, in centimetres.

(5) MNIST Dataset [19]
The MNIST database of handwritten digits. It has a training set of 60,000 examples, and a test set of 10,000 examples. Each image has 28 * 28 pixels. These pixels form the 784 columns of every example, each column referring to a separate parameter. It is a subset of a larger set available from NIST. The digits have been size-normalized and centered in a fixed-size image. An example of the images is shown in Fig. 2.

Fig. 2. Example of handwritten digits in MNIST

6 Proposed Methodology

The method being proposed here makes the use of genetic algorithm to optimise the weights and biases of the neural network. The neural network takes the high dimensionality data as input and produces an output of lower dimensionality which ANFIS uses to classify.

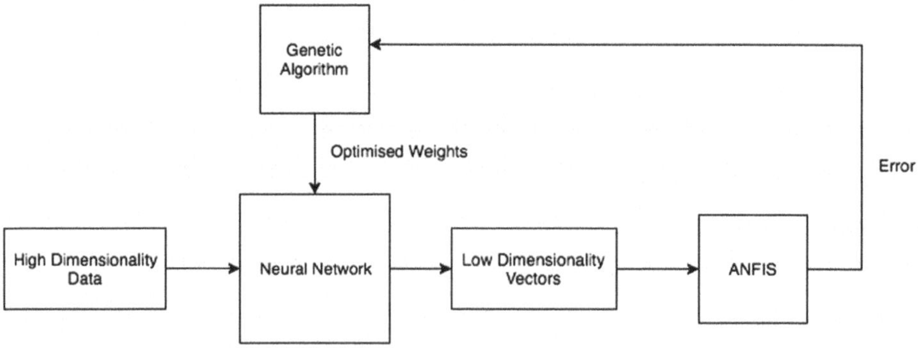

Fig. 3. Flowchart explaining the proposed methodology

The ANFIS classifier uses a neural network that tries to approximate the "if-then" rules of fuzzy logic. Following this ANFIS returns the error to the genetic algorithm, which alters the weights and biases of the neural network in an attempt to minimize the error. A brief description of the steps carried out in this process is given below. Figure 3 shows a conceptual map of the same.

- Step 1: A neural network is initiated with n input nodes, where n is the dimension of the input data, one hidden layer with m nodes, and an output layer with 3 nodes.
- Step 2: The ANFIS network is created, that takes neural nets output as input. And takes the output labels and returns the error to the Genetic Algorithm.
- Step 3: The genetic algorithm is initiated. This GA optimises the weights and biases of the neural network, and tries to lower the error of ANFIS.

  The Pseudo code mentioned below illustrates how the algorithm was implemented.

6.1 Pseudo Code

Algorithm 1. GA-NN-ANFIS

```
procedure GA_NN_ANFIS
    InputData,OutputLabels=LoadData()
    Net = neuralNetwork(m)
    geneticAlgo = GA()
    for i = 0/MAX_NO_OF_ITERATIONS do
        NetOutput = Net(InputData)
        error = anfis(NetOutput, OutputLabels)
        Net.weights = geneticAlgo.minimize(error)

```

7 Experiments and Results

Experiments were conducted to classify data using ANFIS present in the fuzzy logic toolbox of MATLAB2015a. The experiments were performed on a windows 10 machine, with 16 GB RAM and 4 core CPU. The experiments were done in two parts. In the first part the data was reduced to 3 dimensions using t-SNE and then the reduced data was classified using ANFIS. The accuracy and the RAM used were noted. In the second part the data was fed into GA-NN-ANFIS and the accuracy and RAM were again noted. Table 1 shows a comparison of the RAM used by t-SNE vs that used by GA-NN-ANFIS.

It can be noted that the difference in RAM used was not appreciable in datasets like iris and sonar due to their size, but on larger datasets like MNIST and keystroke benchmark, the difference in RAM used was noted to be much bigger. t-SNE could not be completed on MNIST dataset, because of the huge memory requirement. Table 2 shows a comparison between the accuracies given by ANFIS using t-SNE reduced data vs that given by GA-NN-ANFIS.

The accuracies of both the techniques are similar. Yet the difference in RAM used is much bigger. Hence, it can be concluded that the method proposed in this paper gives nearly the same accuracy but is much less resource intensive compared to Dimensionality Reduction algorithms such as t-SNE.

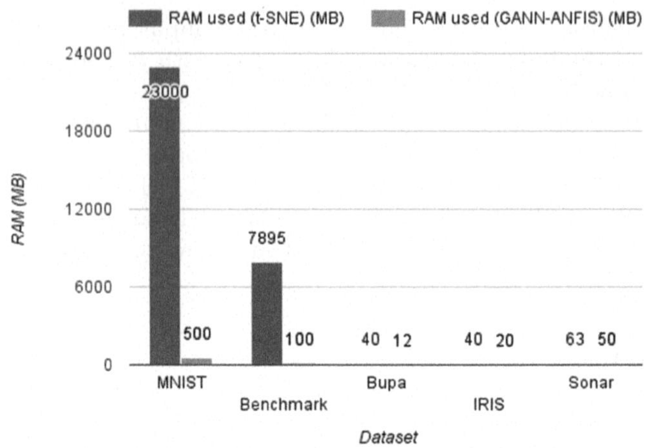

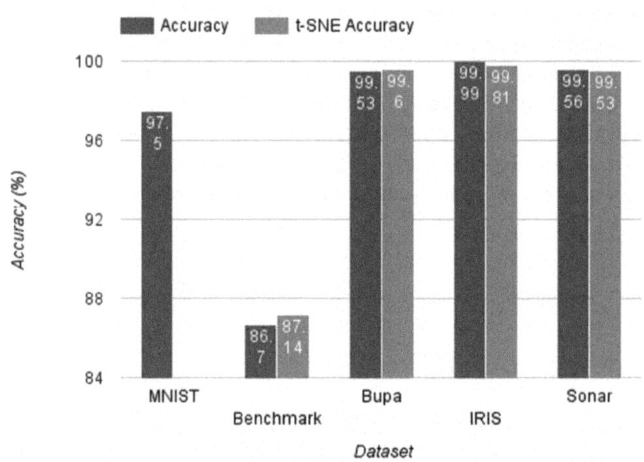

Fig. 4. RAM and accuracy comparison of GA-NN-ANFIS and t-SNE ANFIS on different datasets

Table 1. Comparison of RAM used, t-SNE vs GA-NN-ANFIS

Dataset	RAM used (t-SNE) (MB)	RAM used (GANN-ANFIS) (MB)
MNIST	23000+	500
Keystroke benchmark	7895	100
Bupa	40	12
Iris	40	20
Sonar	63	50

Table 2. Accuracies given by ANFIS using t-SNE and GA-NN

Dataset	GA-NN-ANFIS (%)	t-SNE (%)
MNIST	97.5	N/A
Keystroke benchmark	86.7	87.14
Bupa	99.53	99.6
Iris	99.99	99.81
Sonar	99.56	99.5

8 Conclusion and Future Work

In this paper, we proposed a novel and scalable approach to perform classification using resource intensive algorithms. By means of the proposed method we can use highly accurate algorithms such as ANFIS on high dimensional data, which was otherwise difficult under limited resource conditions. The results from 5 different datasets of varying dimensionality confirm the effectiveness of proposed method. Figure 4 compares performance of the two algorithms on these datasets. The future work may include using other evolutionary algorithms as an optimiser instead of Genetic Algorithm. Research may also be aimed at optimising the number of output nodes of the neural network through GA. Other classifying algorithms may also be plugged into the proposed model, and their performance may then be studied.

References

1. Ishibuchi, H., Nakashima, T., Murata, T.: Performance evaluation of fuzzy classifier systems for multidimensional pattern classification problems. IEEE Trans. Syst. Man Cybern. B Cybern. **29**(5), 601–618 (1999)
2. sorend, sorend/fylearn, GitHub. https://github.com/sorend/fylearn. Accessed 30 Jan 2017
3. Jang, J.-S.R.: ANFIS: adaptive-network-based fuzzy inference system. IEEE Trans. Syst. Man Cybern. **23**(3), 665–685 (1993)
4. Obaidat, M.S., Sadoun, B.: Verification of computer users using keystroke dynamics. IEEE Trans. Syst. Man Cybern. B Cybern. **27**(2), 261–269 (1997)
5. Jamieson, A.R., Giger, M.L., Drukker, K., Li, H., Yuan, Y., Bhooshan, N.: Exploring nonlinear feature space dimension reduction and data representation in breast Cadx with Laplacian eigenmaps and t-SNE. Med. Phys. **37**(1), 339–351 (2010)
6. Herrera, F.: Genetic fuzzy systems: taxonomy, current research trends and prospects. Evol. Intell. **1**(1), 27–46 (2008)
7. Derrac, J., Cornelis, C., Garca, S., Herrera, F.: Enhancing evolutionary instance selection algorithms by means of fuzzy rough set based feature selection. Inf. Sci. **186**(1), 73–92 (2012)
8. Pedrycz, W.: Granular Computing: Analysis and Design of Intelligent Systems. CRC Press, Boca Raton (2016)
9. Jin, Y.: Fuzzy modeling of high-dimensional systems: complexity reduction and interpretability improvement. IEEE Trans. Fuzzy Syst. **8**(2), 212–221 (2000)

10. Wang, D., Zeng, X.-J., Keane, J.A.: Simplified structure evolving method for Mamdani fuzzy system identification and its application to high-dimensional problems. Inf. Sci. **220**, 110–123 (2013)
11. Coello, C.C., Lamont, G.B., van Veldhuizen, D.A.: Evolutionary Algorithms for Solving Multi-Objective Problems. Springer Science & Business Media, New York (2007). https://doi.org/10.1007/978-0-387-36797-2
12. Deb, K.: Multi-objective Optimization Using Evolutionary Algorithms. Wiley, Hoboken (2001)
13. Fazzolari, M., Alcala, R., Nojima, Y., Ishibuchi, H., Herrera, F.: Review of the application of multiobjective evolutionary fuzzy systems: current status and further directions. IEEE Trans. Fuzzy Syst. **21**(1), 45–65 (2013)
14. Azar, A.T., Hassanien, A.E.: Dimensionality reduction of medical big data using neural-fuzzy classifier. Soft. Comput. **19**(4), 1115–1127 (2014)
15. Tomaev, N., Buza, K.: Hubness-aware kNN classification of high-dimensional data in presence of label noise. Neurocomputing **160**, 157–172 (2015)
16. Mansoori, E.G., Shafiee, K.S.: On fuzzy feature selection in designing fuzzy classifiers for high-dimensional data. Evol. Syst. **7**(4), 255–265 (2015)
17. Olson, D.L., Wu, D.: Data sets. Predictive Data Mining Models. CRM, pp. 9–15. Springer, Singapore (2017). https://doi.org/10.1007/978-981-10-2543-3_2
18. Killourhy, K.S., Maxion, R.A.: Comparing anomaly-detection algorithms for keystroke dynamics. In: 2009 IEEE/IFIP International Conference on Dependable Systems & Networks (2009)
19. Lecun, Y., Bottou, L., Bengio, Y., Haffner, P.: Gradient-based learning applied to document recognition. Proc. IEEE **86**(11), 2278–2324 (1998)
20. Gorman, R.P., Sejnowski, T.J.: Analysis of hidden units in a layered network trained to classify sonar targets. Neural Netw. **1**(1), 75–89 (1988)
21. Fisher, R.A.: The use of multiple measurements in taxonomic problems. Ann. Eugen. **7**(2), 179–188 (1936)
22. Parekh, V.S., Jacobs, J.R., Jacobs, M.A.: Unsupervised Non Linear Dimensionality Reduction Machine Learning methods applied to Multiparametric MRI in cerebral ischemia: Preliminary Results, arXiv [cs.CV], 13 June 2016
23. Petscharnig, S., Lux, M., Chatzichristofis, S.: Dimensionality reduction for image features using deep learning and autoencoders. In: Proceedings of the 15th International Workshop on Content-Based Multimedia Indexing, Florence, Italy, pp. 23:1–23:6 (2017)

Improving Road Safety in India Using Data Mining Techniques

Gaurav(✉) and Zunaid Alam(✉)

SGT University, Gurugram, India
gauravsingla31@gmail.com, zunaid.aalam6194@gmail.com

Abstract. Road accidents are very common in India. World Health Organization (WHO) has revealed that India the worst road traffic accident rate worldwide. According to the report, poor driving pattern, drunk driving, badly maintained roads and vehicles are the main triggering factors to road casualties. Statistics shows that one serious road accident in the country occurs every minute. The national capital, Delhi is among the deadliest. To achieve aim of reducing road accidents, novel and robust prevention strategies for improved road severity have to be developed. In this work, we propose use of data mining frame work to analyze traffic on National Highways of India. Using real data set of National Highway of India, we will mine important patterns for accidental data on National Highways of India and, identify key causes to road casualties. The discovered knowledge can be used by Ministry of road transport & highways of India to take effective decisions to reduce road severity.

Keywords: Data mining · Association rules · Road safety

1 Introduction

Road accident is one of the undesirable events that are uncertain and unpredictable. Road accident is one of the major causes of unnatural deaths, disability and property damage [2]. Many people die daily due to road accidents. World Health Organization has revealed India the worst road traffic accident worldwide. Statistics shows that one serious road accident in the country occurs every minute and 16 die on Indian roads every hour. According to the WHO report, poor driving pattern, drunk driving, low use of helmets, badly maintained roads and vehicles are the main contributing factors to road casualties. Road safety improvements can be achieved within the three components of the road safety system through changes in infrastructure design, vehicle safety and road user behavior [11]. However the main cause of road accidents also depends on the area in which it happens but still there may be some other reasons. So we can't be assure of road safety by considering only one or two reasons for road accidents in an area. It's very important to be accurate in case of finding reasons for road accidents in an area. India has 1% of vehicles in the world; but it accounts for about 6% of the total cases of unintentional injuries. According to the survey, male victims involved in the accidents are 78% and rest are females victims [3].

Data mining algorithms are extremely useful in prediction. Once we have the accurate accidental data, we can use data mining approach to find the main causes of

B. Panda et al. (Eds.): REDSET 2017, CCIS 799, pp. 187–194, 2018.
https://doi.org/10.1007/978-981-10-8527-7_17

road accidents in a specific area. In this paper, we have taken the accidental data from National Highway Authority of India (NHAI). As a sample, we applied the algorithm on accidental data from Panipat (Haryana) to Jalandhar (Punjab). In dataset, we had valuable information such as Time, Accident Location, Nature of Accident, Road feature, Road condition, Vehicle responsible for accident, Accident Type etc. We applied data mining methods such as association rule to determine the major factors for the accident.

2 Methodology and Tools

The following figure shows the general path/way which we have followed for mining association rules (Fig. 1):

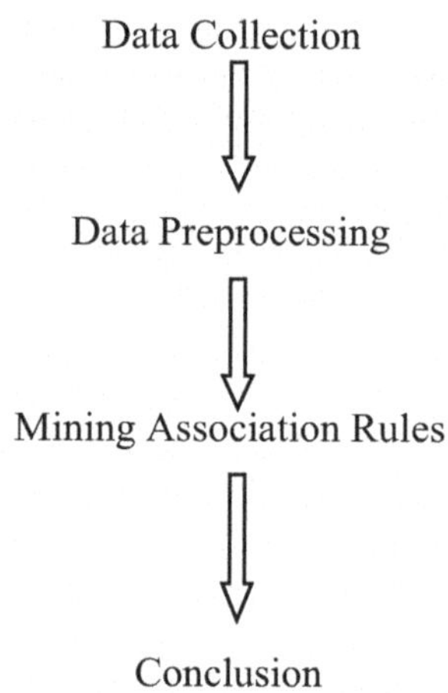

Fig. 1. Steps for mining association rules

As preprocessing of the data set takes 70% of the time to make data set useful and according to as per requirement of algorithms. The goal of data preprocessing is to choose cardinal features then remove irrelevant information and finally transform raw data into sessions. To achieve its goal Data preprocessing is divided into Data Cleaning, user identification, and Session Identification and Path Completion steps [6]. Noisy and erroneous data makes algorithms useless which we apply to mine data. So before processing, data needs to be investigated and preprocessed. Then only it makes it useful [7]. The most common issue that comes during the process of knowledge discovery through data mining includes the missing values. A dataset with 1–5% missing values may not impact as much whereby from 5–15% range requires sensitive algorithms to apply [9] (Fig. 2).

We applied preprocessing on almost every feature of the dataset to make it as per requirement, e.g. we extracted only year from the feature Date. Then we converted the time feature into six zones like early morning, morning, afternoon, evening, night, late night on the basis of timing of accidents.

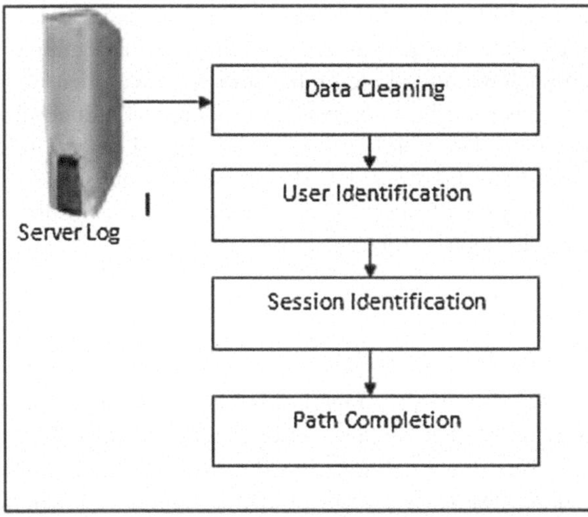

Fig. 2. Steps involved in data preprocessing [6]

Then there are some features such as Nature of accident, Causes of accident, Road features, Road conditions, weather conditions etc. which were in numeric form. We converted them according to their actual values. It's important because while mining association rules, without conversion, it's not possible to determine the actual value of the antecedent and consequent. Then we worked on the feature Accident type. Originally the accident type feature was partitioned into four features such as fatal, grievous, minor, injured. We converted these four features into one to indicate the kind of accident. Here we applied data preprocessing for data mining purpose. But it can also used be used for constructing on data warehouses, www etc. [8].

Once the data was prepared, we mined association rules. Association rule mining method is the most efficient data mining approach to find out patterns among the high volume of data. It is responsible to find correlation relationships among various data attributes in a huge set of items in a database [10]. The data set of association rules is denoted by T, T is the transaction database, T = {t1, t2… tk… tn}, tk = {i1, i2,… im… ip}, tk (k = 1,2,… n) is called a transaction, im(m = 1, 2,… p) is called a item. In the transaction database, item is the name of goods or services, transaction also includes other information such as date, customer number and so on. Simply put, transaction is a collection of items [1]. While mining association rules, we prioritize the most important parameters of association rules and these are support and confidence. However there are some other parameters as well but we have focused on support and confidence. *Support* is an indication of how frequently the items appear in the database. *Confidence* indicates the number of times the if/then statements have been found to be true.

An association rule has two parts, an antecedent (if) and a consequent (then). An antecedent is an item found in the data. A consequent is an item that is found in combination with the antecedent. The major factor of accidents are shown in the result section for the data which we have uses for mining association rules. As far as tools are concerned we used Rstudio for preprocessing of the data. Initially we imported the data from excel to Rstudio and then we preprocessed the data using R Language as per the requirement. Once the data was prepared, then we mined association rules.

The rules which we have mined are in the form X- > Y, where X is antecedent and Y is consequent. We have used all combination of support and confidence for mining association rules such as HS (High support) and LC (Low confidence), LS (Low support) and HC (High confidence), HS (High support) and HC (High confidence). Using different combination of support and confidence, the result which have been mined are accurate and effective for future use.

3 Results

As we mentioned earlier, we have applied different combination of support and confidence to mine association rules. So here in this section, we will see the rules which are mined from the data. First result/table shows the rules for high support and low confidence. Second result/table shows the rules for low support and high confidence. Third result shows the result/table for high support and high confidence. We will see the major factors involved in road accidents. As far as percentage for support and confidence is concerned, we have taken low support as 5–10% and high support as nearby 40%. In case of confidence, we have taken low confidence as 5–10% but high confidence as 80–90% that we can find some closely related data. As there is different role of support and confidence, we have taken all kinds of values so that we can check each angle of data and best association rules can be mined.

3.1 Following is the Table for High Support and Low Confidence

See Fig. 3.

Data	
# Transactions in Input Data	2869
# Columns in Input Data	8
# Items in Input Data	138
# Association Rules	10
Minimum Support	1100
Minimum Confidence	10.00%

Row ID	Confidence %	Antecedent (A)	Consequent (C)	Support for A	Support for C	Support for A & C	Lift Ratio
1	81.2284334	Injured	Petrol Vehicle	1449	1502	1177	1.551560422
2	78.36218375	PetrolVehicle	Injured	1502	1449	1177	1.551560422
3	76.16511318	Petrol Vehicle	Punjab	1502	2032	1144	1.07538243
4	56.2992126	Punjab	Petrol Vehicle	2032	1502	1144	1.07538243
5	93.44375431	Injured	Four lanes	1449	2659	1354	1.008236672
6	50.92139902	Four lanes	Injured	2659	1449	1354	1.008236672
7	93.06102362	Punjab	Four lanes	2032	2659	1891	1.004107096
8	71.11696126	Four lanes	Punjab	2659	2032	1891	1.004107096
9	51.93681835	Four lanes	Petrol Vehicle	2659	1502	1381	0.992055472
10	91.94407457	Petrol Vehicle	Four lanes	1502	2659	1381	0.992055472

Fig. 3. Result for High support and Low confidence

Here we can see that mostly accidents are injured based accidents and happened by petrol vehicle. As the accidental data is from Panipat to Jalandhar wherein two states are involved (Haryana and Punjab), so we can clearly see that the high percentage of accidents are happened in Punjab state as compared to Haryana. On the highway, there are four lanes and at some place there are two lanes but statistics shows that the accident rate is high on four lanes. Statistics shows that there are more number of average accidents in Haryana as compared to other states [5]. So here it's important look over this matter.

Following is the Table for Low Support and High Confidence:

See Fig. 4.

Data	
# Transactions in Input Data	2869
# Columns in Input Data	8
# Items in Input Data	138
# Association Rules	25
Minimum Support	500
Minimum Confidence	85.00%

Row ID	Confidence %	Antecedent (A)	Consequent (C)	Support for A	Support for C	Support for A & C	Lift Ratio
1	98.87429644	Left turn collision	Four lanes	533	2659	527	1.066830976
2	98.42406877	Fault of other driver & Punjab	Four lanes	698	2659	687	1.061973123
3	97.98994975	Fault of other driver	Four lanes	995	2659	975	1.057289078
4	97.34345351	Fault of other driver	Four lanes	527	2659	513	1.050313532
5	93.82488479	Injured & Punjab	Four lanes	1085	2659	1018	1.012348983
6	93.48127601	Car	Four lanes	721	2659	674	1.008641523
7	93.44375431	Injured	Four lanes	1449	2659	1354	1.008236672
8	93.37016575	Injured & Petrol Vehicle & Punjab	Four lanes	905	2659	845	1.007442668
9	93.06102362	Punjab	Four lanes	2032	2659	1891	1.004107096
10	92.97597043	Overturning	Four lanes	541	2659	503	1.003189391
11	92.83088235	LN1	Four lanes	544	2659	505	1.001623924
12	92.65734266	Petrol Vehicle & Punjab	Four lanes	1144	2659	1060	0.999751471
13	92.60832625	Injured & Petrol Vehicle	Four lanes	1177	2659	1090	0.999222595
14	92.17809868	M	Four lanes	831	2659	766	0.994580538
15	91.94407457	Petrol Vehicle	Four lanes	1502	2659	1381	0.992055472
16	91.89655172	M & Punjab	Four lanes	580	2659	533	0.991542711
17	91.7562724	Haryana	Four lanes	837	2659	768	0.990029129
18	91.58415842	Ambulance & Punjab	Four lanes	606	2659	555	0.988172059
19	91.40708915	Ambulance	Four lanes	931	2659	851	0.986261522
20	90.99249374	Rear end Collision	Four lanes	1199	2659	1091	0.981788133
21	90.98765432	Punjab & Rear end Collision	Four lanes	810	2659	737	0.981735917
22	90.28960818	Minor & Punjab	Four lanes	587	2659	530	0.974204159
23	89.33649289	Minor	Four lanes	844	2659	754	0.963920264
24	85.10452962	Overspeeding	Four lanes	1148	2659	977	0.918258351
25	85.07078507	Overspeeding & Punjab	Four lanes	777	2659	661	0.917894255

Fig. 4. Result for low support and High confidence

Here we have found some more interesting features involved in accidents for given specific data. This result shows that almost all accidents happened on four lanes but antecedents are different. As far as timing is concerned, Late night (LN) and morning (M) sessions are more dangerous time for accidents. Over speed is a dangerous factor for accidents and it can be seen here clearly. Other major reasons can be seen that while overturning or because of fault of other drivers there have been many accidents. Rear end collision is also an important feature that can be seen from the statistics. Unlike in previous statistics, here both states can be seen in statistics. Here one interesting feature can be seen that mostly vehicles are petrol vehicles as in previous case. Here we have taken low support but high confidence, it means whenever a rule occur, it occurs very strongly.

Following is the Table for High Support and High Confidence:
See Fig. 5.

Data	
# Transactions in Input Data	2869
# Columns in Input Data	8
# Items in Input Data	138
# Association Rules	9
Minimum Support	1000
Minimum Confidence	80.00%

Row ID	Confidence %	Antecedent (A)	Consequent (C)	Support for A	Support for C	Support for A & C	Lift Ratio
1	81.2284334	Injured	Petrol Vehicle	1449	1502	1177	1.551560422
2	80.50221566	Four lanes & Injured	Petrol Vehicle	1354	1502	1090	1.537688793
3	93.82488479	Injured & Punjab	Four lanes	1085	2659	1018	1.012348983
4	93.44375431	Injured	Four lanes	1449	2659	1354	1.008236672
5	93.06102362	Punjab	Four lanes	2032	2659	1891	1.004107096
6	92.65734266	Petrol Vehicle & Punjab	Four lanes	1144	2659	1060	0.999751471
7	92.60832625	Injured & Petrol Vehicle	Four lanes	1177	2659	1090	0.999222595
8	91.94407457	Petrol Vehicle	Four lanes	1502	2659	1381	0.992055472
9	90.99249374	Rear end Collision	Four lanes	1199	2659	1091	0.981788133

Fig. 5. Result for High support and Low confidence

This statistics is for high support and high confidence. This result is almost as like derived from two previous results. Road feature is four lanes, vehicle involved are petrol vehicles. Accidents happened are injured based. There are some rear end collisions. As far as state is concerned, mostly accidents happened in Punjab instead of Haryana. As far as exact black spot is to be identified we have many spatial analysis methods. Different spatial analysis methods have been used in recent years for pedestrian safety studies. But KDE (Kernel Density Estimation) is the most used method for finding the Black spot and is effectively visualize and helps analysing the accident events spread across the Geography [4].

4 Conclusion

On the basis of association rules which are mined, we can conclude that on the four lanes, the major accidents are during late night and morning sessions. As far as vehicles are concerned, petrol vehicles are more involved in accidents as compared to other vehicles. Many of the accidents are due to fault of other drivers but it's not possible to control driving of others. Rear end collisions have occurred in many cases. So as per result, while using petrol vehicles, we should avoid over speed as this is also one of the major factors especially in late night or morning sessions. However most of the accidents are minor and injured based and very less serious accidents but still these may be reduced if we have prior intimation or information about such happenings. Now some algorithms such as Support vector machine can be used to build a model for traffic accident detection [12]. By using the model based on historical data, prediction can be performed on future data. Now this predictive information can be used by passengers as well as government to check if such are the cases then accident may occur. Govt. can apply some rules or protocols for such cases, in the conclusion of that there will definitely be less accidents.

References

1. Zhong, R., Wang, H.: Research of commonly used association rules mining algorithm in data mining. In: IEEE International Conference on Internet Computing and Information Services (2011). ISBN 978-0-7695-4539-4/11
2. Kumar, S., Toshniwal, D.: Analysing road accident data using association rule mining. In: IEEE International Conference on Computing, Communication and Security, December 2015. ISBN 978-1-4673-9354-6/15
3. Shruthi, P., Vanketesh, V.T., Viswakanth, B., Ramesh, C., Sujatha, P.L., Dominic, I.R.: Analysis of fatal road traffic accidents in a metropolitan city of South India. J. Indian Acad. Forensic Med. **35**(4) 2013
4. Raut, U.M., Nalawade, D.B., Kale, K.V.: Mapping and analysis of accident black spot in Aurangabad city using geographic information system. Int. J. Adv. Res. Comput. Sci. Softw. Eng. **6**(1) (2016)
5. Shah, K.D., Sachdeva, S.N.: A comparative study of accident safety on Haryana road. IOSR J. Mech. Civil Eng., 13–16. e-ISSN 2278-1684, p-ISSN 2320-334X
6. Prince Mary, S., Baburaj, E.: An efficient approach to perform pre-processing. Indian J. Comput. Sci. Eng. **4**(5) (2013). ISSN 0976-5166
7. Aubrecht, P., Koub, Z.: A universal data preprocessing system. In: Popelínský, L. (ed.) DATAKON 2003, Brno, pp. 1–3, 18–21 October 2003
8. Pandey, K.K., Pradhan, N.: An analytical and comparative study of various data preprocessing method in data mining. Int. J. Emerg. Technol. Adv. Eng. **4**(10) (2014). ISSN 2250-2459
9. Aleem, A.S., Asif, K.H., Ali, A., Awan, S.M.: Pre processing methods of data mining. In: IEEE/ACM 7th International Conference on Utility and Cloud Computing (2014). ISBN 978-1-4799-7881-6/14
10. Somkunwar, R.: A study on various data mining approaches of association rules. Int. J. Adv. Res. Comput. Sci. Softw. Eng. **2**(9) (2012)

11. Beshah, T., Ejigu, D., Abraham, A., Snasel, V., kromer, P.: Mining pattern from road accident data: role of road user's behavior and implications for improving road safety. Int. J. Tomography Simul. **22**(1) (2013). ISSN 2319-3336
12. Liang, G.J.: Automatic traffic accident detection based on Internet of things and Support vector machine. Int. J. Smart Home **9**(4), 97–106 (2015)

An Analytical Study to Find the Major Factors Behind the Great Smog of Delhi, 2016: Using Fundamental Data Sciences

Deepak Kumar Sharma, Arushi Bhatt(✉), and Aditi Kumar

Division of Information Technology, Netaji Subhas Institute of Technology, University of Delhi, Delhi, India
dk.sharma1982@yahoo.com,
{arushib.it,aditikl.it}@nsit.net.in

Abstract. Concerns over the alarming situation of Smog Pollution have come under the broad and current interests of masses since past few decades. Exposure to augmented levels of pollutants forming Photochemical Smog poses threat to human life, plants, animals and property as well. The effects of Smog on health can be felt instantaneously, ranging from minor pains to deadly pulmonary diseases such as lung cancer. The Great Smog of Delhi, 2016 was a manifestation of such situations. The air quality dipped to hazardous levels posing a health emergency situation. With an aim to know the intricacies of the problem, an Analytical study of the factors that contributed to Smog Pollution in Delhi was carried out using fundamental Data Sciences in R programming language. The study covers the major Pollutant analysis and Meteorological factors from the data of two pollution monitoring stations viz. R.K. Puram and Mandir Marg. Statistical Analysis and simple Linear Regression models were used for the correlation study between pollutants' concentration levels and meteorological factors. Also, the comparative analysis was executed over the conditions of monitoring stations under study. It was found that the Particulate Matter (PM10) turned up as the major pollutant. Concentrations of pollutants are also affected by the meteorological factors. Less greenery and exposure to more vehicular pollution resulted in R.K. Puram being more polluted than Mandir Marg.

Keywords: Photochemical smog · Data science · R programming language · Pollutants · Meteorological factors · Statistical analysis · Linear regression models · Correlation analysis · Comparative study · Particulate matter

1 Introduction

1.1 Background

Various kinds of respiratory illnesses are the direct consequences of Photochemical Smog, a type of air pollutant. The word 'Smog' is derived from two words i.e. Smoke + Fog. A number of complex photochemical reactions comprising Volatile Organic Compounds (VOCs), oxides of nitrogen and sunlight results in the formation of ozone (a harmful constituent of smog) at ground level and other airborne particles.

B. Panda et al. (Eds.): REDSET 2017, CCIS 799, pp. 195–207, 2018.
https://doi.org/10.1007/978-981-10-8527-7_18

Such pollutants are released from sources like vehicular emissions, power plants, factories and many commercial products, such as paint, hairspray, charcoal starter fluid, chemical solvents. Extreme smog occurrences are often associated with heavy motor vehicle traffic, high temperatures, solar radiations, and low wind speed. Weather and topology affect the location and severity of smog.

If pollutants are emitted directly from a source, they come under the category of Primary Pollutants. Their further reactions in the atmosphere form Secondary Pollutants like ozone, nitrogen dioxide, acid rain, etc. Since the onset of industrialization, Photochemical smog has been a major point of botheration.

Exposure to harmful levels of Smog in the troposphere is posing a great threat to the lives of children, senior citizens and people with lung and heart conditions such as asthma, emphysema and bronchitis. It has a direct and immediate effect on health such as irritation in eyes and nose, dryness in the protective membranes of nose and throat and interference with the immune system. All this has increased susceptibility to illness. These issues have drawn a serious attention all over the world.

Marked as 11th worst polluted city on the globe, Delhi's air quality hit dangerous levels after celebration of Diwali, the Hindu festival of lights on 30th October, 2016.

The Environment Pollution Control Authority (EPCA) for NCR submitted a report to the Supreme Court and said that pollution levels of Delhi had been worse than The Great London smog of 1952 [1]. Also, it was reported as one of the worst levels of Air Quality in Delhi since 1999. Even before the festival, the Delhi government had released a NASA image dated October 26 showing a haze blanket across north India due to crop residue burning in Haryana and Punjab, saying it was having a major adverse effect on the city's air quality [2]. Added to that, the reckless bursting of crackers during the festival aggravated the situation.

The level of Particulate Matter in the air was more than double as compared to that of last year, 2015 [3]. The problem was accentuated by low temperatures and relatively lower wind speed, thereby hampering the dispersion of suspended pollutants. Low visibility was also apparent.

1.2 Overview

This Paper covers two contrasting pollution monitoring stations of Delhi viz. R.K. Puram and Mandir Marg. R.K. Puram is the one of the most polluted areas as evident by the fact that PM10 readings went up by over 42 times from the National Ambience Air Quality Standard. On the other hand, Mandir Marg is counted amongst the less polluted areas. For an efficient coverage of the situation, data for 3 months starting from 1st October 2016 to 31st December 2016 was considered. This ensured the coverability of both the pre-Diwali and post-Diwali conditions.

The study's focus was on Correlation of Meteorological factors with Pollutants using Statistical Analysis for both monitoring stations. This was followed by a Comparative Study of the two monitoring stations.

All this analysis was done in R programming language used for statistical computing under R Studio environment.

1.3 Analytical Approach

Figure 1 summarizes the sequence of steps followed throughout the study[1]:

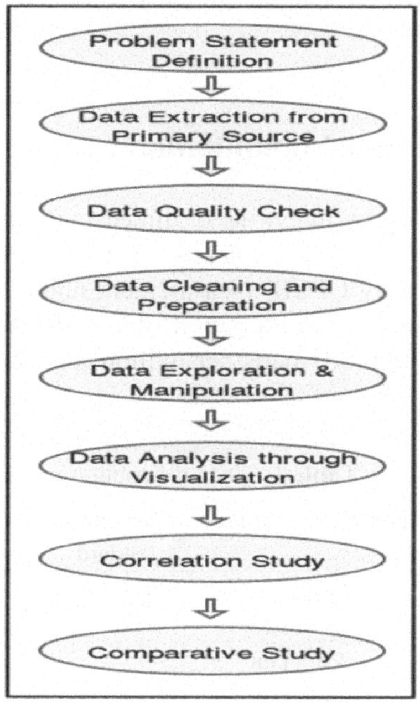

Fig. 1. Analytic approach

- **Problem Statement Definition**. A clear and concise description of the existing problem and objective of the study was identified as: *To perform analysis of major pollutants behind 'Diwali Smog 2016' and find out their correlation with meteorological factors. Also compare the results of the two monitoring stations viz. R.K. Puram and Mandir Marg.*
- **Data Extraction from Primary Source**. The data was obtained from the Central Pollution Control Board (CPCB) real time air quality data monitoring application that is available on-line [4]. Some major pollutants were selected viz. Particulate Matter (PM10), Nitrogen Dioxide (NO_2), Sulphur Dioxide (SO_2) and Ozone (O_3). Also, Meteorological Factors like Wind Speed, Relative Humidity, Temperature and Solar Radiation were preferred. Hence, datasets of total 8 variables for each station for the duration of 3 months were collected. Although the data for Ozone for Mandir Marg was not available.
- **Data Quality Check**. Extracted data had some missing values, and some of the attributes were not in the desired format.

[1] All the empirical data sets and the experimental works in the form of the code in R language or the 'R Scripts', and the plots generated by the codes are available at our GITHUB repository: https://github.com/A-Infinite/DataScience-DelhiSmog2016Analysis

- **Data Cleaning and Preparation.** Missing values of the concentrations were dealt by imputing the median values. Data format of various attributes were changed into specified format for the ease in computation. For instance, the date format was changed, so that individual fields like 'months' could be extracted. This resulted in tidy datasets.

2 Data Exploration and Manipulation

Exploration of data was done by the virtue of dimensions, structure, types of variables along with the overall summary. Table 1 describes all the variables, abbreviations used, types, Prescribed Standards by CPCB, measurement units, and type of data which is continuous for all. The unit for concentration of pollutants is micrograms per cubic meter which is equivalent to 0.001 parts per million (ppm).

Table 1. Data description

Variables	Abbreviations	Variable type	Prescribed standard in $\mu g/m^3$	Unit	Data type
Particulate matter	PM10	Pollutant	100	$\mu g/m^3$	Continuous
Nitrogen dioxide	NO_2	Pollutant	80	$\mu g/m^3$	Continuous
Sulphur dioxide	SO_2	Pollutant	80	$\mu g/m^3$	Continuous
Ozone	O_3	Pollutant	100	$\mu g/m^3$	Continuous
Wind speed	ws	Meteorological	–	m/s	Continuous
Relative humidity	rh	Meteorological	–	%	Continuous
Temperature	t or temp	Meteorological	–	°C	Continuous
Solar radiation	sr	Meteorological	–	watt/m^2	Continuous

A new attribute for the pollutants dataset, 'Exceedance Factor' was computed using Eq. (1). Exceedance Factor is the ratio of mean concentration of a pollutant with its prescribed standard. Exceedance Factor depicts the severity of air pollution caused by a particular pollutant. Higher the Exceedance Factor, lower is the air quality.

$$EF = c / ps \tag{1}$$

Where

EF = Exceedance Factor,
c = Concentration of Pollutant in $\mu g/m^3$ and,
ps = Prescribed Standard as suggested by CPCB

A new Categorical type attribute 'Pollution Category' was added in the datasets according to the Exceedance Factor (EF) calculated in Eq. (1). Table 2 shows the four air quality categories defined by CPCB [5]:

Table 2. Pollution categories and their criteria

S. No.	Pollution category	Criteria
1.	Critical pollution (C)	EF > = 1.5
2.	High pollution (H)	EF = [1.0–1.5)
3.	Moderate pollution (M)	EF = [0.5–1.0)
4.	Low pollution (L)	EF < 0.5

3 Data Visualization and Analysis

For Analysis and Visualization purpose, Bar Graphs, Box Plots and Line Charts were used. Execution of 'R scripts' generated the following graphs:

3.1 R.K. Puram

Figures 2, 3, 4 and 5 show the analysis of various pollutants for R.K. Puram area.

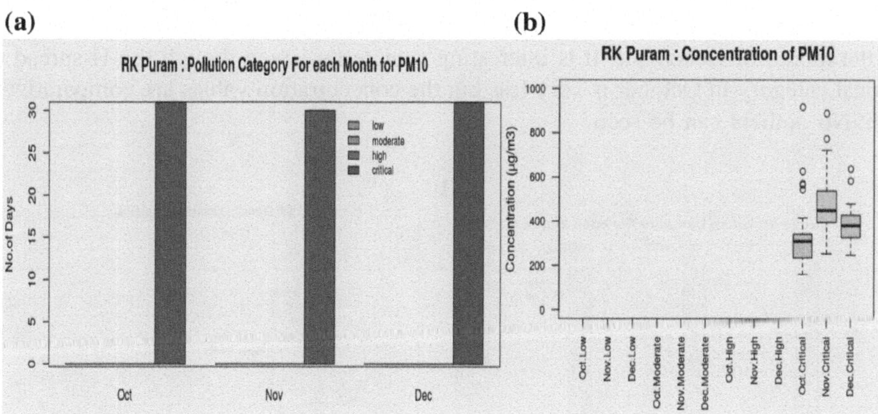

Fig. 2. (a) Pollution category for each month (b) Concentration of PM10

Figure 2a shows that the pollution category for PM10 is always 'Critical'. While Fig. 2b depicts the Box plots showing the concentration range of PM10 from 200 to 700 µg/m^3 which is much higher than the prescribed standard (100 µg/m^3). Box plots basically show the quartile distribution. It can be observed clearly that the median value is highest in November (owing to the bad situations after Diwali), which has later come down in December. Box plot is skewed for all the 3 months, because of the presence of outliers.

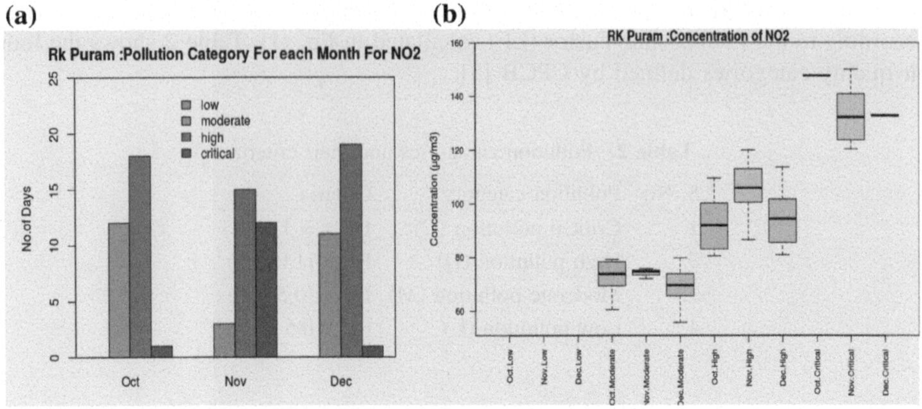

Fig. 3. (a) Pollution category for each month (b) Concentration of NO_2

Figure 3a shows that pollution category for NO_2 varies from Moderate to High and to Critical throughout the duration under study. Before Diwali, there are significant number of cases of Low and Moderate pollution. It can be easily seen that there are more number of critical cases in November just after Diwali. While more cases lie in Moderate category in December, owing to the dispersion of pollutants.

In Fig. 3b, for October, the H-spread of Box plot is the largest for High pollution category and for Critical pollution type in November. And the conditions remain same for the month of December. It is interesting to note that even though the H-spread of Critical category in October is very less but the concentration values are comparatively high. No outliers can be seen.

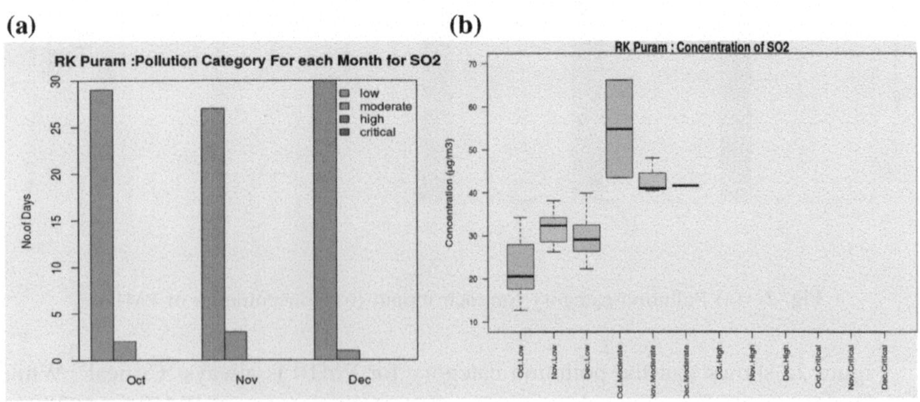

Fig. 4. (a) Pollution category for each month for SO_2 (b) Concentration of SO_2

In Fig. 4a, only instances of Low and Moderate type pollution are there for SO_2. Though there is a rise in number of Moderate cases in November which decreases in December, owing to the dispersion of pollutants.

Figure 4b shows that in October, the H-spread is the largest for Moderate pollution type. Also the median value is high for this category. Here also, no outliers can be seen.

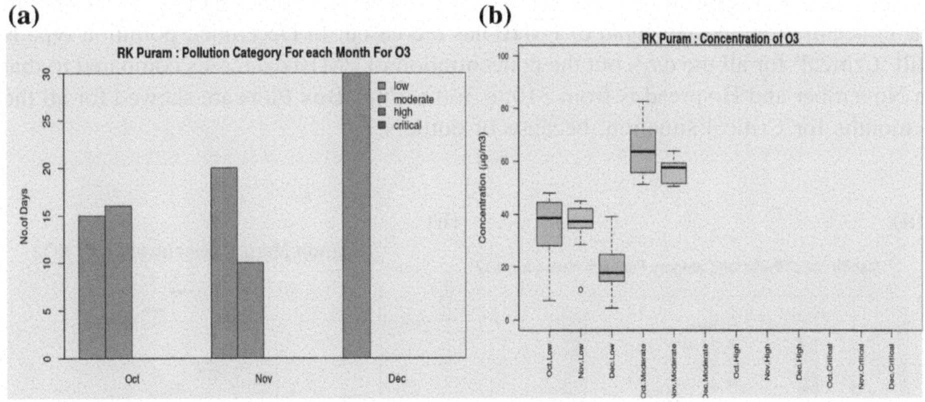

Fig. 5. (a) Pollution category for each month for O_3 (b) Concentration of O_3

In Fig. 5a, only instances of Low and Moderate type pollution are there for O_3. For October, Low and Moderate number of cases are very close. It's interesting to note that in November, Low pollution cases are more than the Moderate ones. This trend isn't noticed for other pollutants. The Moderate cases disappear in December, owing to the dispersion of pollutants. So, only Low pollution cases are seen.

In Fig. 5b, for the month of November, the H-spread is almost same for Low and Moderate pollution type, although concentration values increases. One exceptional reading dipped the most than the general range of low cases.

3.2 Mandir Marg

Figures 6, 7 and 8 show the analysis of various pollutants for Mandir Marg area.

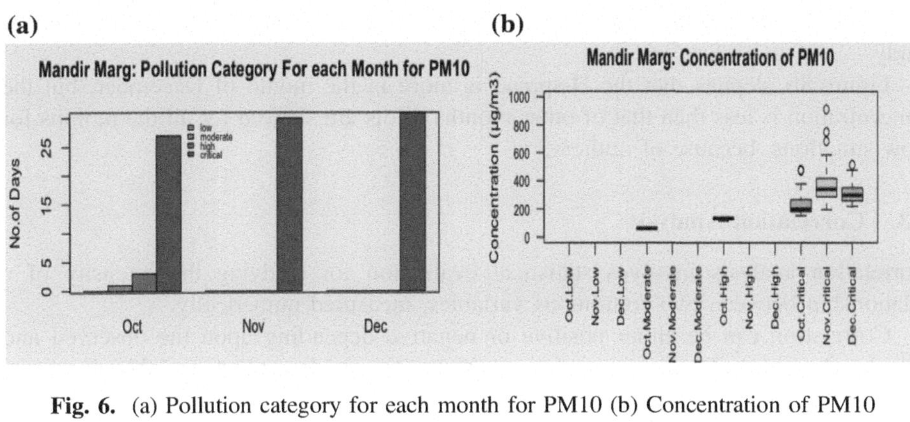

Fig. 6. (a) Pollution category for each month for PM10 (b) Concentration of PM10

Figure 6a depicts that pollution category for PM10 is mainly critical. In the first week of October pollution category is Moderate as well as High for few days.

In Fig. 6b for the month of October the situation is mostly Critical but the H-spread is less. Soon after Diwali i.e. in November the situation becomes more Critical as both the concentration and H-spread of PM10 has increased. In December, pollution type is still 'Critical' for all the days but the concentration of PM10 decreases compared to that in November and H-spread is from 310 to 360 μg/m^3. Box Plots are skewed for all the 3 months for Critical situation, because of outliers.

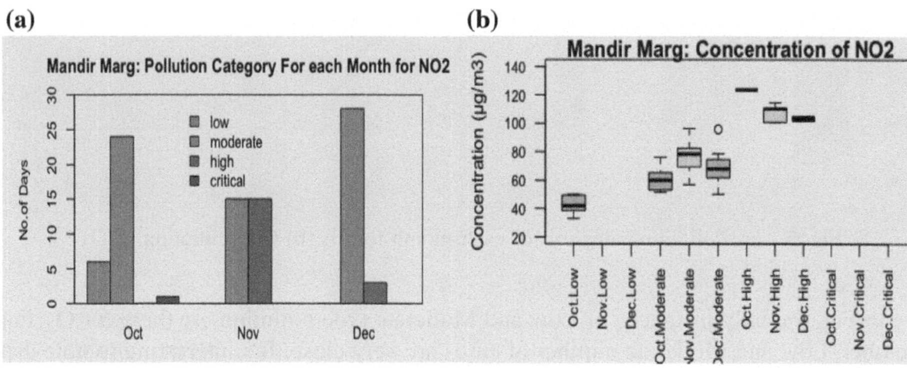

Fig. 7. (a) Pollution category for each month for NO_2 (b) Concentration of NO_2

In Fig. 7a, the pollution category is mostly Low and Moderate but also Critical for few days in October. In November the pollution category varies between Moderate and High owing to the Diwali. Whereas in December the pollution category is Moderate for most of the days and High only for few days.

In Fig. 7b, the H-spread for all the 3 months for Moderate pollution category is same but the concentration is High in the month of November. In case of High pollution category the H-spread is only observed in November. Although in October also, pollution type is High with maximum concentration.

Figure 8a, depicts that the pollution category is Low throughout the duration under study.

Figure 8b, depicts that the H-spread is more in the month of December, but the concentration is less than that of other months. Plots are skewed for all the months for Low situations, because of outliers.

3.3 Correlation Analysis

Correlation analysis involves statistical evaluation for studying the intensity of a relationship between two continuous variables, measured numerically.

Correlation can be either positive or negative depending upon the observed and calculated values. Positive correlation exists if one dependent variable increases

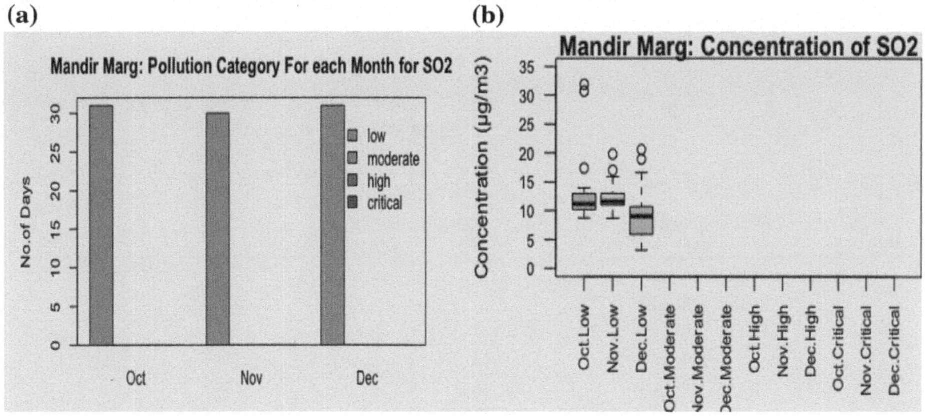

Fig. 8. (a) Pollution category for each month for SO_2 (b) Concentration of SO_2

simultaneously with the other independent variable, whereas Negative correlation depicts inverse proportionality.

Pearson's product-moment coefficient is the measurement of correlation and ranges (depending on the correlation) between +1 and −1. +1 indicates the strongest positive correlation possible, and −1 indicates the strongest negative correlation possible. Therefore, the closer the coefficient is to either of these numbers, the stronger is the correlation of the data it represents. On this scale, 0 indicates no correlation. Hence, values closer to zero highlight weaker/poorer correlation than those closer to +1/−1 [6].

In this section, effects on a dependent variable (each pollutant under observation) due to the Meteorological Factors (Independent Variable) are analyzed. Linear regression models are shown using scatterplots.

Assumptions are:

NULL HYPOTHESIS (H_o): Pollutant Concentration is not influenced by the Weather elements.

ALTERNATE HYPOTHESIS (H_a): Weather Elements have influence on the Concentration of Pollutants.

Figure 9a is showing all the results in which Null Hypothesis was rejected and Alternate Hypothesis was accepted. This establishes the following aspects:

- *Positive relation amongst Ozone, Temperature and Solar radiation:* The photochemical reactions rate increases in the presence of high intensity solar radiations. Ozone, being the major constituent of Smog, is formed at a faster rate.
- *Negative Correlation of NO_2 and PM10* can be seen with the wind speed. If air is calm, then the pollutants cannot disperse, hence their concentration builds up.
- *Negative Correlation of O_3 with Relative Humidity.* Water vapour content of air is reported as a percentage of the saturation of vapour pressure of water at a given temperature. This is the Relative Humidity [7]. The water vapours, having dipolar nature binds with the pollutants, resulting in lower visibility. Also they react with primary pollutants like NO_2 to form O_3. Therefore, rapid consumption of water molecules will form more ozone.

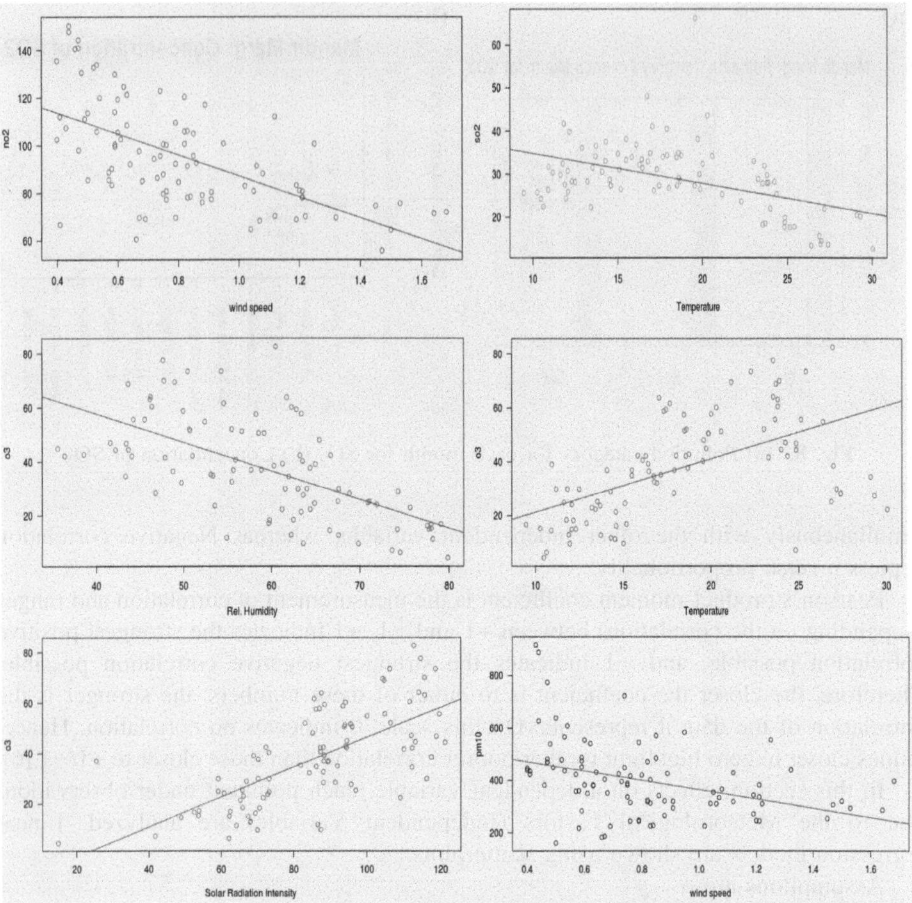

Fig. 9. (a) Linear regression models for R.K. Puram

- *Negative Correlation of SO_2 with Temperature:* Low temperatures results in fog lying at lower levels of troposphere and pollutants are not able to get dispersed. Also, SO_2 combines with water molecules to form sulphuric acid which is equivalent to acid rain [8].

Figure 9b is showing the regression models obtained for Mandir Marg, where alternate hypothesis was accepted. Following additional points were noticed:

- *NO_2 and PM10 are Negatively Correlated with Temperature*, owing to the prevalence of foggy weather due to low temperatures.
- *SO_2 is Negatively Correlated to Wind Speed* as stable wind speed leads to stagnancy of pollutants above the ground.
- *PM10 and Relative Humidity are Positively Correlated* as PM10 binds with water molecules and remain suspended in the air. This again leads to lower visibility.

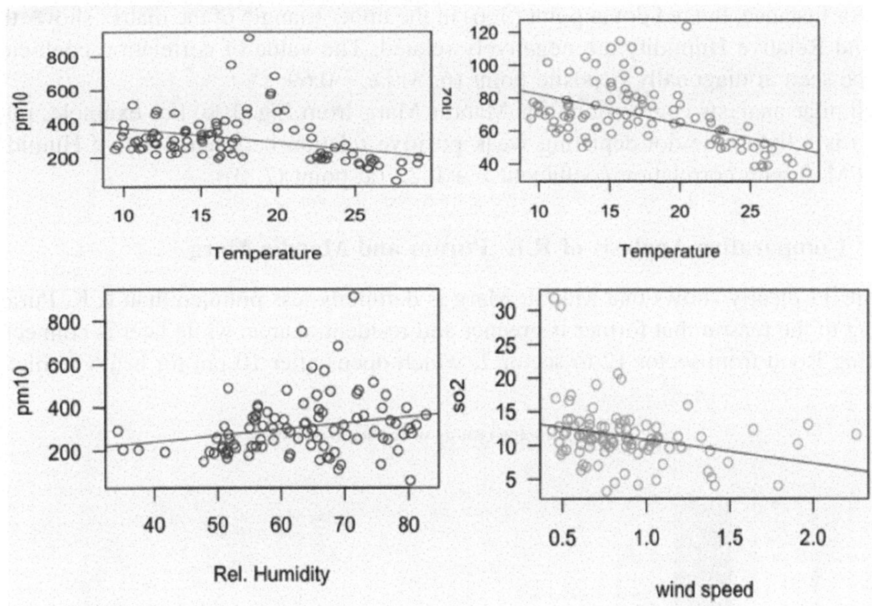

Fig. 9. (b) Linear regression models for Mandir Marg

Figure 10a is an 8 × 8 correlation matrix showing the correlation of 8 variables with each other. This provides summary of the correlation analysis in the most efficient way. Red dots depict negative correlation while blue dots depict positive correlation. The intensity of the colour corresponds to the intensity of relation.

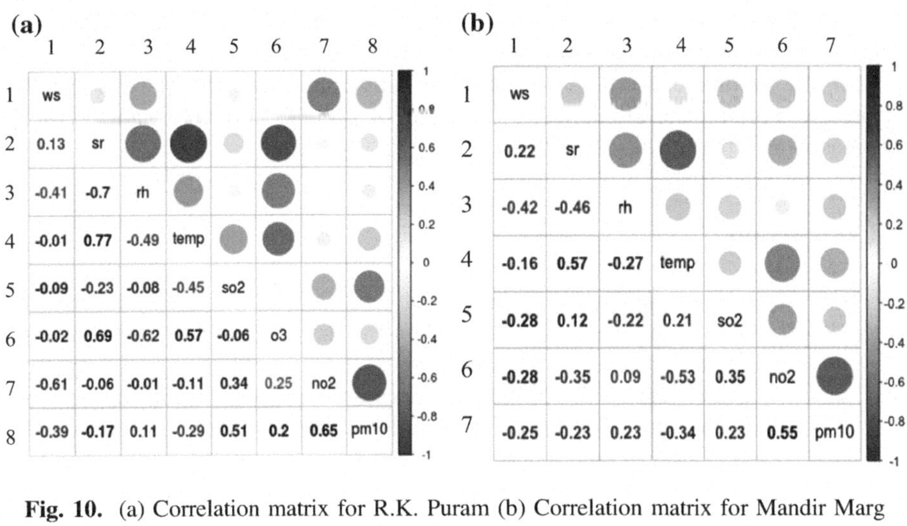

Fig. 10. (a) Correlation matrix for R.K. Puram (b) Correlation matrix for Mandir Marg

For instance, the red dot at point (3, 6) in the upper triangle of the matrix shows that O_3 and Relative Humidity are negatively related. The value of correlation coefficient can be seen at diagonally opposite point (6, 3) i.e. −0.69.

Similar analysis can be done for Mandir Marg from Fig. 10b. For example, point (3, 7) is a light blue dot depicting weak positive relation between Relative Humidity and PM10 with correlation coefficient = + 0.23 (at point (7, 3)).

3.4 Comparative Analysis of R.K. Puram and Mandir Marg

Figure 11 clearly shows that Mandir Marg is definitely less polluted than R.K. Puram, owing to the reason that former is greener and residential area, while later is connected to Ring Road from sector 12 to sector 2, which opens after 10 pm for heavy vehicles.

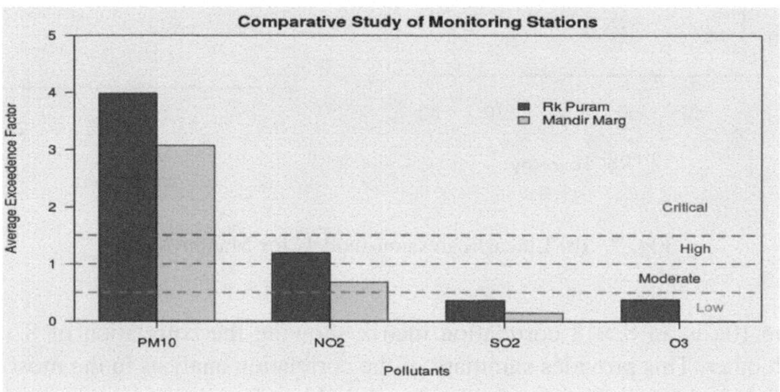

Fig. 11. Comparative analysis

It can be seen that major pollutant (amongst the selected four pollutants) for both the areas is PM10. The average exceedance factor of pollutants other than PM10 hasn't reached the critical region for both the monitoring stations.

Also, the average exceedance factor of all pollutants of Mandir Marg is less than that of R.K. Puram. The difference in the value of average exceedance factor for the two areas is also the greatest for PM10.

4 Conclusion

From the results of this study, it is clear that at R.K. Puram, the levels of Particulate Matter (PM10) were dangerously higher (nearly 40%) than normal level and it emerged as the major pollutant. Situations at Mandir Marg were less problematic as compared to R.K. Puram. Though, hike in the pollutants concentrations post Diwali turned whole Delhi into a 'gas chamber'. Moreover, meteorological factors were too unfavorable. Low wind speed, lower temperatures and high relative humidity, all caused the envelope of pollutants to stay near the ground for a longer duration. Hospitals reported rise in cases of respiratory distress amongst the elderly people and children. Facing an emergency situation, immediate actions by the government included ban on construction activity and shutting down of the Badarpur power plant for 10 days [9]. Though the magnitude of the problem came down in December. But it can't be said that the situation was under the prescribed level mark. Also if long term measures are not taken at the earliest, the problem of Smog Pollution may aggravate even more. The criticality of Air Pollution in Delhi is already evident by the study presented in this paper.

References

1. Soumya Pillai on November 8, 2016: Delhi's pollution levels worse than the great London smog of 1952: EPA. http://www.hindustantimes.com/delhi-news/delhi-s-pollution-levels-worse-than-the-great-london-smog-of-1952-epa/story-Wv54jr5rMSAojqRZ85zdWO.html
2. India Today Article by Prabahsh K. Dutta, October 29, 2016. http://indiatoday.intoday.in/story/haze-descends-in-delhi-ahead-of-diwali-air-hazardous/1/798553.html
3. The Wall Street Journal of November 1, 2106 By Karan Deep Singh. https://blogs.wsj.com/indiarealtime/2016/11/01/air-pollution-in-new-delhi-gets-dangerously-high-during-diwali-celebrations/
4. Data Source: Central Pollution Control Board. http://www.cpcb.gov.in/CAAQM/frmUserAvgReportCriteria.aspx
5. Comprehensive Environmental Assessment of Industrial Clusters by J. S. Kamyotra, Member Secretary, Central Pollution Control Board, Delhi – 110 032
6. At ENVIS Centre – 01. cpcb.nic.in/divisionsofheadoffice/ess/NewItem_152_Final-Book_2.pdf
7. Correlation Analysis from DjsResearch website. Link. http://www.djsresearch.co.uk/glossary/item/correlation-analysis-market-research
8. Influence of Meteorological Factors on Air Quality from Queensland Government Website. https://www.qld.gov.au/environment/pollution/monitoring/airmonitoring/meteorology-factors/
9. Sulphur Dioxide: It's Role in Climatic Change. http://esseacourses.strategies.org/module.php?module_id=168
10. Hindustan Times, November 8, 2016. http://www.hindustantimes.com/delhi-news/all-you-wanted-to-know-about-delhi-air-pollution-cleared-up-here/story-V7EkSU7xtNdnlimBYxGg6K.html
11. All the Empirical Data and the Experiments Work in the form of the code in R Language or the 'R Scripts', and the Plots Generated by the Codes are Available at our GITHUB Repository. https://github.com/A-Infinite/DataScience-DelhiSmog2016Analysis

Check for updates

Effects of Partial Dependency of Features and Feature Selection Procedure Over the Plant Leaf Image Classification

Arun Kumar(✉) and Poonam Saini

Sir Padampat Singhania University, Udaipur, India
arunkumarsai@gmail.com

Abstract. The process of taxonomic classification of plant species has been carried out by the botanist since centuries, by observing their roots, shoots and flowers. It is the age of modernization; roads, buildings and bridges are fast replacing the vegetation, even before the botanist might personally get a chance to look at them. Therefore, the role of computer vision is justified for fast classification of plant species before they become extinct. The sole purpose of this research work is to increase the predictive classification accuracy of plant species by using their shape and texture features obtained from the digital leaf images of dorsal sides. Since the geometrical shape features of the leaves alone are not able to provide better predictive classification accuracy results, therefore, the texture features have been clubbed together to achieve higher order of accuracy results. This leads to increase in the data size. Therefore, in order to reduce the feature dataset, random feature selection procedure has been adopted, which selects features on the basis of weights of attributes. The justifiability of the features selected has been carried out by using the feature importance plots and strengthened further by the partial dependency plots having been drawn to see their final inclusion into the final feature selection dataset. The results exhibited by the shape, shape subset, texture, texture subset of feature dataset as well as the combined dataset are quite exemplary and worth showcasing. In spite of the fact that the geometrical shapes of many of the leaves may be the same or almost same, the combined shape and texture features can be a suitable alternative for improvement in predictive accuracy results.

Keywords: Computer vision · Leaf image · Dorsal · Shape
Texture feature selection · Partial dependency

1 Introduction

The concept of process of identification of objects, plants and human faces is as old as the human history. In fact, man is the best pattern recognition instrument. Man has been recognizing the objects through his naked eyes, and keeping the unique cues of the objects in his brain for future reference. The cues are the color of the objects, shapes of the objects, their texture or feeling of touch or smell etc. Our eyes identify these unique patterns or a combination of the patterns on the objects and form the visual cues.

B. Panda et al. (Eds.): REDSET 2017, CCIS 799, pp. 208–225, 2018.
https://doi.org/10.1007/978-981-10-8527-7_19

Therefore, the study of patterns or pattern matching is not a new concept but presently it has attained new dimensions by using the modern day tools like computers and cameras. When our brain responds by informing that the present object that the eye is seeing is similar to the one seen some times back, the term used is template matching. But, when the brain responds on seeing a baby chicken looking more like a bird, then the term used is prototype matching. While analyzing the features, the brain breaks down the incoming stimulus into individual fragments of patterns as shown in Fig. 1.

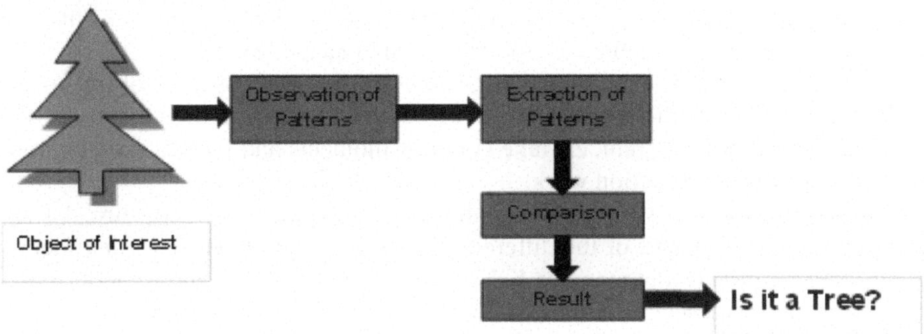

Fig. 1. Pattern recognition pipeline.

The study of flora and fauna has been the part and parcel of human evolution process. Plants have been the prime source of food and energy since centuries, therefore, the study of plants and their identification cannot be chronologised, but the advancement in other fields of knowledge has helped in understanding the plants in a better way. The modernization of the world with the building of roads, bridges, buildings have led to the reckless cutting of plants, trees and shrubs. Some of the vegetation has gone or become extinct even without getting to know them. Therefore the biologists and the computer visionists have to adopt automatic methods of recognition of plants. Plants have been identified and studied using their roots, stems, leaves, flowers and fruits.

The study of plants through their digital leaf images is a recent phenomenon. The term image of the leaf of a plant has been buzzing around in the computer vision field. There are various characteristic features of the leaf like color of the leaf, geometric shape of the leaf, texture of the epidermal layer, presence or absence of the venation pattern, the arrangement of leaves on the plant, describing the structure as simple, compound or complex arrangement etc.

The work carried out by [1] involves use of Gabor features extracted from digital leaf images of dorsal sides. The work provides in-depth comparison for predictive accuracy using complete as well as the subset of features. The subset of features provide an accuracy value of 90.5% using Random Forest for feature selection and classification purpose.

The work carried out by [2] involves use of morphological characters that describe the characteristics features like shape, color and size of a pathogen structure. The morphology based features extracted were area, perimeter, convex area, convex perimeter, compactness, solidity, convexity, and roundness for Jabon's leaf seedling pathogen using microscopic image set. The major outcome of this work has been the use of compactness and roundness features to differentiate each pathogen.

The work carried out by [3], involves the literature survey for automatic quantification and classification of leukocytes in microscopic images for disease identification. The work involves efforts in quantification of these cells include normalization of images, segmentation of its nuclei and cytoplasm followed by their classification.

The researchers in [4] described about essential shape properties as identifiability, invariance to geometrical transformational process, invariance to affine transforms, noise resistance, occultation invariance, statistically independent and reliable. This work has described about forty techniques for extraction of shape features.

The researchers in [5] have used color, shape and texture properties of ornamental leaf with medicinal functionalities for the preparation of image retrieval system. This work has used color histogram, Zernike complex moments and Dyadic wavelet transformation for feature extraction work.

The present research work involves the use of extraction of geometrical shape features for the leaf images of the different plant species and then subjecting them to various classification techniques like K-Nearest Neighbor (KNN) and Random Forest (RF). Since, the classification results obtained by using the shape features alone do not provide with good accuracy results as two or more plant species or subspecies may have the same or more general the same type of shape features. Therefore, the present work involves the use of another characteristic feature of plant leaves, i.e. their texture of the upper epidermal layer. The accuracy results were computed with texture features and a combination of shape and texture features.

The Sect. 2 describes about the detailed methodology adopted to prepare a leaf image dataset for different plant species. It also describes about extraction of geometrical shape features and texture features. Preparation of different datasets and feature subsets has been done in Sect. 2. Finally, the Sect. 2, discusses about the role of partial dependency plots on features. The results and their analysis has been discussed in Sect. 3 followed by conclusions drawn in Sect. 4.

2 Methodology Adopted

The first and the foremost task of any image based work is to have an image database and in the present case the colored leaf image data base has been adopted from [1] and has been shown in Fig. 2. This leaf image database consists of 500 leaf images for 10 different plant species. But, the unique characteristic about this image set is that it consists of 250 dorsal and 250 ventral leaf images for the 10 plant species under observation. But, the present research work has adopted 250 dorsal image dataset.

The initial image processing task involves cropping the image from 640×1024 pixels to 256×256 pixels. This is necessary to avoid unnecessary side images also it reduces the overall image data size and reduces the computational time. The process of background removal has been carried out. For many of the digital images, the object of interest is light in color and the background in which the object has been placed is dark, in such a way that object and background pixels have gray levels grouped into two

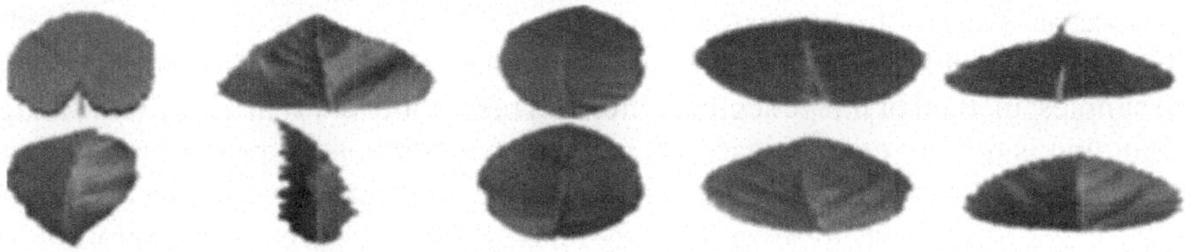

Fig. 2. Sample of leaf images with dorsal sides. (Color figure online)

dominant modes. Therefore, in order to extract the objects from its background, there is a need to select a threshold T, that separates these modes as shown in Eq. (1)

$$g(x,y) = \begin{cases} 1 & \text{if f(x,y)} > \text{T} \\ 0 & \text{otherwise} \end{cases} \tag{1}$$

Where $g(x, y)$ is the thresholded image of f(x,y).

The process of RGB to Gray conversion [6] follows the Eq. (2) mentioned below where R, G and B stand for Red, Green and Blue Channels respectively. The copies of both RGB and Gray image have been kept safe for future work.

$$Gray = 0.299 * R + 0.578 * G + 0.114 * B \tag{2}$$

The present work involves extraction of shape and geometrical features of the object of our concern leaf images.

2.1 Geometrical Shape Based Feature Extraction

The process of recognizing objects through their shapes have been an age old technique adopted by human brain. But, can the technique of recognizing the objects through their individual shapes be relied upon in the computer vision world? The general perception about the shape of the objects is that they have circular, rectangular or oval shapes with minor degrees of fuzziness for their shape classes [7]. But, the general concept of the shapes cannot be applied to the leaf image dataset as the leaves may have varying shapes that may not fall exactly in to general perception about shapes.

The process of image boundary enhancement is an essential initial preprocess as the boundary of the leaves plays an important part in distinguishing the leaf from the background part of the image. This boundary must be dark and distinguishable from the white background. Therefore, all the gray images in the dataset have been subjected to convolution with Laplacian filter with convolution matrix as mentioned in Eq. (3).

$$\begin{bmatrix} 0 & 1 & 0 \\ 1 & -4 & 1 \\ 0 & 1 & 0 \end{bmatrix} \tag{3}$$

The above matrix has been used to swap the pixel values from 1 to 0 and vice versa.

Before, actually starting up extraction of the shape based features, there is a need to apply threshold algorithm on the collected gray dorsal images set. Thresholding which is the simplest method of image segmentation has been applied. From a gray scale image, thresholding is used to create binary images. Segmentation is the process of assigning each pixel in the source image to two or more classes. If there are more than two classes then the usual result leads to several binary images. In image processing, thresholding is used to split an image into smaller segments, or chunks, using at least one color or gray scale value to define their boundary. Thresholding works by separating pixels which fall within a desired range of intensity values from those which do not adhere to the boundary values. Thresholding can be a very effective method of measuring complex or disjointed features in an image. In the present work, the geometrical shapes have been computed for the leaf images. The Fig. 2 shows different shapes of leaves for different plant species.

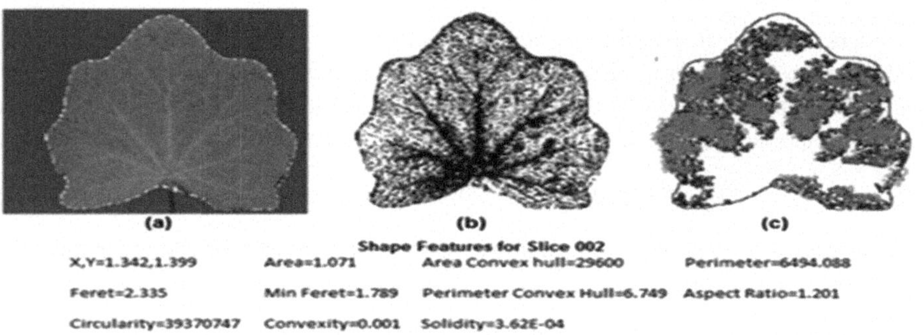

Fig. 3. Shape Features for slice 002 (a) Colored image (b) Gray scale image (c) Thresholded image. (Color figure online)

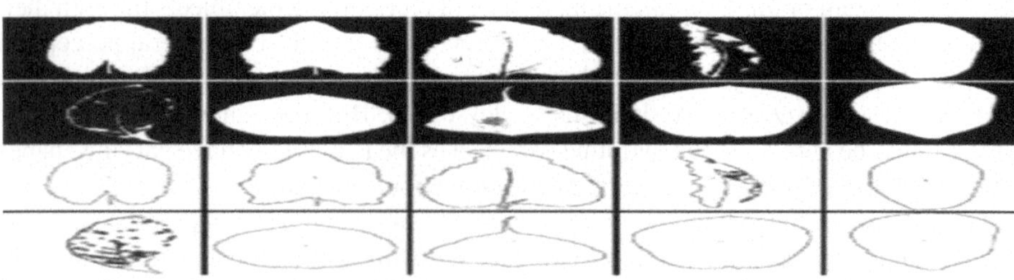

Fig. 4. Images of different leaves after the extraction of different shapes.

In the present work, the following geometrical shape features have been considered for the present study: Area, Perimeter, Angle, Form Factor, Round, Comp, AR, Major, Minor, Effect. Diam, Ferret, Min Ferret, Ferret Angle, Solidity. The detailed explanation and definition can be obtained from [8, 9].

The Fig. 3 shows the slice 002 for which various shape features have been extracted. The slice 002 has been converted from color to gray scale, then converted to binary and then the values have been computed for various shape features. The Fig. 4 shows, the sample of the shapes extracted from the entire ten species of plants used for this research work.

2.2 Extraction of Image Texture Features

The texture of an object is a feeling of touch for us human beings. The object may seem to be smooth or rough to touch. But in the case of digital images, it is the variation in the pixel value patterns which provide a feeling of roughness or smoothness of the object of concern. The gray level co-occurrence matrix has been utilized for calculating the texture features of the digital leaf images of 10 different plant species used for this work.

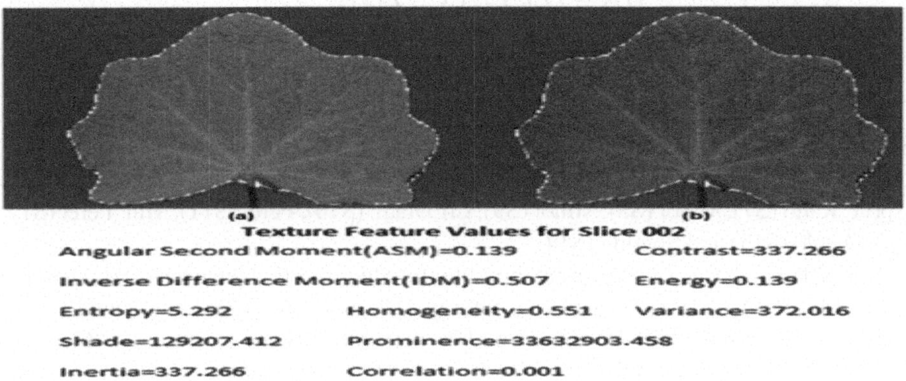

Fig. 5. Extracted texture features for slice 002 (a) Colored image (b) Gray scale image. (Color figure online)

The researchers in [10] has proposed 14 texture features, of which 11 have been chosen and they are Contrast (Contr), Homogeneity, Angular Second Moment (ASM), IDM, Energy, Entropy, Variance, correlation, Inertia, Shade and Prominance. The GLCM matrix was prepared for $0^{\circ}, 45^{\circ}, 90^{\circ}, 135^{\circ}$ with an offset of unity.

The Fig. 5 shows the different texture features extracted for slice 002 of the ten plant species used for this work.

Due to different units of scale, all the shape and texture features obtained above have been normalized by using the Eq. from (4) to (6).

$$Normalization = \frac{f_i - \mu}{\sigma} \tag{4}$$

Where i = 1, 2, 3 … n and μ is the mean value and σ is the standard deviation expressed through Eqs. (5) and (6).

$$\mu = \frac{1}{n}\sum_{i=1}^{n} f_i \tag{5}$$

$$\sigma = sqrt\left(\frac{1}{n}\sum_{i=1}^{n}(f_i - \mu)^2\right) \tag{6}$$

2.3 Preparation of Different Datasets

In the present work 14 shapes based geometrical features and 11 texture based features have been extracted and they are represented through the Eqs. (7) to (9).

$$SDS = \{S1, S2, S3 \ldots S14\} \tag{7}$$

$$TDS = \{T1, T2, T3 \ldots T11\} \tag{8}$$

$$CSTDS = \{S1, S2, S3 \ldots S14\} + \{T1, T2, T3 \ldots T11\} \tag{9}$$

Here *SDS* and *TDS* represent the Shape_Feature_Dataset and Texture_Feature_Dataset respectively. Here $S1, S2, S3 \ldots S14$ represents the 14 shape features extracted and they are: Area (S1), Perimeter (S2), Angle (S3), Form_Factor (S4), Round (S5), Comp (S6), Aspect_Ratio (S7), Major (S8), Minor (S9), Eff.Diam. (S10), Feret (S11), Min_Feret (S12), Feret_Angle (S13) and Solidity (S14).

Here $T1, T2, T3 \ldots T11$ represent the 11 texture features that have been extracted are: ASM (T1), IDM (T2), Contrast (T3), Energy (T4),Entropy (T5), Homogeneity (T6), Variance (T7), Shade (T8), Prominence (T9), Inertia (T10) and Correlation (T11).

Here *CSTDS* represents the Combined_Shape_Texture_Dataset, which has 14 shape based and 11 texture based features and a total of 25 features altogether and this makes the combined dataset a huge one to handle with.

2.4 Feature Subset Selection

As in the present work, 14 shape based geometrical features and 11 texture based features have been extracted from the digital images of 10 different plant species. In order to reduce the size of the dataset, there is a need to choose some unique features to avoid redundancy of the data.

To choose the important features, *SDS* and *TDS* were subjected to the process of Random Forest Feature selection process and by using this algorithm 7 best features have been extracted from Shape based feature dataset (*SDS*), Texture based Feature Dataset (*TDS*) and Combined Shape & Texture based Dataset(*CSTDS*). The individual datasets have been named as Subset Shape based Dataset (*SSDS*), Subset Texture based Dataset (*STDS*) and Combined Subset Shape- Texture Dataset (*CSSTDS*) and have been represented through the Eqs. (10) to (12).

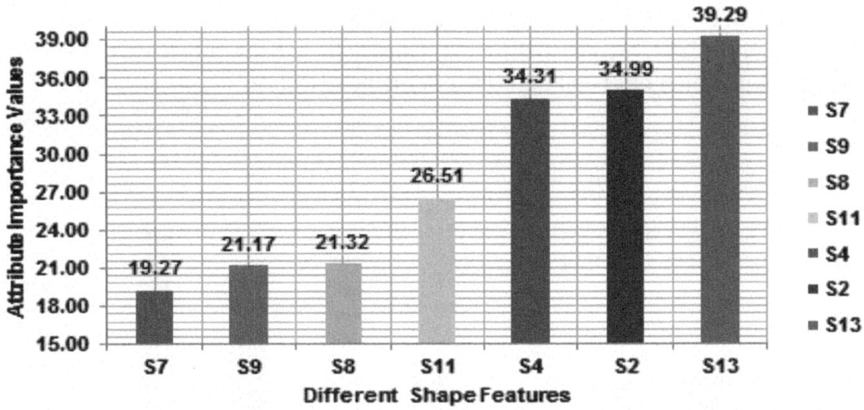

Fig. 6. Seven attribute importance values for different shape features.

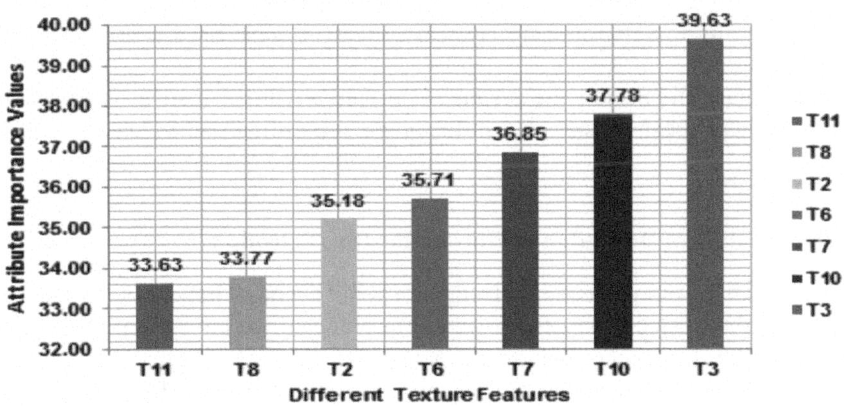

Fig. 7. Seven attribute importance values for different texture features.

The subset of features have been extracted using the FSelector package as described by [11]. Data can contain attributes that are highly correlated with each other. This shall lead to redundancy of data and predictive accuracy results don not perform better for large datasets, therefore highly correlated attributes are removed. The feature ranking or attribute importance values have been individually shown through Figs. 6, 7 and 8 for shape based feature set, texture based feature set and combined shape and texture based feature set.

$$SSDS = \{S7, S8, S9, S11, S4, S2, S13\} \tag{10}$$

$$STDS = \{T11, T8, T2, T6, T7, T10, T3\} \tag{11}$$

$$CSSTDS = \{S3\} + \{T11, T8, T2, T6, T7, T10, T3\} \tag{12}$$

Therefore, in totality 6 different datasets have been prepared viz: *SDS*, *TDS*, *CSTDS*, *SSDS*, *STDS*, and *CSSTDS*. These different datasets have been subjected to the process of classification which has been described in the next section.

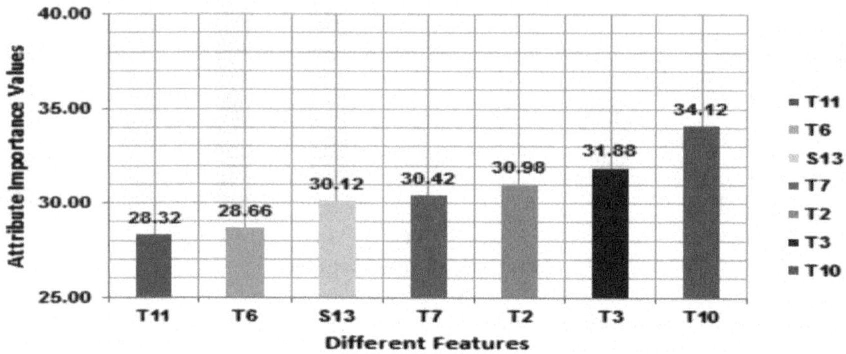

Fig. 8. Seven attribute importance values for combined dataset.

The Figs. 6, 7 and 8 show the attribute importance values for seven different shape features that have been further chosen for preparation of SSDS, STDS and CSSTDS respectively.

2.5 Role of Partial Dependency Plots on Feature Selection

Once the process of unique feature selection is over, it becomes imperative to understand the impact of these selected few features over the outcome. To solve this problem, partial dependency plots have been constructed to visualize the marginal effect of one or many variables upon the overall outcome. The partial dependency plots help in visualizing the average relationship between the predicted responses of one or more variables. These plots have been used for knowledge discovery in the case of large datasets. In the case of partial dependency plots, at each plotted point, the net effect of the background variables is averaged.

According to researchers in [12], suppose S is a subset of p predictor variables, such that $S = \{X_1, X_2, \ldots, X_p\}$. Let C be a complement to S, such that $S \cup C = \{X_1, X_2, \ldots, X_p\}$. The random forest predictor function, $f(x)$ will depend upon all p predictor variables. Therefore,

$$f(x) = f(X_s, X_c) \tag{13}$$

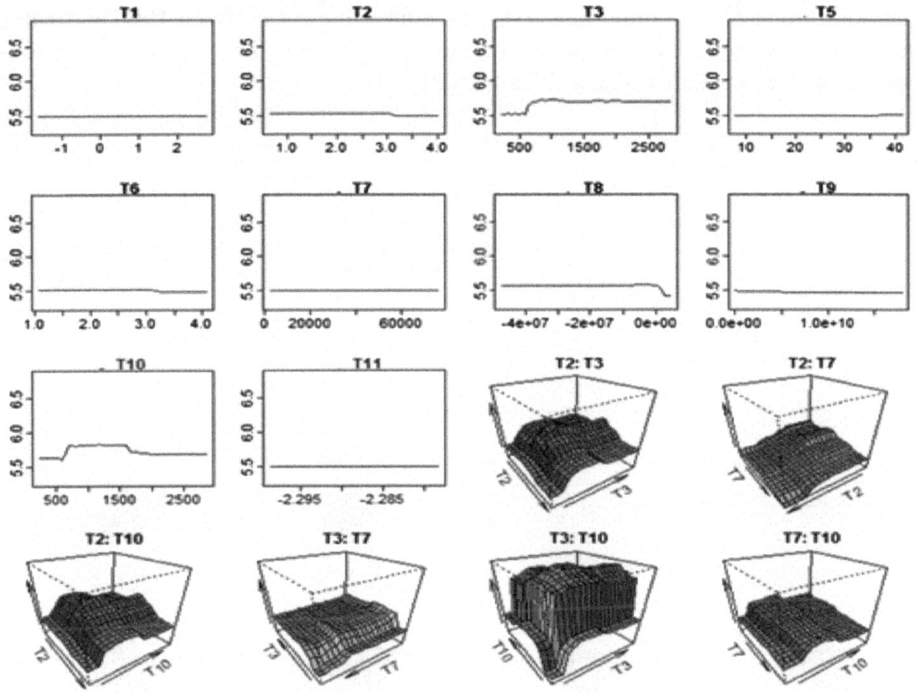

Fig. 9. Effect of partial dependency plots for the texture features.

The partial dependence of the S predictors on the predictive function $f(x)$ can be computed using Eq. (14).

$$f_S = E_{X_C}\left[f(X_S, X_C)\right] = \int f(X_S, X_C)dP(X_C) \tag{14}$$

This can be further written as Eq. (15).

$$\overline{f_S} = \frac{1}{N}\sum_{i=1}^{N}\left[f(X_S, x_{iC})\right] \tag{15}$$

Where $(x_{1C}, x_{2C}, \ldots, x_{nC})$ represent the different values of X_C occurring in the training data.

The partial dependency plots have been prepared using "plotmo" package as described by [13]. In the Fig. 9, it can be observed that the partial dependency plot have been created for different variables of the texture dataset that has been already selected through feature selection procedure adopted earlier. For T2 variable, the values on x-axis greater than 1.0 to 3.4 predict the outcome more strongly and after x > 4.0 on x-axis, there is slight decrease in the positive influence on the classification model created in this research work. For the variable T3, the values on x-axis less than 500 influence the output negatively and the values in between 1000 and 1500, there is positive influence on the classification model. For the variable T6, there is negative influence at around x > 3.5 on x-axis.

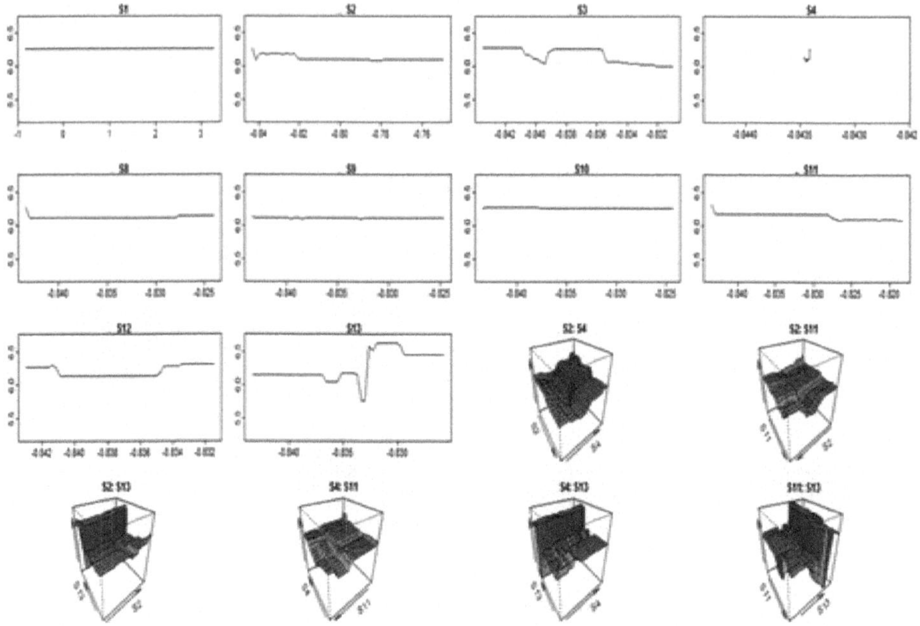

Fig. 10. Effect of partial dependency plots for the shape features.

For Variable T7, the x-values less than 20,000 have more positive influence on the classification model but have a negative effect after 35000 on the classification model. Almost similar nature has been exhibited by variables T8, T10 and T11. As set of regression surfaces have been constructed for various variables, T2:T6, T2:T7, T2:T11, T6:T7, T6:T11 and T7:T11. They show strong interaction between the variables.

In Fig. 9, the partial dependency plots plotted for texture features indicate that all the features have their y-axis values centered around 5.5 and higher which makes them positively effective in boosting the overall predictive accuracy results. Therefore their membership for the final feature selection process is fairly positive and others can be rejected.

In Fig. 10, the partial dependency plots for different shape features indicate that all the features have their y-axis values are centred around 0.0 to 0.5 which makes them less suitable for the final choice of selected features for the combined dataset. In Fig. 10, it has been observed that the S13 (Feret_Angle) shows sharp increase in the y-axis values and therefore, it is the only member suitable for the choice of selected variables from shape based feature dataset.

In both the Figs. 9 and 10, T2, T3, T6, T7, T10, T11, S13, have their y-axis i.e. the response values averaged around 5 to 6. The x-axis shows the actual value of the variable. The details about these features have already been described in the previous sections.

These features have a positive impact over the classification model generated earlier and boost the predictive accuracy results. These features have been used further for test dataset for testing purpose. The Fig. 11 shows the subset of unique texture features plotted for their partial dependency plots. The selected features T2, T3, T6, T7, T8, T10 and T11 have their y-axis value centered around 5.6 and above, and therefore, their selection in the subset feature dataset is appropriate.

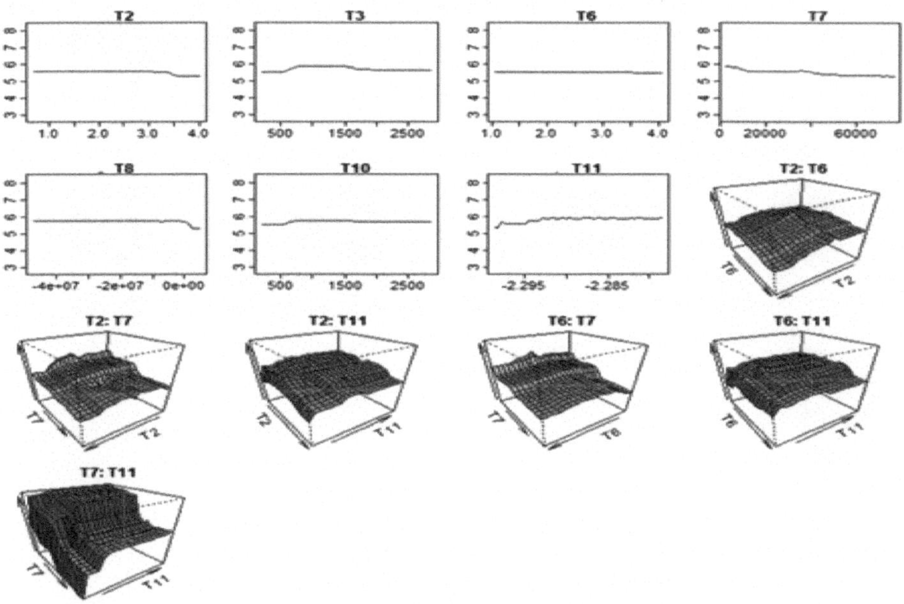

Fig. 11. Effect of partial dependency plots for unique texture features selected.

It has been observed from the feature importance plots (refer Figs. 6, 7 and 8) and from the partial dependency plots (refer to Figs. 9, 10, 11 and 12) that the variables chosen for feature selection set are appropriate and they are amicably suitable for the final feature dataset to be used for final predictive accuracy results. Similar types of the partial dependency plots have been shown in Fig. 12 for the combined set of features (containing both texture and shape based features) and the same can be interpreted on the basis of their average influence on the overall classification model.

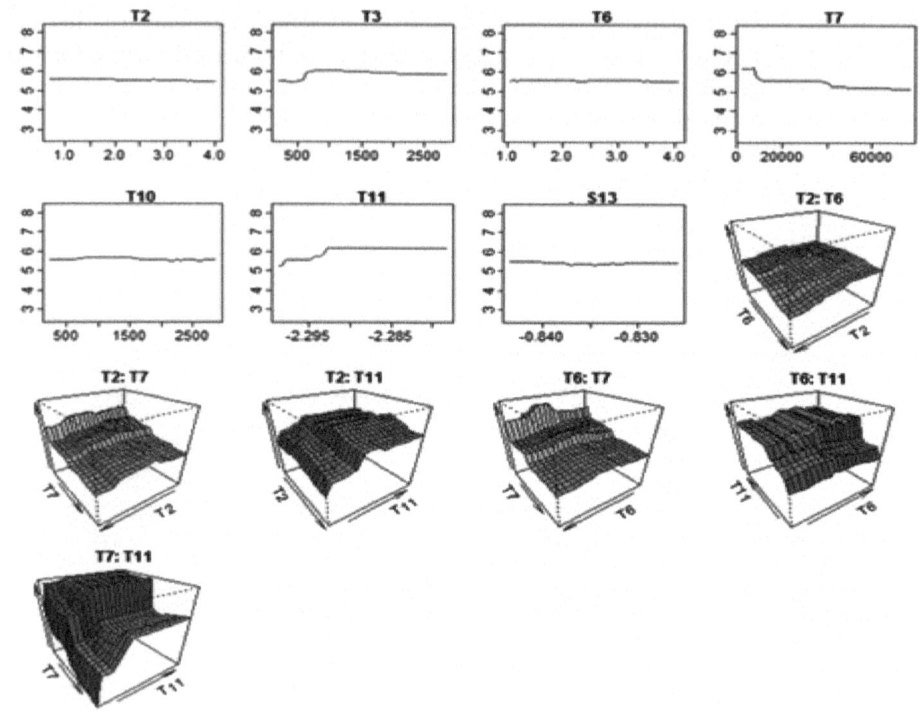

Fig. 12. Effect of partial dependency plots for unique texture and shape features selected (combined type).

3 Results and Analysis

From the results obtained for the shape based feature selection process, it has been observed that the shape features alone themselves do not provide a good accuracy result for the classification of plant species using their dorsal digital images.

By using the KNN based algorithm for SDS, an accuracy value of 63.3% has been achieved with a kappa value of 59.2%. By using the Random Forest Based algorithm for SDS, an accuracy value of 74.8% with a kappa value of 71.9% has been achieved as shown in the Fig. 13.

By using the KNN based algorithm for the TDS, an accuracy value of 80% with a kappa value of 77.8% has been achieved. By using Random forest based algorithm for TDS, an accuracy value of 87.9% with a kappa value of 86.5% has been achieved, as shown in the Fig. 14.

By using the subset of features for shape dataset (SSDS), by using the KNN based algorithm, a predictive accuracy value of 63.8% with a kappa value of 59.7% has been achieved. By using the Random Forest based algorithm, a predictive accuracy value of 73.6% with a kappa value of 70.6% has been achieved, as shown in the Fig. 13.

By using the subset of features for texture dataset (STDS), by using the KNN based algorithm, a predictive accuracy value of 82.3% with a kappa value of 80.4% has been achieved. By using the Random Forest based algorithm, a predictive accuracy value of 88.7% with a kappa value of 87.4% has been achieved, as shown in the Fig. 14.

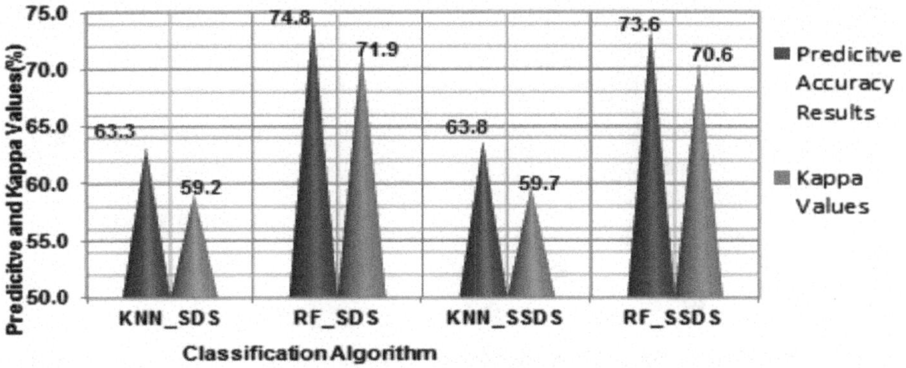

Fig. 13. Results for shape dataset.

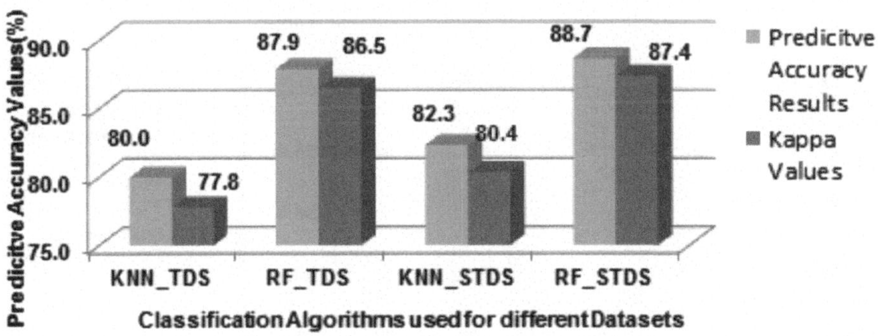

Fig. 14. Results for Texture dataset.

By using the KNN based algorithm for combined shape-texture feature dataset (CSTDS), an accuracy value of 75.5% has been achieved with a kappa value of 72.7%. By using the Random Forest Based algorithm for CSTDS, an accuracy value of 90.6% with a kappa value of 89.6% has been achieved as shown in the Fig. 15.

By using the KNN based algorithm for combined shape-texture feature dataset(CSSTDS), an accuracy value of 82.8% has been achieved with a kappa value of 80.9%. By using the Random Forest Based algorithm for CSSTDS, an accuracy value of 88% with a kappa value of 86.6% has been achieved as shown in the Fig. 15.

The Fig. 16 shows a chart that has been plotted with types of features used on the x-axis, number of features used on one y-axis and percentage predictive accuracy values on the other secondary axis. It shows the maximum achievable accuracy values plotted against the number of features and the type of the dataset used. When 25 features (both shape and texture features) are used then an accuracy value of 90.6% has been achieved with combined dataset. But, it has been observed that when seven features have been used, the maximum achievable accuracy value is 88.7% using texture subset features and 88% using combined subset features.

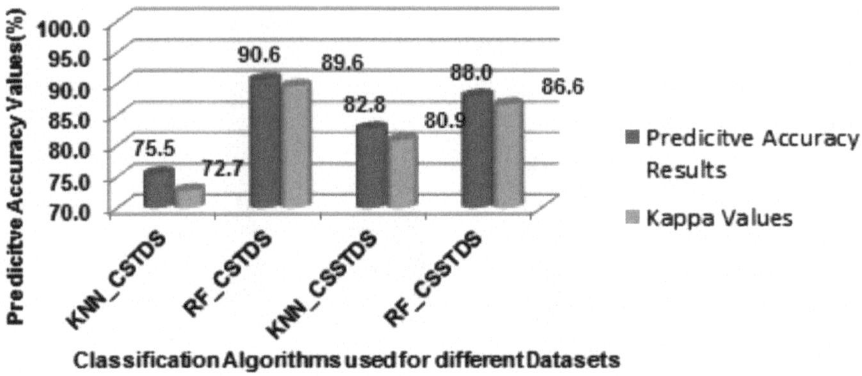

Fig. 15. Results for combined dataset.

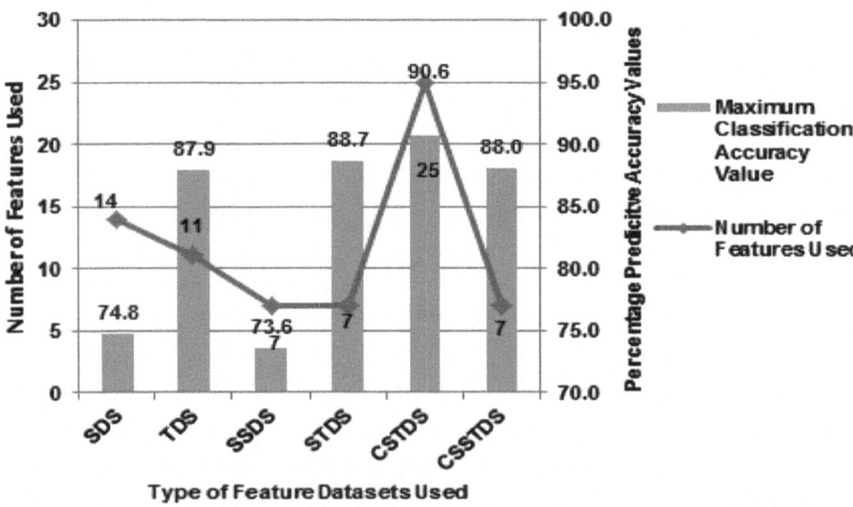

Fig. 16. Predictive accuracy results versus number of features used versus different datasets.

The work carried in this research has been compared with the work of [14–16], where the concept of geometrical shape features have been applied to leaf images for different plant species classification. The comparison chart is represented in Fig. 17. The comparative analysis of the present work with the other researchers cannot be compared directly because of the use of different datasets and classification techniques. The present work has been compared on the basis of digital leaf images and shape features used for classification purpose. The researchers in [14] have worked with 1800 leaf images of 32 different classes and used Probabilistic Neural Networks for the classification work with five different principal components. The maximum achievable accuracy is 90%.

The researchers in [15] have utilized Random Forest (RF) and Linear Discriminant Analysis (LDA) for classifying 340 plant images. This work has been able to achieve an accuracy value of 88.2% using RF algorithm. The researchers in [16] have utilized Probabilistic Neural Network for classifying 1200 simple leaves from 30 different plant species and able to achieve an accuracy of 91.41%.

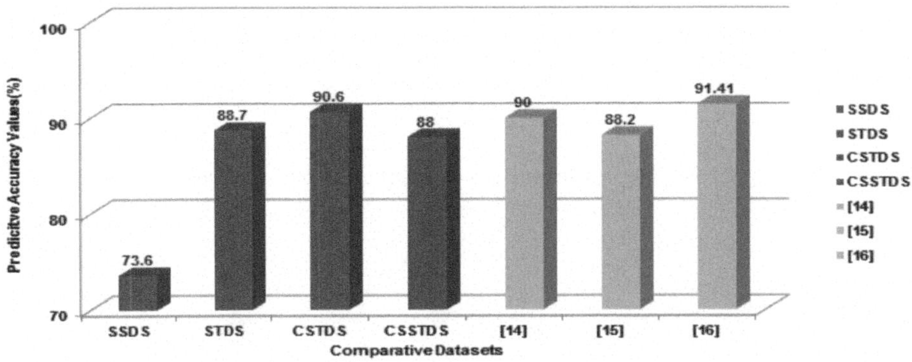

Fig. 17. Comparison of results of present work with the work of [14–16].

From the Fig. 17, it has been observed that the results obtained by this work are more or less in comparison with the works carried out by [14–16]. The PNN algorithm is providing slightly better accuracy as in the case of [14, 15].

The Fig. 18 clearly demonstrates the fact that the process of feature selection does have an impact over the overall classification rates and this chart has been prepared from the different percentage predictive accuracy values obtained and shown through Figs. 13, 14 and 15. There is a negative impact on classification accuracy values in the case of SDS, SSDS, CSTDS and CSSTDS when Random Forest algorithm is used for classification of the dataset. Rest for all the cases when KNN algorithm is used for classification purpose, there is positive impact over the classification results. Maximum effect has been observed in the case of CSTDS and CSSTDS using KNN algorithm.

From the Fig. 19, it is clear that there is a definite positive improvement by computing the percentage predictive accuracy results by combining the texture and shape features together. When the shape feature and texture feature have been added together and then the percentage improvement is around 21.12%, when the RF algorithm is used, and it 16.31% when KNN algorithm is used. When the subset of features is used, RF algorithm improves the results by 19.57% and when KNN algorithm is used for subset of features, the model shows a value of 25.82% as the improvement.

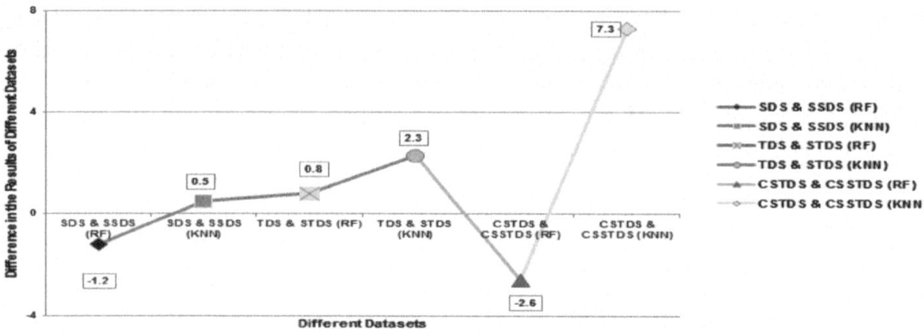

Fig. 18. Studying the net effect of feature selection on classification accuracy values obtained from different datasets.

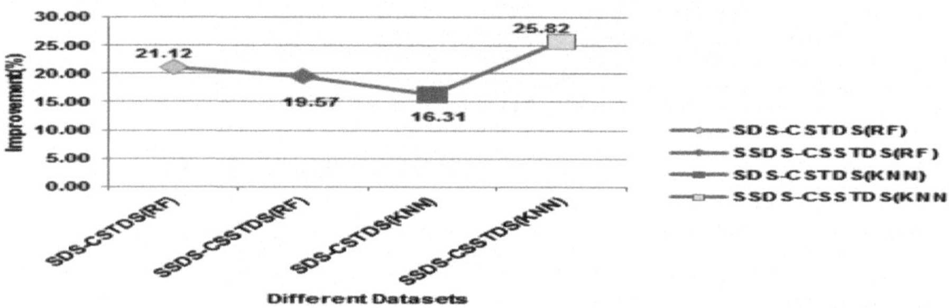

Fig. 19. Improvement in Percentage Predictive Accuracy Results on the addition of Texture Feature dataset to Shape feature dataset.

4 Conclusions

This work utilizes the concept of shape and texture features, testing their ability to classify, independently and in combination. Further, the concept of feature selection for data reduction has been carried out to check whether there is an improvement or downfall in the classification accuracy results. The use of partial dependency plots help in choosing the appropriate features to be selected for inclusion into the feature subset dataset. From the predictive accuracy results, it can be inferred that the shape feature alone will not serve the purpose of plant leaf image classification. There is a need to combine the texture features to improve upon the predictive accuracy values. In the near future, it is proposed to adopt Probabilistic Neural Network (PNN) for the classification purpose.

References

1. Kumar, A., Patidar, V., Khazanchi, D., Saini, P.: Role of feature selection on leaf image classification. J. Data Anal. Inf. Process. **3**, 175–183 (2015). https://doi.org/10.4236/jdaip.2015.34018
2. Bangun, M.B., Herdiyeni, Y., Herliyana, E.N.: Morphological feature extraction of Jabon's leaf seedling pathogen using microscopic image. TELKOMNIKA **14**(1), 254–261 (2016)
3. Saraswat, M., Arya, K.V.: Automated microscopic image analysis for leukocytes identification: a survey. Micron **65**, 20–33 (2014)
4. Yang, M., Kpalma, K., Ronsin, J.: A survey of shape feature extraction techniques. In: Yin, P.-Y. (ed.) Pattern Recognition, IN-TECH 2008, pp. 43–90 (2008). https://hal.archives-ouvertes.fr/hal-00446037
5. Arai, K., Abdullah, I.N., Okumura, H.: Image retrieval based on color, shape and texture for ornamental leaf with medicinal functionality images. Int. J. Image Graph. Sig. Process. **7**, 10–18 (2014)
6. Gonzalez, R.C., Woods, R.E.: Digital Image Processing, 2nd edn. Publishing House of Electronics Industry, Beijing (2004)
7. Geneve, R.: Introduction to Plant Identification. http://dept.ca.uky.edu/PLS220/taxonomymainpage.pdf. Accessed 15 Apr 2017
8. Olson, E.: http://www.ivtnetwork.com/sites/default/files/ImageAnalysis_01.pdf
9. Sonka, M., Hlavac, V., Boyle, R.: Image Processing, Analysis, and Machine Vision, 2nd edn. People's Post & Telecommunications Publishing House, Beijing (2003)
10. Haralick, R.M., Shanmugam, K., Dinstein, I.: Texture features for image classification. IEEE Trans. Syst. Man Cybern. **3**(6), 610–621 (1973)
11. Romanski, P., Kotthoff, L.: FSelector: Selecting Attributes. R package version 0.21. (2016). https://CRAN.R-project.org/package=FSelector. Accessed 5 Apr 2017
12. Hastie, T., Tibshirani, R., Friedman, J.H.: The Elements of Statistical Learning: Data Mining, Inference, and Prediction. Springer, New York (2009). https://doi.org/10.1007/978-0-387-84858-7
13. Milborrow, S.: plotmo: Plot a Model's Response and Residuals. R package version 3.3.3 (2017). https://CRAN.R-project.org/package=plotmo. Accessed 3 June 2017
14. Wu, S.G., Bao, F.S., Xu, E.Y., Wang, Y.-X., Chang, Y.-F., Xiang, Q.-L.: A leaf recognition algorithm for plant classification using probabilistic neural network. In: IEEE International Symposium on Signal Processing and Information Technology, pp. 11–16. IEEE Explore Library (2007)
15. Elhariri, E., Bendary, N.E., Hassanien, A.E.: Plant classification system based on leaf features. In: Ninth International Conference on Computer Engineering & Systems, ICCES, Cairo, Egypt, pp. 271–276 (2014)
16. Hossain, J., Amin, M.A.: Leaf shape identification based plant biometrics. In: Thirteenth International Conference on Computer and Information Technology, ICCIT 2010, Dhaka, Bangladesh (2010)

Performance Measure Based Segmentation Techniques for Skin Cancer Detection

Ginni Arora[1], Ashwani Kumar Dubey[2(✉)], and Zainul Abdin Jaffery[3(✉)]

[1] Amity Institute of Information Technology, Amity University Uttar Pradesh, Noida, UP, India
garora@amity.edu
[2] Amity School of Engineering and Technology, Amity University Uttar Pradesh, Noida, India
dubey1ak@gmail.com
[3] Department of Electrical Engineering, Jamia Millia Islamia, New Delhi, India
zjaffery@jmi.ac.in

Abstract. Skin Cancer is a very common form of cancer which initially starts with investigation and analysis going through biopsy and examination. Doing analysis is the most challenging task as it depends on appearance of skin lesion. Computer Aided Diagnostic (CAD) system have been developed for skin cancer detection which goes through various phases starting from pre-processing, segmentation, feature extraction & selection and classification of cancer type. Segmentation is an important as well as difficult phase which extracts the lesion from non-lesion area depending on variation in terms of color, texture, size and shape. In this paper, different segmentation techniques have been discussed, Otsu thresholding as Pixel Based Segmentation, Canny edge detection as Edge based Segmentation, Watershed as Region Based Segmentation and K-Means as Clustering based Segmentation. The performance of techniques have been measured by Peak Signal Noise Ratio (PSNR), Mean Square Error (MSE) and Structure Similarity Index Measure (SSIM) using MATLAB.

Keywords: MSE · PSNR · Skin cancer · Segmentation · SSIM

1 Introduction

Skin cancer is a type of cancer which is more common that usually begins within the skin cell. This type of skin disease (non-melanoma) is usually started in the basal cells or squamous cells. These cells are found at the base of the outer layer of the skin. The exposure of the skin to sunlight is considered the main cause of the development of the most basal and squamous cell cancers. Dermoscopy is a predominantly and a very helpful standard method to diagnose the malignancy [1].

An expected 87,110 new instances of melanoma will be analyzed in the US in 2017. Frequency rates are higher in ladies than in men before age 50, however by age 65, rates in men are twofold those in ladies, and by age 80 they are triple. This example reflects age and sex contrasts in word related and recreational presentation to bright radiation (counting the utilization of indoor tanning), and maybe early discovery practices and utilization of human services. In 2017, an expected 9,730 passing's from melanoma will

B. Panda et al. (Eds.): REDSET 2017, CCIS 799, pp. 226–233, 2018.
https://doi.org/10.1007/978-981-10-8527-7_20

happen. Despite the fact that the US Preventive Services Task Force as of late announced that there is deficient proof to prescribe for or against visual skin examination by a clinician for individuals at normal danger of skin tumor, the most ideal approach to distinguish skin malignancy early is to know about new or changing skin developments, especially those that look abnormal. Any new sores, or a dynamic change in an injury's appearance (size, shape, or shading, and so on), ought to be assessed instantly by a doctor. The ABCDE run plots cautioning indications of the most well-known kind of melanoma: A is for asymmetry (one portion of the mole does not coordinate the other half); B is for fringe anomaly (the edges are battered, indented, or obscured); C is for shading (the pigmentation is not uniform, with variable degrees of tan, darker, or dark); D is for distance across more noteworthy than 6 mm (about the measure of a pencil eraser); and E is for advancement, which means an adjustment in the mole's appearance [2].

Initially skin cancer starts with investigation and analysis, a biopsy and examination. Analysis through images is a challenging task as appearance of skin lesion can make the difference. CAD (Computer Aided Diagnostic System) is built for automated analysis of skin lesion but accuracy is still a demanding factor. These systems constitutes of following phases: 1. Pre-processing, 2. Segmentation, 3. Feature Extraction, and 4. Classification. Segmentation is an important as well as difficult phase which extracts the lesion from non-lesion area depending on variation in terms of color, texture, size and shape. Figure 1 shows sample images of different skin cancer types from ISIC (International Skin Imaging Collaboration) Archive [3]. These images are further used for

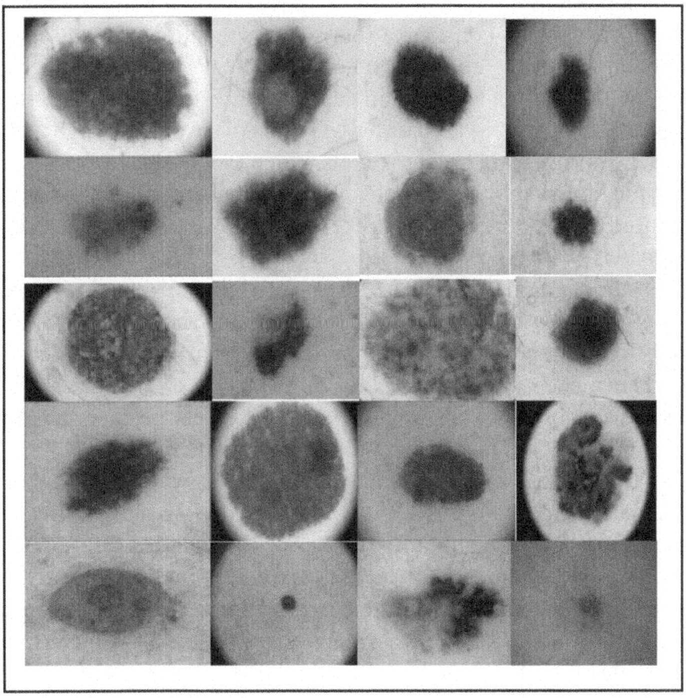

Fig. 1. Skin cancer images

segmentation process. These segmentation techniques broadly classified as: Pixel Based, Edge Based, Region Based and Clustering Based segmentation. In this paper focus has been given on standard techniques defined under broad categories.

2 Segmentation Techniques

Image segmentation is a division process in which digital images are divided into multiple segments in such a way that it is more meaningful as well as easier to evaluate. It is particularly used in finding the object and boundary of an image which is processed by allotting a tag to each and every pixel of the image, thus pixels having similar tag shares a certain characteristic. Otsu thresholding is Pixel based segmentation, Canny edge detection is Edge based Segmentation, Watershed as Region Based Segmentation and K-Means as Clustering based Segmentation. Each of these techniques has different methods of segmentation.

Otsu Thresholding skin lesion image, on the basis of gray level distribution separate the objects of interest from the background selection of an optimal gray level threshold value have become a basic objective. In thresholding, binary images is created based on grey level by converting pixels having below threshold to zero whereas pixel having about that threshold to one. Otsu's thresholding chooses the threshold in order to minimise the variation in intraclass of white and black pixels of threshold [4].

Canny edge detector is defined as the standard benchmark for comparing with other edge detection methods.

Canny detector algorithm consists of four steps as mentioned: (1) usage of Gaussian convolution to blur the image and reduce noise effects (2) usage of Sobel operator and finding the 2D spatial gradient to determine the edge directions and strength (3) use edge direction to search and suppress the non-edge pixels (4) using two high and low thresholds, eliminate edges which are broken, pixels which crosses the high threshold and also lies in between the high and low thresholds that are adjacent to the edge are edge pixels. However Canny edge detector can detect pixels which is near to the edge, but its accuracy is low in finding the exact edges [5].

Watershed segmentation algorithm is considered as half breed technique between group based segmentation and edge based segmentation. The objective of the watershed segmentation is to find the watershed line in the image provided in order to find prominent regions. The concept behind this algorithm is based on flooding water process in topographic surface, flowing from lowest basin to highest peak, water flows into the holes and flood the surface. Thus dam is built to prevent merging of two different basins in which boundary of two connected dam is considered as watershed edges. Though the resultant segmented image leads to the over divided of regions and the time consumption is high, it has advantage over continuity of region's boundaries [4].

As compared to other segmentation techniques, k-means clustering differs from other types of segmentation techniques that the desired numbers of segment or cluster were specified by the analyst. During the classification procedure in K-means, the distances of cluster centers from each respondent are calculated. This procedure is repeated until the distance between skin lesion cluster centers is maximized while respondents are assigned to the cluster with the nearest Centre. Conversion of RGB to any other color requires number of clusters and sensitive to noise. The K-means technique is highly preferred over other techniques because it is simple, easy and versatile in its implementation. And, it is also computationally faster than hierarchical clustering with linear time and storage complexity. However, one of the most disadvantages of this technique is that it requires number of clusters and is sensitive to noise [5].

3 Performance Measures

There are many types of performance measurement available to evaluate on the performance analysis of different methods in image segmentation. Among those methods, the most efficient technique is selected with the help of performance analysis. This analyses thoroughly on the parameters value which can be either low or high with respective to the type of parameter used.
List of quality parameters used for image segmentation are as follow:

- PSNR (Peak Signal to noise)
- MSE (Mean Square Error)
- SSIM (Structural Similarity Index)

3.1 PSNR

It is a measurement of quality of image in mathematical form which is based on pixel difference between two images and is measured in terms of decibels scale [6]. PSNR value of image is directly proportional to the quality of an image i.e. higher the value betters the quality. It is usually used as a measure to reconstruct the quality of an image. In case, if, the value of PSNR is above 30, clarity in output image is 100%. PSNR of two images is calculated as given by [7] shown in (1):

$$Y_{PSNR} = 10\log_{10}\left(\frac{MAX}{X_{MSE}}\right) \tag{1}$$

Where,

MSE = Mean Square error
MAX = value of maximum pixel in the image, usually it's 255 for 8 bit image

3.2 MSE (Mean Square Error)

It is calculated by every picture element in which squared differences of all the pixels are added and divides it by total number of pixel count. In segmented image MSE can be calculated by using the equation given by [8] shown in (2):

$$MSE = \frac{1}{MN}\sum_{y=1}^{M}\sum_{x=1}^{N}\left[I(x,y) - I'(x,y)\right]^2 \tag{2}$$

Where, M and N are number of rows and columns in the given image. I(x, y) is the original image, I'(x, y) is the approximated version. Unlike PSNR, in MSE lower the value leads to the less error obtain higher quality of segmented image.

3.3 SSIM (Structural Similarity Index)

It is a strategy for measuring the similarity between two images based on its structure, contrast and luminance from the same image captured. The SSIM measures the image quality by referencing the uncompressed image so it is also called as reference metric. SSIM is calculated using the following equation given by [9] shown in (3):

$$\mathrm{SSIM}(x,y) = \left(2\mu_x\mu_y + c1\right)(2\sigma_{xy} + c2)/\left(\mu_x^2 + \mu_y^2 + c1\right)(\sigma_x^2 + \sigma_y^2 + c2) \tag{3}$$

Where μ_x is the average of x, μ_y is the average of y, σ_{xy} is covariance of x and y, σ_y^2 is the variance of y and σ_x^2 is the variance of x.

4 Experimentation and Results

Based on the selected 10 images from Fig. 1, performance measures are calculated for each of the different type of segmentation techniques. As discussed above the property of each performance technique, the value of mean square error should be less, while the higher the value of PSNR, the better it is. The MSE and the PSNR mainly estimate the absolute error while the SSIM takes into consideration the image degradation as perceived change in structural information. The value of SSIM should be lower. In the above calculations, canny segmentation technique produces the desired result. The MSE value is the less; PSNR is high while the SSIM is also less as desired. This means canny gives a closer view of segmented skin cancer image. Table 1 shows different segmentation techniques with their MSE, PSNR and SSIM values. Lowest MSE, higher PSNR and closest to 1 SSIM is highlighted in bold for each segmentation. Figure 2 represents the graphical view of segmentation techniques based on performance measures. Lowest MSE with redline, higher PSNR with blue line and SSIM nearest to 1 with green line is accurate through canny segmentation technique.

Table 1. Segmentation techniques with performance measures

Segmentation technique	Image sample no	MSE	PSNR	SSIM
Threshold	S1	255	24.0994	1
	S2	254.84	24.1021	1
	S3	255	24.0994	1
	S4	255	24.0994	1
	S5	255	24.0994	1
	S6	255.02	24.09913	1
	S7	255.03	24.09886	1
	S8	255.047	24.09859	1
	S9	255.06	24.09832	1
	S10	255.078	24.09805	1
Canny	S1	0.5816	50.5187	0.3583
	S2	0.5569	50.7069	0.3738
	S3	0.9309	48.4759	0.0484
	S4	0.9315	48.4728	0.0354
	S5	0.7749	49.2726	0.1828
	S6	0.8052	49.1055	0.156
	S7	0.6349	50.1379	0.3109
	S8	0.9413	48.4277	0.0359
	S9	0.8398	48.9233	0.1223
	S10	0.7832	49.226	0.1607
Watershed	S1	30.8132	33.2774	0.9491
	S2	73.7266	29.4886	0.9212
	S3	70.0962	29.7079	0.846
	S4	63.698	30.1235	0.8451
	S5	90.4841	28.5991	0.901
	S6	117.498	27.4645	0.8147
	S7	118.3323	27.4338	0.8809
	S8	147.3902	26.4801	0.7437
	S9	60.6543	30.3362	0.9196
	S10	91.4905	28.551	0.8001
K-means	S1	234.2328	24.4683	0.0195
	S2	188.9799	25.4006	0.1673
	S3	167.9884	25.912	0.2232
	S4	241.1214	24.3424	0.0403
	S5	215.7924	24.8242	0.0767
	S6	220.0032	24.7405	0.0677
	S7	213.1593	24.8778	0.1145
	S8	171.3275	25.8265	0.2652
	S9	209.9161	24.9443	0.1445
	S10	220.1154	24.7383	0.0619

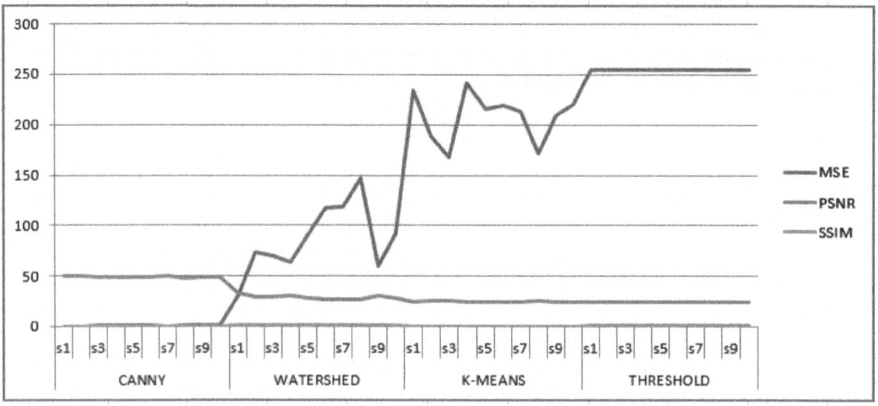

Fig. 2. Analysis of segmentation techniques (Color figure online)

5 Conclusion

Skin cancer cases are increasing day by day so early detection can reduce the chances to avoid deadliest stage. Computer Aided Diagnostic systems are used for this purpose in which segmentation process plays a major role for further classification. This paper highlights major segmentation techniques for differentiating skin lesion area. Further, analyses of these techniques are done through the Mean Square Error, Peak Signal Noise Ratio and Structure Similarity Index performance measures. Canny Segmentation technique resulted to be the best for segmentation of skin cancer images due to low MSE value, high PSNR value and SSIM nearest to 1.

References

1. Urooj, S., Singh, S.: A novel computer assisted approach for diagnosis of skin disease. In: International Conference on Computing for Sustainable Global Development, pp. 1585–1590 (2015)
2. Cancer Facts and Figures. (2017). American Cancer Society. https://www.cancer.org/research/cancer-facts-statistics/all-cancer-facts-figures/cancer-facts-figures-2017.html. Accessed 31 July 2017
3. https://isic-archive.com/. Accessed 31 July 2017
4. Farooq, M.A., Azhar, M.M., Raza, R.H.: Automatic Lesion Detection System (ALDS) for skin cancer classification using SVM and neural classifiers. In: International Conference on Bioinformatics and Bioengineering, pp. 302–308 (2016)
5. Revathi, V.L., Chithra, A.S.: A review on segmentation techniques in skin lesion images. Int. Res. J. Eng. Technol. **2**(9), 2598–2603 (2015)
6. Iqbal, S., Sheetlani, J.: Application of modified K means clustering algorithm in segmentation of medical images of brain tumor. Biosci., Biotechnol. Res. Asia **14**, 735–739 (2017)

7. Jain, S., Goswami, S.: An efficient approach of segmentation and blind deconvolution in image restoration. IOSR J. Comput. Eng. **17**(6), 41–46 (2015)
8. Wang, Z., Bovik, A.C.: Mean squared error: love it or leave it? IEEE Sig. Process. Mag. 99–117 (2009)
9. Gobindchandra, K., Kumar, S.: Analysis of image segmentation techniques. Int. Res. J. Comput. Sci. **2**(6), 45–53 (2015)

Effectiveness of Region Growing Based Segmentation Technique for Various Medical Images - A Study

Manju Dabass(✉), Sharda Vashisth(✉), and Rekha Vig

The NorthCap University, Gurgaon 121102, Haryana, India
manjurashi87@gmail.com,
{shardavashisth, rekhavig}@ncuindia.edu

Abstract. Due to rapid and continuous progress along with higher fidelity rate, medical imaging is becoming one of the most crucial fields in scientific imaging. Both microscopic and macroscopic modalities are probed and their resulting images are analyzed and interpreted in medical imaging for the early detection, diagnosis, and treatment of various ailments like a tumor, cancer, gallstones, etc. Although the field of medical image processing is growing significantly and persistently, there still exist a number of challenges in this field. Among these challenges, the frequently occurring and critically significant one is image segmentation. The theme work presented in this paper includes challenges involved and comparative analysis of segmentation using region growing techniques frequently utilized in various biomedical images like retinal vessel image, mammograms, magnetic resonance images, PET-CT image, coronary artery image, microscopy image, ultrasound image, etc. It discusses the effectiveness of the region growing technique applied on various medical images.

Keywords: Biomedical image processing · Image segmentation
Threshold · Region growing

1 Introduction

Medical Imaging is the process of creating visual representation at the microscopic level i.e. cells and tissues and at the macroscopic level i.e. organs and systems of the human body (a term coined as bio-medical images) and then applying set of image processing techniques for diagnostic as well as therapeutic purposes. Bio-medical images are captured using different imaging techniques utilizing either light (endoscopy, OCT), magnetism (MRI), radioactive pharmaceuticals (nuclear medicine: PET, SPECT), X-rays (CT scan) or sound (ultrasound). These biomedical images are used for assessment of the current condition of the tissue or organs and thus aid in diagnosis with high accuracy.

The term biomedical image processing means applying digital image processing techniques for biomedical science. All the major areas covered in image processing used for biomedical images are shown in Fig. 1.

In biomedical imaging, a lot of research has been done but still, there are some challenges left on which progressive work is continuously going on. The various

B. Panda et al. (Eds.): REDSET 2017, CCIS 799, pp. 234–259, 2018.
https://doi.org/10.1007/978-981-10-8527-7_21

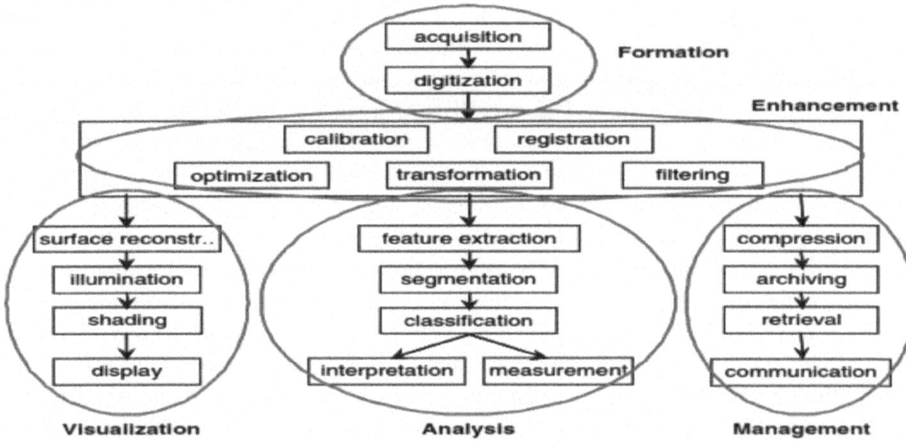

Fig. 1. Modules of image processing. In general, image processing covers four main areas: image formation, visualization, analysis, and management. The algorithms of image enhancement can be assigned as pre- and post processing in all areas.

challenges present in medical imaging are in restoration, enhancement, segmentation, registration as well as fusion of multimodality images, classification along with quantitative measurement of image features and their interpretation and lastly the development of an integrated system which can work for clinical use. From all these challenges, the proper segmentation technique for biomedical images is quite a critical one.

Segmentation can be termed as partitioning an image into its constituent regions or objects or, it can be defined as dividing the individual elements present in an image or volume into a set of groups in which all elements of a group have a common property. In the medical domain, image segmentation is usually done to partition the elements of medical images which belong to the same tissue type or organ. There are following few concerns related to medical image segmentation:

1. Usually, only a few structures are of main interest in medical images which contain not only a lot of information but also noise and other image artifacts. Thus, the complete segmentation process should not be only about segmenting the images but it must also include the application of enhancement techniques for preprocessing step to remove unwanted elements along with visual enhancement of certain features and application of filtering and conditioning as post-processing step for further removal of certain imperfections which appear as undesirable objects in addition to segmentation techniques. Hence, the basic segmentation process should incorporate noise removal first, and then initial segmentation and knowledge-based information refinements. In this way, segmentation would result in visualization of the relevant structures along with the removal of the unnecessary information.
2. The other main concern is the level to which this subdivision is carried out i.e., it should stop when the required objects or regions of interest present in images are detected. For example in EEG images, segmentation should stop when the tumor affected cells present in the brain are detected. For this purpose, stopping criteria should also be included in the segmentation process.

Hence, overall segmentation is a difficult, labor-intensive, error-prone and very time-consuming procedure. Due to all these factors, segmentation comes under one of the most tedious and complicated task categories and calls for the considerable amount of care in its whole procedure. The overall success and failure of any computerized analysis procedure depend on the accuracy with which segmentation is done. The application areas of image segmentation for biomedical imaging are quite wide. It is used for segmenting various region of interest like a tumor, gallstones, cancer, etc. which is the basic requirement for the diagnosis. Apart from partitioning the image, segmentation is also useful in image registration as well as structure analysis, for example, in the calculation of tumor volume in organs. Also, nowadays telemedicine is used for transmission of medical images as well as videos of patients to physicians for their opinion on the diagnosis. Thus, medical imaging plays a very vital role in the medical field especially in surgical planning process along with the diagnosis. But, the various imaging device used in this field generate a very large amount of data and that also for a single patient which further has the requirement of a long-term storage as well as a very efficient transmission. The currently used compression schemes have the capability of producing high compression rates but only with some loss of quality. But for the proper and accurate diagnosis, any kind of missing information present in diagnostically critical regions in biomedical images can't be afforded. Thus, it is quite necessary to preserve good quality for the ROI along with high compression rate. The approach for achieving this goal is to use lossless encoding for diagnostically important regions and lossy encoding for the remaining regions. This can't be achieved without segmentation process. Thus, segmentation is critically important and unavoidable step in biomedical imaging.

Currently, there are many different segmentation techniques used for biomedical images like region based, threshold, edges based, recognition based, deformable models, atlas-based, radiation active contour, wavelets based etc. But still, no one is able to say exactly which method for segmentation is best and can give an accurate result. The choice of method for segmentation depends solely on the application area, the type of image taken and the structure which is to be segmented.

In this paper, the aim is primarily focused on the use of one of the regions based segmentation technique known as region growing for the various biomedical images. Thus, this technique will be discussed at length over here.

2 Basic Concepts of Region Growing Segmentation

As the name implies, region growing is a procedure in which pixels are grouped into larger regions based on some predefined conditions. For this purpose, a region is defined as a connected set of pixels i.e., a set where all the pixels are adjacent or touching. For finding connectivity there are mainly two criteria used, four-connectivity and eight-connectivity and either of these can be adopted. To find the four-connectivity, only lateral adjacent pixels i.e., up, down, left and right are considered to be connected. Thus, only four neighbors would be there for each pixel. On the other hand for finding eight-connectivity, diagonally adjacent i.e., forty-five degree eight neighboring pixels are also checked for connectedness in addition to four neighbors, due to which each pixel now has eight neighbors to which it can be connected.

The basic approach used in a region growing segmentation is to select a seed point (a pixel from where segmentation would begin) and then grow regions from this seed pixel. The process begins by dividing an image into many tiny regions which can be a small neighborhood or even single pixel. Thus, the whole process is divided into two parts and these are:

1. **Selection of Seed Pixel:** This can be done by picking up an arbitrary pixel from the image that needs to be segmented.
2. **Region Growing:** For this connectivity (either four or eight connectivity) of the nearest neighbors of the seed pixel is examined one by one. The neighboring pixel is accepted in the same region if they together satisfy the homogeneity criterion. For example, if the condition $|X_g - X_c| < e$ is satisfied then only the neighboring pixels would add to the region, where X_g denotes the intensity of the compared neighborhood pixel, X_c denotes the intensity of the seed pixel and 'e' is some threshold value. This 'e' plays an important role in segmentation as the bigger value of 'e' can lead to overgrowth of the segmented region while its smaller value can limit the extension of the seed point set. This whole procedure goes on recursively until no new pixel is accepted. This region growing process is continued until stopping criteria would not meet and the threshold is achieved and thus, no new pixel can be accepted further. In this way, the segmentation gets completed.

The region growing algorithms are more expensive in terms of computation than the other simpler techniques but it is able to utilize several image properties directly as well as simultaneously for determining the various objects' boundary. Also, it shows the greatest promise in the segmentation of complex scene where strong a priori knowledge is not available. The various methods for finding the accuracy of the region growing technique are as follows:

(i) **First method**: In this method, first the following metrics are calculated,

TP: true positive, the classification result is positive in presence of malignancy.
TN: true negative, the classification result is negative in being benign.
FP: false positive, the classification result is positive in being benign.
FN: false negative, the classification result is negative in presence of malignancy.
According to above definitions the equation for accuracy is calculated as follows:

$$Accuracy = \frac{TP + TN}{TP + TN + FP + FN} \tag{1}$$

Based upon this equation, the accuracy rate is measured in retinal images, mammograms, and angiograms.

(ii) **Second method**: In this, four error metrics are used: XOR measure coefficient, *Hausdorff* distance, Jaccard similarity coefficient and Volumetric overlap fraction (VOF). Let *X* be manual segmentation region observed by the expert and *Y* be the segmentation region comes out by automatic algorithm, thus

$$XOR = (region(X \cup Y) - region(X \cap Y))/region(X) \tag{2}$$

$$Jaccard = region(X \cap Y)/region(X \cup Y) \tag{3}$$

where *region(I)* is denoting the number of pixels in *I*.

Let *borderX* be the border pixels of *X* and *borderY* be the border pixels of *Y*, thus, Hausdorff distance is calculated as

$$Hausdorff = \max(h(X,Y), h(Y,X)) \tag{4}$$

in which

$$h(X,Y) = max_{x \in borderX} min_{y \in borderY} \|x - y\| \tag{5}$$

where x is a point on the border of X, y is the point on the border of Y and $\|x - y\|$ denotes the Euclidean distance between x and y.

The VOF between the volume of X and Y is given by:

$$VOF(V_X, V_Y) = |V_X \cap V_Y|/|V_X \cup V_Y| \tag{6}$$

where V_X is the volume of the segmented image by the expert and V_Y is the volume calculated by the automated segmentation method.

In general, a low XOR and Hausdorff distance signify a better segmentation result whereas a high Jaccard and VOF represent a better segmentation result.

3 Region Growing Segmentation in Various Medical Images

3.1 Retinal Images

There are many diseases like diabetes, stroke, hypertension etc. where the change in retinal vessels occurs and can lead to the vision loss [1–5]. But this situation can be prevented by a proper and periodic screening of retinal vessels and analyze them for recognition of any changes in their structure. Thus, a pre-requisite for diagnosis of any retinal disease is the accurate segmentation of the retinal vessels. But there exist several challenges in the segmentation process like, the existence of other structures like fovea, optic disc, etc. along with retinal vessels in the retinal image due to which automatic segmentation of having only retinal vessels becomes difficult. The other challenge is the presence of wide range of the retinal vessel's width in which thin vessels are having a low contrast in comparison to the background, thus making the object detection a harder task.

There have been many methods proposed for the accurate segmentation of retinal vessels from using matched filters and adaptive thresholding to use of zero-mean Gaussian function and first-order derivative of Gaussian (FDOG) [6–8]. In [9], authors proposed an improved segmentation method based on graph theory approach for segmenting 3D retina layers from low-quality Optical Coherence Tomography (OCT) images. In [10], authors used a segmentation algorithm based on level set and region growing. The whole process is divided into three parts: pre-processing, segmentation and post-processing. For pre-processing, contrast limited adaptive histogram equalization (CLAHE) is applied so that the adverse effects of non-uniform lighting can be compensated. The CLAHE first computes the local histogram mapping function and then determines the clipping level for histogram flexibility, which further helps in reducing the unwanted noise amplification of retinal image. This is followed by 2D Gabor wavelet transformation which enhances the contrast in the frequency domain for the retinal image.

After this, the segmentation of retinal vessel is conducted in two simultaneous ways. The first way is for extracting wide retinal vessels by the application of active contour model in which anisotropic diffusion filter is used to smoothened the retinal image while preserving the boundaries of retinal vessels, thus contributing to efficient and accurate segmentation for retinal vessels while the second parallel way is for detecting thin vessels by directly applying region growing which was not possible by the earlier way of level set method. Then, by the inclusion of a post-processing stage, the final segmented results are obtained in which first results of different retinal vessel segmentation from both processes are combined and then isolated vessel pixels are removed which are detected falsely. The comparison of level set and region growing techniques for the segmentation of thin vessels discussed in this paper is shown in Fig. 2.

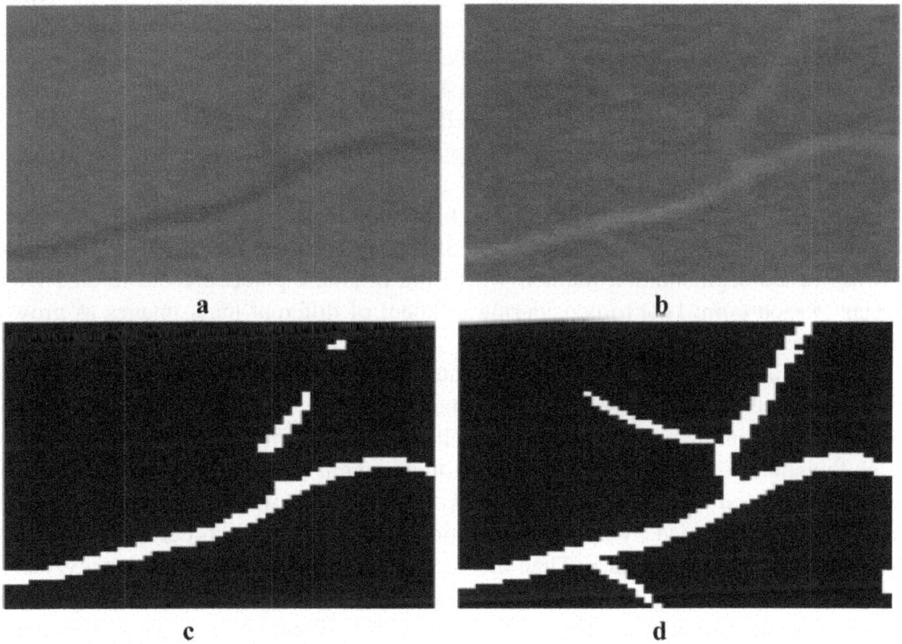

Fig. 2. Comparison of level set and region growing for thin retinal vessel segmentation: (a) and (b) amplified fragment of the original retinal image and the green channel image, (c)–(d) segmentation results by level set and region growing, respectively [10]

3.2 Mammograms

One of the most frequent causes of death in women is breast cancer. Due to breast cancer, abnormal multiplication of cells occurs in breast tissue. The only effective diagnosis for it is early detection and effective treatment. And this can be done by the accurate study of mammograms and efficient segmentation of tumor where its main characteristics, especially boundaries are preserved. In mammograms, there are different types of abnormalities such as micro-calcifications and masses are present where the micro-calcifications are the calcium deposits mainly due to the secretion of milk glands present in the breast and appear as individual clusters and on the other hand, masses are attributes such as lumps, lesion or protuberance occurred in the breast. The range of individual micro-calcifications can vary from twenty microns in diameter to hundreds of microns in diameter. Since masses have lower contrast than micro-calcifications in mammograms, their efficient detection and accurate diagnose becomes a challenging problem.

There have been a lot of recent developments made aiming at better diagnosis for various abnormalities present in breast and thus increasing the survival chance. One of them is CAD (computer-aided diagnosis) which is mainly a set of semi-automatic or fully-automatic tools with the use of computer technology which helps radiologists in the detection and proper classification of abnormalities present in breast [12]. As a result, radiologists now are more interested in using CAD systems. Mainly, a CAD system consists of three main stages and these are segmentation, feature extraction and classification stage [13]. Thus, efficient segmentation becomes the most influential stage of all and overall success of a CAD system is totally dependent on this.

In mammograms, there are generally two types of regions i.e., breast and non-breast. For diagnosis masses, the first step is cropping the region of interest (ROI) from the breast area. Usually, in an ROI, pixels present inside the masses have the highest intensity due to which they appear as visual continuous variations. Thus, a region growing procedure must segment masses in ROIs in order to imply these characteristics. A lot of advancement has happened in the region growing procedure from detecting a seed point to the selection of appropriate threshold value [11] to region growing based segmentation method where the brightest pixels present in an ROI is chosen as seed point [14] to considering gradient of different mass images as growth criteria.

In [15], authors proposed two automated segmentation approaches to diagnose benign and malign mass types present in mammograms. Their first approach is based on automated region growing. It is basically an improvement of region growing in which threshold is obtained by a trained artificial neural network (ANN). Their second approach is based on cellular neural network (CNN) in which parameters for segmentation are calculated by applying genetic algorithm (GA) in order to preserve the information of tumor boundary. Then the various features like textural, intensity, shape features are extracted from the segmented tumor and from that set of various extracted features, selection of appropriate features is done by utilizing genetic algorithm. In the next stage, ANNs are used to detect benign and malignant mammograms. The last stage is the classification stage for detecting the benign and malignant tumor. In this way, the improvement of region growing based segmentation is performed by extracting intensity features from the ROIs and then ANN is applied to generate an adaptive threshold for proper and efficient segmentation of tumor. The result of region growing technique is shown in Fig. 3.

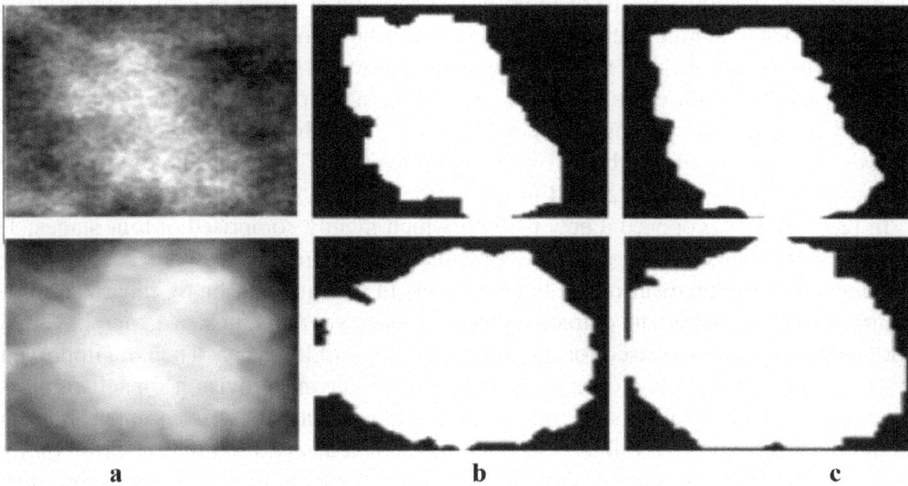

Fig. 3. Results of segmentation based on region growing corresponding two images: (a) original images, (b) segmented images, and (c) target images [15].

3.3 PET-CT Image

The highest mortality rate among all the cancers is of lung cancer. Every year lot of death are recorded owing to this cancer. Thus to improve this scenario, it is crucial for lung cancer affected patients to have the early diagnosis and effective treatment in order to have an increment in their survival rate. For early detection of lung cancer, a CAD system plays a very pivotal role [16]. Many medical imaging modalities like Ultra-Sonography, Computed Tomography (CT), Magnetic Resonance Imaging (MRI) and Positron Emission Tomography (PET) are used to detect lung cancer. Out of all imaging modalities, the most robust one is PET-CT.

For lung cancer analysis, the very first step for a CAD system is the segmentation of pulmonary parenchyma which further becomes the basis for various post-processing like pulmonary nodules detection, in 3-D reconstruction and for visualization analysis. Thus, the high efficiency and accuracy are the critical requirement in the lung segmentation for the detection of lung edges along with complete preservation of lung region.

Earlier threshold-based segmentation methods based were used for easy as well as quick extraction of pulmonary parenchyma. But these methods inhibit some limitations: 1. The density of lesion area is quite close to pleura, thus there remains the possibility of its removal from lung region. 2. The removal of the tracheal bronchus areas is quite difficult. In recent years, lots of segmentation techniques are proposed to solve these problems. Some methods applied the artificial auxiliary strategy of refining for accurate lung segmentation and then merging the lesion area into a region of the lung which was present near pleura [17, 18]. The results got with this segmentation were quite accurate but being time-consuming, failed to meet the CAD systems requirement. After this, in [19], authors proposed a 3-D method for lung volume segmentation by the use of adaptive 3-D based region growing algorithm in which automatic seed location by fuzzy logic was incorporated. Then in [20], authors gave adaptive border marching method based on a threshold for correcting lung boundary. But this was not applicable to CT sequences. So in [21], authors gave hybrid segmentation method with error detection. After this, a lot of other methods have been proposed for using morphological operation along with threshold-based segmentation methods to using methods based on a combination of 3-D thresholding and 2-D wavelet edge highlighting [22] and much more.

In [23], authors proposed a new method which mainly comprised of four stages: 1. Binarization of image, 2. Rough lung segmentation using region growing, 3. Denoising of image and 4. Refinement of the lung contour. In this method, firstly binarization of CT images is performed to extract regions of interest. After this, a general seeded region growing method is used for rough segmentation of lung area. Then the improved region growing method based on eight connectivity having provision for left-right as well as four corners rotating scanning is applied to eradicate noise from upper, bottom and middle lung region for different morphological characteristics. Finally, morphology operations like corrosion, expansion are used for refinement of lung contour and thus getting the final lung segmentation results. This is a more efficient as well as accurate method as compared with other methods.

The comparison of images resulted in the manual as well as automated segmentation is shown in Fig. 4.

3.4 2-D X-Ray Angiograms

The gold standard used for the assessment of coronary artery diseases is X-Ray Coronary Angiography (XCA) in which the obtained angiograms revealed the initial symptoms of coronary artery diseases with the use of various morphological features like length, branching angle, diameter, tortuosity of coronary arteries. However, vessel tracking in XCA is a very complicated task because of various factors such as image noise, in-homogenous illumination, complex vessel structure and poor contrast. Thus, accurate detection of coronary vessels comes in the category of fundamental steps for success in many applications of medical imaging like stenosis detection [25], assessment of cardiac dynamics [27] and 3-D reconstruction [26].

Two important tasks for accurate vessel detection are an enhancement of features and segmentation of blood. The main aim of enhancement step is a reduction of artifacts present in the background with an improvement in vessels delineation. A wide variety of enhancement methods especially for vessels have been proposed which are classified by Truc et al. as (i) Linear Filtering, (ii) Non-Linear anisotropic Filtering (iii) Hessian-based Multi-scale Filtering. Anyone of them can be chosen according to the application required.

After enhancement, the next step applied for vascular analysis is the segmentation of vessels. For angiograms, two classes are there for all existing segmentation methods i.e., based on skeleton and non-skeleton [28]. In the skeleton based methods, first

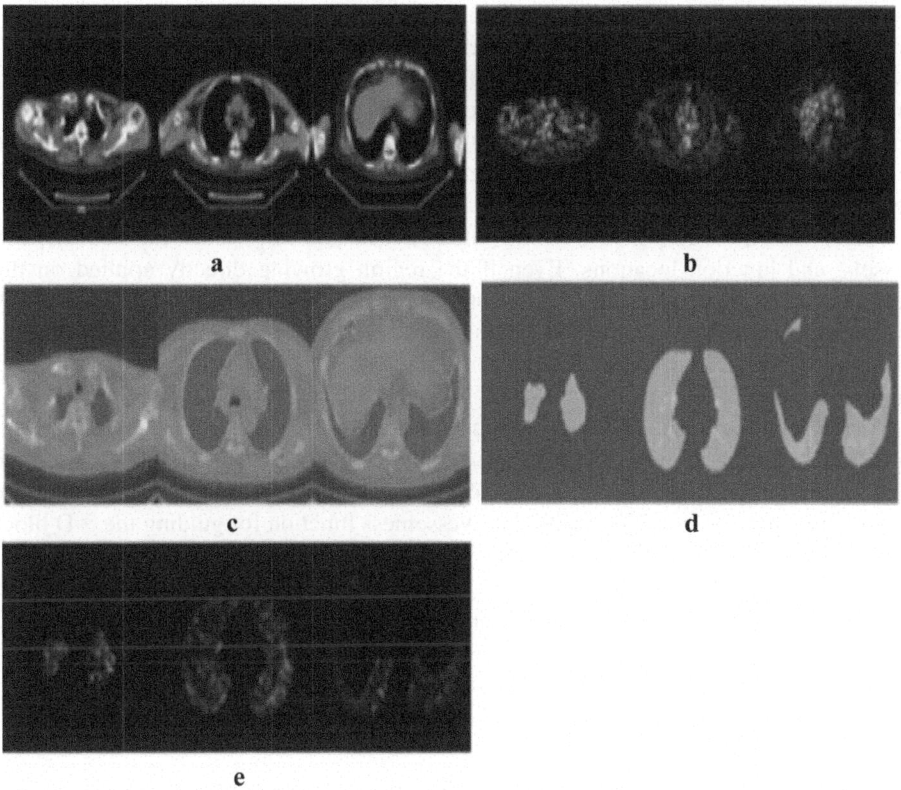

Fig. 4. The results of manual segmentation and automatic segmentation. (a) The upper, middle, and bottom part of lung in original CT images; (b) the original PET images; (c) the segmentation results in CT images by the expert; (d) the segmentation results in CT using the proposed method; (e) the segmentation results in PET by our method [24].

centrelines are detected and after this, vessel-width is estimated. But this method is suffered from limitations i.e., failed in vessels segmentation's approximation where stenosis and bifurcations are present. Quite opposite to this are the segmentation techniques based on non-skeleton where the vessels are extracted directly. The various methods which come under this category are fuzzy clustering, deformable models based on level set and active contour, thresholding, graph cuts, morphology, and region growing.

Region growing technique is widely popular for particular medical imaging applications like vessel extraction as being a connectivity-based technique suits the vascular trees favorably. There are many factors like stenosis, noise and image artifacts, etc. present in coronary artery angiograms that result in discontinuities. Due to all these factors, region growing often leads to over-segmentation and introduction of false negatives known as holes [31]. To overcome such limitations, many techniques for growing process have been proposed. Like in [29], the region growing process was performed for many frames utilizing the same sequence. Although temporal tracking usage had avoided the problem of discontinuities, the challenges like the requirement of user interaction for each step and centreline matching were left unattended. To overcome these limitations, authors in [32] used a frangi-vesselness filter in order to introduce more seed points in growth process when stopping threshold was attained by one seed point. After this, authors in [30] gave a new vesselness function and hence, proposed a vessel segmentation which comprised of two steps. In its first step, large vessels were extracted by region growing from the maximum vesselness response. But this final vesselness response was still inflicted with the low values for stenosis, thin vessels, and junction locations. Even if the region growing directly applied on this vesselness image, the occurrence of discontinuities cannot be marginalized. Due to this, a repairing process was launched where thin vessels were extracted by the use of direction information given by the intensity gradient of the image which was basically the first directional directives.

It seems to be a good idea in which vessel tracking is performed by combining directional information with the vesselness function. Thus, the authors in [33] used this idea and proposed a technique where the hessian Eigenvector gave the line direction information that was combined with Sato vesselness function for guiding the 3-D blood segmentation.

By taking all these ideas, authors in [34] proposed a technique where they introduced the multi-scale vessel segmentation. Normally, two major problems occur in vessel segmentation i.e., difficulty in detection of poorly enhanced vessels and occurrence of holes i.e., false positives. This method overcomes these problems by using the multi-scale strength analysis of Hessian matrix. Mainly, this paper has given the following findings:

1. A novel region growing technique based on features like Eigenvectors and Eigenvalues of hessian matrix integrated with multi-scale analysis for ensuring the proper detection of vessels which are of different sizes,
2. An Evaluation database is proposed where two datasets of different challenging degrees are there for doing the quantitative evaluation in terms of precision, region-overlapping, and sensitivity of the region growing methods.
3. Enhancement is done by frangi vesselness filter which removes background noise in more efficient way than the others filters such as Sato filter, median filter, etc.

The resulted image from various segmented techniques along with of region growing technique is shown in Fig. 5.

3.5 Magnetic Resonance Imaging (MRI)

For treating thalassemia suffering patients, the regular transfusion of blood is a crucial requirement. But these repetitive transfusions of blood also lead to the problem of iron-overload and putting the patient at a significant risk of heart diseases which can further result in heart failure. This iron-overload cardiomyopathy can be reversed if treatment for intensive iron chelation is performed on time. But as the deposition of cardiac iron is quite unpredictable in nature and also its symptoms are detected quite late, so the diagnosis for this is often get delayed. There is a number of ways which are employed for assessing this tissue iron overload such as superconducting quantum

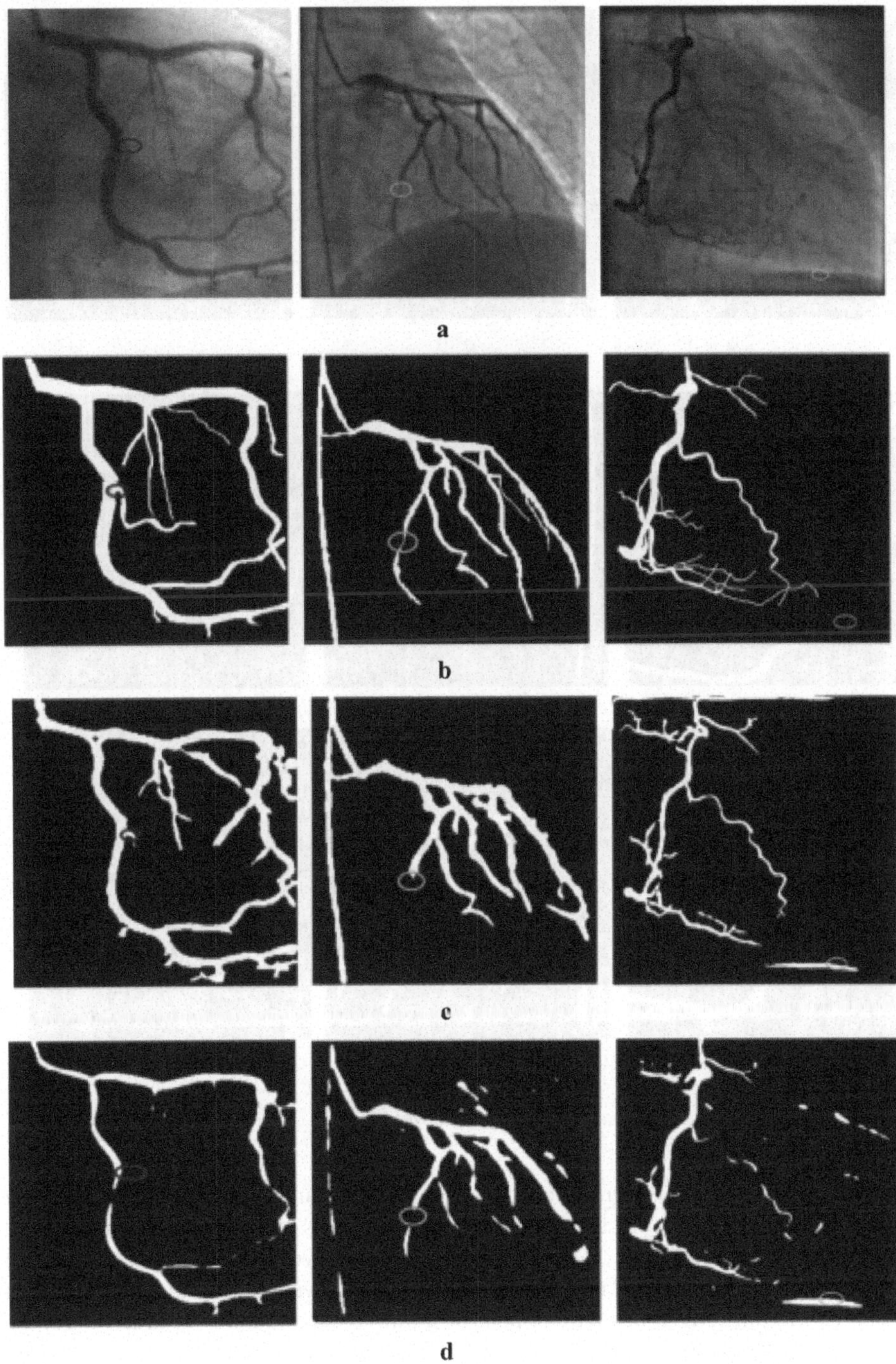

Fig. 5. Segmentation Results. Top to bottom: (a) real angiograms; (b) ground truth; (c) hysteresis thresholding; (d) fuzzy clustering; (e) region growing; (f) AQCA and (g) the method proposed [34]

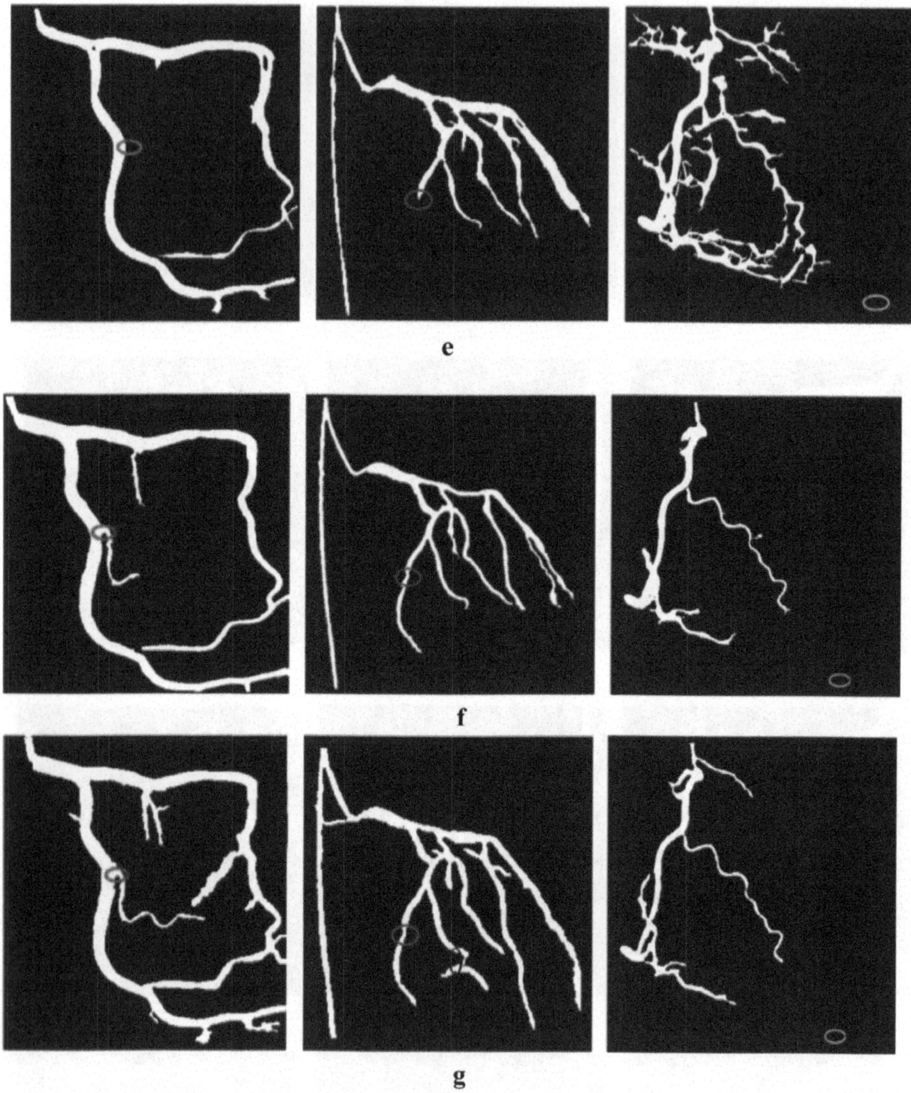

Fig. 5. (*continued*)

interface device (SQUID), serum ferritin, magnetic resonance imaging (MRI) and liver iron concentration (LIC). In all of these methods, LIC is a most reliable process but being an invasive technique due to the requirement of liver biopsy, the occurrence of infection is probable. The all other techniques are non-invasive but have limitations of their own. Serum ferritin has requirement of multiple examinations in order to get the follow-up of the symptoms. While in SQUID, the machine required for detection need an operator along with limited supply. But MRI requires the only investigation of parameters i.e., relaxation rates (R2*) and relation time constant (T2*). The T2* is basically a relaxation parameter which arises from the local magnetic field homogeneities. Its value decreases due to iron concentration in internal organs such as liver and heart. R2* is only the reciprocal value of T2*. The normal range of T2* value is greater than 20 ms. And thus, the patients having a smaller value of T2*(>20 ms) have the myocardial iron overloading which puts them at a higher risk of suffering from resting systolic dysfunction. There have been many techniques proposed for estimating the T2* value accurately.

In [35], authors proposed a technique in which comparison of cardiac T2* measurements was done where one T2* was measured by using established multiple breath-hold techniques having variable TR and other was measured by using a multi-echo sequence in which all images were acquired within a single breath-hold having a constant TR. The results got in this paper showed that a multi-echo acquisition method with a single breath-hold had higher accuracy, more reliability of quantized cardiac T2*, fast patient throughput, good speed and reproducibility along with the reduction in costs. After this, several methods were proposed in which T2* values measured from different data acquisition methods like black-blood and white blood methods were compared and it was established that black blood methods have better reproducibility in comparison to white blood methods.

Another concern related to the accuracy of T2* is the proper selection of curve fitting models. The three models which are quite popular for fitting the T2* decay are bi-exponential, offset and mono-exponential models. In addition to all these, one other model was proposed named as truncation model where the complicated points evaluation are discarded first and then remaining points are fitted using a mono-exponential model. These complicated points are known as late plateau points arising due to motion and noise which introduces errors in T2* measurement. With the help of this model, there results in a significant reduction in problems aroused in heavily iron-loaded hearts in which a very small value normally less than 10 ms of T2* results in rapid decaying of signal intensity which further leads to low SNR i.e., signal to noise ratio in echo time (TE) images.

For computing T2* values, earlier there was a requirement of manual selection of a region of interest (ROI) which was quite a time-consuming task. But this limitation can be solved by using automatic segmentation techniques. There are two fundamental methods for selecting ROIs in cardiac MR images and these are pixel-wise methods and region based methods. In region-based methods, ROI is selected first, then the mean of all the signal intensity (SI) which are presented in that selected ROI, is calculated. After this, a decay model is created by using the mean of ROI's signal intensity calculated from all the TEs and then, by fitting the resulted decay model evaluation of T2* is done. On the other hand in the pixel-wise method, the ROI is selected just like the region based method but unlike it, here the decay model is created by using each pixel present in the ROI from all the TEs and then by fitting those decay models, evaluation of T2* is done. After this, the mean of all the estimated T2*s is calculated and in this way, a final T2* value is estimated which represent all the pixels present in ROIs.

The main advantage of the pixel-wise method is the rejection of undesirable pixels like vessel pixels present in the liver or bad pixels resulting from susceptible artifacts which can lead to small values of R^2 or poor fitting case. But as this method has a lot of computations, it is quite an expensive method. Contrary to this, the region based method is computationally more feasible because of its simplicity but as there is no provision for rejection of any poor or undesirable pixel, the good fitting quality cannot be a guarantee. Thus, it is suited more for those regions where rapidity is required. The other limitation of region growing method is the need for uniformity in intensity variations in the selected region. But this can be removed by the use of a median filter as it gives decent performance and is a smoothing filter which preserves the edges.

Several methods are there for segmentation such as thresholding, dynamic programming, active contour model, graph cuts, matching of convex relaxed distributions, region growing, deformable models, edge modelling, level set, KNN classifier and clustering where automatic or semi-automatic techniques are used for left-ventricle (LV) segmentation and thus analysis of epicardial and endocardial contours is done. Most of the automatic methods for LV segmentation were focused only on the calculation of cardiac function like ejection function, stroke volume or mass but only a few were focused on T2* value calculations.

After this, the semi-automatic technique was proposed for assessing the T2* values in cardiac MRI [36] where the manual segmentation of ROIs by a user was there for calculation of T2* values. Then, in [37] fully automatic technique for the measurement of myocardial T2* was proposed in which improved Chan-Vese (I-CV) model followed by circular Hough transform (CHT) was used to locate the endocardium and epicardium in order to extract the myocardial. Then by using the thresholding method where the calculation of threshold value is done automatically from the segmented LV, the segmentation of right ventricle (RV) is done. After this, finally by the use of geometrical relation which exists between RV and myocardium, the analysis of interventricular septum was done.

In [38], a fully automatic assessment method for cardiac T2* is proposed by the use of region growing algorithm and the mathematical morphologies for myocardium segmentation in cardiac MR images without manual process is required during the segmentation of ROI and calculation of T2* value. As this is a very fast technique, hence it is quite beneficial in a busy center for a faster reporting result. In this, the results are compared with the manual process done by the experts for the segmentation process as well as T2* value estimation. Here, the automatic selection of seed points is done by the following steps:

(1) By the use of global thresholding method, the background is extracted from each MR image to form a binary image.
(2) By the use of the morphological opening, removal of small patches with the breaking of joint objects is done.
(3) By considering the edge of other objects got from step 2, the selection of LV area around each remaining candidate object is done iteratively until no candidate object is left.
(4) After the selection of LV, the seed point which used to find the exhaustive LV areas is calculated by finding the centroid of the selected LV.

(5) Then to confine the desirable area, a circle is created by the use of LV centroid as the center which covers whole LV area including its wall. Thus, by applying the four-connectivity rule in LV endocardium the other seed points used in the growth of LVs' wall are selected and this process goes on.

(6) Edges are smoothened, small gaps are filled and protrusions are stripped away from LV area using mathematical morphological operators.

The result of various steps discussed in this paper is shown in Fig. 6.

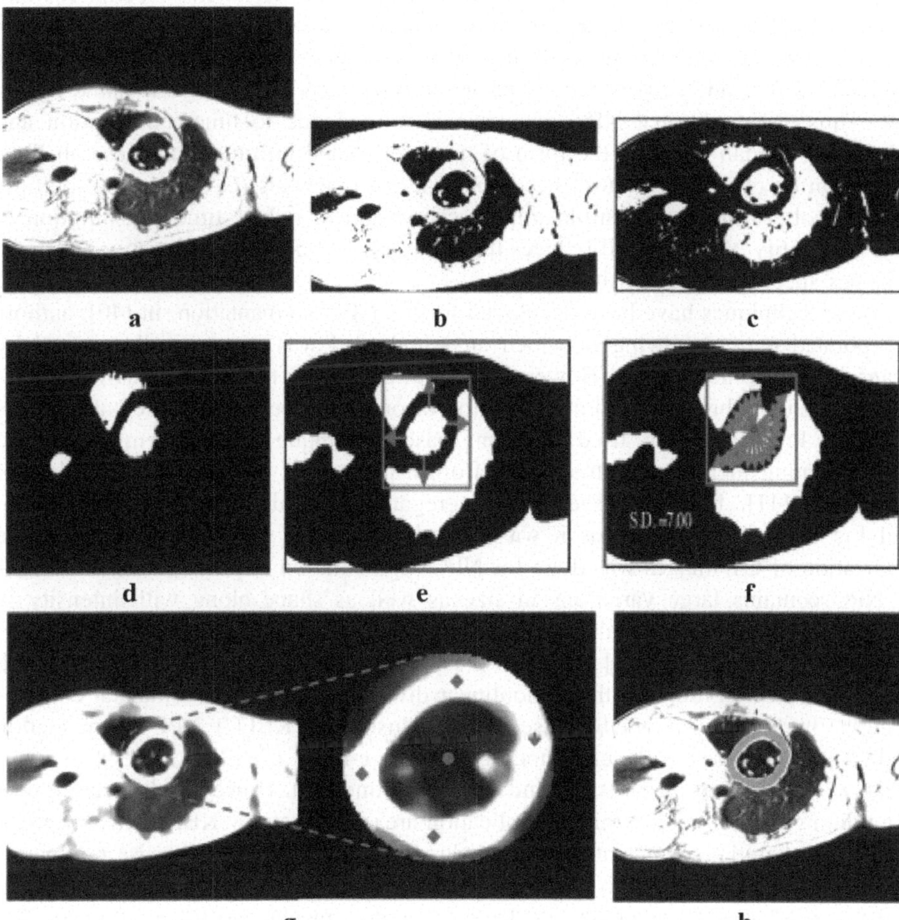

Fig. 6. The myocardium segmentation step by region growing method, (a) original image, (b) binary image after thresholding, (c) binary image is converted the binary pixels value and removed some background, (d) candidate objects which may be defined as left ventricle, (e) rectangle around a candidate object to limit distance calculation, (f) and (g) calculation of standard deviation (S.D.) of all distances between object's centroid and the edge pixels, (h) seed points initialization for region growing, (i) myocardium labeled in green superimposed on the original image [38]. (Color figure online)

3.6 Microscopy Image

Nasopharyngeal carcinoma (NPC) is a type of cancer found between nasal cavity and pharynx of the throat region. When a microscopic image is taken to detect the presence of NPC, it contains both the related data as well as unrelated data to NPC. In traditional diagnosis, the quantification of the region of interest for NPC as well as the discrimination between negative and positive cases in tumor areas based on that are done manually by the physicians. Thus, the whole diagnostic procedure involves many subjective decisions and depends entirely only on physician's experience. But this can lead to intra- and interobserver variations. Inter-observer variations account for that amount of difference which occurs when outcomes are recorded by the different observers for the same image while the intra-observer variations are that amount of difference which one observer acquired while repeatedly observing the same region [39]. Thus, the traditional NPC diagnosis is limited due to time-consumption and presence of human errors in the form of missed detailed information. These all limitations can be overcome by use of computer-aided diagnosis (CAD) having multiple support tools to increase identification precision and to reduce time consumption in order to identify NPC cases. It reduces the occurrence of positive or negative false and enhances specificity and sensitivity.

Many techniques have been developed for the NPC segmentation. In [40], authors incorporated region growing in which an initial seed was automatically created by means of probabilistic maps. However, this suffered from two limitations i.e., unexplained intensity threshold and an indication of only one seed point which affected its adequacy. In [40], authors used clustering based technique utilizing semi-supervised metric learning method to extract NPC from a pivotal set of different patient's MR images. In [41], beginning seed was segregated from dictated intensities before applying region growing. Thus it was a modified region growing technique where localization of CT images was done for NPC segmentation step.

NPC contains large variations in size as well as shape along with intensity in adjacent tissues. Owing to this, new methods were developed like one-class support vector machine (SVM) [42] and two-class support vector machine (SVM) [43]. The SVM detected tumor with the nonlinear division but it required manual communication. In [44], a knowledge-based fuzzy clustering (KBFC) NPC segmentation method was proposed with semi-supervised fuzzy c-mean (SFCM) where error minimization was done by progressive and iterative refinement. However, the requirement of a training dataset could limit its application area. Thus, a new KBFC was proposed incorporating initial segmentation, knowledge-based refinement, and noise removal.

In [45], a novel approach was proposed in which generation of initial seed and hence region based segmentation of the microscopic images was done automatically. This system included many phases. In the first phase, microscopy image was formed with the aid of sound lessening processes. Then, high ratio sub-bands are removed by utilizing wavelet transform which is an image enhancement technique, for reducing noise. After this, segmentation is performed in many steps. In the first step, a binary image is created using threshold which gave a dual imagery of microscopic image comprising NPC as a white area along with the presence of other different objects in a substantial amount. These little objects were then deleted by using morphological methods. After this, non-NPC objects are liquidated out by use of geometrical features like object area, circularity and object mean of gray-scale value. Then region growing is performed to segment the NPC area by utilizing the area as a seed point. All the results obtained in various steps of [45] are shown in the Fig. 7.

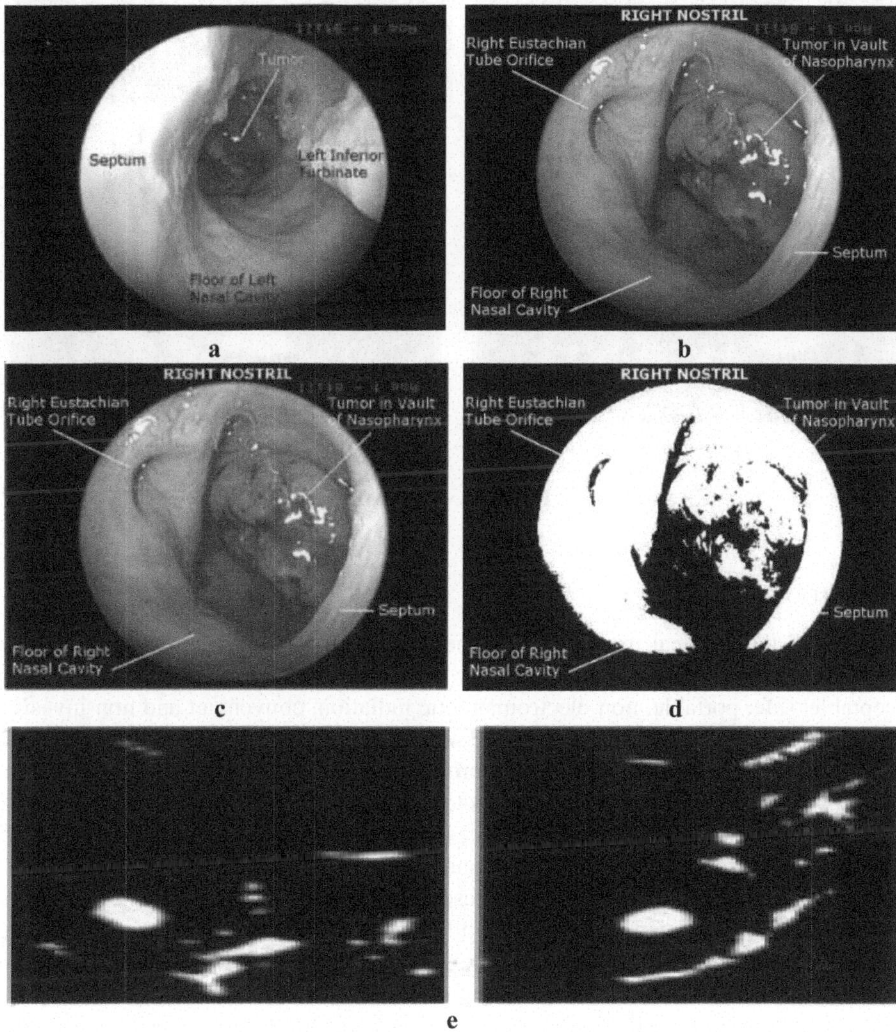

Fig. 7. NPC segmentation operations (a) original image (b) enhanced image (c) Seed point output (d) Object Segmentation output (e) threshold output (f) clean image (g) Filtering Out Non NPC Object [45].

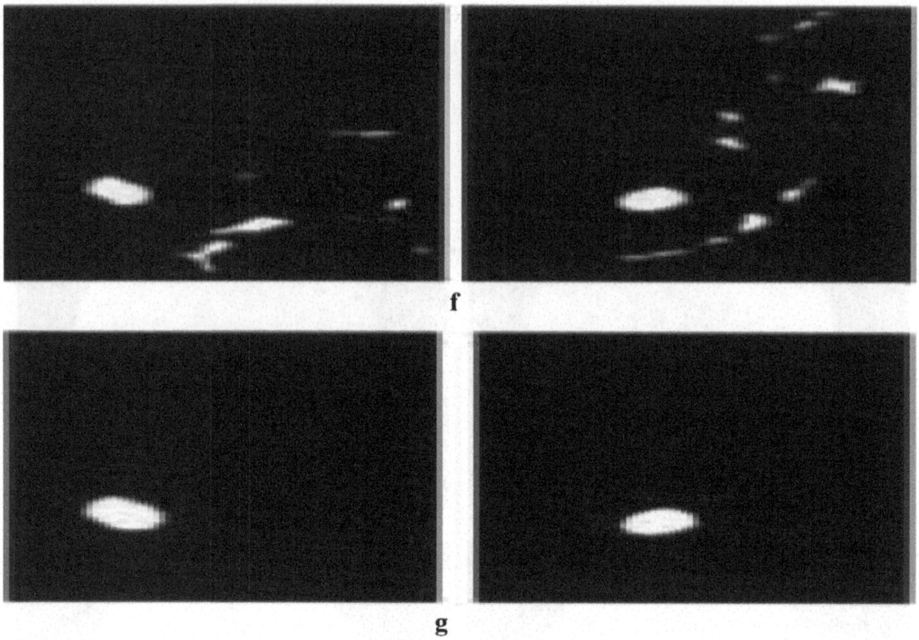

Fig. 7. (*continued*)

3.7 Ultrasound

Amongst all the medical imaging modalities, the most widely used is the ultrasound imaging because of its various advantages like being real-time, cost-effective, widely acceptable, safe, portable, non-electromagnetic radiation, convenient and non-invasive. It is used by the radiologists to assess the internal organs of humans in order to detect gallstones, tumors, etc. But the images produced by ultrasound imaging systems are generally of poor quality as they are inflicted with low contrast and speckles which is basically a granular noise type that reduces the image quality. Thus, segmentation of ultrasound images is quite a tedious and challenging task due to its intensity's in-homogeneity nature along with the presence of low contrast. For clinical practice, the task of segmenting is basically done by radiologists by the use of manual tracing. Due to this, it becomes a subjective and mostly skill-dependent task as there are chances of mismatch in the manual tracing done by radiologists. Thus, a segmentation tool fully supported by either automatic or semi-automatic technique will prove to be quite helpful in the realization of ultrasound images using computer-aided diagnostic process. Till now, several methods are timely proposed to meet this requirement. Ultrasound is also used in gallbladder diagnosis. However, for quantification of the gallbladder as well as the gallstone size, the manual delineation is very time consuming as well as labor-intensive. Thus, the requirement of the automatic region segmentation for gallbladder and gallstone region is of great importance.

In [46], authors presented modified snake model for searching the boundaries of the gallstones and gallbladder. In [47], authors have done the segmentation of gallstone by level set. In [48], a hybrid method for segmenting ultrasound medical images was proposed that incorporated the Gaussian kernel fuzzy C-means (GKFCM) clustering. The result obtained from this was utilized for initializing contour that would spread in order to identify the estimated regions. This further helped in estimating controlling parameters which were used in curve evolution process. Finally, the active contour model based on region-scalable fitting (RSF) energy function was used for the eliminating the requirement of the re-initialization process that was responsible for the contour attraction toward the object boundaries.

In [49], authors proposed a method which includes five steps.

1. By the use of the modified Otsu algorithm and anisotropic diffusion, speckle noise reduction and image contrast enhancement are done. The Otsu algorithm separately distinct the region of weak edges from the central gallbladder region.
2. The fine gallbladder region is acquired by the use of global morphology filtering algorithm.
3. A parameter adaptive pulse-coupled neural network (PA-PCNN) is employed for obtaining the high-intensity regions including gallstones.
4. Elimination of physicians' labeled regions is done by the use of modified region growing algorithm which also avoids the over-segmentation of gallstones. The modified region growing has specified conditions for region growing and termination which make it self-adaptable in the growth cycle.
5. By the use of locally weighted regression smoothing (LOESS), the smoothing contours are obtained from the detected gallbladder and gallstones. This contour information helps in performing feature extraction and determining stone types.

The results got by the region growing segmentation technique discussed in this paper is shown in Figs. 8 and 9.

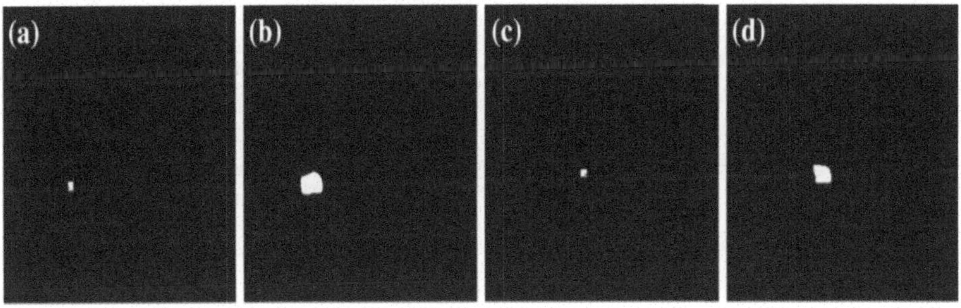

Fig. 8. Initial seed regions and region-growing results: a, c Initial seed region; b, d Final growing results from (a) and (c), respectively [49]

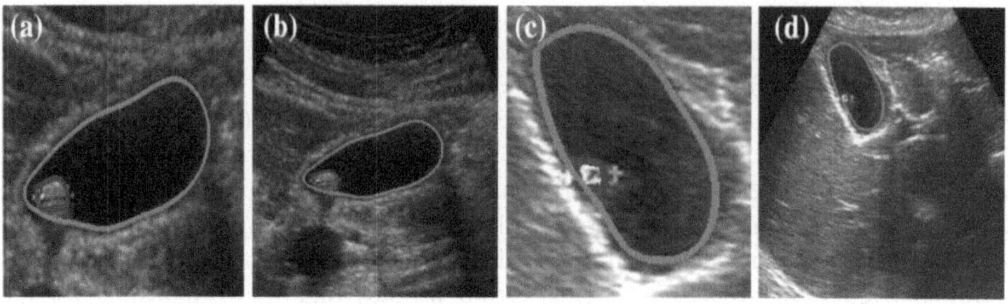

Fig. 9. The final segmentation results (the *red lines* and the *blue ones* denote the contours of the final results for the gallbladder and gallstones, respectively) [49]. (Color figure online)

Table 1. Summarization of region growing technique for segmentation used in various medical images

Medical image	Types of segmentation used	Accuracy	Features extracted	Advantages	Disadvantages	Future work
Retinal image [10]	Level set and region growing	94.77% to 95.09%	Intensity of retinal vessels	1. Use of level set for wide retinal vessel segmentation led to a convergence of the boundary of wide vessels while region growing helps in thin retinal vessel's segmentation 2. It is an unsupervised method which does not require any manual segmentation 3. It gives good performance in obtaining retinal vessel's connectivity 4. It gives more accuracy than the other existing supervised methods	1. The active contour method used here results in the movement of pathological regions if some abnormality comes in the retinal image	To solve the disadvantages present in this and to include techniques for assessing the segmented retinal vessel's connectivity
Mammograms [15]	Region growing and cellular neural network	96.47%	Intensity, textural and shape features of tumor	1. It is an improvement of region growing and CNN methods for segmentation 2. Performance in terms of specificity, AVC, sensitivity, and accuracy to recognize malignant and benign breast tumor is quite comparable with the other existing methods	1. If used on a different database, it will give variable results 2. In this, less emphasis is given on pre-processing techniques	Further study can be conducted with giving more emphasis on different pre-processing methods. Also, other neural networks such as SOM, SVM and radial basis function(RBF) along with different evolutionary algorithms such as particle swarm, harmony, ant colony, tabu search, etc. can be applied to determine CNN templates and the adaptive threshold for region growing

(*continued*)

Table 1. *(continued)*

Medical image	Types of segmentation used	Accuracy	Features extracted	Advantages	Disadvantages	Future work
PET-CT image [23]	Seeded region growing based on eight connectivity	96.21 ± 0.39%	Lung contour	1. It is able to produce segmentation results of high quality while ensuring low computation complexity in the integration of lung 2. Accuracy and efficiency of segmentation achieved by this method are much better than other existing methods 3. It performs accurate lung segmentation method which helps in volume measurement in clinical practice	1. Its overall efficiency is greatly impacted because of the last step used for refining edges as it involves performing a large number of iterative convolution computations	Further optimization of the edge refining algorithm should be done to reduce complexity and improving accuracy
2-D X-Ray angiograms [34]	Multiple Region Growing by combining both vesselness and direction information at different scale	82%	Thin and peripheral vessels of coronary artery	1. It gives an acceptable performance while dealing with challenging situations such as stenosis, noise and poor contrast 2. The multi-scale region growing is robust especially when dealing with discontinuity factors 3. It generates a better performance than fuzzy clustering, hysteresis thresholding and region growing in terms of vessel overlap, sensitivity, and precision	1. The results obtained by this algorithm seem to represent a significant misalignment 2. Non-Vascular structures like background structures which are adjacent to vessels can't be detected 3. Almost the false negatives occur in vessels boundaries due to which border detection, especially for thin arteries, are inaccurate	Work should be done for automatic detection of non-vascular structures and better vessel border delineation in order to overcome its limitations
Magnetic Resonance Image (MRI) [38]	Automatically initialized seeded region growing	76%	Myocardium	1. It corrects motions along with significant reduction in motion artifacts between images in 3-D MRIs which is not sufficiently corrected by rigid or affine registration techniques 2. When the CHT can correctly detect the circles representing LV contours, this method is quite superior 3. It gives much better values for evaluation measures like positive predictive value (PPV), Sensitivity, Hausdorff distance and Dice similarity coefficient (DSC) 4. It gives fully automatic T2* relaxation time estimation algorithm	1. There still exist some dissimilarities and disagreements in which most segmentation errors occur due to the unnecessary segmentation of some trabeculae of left ventricular endocardium as the signal intensities of these are quite similar to that of the myocardium	To incorporate shape considerations, for example, round like shape of left ventride to minimize the inclusion of trabeculae of left ventricular endocardium in the segmentation process

(continued)

Table 1. (*continued*)

Medical image	Types of segmentation used	Accuracy	Features extracted	Advantages	Disadvantages	Future work
				5. It can segment the areas of myocardium very well		
Microscopy images [45]	Automatic seed point selection based region growing technique	83.89% to 92.04%	Geometric features like circularity, object area and mean of grayscale objects for Nasopharyngeal carcinoma cancer segmentation	1. The segmentation used here registers very high accuracy because a lot of research has been done to study a wide range of limitations and steps to curb them 2. The automatic measurement obtained here is very close to the expert measurements	1. The limited size of database and variability is used which makes the results less reliable 2. Here only three features i.e., circularity, mean of grayscale objects and object area are extracted to select the NPC but these features are not quite enough to select Region of interest which negatively impact the segmentation process	To Extend the test of this method on a larger database, improving its efficiency and developing a hybrid framework to solve its limitations
Ultra-sound [49]	Modified region growing	86.01%	Contour information of gall-bladder and gallstone	1. Segmentation result is quite close to that of the manual drawing result obtained by a physician 2. It has better performance. 3. It avoids over-segmentation of gallstones 4. All parameters in each step are obtained by self-adaptive ways, thus this has better testing results than various semi-automatic techniques	1. The method is still unable to process several cases like stones with acoustic shadows 2. There is no inclusion of shape features and texture features for further analysis of stone	The further need of deduction of image feature extraction like shape feature such as area, eccentricity, extent, perimeter, solidity, circularity, etc., and texture features such as variance, entropy, mean, contrast, skewness, etc., for automatic determination of the stone type

4 Conclusion

Nowadays, medical imaging systems exhibit a very important role in the diagnosis of various contemporary medical problems as they have a high degree of precision as well as speed and thus, the success or failure of diagnosis procedure is dependent on them. Medical images gained from various viable and non-obtrusive techniques not only contain tumor-related data such as tumor size, the affected area, its volume and its degree of seriousness but the unrelated tumor data also. In order to give an effective and accurate diagnosis, doctors are required to physically recognize the affected region of interest slice by slice which is laborious, time-consuming, tedious and error-prone. Thus, an Extensive study has been done to study the use of region growing technique of segmentation in various medical images. The advantages, as well as disadvantages of region growing segmentation, are studied for each medical image and thus possible future work which can be done for improvement are formed. Also, it is concluded that region growing segmentation is better for various biomedical images. So still, a lot of work is needed for improving its accuracy rate.

References

1. Jiang, X., Mojon, D.: Adaptive local thresholding by verification based multi-threshold probing with application to vessel detection in retinal images. IEEE Trans. Pattern Anal. Mach. Intell. **25**(1), 131–137 (2003)
2. Mendonca, A.M., Campilho, A.: Segmentation of retinal blood vessels by combing the detection of centerlines and morphological reconstruction. IEEE Trans. Med. Imaging **25**(9), 1200–1213 (2006)
3. Martinez-Perez, M.E., Hughes, A.D., Thom, S.A., Bharath, A.A., Parker, K.H.: Segmentation of blood vessels from red-free and fluorescein retinal images. Med. Image Anal. **11**(1), 47–61 (2007)
4. You, X., Peng, Q., Yuan, Y., Cheung, Y., Lei, J.: A segmentation of retinal blood vessels using the radial projection and semi-supervised approach. Pattern Recogn. **44**(10), 2314–2324 (2011)
5. Marin, D., Aquino, A., Gegundez-Arias, M.E., Bravo, J.M.: A new supervised method for blood vessel segmentation in retinal images by using gray-level and moment invariants-based features. IEEE Trans. Med. Imaging **30**(1), 146–158 (2011)
6. Chaudhuri, S., Chatterjee, S., Katz, N., Nelson, M., Goldbaum, M.: Detection of blood vessels in retinal images using two-dimensional matched filters. IEEE Trans. Med. Imaging **8**(3), 263–269 (1989)
7. Hoover, A., Kouznetsova, V., Goldbaum, M.: Locating blood vessels in retinal images by the piecewise threshold of a matched filter response. IEEE Trans. Med. Imaging **19**(3), 203–210 (2000)
8. Zhang, B., Zhang, L., Zhang, L., Karray, F.: Retinal vessel extraction by matched filter with a first-order derivative of Gaussian. Comput. Biol. Med. **40**(4), 438–445 (2010)
9. Stankiewicz, A., Marciniak, T., Dabrowski, A., Stopa, M., Rakowicz, P., Marciniak, E.: Improving segmentation of 3D retina layers based on graph theory approach for low-quality OCT images. Metrol. Meas. Syst. **23**(2), 269–280 (2016)
10. Zhao, Y.Q., Wang, X.H., Wang, X.F., Shih, F.Y.: Retinal vessels segmentation based on level set and region growing. Pattern Recogn. **47**, 2437–2446 (2014)
11. Cao, Y., Hao, X., Zhu, X., Xia, S.: An adaptive region growing algorithm for breast masses in mammograms. Front. Electr. Electron. Eng. China **5**(2), 128–136 (2014)
12. Freer, T.W., Ullissey, M.J.: Screening mammography with the computer-aided detection-perspective study of 12,860 patients in a community breast center. Radiology **220**(3), 781–786 (2001)
13. Tahmasbi, A., Saki, F., Shokouhi, S.B.: Classification of benign and malignant masses based on Zernike moments. Comput. Biol. Med. **41**(8), 726–735 (2011)
14. Wei, C.H., Chen, S.Y., Liu, X.: Mammogram retrieval on similar mass lesions. Comput. Methods Programs Biomed. **106**(3), 234–248 (2012)
15. Rouhi, R., Jafari, M., Kasaei, S., Keshavarzian, P.: Benign and malignant breast tumors classification based on region growing and CNN segmentation. Expert Syst. Appl. **42**(3), 990–1002 (2015)
16. McNitt-Gray, M.: Lung nodules and beyond-approaches, challenges and opportunities in thoracic CAD. In: Proceedings of 18th International Congress and Exhibition on Computer Assisted Radiology and Surgery, pp. 896–901 (2004)
17. Denison, D.M., Morgan, M.D., Milla, A.B.: Estimation of regional gas and tissue volumes of the lung in supine man using computed tomography. Thorax **41**(8), 620–628 (1986)
18. Kalender, W.A., Fichte, H., Bautz, W., Skalej, M.: Semiautomatic evaluation procedures for quantitative CT of the lung. J. Comput. Assist. Tomogr. **15**(2), 248–255 (1991)

19. Sun, X., Zhang, H., Duan, H.: 3D computerized segmentation of lung volume with computed tomography. Acad. Radiol. **13**(6), 670–677 (2006)
20. Pu, J., Roos, J., Chin, A.Y., Napel, S., Rubin, G.D., Paik, D.S.: Adaptive border marching algorithm: automatic lung segmentation on chest CT images. Comput. Med. Imaging Graph. **32**(6), 452–462 (2008)
21. Van Rikxoort, E.M., de Hoop, B., Viergever, M.A., Prokop, M., Ginneken, B.V.: Automatic lung segmentation from thoracic computed tomography scans using a hybrid approach with error detection. Med. Phys. **36**(7), 2934–2947 (2009)
22. Korfiatis, P., Skiadopoulos, S., Sakellaropoulos, P., Kalogeropoulou, C., Costaridou, L.: Combining 2D wavelet edge highlighting and 3D thresholding for lung segmentation in thin-slice CT. Br. J. Radiol. **80**(960), 996–1004 (2014)
23. Zhao, J., Ji, G., Han, X., Qiang, Y., Liao, X.: An automated pulmonary parenchyma segmentation method based on an improved region growing algorithm in PET-CT imaging. Front. Comput. Sci. **10**(1), 189–200 (2016)
24. Li, Z., Zhang, Y., Liu, G., Shao, H., Li, W., Tang, X.: A robust coronary artery identification and centerline extraction method in angiographies. Biomed. Sig. Process. Control **16**, 1–8 (2015)
25. Sato, Y., Araki, T., Hanayama, M., Naito, H., Tamura, S.: A viewpoint determination system for stenosis diagnosis and quantification in coronary angiographic image acquisition. IEEE Trans. Med. Imaging **17**(1), 37–121 (1998)
26. Liao, R., Luc, D., Sun, Y., Kirchberg, K.: 3-D reconstruction of the coronary artery tree from multiple views of a rotational X-ray angiography. Int. J. Cardiovasc. Imaging **26**, 49–733 (2010)
27. Zheng, S., Zhou, Y.: Assessing cardiac dynamics based on X-ray coronary angiogram. J. Multimedia **8**(1), 48–55 (2013)
28. Suri, J., Liu, K., Reden, L., Laxminarayan, S.: A review on MR vascular image processing: skeleton versus non-skeleton approaches: part II. IEEE Trans. Inf. Technol. Biomed. **6**(4), 50–338 (2002)
29. O'Brien, J.F., Ezquerra, N.F.: Automated segmentation of coronary vessels in angiographic image sequences utilizing temporal, spatial, and structural constraints. In: Visualization in Biomedical Computing 1994, pp. 25–37. International Society for Optics and Photonics (1994)
30. Li, Y., Zhou, S., Wu, J., Ma, X., Peng, K.: A novel method of vessel segmentation for X-ray coronary angiography images. In: 2012 Fourth International Conference on Computational and Information Sciences (ICCIS), pp. 468–471. IEEE (2012)
31. Lesage, D., Angelini, E.D., Bloch, I., Funka-Lea, G.: A review of 3D vessel lumen segmentation techniques-models, features and extraction schemes. Med. Image Anal. **13**(6), 819–845 (2009)
32. Lara, D.S., Faria, A.W., Araújo, A., Menotti, D.: A semi-automatic method for segmentation of the coronary artery tree from angiography. In: XXII Brazilian Symposium on Computer Graphics and Image Processing, pp. 194–201. IEEE (2009)
33. Nimura, Y., Kitasaka, T., Mori, K.: Blood vessel segmentation using line-direction vector based on the Hessian analysis. In: SPIE Medical Imaging, p. 76233Q. International Society for Optics and Photonics (2010)
34. Kerkeni, A., Benabdallah, A., Manzanera, A., Bedoui, M.H.: A coronary artery segmentation method based on multiscale analysis and region growing. Computer. Med. Imaging Graph. **48**, 49–61 (2016)

35. Westwood, M., Anderson, L.J., Firmin, D.N., Gatehouse, P.D., Charrier, C.C., Wonke, B., Pennell, D.J.: A single breath-hold multiecho T2* cardiovascular magnetic resonance technique for diagnosis of myocardial iron overload. J. Magn. Reson. Imaging **18**, 33–39 (2003)
36. Boon-Chieng, E., Duangchaemkarn, K.: Myocardial iron measurement in thalassemia using cardiac magnetic resonance image processing software. In: Biomedical Engineering International Conference (BMEiCON), pp. 1–4 (2012)
37. Zheng, Q., Feng, Y., Wei, X., Feng, M., Chen, W., Lu, Z., Xu, Y., Chen, H., He, T.: Automated interventricular septum segmentation for black-blood myocardial T2* measurement in thalassemia. J. Magn. Reson. Imaging **41**, 1242–1250 (2015)
38. Wantanajittikul, K., Theera-Umpon, N., Saekho, S., Auephanwiriyakul, S., Phrommintikul, A., Leemasawat, K.: Automatic cardiac T2* relaxation time estimation from magnetic resonance images using region growing method with automatically initialized seed points. Comput. Methods Programs Biomed. **130**, 76–86 (2016)
39. Tatanun, C., Ritthipravat, P., Bhongmakapat, T., Tuntiyatorn, L.: Automatic segmentation of nasopharyngeal carcinoma from CT images: region growing based technique. In: 2010 2nd International Conference on Signal Processing Systems (ICSPS), pp. V2-537–V2-541 (2010)
40. Huang, W., Chan, K.L., Chong, V.: Nasopharyngeal carcinoma lesion extraction using clustering via semi-supervised metric learning with side-information. In: 2008 5th International Conference on Visual Information Engineering (VIE 2008) (2008)
41. Chanapai, W., Bhongmakapat, T., Tuntiyatorn, L., Ritthipravat, P.: Nasopharyngeal carcinoma segmentation using a region growing technique. Int. J. Comput. Assist. Radiol. Surg. **7**, 413–422 (2012)
42. Zhang, J., Ma, K.-K., Er, M.-H., Chong, V.: Tumor segmentation from magnetic resonance imaging by learning via one-class support vector machine. In: International Workshop on Advanced Image Technology (IWAIT 2004), pp. 207–211 (2004)
43. Zhou, J., Chan, K.L., Xu, P., Chong, V.F.: Nasopharyngeal carcinoma lesion segmentation from MR images by support vector machine. In: 3rd IEEE International Symposium on Biomedical Imaging: Nano to Macro 2006, pp. 1364–1367 (2006)
44. Zhou, J., Chong, V., Lim, T.-K., Houng, J.: MRI tumor segmentation for nasopharyngeal carcinoma using knowledge-based fuzzy clustering. Int. J. Inf. Technol. **8** (2002)
45. Mohammed, M.A., Ghani, M.K.A., Hamed, R.I., Abdullah, M.K., Ibrahim, D.A.: Automatic segmentation and automatic seed point selection of nasopharyngeal carcinoma from microscopy images using region growing based approach. J. Comput. Sci. **20**(5), 61–69 (2017)
46. Ciecholewski, M., Chocholowicz, J.: Gallbladder shape extraction from ultrasound images using active contour models. Comput. Biol. Med. **43**(12), 2238–2255 (2013)
47. Xie, W., Ma, Y., Shi, B., Wang, Z.: Gallstone segmentation and extraction from ultrasound images using the level set method. In: IEEE Bio-signals and Bio-robotics Conference (2013)
48. Gupta, D., Anand, R.S., Tyagi, B.: A hybrid segmentation method based on Gaussian kernel fuzzy clustering and region-based active contour model for ultrasound medical images. Biomed. Sig. Process. Control **16**, 98–112 (2015)
49. Lian, J., Ma, Y., Ma, Y., Shi, B., Liu, J., Yang, Z., Guo, Y.: Automatic gallbladder and gallstone regions segmentation in the ultrasound image. Int. J. Comput. Assist. Radiol. Surg. **12**(4), 553–568 (2017)

Biomedical Image Enhancement Using Different Techniques - A Comparative Study

Jyoti Dabass(✉) and Rekha Vig(✉)

The NorthCap University, Gurgaon, India
jyotidabas91@gmail.com, rekhavig@ncuindia.edu

Abstract. In medical applications, processing of various medical images like chest X-rays, projection images of trans-axial tomography, cineangiograms and other medical images that occur in radiology, ultrasonic scanning and nuclear magnetic resonance (NMR) is required. These images may be used for patients' screening and monitoring for detection of diseases in patients. Image enhancement algorithms are employed to emphasize, smoothen or sharpen image features for display and analysis. In the biomedical field, image enhancement faces the greatest difficulty in quantifying the criterion for enhancement. Enhancement methods are application specific and often developed empirically. The theme work presented in this paper is a detailed analysis of enhancement of medical images using contrast manipulation, noise reduction, edge sharpening, gray level slicing, edge crispening, magnification, interpolation, and pseudo-coloring. Comparison of these techniques is necessary for deciding an apt algorithm applicable for enhancement of all medical images and further processing. This paper reviews the background of enhancement techniques in three domains i.e. spatial, frequency and fuzzy domain. The comparative analysis of different techniques is shown using results that are obtained by applying these techniques to medical images.

Keywords: Biomedical images · Image enhancement · Frequency Fuzzy and spatial domain techniques

1 Introduction

Biomedical image processing is a very broad field. It includes collecting biomedical signals, forming images, processing pictures and displaying images to medical diagnosis on the basis of feature extracted from the image. The existence of image acquisition artifacts, fuzziness, and non-homogeneity of luminance and contrast levels, form, and size of images determines the specificity of biomedical images [1]. In last few years, biomedical image processing has experienced dramatic expansion owing to use of computational resources, magnetic resonance imaging (MRI), Doppler ultrasound, computed tomography (CT), X-ray, optical imaging technologies and nuclear emission based techniques- PET (positron emission tomography), SPECT (single photon emission computed tomography) in medical field.

Biomedical imaging focuses on the acquisition of images for both therapeutic and diagnostic purposes. Digital imaging gave rise to CT scanner and allows doctors to

B. Panda et al. (Eds.): REDSET 2017, CCIS 799, pp. 260–286, 2018.
https://doi.org/10.1007/978-981-10-8527-7_22

watch real-time X-rays on a monitor-a technique called as X-ray fluoroscopy. It helps in guiding invasive procedures such as biopsies and angiograms. A catheter is put into a vein or an artery in the groin to produce images (known as angiograms of blood vessels) in angiography. It is threaded into the blood vessel and is guided to the area to be studied by injecting an X-ray contrast medium through the catheter. This increases the contrast of blood vessels so that the radiologist is capable to visualize the irregularities or blockages [1]. Compared to X-ray, biological tissues in MRI are more opaque and transparent to radiation with intermediate wavelengths when proceeding from the shorter to the longer wavelength. This is true for visible, ultraviolet and to some extent, microwaves, and infrared light. Magnetic resonance imaging emerging as a valuable medical imaging modality owing to the combined effects of unprecedented information available from nuclear signals and the benefits derived from low energy radiation. Although computerized algorithms provide spatial and temporal analysis to detect characteristics and patterns indicative of tumor and other diseases still low contrast, noise, other data acquisition devices, illumination condition and poor quality affect the human perception in analyzing medical images. A lot of researchers are working on enhancement of the images obtained by MRI in the fuzzy domain. Surgeons also find enhanced medical image useful in reliable detection and diagnosis of diseases.

Enhanced images inhibit higher quality image and low level of noise to avoid problematic and unreliable feature extraction, analysis and recognition. Enhancement solves the problem of low contrast by enhancing the region of interest using technique of contrast enhancement. This technique calculates the difference in the brightness and color of the object's background to aid better perception of the human visual system. Biomedical enhancement technique such as Contrast Stretching uses a predetermined transformation to map each gray level into another gray level [1]. To quantify the image quality and purity of view Local Contrast C_{local} is calculated as given below:

$$C_{local} = \frac{\left|\mu_{target-\mu_{background}}\right|}{\left|\mu_{target} + \mu_{background}\right|} \tag{1}$$

Here μ_{target} and $\mu_{background}$ are the mean grey levels of the target and background image in the local region of interest. Bigger value of C_{local} represents more purity of the image [34]. But traditional spatial domain enhancement methods do not embed any high-quality background information. It is because, in dark biomedical images, the information is already lost in those regions which are so dark. No matter how many enhancement algorithms are applied on these medical images, they will not be able to bring back the lost information. So it becomes imperative to assure that no information is lost before enhancing the contrast. Major challenges faced by researchers in enhancing the medical images include a selection of proper imaging technique to process and analyze a large volume of data without compromising the quality of the image. It is because of the fact that image enhancement techniques are application specific i.e. image enhancement technique that works well for MR images may not work well for X-ray topographic images. For low contrast images like Cephalometric images, fully automatic and non-linear histogram equalization is powerful. However, it suffers from lack of brightness preservation, excessive enhancement, and spikes. Furthermore, it is not suitable for retaining local detail due to its global treatment of the image. Image Subtraction is used to enhance the blood vessels under observation in case of angiography. Other enhancement techniques perform transform operations as in the discrete Fourier transform, local neighborhood operations as in convolution and other operations as in pseudo coloring where a gray level image is mapped into a color image by assigning different color to different features. Fusion of different techniques proved efficient in providing a high quality of images.

2 Objectives of Biomedical Image Enhancement Techniques

Enhancement of Biomedical images has become an interdisciplinary research field attracting expertise from computer science, statistics, physics, engineering, applied mathematics, and biology. Computer-aided diagnostic has already become an important essence of clinical routine. Image Enhancement techniques are found extremely useful in attaining the following objectives.

1. To improve the quality of biomedical images as perceived by the doctors either by enhancing the image contrast or suppressing the noise [2].
2. To emphasize, smoothen or sharpen or smoothen or enhance the medical image features for analysis and display.
3. To improve the dynamic range of selected features.
4. To obtain contrast in both dark and bright regions.
5. To obtain details with more natural frequency.
6. To provide contrast enhancement with a minimum number of artifacts.
7. To enhance contrast with the reversible hiding of data and tamper localization in order to transmit medical images digitally [3].
8. To provide convenient implementation and preservation of brightness.

Enhanced medical images are utilized in the process of diagnosis of diseases in the patients. Image modeling and reconstruction techniques create 3D images by instant processing of 2D signals. Image processing software aids to identify and analyze what might not be apparent to the human eye. Image enhancement techniques can be applied effectively only when we have the prior knowledge of the required image quality. Before reviewing image enhancement techniques it becomes imperative to review the image perception to understand the scales that decide the image quality.

3 Parameters for Image Perception

It is essential to consider how the output of a medical imaging system is transformed into information by the viewer. For developing measures of medical image fidelity which helps in the evaluation and design of medical image processing algorithms and imaging system, understanding of visual perception model is important. Visual medical image data present spatial distribution of physical qualities such as spatial frequencies and luminance of an object. Attributes such as brightness, color, and edges represent the perceived information. The perceptual information is represented quantitatively using the information given in Tables 1 and 2.

Image perception plays a major role in Biomedical Image processing because Image enhancement merely improves the subjective quality of the medical images by applying algorithms to existing data. The enhanced medical images require an optimal trade-off between noise and sharpness for balancing the PSNR values and sharpness measure. It is because when a large part of the image or entire image contains additive white Gaussian noise then image quality degrades but the image looks sharper [4].

Luminance to Contrast Models: Luminance or intensity of a spatially distributed object having light distribution $\mathcal{J}(x, y, \lambda)$ can be mathematically defined as

$$f(x, y) = \int_0^{\infty} \mathcal{J}(x, y, \lambda *)\mathcal{V}(\lambda)d\lambda \tag{2}$$

where $\mathcal{V}(\lambda)$ is the relative luminous efficiency function of the visual system. Contrast can be defined as

$$c = a_1 + a_2 log f \tag{3}$$

Here a_1 and a_2 are constant.

Luminous to contrast models can be explained better using the following laws:

- Logarithmic Law: It defines the relation between contrast and log of the luminance using the equation

$$c = 50log_{10}f \quad 1 \leq f \leq 100 \tag{4}$$

- Power Law: According to Power Law relative change in contrast results in a proportional relative change in luminance which can be mathematically defined as

$$c = \alpha_{nf^{1/n}},\ n = 2, 3 - - - -;\ \alpha_2 = 10;\ \alpha_3 = 21.9 \tag{5}$$

- Background Ratio: Background ratio relates contrast and luminance using the expression

$$c = f(f_B + 100)(f_B + f) \tag{6}$$

where f_B = background luminance

Except in the Logarithm Law, the luminance f lies in the interval [0, 100]. Contrast Scale is over [0,100].

Image fidelity criteria aids in determining image quality and in rating the performance of a processing technique or a vision system. To evaluate image quality two types of criteria are utilized. One is subjective and the other is quantitative. The subjective rating criterion includes scales such as impairment scales and goodness scales.

Image Goodness Scale: A goodness scale can be a global scale or a group scale. The overall goodness criteria measure image quality on a scale ranging from excellent to unsatisfactory. Table 1 shows the scale calibrated by the training set of images.

Table 1. Image goodness scale

Overall goodness scale	Group goodness scale
Excellent (5^)	Best (7^)
Good (4^)	Well above average (6^)
Fair (3^)	Slightly above average (5^)
Poor (2^)	Average (4^)
Unsatisfactory (1^)	Slightly below average (3^)
	Well below average (2^)
	Worst (1^)

^Quantitative weights associated with rating are represented by the numbers in parenthesis.

Impairment Scale: Impairment scale provides the image rating of evaluated performance in terms of degradation level available in biomedical images when compared with a reference image. Table 2 shows how the images are rated in impairment scale.

Table 2. Scale for impairment of biomedical images.

Not Noticeable (1^)
Just Noticeable (2^)
Definitely noticeable but only slight impairment (3^)
Impairment not objectionable (4^)
Somewhat objectionable (5^)
Definitely objectionable (6^)
Extremely objectionable (7^)

4 Image Enhancement Techniques [5]

As the name suggests, in order to get enhanced the image, input biomedical image is pre-processed to make it more suitable compared with input image for particular applications i.e. the contrast and details of the biomedical image are improved or enhanced It is a totally subjective technique for processing the outcomes may vary from people to people. In order to understand the specific requirements of the enhancement techniques, we exemplify few areas where medical images are enhanced.

1. Transthoracic echocardiography suffers from artifacts, reduced contrast and acoustical noise because of the interaction of structures such as bone, lung, and fat with transmitted ultrasound which limits the diagnostic value and effectiveness of

post-processing tools on cardiac ultrasound images. Spatial compounding combines partially correlated images generated by imaging the target region of interest from different angles to suppress noise and artifacts and also to enhance the tissue structures present in all partially de-correlated views [6].

2. According to the anatomical structure information of the reflected image, the MRI image of the brain has the soft tissue structure characteristics of the brain but in MRI, there are more complicated events where the WMH (White matter hyper-sensitivities) signal is high but it might erroneously be categorized as other brain tissues such as CSF (cerebrospinal fluid). Average intensity replacement based on Adaptive Histogram Equalization utilizes segmentation and contrast enhancement to classify a possible WMH regions [7].
3. Magnetic Resonance Imaging with enhanced contrast provides profusion in tumor-related biomarkers. It is permeable to provide enlarged details of the microenvironment around tumor concerning the Vasculator. It is useful for finding malignancy in breast and to contrast lesion morphology [8].

Biomedical image Enhancement techniques are applicable for following domains.

I. Spatial Domain
II. Frequency/Transform Domain
III. Fuzzy Domain.

4.1 Techniques in Spatial Domain

By spatial domain, we simply dealing with particularly given space, in the reference case, the input image i.e. we are working with the values of pixels. Suppose f(x, y) is the original input image where f denotes the value of grey level and (x, y) are the coordinates of the image. For one byte image, r can have values ranging from 0–255 where 255 means white and 0 means black and all the other values present shades of grey. So the modified version of image can be represented as

$$g(x, y) = T[f(x, y)] \tag{7}$$

Here original image is represented by $f(x, y)$ and $g(x, y)$ represents modified image after applying the transformation. In case of all techniques used in spatial domain, only transformation operator changes and the rest of the equation is left unchanged.

Enhancement in spatial domain can be done in following ways.

1. By processing points
2. By processing in neighborhood

1. A technique based on processing point: In case of point processing technique, T is 1*1 operator. It means we work on one pixel only. It implies that modified value of f (x, y) depends on the current value of f(x, y) and on the transformation operator T.

Some of the common methods of point processing are given below. The technique to be used depends on the results desired and the type of image.

Background of the Conventional Techniques for Enhancement of Biomedical image [4]

- *Stretching the Contrast:* It is required to improve overall visibility of poor contrast medical images encountered due to poor conditions of lightning or due to the less dynamic range or nonlinearities of imaging sensors. Linear contrast stretching method can hardly enhance all parts of the image simultaneously [33]. Mathematically,

$$s = \begin{cases} x(t), 0 \leq t < p \\ y(t-p) + f, p \leq t < q \\ z(t-q) + g, q \leq t < L-1 \end{cases} \tag{8}$$

The slopes x and z should be less than one to make dark grey levels darker and y > 1 to make bright levels brighter.

- *Noise Clipping and Thresholding:* Its purpose is to highlight the region of interest. It gives the maximum value of contrast for it has only white and black grey values in case of binary images that have a bimodal distribution of grey levels. It can be written as

$$s = \begin{cases} 0 \; if \; t < p \\ \mathcal{L} - 1 \; if \; t \geq p \end{cases} \tag{9}$$

  Here $\mathcal{L}$ is the number of grey levels.
- *Digital Negative:* It is used to highlight a particular range of grey values like for example enhancing the flaws in the images of computed tomography or X-ray. In this, we choose a band of all values of grey level. To find digital negative we use the expression:

$$s = (\mathcal{L} - 1) - t \tag{10}$$

- *Gray Level window slicing:* It helps in highlighting a specific range of grey values like for example enhancing the flaws in an X-ray or a CT image. In this, we select a band of grey level values. Mathematically

$$s = \begin{cases} \mathcal{L} - 1, & p \leq t \leq q \\ 0, & \textit{for all other conditions} \end{cases} \tag{11}$$

- *Bitplane slicing:* In this, we find the contribution of each bit in producing the final image. Majority of visually significant data is represented by higher order bits while the lower bits comprise suitable information in the image. It is useful in hiding the data. If we replace more than 2 LSB's with 2 MSB's we get the secret data imposed on the original image

- *Power Law Transformation:* Gamma correction improves the nonlinearities encountered during the process of capturing, printing and displaying the images. Mathematically,

$$g(x, y) = c * f(x, y)\gamma \tag{12}$$

Here c & γ denotes positive constants.

- *Dynamic Range Compression:* It is achieved using log operator. Useful when the dynamic range of the image is more than the range of the device used for display. Mathematically (Fig. 1),

$$S = c * x * log(1 + r) \tag{13}$$

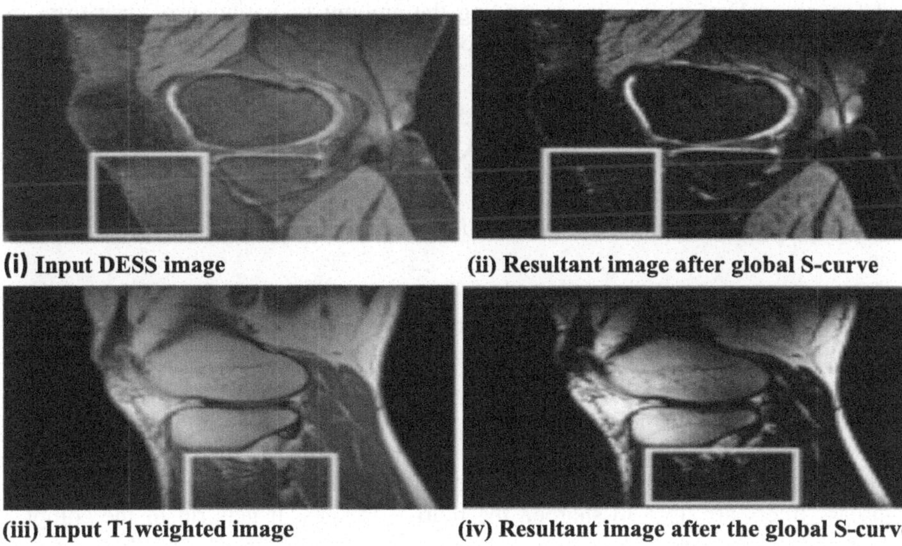

Fig. 1. (i) original image of DESS (ii) resultant image after applying global S-curve (iii) input T1 weighted image, and (iv) result of global S-curve enhancement technique (loss in details can be seen in the highlighted region) [29]

2. Neighbourhood processing: In point processing technique, we take a single pixel at a time and modify it according to our requirement. But it neighborhood processing, we consider single pixel and its immediate neighbors. To achieve neighborhood processing first consider a mask say 3*3(it could also be a 5*5 or a 7*7 ....) mask and add up the values got by multiplying the component of the mask with its corresponding value in the image and finally place the value at the center. This operation is the same as convolution. In images, regions where the grey levels change slowly or the background are low-frequency regions and regions which have abrupt grey level changes or the edges, are high-frequency regions. Hence low pass filtering implies removing (blurring) the edges while high-pass filtering implies removing the background. Image

Entropy determines the amount of information present in the image. It takes value from 0 to 8 and it can be mathematically defined as:

$$E = -\sum\nolimits_{i=0}^{N} p(x_i) logp(x_i) \tag{14}$$

Here p is the probability and X_i represent grey scale values. To get better quality image value of E should be large.

Averaging filters are excellent when the image contains Gaussian noise. The new selective average filter is used for smoothing the ultrasound images affected by speckle noise. This filter applies a reduced smoothing to the pixels belonging to the border of the structures of interest in the image whilst applying more intense smoothing to the remaining pixels in order to remove speckle noise [29]. But in the process, it corrupts the image leads to blurring of edges. Amount of blurring depends on the size of the mask. Standard Deviation helps in finding the amount of variation of data from the average or mean value. A Larger value of STD indicates clear image. STD can be calculated using the equation:

$$STD = \sqrt{\sum\nolimits_{x=1}^{A} \sum\nolimits_{y=1}^{B} \frac{|F(x,y) - \mu|^2}{AB}} \tag{15}$$

Here A and B represent the dimensions of the image F(x, y) and μ represents the mean value.

When we need to eliminate the salt and pepper noise, we work with a non-linear filter known as the Median filter. They are also known called order-statistics filters because their response is based on the ordering or ranking of the pixels contained within the mask. The median filter removes outliers and achieves the highest percentage in recognizing the surgical situs in minimally invasive hip arthroplasty as compared with other filtering techniques [35]. High pass filtering eliminates the low-frequency regions while retaining or enhancing the high-frequency components. High-pass filters are used to sharpen the blurred images. It gets rid of the complete background. These versatile edge preserving filters along with guided filters enhance the medical image to overcome the challenge of acquiring medical images accurately [36]. There are times when we need to enhance the edges but also retain some of the backgrounds. To do that, we use the modified form of the high-pass filter known as High boost filtering.

Edges are abrupt discontinuities in the grey levels and hence are high-frequency regions. Derivative filters calculate the gradient of the image. They are very sensitive to noise. Both Prewitt and Sobel operators provide a smoothing effect along with providing differentiation. They perform well even when the image is noisy because they smoothen up the noise. Prewitt operator performs uniform smoothing in one direction with edge detection in the perpendicular direction. Average Gradient [34] is used in calculating the amount of texture variation in the image using the equation: [34]

$$G = \frac{1}{(A-1)(B-1)} \sum_{i=1}^{(A-1)(B-1)} \sqrt{\frac{\frac{\partial f^2}{\partial x} + \frac{\partial f^2}{\partial y}}{z}} \tag{16}$$

Sobel, Prewitt, and Canny edge detectors are used to produce edge maps of two-dimensional images useful in encryption of medical images [30]. It is because medical images comprising a lot of confidential information in relation to patient privacy are distributed via internet or intranet making them vulnerable to privacy leakage and malicious tampering [30]. To detect derivative approximation of its rows and columns, $\mathcal{GD}_r$ and $\mathcal{GD}_c$ these detectors utilize two masks $\mathcal{MD}_r$ and $\mathcal{MD}_c$ convolved with an image. Mathematically, the function can be written as

$$\mathcal{GD}_r = \mathcal{MD}_r^* \mathcal{I}_i \tag{17}$$

$$\mathcal{GD}_c = \mathcal{MD}_c^* \mathcal{I}_i \tag{18}$$

where * implies one-dimensional convolution operator.

After that, the gradient magnitude or the edge Intensity $\mathcal{GD}$ at every point and the direction ω of that gradient are calculated as

$$\mathcal{GD} = \sqrt{\mathcal{GD}_r^2 + \mathcal{GD}_c^2} \tag{19}$$

And

$$\phi = \tan^{-1} \frac{GD_r}{GD_c} \tag{20}$$

Different edge detectors are utilized to plot the gradient magnitude. Prewitt operator performs uniform smoothing in one direction with edge detection in the perpendicular direction.

Canny edge detector being gaussian function's derivative is considered as best edge detector owing to its low error rate, strong denoising capability and to get a good balance between the edge detection and noise suppression. In this firstly gauss filter is used to smoothen the image and then the masks for the convolution of edge detectors e.g. Prewitt and Sobel detectors are used to find the intensity gradient of the image [30]. It utilizes the concept of an- maxima suppression and algorithms based on thresholding to detect edges and to calculate the gradient information. Edge maps generated by various edge detectors are selected as the keys for security in case of EMMIE [30]. High pass sharpening filters i.e. Laplacian filter enhances edges and improves line structure of fused medical images [34]. For the medical diagnosis combination of Additive Wavelet Transform and Dual-Tree Complex Wavelet Transform provides the best result [34]. It provides shortest processing time, better visual perception, fine details and better quality in the image.

Table 3. Review of spatial domain-based image enhancement techniques.

Method	Functionality/description
Spline concept [6]	Enhances medical images similarly to BBCCE by using Spline functions to modify the Cumulative distribution function
Histogram Equalization (HE) [11]	Enhances the medical image by flattening and stretching the histogram of the original image across the complete grayscale range (0–255)
Bi-histogram based HE (BBHE) [11]	It divides the histogram into two sub-histograms on the basis of a mean grey scale value and then separately equalizes them to enhance the contrast of the image
Recursive mean-separate HE (RMSHE) [11]	Enhancement is obtained similarly to BBHE by dividing the image histogram based on mean grey values present in medical images recursively into sub-histograms
Recursive sub-image HE [46]	Provides enhancement similarly to RMSHE but after setting the probability cumulative density function to 0.5, the histogram is divided recursively
Edge-based de-noising and adaptive HE [45]	Enhancement is done in two stages: using the wavelet-based de-noising technique initial image de-noising is done and contrast enhancement with certain control parameters by adaptively stretching the histogram
Inverse sigmoid [15]	Enhances X-ray images to recover bright regions using the inverse sigmoid function instead of log function as a tone mapping in the retinex processing
Contrast enhancement using Bezier curve based on Bi-histogram (BBCCE) [7]	Enhance the contrast of images by utilizing a Bezier curve function to modify the cumulative distribution function
Exposure-based Sub-image histogram equalization [47]	Enhance contrast and preserve entropy by equalizing the histogram of sub-images independently and using a threshold value to clip the histogram
Hierarchical correlation histogram analysis [7]	Based on the gray scale distribution of pixel intensity, it enhances medical images by constructing a hierarchical correlation histogram
Un-sharp masking [12]	Details enhancement by focusing on high-frequency contents
Nonlinear transfer function and Un-sharp masking [12]	Local brightness enhancement algorithm divides the V-space image into smaller windows and then do a calculation of the non-linear transfer function of each window to enhance the pixels in the window and finally to restore the contrast of brightness enhanced image

(*continued*)

Table 3. (*continued*)

Method	Functionality/description
Optimum scale value [44]	Enhances contrast with Un-sharp masking but it combats the limitation of using fixed scale value irrespective of the input medical images where scale values are selected randomly
Cuckoo search algorithm [16]	Based on adaptive mutation and adaptive cross-over. To calculate the probability of building a nest and to adapt operators of genetic, it uses same threshold value
Detail synthesis [41]	It enhances the image super-resolution. To obtain details with the more natural frequency it combines singular decomposition of patches and local self-similarity search together
LCS [44]	Enhances range of intensity level but degrade image quality by providing artifacts like saturation
Other techniques [8]	Multi-contrast imaging and other techniques

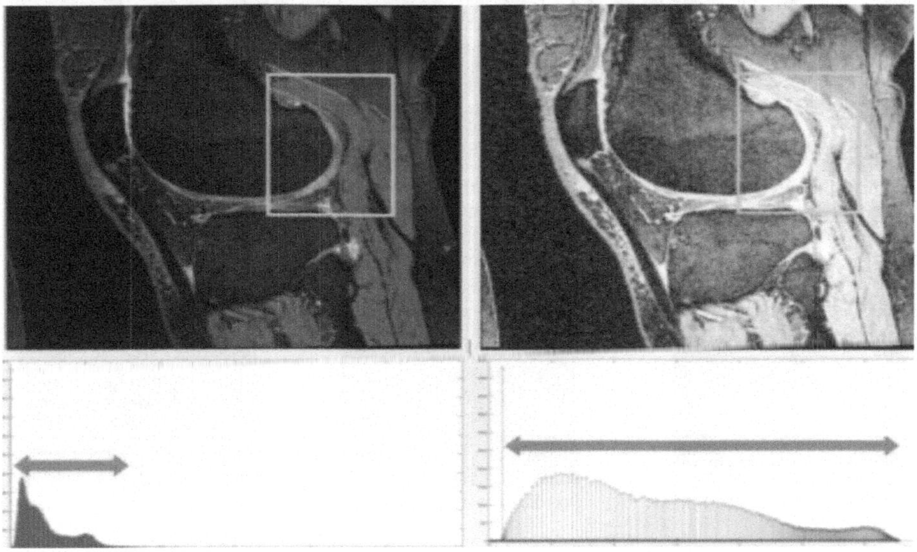

(a) Original image **(b) Histogram equalization**

Fig. 2. Example of over-brightness obtained by histogram equalization (HE) [28]

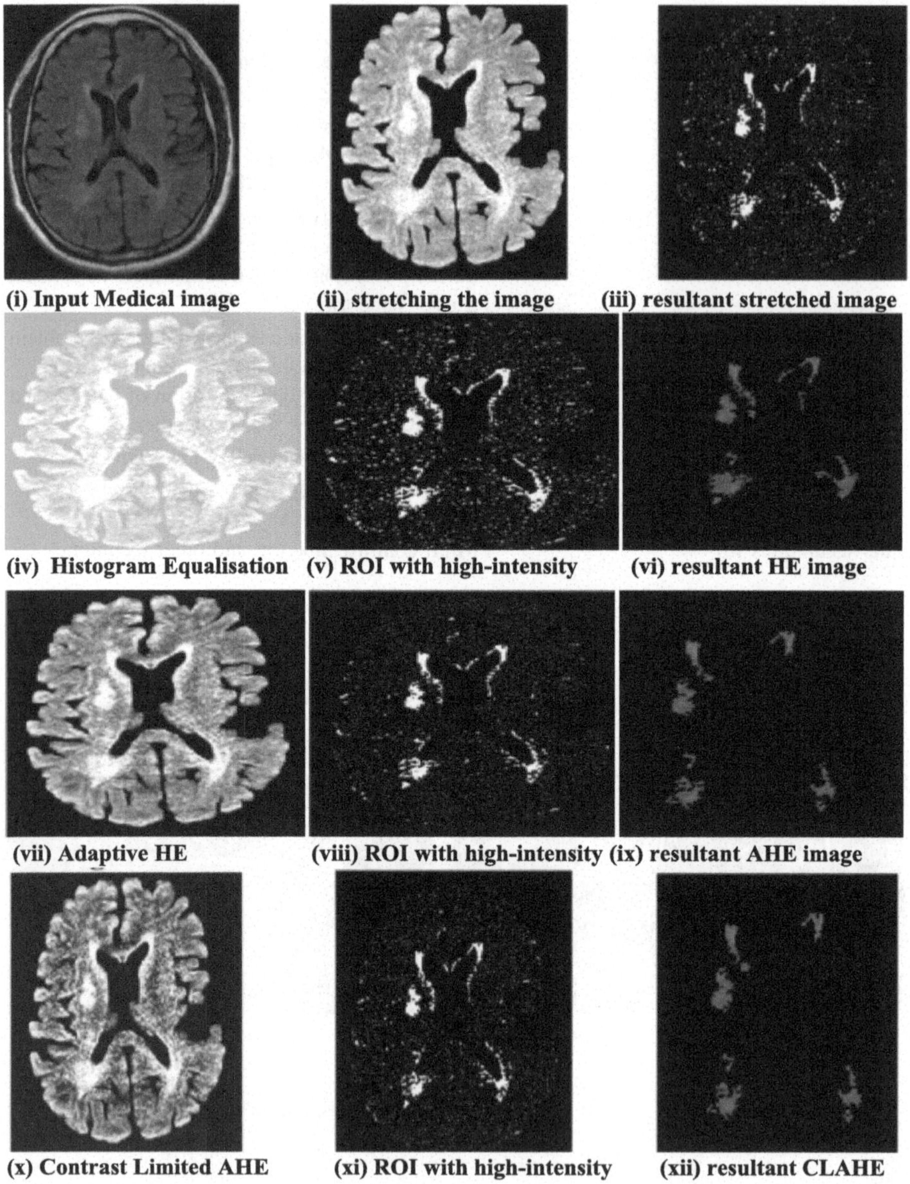

Fig. 3. Comparison outcomes of different algorithms for enhancing contrast in spatial domain depicting AIR-AHE enhanced image better than the rest enhanced image shown above [2]

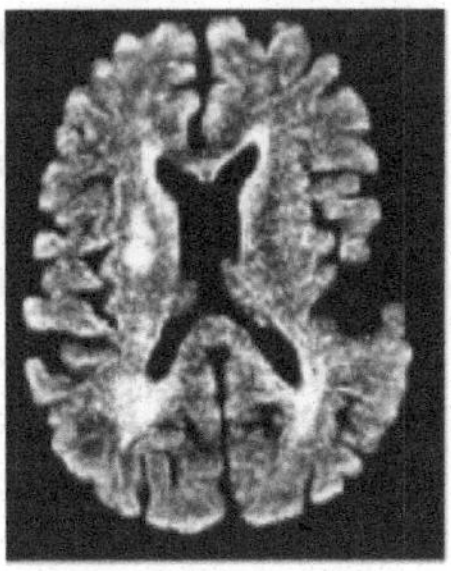

(xiii) AIR-AHE Image

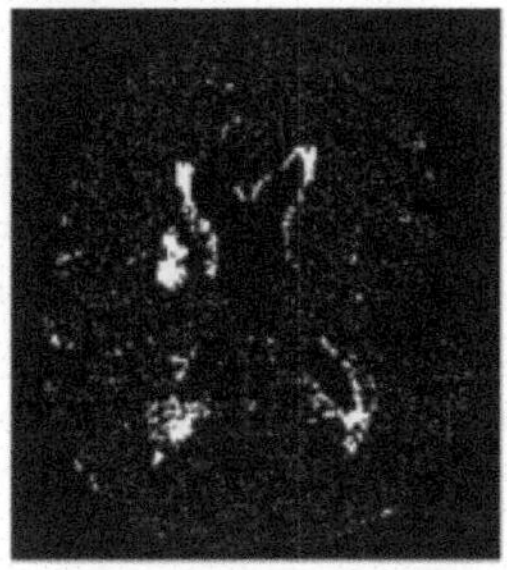

(xiv) ROI with high-intensity

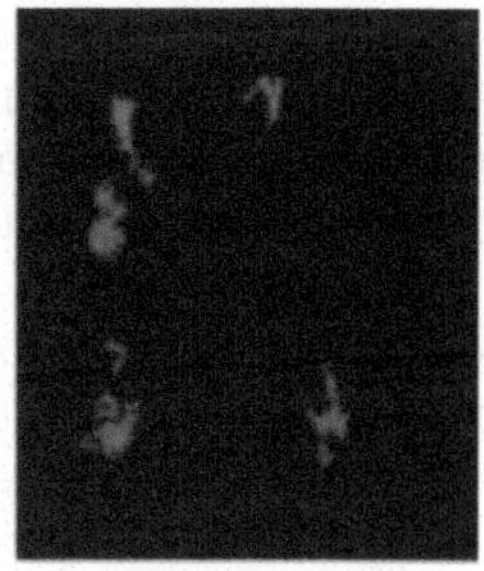

(xv) Resultant AIR-AHE

Fig. 3. (*continued*)

Histogram modeling: Histogram of the biomedical images gives global information about the appearance of the image. There are many areas, wherein we require a flat histogram. Histogram stretching fails to achieve it so we use histogram equalization (HE). HE is automatic and not always provides one result i.e. not interactive. So we use Histogram specification. Table 3 gives a brief review of various techniques in the spatial domain (Figs. 2 and 3).

4.2 Techniques of Frequency Domain

In case of the frequency domain, when we calculate Discrete Fourier Transform, the value of the dc component is very large compared to the higher frequency. No display device has such a large dynamic range; hence there is a need for dynamic range compression. Using high pass butter-worth filter, ringing effects are removed and the transition is smoothened. Traditional Homomorphic filtering uses this illumination-reflectance model to filter images in the frequency domain [9] (Figs. 4 and 5).

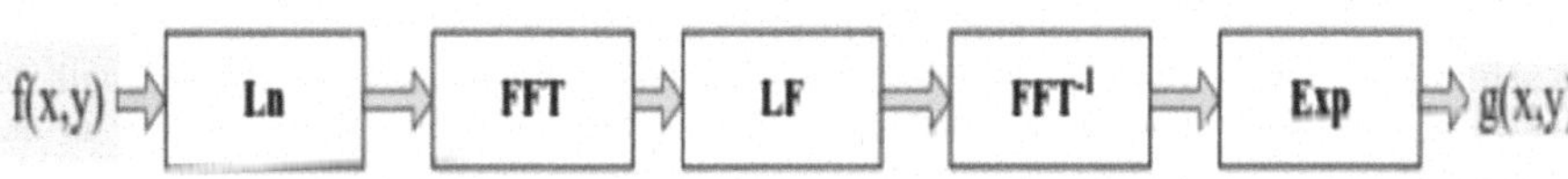

Fig. 4. Traditional homomorphic filtering procedure [33].

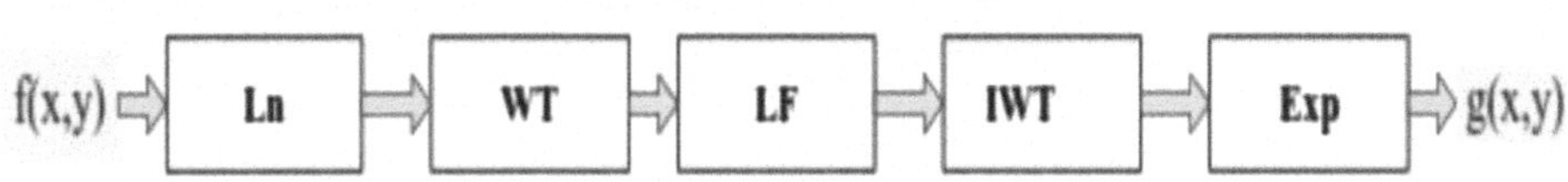

Fig. 5. Wavelets homomorphic filtering transforms procedure [33]

While wavelet-based Homomorphic filtering [33] proposed by Xinmin Zhou performs a filtering operation in the spatial domain to remove non-uniformity luminance distribution of medical images.

Medical images have low spatial resolution and low contrast between two distinct structures. Noise to signal ratio of medical images is low owing to the availability of artifacts (e.g. bias and motion field in MRI). There is no problem in filtering out local bright noise patches but in case of mammography, we are required to be extra conscious to preserve micro-calcifications. Due to the stability of low flip angle, out of field count in the scanning of PET, low flip angle stability in MRI acquisition, Medical imaging modalities generate noise. To remove the noise using the concept of local averaging, wavelet-based filter is utilized. The nearest neighbor or visualization-driven filtering or bi-cubic interpolation provide extremely zoomed image and low-resolution data [10] Image transform implies class of unitary matrices utilized to represent biomedical images. Just as a signal of 1D can be expanded in terms of an orthogonal set of basis functions, a biomedical image can be represented by basis images or set consists of basis arrays.

Background of Transforms:

✓ **Sinusoidal transforms**	Many members have a fast implementation, useful in finding a practical replacement for Karhunen Loeve Transform, analyzing Toeplitz systems, mathematical modeling of signals, excellent energy compaction in case of the optimum fast transform.
✓ **FFT**	It refers to a class of algorithms used to compute discrete Fourier transform efficiently.
✓ **DCT**	Fourier transform utilizes cosines and sine waves to present the signal, but the DCT utilizes only waves of cosine.
✓ **Hartley Transform**	It jointly utilizes both sines and cosines basis functions but its coefficients are real numbers
✓ **DST**	About twice as fast as the cosine transform. Good energy compaction. useful for coding and filtering
✓ **DFT**	It transforms N real numbers into N complex numbers with conjugate symmetry.
✓ **Haar**	Its basis functions vary in both scale (width) and position. It samples the input data sequence in coarse to fine resolution and takes the difference between adjacent pairs. It provides multi-resolution analysis.
✓ **Slant**	It was designed to have not only a constant first basis function but a linear second basis function as well.
✓ **Karhunen Loeve Transform(Hotelling Transform)**	Because of the concept of using eigenvectors associated with the largest eigenvalues to reduce the error, the KL transform is also known as the "Principal components Transform". It is linear transformation whose basis functions are the eigenvectors calculated for the covariance matrix of the biomedical image. As it diagonalizes the matrix of covariance, it decorrelates the data, thus making it suitable for compression

Table 4 compares the transforms utilized in the field of biomedical image processing.

Transforms are utilized in providing robust and imperceptible multiple watermarking of digital images [31]. Morphological transforms enhance the contrast improve the quality of biomedical images. Being non-linear, they are efficient in sharpening medical images utilizing the concept of a bottom hat and top-hat transforms [32]. It includes opening operation i.e. application of the erosion and dilation operations on the same image respectively and closing operation. The opening operator (AoB) helps to

Table 4. Comparison of transforms

Properties	DCT	DFT	Slant	Hadamard	KL	Haar
Energy compaction	Better than DFT	Better than Hadamard	Better than Hadamard	Better than Haar	Best	Fair
Complexity in computation	Better than Slant	Excellent	Better than Haar	Better than Slant	Best	Less than Slant
Applications	Designing Weiner filters and transform coders	Digital filtering	Coding image	Compressing data, filtering and designing codes	Useful for multispectral colors	Extracting feature, coding, and analysis of the image and in wavelet transform

remove connections between objects while the closing operation (A, B) eradicates small holes and fills cracks. Bottom hat eliminate the background of the image. Top hat or white top hat used to remove the image background can be defined as

$$Top - Hat(A) = ATH = A - (AoB) \tag{21}$$

Morphological transform acts like a high-pass filter and filters out the bright areas of the image. To improve the contrast between dark and bright areas we add the bright areas (the result of the opening operator) to the image and subtract the dark areas (the result of the closing operator) from it. Mathematically,

$$A_{q1} = A + ATH - ABH \tag{22}$$

The Fourier transform breaks down a signal into the constituent sinusoids of different frequencies. It tells us which frequencies are present in the signal and transforms a signal from the time domain to the frequency domain. For functions of two dimensions, the direct and inverse Fourier transforms are respectively defined as:

$$F(u, v) = \int_{-\infty}^{\infty} \int_{-\infty}^{\infty} e^{-j2\pi(ux+vy)} dxdy \tag{23}$$

and

$$f(x, y) = \int_{-\infty}^{\infty} \int_{-\infty}^{\infty} e^{j2\pi(ux+vy)} dudv \tag{24}$$

where f(x, y) is an image and F (u, v) is its spectrum. Just by looking at the Fourier transform of a signal, one can tell which frequencies are present but it is impossible to tell when a particular event took place. Because of this limitation Fourier transforms is not suitable for medical image signals which contain numerous transitory characteristics viz. drift abrupt changes, beginning, and end of events. To correct this deficiency, a small window is placed over the signal and the Fourier transform is computed only on windowed signal. The window is then moved over the entire signal. STFT provides some information about both time and frequency but it offers limited precision which is determined by the size of the window. So we moved to Wavelet analysis that aims to tell us which frequency at what time. Using it, it was possible to resolve high-frequency components within a small time window and low-frequency components within a large time window [4].

Modified histogram equalization for a medical image with a minimum number of artifacts uses stationary wavelet transform and histogram mapping [14]. Noise problems of medical images led to the decrease in the image quality and contrast as well as the fuzziness of some image details. Such images have to be enhanced to meet the requirements of clinical diagnosis using Multi-Resolution Analysis. As the name suggests, the Multi-Resolution analysis allows us to study a signal at different scales. A simple analogy is looking at an object from different distances. Viewed from a great distance, a large scale representation of the object is perceived in which only the global (non-detailed) information about the object is available. As we get closer, the object is perceived at smaller scales and more details become available. In a similar way, a

Table 5. Review of transform domain based enhancement techniques:

Method	Functionality/description
Wavelet Transform Fusion Techniques [13]	Being an extension of Fourier Transformation idea, it can carry out local analysis on signals in terms of frequency and time which are frequency sub-division on low-frequency signals and time subdivision on high-frequency signals. It avoids loss of image details and amplification of noise
Transform based Enhancement techniques [13]	To provide the best contrast and to enhance the image visualization histogram of the original image is modified based on the threshold values and gradient information with a minimum number of artifacts. MHE uses histogram mapping and stationary wavelet transform
Rayleigh Maximum Likelihood bilateral filter [43]	Enhances ultrasound images and improves SNR by following two steps: speckle, noise and edge detection followed by filtering. The bilateral filter removes noise while Rayleigh maximum likelihood filter suppresses the speckle
Edge Preserve Filter [14]	Enhances Medical images by Combining Edge preserving filter for image enhancement and smoothing and multi-scale transform to construct a fused image
Multi-scale edge representation [42]	Enhancement of the medical images is obtained in the wavelet domain using a multi-scale decomposition of the image

signal can also be analyzed at different scales where large-scale deals with global information while small scales deal with detailed information. The continuous wavelet transforms of the signal $x(t)$ and $\psi(t)$ is defined as,

$$W_{\Psi(p,q)} = \int_{-\infty}^{+\infty} x(t) * \Psi_{p,q(t)} dx \tag{25}$$

where

$$\psi_{p,q(t)} = \frac{1}{\sqrt{|p|}} \psi(t - p/q) \tag{26}$$

And the wavelet $\Psi p, q$ is calculated from the mother wavelet ψ using dilation and translation. Also p is the dilation factor and q is translation parameter (both being real positive numbers). The mother wavelet Ψ fulfils the condition of having zero mean under some mild assumptions (Daubechies 1992). Combination of thresholding, DWT, dual tree and double density DWT provides good visual perception of the image [38]. Table 5 describe the review of transform based enhancement techniques.

5 Color Biomedical Image Enhancement

Human beings have the ability to perceive and differentiate few hundreds of color intensities and shades instead of limited shades of gray. The retina is covered with photoreceptor cells (rods cones). Rods provide us with monochromatic night vision while cones are responsible for color vision. These cones divide the visible portion of the electromagnetic spectrum into three bands viz. Red, Green, and Blue. Similar to RGB model, NTSC model consists of three components viz Luminance, Hue, and Saturation. In this model, Luminance component represents the grey scale information while the Hue and Saturation carry the color information. When color images are applied in the quaternion space then we apply the 2-D quaternion discrete Fourier transform (2-D QDFT). The quaternion numbers are basically four-dimensional hypercomplex numbers. Quaternion representation of color image aids to visualize the color of the image as the single unit by representing each color as a vector. Retinal imaging helps in diagnosing common eye diseases and cardiovascular diseases. Quality of retinal images degrades due to uneven illumination, image blurring and low contrast. It becomes imperative to use enhancement techniques to improve color retinal image luminosity and contrast. Color retinal image enhancement helps ophthalmologists' inefficient screening of retinal diseases. It also aids in improving automated image analysis for clinical diagnosis. DCT is used in biomedical image processing owing to its strong energy compaction property. The two-dimensional DCT transform formula is defined as [39]

$$F(x, y) = c(x)c(y)\frac{2}{N}\sum_{i=0}^{N-1} \cos\left(\frac{2i+1}{2N} x\Pi\right) \cos\left(\frac{2j+1}{2N} y\Pi\right) \tag{27}$$

where x, y, i, j *(varies from 0 to N-1)* and

$$c(x) = c(y) = \begin{cases} \frac{1}{\sqrt{2}} x = 0, y = 0 \\ 1 \; in \; other \; cases \end{cases} \quad (28)$$

The inverse discrete cosine transform can be mathematically defined as in [40]

$$f(i,j) = \frac{2}{N} \sum_{x=0}^{N-1} c(x)\, c(y) \sum_{y=0}^{N-1} F(x,y) \cos\left(\frac{2i+1}{2N} x\Pi\right) \cos\left(\frac{2j+1}{2N} y\pi\right) \quad (29)$$

where $f(i,j)$ is grey-value of the pixel and $F(x,y)$ is the DCT coefficient

Common geometric transformation attacks (like rotation, cropping, scaling and deletion of lines/columns), common enhancement technique attacks (like low pass filtering, histogram equalization, sharpening, gamma correction, noise addition) and JPEG compression attacks are applied in a blind DCT based color watermarking algorithm for embedding multiple watermarks [37]. Table 6 reviews the enhancement techniques in color domain.

Table 6. Review of color image enhancement techniques.

Method	Functionality/description
Zonal rooting and alpha rooting methods applied on 2D- QDFT [17]	Zonal alpha rooting method segregates the frequency spectrum into various zones. For different zones, it then applies the alpha rooting with different alpha values. Enhances or improves the visual perception by modifying the reference grey lines
Dark channel prior method [18]	Enhances the contrast and highlights the details in X-ray image deteriorated by X-ray scattering same as haze scattering by dark channel prior method
Enhancing Color retinal images on the basis of contrast and Luminosity adjustment [19]	It utilizes the value calculated after applying gamma correction on HSV (Hue, Saturation, and value) channel to obtain luminance gain matrix and color space in order to increase the contrast of channels of RGB (Red, Green, and Blue) plane. Contrast Limited adaptive histogram equalization increases the contrast in case of the channel of luminosity in L*a*b color space
Mammography Malignancy detection algorithm [20]	Increases the mammographic feature representation, discerns the malignancy and classifies the full mammogram image. It utilizes dual deep CNN (Convolution Neural Network) and genetically searched pseudocolor for enhancing the input

Pseudo Coloring: Pseudo simply means fake; hence fake coloring. It is known that the human eye can discern thousands of colors and intensities as opposed to only one or two dozen shades of grey. Hence in pseudocoloring, grey scale images are given color based on their values of the grey levels. There are two different approaches to color image processing [4]:

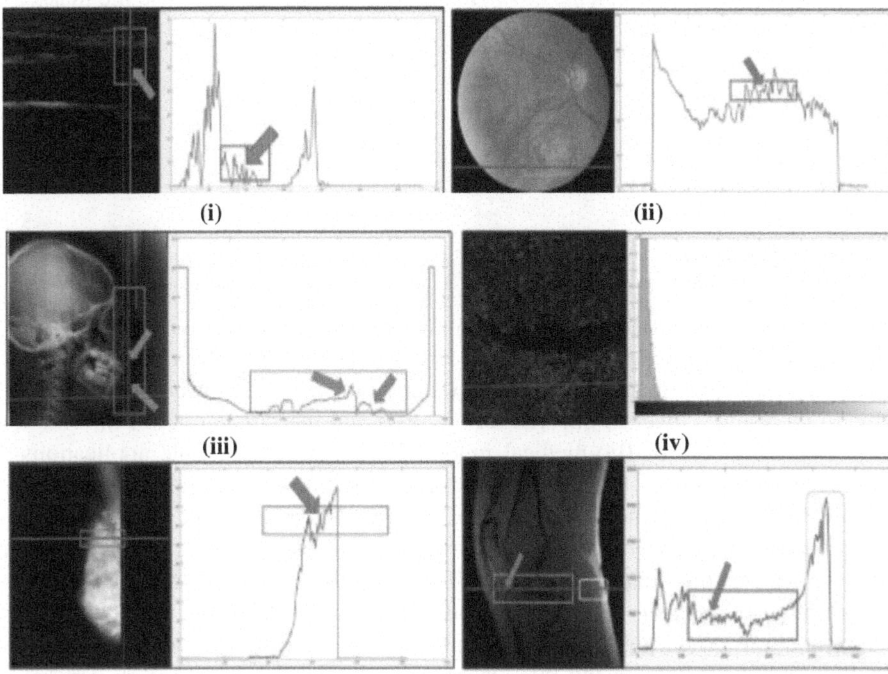

Fig. 6. Contrast and brightness in medical image: inadequate tissue contrast leading to weak edges in (i) ultrasound (ii) fundus images (iii) inadequate contrast between the background and tissue in an X-ray radiograph (iv) very low brightness in a fluorescent image, and inadequate contrast leading to difficulty in differentiating surrounding tissues in (v) mammograms and (vi) MRI images [28]

1. We process each of the 3 color planes individually and then combine the modified 3 planes to get a processed color image. This is similar to grey scale processing as each of the 3 planes is 8 bit.
2. We directly process the color image.

   As for medical image smoothing, we can perform sharpening by implementing the Laplacian on three color planes individually. We could use a Laplacian mask $\mathcal{M}_\ell$ shown below:

$$\mathcal{M}_{\ell} = \begin{bmatrix} 0 & -1 & 0 \\ -1 & 4 & -1 \\ 0 & -1 & 0 \end{bmatrix} \tag{30}$$

But if we are interested in preserving the low-frequency components, we make sure that the sum of the coefficients of the mask is not zero. We hence use the mask $\mathcal{M}_{k}$ given below (Fig. 6):

$$\mathcal{M}_{k} = \begin{bmatrix} 0 & -1 & 0 \\ -1 & 5 & -1 \\ 0 & -1 & 0 \end{bmatrix} \tag{31}$$

6 Fuzzy Domain

Fuzzification means an association of fuzzy membership functions with variables [15]. Image enhancement problems of some uncertain and inaccurate image are dealt with the fuzzy set. Medical image enhancement diverted his attention towards fuzzy set as it is able to represent a diverse, uncertain, non-exact and inaccurate pool of information. Contrast enhancement of Bio-medical images is one of the principle applications of intensity transformations. For spatial filtering, first, the neighborhood properties of fuzzy are defined that catches the essence of what the filters are supposed to detect. It is a computationally intensive process. It is because, at every location in the medical image, we apply the fuzzy operations. To apply Rule-based fuzzy logic for the transformation of intensity, first, the inputs are fuzzified using the applicable membership functions. Then to perform any required fuzzy logical operations, for example, to yield a maximum value using max or min operations, the outputs of all parts of an antecedent is combined. After this implication and aggregation method is applied. Finally, we defuzzify the final output fuzzy set. The fuzzification and defuzzification are because of the fact that we do not possess fuzzy hardware. Processing of images with fuzzy techniques is possible through the coding of image data (fuzzification) and decoding of the results (defuzzification). The middle step (modification of membership values) that comes after the transformation of data from gray- level plane to membership plane (fuzzification) is the main power of fuzzy image processing. An appropriate fuzzy technique such as fuzzy rule-based approach; fuzzy clustering or a fuzzy integration approach is required to modify the membership values. Fuzzy logic is a powerful tool for the representation and processing of human knowledge in the form of fuzzy if-then rules. These techniques are utilized for bio-medical image processing chain, image understanding, and object recognition. Fuzzy logic image processing is more informative compared with binary image processing. To reduce the noise in an image and to reduce the disparity between pixel values one can introduce an adaptive fuzzy morphology filter in the future. Fuzzy clustering plays a pivotal role in pattern recognition, data analysis, and fuzzy modeling because of its capabilities to reveal structural relationship in data. Owing to the support of unsupervised mode of learning,

Table 7. Review of contrast enhancement techniques in the fuzzy domain.

Method	Functionality/description
Brightness preserving bi-level fuzzy histogram equalization (BPFHE) [21]	Better visual quality, preserve the original brightness, enhances the contrast of MRI brain images. To overcome the washed out appearance and false contouring problems, brightness preserving HE based techniques divide the histogram of the real image into sub-histograms and then separately equalize each sub-histogram
Improved fuzzy set combined with adaptive threshold in NSCT (Non-sub sampled contourlet transform) [22]	Fuzzy set enhances global contrast and Laplace operator enhances details in the medical image. Remove noise by decomposing the image into the NSCT domain with a low-frequency sub-band and various high-frequency sub-bands. Then apply the linear transformation for the low-frequency components and adaptive threshold method to remove the high-frequency noise
Fuzzy logic and cellular automata [23]	To detect microcalcifications in mammography, X and Y gradient operators are used to process the image. Fuzzy system after getting the output of each filter detects areas with high tone variation. Cellular automaton utilizes local rules to remove noise and keep the pixels with high probabilities to a microcalcification region
Contrast enhancement based forensics method (MCEF) based on fuzzy fusion [24]	Uses artificial neural network instead of SVM to increase the robustness of tamper detection methods, accuracy and threshold value for contrast detection. In this, gaps are removed and sudden peaks are introduced using CE trace hiding attack and CE trace forging attack. Integration of local random dithering in the form of pixel value mapping is done to implement CE trace hiding. Grey level histogram of target pixel region is modified in the form of fraudulent peak/gap artifacts. Then both attacks are added to obtain enhanced the security against attacks in forensic detection framework
Contrast limited fuzzy adaptive histogram equalization (CLFAHE) [25]	Better contrast, preserve local information and improve the contrast of MRI brain images. In this first do the transformation of grey level intensities into membership plane which is modified with contrast

(*continued*)

Table 7. (*continued*)

Method	Functionality/description
	intensification operator. To prevent excessive contrast enhancement CLAHE is applied to modified membership plane which is finally mapped back to grey level intensities
Refinements of prototypes to enhance the Classification and reconstruction performance of fuzzy C-means algorithm (FCM) [26]	Performance index is optimized by aggregating clusters (information modules) produced by FCM in the supervised mode with the help of Differential Evolution (DE)
Type II Fuzzy set [27]	It is used to enhance the contrast of medical images with uncertainties. It uses Hamacher T Co to frame new membership function and considers the membership function of type I fuzzy set

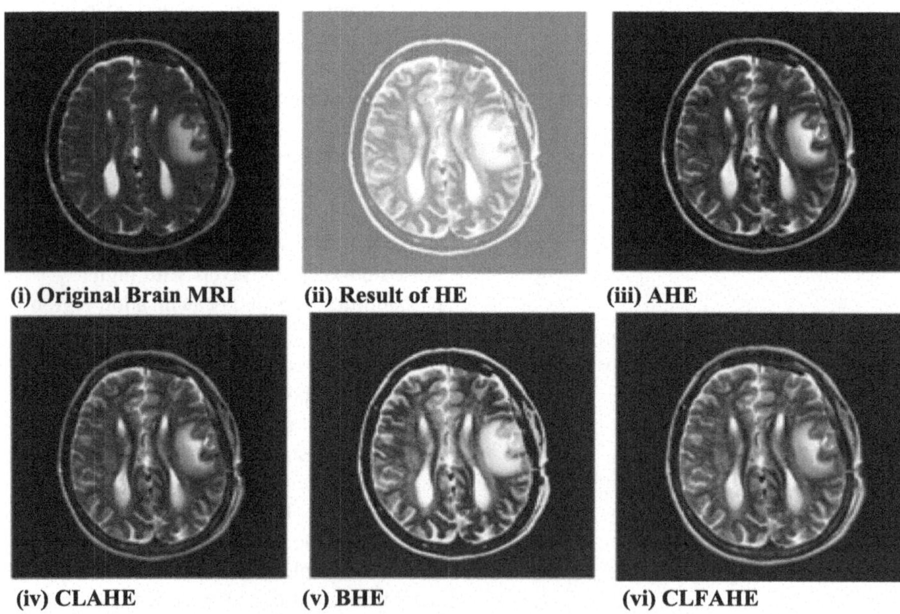

Fig. 7. Comparison result that proves ClFAHE technique is better than other histogram based techniques [25].

fuzzy clustering provides many opportunities in the data analysis. Table 7 reviews the enhancement techniques used for improving the quality of the image in the fuzzy domain (Fig. 7).

Gaps found in Literature Review of these domains: After reviewing the literature of enhancement techniques in three domains the following literature gaps are analyzed which can be removed in the time to come.

1. It has been found from the survey that biomedical image enhancement in the spatial domain using filters, histogram equalization and so on leads to degraded images.
2. Traditional Transform domain methods introduce the Gaussian Noise and the Color artifacts result in a color imbalance of output images [15].
3. Conventional Fuzzy based image enhancement techniques satisfactory adjustment factor k = 128 which is feasible only for low contrast images. Information is lost when applied for over contrast images.
4. Conventional biomedical image enhancement techniques are subjective, arbitrary and snot precise [10].

7 Conclusions

Enhancement of image is one of the first steps in image processing and is utilized in every field of image analysis of the biomedical field. It is extremely useful for the doctors in the treatment of diseases. Every technique of enhancement is unique in one or other aspect. Through this paper, we highlighted the main aspects of enhancement techniques to be useful in enhancing the contrast of fused medical image according to the requirement. It has been observed that large variety of methods used to enhance the image prior to their morphological and/or statistical analysis for biomedical or technological purposes causes a requirement for comparative evaluation of the methods in order to choose the most effective ones.

Till now visual comparison of images subjective to enhancement procedures are used to do a comparative evaluation of medical images. In this paper, we discussed the limitation, application, conventional and recent enhancement techniques in three domains in the field of biomedical image processing. Utilizing the enhancement techniques, it is possible for doctors to see the interior portions of the human body with extreme clarity ease and detail thus facilitating easy detection and diagnosis of various diseases and helping them make keyhole surgeries with minimal opening of body parts.

Based on the requirement of the image, different and best medical image enhancement techniques are combined to provide effective results. The future scope will be in medical image fusion of enhancement techniques in multiple domains for increasing contrast, detecting texture, removing noise and thus improving the image quality.

References

1. Przytulska, M., Kulikowski, J.L.: Quantitative test-based assessment of biomedical image enhancement procedures. Biocybern. Biomed. Eng. **36**(1), 205–216 (2016)
2. Isa, I.S., Sulaiman, S.N., Mustapha, M., Karim, N.K.A.: Automatic contrast enhancement of brain MR images using Average Intensity Replacement based on Adaptive Histogram Equalization (AIR-AHE). Biocybern. Biomed. Eng. **37**(1), 24–34 (2017)
3. Gao, G., Wan, X., Yao, S., Cui, Z., Zhou, C., Sun, X.: Reversible data hiding with contrast enhancement and tamper localization for medical images. Inf. Sci. **385**, 250–265 (2017)
4. Gonzalez, R.C., Woods, R.E.: Image processing. Digital image processing, 2nd edn. (2007)
5. Wu, Q., Merchant, F., Castleman, K.: Microscope Image Processing. Academic Press, Boston (2013)
6. Perperidis, A., Cusack, D., White, A., McDicken, N., MacGillivray, T., Anderson, T.: Dynamic enhancement of B-mode cardiac ultrasound image sequences. Ultrasound Med. Biol. **43**(7), 1533–1548 (2017)
7. Maurya, L., Mahapatra, P.K., Kumar, A.: A social spider optimized image fusion approach for contrast enhancement and brightness preservation. Appl. Soft Comput. **52**, 575–592 (2017)
8. Chou, G.Y., Moy, L., Kim, S.G., Leite, A.P.K., Baete, S.H., Babb, J.S., Sodickson, D.K., Sigmund, E.E.: Comparison of contrast enhancement and diffusion-weighted magnetic resonance imaging in healthy and cancerous tissue. Eur. J. Radiol. **84**, 1888–1893 (2015)
9. Pratt, W.K.: Introduction to Digital Image Processing. CRC Press, Boco Raton (2013)
10. Milanfar, P.: A tour of modern image filtering: new insights and methods, both practical and theoretical. IEEE Sig. Process. Mag. **30**(1), 106–128 (2013)
11. Akila, K., Jayashree, L.S., Vasuki, A.: Mammographic image enhancement using indirect contrast enhancement techniques–a comparative study. Procedia Comput. Sci. **47**, 255–261 (2015)
12. Zhang, K., Wang, H., Yuan, B., Wang, L.: An image enhancement technique using nonlinear transfer function and unsharp masking in the multispectral endoscope. In: International Conference on Innovative Optical Health Science, p. 1024504. International Society for Optics and Photonics, January 2017
13. Liu, S.: Study on medical image enhancement based on wavelet transform fusion algorithm. J. Med. Imaging Health Inform. **7**(2), 388–392 (2017)
14. Li, W., Zhao, Z., Du, J., Wang, Y.: Edge-preserve filter image enhancement with application to medical image fusion. J. Med. Imaging Health Inform. **7**(1), 16–24 (2017)
15. Ko, J., Hong, W.K.: Inverse sigmoid-based X-Ray image enhancement. Indian J. Sci. Technol. **9**(47) (2016)
16. Daniel, E., Anitha, J.: Optimum wavelet-based masking for the contrast enhancement of medical images using enhanced cuckoo search algorithm. Comput. Biol. Med. **71**, 149–155 (2016)
17. Grigoryan, A.M., Johna, A., Agaian, S.S.: Color image enhancement of medical images using alpha-rooting and zonal alpha-rooting methods on 2-D QDFT. In: SPIE Medical Imaging, p. 1013618. International Society for Optics and Photonics, March 2017
18. Rui, W., Guoyu, W.: Medical X-ray image enhancement method based on dark channel prior. In: Proceedings of the 5th International Conference on Bioinformatics and Computational Biology, pp. 38–41. ACM, January 2017
19. Zhou, M., Jin, K., Wang, S., Ye, J., Qian, D.: Color retinal image enhancement based on luminosity and contrast adjustment. IEEE Trans. Biomed. Eng. (2017)

20. Teare, P., Fishman, M., Benzaquen, O., Toledano, E., Elnekave, E.: Malignancy detection on mammography using dual deep convolutional neural networks and genetically discovered false color input enhancement. J. Digit. Imaging **30**, 1–7 (2017)
21. Magudeeswaran, V., Ravichandran, C.G., Thirumurugan, P.: Brightness preserving bi-level fuzzy histogram equalization for MRI brain image contrast enhancement. Int. J. Imaging Syst. Technol. **27**(2), 153–161 (2017)
22. Zhou, F., Jia, Z., Yang, J., Kasabov, N.: Method of improved fuzzy contrast combined adaptive threshold in NSCT for medical image enhancement. BioMed. Res. Int. (2017)
23. Rubio, Y., Montiel, O., Sepúlveda, R.: Microcalcification detection in mammograms based on fuzzy logic and cellular automata. In: Melin, P., Castillo, O., Kacprzyk, J. (eds.) Nature-Inspired Design of Hybrid Intelligent Systems. SCI, vol. 667, pp. 583–602. Springer, Cham (2017). https://doi.org/10.1007/978-3-319-47054-2_38
24. Rao, B.S.: A fuzzy fusion approach for modified contrast enhancement based image forensics against attacks. Multimedia Tools Appl. 1–21 (2017)
25. Magudeeswaran, V., Singh, J.F.: Contrast limited fuzzy adaptive histogram equalization for enhancement of brain images. Int. J. Imaging Syst. Technol. **27**(1), 98–103 (2017)
26. Reyes-Galaviz, O.F., Pedrycz, W.: Enhancement of the classification and reconstruction performance of fuzzy C-means with refinements of prototypes. Fuzzy Sets Syst. **318**, 80–99 (2017)
27. Chaira, T.: An improved medical image enhancement scheme using type II fuzzy set. Appl. Soft Comput. **25**, 293–308 (2014)
28. Gandhamal, A., Talbar, S., Gajre, S., Hani, A.F.M., Kumar, D.: Local gray level S-curve transformation–a generalized contrast enhancement technique for medical images. Comput. Biol. Med. **83**, 120–133 (2017)
29. deAraujo, A.F., Constantinou, C.E., Tavares, J.M.R.: Smoothing of ultrasound images using a new selective average filter. Expert Syst. Appl. **60**, 96–106 (2016)
30. Cao, W., Zhou, Y., Chen, C.P., Xia, L.: Medical image encryption using edge maps. Sig. Process. **132**, 96–109 (2017)
31. Singh, A.K., Dave, M., Mohan, A.: Hybrid technique for robust and imperceptible image watermarking in DWT–DCT–SVD domain. Natl. Acad. Sci. Lett. **37**(4), 351–358 (2014)
32. Firoz, R., Ali, M.S., Khan, M.N.U., Hossain, M.K., Islam, M.K., Shahinuzzaman, M.: Medical image enhancement using morphological transformation. J. Data Anal. Inf. Process. **4**(01), 1 (2016)
33. Zhou, X., Zheng, Y., Tan, L., Zhao, J.: medical image contrast enhancement via wavelet homomorphic filtering transform. TELKOMNIKA (Telecommun. Comput. Electron. Control) **14**(3), 1203–1212 (2016)
34. Yang, Y., Que, Y., Huang, S., Lin, P.: Multimodal sensor medical image fusion based on type-2 fuzzy logic in NSCT domain. IEEE Sens. J. **16**(10), 3735–3745 (2016)
35. Putzer, D., Pizzini, A., Liebensteiner, M., Moctezuma, J.L., Nogler, M.: Recognizing the surgical situs in minimally invasive hip arthroplasty: a comparison of different filtering techniques. Biocybern. Biomed. Eng. **36**(1), 182–192 (2016)
36. Rajendran, R., Rao, S.P., Agaian, S.S., Panetta, K.: A versatile edge-preserving image enhancement approach for medical images using a guided filter. In: 2016 IEEE International Conference on Systems, Man, and Cybernetics (SMC), pp. 002341–002346. IEEE, October 2016
37. Roy, S., Pal, A.K.: A blind DCT based color watermarking algorithm for embedding multiple watermarks. AEU-Int. J. Electron. Commun. **72**, 149–161 (2017)
38. Vimala, C., Priya, P.A.: Degraded image enhancement through double density dual tree discrete wavelet transform. Indian J. Sci. Technol. **9**(28) (2016)

39. Akansu, A.N., Serdijn, W.A., Selesnick, I.W.: Emerging applications of wavelets: a review. Phys. Commun. **3**(1), 1–18 (2010)
40. Ali, M., Ahn, C.W.: An optimized watermarking technique based on self-adaptive DE in DWT–SVD transform domain. Sig. Process. **94**, 545–556 (2014)
41. Xiao, J., Liu, E., Zhao, L., Wang, Y.F., Jiang, W.: Detail enhancement of image super-resolution based on detail synthesis. Sig. Process. Image Commun. **50**, 21–33 (2017)
42. Luo, Z., Jia, Y.: MR image contrast enhancement by wavelet-based contourlet transform. Int. J. Bioautom. **20**(2) (2016)
43. Li, H., Wu, J., Miao, A., Yu, P., Chen, J., Zhang, Y.: Rayleigh-maximum-likelihood bilateral filter for ultrasound image enhancement. Biomed. Eng. Online **16**(1), 46 (2017)
44. Verma, H.K., Pal, S.: Modified sigmoid function based gray scale image contrast enhancement using particle swarm optimization. J. Inst. Eng. (India) Ser. B **97**(2), 243–251 (2016)
45. Hu, H.M., Gao, Y., Guo, Q., Li, B.: A region-based video de-noising algorithm based on temporal and spatial correlations. Neurocomputing **266**, 361–374 (2017)
46. Koh, N.C.Y., Sim, K.S., Tso, C.P.: CT brain lesion detection through a combination of recursive sub-image histogram equalization in wavelet domain and adaptive gamma correction with weighting distribution. In: International Conference on Robotics, Automation and Sciences (ICORAS), pp. 1–6. IEEE, November 2016
47. Vig, N., Budhiraja, S., Singh, J.: Hue preserving color image enhancement using a guided filter based sub image histogram equalization. In: 2016 Ninth International Conference on Contemporary Computing (IC3), pp. 1–6. IEEE, August 2016

Using Variant Directional Dis(similarity) Measures for the Task of Textual Entailment

Anand Gupta[1], Manpreet Kaur[1], Disha Garg[2], and Karuna Saini[2](✉)

[1] Department of Computer Science, NSIT, New Delhi, India
[2] Department of Information Technology, NSIT, New Delhi, India
karuna.saini07@gmail.com

Abstract. Textual entailment (TE) is a task used to determine degree of semantic inference between a pair of text fragments in many natural language processing applications. In literature, a single document summarization framework has exploited TE to establish degree of connectedness between pair of sentences in a text summarization method. Despite noteworthy performance of the method, the extensive resource requirements and slow speed of the TE tool render it impractical to generate summaries in real time scenarios. This has stimulated the authors to propose the use of available directional dis(similarity) (distance and similarity) measures in place of TE system. The present paper aims to find a suitable directional measure which can successfully replace the TE system and decrease the overall runtime of the summarization method. Therefore, state-of-the-art directional dis(similarity) measures are implemented in the same summarization framework to present a comparative analysis of performance of all the measures. The experiments are conducted on DUC 2002 dataset and the results are evaluated using ROUGE tool to find the most suitable directional measure of textual entailment.

1 Introduction

Textual entailment is a task of predicting semantic inference between two text fragments i.e. whether the meaning of one fragment can be inferred or entailed from the other text. The formal definition of textual entailment is given in [1] as a directional relationship between two fragments-T, the entailing text and H, the entailed text- so that *T entails H if, typically, a human reading T would infer that H is most likely true*. The essence of textual entailment is in its unidirectional nature. The hypothesis must be entailed by the given text, but the text need not be entailed by the hypothesis.

For example:

Text: The Aztec Indians founded a city on the site of modern-day Mexico City in the 14th century.
Hypothesis: The Aztecs arrived in the Valley of Mexico in the 13th century.

B. Panda et al. (Eds.): REDSET 2017, CCIS 799, pp. 287–297, 2018.
https://doi.org/10.1007/978-981-10-8527-7_23

Textual entailment plays a vital role in many NLP applications like Machine Translation, Information Extraction, Information Retrieval, Question Answering, Paraphrasing, Text Summarization etc. Many lexical, syntactic and semantic matching approaches of recognizing textual entailment have been proposed till now. The traditional string matching measures also have been used for the same purpose. But string similarity measures can't be exploited alone for semantic inference mainly because predicting degree of textual entailment between two texts require knowledge which is not explicitly embedded in the texts [2].

However, string similarity measures in [3] have been used for determining semantic inference at lexical and shallow-syntactic level. They have used ten similarity measures to capture different kinds of similarity of strings. It has worked well, atleast for the task of Question Answering.

It has been stated in [4] also that similarity measures can't be used directly for predicting the degree of entailment. Also, high similarity value between two texts doesn't necessarily mean high degree of entailment. Some kind of transformation function is required for converting the similarity values to the degree of entailment. It has been proved through experiments also in [5] that the most sentence similarity measures do not produce satisfactory results for TE. String similarity measures have been used in [6] like word overlap along with synonymy and morphological relations to find relation between text and hypothesis. But string similarity matching is combined with a deeper semantic analysis and theorem proving to find the entailment relation. Futhermore, the string similarity measures are symmetric in nature, while TE is an asymmetric relation.

Henceforth, it is required to investigate directional dis(similarity) measures to find a suitable measure which could compute degree of textual entailment between sentences in [7].

This paper attempts to perform comparative analysis of various directional dissimilarity measures available in literature. The experiments are conducted by employing different directional measures in Gupta et al. summarization framework in [7] in order to study the behaviour of individual measures.

The rest of the paper is organized as follows: Gupta et al. [7] summarization method is elaborated in Sect. 2. The related work about directional dis(similarity) measures is discussed in Sect. 3. Next, all the directional measures are formally introduced in Sect. 4. The Experiments and results are presented in Sect. 5, and finally, the conclusion and future work are outlined in Sect. 6.

2 Gupta et al. [7] Text Summarization Method

This section discusses the Gupta et al. summarization method proposed in [7] which formulates single document text summarization problem as weighted minimum vertex cover problem.

The source document to be summarized is represented as a weighted graph $G = (V, E, w)$, where each of $v \in V$ corresponds to a sentence in the document; an edge $(u, v) \in E$ exists if either u strongly entails v or v strongly entails u. The vertices are further assigned a weight w_i based on (negated) TE values.

When applied, wMVC returns a cover C which is a subset of the vertices having a minimal total weight. The sentences corresponding to the vertices in the cover forms the summary of the input document. The whole method is pictorially depicted in Fig. 1. The steps of the method are outlined as below:

1. Computing TE scores
2. Computing connectivity scores
3. Entailment connectivity graph construction
4. Applying wMVC to graph

The method is discussed in detail in the following subsections.

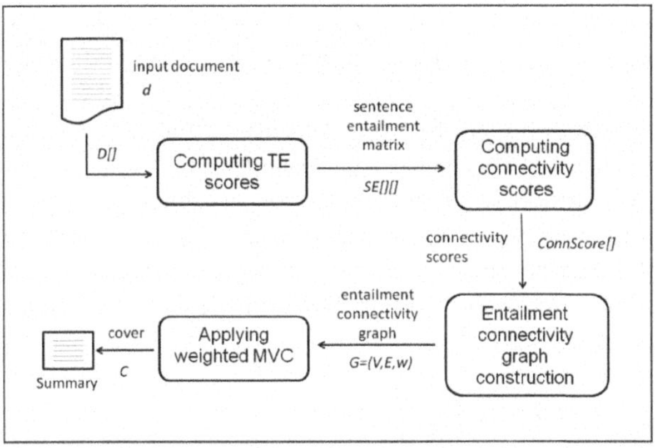

Fig. 1. Gupta et al. method in [7]

2.1 Computing TE Scores

The source document d is stored in an array $D_{1 \times N}$. This step calculates degree of textual entailment between each and every pair of sentences in D using a TE tool. The TE scores for all the sentence pairs are stored in a *sentence entailment matrix*, $SE_{N \times N}$. where each entry $SE[i, j]$ indicates the extent by which sentence i entails j.

2.2 Connectivity Scores

This step computes connectedness scores for each sentence by adding the entailment scores of the sentence with respect to the rest of the sentences in the document, denoted as $ConnScore$. Formally, $ConnScore$ for sentence i is computed as follows.

$$ConnScore_i = \sum_{i \neq j} SE_{i,j} \tag{1}$$

After applying above formula to each sentence in the document, the $ConnScore_{1 \times N}$ vector is obtained.

2.3 Entailment Connectivity Graph Construction

This step constructs sentence entailment connectivity graph by using sentence entailment scores SE[i,j] to add an edge between two vertices v_i and v_j corresponding to two sentences S_i and S_j and assigning weights to the vertices that are calculated using sentence connectivity scores $ConnScore$. The connectivity scores are converted into positive weights by inverting them in order to make the weights comply with the wMVC algorithm that searches for a minimal solution. The scores are converted to positive weights in the following way:

$$w_i = -ConnScore_i + Z \quad (2)$$

where w_i is the weight assigned to the vertex v_i; Z is a large constant (set to value = 100 in present paper) used to assign positive weights. It tells that a well connected sentence is going to have higher sentence entailment scores whereas lower weights.

This process leads to an undirected weighted sentence entailment connectivity graph, $G(V, E, w)$, for the source document.

An edge (i, j) is added to G between two vertices v_i and v_j with entailment scores $SE[i, j]$ and $SE[j, i]$ between them if $SE[i, j] \geqslant \tau$ OR $SE[j, i] \geqslant \tau$, i.e. if at least one of them is equal or highest than the empirically set threshold τ. The threshold is calculated by taking mean of all the entailment scores entries in the entailment matrix SE.

2.4 Applying wMVC to Graph

Finally, we apply the weighted minimum vertex cover algorithm to the sentence entailment connectivity graph to determine the minimal vertex cover, which forms the minimal set of sentences covering the document. The vertex cover C corresponds to the document's summary. The whole weighted graph $G = (V, E, w)$ is given as input to wMVC algorithm where each vertex $v_i \in V (1 \leq i \leq n)$ is assigned weight w_i. The output of the algorithm is a minimal vertex cover C of G which comprises a subset of vertices V. The sentences corresponding to the selected vertices are rearranged in original order to form a summary.

In citemvc, BIUTEE[1], which is a transformation based tool has been used for calculating TE scores. But slow speed and extensive resource requirements of BIUTEE tool make it practically infeasible to generate summaries in real time scenarios like in summarization apps on smart phones, tabloids etc. This has motivated us to investigate directional similarity measures and pick the best one for calculating the degree of entailment between sentences. We discuss the state-of-the-art directional similarity measures in next section.

3 State-of-the-Art Work

A directional dis(similarity) measure has an asymmetric property, which makes it well suited to the tasks of predicting degree of textual entailment which itself

[1] Can be downloaded at: http://www.cs.biu.ac.il/~nlp/downloads/biutee.

is an asymmetrical relation. Next, we discuss the state-of-the-art work in directional similarity measures. First and foremost work on directional measures for entailment relates to [8] who compute entailment relations between segments of documents. They propose a directional similarity measure called *entailment score* based on the most commonly used information retrieval metric called *inverse document frequency* (idf). It is a measure of term importance. The entailment score of two document d and d' is calculated by comparing sum of the weights (idf) of the terms that appear in both documents to the sum of the weights of all terms in d'. Another measure called *entailment score* has been presented in [9] which is based on edit distance between dependency trees of text T and H. The Edit distance between T and H is basically cost of edit operations i.e. insertion, deletion and substitution to transform T into H. Another measure which is a variant of Levenshtien distance called modified Levenshtien distance has been proposed in [10]. It is defined as the minimal number of transformations (deletions, insertions and substitutions) required to convert T into H.

The authors in [10] have also proposed *cosine directional similarity measure* based on common words between T and H. A measure has been proposed in [11] which combines the word-to-word similarities of T and H into text-to-text similarities. It calculates the semantic similarity of the words using wordnet. All of the above directional measures are discussed in detail in the next section.

4 Directional Dis(similarity) measures

This section formally discusses all the directional dis(similarity) measures as below:

1. IDF based ***entscore:*** The entailment score [8], *entscore* $(s_{i,d}, s_{j,d'})$, of two segments $s_{i,d}$ in document d and $s_{j,d'}$ in document d' is calculated by comparing the sum of the weights of terms that appear in both the segments to the sum of the weights of all terms in $s_{j,d}$:

$$entscore(s_{i,d}, s_{j,d'}) = \frac{t_k \in (s_{i,d} \bigcap s_{j,d'}) idf_k}{t_k \in s_{j,d'} idf_k} \tag{3}$$

   where *idf* (inverse document frequency) of each term t_i is calculated as:

$$idf_i = log(\frac{N}{n_i}) \tag{4}$$

   where N refers to total number of segments where each segment is a bag of weighted words and n_i refers to the number of segments in which term t_i occurs. In this paper, d, d' refer to the T and H respectively, n_i refers to the number of sentences in which term t_i occurs and N refers to the number of sentences in the document.
2. **Tree Edit Distance based *entailment score:*** The Edit Distance entailment score [10] is a useful distance measure to calculate the degree of textual entailment by applying a sequence of transformations to T to obtain H with

an overall score below a certain threshold. A tree edit distance algorithm is applied to the syntactic representations (i.e. dependency trees) of both T and H. The scores obtained give a measure of the extent to which T entails H. Following are the transformations that are applied on T to obtain H along with their costs:

(a) Insertion: insert a node from the dependency tree of H into the dependency tree of T (cost = 3)
(b) Deletion: delete a note from the dependency tree of T. When a node is deleted all its children are attached to their parent (cost = 3)
(c) Substitution: change a node in the T into a node of H (cost = 5)
(d) Swapping: Swap two nodes of dependency trees of T so that the current node of T is same as current node of H (cost = 2)
(e) Changing Case: Change the case of the node in dependency tree of T from uppercase to lowercase or vice-versa (cost = 1)

More the number of transformations needed to be applied, lesser is the extent by which T entails H, i.e., an inverse relation exists. The entailment score of a given pair is calculated as:

$$Entailmentscore(T, H) = \frac{ed(T, H)}{ed(, H)} \tag{5}$$

where *ed(T,H)* is the sum of cost of all applied transformations and ed(,H) is the cost of inserting the entire tree.

3. **Modified Levenshtien distance score:** The modified Levenshtien distance score $LD(T, H)$ is defined in [10] as the minimal number of transformations such that T is transformed into H, reflecting quantity of information of H with respect to T. It gives the entailment score between T and H. The transformation costs are as follows:
   (a) Insertion: Inserting a character from H into T (cost = 3)
   (b) Deletion: Deleting a character from T (cost = 3)
   (c) Substitution: Substituting a character from H into T (cost = 5)
   (d) Swap: Swapping two letters of T so that the current letter of T is same as current letter of H (cost = 2)
   (e) Change Case: Changing the case of the letter of T from uppercase to lowercase or vice-versa (cost = 1)
4. **Cosine directional similarity measure:** Cosine directional similarity measure [10] is based on the concept of number of overlapping words between T and H. To find out the extent by which T entails H, it is given by the relation:

$$Cos_T(T \cup H) = \sqrt{\frac{c}{m}} \tag{6}$$

where c is the number of overlapping words between T and H, and m is the number of words in T. More the number of overlapping words, more is the degree of textual entailment between T and H.

5. **Text-to-Text similarity score:** The similarity score [11] for a text segment T_i with respect to another text segment T_j is determined by using a score function that combines the word to word similarities:

$$sim(T,H)_T = \frac{\sum_{pos} \sum_{w_k \in WS^T_{pos}} maxSim(w_k).idf_{w_k}}{\sum_{pos} \sum_{w_k \in WS^T_{pos}} idf_{w_k}} \tag{7}$$

where WS^T_{pos} and WS^H_{pos} are the sets of open-class words (nouns, verbs, adjectives and adverbs) in each text segment. For a word w_k with a given pos in T_i, the highest similarity of the words with the same pos in the other text T_j is denoted by $maxSim(w_k)$.
All the measures return entailment score between 0 and 1.
In the next section, all the measures are implemented in text summarization framework discussed in Sect. 2 and corresponding generated summaries are evaluated and compared with those generated in [7].

5 Experiments

5.1 Experimental Settings and Dataset

The experiments are performed on the task based on single document summarization of Document Understanding conference (DUC-2002). The results have been collected on DUC-2002 [12] dataset which contains 567 news articles. The results have been collected on 60 news articles which are randomly but uniformly chosen from 60 clusters of articles in the dataset. The average length of the documents of dataset taken is 21 sentences per document. The final summary length has been fixed to 100 words. All the scripts for the implementation of directional measures have been developed in *Python* language.

Evaluation Metrics. The performance evaluation of the method using different similarity measures have been done using *ROUGE* (Recall-Oriented Understudy of Gisting Evaluations) [13] tool. ROUGE compares the system generated summary with a set of reference summaries that are typically human generated. *ROUGE-n* is defined as the n-gram recall of a system generated summary when compared to a set of *reference summaries* and ROUGE-*SU*4 is the skip bigrams (with maximum gap of length 4). The ROUGE results are collected in the paper by comparing each of the 60 articles of the dataset with a set of two reference summaries for *ROUGE*-1, *ROUGE*-2 and *ROUGE-SU*4[2] metrics. These metrics have been reported to perform well for short summaries in the case of single document summarization. Also, *ROUGE-1* has shown high correlation with human judgements in [14].

[2] See [13] for formal definitions of these metrics.

5.2 Results and Analysis

This section performs a detailed analysis of the behaviour of different directional measures on the basis of their performance characteristics and runtime behaviour.

1. **Performance Comparison:** The results for the precision (P), recall (R) and F_1 scores for each ROUGE metric are presented in Table 1. It can be clearly seen from the results that the *idf based entscore* outperforms all the measures including BIUTEE based entailment score with best scores for recall and F_1. The performance of Tree edit distance score is also comparable to that of *idf based entscore* but its poor runtime behaviour makes it a poor choice in the text summarization framework. The authors have manually analyzed and compared the best and the worst summaries of [7] using different directional measures. The comparative analysis had given some useful insights into the behaviour of all the measures. Thus, the best performance of *idf based entscore* is attributed to the following facts:
   - It is to be understood that *idf based entscore* computes degree of textual entailment as a function of highly relevant and similar words present in them. Eventually, it assigns higher weights to more relevant sentences. While *text-to-text similarity measure* computes degree of textual entailment as a function of nouns, verbs, adjectives and adverbs present in T and H, whatever their importance may be in the whole document. Thus, it leads to high scoring of the sentences only due to presence of nouns, verbs, adjectives and adverbs inspite of their importance.
   - The *idf based entscore* is the weighted version of *Cosine directional similarity* measure. In the latter, weight of each word is considered to be 1.

Table 1. *ROUGE-1* results.

Measure	ROUGE-1			ROUGE-2			ROUGE-SU4		
	P (%)	R (%)	F_1 (%)	P (%)	R (%)	F_1 (%)	P (%)	R (%)	F_1 (%)
Gupta et al. method [7]	42.8	35.9	39.03	15.6	19.1	17.1	12.1	16.8	14.1
IDF based entscore	**42.5**	**43.8**	**43.2**	**20.6**	**21**	**20.8**	**17.3**	**17.6**	**17.5**
Tree edit dist. score	**41.8.2**	**43.3**	**42.6**	**20.2**	**20.9**	**20.5**	**17.1**	**16.1**	**16.6**
Mod. Levenshtien distance score	40.3	42.03	41.1	19.7	20.8	20.3	15.6	17.3	16.4
Cosine directional similarity score	40.3	41.3	40.8	18.9	19.3	19.1	15.7	16.2	15.9
Text-to-text similarity score	39.2	41.7	41.7	19.9	21.8	20.8	14.8	16.4	15.5

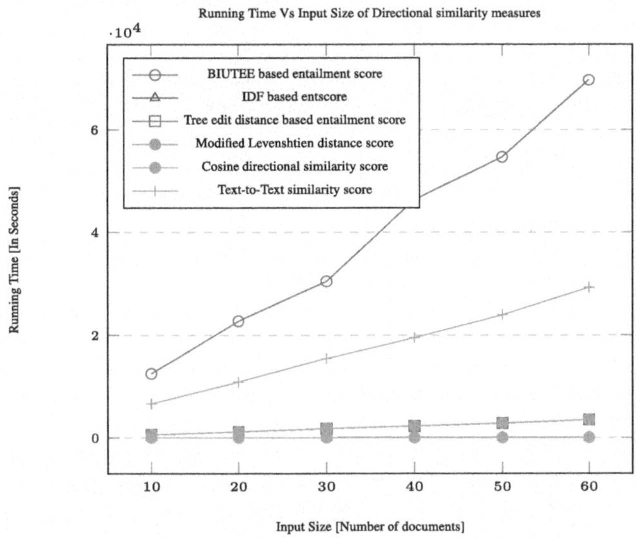

Fig. 2. Running time vs input size

Therefore it is concerned only with the number of words. This is another major reason for the *idf based entscore*'s better performance over the *Cosine directional similarity measure.*

- The performance of *idf based entscore* and distance based measures (*Modified Levenshtien distance* and *Tree Edit Distance score*) is almost comparable but in some instances, the later performs worse due to its sensitivity to word order of the sentence. The *idf based entscore* will give the same score whatever be the order of words of the sentence but cost of transformations for the distance measure will greatly vary with order of words in a sentence.

2. **Runtime complexity:** The aim of using directional measures in Gupta et al. summarization method is to improve its runtime of [7] summarization method. Its sole purpose is to generate summaries in real time for the users. The Fig. 2 clearly shows the runtime performance of various measures used for comparison. It is important to specify here that curves for *entscore* and *cosine directional score* overlap and that of *Tree Edit dist. score* and *Mod. Levenshtien Distance score* overlap in the graph. A careful analysis shows that *entscore* outperforms all the measures in terms of both rouge scores and execution times. Though the rouge scores of Tree Edit Distance score are comparable to those of *entscore* but the run time performance lags behind significantly. The Table 2 also shows that execution time taken per document by *entscore* makes it the most appropriate choice for the real time scenarios.

Table 2. *Runtime comparison* results.

Measure	Runtime (in sec/document)
Gupta et al. method [7]	2867
IDF based entscore	**1.1**
Tree edit dist. score	57.8
Mod. Levenshtien distance	58.4
Cosine directional similarity score	**0.3**
Text-to-text similarity score	487.52

6 Conclusions and Future Work

This paper has implemented directional dis(similarity) measures in a text summarization method proposed in [7] and conducted experiments on DUC 2002 dataset. It is observed that *entscore* has shown notable performance in terms of runtime as compared to TE system. However, for certain input documents, which contain simple and short sentences, the later system has produced better quality summaries than *entscore* measure. Thus, it may be said that characteristics of a sentence, or characteristics of an article may also affect the performance of the measures. Therefore, this finding gives a new direction of experimenting with all the measures in different domains of articles like fiction, science and healthcare literature apart from the news articles in the future.

References

1. Bentivogli, L., Dagan, I., Dang, H.T., Giampiccolo, D., Magnini, B.: The fifth PASCAL recognizing textual entailment challenge. In: Proceedings of Text Analysis Conference, Gaithersburg, Maryland, USA, pp. 14–24, 16–17 November 2009
2. LoBue, P., Yates, A.: Types of common-sense knowledge needed for recognizing textual entailment. In: Proceedings of the 49th Annual Meeting of the Association for Computational Linguistics: Human Language Technologies: Short Papers, vol. 2, pp. 329–334. Association for Computational Linguistics (2011)
3. Malakasiotis, P., Androutsopoulos, I.: Learning textual entailment using SVMs and string similarity measures. In: Proceedings of the ACL-PASCAL Workshop on Textual Entailment and Paraphrasing, pp. 42–47. Association for Computational Linguistics (2007)
4. Yokote, K.I., Bollegala, D., Ishizuka, M.: Similarity is not entailment-jointly learning similarity transformation for textual entailment. In: AAAI (2012)
5. Achananuparp, P., Hu, X., Shen, X.: The evaluation of sentence similarity measures. In: Song, I.-Y., Eder, J., Nguyen, T.M. (eds.) DaWaK 2008. LNCS, vol. 5182, pp. 305–316. Springer, Heidelberg (2008). https://doi.org/10.1007/978-3-540-85836-2_29
6. Bos, J., Markert, K.: Recognising textual entailment with logical inference. In: Proceedings of the Conference on Human Language Technology and Empirical Methods in Natural Language Processing, pp. 628–635. Association for Computational Linguistics (2005)

7. Gupta, A., Kaur, M., Singh, A., Goel, A., Mirkin, S.: Text summarization through entailment-based minimum vertex cover. In: Lexical and Computational Semantics (*SEM 2014), p. 75 (2014)
8. Monz, C., de Rijke, M.: Light-weight entailment checking for computational semantics. In: Proceedings of the Third Workshop on Inference in Computational Semantics (ICoS-3) (2001)
9. Kouylekov, M., Magnini, B.: Tree edit distance for recognizing textual entailment: estimating the cost of insertion. In: Proceedings of the PASCAL RTE-2 Challenge, pp. 68–73 (2006)
10. Tatar, D., Serban, G., Mihis, A.D., Mihalcea, R., et al.: Textual entailment as a directional relation. J. Res. Pract. Inf. Technol. **41**(1), 53 (2009)
11. Corley, C., Mihalcea, R.: Measuring the semantic similarity of texts. In: Proceedings of the ACL Workshop on Empirical Modeling of Semantic Equivalence and Entailment, pp. 13–18. Association for Computational Linguistics (2005)
12. DUC: Document understanding conference. In: HLT/NAACL Workshop on Text Summarization, pp. 22–31 (2002). http://duc.nist.gov/
13. Lin, C.Y.: ROUGE: a package for automatic evaluation of summaries. In: Proceedings of the Workshop on Text Summarization Branches Out, Post-Conference Workshop of ACL 2004, Barcelona, Spain (2004)
14. Lin, C.Y., Hovy, E.: Automatic evaluation of summaries using n-gram cooccurrence statistics. In: Proceedings of the 2003 Conference of the North American Chapter of the Association for Computational Linguistics on Human Language Technology (HLT-NAACL 2003), Edmonta, Canada, pp. 71–78, 27 May–1 June 2003

Image Enhancement of Lemon Grasses Using Image Processing Techniques (Histogram Equalization)

Ofeoritse S. Temiatse[1], Sanjay Misra[1](✉), Chitra Dhawale[2], Ravin Ahuja[3], and Victor Matthews[1]

[1] Department of Electrical and Information Engineering, Covenant University, Ota, Nigeria
ofetemiatse1@gmail.com, sanjay.misra@covenantuniversity.edu.ng
[2] Amravati University, Amravati, India
[3] University of Delhi, Delhi, India

Abstract. Lemon grass a type of medicinal plants has been part of human existence and has been applied in so many ways, like for healing, for drugs and for protection. In this paper, the conventional Histogram Equalization has been used to improve the images of the lemon grasses. MATLAB software was used to display the Histogram as well as the Histogram Equalization of the image of the lemon grasses. Image processing techniques to be used here is Histogram Equalization. The Histogram Equalization is considered, since it is one of the techniques in the enhancement of images and as such is being applied to the medicinal herb which in particular is the lemon grasses. The Histogram Equalization technique used may be seen as a conventional technique but the results obtained demonstrates its capability to improve the appearance of images by bringing out hidden details. The performance of the technique also shows that it is a better method in comparison to other types of Histogram Equalization methods.

Keywords: Lemon grasses · Medicinal plants · Image processing techniques MATLAB · Histogram and conventional histogram equalization

1 Introduction

Lemon grass which is a type of medicinal herb plants are of immense significance in the existence of humans and animals alike. It is found in every part of the world which gives therapeutic and medical benefits; it also is being used as flavouring in some countries in Asia for cooking. Although lemon grass has been known for its uses as tea and soups as well. It is a plant that is used to ease unwanted symptoms or improve overall wellbeing [1]. Image processing is composed by a set of techniques aiming at manipulating image using computational algorithm in order to extract information from them [2]. The most commonly used approach is histogram equalization based on the assumption that the uniformly distributed gray scale histogram has the best visible contrast [10]. Note: Image processing is a process of changing an image to digital form and it allows other operations to be carried on it so that the image becomes enhanced. It is clear how importance histogram equalization is, and so it is needed for the implementation of the paper. For the concluding division of this paper, it is structured in the subsequent ways, which are

B. Panda et al. (Eds.): REDSET 2017, CCIS 799, pp. 298–308, 2018.
https://doi.org/10.1007/978-981-10-8527-7_24

Sect. 2 which shows related works that have been carried out then Sect. 3 explains what the lemon grass is, and also explains what histogram and histogram equalization does which has the image processing techniques-histogram equalization explained and Sect. 4 shows the results and analysis gotten and Sect. 5 has the conclusion.

2 Literature Review

In image processing, works have been done in this area. It has various techniques but in this paper, histogram equalization is used here. Below shows the works using image processing. This paper is on adaptive histogram-based algorithm where the information entropy gotten from the system doesn't change. Here the algorithm made brings parameters in the gray mapping formula whereby it sees the information entropy as a goal to adaptively change slightly the spacing of the two gray levels placed adjacently in the new histogram made. This avoids undue and unwanted bright areas of the image. The experiments gained show that the algorithm brings about an improvement visual effect under on account of the unchanged information entropy [9]. In this study, it shows the importance as well as the difficulties of recognition of plant leaf image. It has been discovered that bringing out the feature of the texture of the leaf images is a paramount key to solve the problem. Both the wavelet procedures which focus on low-frequency of the images and fractal methods can't identify the images accurately. The proposed topic known as a novel wavelet fractal feature based approach for plant leaf images recognition is discussed in this paper. There are steps involved in this paper, first step is; the leaf image which is pre-processed undergoes decomposition accompanied with 5/3 lifting wavelet which brings about sub images. The next step involves fractal sizes of the individual sub images which are calculated to be the exact wavelet of the leaf image. The last but certainly not the least involves adoption of artificial neural network which is used for classification of the plant leaf. After the experiment, the results obtained show that the proposed procedure sure enhances the performance for the plant image recognition as compared with the other procedures using wavelet sizes [3]. Agriculture research on disease detection of leaf plays a fundamental role because it brings benefit in the checking of numerous crops of all kind and does detect disease symptoms automatically immediately they are detected on the plant leaves. Disease basically causes destruction to farm crops. This paper focuses on various methods that can be applied in studying the detection of leaf disease using image processing as an area. These procedures are used are rising throughput and reducing the arising from the experts who detect leaf diseases [4]. According to Pande Ankita he proposes a procedure for the leaf identification that will be based on computer aided plant class. He used a chain code procedure as well as linear computer method where the linear method will be used with dual sets of dataset [5]. As for Valliammai he came up with a hybrid to enhance the plant leaf recognition. He used histogram equalization to enhance the image specifically. Different thresholds were used in different regions [6]. In this paper it shows a review histogram forms that are new for the image enhancement. Various differences of this method is applied to divide the input histogram [11]. The improvement of the characteristic of an image is the goal of the image enhancement procedure which results in the resulting image been better than the real image. In this paper, a new smoothing histogram modification method is proposed to improve the quality of digital medical image which is done by smoothing the histogram of the input image using the band pass filtering, detecting the spike regions in the histogram and removing them, and then modifying the histogram according to the mapping function to generate the output histogram. The experimental results show that the proposed technique adds an increase in visibility of the variety of embedded structures. It shows also that the performance is far better than the already existing conventional [12]. The image enhancement brings an improvement to any image. It consists of a collection of methods which provides improvement of the appearance of the image in order to make it look more suitable. There are several reasons why it is sorted after. It assists the increase of the image visually [13]. For this paper, the author proposes an adaptive histogram equalization method as well as contrast limited adaptive histogram equalization technique for normal and abnormal light design for the image which is based on a generalization of histogram equalization [14]. He formulated a novel procedure multi-decomposition histogram equalization to remove the setbacks of the past methods. In multi-decomposition histogram equalization, the image is decayed using a unique logic. The ultimate image after multi-decomposition histogram equalization gives a better result which is based on contrast enhancement and brightness preservation aspect as compared to all other procedures [15]. This author proposes entropy-based local histogram equalization algorithm by applying local entropy quality to know if the local histogram equalization is applied on the center, this method can increase the speed of processing and decrease the background significantly [16]. The paper proposes a novel method to enhance the value of images that are medical that will be based on histogram equalization. The first thing done is applying noise decrease method as well as applying some preprocessing on the histogram of the images that are medical ones, and then histogram equalization will be applied on the new one. [17].

3 Lemon Grass and Image Processing Technique (Histogram Equalization)

It has health benefits, like relieving certain throat disorders; also it helps to reduce high fevers because of this property called anti-pyretic, it aids in removing ache because of its dismissing properties. It aids in relieving muscle thus a decrease in ache-related indicators and headaches, joint pains, abdominal pain, muscle cramps, stomachache and others. Additional associated value is for increase in blood circulation. The existence of vitamins like vitamin A in lemongrass makes it ready to lend a hand in skin concerns such as acne pimples. It aids in the brightening of the skin thus by improving acne. It also aids in the improvement of poor body odor by regulating extreme perspiring. A histogram is a plot between the pixels (picture element) and its intensities. While histogram equalization is a processing enhancement technique that pursues to optimize the disparity of an image at all levels and is used to improve the particular image, with this explained the grayscale values in the output image are evenly distributed. As the name suggests, its purpose is to increase image contrast by leveling, or equalizing of the image.

In gray scale image, an 8-bit image is considered to have 256 possible intensities, which the histogram then graphically displays by reflecting each pixel, by its distributions [7]. Looking at the histogram of the image shows the occurrence of the individual intensity value. It has been stated before that the histogram is a graph which shows the individual numbers of pixels at different intensity values of the image [8]. It is known that the histogram equalization is a procedure which produces a gray map which alters the image by its histogram and making a change in the pixel values to make them near to the user. It shows the transformation function which produces the output image on the histogram. It is used in image processing to cause an adjustment using the image histogram [13]. In summary the histogram can be seen as a table which shows the amount of time a value comes to view.

4 Results and Discussion

This area shows the results of applying on the images gotten from the camera the technique called histogram equalization. Figure 1 shows the input image taken and using MATLAB to read the image into the system and getting the histogram equalization of it as well. The following shows the MATLAB codes used to represent the reading and

Fig. 1. Input image for the lemon grasses

plotting of both the histograms and histogram equalization of the lemon grasses image shown in all figures below.

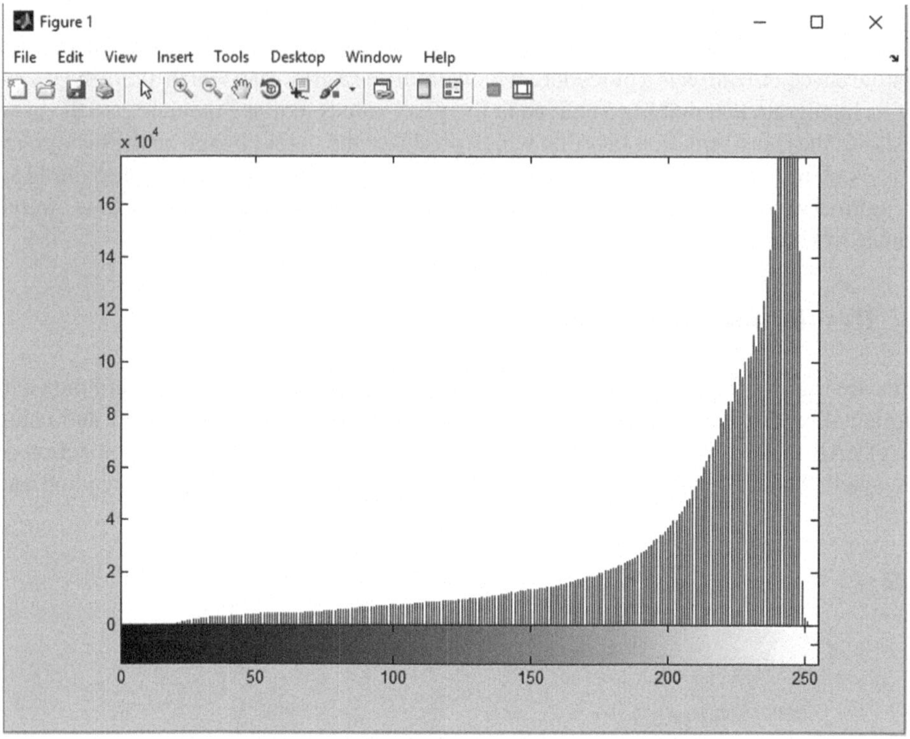

Fig. 2. The graph

```
% This is a program to read the image of the lemon grasses
Image1 = imread('lemon4.jpg');
imshow(Image1);
```

Then, Fig. 2 display the plot gotten from the histogram of the input lemon grasses image.

```
% A program to display the histogram of the image of the lemon grasses
% imread denotes reading the image
% lemon4.jpg is the name of the image
I = imread('lemon4.jpg');
% converting from RGB to grayscale
I_gray = rgb2gray (I);
% The histogram of the input image
imhist( I_gray);
```

The figures below show the histogram equalization of three samples test images gotten.

The first sample test image which is displayed at Fig. 3, the image was taken in a dark. It is seen that the input image was so dark and from the histogram gotten, it shows the concentration of the intensities was only at (0–50) on a scale of (0–255) whereas the histogram equalization of the dark image shows an enhanced and bright image and from the histogram of the Histogram Equalization image, it was distributed evenly. The following codes in MATLAB represent it below.

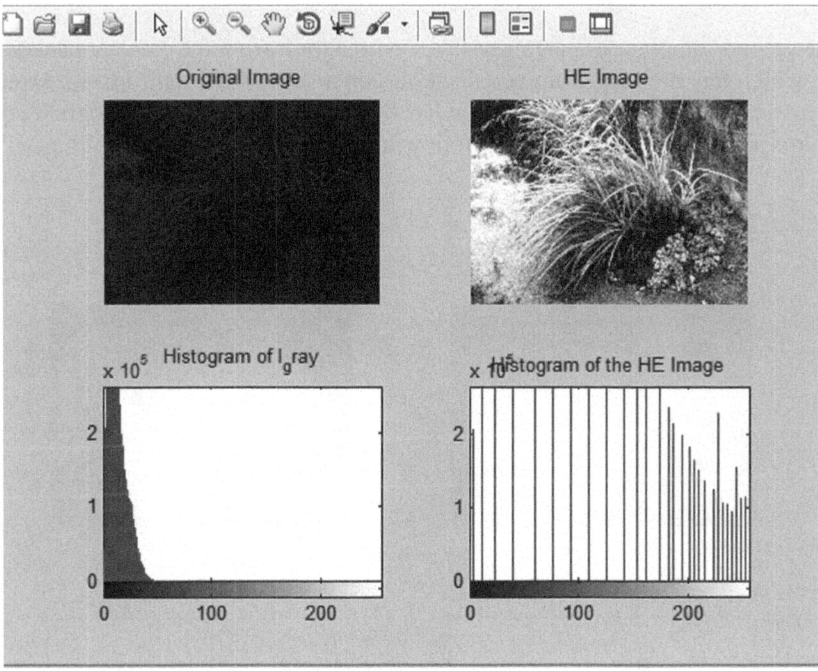

Fig. 3. The image was taken in the dark

```
% A program to show the histogram and histogram equalization of the image of
the lemon grasses
% imread denotes reading the image
% The name of the image is lemon5.jpg
I = imread('lemon5.jpg');
% converting from rgb to grayscale
%The coloured image has to be converted to grayscale since histogram
equalization works well with it
I_gray = rgb2gray (I);
% Histogram
%Histogram equalization of I_gray
I_histeq = histeq(I_gray);
%The plots
subplot(2,2,1), imshow(I_gray), title('Original Image');
subplot(2,2,2), imshow(I_histeq), title('HE Image');
subplot(2,2,3), imhist(I_gray), title('Histogram of I_gray');
subplot(2,2,4), imhist(I_histeq), title('Histogram of the HE
Image');
```

Unlike other image processing techniques which uses or applies the histogram equalization techniques, for this paper the conventional histogram equalization without using its techniques was applied because it displayed the image of the lemon grasses efficiently and clearly. The results gotten from the three samples of the lemon grasses which were the dark image, bright image and moderate image of the lemon grasses image.

The second sample test image was taken with a flash from the camera displayed on Fig. 4, which has the histogram equalization gotten from the bright image. From the Fig. 4 again, the histogram of the image has been displayed and the histogram equalization image reflects very bright. The following is the MATLAB codes of Fig. 4.

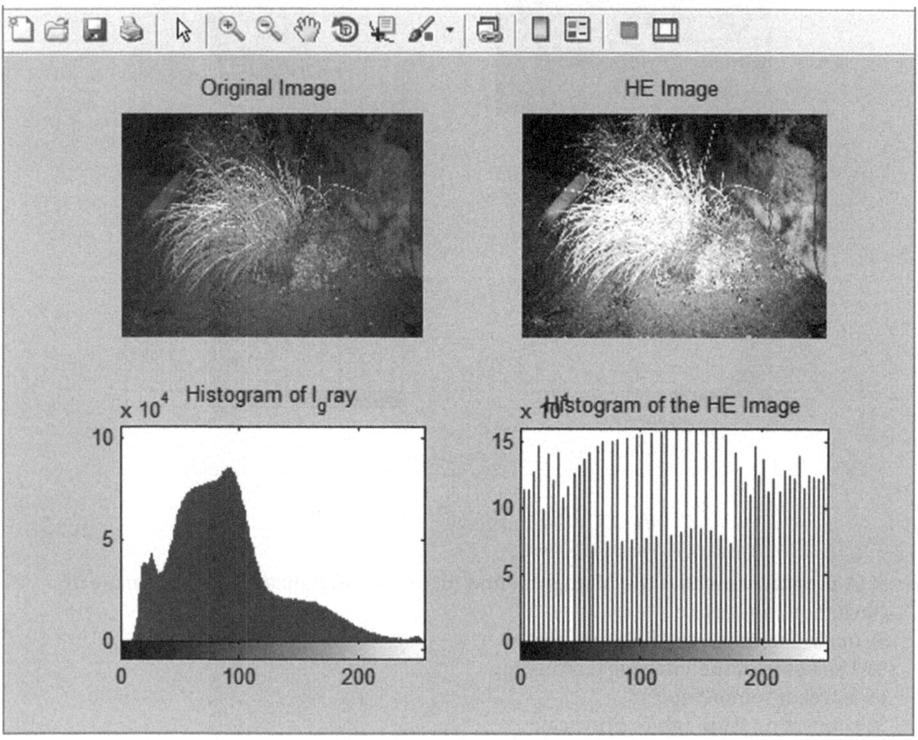

Fig. 4. The histogram equalization of the bright image

```
% A program to show the histogram of the image of the lemon grasses
% imread denotes reading the image
% lemon12.jpg is the name of the image
I = imread('lemon12.jpg');
% converting from rgb to grayscale
I_gray = rgb2gray (I);
% The histogram of the image here
%Also the h istogram equalization of I_gray
I_histeq = histeq(I_gray);
%The plots
subplot(2,2,1), imshow(I_gray), title('Original Image');
subplot(2,2,2), imshow(I_histeq), title('HE Image');
subplot(2,2,3), imhist(I_gray), title('Histogram of I_gray');
subplot(2,2,4), imhist(I_histeq), title('Histogram of the HE
Image');
```

The third sample test image was taken in a moderate environment, Fig. 5 show both the histogram and histogram equalization of the test image, which was so enhanced that the details was displayed. The following is the MATLAB codes of Fig. 5.

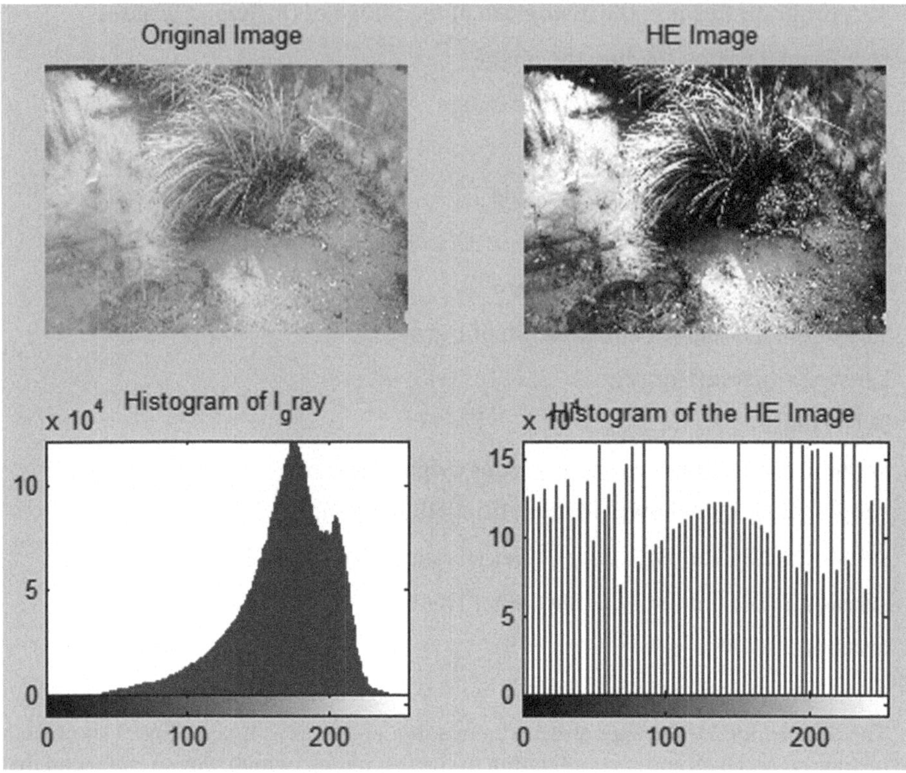

Fig. 5. Histogram and histogram equalization of the image

```
% A program to show the histogram of the image of the lemon grasses
% imread denotes reading the image
I = imread('lemon11.jpg');
% converting from rgb to grayscale
I_gray = rgb2gray (I);
% The histogram of the image
%The histogram equalization of I_gray
I_histeq = histeq(I_gray);
%The plots
subplot(2,2,1), imshow(I_gray), title('Original Image');
subplot(2,2,2), imshow(I_histeq), title('HE Image');
subplot(2,2,3), imhist(I_gray), title('Histogram of I_gray');
subplot(2,2,4), imhist(I_histeq), title('Histogram of the HE Image');
```

From these results acquired for the dark, moderate and bright images of the lemon grass it is clearly perceived that in comparison to other methods, conventional histogram equalization produces the images having high clarity and more brightness which leads to enhancement of the test image.

5 Conclusion

In this paper, three samples of the lemon grass were taken and the conventional histogram equalization was applied to get the brightness and efficiency. It was used to test the quality and effectiveness of each of them using MATLAB and from the simulation, it clearly shows that for each sample of the lemon grass image taken, it effectively enhanced each and brought out its details as compared to the types of histogram techniques.

Acknowledgement. We acknowledge the support and sponsorship provided by Covenant University through the Centre for Research, Innovation and Discovery (CUCRID).

References

1. Lili, N.A., Khalid, F., Borhan, N.M.: Classification of herbs plant diseases via hierarchical dynamic artificial neural network after image removal using kernel regression framework. Int. J. Comput. Sci. Eng. (IJCSE) **3**, 15–20 (2011)
2. Nithiyanandhan, K., Mathpati, S.: Analysis of fractal dimension of medicinal leaves by using techniques of image processing. Int. Res. J. Eng. Technol. (IRJET) **3**(8), 1531–1535 (2016)
3. Zhang, H., Tao, X.: Leaf image recognition based on wavelet and fractal dimension. J. Comput. Inf. Syst. **11**(1), 141–148 (2015)
4. Rathod, A.N., Tanawal, B., Shah, V.: Image processing techniques for detection of leaf disease. Int. J. Adv. Res. Comput. Sci. Softw. Eng. **3**(11), 397–399 (2013)
5. Pande Ankita, V., Shandilya, V.K.: Digital image processing approach for fruit and flower leaf identification and recognition. Int. J. Eng. Comput. Sci. **2**(4), 1280–1285 (2013). ISSN 23197242
6. Valliammai, N., Geethalakshmi, S.N.: A hybrid method for enhancement of plant leaf recognition. World Comput. Sci. Inf. Technol. J. **1**(9), 370–375 (2011). ISSN 2221-0741
7. Gonzalez, R.C., Woods, R.E.: Digital Image Processing Using MATLAB. Pearson Education Inc., Upper Saddle River (2009)
8. Paragi, A.N.S.: Image contrast enhancement using histogram equalization. Accent J. Econ. Ecol. Eng. **2**(3) (2017)
9. Zhu, Y., Huang, C.: An adaptive histogram equalization algorithm on the image gray level mapping. Phys. Procedia **25**, 601–608 (2012)
10. Kaura, T., Sidhub, R.K.: Second international symposium on computer vision and the internet (VisionNet 2015). Procedia Comput. Sci. **58**, 470–477 (2015)
11. Kaur, M., Kaur, J., Kaur, J.: Survey of contrast enhancement techniques based on histogram equalization. (IJACSA) Int. J. Adv. Comput. Sci. Appl., **2**(7), 137–141 (2011)
12. Rathi, M.S., Karode, A.H., Suralkar, S.R.: Contrast enhancement and smoothing using histogram modification method for medical images. Int. J. Comput. Technol. Appl. **3**(5), 1789–1798

13. Vij, K., Singh, Y.: Enhancement of images using histogram processing techniques. Int. J. Comp. Tech. Appl. **2**(2), 309–313 (2011)
14. Sonker, D.: Comparison of histogram equalization techniques for image enhancement of grayscale images in natural and unnatural light. Int. J. Eng. Res. Dev. **8**(9), 2476–2480 (2013)
15. Nimkar, S., Shrivastava, S., Varghese, S.: Contrast enhancement and brightness preservation using multi-decomposition histogram equalization. Sig. Image Process. Int. J. (SIPIJ) **4**(3), 83–93 (2013)
16. Zhang, X.Y., Ge, L., Wang, T.F.: Entropy-based local histogram equalization for medical ultrasound image enhancement. In: 2nd International Conference on Bioinformatics and Biomedical Engineering, (2008)
17. Ziaei, A., Yeganeh, H., Faez K., Sargolzaei, S.: A novel approach for contrast enhancement in biomedical images based on histogram equalization. In: 2nd International Conference on Bioinformatics and Biomedical Engineering (2008)

Unit Testing in Global Software Development Environment

Sanjay Misra[1(✉)], Adewole Adewumi[1], Rytis Maskeliūnas[2], Robertas Damaševičius[2], and Ferid Cafer[3]

[1] Covenant University, Ota, Nigeria
Sanjay.misra@covenantuniversity.edu.ng
[2] Kaunas University of Technology, Kaunas, Lithuania
[3] Turkcell, Istanbul, Turkey

Abstract. Global software development has many challenges. Amongst them maintaining quality in the code developed in distributed sites is also a challenge. One of effective way to control the quality of the code is the unit testing. It removes defects at the early stage of development and further reduces the testing and maintenance efforts at the later phase of the development lifecycle. In this paper, a class complexity metric for testing the class, which is normally treated as a unit in object-oriented programming is proposed. The applicability of class complexity metrics for unit testing is demonstrated through a project in JAVA.

Keywords: Global software development · Unit testing · Software metrics

1 Introduction

Global software development (GSD) is a common trend of present software development. The economy of several countries as India, heavily depends on software industries and majority of those companies are involved in global software development. This trend is expanding in all over the world as more software companies continue to adopt GSD for large projects. The successes recorded thus far for GSD is due to a number of factors which include: provision of solution to the challenges of IT skills, cost efficiency, competitive advantages, round the clock software development and availability of new market. On the flip side, there are also risks and challenges associated with GSD; an instance of this is, the uncertainty surrounding a project team's ability to communicate accurately, precisely and unambiguously [1]. Further, different cultures have varied approaches to development [4]. Therefore, one of the major issues in GSD is, the loss of control on the quality of software developed by the software professionals from different locations and cultures, having different skills and responsibilities [2, 5]. Sometimes, the development team members fail to realize the advantages of the quality aspects, which must be controlled during the early phases of software development. Presently, most of the organizations are adopting the agile strategy for GSD. In this case, they apply iterative techniques, but in most of the cases, the development team members neglect to evaluate the quality of the code after each iteration process [3]. In other words, instead of performing unit test of code after each iteration, they leave it for testing at

B. Panda et al. (Eds.): REDSET 2017, CCIS 799, pp. 309–317, 2018.
https://doi.org/10.1007/978-981-10-8527-7_25

later phases. However, this practice is not acceptable for several reasons. First, the average cost of detecting defects rises exponentially [6] at each later stage. Also, if fault is overlooked due to any reason during testing phase, it may create severe complications after delivery of the product.

Unit is, the fundamental entity of software and therefore its correctness plays an important role in ensuring quality of final system. It has been proved by several researchers [22–25], that continuous unit testing is a very effective component for producing high quality software and reducing defect rates [23].

Object Oriented (OO) languages are most preferred languages for software development in the software industry. In OO software development, the class is treated as fundamental unit. In this point of view, for unit testing purpose in OO software development environment we consider to test classes.

The present study proposes to apply a metric on class level to perform unit test in OO systems. We have searched to get metrics [7–12] at class level. Some of the metrics at class level are Weighted class complexity [7], CK metric suites [8] and Costagliola and Tortora's Class points metric [9] and Kim et al. [10] complexity metrics based on entropy. Amongst available metrics at class level, we selected to apply the Weighted Class Complexity (WCC), because WCC metric computes the structural and cognitive complexity of class by associating a weight to the class. WCC includes the complexity of operations and messages in a method in terms of cognitive weights. It also considers the complexity due to data members (attributes). The data members are equally important in design consideration.

In the next section, we are summarizing the motivation for the work. A brief summary of WCC is in Sect. 3. In Sect. 4, we demonstrate that how WCC can be used for unit testing. We have considered a JAVA project for this purpose. We have summarized our findings and conclusion in Sect. 5.

2 Motivation of the Work

It is general observation that developers do not care about unit testing. Once it is global software development, it becomes more crucial because the managers lose their control on the quality development. There are several reasons for not using quality guidelines during code development. One of the reasons is that, the software developers do not find the proper tools and metrics for this purpose [12]. Further, one of the features of the unit testing (i.e. the complexity of the code) can be evaluated by the conventional software metrics [19–21], but, most of the metrics are language dependent, do not care about the cognitive complexity and also not capable of evaluating the internal architecture of code, therefore not suitable for unit testing. At present, most of the software is developed in object-oriented languages like Java and C++. Therefore, the metrics developed for procedural languages cannot be applicable for unit testing of object-oriented code. In addition, most of metrics evaluate the complexity of code from some specific attribute. For example, cyclomatic complexity is based on control flow structured ness and do not care about internal architecture and the size of the code. Similarly, line of code indicates only the size of code. Because the current software metrics are subject to these criticisms, it seems appropriate to develop a new metric, which can be applicable at the level of unit testing and satisfy most of the parameters required for calculating complexity of code. By keeping these issues in mind, we propose to apply the WCC for the unit testing of GSD, which is capable to evaluate the complexity of code from cognitive and architectural point of view and consider the complexity due to attributes. In a related work author [13] has suggested to utilize the cognitive weight [14] for unit testing. We are extending the work by considering all the factors, which are responsible for complexity of class. We feel that class complexity cannot be computed only by computing the complexity of methods but attributes are also responsible.

3 Metric Under Consideration: Weighted Class Complexity

Weighted class complexity (WCC) is developed on the concept of object orientation programming i.e. object orientation is a form of expression relation between the data and function and the class can be assumed as a set of data and set of method accessing them [7]. Hence, the complexity of the class should be measured by complexity of methods and attributes. Accordingly, WCC is computed by adding the complexity of methods and complexity of attributes.

The method complexity is computed by

$$MC = \sum_{j=1}^{q} \left[\prod_{k=1}^{m} \sum_{i=1}^{n} W_c(j, k, i) \right] \quad (1)$$

where W_c is the cognitive weight of the concerned Basic Control Structure (BCS).

If there are s methods in a class/object, then complexity due to all methods of class/object is given by total method complexity

$$= \sum_{p=1}^{s} MC_p \quad (2)$$

The complexity of Attributes is computed by summing the total number of attributes in that class/object. It reflects the complexity due to data members (attributes). In other words, the complexity due to data members for a class/object equal to total number data members in that class. The attributes are not local to one procedure but local to objects and can be accessed by several procedures. We represent the complexity due to attributes is $N_{a.}$

For computing Weighted Class Complexity (WCC), the complexity of a single class/object is

$$WCC = N_a + \sum_{p=1}^{s} MC_p \quad (3)$$

The unit of WCC is defined as the cognitive weight of the simplest software component i.e. only a linear structure BCS is taken as one Weighted Class Complexity unit (WCCU).

The WCC was theoretically evaluated through Weyuker's measurement properties [16]. It was found that WCC satisfy seven (7) Weyuker's properties. WCC was also examined through principles of measurement theory developed by Briand et al. [17]. Briand et al. have specially developed five properties to examine the additive and scale of the complexity metrics. After examination through Briand et al. properties it was found that WCC is an additive measure and on ratio scale. WCC was also examined through Kaner's practical framework [18]. All these evaluation criteria prove the theoretical soundness of the WCC. This was also one of the reasons for considering WCC for unit testing in GSD environment. It is worth mentioning here that in the original paper [7], WCC was demonstrated only by a example program developed in C++ and not applied on a real project. In fact, we also want to evaluate the applicability of WCC on JAVA.

4 Application of WCC on a Project in JAVA

For unit test in GSD environment, one have to choose class as a unit in the object oriented software development environment. Further for demonstration of the application of WCC on a class as a unit test in GSD environment, we have selected a small project developed in JAVA [15]. The project is demonstrated in Fig. 1 and one can find the full source code on [15]. We have selected the open source project because it is our belief that the open source is beneficial because the reader can easily access to the original code and if they (reader) want they can check the computation and other claims of author (regarding projects).

The project is developed for vehicle. The vehicle project consists of seven classes with varieties of characteristics. The considered project is small but, it includes most of the characteristics of object-oriented project. The class diagram of this project is shown in Fig. 1. We have shown all the methods and attributes inside the classes in each class diagram.

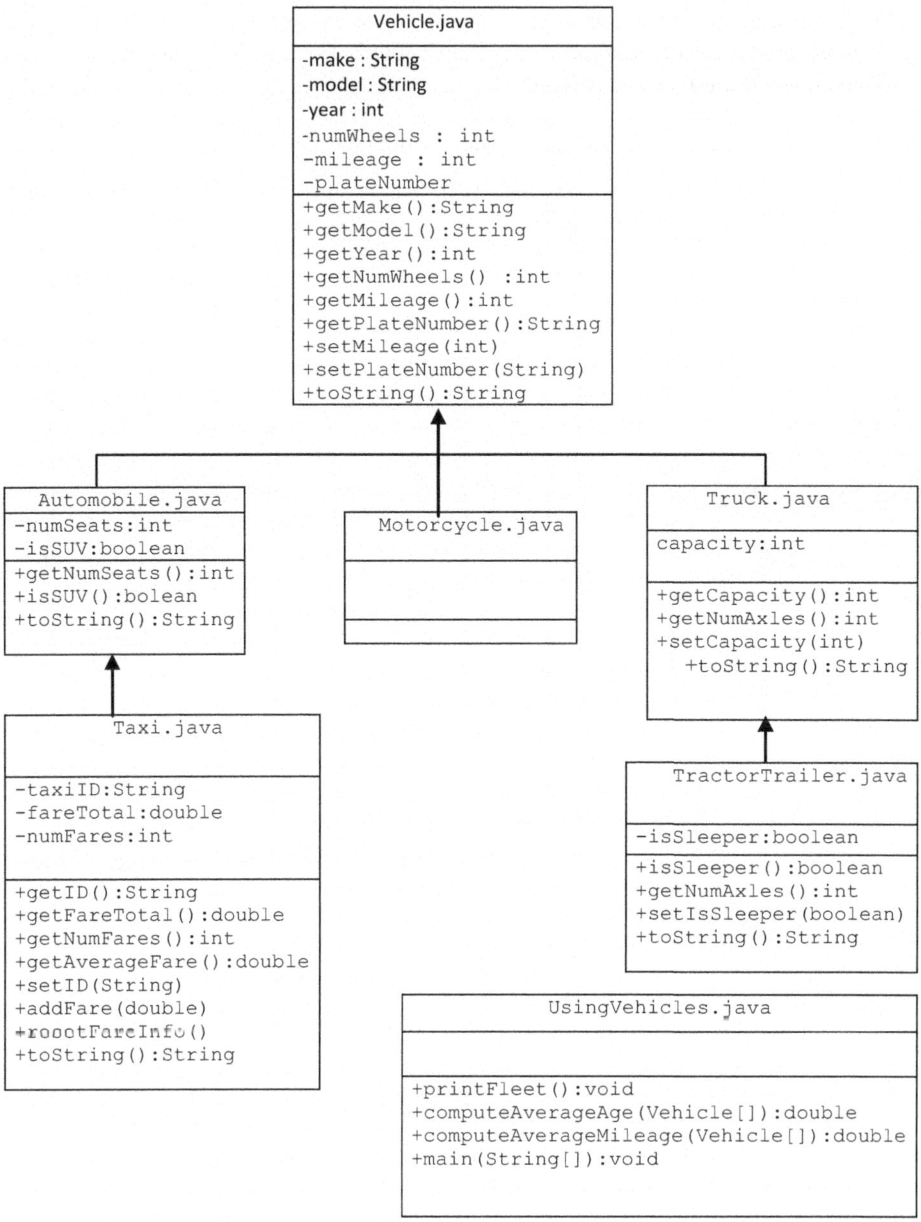

Fig. 1. An object oriented project developed in JAVA

We have applied WCC for computing the class complexity of each class. The component count for each unit/class is given in Table 1. The data WCC and its two major components are demonstrated in Table 2.

Table 1. Component counts for different classes/units.

Classes Counts	using vehicles	Tractor trailer	Taxi	Automobile	Motorcycle	Truck	Vehicle
If	0	0	2	0	0	0	2
For	3	0	0	0	0	0	0
While	0	0	0	0	0	0	0
intMethod	3	4	8	3	0	4	9
intField	0	1	3	2	0	1	6
Class_Level	*	3	3	2	2	2	1
Child	NA	0	0	1	0	1	3
Field_UsedBy_Met	0	3	10	4	0	4	10
Used_Other_Class	1	1	1	1	1	1	0
Used_Other_Field	0	0	0	3	3	4	0
IntCallMet	0	0	0	0	0	0	0
ExtCallMet	2	2	0	1	0	2	0
Methods used common attributes/attributes	0	3	8	0	0	3	4
AllMethods	5	6	8	4	0	6	9

Table 2. WCC and its major component metrics

Classes Metric	Using vehicles	Tractor trailer	Taxi	Automobile	Motorcycle	Truck	Vehicle
Attribute complexity	0	1	3	2	0	1	6
Total method complexity	20	10	12	6	1	10	14
WCC	20	11	15	8	1	11	20

In the parent directory, there are seven different files, which belong for seven classes. A class, which is on the top in the hierarchy, is Vehicle class. It is a super class of the other classes: Automobile, Motorcycle, Truck, and their subclasses. Vehicle class has 9 methods and one constructor. In constructor and in one methods two if statements have been used. Accordingly, the complexities of this class due to methods are computed as 14. This class consists of 6 attributes. Finally the total complexity of this class i.e. WCC is computed 20.

The next class in the hierarchy is Automobile class. It is a subclass of Vehicle and super class of Taxi. It includes 3 methods, which are simple in structure. However, 1 more method is invoked from Vehicle class. Due to this reason, the weight of this all the methods for this class is $3 + 2 + 1 = 6$ (3 for three methods of Automobile class, 2 for method call and 1 is the complexity of called methods from Vehicle class). This class consists of two variables. Accordingly, the WCC for this class is 8.

In the same level of Automobile class, there exists Motorcycle class. It is subclass of Vehicle. It includes only one method. The complexity of methods for this class is 1. This class has no attributes, therefore the WCC values for this class is only due to method complexity, which is 1.

Another class Truck, which is a subclass of Vehicle and super class Tractor-Trailer). It has four methods and also calling two methods getNumWheels() and toString() from Vehicle Class. Accordingly, its method complexity is 10. This class has only one attribute. The total complexity of this class is 11.

Taxi, subclass of Automobile is at second level of hierarchy. It includes 8 internal methods. Two if statements are used in two of its methods. Accordingly, the method complexity of this class is 12. This class has three attributes. Therefore, the WCC for this class is computed as 15.

The class TractorTrailer is subclass of class Truck. It includes 4 internal methods and invokes method getNumWheel() two times from Vehicle class. Its method complexity is computed as 10(4(for its internal methods + 4(for two calls) + 2(weight of two called methods). This class has only one attribute. Accordingly, the WCC is computed as 11.

UsingVehicles is independent class. It has 3 internal methods. Two of them are using two methods getYear() and getMilage() from Vehicle class. In addition, this class uses 3 for statements. Accordingly the complexity of the all methods is 20 (3(for its internal methods) + 9 (3 for statements) + 4 (for 2 calls) + 4 (weight of two called methods getYear() = 1 and getMilage() = 3)). This class has no attributes; therefore the WCC is only due to its method complexity. This is to worth mention that calculation for classes given here is only to help in understanding for readers, how to estimates the complexity of a class. On the other hand, the proper way is to calculate the complexity of each method in a class and then add them to get the complexity of entire class. Obviously, both approach for calculating complexity provides the same values.

5 Conclusion

Object orientated software development is a widely accepted in Global software development environment. Majority of companies are using object oriented languages particularly JAVA in their software development process. Unit testing is the basic and fundamental testing of classes at the developer level. The WCC is found to be effective metric for unit testing of Class. Since the complexity of the class depends on these two factors: methods and the attributes. We calculate the cognitive complexity of the class due to these factors. It considers the internal architecture of method and the complexity due to attributes also. The computation of WCC is easy and straightforward. The software development in GSD environment is not similar as in in-house development. The developers at different sites works in different environment so if they will not get easy metrics for testing their units, they may skip this process, which may complicate the whole process if any problem will arises in next phase or in future.

Acknowledgements. We acknowledge the support and sponsorship provided by Covenant University through the Centre for Research, Innovation and Discovery (CUCRID).

References

1. Cammarano, B.: Geographically distributed development with the IBM software development platform: a unified life cycle approach. In: Global Communication, Global Development, Global Success, Rational Software IBM, pp. 1–19 (2004)
2. Anschuetz, L.: Managing geographically distributed team. In: Proceedings of the IEEE IPCC 1998, pp. 1–10 (1998)
3. Ambler, S.W.: Agile strategies for geographically distributed quality management. Agile J. 1–4 (2007)
4. Richardson, I., Casey, V., Zage, D., Zage, W.: Global Software development – the challenges (2004). www.serc.net/report/tr278.pdf
5. Wade, K.: Successfully managing geographically distributed development. In: Rational Software IBM, pp. 1–12, August 2004
6. Boehm, B.: Software Engineering Economics. Prentice Hall, Englewood Cliffs (1981)
7. Misra, S., Akman, I.: Weighted class complexity: a measure of complexity for object-oriented system. J. Inf. Sci. Eng. **24**, 1689–1708 (2008)
8. Costagliola, G., Tortora, G.: Class points: an approach for the size estimation of object-oriented systems. IEEE Trans. Soft. Eng. **31**, 52–74 (2005)
9. Chidamber, S.R., Kermer, C.F.: A metric suite for object oriented design. IEEE Trans. Softw. Eng. **20**(6), 476–493 (1994)
10. Kim, K., Shin, Y., Wu, C.: Complexity measures for object-oriented program based on the entropy. In: Proceedings of APSEC, pp. 127–136 (1995)
11. Binder, R.V.: Object-oriented software testing. CACM **37**(9), 29 (1994)
12. Basily, V.R., Briand, L.C., Melo, W.L.: A validation of object oriented design metrics as quality indicators. IEEE Trans. Softw. Eng. **22**(1), 751–761 (1996)
13. Misra, S.: A metric for global software development environments. Proc. Indian Nat. Sci. Acad. **75**(4), 145–158 (2009)
14. Wang, Y., Shao, J.: A new measure of software complexity based on cognitive weights. Can. J. Electr. Comput. Eng. **28**(2), 69–74 (2003)
15. http://cspeople.bu.edu/dgs/courses/cs111/lectures/inheritance/vehicles/
16. Weyuker, E.: Evaluating software complexity measures. IEEE Trans. Softw. Eng. **14**, 1357–1365 (1988)
17. Briand, L.C., Morasca, S., Basily, V.R.: Property based software engineering measurement. IEEE Trans. Softw. Eng. **22**, 68–86 (1996)
18. Kaner, C.: Software engineering metrics: what do they measure and how do we know? In: Proceedings of 10th International Software Metrics Symposium, Metrics (2004)
19. McCabe, T.J.: A complexity measure. IEEE Trans. Softw. Eng. **2**(6), 308–320 (1976)
20. Halstead, M.H.: Elements of Software Science. Elsevier North-Holland, New York (1997)
21. Mackinnon, T., Freeman, S., Craig, P.: Endo-testing: unit testing with mock objects. In: Succi, G., Marchesi, M. (eds.) Extreme Programming Examined, pp. 287–302. Addison Wesley Longman, Reading (2001). chapter 17
22. Cheon, Y., Leavens, Gary T.: A simple and practical approach to unit testing: the JML and JUnit way. In: Magnusson, B. (ed.) ECOOP 2002. LNCS, vol. 2374, pp. 231–255. Springer, Heidelberg (2002). https://doi.org/10.1007/3-540-47993-7_10

23. Link, J., Fröhlich, P.: Unit testing in Java: how tests drive the code. Morgan Kaufmann, Los Altos (2003)
24. Fiedler, S.P.: Object-oriented unit testing-HP's Waltham div-technical, pp. 69–74. Hewlett-Packard J. (1989)
25. Hunt, A., Thomos, D, Hargett, M.: Pragematic unit test in C# with NUnit. The PragmaticBookself, USA. ISBN-13 978-0-9776166-7-4

Next Generation Computing

Comparative Analysis of Different Load Balancing Algorithm Using Cloud Analyst

Meeta Singh(✉), Poonam Nandal, and Deepa Bura

Department of Computer Science and Engineering, Faculty of Engineering and Technology, Manav Rachna International Institute of Research and Studies, Faridabad, India
{meeta.fet,poonamnandal.fet,deepa.fet}@mriu.edu.in

Abstract. Cloud computing is the emerging trend for effective allocation of hardware, platform and software over the internet, but there are many advantages and disadvantages of using cloud computing in today's world. The main features of cloud computing are reduced cost, uninterrupted pervasive accessibility, backup retrieval, throughput and efficiency and improved storage competence. Data security, privacy, cloud infrastructure, monitoring and load balancing are also the major concern. This paper focuses on load balancing for improving the performance of the resources available and distributes the load uniformly across the servers.

Keywords: Cloud computing · Data security · Load balancing · Response time Internet

1 Introduction

In the past, few years, cloud computing has gained significant importance, as it offers flexibility in retrieving data from internet. Cloud Computing is accomplishment of various activities over internet. It encourages allocation of hardware, software and platform over internet. It aims to provides various services such that in the case of unavailability of required infrastructure, software and platform, cloud service provider can provide these services on payment basis to the user. With increasing number of users on internet, it is required to provide users with rapid availability of large data sets with optimized techniques [1]. These requirements generate the necessity of cloud computing environment. Cloud computing provides helps in providing these services to the users. Moreover, it becomes imperative to identify areas in cloud computing which requires major attention in the field of storage and performance offered. One of the areas that has been identified in the past several years is load balancing for efficient resource utilization. Load balancing has been efficiently used in other fields, however it needs special attention in terms of cloud environment. Load balancing in cloud has some extra challenges, which needs to be solved for enhancing efficiency and throughput. In cloud environment, the main issue involves competently allocating requests to the Cloud nodes, wherein effort and request handling should be done at an efficient rate. Secondly cloud should be able to deal with heterogeneous traffic and large communication delay [2, 3].

B. Panda et al. (Eds.): REDSET 2017, CCIS 799, pp. 321–329, 2018.
https://doi.org/10.1007/978-981-10-8527-7_26

The process of distributing load in a uniform manner in cloud computing is termed as load balancing. All the workload requests are managed by proper allocation of available resources using load balancing algorithms. The primary aim behind this concept is to reduce average response time, such that the requests does not get queued and are allocated resources evenly [4]. Moreover, it serves other purposes also such as: (i) it enhances the performance and throughput by proper allocation of available resources. (ii) it enhances the stability of systems. (iii) And also, helps in accommodating instable traffic flow. (iv) In the case of system crash, it provides appropriate backup. (v) It ensures proper utilization of resources such that resources are not under-utilized and over-utilized. Based upon traffic flow and operating environments Load Balancing algorithms are classified as static and dynamic load balancing algorithms. Static algorithms works well with homogeneous traffic flow and stable environments, however these algorithms are less flexible. And cannot work well with frequent changes in the subsequent environment. On the other hand, dynamic algorithms works in unstable environment [5].

2 Attributes and Strategies of Load Balancing

An attribute is defined as a metric which should be considered before using any algorithm. The following attributes are measured to find the accuracy and optimality of any load balancing algorithm:

Wait time: It is the measure of time of a process that is in ready state but is queued.

Reaction Time: It is the measure of time used by resource when a resource is allocated to it.

Context switch: It is the measure of time used by resource when a resource is allocated to it.

There are different rules for evaluating the load on the virtual machine in a data center [6]. There are three policies which should be considered for evaluating the load.

(1) Closest Data Center: Location of cloud service providers plays a major role as it is one of the most significant policy in determining the performance of the cloud around the data center. In ideal situation, the nearest data center is chosen for routing the request.
(2) Optimize Response Time: The best response time that is experienced by the cloud for providing services is known as Optimize Response Time.

3 Literature Review

In general, cloud computing has given the boom to the usage of services provided by the internet. Further, it has also enhanced the services provided by the network in which one node utilizes the services of the other nodes of the network. Many researchers have given various approaches for balancing of load using cloud analyst as it is the most vital task for effective utilization of cloud.

[7] has discussed the issue of load balancing for effective utilization of all the resources given by the service provider. The authors discussed the various load

balancing policies using cloud analyst given by various researchers. The cloud analyst is a tool which is used for analysis of different load balancing algorithms. The widely known architectures SoA and IS raises the issue of performance efficiency and complexity existing in cloud environment. In view of this, the authors focused that the balancing of jobs given or submitted by the service provider is significant.

[8] also discussed the load balancing methodologies. In today era the distributed and parallel computing systems the technology like cloud computing has changed significantly. It empowers an extensive range of users to access distributed, scalable, virtualized hardware and/or software infrastructure over the Internet. The authors explained methodology used in load balancing for workload distribution across multiple nodes or resources available in the network. This load balancing is required to attain the optimal utilization of all the network resources, to increase the throughput for maximum efficiency, to decrease the response time of any resource in the network. The authors have given an analysis of some load balancing algorithms to recognize the significant components required for simulation in the environment of cloud. These significant components are further used by the authors for presenting the execution analysis of all the discussed algorithms.

[9] have given all the significant issues related to the performance of business applications. These are important to analyze to enhance the overall growth of business in an organization. Current research specifies that organizations could lose important amount of the organization revenues due to deferment from the already defined threshold decided by the experts for enactment of different and wide applications of web. The authors has discussed that users threshold for waiting is approximate 4–6 s for opening single page. The analysis given by the authors focus on the response time and the delay which is reduced which helps in an organization to overcome the loss in revenue.

4 Load Balancing Algorithms

Cloud computing is the independent of business sizes as it provides services of all types for every business [10]. The main benefit of cloud is that it is independent of infrastructure set up and there is no pre- requisite of any knowledge base for using cloud services. All these help business owners to focus on their own business processes. The main features of cloud are as mentioned below:

i. Reduced Cost: As cloud computing eliminates the requirement of stand-alone servers and independent infrastructure, it helps in reducing the overall cost.
ii. Uninterrupted Pervasive Accessibility: Irrespective of physical location and time zone, the cloud service providers provide the user an uninterrupted pervasive accessibility to the cloud.
iii. Backup Retrieval: Since the data is stored on clouds and not on physical devices, the process of recovering data becomes simpler.
iv. Throughput and Efficiency: cloud services are arranged when required only, this reduces the payment as the user has to pay only.

v. Enhancement and Performance: Whenever required the deployment of cloud can be done automatically and there is a policy of usage based payment scheme i.e. user can pay per usage only.
vi. Improved storage competence: For the improvement in the storage capacity user can freely use cloud computing as per their requirements.

As cloud computing is the emerging trend it has many pros and cons. Most of the pros are stated above [11]. As Cloud computing is fully relied on Internet, any problem encountered in the Internet connection will directly affect the performance of cloud computing. In today's era data security is the most critical issue and thus the important concern for the competitive cloud environment, so the maximum vendors of cloud make sure that the data security systems should be appropriate to avoid the secure data leakage. Other than data security, privacy, cloud infrastructure, monitoring and load balancing are also the major concern. This paper focus on load balancing for improving the performance of the resources available and distribute the load uniformly across the servers.

Load balancing helps in the optimizing the execution of jobs in minimum time without waiting in a queue. This will further helps to reduce the overall response time of the job request [12]. Load balancing will improve the overall performance of cloud computing by improving the stability, uniform traffic distribution, managing resources for optimal utilization.

As there are many algorithms in cloud computing which can be used to improve the performance by managing uniform load distribution. Different load balancing algorithms are discussed below:

Round Robin: This algorithm basically work on time slots given for the jobs in a circular motion.

Equally Spread: This algorithm works on the uniform distribution of the loads among the idle servers.

Throttled: This algorithm is dynamic in nature as it allocates the to the best suited virtual machine as per the received job.

5 Load Balancing Algorithms

In this paper simulation environment is created for five different user bases and three data centers. Every user bases have their specific peak load time and costing plan as shown in Tables 1 and 2. Simulation is done with × 86 hardware architecture using Linux OS with VM or hypervisor Xen. The total Virtual machine cost is $ 3.00 whereas total data transfer cost is $ 0.32 which makes grand total of $ 3.34. VM s at DC1 & DC2 are having 1 GB RAM whereas, DC3 is having 512 MB. Number of simultaneous users is the factor of 10 and Simultaneous requests are also a factor of 10. Executable instruction length per request is 100. Figures 1 and 2 shows the region boundaries and data centre configuration respectively.

Table 1. Simulation parameters

User base	Request per user/hr	Data size per request (BITS)	Peak hours start (GMT)	Peak hours ends (GMT)	Average peak users	Average off peak users
UB1	60	100	3:00	9:00	1000	100
UB2	60	100	4:00	10:00	1000	100
UB3	60	100	5:00	11:00	1000	100
UB4	60	100	6:00	12:00	1000	100
UB5	60	100	7:00	1:00	1000	100

Table 2. Costing plan

User base	VM cost $	Data transfer cost $	Total $
DC1	1	0.06	1.07
DC2	1	0.07	1.07
DC3	1	0.19	1.2

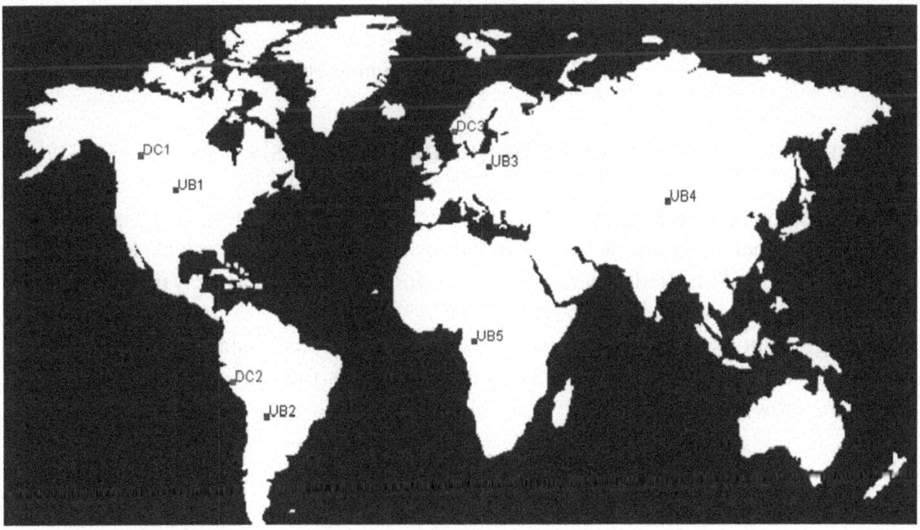

Fig. 1. Region boundaries

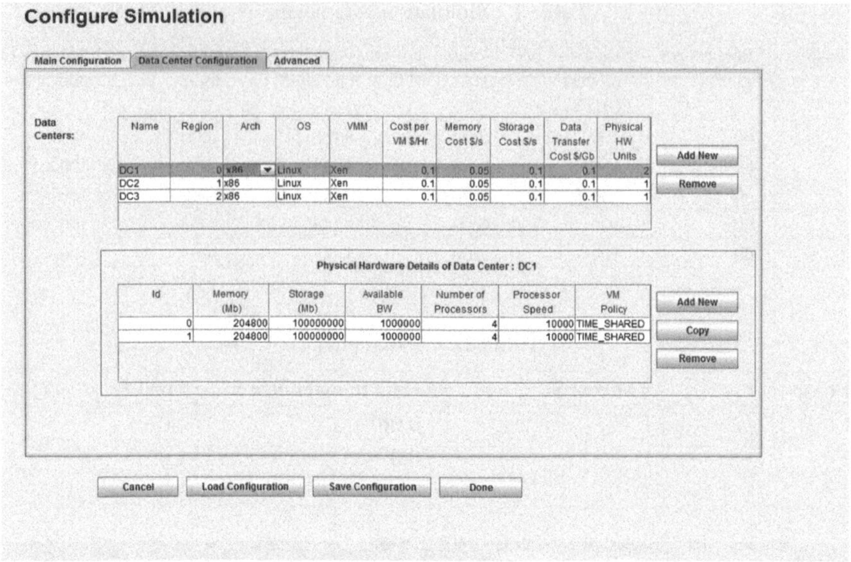

Fig. 2. Data center configuration

6 Simulation Results and Comparative Analysis

Virtual machines are used to handle the traffic load between the user bases and data centers. This paper analyses the behavior of three load balancing algorithm Round robin, Equally spread & Throttled in terms of the performance and cost of Virtual Machines across the Data Centers using Cloud Analyst.

Average response time (in milliseconds) of different load balancing polices which are used by different load balancing algorithms across the Virtual Machines in data centers are shown in Table 3.

Table 3. Average response time

Algorithm name	Closest data center	Optimize response time	Reconfigure dynamic with load
Round robin	150.85	150.67	152.58
Equally spread execution load	150.86	150.69	151.43
Throttled	150.85	150.68	151.41

Average response time of load balancing algorithms improves if data centers reconfigure itself dynamically with the increase or decreasing of the traffic load. Response time of Round robin algorithm is best as compared with the other two algorithms if reconfigure dynamic with load policy of load balancing is used.

Data processing time taken by Virtual Machines for all the algorithms for different load balancing policies are shown in Table 4. Data processing time taken in Closest Data

Center and Optimize Response Time in same in all the three load balancing algorithm. If Virtual Machines are configured dynamically according to the traffic load then the time taken In this paper, it is concluded that the data processing time taken in Closest Data Center and Optimize Response Time is same in the entire three load balancing algorithm. If Virtual Machines are configured dynamically according to the traffic load then the time taken to process the data is less in Throttled load balancing algorithm as compared with the other two algorithms. Data processing time of Round Robin is maximum in the comparative analysis of the results. to process the data is less in Throttled load balancing algorithm as compared with the other two algorithms. Data processing time of Round Robin is maximum (Figs. 3 and 4).

Table 4. Data center processing time

Algorithm name	Closest data center	Optimize response time	Reconfigure dynamic with load
Round robin	0.54	0.54	2.30
Equally spread execution load	0.54	0.54	1.12
Throttled	0.54	0.54	1.10

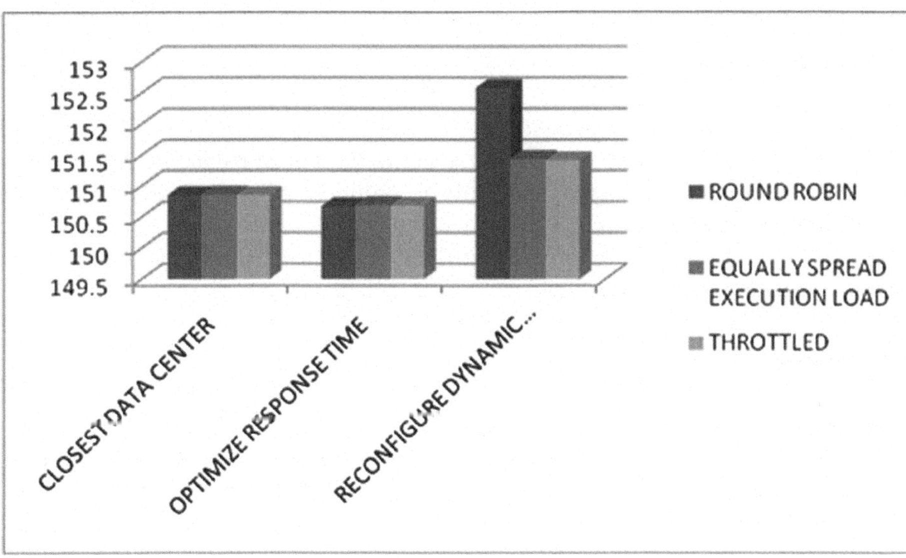

Fig. 3. Average response time

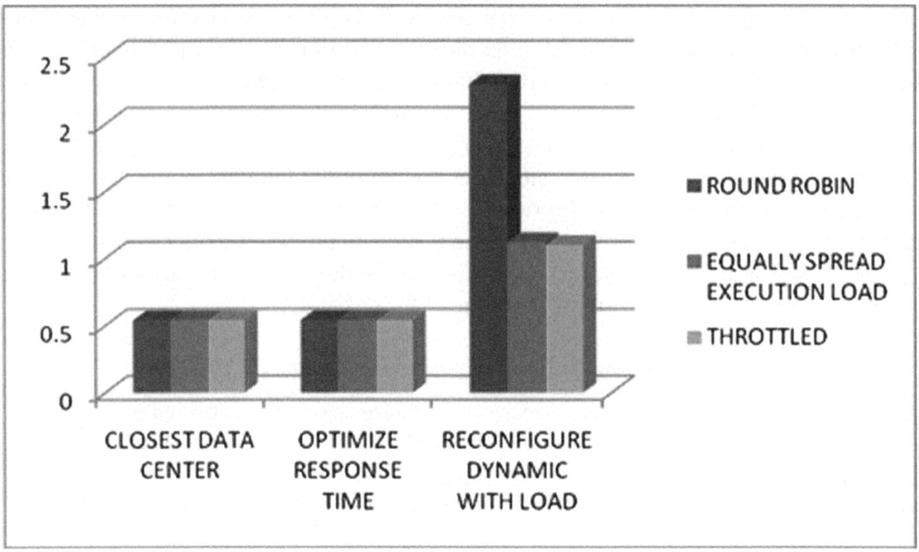

Fig. 4. Data center processing time

7 Conclusion

In this paper, it is concluded that the data processing time taken in Closest Data Center and Optimize Response Time is same in the entire three load balancing algorithm. If Virtual Machines are configured dynamically according to the traffic load then the time taken to process the data is less in Throttled load balancing algorithm as compared with the other two algorithms. Data processing time of Round Robin is maximum in the comparative analysis of the results.

References

1. Wickremasinghe, B., Calheiros, R.N., Buyya, R.: Cloudanalyst: a cloudsim-based visual modeller for analysing cloud computing environments and applications. In: 2010 24th IEEE International Conference on Advanced Information Networking and Applications, pp. 446–452. IEEE, April 2010
2. Mohapatra, S., Rekha, K.S., Mohanty, S.: A comparison of four popular heuristics for load balancing of virtual machines in cloud computing. Int. J. Comput. App. **68**(6), 33–38 (2013)
3. Calheiros, R.N., Ranjan, R., Beloglazov, A., De Rose, C.A., Buyya, R.: CloudSim: a toolkit for modeling and simulation of cloud computing environments and evaluation of resource provisioning algorithms. Softw.: Pract. Exp. **41**(1), 23–50 (2011)
4. Mohapatra, S., Mohanty, S., Rekha, K.S.: Analysis of different variants in round robin algorithms for load balancing in cloud computing. Int. J. Comput. App. **69**(22), 17–21 (2013)
5. Samal, P., Mishra, P.: Analysis of variants in round robin algorithms for load balancing in cloud computing. Int. J. Comput. Sci. Inf. Technol. **4**(3), 416–419 (2013)

6. Florence, A.P., Shanthi, V.: A load balancing model using firefly algorithm in cloud computing. J. Comput. Sci. **10**(7), 1156–1165 (2014)
7. Ahmed, T., Singh, Y.: Analytic study of load balancing techniques using tool cloud analyst. Int. J. Eng. Res. App. **2**(2), 1027–1030 (2012)
8. Ray, S., De Sarkar, A.: Execution analysis of load balancing algorithms in cloud computing environment. Int. J. Cloud Comput.: Serv. Archit. **2**(5), 1–13 (2012)
9. Nitika, M., Shaveta, M., Raj, M.G.: Comparative analysis of load balancing algorithms in cloud computing. Int. J. Adv. Res. Comput. Eng. Technol. **1**(3), 120–124 (2012)
10. Raghava, N.S., Singh, D.: Comparative study on load balancing techniques in cloud computing. Open J. Mobile Comput. Cloud Comput. **1**(1), 352–357 (2014)
11. Dash, M., Mahapatra, A., Chakraborty, N.R.: Cost effective selection of data center in cloud environment. Int. J. Adv. Comput. Theory Eng. (IJACTE) **2**, 2319–2526 (2013)
12. Mishra, R.K., Bhukya, S.N.: Service broker algorithm for cloud-analyst. Int. J. Comput. Sci. Inf. Technol. **5**(3), 3957–3962 (2014)

Performance Analysis of QoS Parameters During Vertical Handover Process Between Wi-Fi and WiMAX Networks

Bhawna Narwal(✉) and Amar K. Mohapatra

Indira Gandhi Delhi Technical University, New Delhi, India
bhawnanarwal@gmail.com, mohapatra.amar@gmail.com

Abstract. To make a seamless handover among heterogeneous networks, the optimal selection of a network is a challenging task. These networks vary in terms of QoS provisioning. The challenge is to select a network which has better QoS. The paper showcases the effects of Hard Handover and Predictive Handover on the QoS parameters with different data rates of application running on the mobile node at different mobile node speeds between Wi-Fi and WiMAX networks.

Keywords: Handover Latency · Packet Loss Ratio · Predictive Handover Qualnet · Throughput · Wi-Fi · WiMAX

1 Introduction

In the Next Generation Wireless Networks (NGWN), for seamless mobility and service continuity the decision of vertical handover is very important as it impacts the QoS (Quality of Service) of the mobile users. The NGWN mobile devices have multiple interfaces; the challenge is to select the best network which improves the QoS. Vertical Handover is the process of switching the connections from one access technology to another such as Wi-Fi to WiMAX, WiMAX to UMTS i.e. Heterogeneous Networks [1–3]. There are three phases of vertical handover; they are Handover Information Gathering, Handover Decision and Handover Execution. In the rest phase, the information about neighboring networks are collected, based on this information the decision in the second phase i.e. Handover Decision phase is take. Decision is dependent on the user needs and should satisfy it. In the last phase which is Handover Execution, the connections are switched. The Vertical Handover Decision can be taken based on different factors such as power consumption, RSS, security and bandwidth etc. Heterogeneous Networks Wi-Fi and WiMAX have different characteristics. IEEE 802.11 is the standard for Wi-Fi which is designed for small coverage such as home, office etc. It uses unlicensed spectrum. Due to small coverage area, it has low mobility. It has typical 6.5 Mbps data rate and maximum 11 Mbps data rate with a coverage area of approximately 30 m. IEEE 802.16 is the standard for WiMAX which is designed for broad-band wireless access. WiMAX is a Wi-Fi with greater range and is optimal for data. WiMAX has a reach of about 50 km of range. It uses the licensed or unlicensed 2 GHz to 11 GHz frequency band. It has typical 15 Mbps data

B. Panda et al. (Eds.): REDSET 2017, CCIS 799, pp. 330–344, 2018.
https://doi.org/10.1007/978-981-10-8527-7_27

rate at 5 MHz channelization. QoS is a defined measure of performance in a data communications system [7]. Different QoS Performance metrics are useful to understand performance of different scenarios.

Hard handover is a handover technique in which the mobile station moving between the wireless cells makes the connection to a new Base Station only when connection with the existing Base station are broken. It means after breaking the connection with the channel in the source cell the mobile node can establish the connection with the channel in the target cell. This is the reason Hard Handover is also known as Break-before-Make Handover. Hard Handover operates on single channel which makes it cheaper. It is instantaneous (takes about 60 ms) which makes it difficult to feel the interruption in the call. This handover technique is suitable for applications/services such as VoIP, Internet etc. because in these slight delay does not create problem.

The rest of the paper is organized as follows; In Sect. 2 related work is presented. Section 3 introduces the proposed predictive handover algorithm between Wi-Fi and WiMAX networks. Section 4 discusses the simulation environment including the General, Application and Performance parameters. Simulation Scenarios are also presented in this section. In Sect. 5 results are analyzed for Wi-Fi to WiMAX and WiMAX to Wi-Fi in both Predictive and Hard Handover. Finally, Conclusions and Future Work are present in Sect. 6.

2 Related Work

In the literature several proposals and approaches have been made for vertical handover decisions. Authors of [4] presents effects on the QoS metrics during the vertical handover process between Wireless networks (Wi-Fi and WiMAX) using MIH concerning speed with which mobile node moves. This paper does not consider the RSS factor. Paper [5] proposed and implemented a vertical handover algorithm using IEEE 802.21 in WiMAX-Wi-Fi heterogeneous environment based on mobile nodes speed for VoIP users; however the paper lacks the consideration if multiple applications runs on the mobile node. In [6] proposed a user centric vertical handover algorithm is proposed which combines a trigger to continuously maintain the connection and another one to maximize the user throughput in IEEE 802.11 and 802.16 hybrid networks. In [7] authors proposed a new vertical handover algorithm between IEEE 802.16e and IEEE 802.11e networks. It uses a decision mechanism based on available bandwidth, signal to noise ratio and access delay. The authors were successful in reducing cost, power consumption and useless handovers and also mitigated ping-pong effects. Authors of [8] proposed an active application oriented scheme for efficient inter-face management in the Mobile Terminals with multiple interfaces. Authors of [11] proposed an energy efficient vertical handover scheme which executes vertical handover based on the value of lifetime parameter.

3 Proposed Algorithm

In the proposed algorithm vertical handover is triggered at the network layer based on Received Signal Strength (RSS) and speed of the mobile node (S). The algorithm is tested for mobile node travelling with low speeds such as 1, 2 and 3 m/s. There is no requirement of doing handover to smaller networks such as Wi-Fi if the mobile node is moving with higher speed as it will be covered in shorter period of time and doing handovers to Wi-Fi at high speeds leads to unnecessary handovers. According to our algorithm if the speed of the mobile node while moving from Network N1 to Network N2 is S (which could be 1, 2 or 3 m/s) then set the RSS threshold (RSSTH) according to this speed. Here N1 and N2 are based on the mobile node direction of movement which can be Wi-Fi to WiMAX network or WiMAX to Wi-Fi network. While approaching the Network N2 from Network N1 if RSS of Network N1 is less than the acceptable threshold of RSS and also if it is lower than RSS of Network N2 then execute the vertical handover and switch the connections to Network N2 otherwise remain with your current network. Our proposed algorithm for Predictive Handover is outlined in Fig. 1.

4 Simulation Environment

In this section we describe the simulation environment of our experiments using Qualnet 6.1 simulator. In the simulations using Wi-Fi and WiMAX technologies we performed hard handover and predictive handover. Simulation and Application Parameters used in simulation are shown in Tables 1 and 2 respectively.

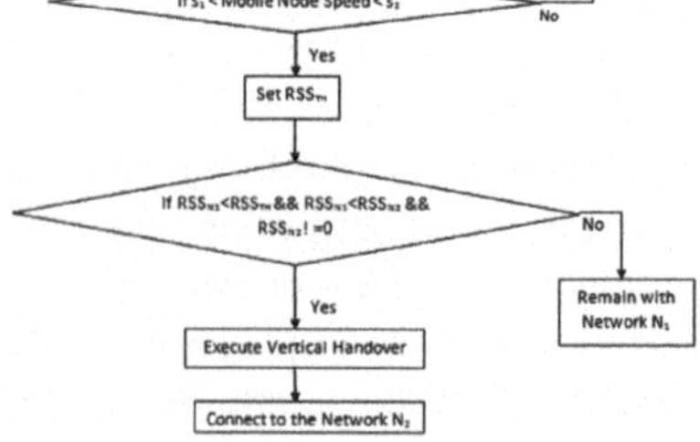

Fig. 1. Block diagram of Predictive Handover

Table 1. Simulation parameters.

General parameters	
Simulation time	900 s (For Wi-Fi to WiMAX Handover)
	882 s (For WiMAX to Wi-Fi Handover)
Area	1500 × 1500 m
Channel frequency	2.4 GHz
Pathloss model	Two Ray
Shadowing Model	Constant
Mobility	(1, 2, 3) m/s
Traffic type	CBR, VoIP
Mobility model	Random waypoint
Wi-Fi parameters	
No. of nodes in Wi-Fi cell	10 (For both Wi-Fi to WiMAX & WiMAX to Wi-Fi Handover)
Radio type	802.11b Radio
Data rate	2 Mbps
Antenna model	Omni directional
MAC protocol	802.11
Network protocol	IPv4
Routing protocol	AODV
WiMAX parameters	
No. of nodes in WiMAX cell	20 (For Wi-Fi to WiMAX Handover)
	10 (For WiMAX to Wi-Fi Handover)
Radio type	802.16 Radio
Transmission power	20 dBm (For Wi-Fi to WiMAX Handover)
	28 dBm (For WiMAX to Wi-Fi Handover)
Channel bandwidth	20 MHz
Antenna model	Omni directional
MAC protocol	802.16
Network protocol	IPv4
Routing protocol	AODV

Table 2. Application parameters.

CBR	
Item size	500 bytes
Interval	40 ms (for 100 kbps)
	4 ms (for 1000 kbps)
VoIP	
Average talking time	20 s
Call status	Accept
Packetization interval	By interval
Encoding codec	G.729 codec
	G.723 codec

4.1 Simulation Scenario

In Wi-Fi to WiMAX, the mobile node is moving from Wi-Fi; the serving PoA to WiMAX, which represents the target PoA with a constant speed and for WiMAX to Wi-Fi; the serving PoA is WiMAX and target PoA is Wi-Fi. For both Wi-Fi to WiMAX and WiMAX to Wi-Fi, two simulation scenarios are created. In the first simulation scenario, CBR application runs on the mobile node and in the second simulation scenario, two applications CBR and VoIP. These simulation scenarios are analyzed for two data rates of application (CBR→100 kbps and 1000 kbps; VoIP→G.723 codec and G.729 codec) at different speeds (1, 2 and 3) m/s in Hard Handover and Predictive Handover. The remaining nodes in both Wi-Fi cell and WiMAX cell are following random waypoint mobility model with a minimum speed of 0 m/s, maximum speed of 0.5 m/s, pause time of 1 min and position granularity of 1 m. Figures 2, 3, 4 and 5 presents the simulation scenarios.

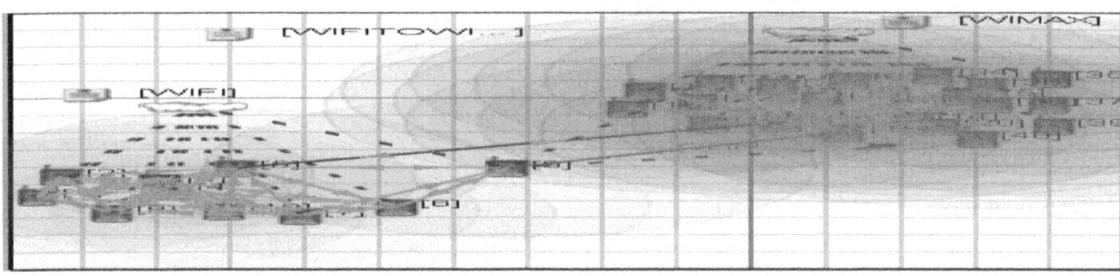

Fig. 2. Wi-Fi to WiMAX with CBR application

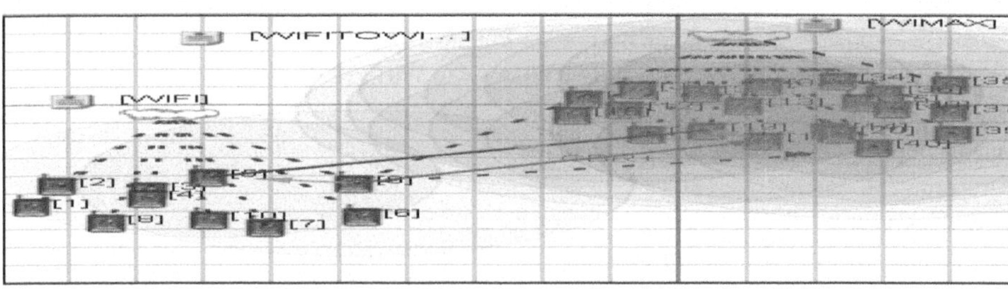

Fig. 3. Wi-Fi to WiMAX with CBR and VoIP application

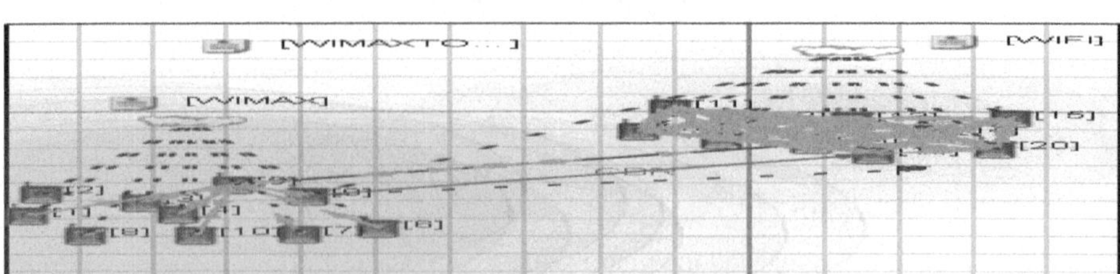

Fig. 4. WiMAX to Wi-Fi with CBR application

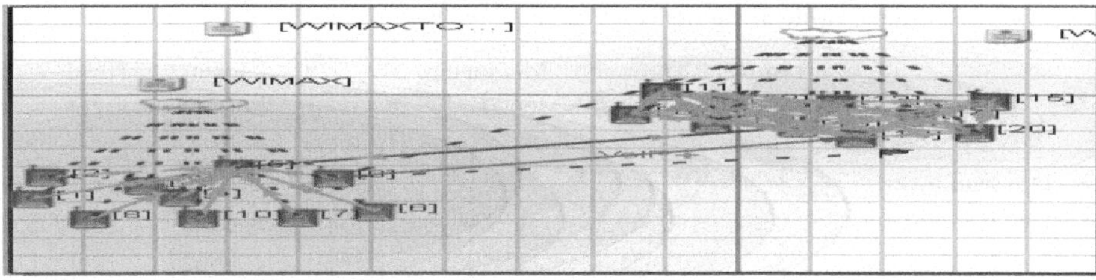

Fig. 5. WiMAX to Wi-Fi with CBR and VoIP application

4.2 Performance Parameters

Three performance parameters Throughput, Packet Loss Ratio and Handover Latency are evaluated for both Hard Handover and Predictive Handover. These three parameters are mentioned as follows:

Throughput: Throughput or network throughput is the average rate of successful message delivery over a communication channel. Throughput is measured in bits per second (bit/s or bps [10]).

$$\text{Throughput} = \frac{\text{Total Bytes Sent} * 8}{\text{Time Last Packet Sent} - \text{Time First Packet Sent}}$$

where 'time' is in seconds [9].

Packet Loss Ratio: It is defined as the difference between the total number of packets sent by the source and the number of the packets received by the mobile node interface divided by the total number of packets generated by the source [4, 9].

$$\text{Packet Loss Ratio} = \frac{\text{Total Packets generated} - \text{No. of Packets Received}}{\text{Total Packets Generated}}$$

Handover latency: It is defined as the amount of time elapsed between one network interface sending redirect request to another network interface and receiving the correspondent redirect acknowledgement from target network interface. It is measured in seconds [4].

$$\text{Handover Latency} = \text{Acknowledgement time from target network} - \text{Request Time from source network}$$

where 'time' is in seconds [4].

Tables 3, 4, 5, 6, 7, 8, 9 and 10 are presented at the end of the paper showcasing the values obtained in each scenario.

Table 3. CBR with 100 Kbps for Wi-Fi-WiMAX

		Move speed (m/s)	Throughput (bits/sec)	Messages sent (Number)	Messages received (Number)	Packet Loss Ratio (%)	Handover Latency (seconds)
1	Hard Handover	1	99418.2	18725	18371	1.8905	21.4058
2	Hard Handover	2	99759.5	10225	9954	2.6503	13.1095
3	Hard Handover	3	99621.4	6850	6579	3.9562	12.9217
4	Predictive Handover	1	100016	18725	18482	1.2977	3.3300
5	Predictive Handover	2	100040	10225	9983	2.4241	2.0900
6	Predictive Handover	3	100045	6850	6606	3.5620	4.5699

Table 4. CBR with 1000 Kbps for Wi-Fi-WiMAX

		Move speed (m/s)	Throughput (bits/sec)	Messages sent (Number)	Messages received (Number)	Packet Loss Ratio (%)	Handover Latency (seconds)
1	Hard Handover	1	971005	187250	179432	4.1751	27.4077
2	Hard Handover	2	958828	102250	95691	6.4146	6.9574
3	Hard Handover	3	953786	68500	62988	8.0467	7.4047
4	Predictive Handover	1	973792	187250	179947	3.9001	3.3380
5	Predictive Handover	2	971492	102250	96950	5.1833	2.0980
6	Predictive Handover	3	968433	68500	63965	6.6204	4.1380

Table 5. CBR with 1000 kbps and VoIP with G.729 Codec for Wi-Fi-WiMAX

		Move speed (m/s)	Throughput (bits/sec)	Messages sent (Number)	Messages received (Number)	Packet Loss Ratio (%)	Handover Latency (seconds)
1	Hard Handover	1	99107	18725	18313	2.2002	19.3735
2	Hard Handover	2	98577	10225	9837	3.7946	8.0819
3	Hard Handover	3	99114.4	6850	6547	4.4233	10.3810
4	Predictive Handover	1	98483.9	18725	18351	1.9973	3.3300
5	Predictive Handover	2	99990	10225	9977	2.4254	2.0924
6	Predictive Handover	3	99901.6	6850	6601	3.6350	4.1699

Table 6. CBR with 1000 kbps and VoIP with G.729 Codec for Wi-Fi-WiMAX

		Move speed (m/s)	Throughput (bits/sec)	Messages sent (Number)	Messages received (Number)	Packet Loss Ratio (%)	Handover Latency (seconds)
1	Hard Handover	1	744235	187250	138863	25.840	37.7666
2	Hard Handover	2	956821	102250	95486	6.6151	5.9542
3	Hard Handover	3	232772	68500	51740	24.467	9.3512
4	Predictive Handover	1	971281	187250	179483	4.1479	3.3380
5	Predictive Handover	2	683548	102250	69592	31.939	2.0980
6	Predictive Handover	3	737399	68500	48967	28.515	4.1740

Table 7. CBR with 100 Kbps for WiMAX-Wi-Fi

		Move speed (m/s)	Throughput (bits/sec)	Messages sent (Number)	Messages received (Number)	Packet Loss Ratio (%)	Handover Latency (seconds)
1	Hard Handover	1	72311.1	22025	15844	28.06356	0.010518
2	Hard Handover	2	36068.8	11000	7903	28.15455	0.012467
3	Hard Handover	3	23988.1	7325	5256	28.24573	0.015612
4	Predictive Handover	1	100461	22025	22011	0.063564	0.009306
5	Predictive Handover	2	100901	11000	10983	0.154545	0.009372
6	Predictive Handover	3	101388	7325	7310	0.204778	0.015532

Table 8. CBR with 1000 Kbps for WiMAX-Wi-Fi

		Move speed (m/s)	Throughput (bits/sec)	Messages sent (Number)	Messages received (Number)	Packet Loss Ratio (%)	Handover Latency (seconds)
1	Hard Handover	1	718460	220250	157421	28.52622	0.021647
2	Hard Handover	2	356407	110000	78092	29.00909	0.011154
3	Hard Handover	3	235691	73250	51642	29.49898	0.018129
4	Predictive Handover	1	1.00E+06	220250	219153	0.49807	0.015827
5	Predictive Handover	2	1.00E+06	110000	108950	0.954545	0.010666
6	Predictive Handover	3	1.00E+06	73250	72191	1.445734	0.01563

Table 9. CBR with 100 kbps and VoIP with G.723 Codec for WiMAX-Wi-Fi

		Move speed (m/s)	Throughput (bits/sec)	Messages sent (Number)	Messages received (Number)	Packet Loss Ratio (%)	Handover Latency (seconds)
1	Hard Handover	1	88922.8	22025	19483	11.54143	0.10974
2	Hard Handover	2	94460.8	11000	10282	6.527273	0.033112
3	Hard Handover	3	71138	7325	5129	29.97952	0.015846
4	Predictive Handover	1	88923.1	22025	19483	11.54143	0.010355
5	Predictive Handover	2	94460.8	11000	10282	6.527273	0.015236
6	Predictive Handover	3	81706.8	7325	5891	19.57679	0.00965

Table 10. CBR with 1000 kbps and VoIP with G.729 Codec for WiMAX-Wi-Fi

		Move speed (m/s)	Throughput (bits/sec)	Messages sent (Number)	Messages received (Number)	Packet Loss Ratio (%)	Handover Latency (seconds)
1	Hard Handover	1	794466	220250	174074	20.96527	0.108164
2	Hard Handover	2	674556	110000	73431	33.24455	0.010857
3	Hard Handover	3	731399	73250	52740	28	0.018118
4	Predictive Handover	1	817970	220250	179224	18.62701	0.016253
5	Predictive Handover	2	738620	110000	80405	26.90455	0.00947
6	Predictive Handover	3	770009	73250	55524	24.19932	0.009765

5 Results and Analysis

5.1 Throughput

Figure 6 shows CBR Throughput at 100 kbps in Wi-Fi to WiMAX, it is seen that the Throughput for Predictive Handover is greater than Hard Handover at all the speeds. For Hard Handover the Throughput increased by 0.002% from 1 m/s to 3 m/s while for Predictive Handover the increase is by 0.0002%. Figure 9 shows CBR Throughput in Wi-Fi to WiMAX, when both CBR and VoIP applications run on the mobile node. Data rate for CBR is 100 kbps and VoIP uses G.723 codec. It is observed that Throughput for Predictive Handover increased with increase of speed then Hard Handover. For Hard Handover the Throughput increased by 0.00007% from 1 m/s to 3 m/s while for Predictive Handover the increase is by 0.01439%. Figure 12 shows CBR Throughput at 100 kbps in WiMAX to Wi-Fi, it is seen that the Throughput for Predictive Handover is greater than Hard Handover at all the speeds. For Hard Handover the Throughput decreased by 6.9972% from 1 m/s to 3 m/s while for Predictive Handover the decrease is by 0.08115%. Figure 15 shows CBR Throughput in WiMAX to Wi-Fi, when both CBR and VoIP applications run on the mobile node. Data rate for CBR is 100 kbps and VoIP uses G.723 codec. It is observed that Throughput for Predictive Handover increased with increase of speed then Hard Handover. For Hard Handover the Throughput decreased by 0.66826% from 1 m/s to 3 m/s while for Predictive Handover the increase is by 0.0092%.

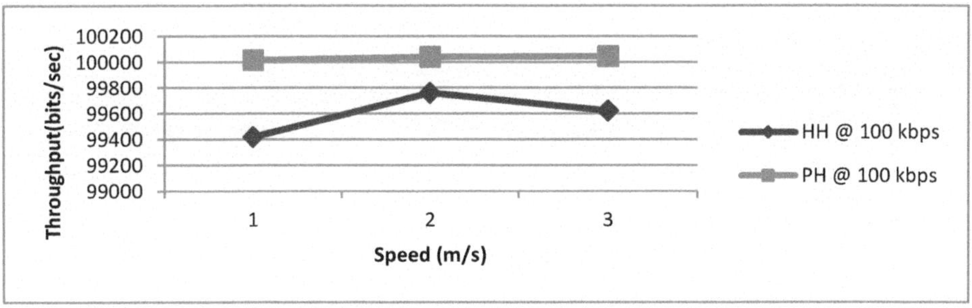

Fig. 6. CBR Throughput at 100 kbps in Wi-Fi to WiMAX

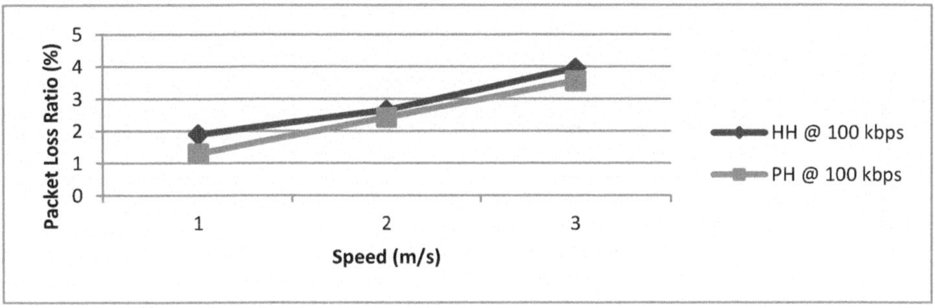

Fig. 7. CBR Packet Loss Ratio at 100 kbps in Wi-Fi to WiMAX

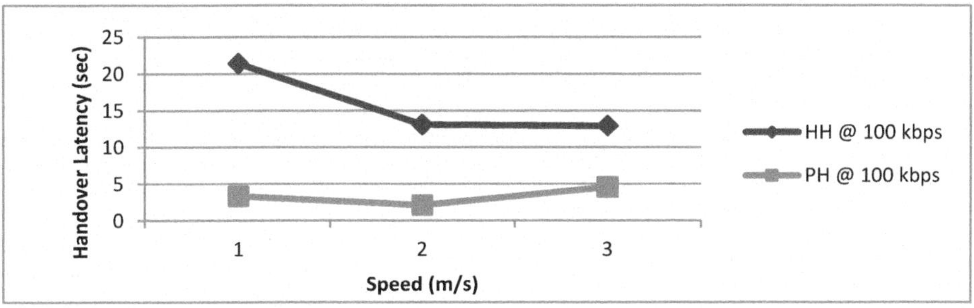

Fig. 8. CBR Handover Latency at 100 kbps in Wi-Fi to WiMAX

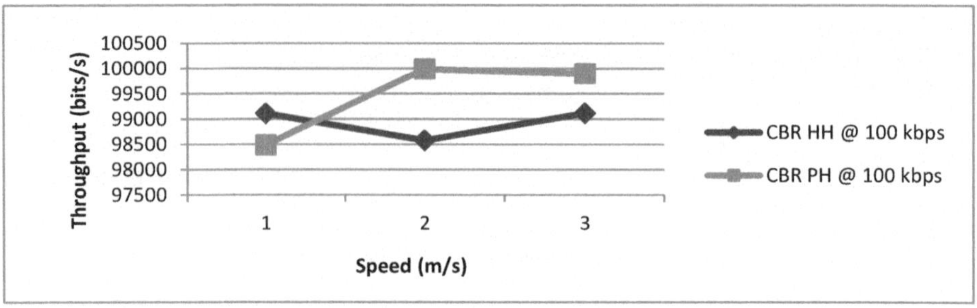

Fig. 9. CBR Throughput at 100 kbps and G.723 codec when CBR and VoIP running on the mobile node in Wi-Fi to WiMAX

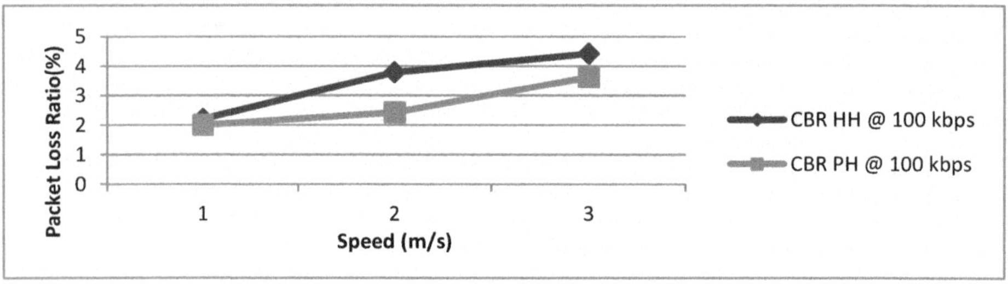

Fig. 10. CBR Packet Loss Ratio at 100 kbps and G.723 codec when CBR and VoIP running on the mobile node in Wi-Fi to WiMAX

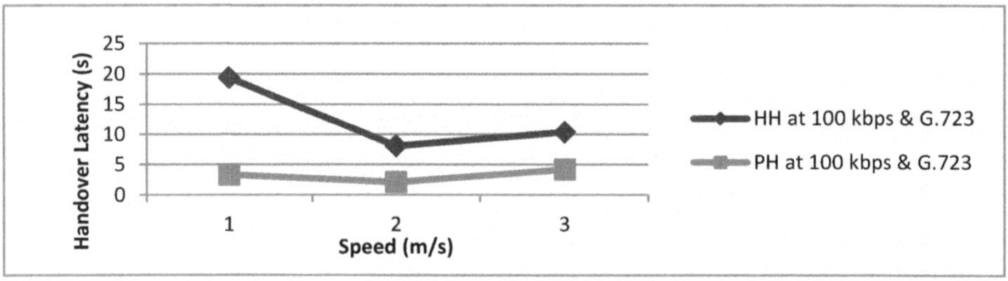

Fig. 11. CBR Handover Latency at 100 kbps and G.723 codec when CBR and VoIP running on the mobile node in Wi-Fi to WiMAX

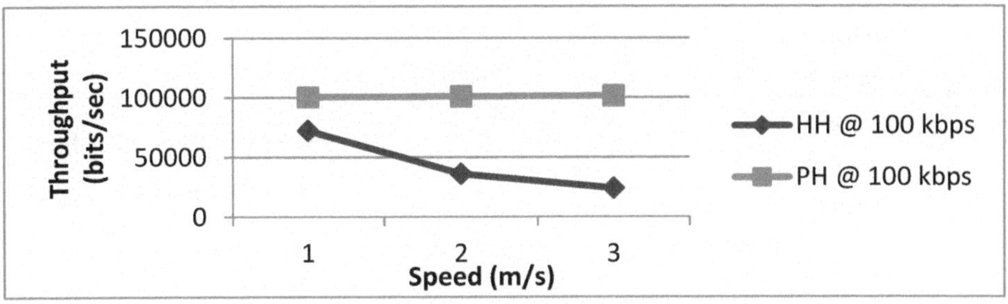

Fig. 12. CBR Throughput at 100 kbps in WiMAX to Wi-Fi

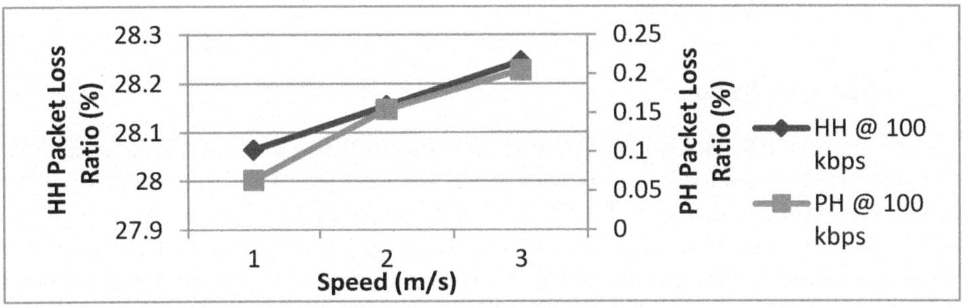

Fig. 13. CBR Packet Loss Ratio at 100 kbps in WiMAX to Wi-Fi

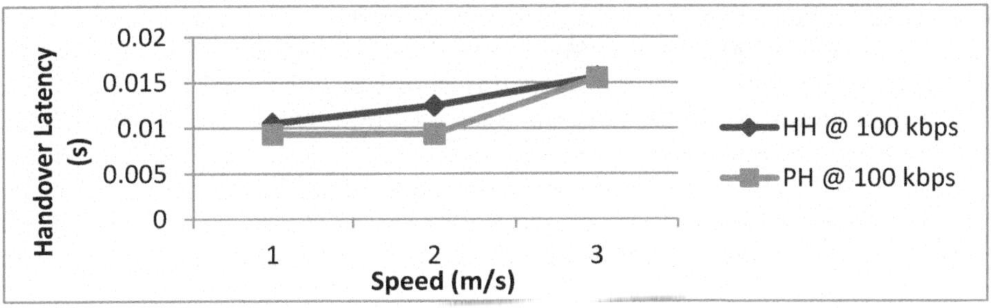

Fig. 14. CBR Handover Latency at 100 kbps in WiMAX to Wi-Fi

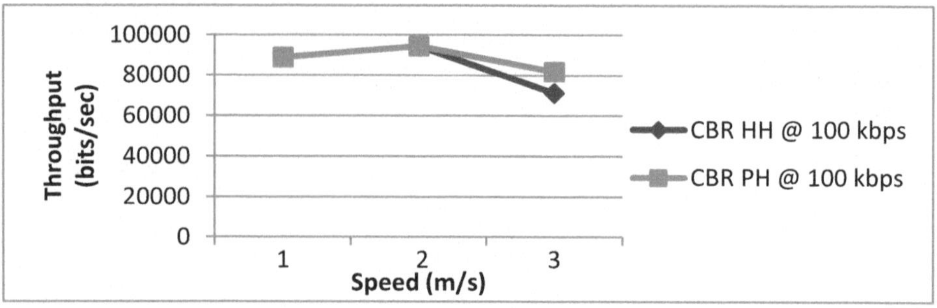

Fig. 15. CBR Throughput at 100 kbps and G.723 codec when CBR and VoIP running on the mobile node in WiMAX to Wi-Fi

5.2 Packet Loss Ratio

Figure 7 shows CBR Packet Loss Ratio at 100 kbps in Wi-Fi to WiMAX, it is seen that the Packet Loss Ratio for Predictive Handover is lower than Hard Handover at all the speeds. For Hard Handover the Packet Loss Ratio increased by 1.0926% from 1 m/s to 3 m/s while for Predictive Handover the increase is by 1.7448%. Figure 10 shows CBR Packet Loss ratio in Wi-Fi to WiMAX, when both CBR and VoIP applications run on the mobile node. Data rate for CBR is 100 kbps and VoIP uses G.723 codec. It is observed that Packet Loss ratio for Predictive Handover is lower than Hard Handover at all the speeds. For Hard Handover the Packet Loss ratio decreased by 0.4641% from 1 m/s to 3 m/s while for Predictive Handover the increase is by 0.2522%. Figure 13 shows CBR Packet Loss ratio at 100 kbps in WiMAX to Wi-Fi, it is seen that the Packet Loss ratio for Predictive Handover is lower than Hard Handover at 1 and 3 m/s but not at 2 m/s. For Hard Handover the Packet Loss ratio increased by 1.5975% from 1 m/s to 3 m/s while for Predictive Handover the increase is by 0.69621%. Figure 16 shows CBR Packet Loss ratio in WiMAX to Wi-Fi, when both CBR and VoIP applications run on the mobile node. Data rate for CBR is 100 kbps and VoIP uses G.723 codec. It is observed that Packet Loss ratio for Predictive Handover is lower at 3 m/s but same at 1 and 2 m/s with

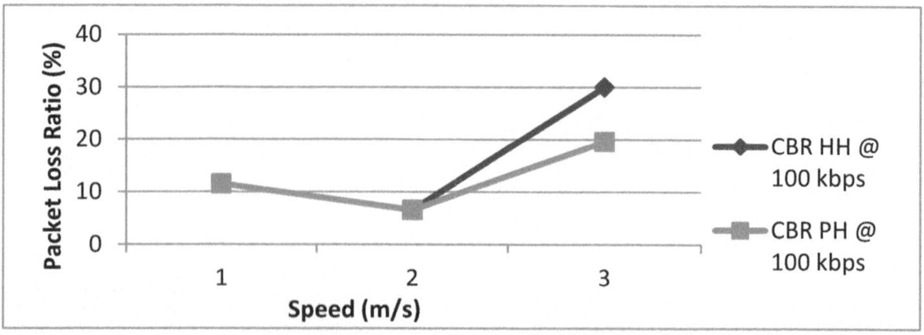

Fig. 16. CBR Packet Loss Ratio at 100 kbps and G.723 codec when CBR and VoIP running on the mobile node in WiMAX to Wi-Fi

respect to Hard Handover. For Hard Handover the Packet Loss ratio increased by 0.0064% from 1 m/s to 3 m/s while for Predictive Handover the increase is by 2.22154%.

5.3 Handover Latency

Figure 8 shows CBR Handover Latency at 100 kbps in Wi-Fi to WiMAX, it is seen that the Handover Latency for Predictive Handover is lower than Hard Handover at all the speeds. For Hard Handover the Handover Latency decreased by 0.39634% from 1 m/s to 3 m/s while for Predictive Handover the increase is by 0.37234%. Figure 11 shows CBR Handover Latency in Wi-Fi to WiMAX, when both CBR and VoIP applications run on the mobile node. Data rate for CBR is 100 kbps and VoIP uses G.723 codec. It is observed that Handover Latency for Predictive Handover is lower than Hard Handover at all the speeds. For Hard Handover the Handover Latency increased by 1.0103% from 1 m/s to 3 m/s while for Predictive Handover the increase is by 0.8199%. Figure 14 shows CBR Handover Latency at 100 kbps in WiMAX to Wi-Fi, it is seen that the Handover Latency for Predictive Handover is lower than Hard Handover at all the speeds. For Hard Handover the Handover Latency decreased by 0.8556% from 1 m/s to 3 m/s while for Predictive Handover the decrease is by 0.06763%. Figure 17 shows CBR Handover Latency in WiMAX to Wi-Fi, when both CBR and VoIP applications run on the mobile node. Data rate for CBR is 100 kbps and VoIP uses G.723 codec. It is observed that Handover Latency for Predictive Handover is lower at speed 1 and 3 m/s but higher at 2 m/s with respect to Hard Handover. For Hard Handover the Handover Latency increased by 0.4852% from 1 m/s to 3 m/s while for Predictive Handover the increase is by 0.6687%.

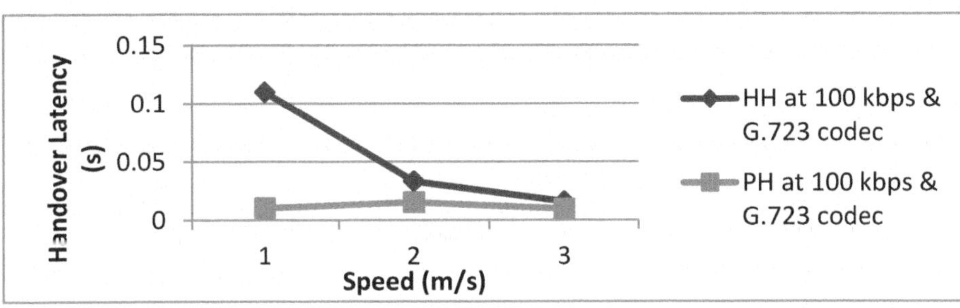

Fig. 17. CBR Handover Latency at 100 kbps and G.723 codec when CBR and VoIP running on the mobile node in WiMAX to Wi-Fi

6 Conclusion and Future Work

In this paper we demonstrated Throughput, Packet Loss Ratio and Handover Latency QoS parameters for Hard Handover and Predictive Handover at different data rates of application in both single CBR application and using both CBR and VoIP application at mobile node, which we tested at different constant speeds (1, 2 and 3) m/s. We analyzed these handovers when the mobile node moves from Wi-Fi to WiMAX and

WiMAX to Wi-Fi. The results show improvement over Hard Handover for all three QoS Parameters. The paper contributes in the improvement of QoS parameters by using Predictive Handover when user is moving from Wi-Fi to WiMAX and vice versa. In future our aim is to enhance the predictive handover algorithm by considering the energy issue as frequent handover between different NICs cause battery discharge. We are also working in the direction of making our algorithm secure.

References

1. Jung, B.: Centralized scheduling mechanism for enhanced end-to-end delay and QoS support in integrated architecture of EPON and WiMAX. J. Light Wave Technol. **28**, 2277–2288 (2010)
2. Islam, M.: Measurement and statistical analysis of QoS parameters for mobile WiMAX network, pp. 818–822 (2008)
3. Abdelkader, S., Salem, N.: QoS metrics modeling and analysis based on dynamic routing. Int. J. Distrib. Parallel Syst. (IJDPS) **3**(2), 43–52 (2012)
4. Hamaydeh, N., Bali, S.: The impact of mobile speed on vertical handover process between Wi-Fi and WiMax networks. In: IEEE International RF and Microwave Conference, pp. 138–143 (2013)
5. Janevski, T., Jakimoski, K.: Mobility sensitive algorithm for vertical handovers from WiMax to WLAN. In: 20th Telecommunications Forum TELFOR (IEEE), pp. 91–94 (2012)
6. Dai, Z., Fracchia, R.: Vertical handover criteria and algorithm in IEEE 802.11 and 802.16 hybrid networks. In: IEEE International conference on Communications, pp. 2480–2484 (2008)
7. Ciccarese, G., Blasi, M.: Vertical handover algorithm for heterogeneous wireless networks. In: INC, IMS and IDC, pp. 1948–1954 (2009)
8. Chen, W., Shu, Y.: Active application oriented vertical handoff in next generation wireless networks. In: IEEE Wireless Communications and Networking Conference, vol. 3, pp. 1383–1388 (2005)
9. Qualnet 6.1 Developer Model Library
10. Kumar, R., Singh, B.: Comparison of vertical handover mechanisms using generic QoS trigger for next generation network. Int. J. Next Gener. Netw. **2**(3), 80–97 (2010)
11. Narwal, B., Mohapatra, A.: Energy efficient vertical handover algorithm for heterogeneous wireless networks. Int. J. Control Theor. Appl. **9**(19), 9221–9225 (2016)

Improving the Performance of Monostatic Pulse RADAR by Changing Waveform Design Using MATLAB

Diksha Prakash[1(✉)] and Shreya Prakash[2]

[1] GD Goenka University, Gurgaon, India
diksha.prakash@gdgu.org
[2] Rutgers University, New Brunswick, New Jersey, USA
shreya.prakash@rutgers.edu

Abstract. This paper describes the designing of a reliable monostatic pulse radar system with improved signal to noise ratio. The waveform transmitted by the radar is varied and the effect of the waveform variation is noted on important radar parameters like peak transmit power and radar range. Also, the validity of the radar range equation for various waveforms has been verified. All the simulations have been done in MATLAB and useful conclusions are drawn about the effect of pulse integration on the reliability of a monostatic pulse radar system and the effect of waveform variation on peak transmit power and radar range.

Keywords: Radar · Waveform · Parameter · Peak power · Range · SNR

1 Introduction

Radar is widely used for military purposes: to locate air, ground and sea targets. It is also applied in the civilian field into applications for aircraft, ships, and roads. Radio Detection (A)nd Ranging (RADAR) [1, 2] is an electromagnetic system for the detection and location of objects. Aircrafts are equipped with radar devices that warn of the presence of other aircrafts or obstacles in or approaching their path. The first commercial device fitted to aircraft was a 1938 Bell Lab unit on a United Air Lines air-craft [3]. It finds its use in the weather prediction and weather analysis, by display-ing weather information and by giving accurate altitude readings. In the modern scenario, the applications of radar are eclectic and diverse [4]. The exhaustive applications include air and terrestrial traffic control, marine radars to locate alien ships and landmarks, radar astronomy, ocean surveillance systems, meteorological precipitation monitoring, altimetry and flight control systems etc. Popularly used, range-controlled radar for public health surveillance [5] helps to create databases and modern computer systems to track and monitor emerging outbreaks of diseases like influenza, HIV, SARS etc. Monostatic radars are also used for early warning of long in-coming threats, migration tracking of birds and insects [6], estimation of vehicle speeds and even for sensing the precipitation and wind speed and direction [7, 8]. Now-a-days, emergency braking systems also employ radar to enhance the safety of the passengers in a vehicle [9]. 'Digital Signal

B. Panda et al. (Eds.): REDSET 2017, CCIS 799, pp. 345–352, 2018.
https://doi.org/10.1007/978-981-10-8527-7_28

Processing' and 'Machine Learning' associated hightech radars are capable of extracting constructive information from very high level noises. Though recently discovered, LADAR [10], which uses pulsed laser light instead of radio-waves, has been used to make high-resolution maps and for controlling the navigation of some autonomous cars [11]. Marine radars are used to prevent collision by keeping a track of the bearing and distance of ships. Vessel traffic service radar systems are used at ports and harbours to monitor and regulate ship movements in busy waters. Radars are also useful in the meteorological departments to monitor precipitation and wind. It is used to make short-term weather forecasts and for watching out for extreme weather. Ground-penetrating radars are used by geologists to map the composition of Earth's crust. Radar guns are used by police forces to monitor vehicle speeds and track human movement. Radars are also used for breathing pattern detection for sleep monitoring [12] and for gesture detection (hand and finger0 for computer interaction [13].

During the operation of radar, a waveform is sent from the transmitter and the nature of the echo signal is analyzed. Radar is primarily constituted of a transmitting antenna, a receiving antenna and an energy detection device. The energy emitted by the radar is in the form of a train of narrow, rectangular shaped pulses (typically) known as 'Radar waveform'. The reflected or echo signal is received by radar antenna, which is then delivered to the receiver. Monostatic radar has the transmitter co-located with the receiver. A pulse is generated by the transmitter which hits the target and an echo is produced. This echo is received by the receiver and is used to analyzed the various parameters of the target object like its shape, size, distance from the radar etc. The range of the target is estimated by measuring the location of echoes in time. The block diagram of a pulse radar system has been shown in Fig. 1.

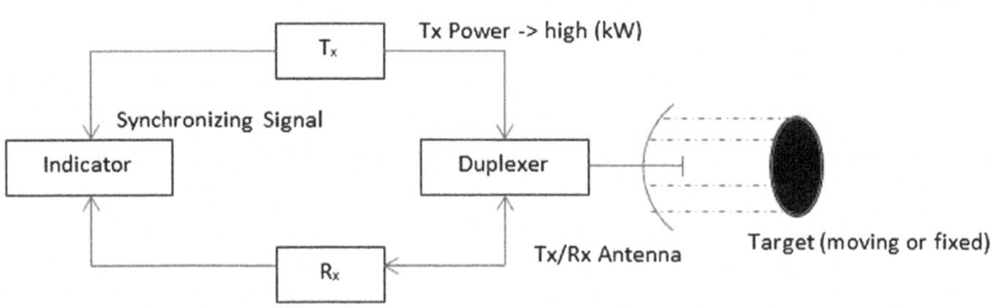

Fig. 1. Block diagram of a pulse RADAR system

Plethora of research work has been done in the field of Radars which are aimed at mitigating the effects of ECM (Electronic Countermeasures) [14–17]. Many of these employ algorithms to clean the acquired data from intentional interference components while others devise detection algorithms to provide the constant false alarm rate property with respect to clutter and thermal noise [18, 19].

Few of the important simulation software that are often employed are Cambridge Pixel, Simtel16, CST Design Studio, FERS and MATLAB. In this paper MATLAB is used to generate important simulation results because of it is very readily available.

2 Methodology

A study of pulse integration method was done and its effect on the signal to noise ratio was analysed to design and develop a more reliable radar system. The analysis of the effect of waveform variation on important radar parameters like peak power and range was performed. The designing of the radar system and the study of the effect of waveform variation was done using the toolbox of MATLAB. The example also assumes a free state environment. To start with, first amongst different types of radars available, particular radar was chosen, in the study undertaken, it was mono-static pulse radar. After that a particular set of parameters is chosen and various values are assigned to them as discussed under (Fig. 2):

```
pd = 0.9; % Probability of detection
pfa  =  1e-6;  %  Probability  of  false  alarm
max_range = 5000; % Maximum unambiguous range
range_res = 50; % Required range resolution
tgt_rcs = 1;        % Required target radar cross section
```

Fig. 2. Design constraints of the pulse radar system

The design goal of this pulse radar system is to detect non-fluctuating targets with at least one square meter radar cross section (RCS) at a distance up to 5000 m from the radar and with a range resolution of 50 m. The desired performance index is decided through 'Probability of Detection (Pd)' of 0.9 and 'Probability of False Alarm (Pfa)' below 1e−6. A noncoherent detection scheme has been adopted as the coherent detection is computationally more expensive as it requires phase information. During the designing of the radar system, three stationary targets are used and hence, Albersheim's equation has been used for computing the SNR in decibels.

After designing the radar, the waveform is defined. Two waveforms are used here for analysis namely, rectangular wave and linear FM wave. The receiver and transmitter characteristics are then defined. Then, two different waveforms are transmitted using the same radar model and the peak power needed in the two cases is calculated. Eventually, the isotropic antenna, the radiator and collector are also defined.

The flowchart of the same has been described below:

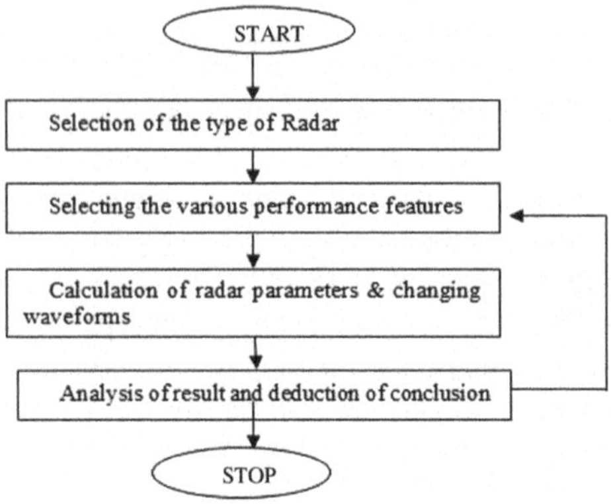

In this paper MATLAB is used to generate important simulation results because of it is very readily available. In order to describe the performance of radar, there are various parameters: Peak Power and Range are some of the important radar parameters. A description of each of these parameters is given.

A. *Peak Power*

Scientifically, peak power is the rate of energy flow every pulse. The maximum power that the waveform provides either in continuous mode (CW) or pulsed mode is known as peak power. It refers to the maximum amplitude of the waveform in the power vs. time graph, as it progresses through the media. In case of a radar, can be calculated using the radar equation. In MATLAB, it is calculated using the keyword 'radareqpow'. The most critical parameter of a transmitter is the peak transmit power. The required peak power is related to many factors including the maximum unambiguous range, the required SNR at the receiver, and the pulse width of the waveform.

B. *Radar Range*

The maximum radar detection range is defined as radar range. The various limiting factors of the radar range include 'Beam path and range', 'Noise', 'Interference', 'clutter' and 'Jamming' [20]. The radar range equation is as under [21]:

$$R_{max} = \sqrt[4]{\frac{P_t G^2 \lambda^2 \sigma}{(4\pi)^3 S_{min}}}$$

Where,

R_{max} is the maximum range of the radar
P_t is the average power of transmitter
G is the gain of transmit/receive antenna
λ is the wavelength of operating frequency
σ is the radar cross-section of the target
S_{min} is the minimum detectable signal power

3 Result

The waveforms of the radar are varied and the effect of this variation is analyzed on radar parameters like Peak Power and Radar Range. These results are obtained using the Toolbox of MATLAB. The results so obtained for two different waveforms have been described.

During the designing of transmitter, ROC (Receiver Operating Characteristics) curve can be plotted to understand the relationship between Pd (Probability of detection), Pfa (Probability of false alarm) and SNR (Signal to Noise Ratio).

Figure 3(L) shows the need for 'pulse integration technique' in the designing of a monostatic radar. According to the generated ROC, to fulfil the design goals of Pfa = 1e −6 and Pd = 0.9, the received signal's SNR must exceed 13 dB. This is quite high and impractical requirement. Thus to make the radar system more feasible, we use a 'pulse integration technique' to reduce the required SNR. If we choose to integrate 10 pulses, the ROC curve can be generated as Fig. 3(R). The curve shows a drop in the required power to about 5 dB. However integration of pulses has a limitation due to the constraints like the motion of target and heterogeneity of environment.

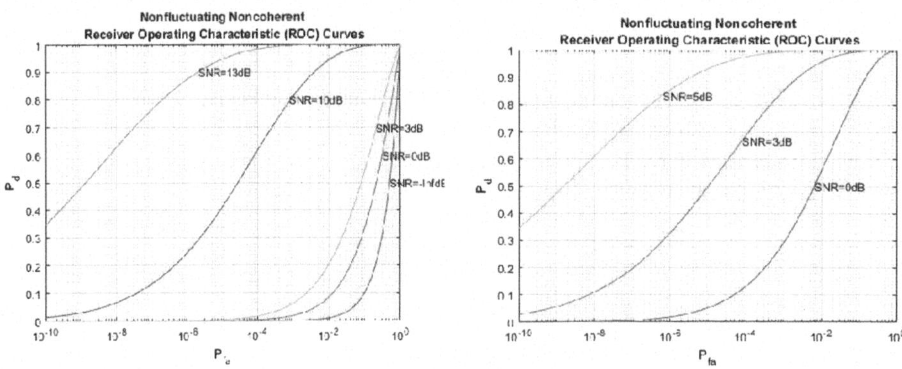

Fig. 3. (L) ROC curve with the minimum signal's SNR = 13 dB (R) ROC curve (post pulse integration technique) with minimum signal's SNR = 5 dB

Now, the previously designed radar is exposed to a new environment having maximum unambiguous range extended up to 8 km and the ability to detect two stationary and one swerling target (initially, all the targets were assumed to be stationary). Due to this new environment, the first affected parameter is the pulse repetition frequency (prf).The targets assumed in this case are not only stationary but also swerling. Thus there is a need to use Shindman's equation, instead of Albersheim's equation. Also, the number of pulse integrations used is 10.

The SNR minimum for the same was obtained to be '6.1583' and was calculated using (Fig. 4):

```
  num_pulse_int    =
10; pfa = 1e-6;
  snr_min = shindman(0.9,pfa,num_pulse_int,2)
```

Fig. 4. Recalculation of SNR minimum for the new environment

Now, a rectangular waveform is used in the existing design and the required peak transmit power is recalculated as under (Fig. 5):

```
fc  =  radiator.OperatingFrequency  ;
lambda = prop_speed/fc;
   peak_power = radareqpow(lambda,max_range,snr_min, ...
 waveform.PulseWidth'RCS',1,'Gain',transmitter.Gain)

   OUTPUT:
   peak_power = 4.4821e+04
```

Fig. 5. Recalculation of peak transmit power for rectangular wave

Now, a linear FM wave is used in the existing design and the required peak transmit power is recalculated to obtain (Fig. 6):

```
peak_power  =  radareqpow(lambda,
max_range,snr_min,pulse_width,...
'RCS,1,'Gain',transmitter.Gain)

   OUTPUT:
   peak_power = 2.2411e+03
```

Fig. 6. Recalculation of peak transmit power for linear FM wave

Thus, the same can be tabulated as under (Table 1):

Table 1. The peak transmit power variation for two different waveforms

Wave	Peak power
Rectangular	4.4821e+04
Linear FM wave	2.2411e+03

The peak transmit power required for a rectangular wave is approximately double to that of Linear FM wave. The probable reason for the same can be that linear FM wave uses longer pulses than the rectangular waveform and hence is capable of travelling longer distance in the same time frame.

Also, the variation in peak power as a result of variation in range can be tabulated as under (Table 2):

Table 2. The peak transmit power variation with variation in range for two different waveforms

Waveform	For range = 8000	For range = 16000
Linear FM wave	2.2411e+03	3.5857e+04
Rectangular wave	4.4821e+04	7.1714e+05

For a range of 16000 m, the peak transmit power required by Linear FM wave is about 16 times as that required for a range of 8000 m. Also, for the Rectangular wave, for a range of 16000 m, the peak power has to be increased by a factor of 16 as compared to that for a range of 8000 m. Thus, for both the Linear FM wave and the Rectangular wave, the peak power has to become 16 times of its initial value in order to increase the range by a factor of 2. This is also in line with the radar range equation which says that in order to increase the range by a factor of two, the peak power has to increase sixteen times [22]. It can be inferred from the table that irrespective of waveform variation, the peak transmit power has to be increased by a factor of 16 to double the range.

4 Conclusion

Radars have a lot of applications from airborne navigation to detection of the pattern of infectious diseases. It is the need of modern communication services which requires more security and high speed. In the study conducted, it can be concluded that the presence of longer pulses reduces the peak transmit power requirement. Thus, it was seen that a Linear FM wave required lesser peak transmit power. Furthermore, the 'Pulse Integration Technique' leads to a significant reduction in the minimum SNR requirement, making the design more feasible. Also, the radar range equation stays valid for different kinds of waveforms.

References

1. Translation Bureau: Radar definition. Public Works and Government Services Canada (2013). Accessed 8 November 2013
2. Lapedes, D.N.: McGraw-Hill Dictionary of Scientific and Technical Terms, A26 p. McGraw-Hill, New York, Montreal (1976). [xv], 1634
3. Hearst Magazines: Popular Mechanics. Hearst Magazines, p. 26, September 1941
4. Levanon, N., Mozeson, E.: Radar Signals. Wiley.com (2004)
5. Liu, L., Popescu, M., Skubic, M., Rantz, M., Yardibi, T., Cuddihy, P.: Automatic fall detection based on Doppler radar motion signature. In: IEEE Pervasive Health (2011)
6. Reynolds, D.R., Smith, A.D., Chapman, J.W.: A radar study of emigatory flight and layer formation by insects at dawn over Southern Britain. Bull. Entomol. Res. **98**, 35–52 (2008). AN02898

7. Zavorotny, V.U., Voronovich, A.G.: Scattering of GPS signals from the ocean with wind remote sensing application. IEEE Trans. Geosci. Remote Sens. **38**, 951–964 (2000)
8. Gleason, S.: Remote sensing of ocean, ice and land surfaces using bistatically scattered GNSS signals from low earth orbit. Doctorate Dissertation, Stanford University (2000)
9. Wu, T.: Pedestrian and vehicle recognition based on radar for autonomous emergency braking. SAE Technical Paper 2017-01-1405 (2017)
10. LIDAR—Light Detection and Ranging—is a remote sensing method used to examine the surface of the Earth. NOAA. Archived from the original on 4 June 2013. Accessed 4 June 2013
11. Cracknell, A.P., Hayes, L.: Introduction to Remote Sensing, 2nd edn. Taylor and Francis, London (2007). ISBN 0-8493-9255-1. OCLC 70765252 (1991)
12. Myplus Homepage. https://sleep.mysplus.com/technology.html
13. Atap Homepage. https://atap.google.com/soli/
14. Wang, Y., Bao, Q., Chen, Z.: Robust mainlobe interference suppression for coherent interference environment. EURASIP J. Adv. Signal Process. **2016**, 135 (2016). Special Issue on Advanced Techniques for Radar Signal Processing
15. Qian, J., He, Z., Xie, J., Zhang, Y.: Null broadening adaptive beamforming based on covariance matrix reconstruction and similarity constraint. EURASIP J. Adv. Signal Process. **2017**, 1 (2017). Special Issue on Advanced Techniques for Radar Signal Processing
16. Wang, Z., Wang, W., Shao, H.: Range-azimuth decouple beamforming for frequency diverse array with Costas-sequence modulated frequency offsets. EURASIP J. Adv. Signal Process. **2016**, 124 (2016). Special Issue on Advanced Techniques for Radar Signal Processing
17. Xiong, W., Zhang, G., Liu, W.: Efficient filter design against interrupted sampling repeater jamming for wideband radar. EURASIP J. Adv. Signal Process. **2017**, 9 (2017). Special Issue on Advanced Techniques for Radar Signal Processing
18. Fortunati, S., Gini, F., Greco, M.S.: Matched, mismatched and robust scatter matrix estimation and hypothesis testing in complex t-distributed data. EURASIP J. Adv. Signal Process. **2016**, 123 (2016). Special Issue on Advanced Techniques for Radar Signal Processing
19. Palamà, R., Greco, M., Gini, F.: Multistatic adaptive CFAR detection in non-Gaussian clutter. EURASIP J. Adv. Signal Process. **2016**, 107 (2016). Special Issue on Advanced Techniques for Radar Signal Processing
20. Stimson, G.: Introduction to Airborne Radar, p. 98. SciTech Publishing Inc. (1998). ISBN 1-891121-01-4
21. Ranney, K.I., Doerry, A.: Radar sensor technology XX. In: Proceedings of SPIE, vol. 9829 (2016). 98290P © 2016 SPIE CCC code: 0277-786X/16/$18. https://doi.org/10.1117/12.2224478
22. Skolnik, M.I. (ed.): Radar Handbook, 2nd edn. McGraw-Hill, New York (1990). ISBN 0-07-057913-X

Analysis and Detection of Ransomware Through Its Delivery Methods

Keertika Gangwar[1(✉)], Subhranshu Mohanty[2], and A. K. Mohapatra[1]

[1] Indira Gandhi Delhi Technical University for Women, Delhi, India
gangwarkeertika@gmail.com, mohapatra.amar@gmail.com
[2] Army Institute of Management and Technology, Greater Noida, India
mohanty77@rediffmail.com

Abstract. Cyber criminals are utilizing diverse approaches to draw money from internet users and organizations. Recently, a malware called ransomware has become effectively accessible for this job due to its ease of availability and distribution methods. Security experts are working to counter ransomware attacks by fixing the vulnerabilities of operating system. In this research work, we have proposed a method to prevent the ransomware attack at its early stages through its delivery channels like Exploit Kits. We have analyzed the crawling patterns (listing of file path, dropped file, network activity, ransom note etc.) of victim's computer. These patterns have been used to extract the features for classification of malicious samples. We have used supervised machine learning algorithms for classification of malwares. Experimental results shows that accuracy of 94% is achieved in tightly bound mode by using random forest algorithm. While, accuracy of 91% is achieved in moderate bound mode by using random forest classification algorithm.

Keywords: Cybercrime · Exploit kit · Malware · Ransomware · Security Vulnerability

1 Introduction

Use of mobile commerce for business transactions is increasing rapidly [1]. When the number of users increases the security becomes a measure concern [2]. Many malicious programs like adware, spyware, banking trojans etc. exist to steal information. Most of the malicious programs exploit existing vulnerabilities present in the operating system, browsers and various programming languages. Ransomware is a type of malware that encrypts victim's computer and demands ransom for release of cryptographic key required for decryption [18]. The conventional malwares extracts user credentials in stealth mode by using social engineering practices while in contrast, ransomware exploit the system's vulnerability to compromise the computer system. Investigation of ransomware attack is difficult due to lack of effective forensic processes and specialized tools [3].

Ransomware comes in various varieties, like locking ransomware which locks desktop and blocks access to the desktop or mobile phones e.g. small, fusob, svpeng [6] etc. This

B. Panda et al. (Eds.): REDSET 2017, CCIS 799, pp. 353–362, 2018.
https://doi.org/10.1007/978-981-10-8527-7_29

type of ransomware mostly targets mobile phones. The other category of ransomware uses cryptographic techniques to perform encryption on user files and resources. This type of ransomware is known as encrypting ransomware, for example, wannacry, teslacrypt, petya, cryptowall etc. Encrypting ransomware is frequently seen, due to its easy modus operandi. According to IBM-X-force [5] report around 4000 attacks per week were measured in the year 2016 and on the top of that most of the legal advisors advised people to just pay the ransom because it is hard to break the ransomware when it is using strong cryptographic algorithm like AES 256 for data encryption and RSA 2048 for key encryption. Phishing, exploit kits, and botnets are most popular methods used by cybercriminals. A survey of 255 organizations in United States, conducted by Information Security Media Group (Trend Micro) [15], found that around sixty five percent of ransomware attacks are caused due to compromised websites, while forty four percent ransomwares are delivered through malvertisments. Malvertisments are malicious advertisements injected in legitimate webpages to lure users. Twenty six percent of ransomware are delivered through spam mail attachments, whereas twenty five percent ransomwares delivered through bots and other malicious derivers as summarized in Fig. 1.

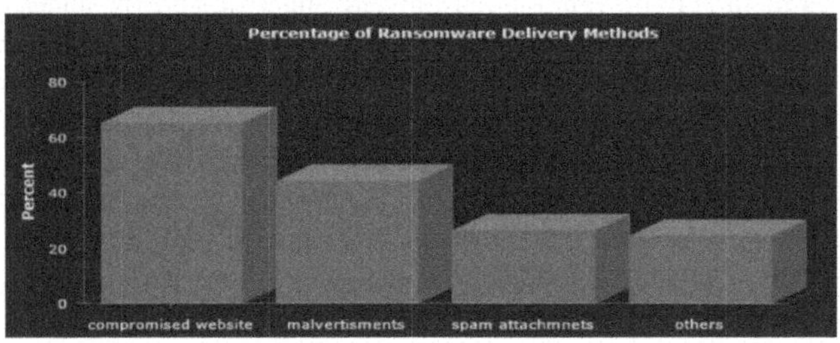

Fig. 1. Percentage of ransomware delivery methods [15]

In this paper we have taken exploit kits as our delivery method to devise an early ransomware detection method. Exploit kits come under category of drive-by-download methods for exploitation which is first discussed by Cova et al. [18]. Recently the latest ransomware "wannacry" attack launched on 20 million companies around the world. It is observed that the above attack was caused due to the vulnerabilities of windows XP systems. The efficient cryptanalysis technique can provide a solution for countering various security issues caused by ransomware [14]. In this research, the simulation has been done by a collection of 1000 malicious samples. The results shows that the accuracy of proposed approach is more than 90%.

The rest of the paper is organized as follows. In Sect. 2 we present related work done by other researchers. Section 3 explains proposed methodology and workflow. Section 4 presents the design and implementation details with results. Finally we present the conclusions and future work in Sect. 5.

2 Related Work

There exist many ways through which cybercriminals can rent a service to perform a successful attack, Grier et al. [16] has analyzed exploit kit as a service through which cyber criminals perform a successful attack. Exploits kits are automated toolkits designed for scanning victim's device. In this type of attack cybercriminals uses browsers vulnerability to perform the attack. After successful exploit, a malicious payload (ransomware in our case) is injected to victim's device, the payload executes and encrypt user's electronic documents.

2.1 Ransomware Prevention Schemes

In 1996 Young and Yung [9] presented a virus that uses methods of cryptography to spread encryption as infection. This crypto virus was build using functionality of existing malware like Trojan horse, and virus with extra feature of malicious cryptography. In 2004 Young et al. [10, 11] came with an idea and implementation of crypto virus using the Microsoft Cryptographic API. This crypto virus was created using public key cryptography as proof of malevolent usage of cryptographic techniques. In year 2015 an extended study of ~1400 samples of ransomware is performed by Kharaz et al. [12] which provided insights of several attack vectors of ransomware families and their variants. In 2016 Kharazz et al. [8] implemented a model called Unveil as an extension of their previous work. Unveil claimed to have detection rates of 96.3%. by setting up a sandboxed environment for testing, a clean image of system is compared with the infected image of system they have used various parameters like entropy, to detect change in current and previous image of system, pollution ratio to find status of ransomware sample, whether it is detected by existing antiviruses or not. Sgandurra et al. [7] build a framework called EldRan using machine learning algorithms. They have analyzed dynamic behavior of ransomware using heuristic analysis in sandboxed environment. In 2016 Scafie et al. [4] implemented a framework for early detection of ransomware in which they have tested their system with 14 families of ransomware and claimed 100% detection rate. In 2016 Netherlands police initiated "NoMoreRansom"[1] campaign which now supported by various AV vendors like Kaspersky, Intel security, AVG etc. is a great initiative to fight against this threat they provide decryption keys for numerus ransomwares.

In the proposed work we have focused on identification of ransomware by analyzing payload of exploit kit at application layer. We have used data in mixed form that include malicious samples as well as legitimate samples. The url is input to the proposed system which goes through a processing step and separates malicious and legitimate samples. We are identifying malicious samples in initial stage to reduce workload at payload discovery stage.

[1] https://www.nomoreransom.org/.

The notations are defined as follows:

U = U is set of URLs
F = Classifier used for classification of URLs
$U_{malicious}$ = URL belongs to malicious sample
IOC = Indicator of Compromise
U_{IOC} = IOC obtained from URL U_i
R = Detected Sample as Ransomware

Mathematically, detection and payload discovery step is represented in Eqs. 1, 2 and 3. In first equation U is an URL sample. The fields of URL are domain name, referrer, user agent, and status code, content type acts as identification vectors or features at step 1.

$$F_{(features)}(U) \rightarrow U_{(malicious)} \tag{1}$$

$$F_{(malicious)}(U) \rightarrow U_{(IOC)} \tag{2}$$

$$F\,(IOC) \rightarrow R \tag{3}$$

3 Proposed Approach

In this section we discuss our proposed methodology, initially the assessment is done by considering the features of payload of an exploit kit. The experimentation has been done using cuckoo sandbox[2] with windows 7 virtual machine for malware analysis. Initially some major features and indicators of compromise are generated through manual selection and analysis. We have integrated tracewrangle[3] and Wireshark (see footnote 3) to find indicator of compromise in a pcap file. Pcap files are generated through well-known network sniffer Wireshark, honeypots.

3.1 Feature Selection

The main aim of this section is to collect all possible information about the malicious samples the features shown in Table 1 are major features which are further divided into sub features called indicators of compromise. We have also considered features mentioned by Frenz and Diaz [13] in anti-ransomware guide of OWASP [13] web security. The high-level view of our proposed methodology is represented in Fig. 2. The network traffic is captured of each URL and samples are tested in virtual machine. Output packet is submitted to virus total for further testing and verification.

---

[2] https://cuckoosandbox.org.
[3] https://www.wireshark.org.

Table 1. Major features

Feature	Description
URL	Analyzing url parameters to find patterns for identification
File type	Type of files transferred over network gives information about the exploit used by exploit kits
IP address	IP address is major feature for detection of source ip address and further redirected ip addresses are stored in data base for static analysis
Web page	Static analysis of compromised web page gives details about redirections, clickjacking, and web application vulnerabilities

Fig. 2. High-level view of proposed work

4 Implementation and Observation

All the implementation of proposed work is done in Linux environment. Python language is used to write scripts. The following steps are used for assessment and experimental setup. Step 1 deals with data collection, data cleaning, step 2 deals with feature extraction while in Step 3 various tools and supervised classification algorithms are deployed which helped in automation and training of proposed model.

Step 1: Data Cleaning

We have deployed Dionaea Honeypot[4] for collection of new samples. The setup is run on the basis of 24 × 7 with automated collection and data pushing to central FRED server[5]. Collected data is fed to a central database on FRED server for the purpose of persistent storage. After that data is sent for processing. Where we have extracted many features from network data. Then we have used Naïve Bayes technique to extract the helpful data. We have used 4 major features that are listed in Table 1, we have also maintained sub features database which falls under category of major features.

Step 2. Extraction of IOCs

In this step, confirmed malicious samples are tested in experimental setup for further analysis and feature extraction. At this stage features like change in file extensions, privilege escalation, open ports, http connections, cpu utilization, process id and services are observed. Payload identification is major task of this step. Identification of payload containing ransomware is the objective of this step. URL, Filetype, Ipaddress have been used as major features to draw IOCs. In major feature URL we have found Http interactions, redirection count, domain names, url parameters and email ids are collected as sub features of URL. These behaviors are tracked and logged in a database through interactive API of Wireshark. Figure 3 shows number of redirections for exploit kit (URL) samples. Redirections in a website can be introduced to a webpage using iframe vulnerability present in JavaScript. We have observed that redirection count plays important role in separating malicious and legitimate sample. It is also observed that redirection counts are varied in rerun of our program in intervals of a week as shown in Fig. 3.

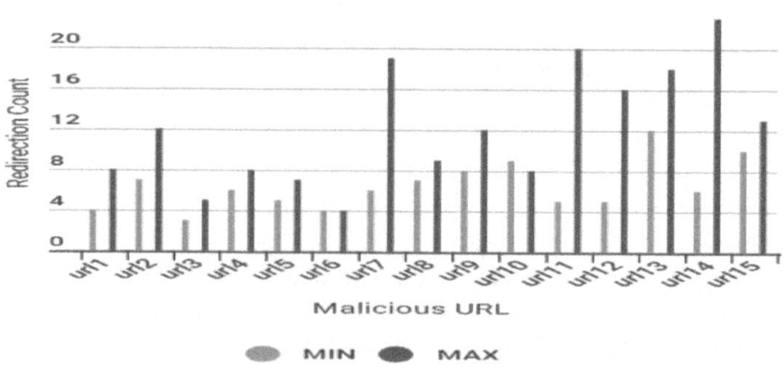

Fig. 3. Redirection counts observed in rerun of samples in a week

4 https://github.com/DinoTools/dionaea.

5 https://www.digitalintelligence.com/products/fred.

By tracking files transferred in network activity mime types are observed. With the help of mime type we can discover type of exploit an exploit kit is carrying, in our methodology file extensions are checked very carefully to detect the compromise of the system. Ransomware attack mostly tracked by the encrypted file extensions. In our case we have found 600 samples of various ransomwares, out of six hundred samples, two hundred and eighty samples were distinct. Figure 4 shows word cloud of ransomware samples found in our data set.

Fig. 4. Word cloud of extensions dropped by ransomware

Hacker's use Domain Generation Algorithms through which domain name keeps on changing and it becomes difficult to detect just on the basis of domain. But ip address remains same for some time, though ip spoofing is not a big deal for cyber criminals but still by maintaining extensive list of ip addresses it can help in blocking these threats. Using list of ipaddresses obtained in each run of a sample we have discovered ipaddresses belonging to hacker server or command and control server. These malicious ipaddresses are used as major features in prevention of ransomwares in this work. Experimental setup of results i.e. discovery of payload is shown in Fig. 5 it is observed that most of payloads dropped by exploit kits are ransomware the data is collected from September 2016–January 2017. URLs from various sources like www.malware-traffic-analysis.net, virus total[6], twitter[7] and dontneedcoffee[8]. We have tested all the samples in cuckoo sandbox. Out of these 1000 samples, 600 samples dropped ransomware, 180 samples turned out to drop Trojan. While 110 payloads belonged to bots, 20 samples dropped spyware while remaining 90 belonged to other malwares. We have extracted sub features which are discovered under major features as given in Table 1. These sub features actually called as indicators of compromise.

[6] https://www.virustotal.com.

[7] https://www.twitter.com/.

[8] http://malware.dontneedcoffee.com/.

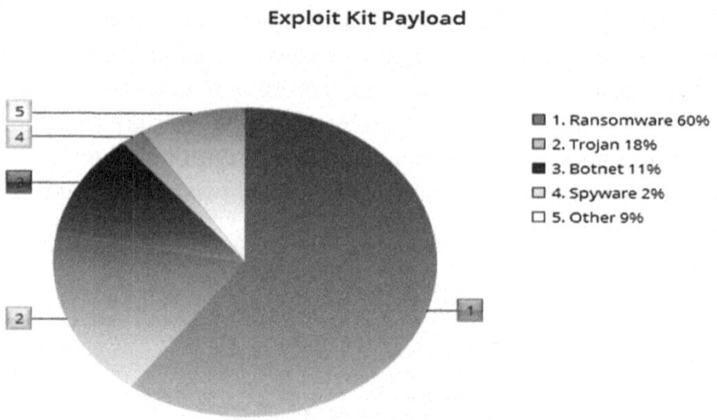

Fig. 5. Payload discovery

Step 3. Classification Results

In this step, we have performed classification on the combined dataset containing training set of 50 normal and 50 malicious URL samples. We have used J48 Decision Tree, Random Forest, and Naive Bayes as the classification algorithm on the combined dataset with indicators of compromise as feature vectors found in step 2 as described in the earlier section. The results are summarized in Tables 2 and 3, we found that random forest classifier works best with features selected and collected in this paper. The summarized results are shown in the Tables 2 and 3 which is given below:

Table 2. Performance in tightly bound mode

Classifier	True positive	False positive	Accuracy
J48 decision tree	94%	0.1%	92%
Random forest	98%	0.1%	94%
Naïve Bayes	96%	0.02%	97%

Table 3. Performance in moderate bound mode

Classifier	True positive	False positive	Accuracy
J48 decision tree	70%	0.00%	85%
Random forest	84%	0.02%	91%
Naïve Bayes	82%	0.00%	91%

5 Conclusion and Future Work

In this paper, the ransomware have been identified by using behavior patterns and features of exploit kits. The features like redirection count, ipaddresses and file type have been used as the major features for classification of malicious samples. Experimental results yields that the proposed approach classified the ransomwares with maximum accuracy of 97% having 0.02% false positives while minimum accuracy attained 92% having 0.01% false positives. The testing was done in very limited amount of resources therefore the result may vary for large dataset. Ransomware is now targeting Internet of Things, therefore, wireless networks are needed to be protected from this threat. Its consequences can be drastic if in future it starts spreading its infection in wearable gadgets. Our proposed work can be extended to IOT's but it will require light wt. processing methods.

References

1. Khandelwal, A., Mohapatra, A.K.: An insight into the security issues and their solutions for android phones. In: 2015 2nd International Conference on Computing for Sustainable Global Development (INDIACom), pp. 106–109. IEEE, March 2015
2. Usmani, K., Mohapatra, A.K., Prakash, N.: An improved framework for incident handling. Inf. Secur. J.: Glob. Perspect. **22**(1), 1–9 (2013)
3. Kumari, N., Mohapatra, A.K.: An insight into digital forensics branches and tools. In: 2016 International Conference on Computational Techniques in Information and Communication Technologies (ICCTICT), pp. 243–250. IEEE, March 2016
4. Scaife, N., Carter, H., Traynor, P., Butler, K.R.B.: Cryptolock (and drop it): stopping ransomware attacks on user data. In: 2016 IEEE 36th International Conference on Distributed Computing Systems (ICDCS), pp. 303–312. IEEE (2016)
5. Ransomware: How consumers and businesses value their data. IBM X-Force® Research, IBM Security. Accessed 15 Jan 2017
6. Kaspersky Lab: KSN Report: Mobile Ransomware in 2014–2016. https://securelist.com/analysis/publications/75183/ksn-report-mobile-ransomware-in-2014-2016/. Accessed 29 June
7. Sgandurra, D., Muñoz-González, L., Mohsen, R., Lupu, E.C.: Automated dynamic analysis of ransomware: benefits, limitations and use for detection. arXiv preprint arXiv:1609.03020 (2016)
8. Kharraz, A., Arshad, S., Mulliner, C., Robertson, W., Kirda, E.: UNVEIL: a large-scale, automated approach to detecting ransomware. In: 25th USENIX Security Symposium (USENIX Security 2016), pp. 757–772. USENIX Association (2016)
9. Young, A., Yung, M.: Cryptovirology: extortion-based security threats and countermeasures. In: Proceedings of the 1996 IEEE Symposium on Security and Privacy. IEEE (1996)
10. Young, A., Yung, M.: Malicious Cryptography: Exposing Cryptovirology. Wiley, Hoboken (2004)
11. Young, A.L.: Cryptoviral extortion using Microsoft's Crypto API. Int. J. Inf. Secur. **5**(2), 67–76 (2006)
12. Kharraz, A., Robertson, W., Balzarotti, D., Bilge, L., Kirda, E.: Cutting the gordian knot: a look under the hood of ransomware attacks. In: Almgren, M., Gulisano, V., Maggi, F. (eds.) DIMVA 2015. LNCS, vol. 9148, pp. 3–24. Springer, Cham (2015). https://doi.org/10.1007/978-3-319-20550-2_1

13. Anti-Ransomware Guide. https://www.owasp.org/images/a/a8/Anti-RansomwareGuide.pdf. Accessed 12 Oct 2016
14. Mohapatra, A.K., Prakash, N.: Wired equivalent privacy reinvestigated. J. Discrete Math. Sci. Crypt. **13**(2), 141–151 (2010)
15. Gilbert Sison (2017). http://blog.trendmicro.com/trendlabs-security-intelligence/cerber-starts-evading-machine-learning/
16. Grier, C., et al.: Manufacturing compromise: the emergence of exploit-as-a-service. In: Proceedings of the 2012 ACM Conference on Computer and Communications Security. ACM (2012)
17. Cova, M., Kruegel, C., Vigna, G.: Detection and analysis of drive-by-download attacks and malicious JavaScript code. In: Proceedings of the 19th International Conference on World Wide Web. ACM (2010)
18. Gazet, A.: Comparative analysis of various ransomware virii. J. Comput. Virol. **6**(1), 77–90 (2010)

A Comparative Analysis of Various Regularization Techniques to Solve Overfitting Problem in Artificial Neural Network

Shrikant Gupta[1(✉)], Rajat Gupta[1], Muneendra Ojha[1], and K. P. Singh[2]

[1] Dr. SPM International Institute of Information Technology Naya Raipur, Naya Raipur, India
{shrikant15101,rajat15101,muneendra}@iiitnr.edu.in
[2] Indian Institute of Information Technology Allahabad, Allahabad, India
kpsingh@iiita.ac.in

Abstract. Neural networks having a large number of parameters are considered as very effective machine learning tool. But as the number of parameters becomes large, the network becomes slow to use and the problem of overfitting arises. Various ways to prevent overfitting of model are further discussed here and a comparative study has been done for the same. The effects of various regularization methods on the performance of neural net models are observed.

Keywords: Dropout · L1 regularization · L2 regularization · Neural network Overfitting

1 Introduction

Artificial neural network contains multiple non-linear hidden layers which makes it possible for them to learn very complicated relationships between inputs and outputs. One of the problems that occur during neural network training is overfitting which causes them to perform very poorly. In case of overfitting it is observed that the error at the time of training the datasets reaches to a very insignificant value, but when new data is presented to the network the error produced is large. This is so because the network has learned the training examples, but it has not learned to generalize to new situations. Regularization is a way to reduce the problem of overfitting. A similar work is also done previously with respect to dropout by Srivastava et al. [1]. They have improvement in performance of models using dropout and obtained state-of-the-art results on many supervised learning tasks.

Performance of different regularization techniques on ImageNet is compared by Evgeny A. Smirnov et al. in the paper [2]. They have shown empirically that performance of Dropout on ImageNet Dataset is better than DropConnect. Implementation of neural network on Airfoil Noise is also shown by Lau et al. in his paper [3]. DropConnect is introduced in paper [4] which is a generalization of Dropout. It is used for large fully-connected hidden layers of the neural network. DropConnect is evaluated in the paper [4] on a range of datasets and it is observed that for some datasets DropConnect outperforms Dropout.

B. Panda et al. (Eds.): REDSET 2017, CCIS 799, pp. 363–371, 2018.
https://doi.org/10.1007/978-981-10-8527-7_30

A brief introduction to various regularization techniques is deliberated in Sect. 2 of this paper. Section 3 contains the features of the overall model that is used here to train the datasets. Section 4 of this paper contains the observations and results after training the datasets using the discussed model. A final conclusion based on observed results has been drawn in Sect. 5 of this paper.

Artificial Neural Network (ANN) is an inspiration from biological neural networks of the human brain. ANN can be applied to wide range of field such as pattern recognition, image processing, financial data, medicine etc. As brain neurons are connected through synapses similarly nodes in neural network model are connected to each other. The ANN model contains several layers both hidden and visible. ANN models can generate a nonlinear function with the help of activation functions. There are different kinds of neural network based on network topologies and the one used here is the feed-forward neural network. The other types include Recurrent Neural Network, Convolutional neural network etc. Hypothesis in a neural network model having weight w, input x and bias b can be defined as Eq. 1.

$$h_\theta(x) = \sum_i w_i x_i + b \tag{1}$$

2 Regularization Techniques

There are several ways of controlling the problem of overfitting in a neural network. Some of them are discussed here.

2.1 L2 Regularization

L2 Regularization is one of the most general forms of regularization. It can be implemented by adding the squared magnitude of all the parameters i.e. weights and biases in the cost/loss function. This total cost function is further minimized using optimizer. That is for every weight *w* we add a term ½ λw^2 where λ is the regularization parameter. A factor of ½ is multiplied to simplify the gradient term. Using the L2 regularization ultimately means that every weight is decayed linearly towards zero.

$$L2{:}\ \frac{\lambda}{2}\sum_{i=1}^{m} w_i^2 \tag{2}$$

2.2 L1 Regularization

L1 is another common form of regularization, where instead of adding the square of the weights we just add the absolute value of the weights to the cost function.

$$L1: \lambda \sum_{i=1}^{m} |w_i| \tag{3}$$

Sometimes both L1 regularization and L2 regularization are applied together (it is called Elastic-net regularization). L2 regularization generally gives better performance than L1 regularization. Comparison between L1 regularization and L2 regularization is done by Ng [5]. In his paper, he compared L1 and L2 regularization and showed how L1 regularization of parameters grows logarithmically while L2 regularization with Neural Networks and SVM worst case sample grows linearly in a number of irrelevant features.

2.3 Dropout

Dropout is a recently introduced regularization technique by Srivastava et al. [1]. Dropout is a simple but extremely effective regularization technique. It prevents complex co-adaptations on training data in a neural net. The term "dropout" refers to dropping out hidden units and visible units in a model i.e. both hidden layer and input layer. The idea behind dropout neural network can be understood by Fig. 1.

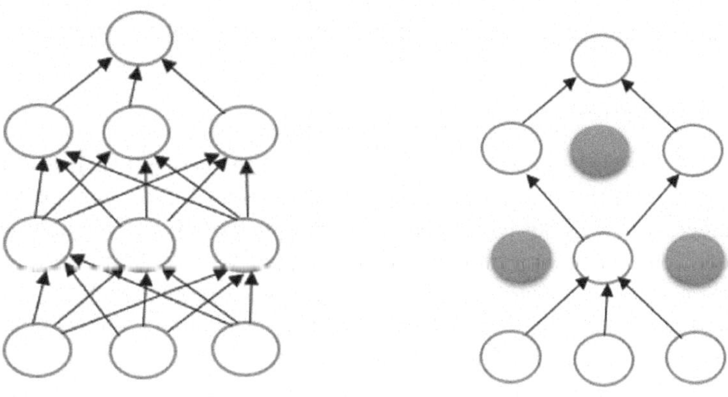

Fig. 1. Dropout neural net model (the black circle represents dropped units)

Dropping a unit means temporarily removing the unit along with all its connections from the network, as shown in Fig. 1. The decision on which unit to drop or remove is totally random. Generally, each unit in the model is kept with a probability p which is fixed and independent of other units in the model. The value of p can simply be set to 0.5 while for input units it is usually kept closer to 1 than to 0.5 (nearly 0.8).

At training time, the unit is present with probability p and is connected with weight w to the units in the next layer while at test time, the units are always present but the weights are multiplied with probability p. Therefore, the output at test time is same as expected output at the time of training.

3 Setting Up of Overall Model

Before running the model on dataset, the model and data needs to be properly processed to yield best result. In this section, we have discussed about the overall model after applying regularization. Following subheading gives a brief info about the additional design choices regarding data preprocessing, weight initialization, and loss functions.

3.1 Data Preprocessing

The two-common techniques of data preprocessing used here are Mean subtraction and Normalization. Preprocessing.scale() function of TensorFlow library does both mean subtraction and normalization.

Mean Subtraction. Mean Subtraction involves subtracting the mean (μ) across every individual feature i.e. replacing x_i with $x_i - \mu_i$. This in turn centralizes the data around origin and makes the features have approximately zero mean.

$$x_i \rightarrow x_i - \mu_i \tag{4}$$

Normalization. Normalization refers to normalizing the data dimensions to bring the data on the same scale. One way to achieve normalization is by dividing each dimension by its standard deviation. The scaled data will have zero mean and unit variance.

3.2 Weight Initialization

Before training the model initialization of the parameters is required. It is important to select appropriate initial values for the weights and biases. A good guess is to initialize all the parameters to zero but there will be no asymmetry between the neurons as they will compute same output and same gradient during backpropagation. As a result, they will go same parameter update and all the neurons will become identical. Therefore, a good solution is to initialize the parameters with small random numbers close to zero. This will make all the neurons random and unique.

3.3 Activation Function

Activation function defines the output of a node when an input or set of input is given to that node. They provide a different type of nonlinearities in the model. There are many known activation functions like linear, tanh, softmax, sigmoid, relu etc. but the activation function used in Sect. 3 for observations are relu and softmax.

Relu stands for Rectified Linear Unit. It returns the maximum of input and zero i.e. if the input of a unit is negative it will output zero else it will pass the input. Relu is used here in the regression problem (Airfoil dataset) and in the hidden layers of the model built for MNIST dataset.

$$Relu(x) = \begin{cases} 0, \; x < 0 \\ x, \; x \geq 0 \end{cases} \tag{5}$$

Softmax activation function is used in the output layer of MNIST dataset. It is used to assign probabilities to the units of output layer in classification problem as they give us a list of values that are between 0 and 1 and sum up to 1. Softmax is the final layer in our model for MNIST dataset.

$$softmax(x)_i = \frac{e^{(x_i)}}{\sum_j e^{(x_j)}} \tag{6}$$

3.4 Regularization

In Sect. 2 various regularization techniques have been discussed. Here we have used regularization functions present in Tensorflow library for implementing regularization. Regularization is applied to the loss/cost function to reduce overfitting.

3.5 Loss Functions

Mean Squared Error (MSE). To calculate loss, the sum of squares of the difference between predicted value and the actual value is taken for all the training example and it is further reduced by taking mean. Squaring the difference makes the error positive as we do not want to add negative error in our cost function. Another benefit is that it results in a function which has a single local minimum i.e. its global minima is same has local minima.

$$J(\theta) = \frac{1}{m} \sum_{i=1}^{m} \left(h_\theta\left(x^{(i)}\right) - y^{(i)}\right)^2 \tag{7}$$

Where,

$$h_\theta\left(x^{(i)}\right) - \text{Predicted output}$$

$$y^{(i)} - Actual\,value$$

Cross-Entropy Error Function. During the process of learning, the neural network model goes through stages in which the reduction of error may become extremely slow. This stagnation period can impact learning time. In order to resolve this problem a better way is to replace the mean squared error (MSE) by cross-entropy function. The bounds of the squared error and cross entropy are further compared by Pavel et al. [6]. They have presented an investigation on the properties of the cross-entropy (CE) and mean squared error (MSE) criteria for training models in Neural net.

$$J(\theta) = -\sum_i h_\theta\left(x^{(i)}\right)\log\left(y^{(i)}\right) \tag{8}$$

The optimizers are used to compute the gradients for loss and apply those gradients to the weights and biases. The optimizers used in this paper are Gradient Descent optimizer and Adam optimizer. Gradient descent optimizer applies the gradient descent algorithm which is a well-known algorithm in machine learning field. On the other hand, Adam optimizer implements Adam algorithm. Both optimizers require a learning rate α to train the data which should neither be too large or too small. Taking a small learning rate will make the algorithm very slow while a large learning rate will result into an algorithm which will never reach to minima. The mathematics behind Adam optimizer is introduced in the paper by Kingma et al. [7].

3.6 Model Evaluation

Error Analysis. Percentage relative error is used for the comparison between different models. The absolute error for each testing example i.e. the |predicted value – true value| is divided by true value and it is then converted it into percentage form. The overall mean of error for each testing example is obtained which gives us the final % error of the model.

$$\frac{|Predicted\ Value - Actual\ Value|}{|Actual\ Value|} \times 100 \tag{9}$$

Accuracy. To figure out that we predicted the label correctly argmax function of TensorFlow is used which gives the index of the highest entry in a tensor along some axis. This function is applied to both actual values and predicted values and the outputs of the function are compared using the equal function in TensorFlow. The Equal function generates a Boolean output which is further cast into float value and its mean is taken.

In Sect. 4 the Airfoil Dataset is a regression problem so the model is evaluated using percentage relative error while MNIST is a classification problem and is evaluated using the accuracy of the model.

4 Implementation on Datasets

4.1 Airfoil Self-noise Data Set

Airfoil Self Noise Dataset is taken from UCL Machine Learning Repository Donated by Thomas et al. [8].

In Air dataset initially preprocessing was done to bring the features on the same scale. Two hidden layers of 100 and 10 units were used respectively. Relu activation function is applied to the hidden layers while the output layer is linearly activated. The model is trained for 10000 epochs with a learning rate of 0.01. Optimizer used for optimizing the cost is Adam Optimizer and the error function used is Mean Squared error (MSE). For evaluating the model error analysis is done by comparing percentage relative error.

On applying various regularization technique in air dataset, it is observed that the performance of L2 Regularization is better when applied to both weights and biases. The percentage relative error of various regularization techniques is shown in Fig. 2. Dropout here yield maximum error percentage and therefore is not suitable for datasets with fewer attributes.

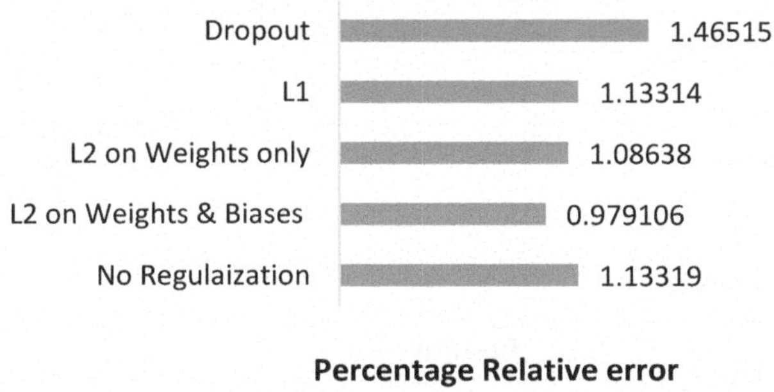

Fig. 2. Percentage relative error in different regularization technique

The performance of the model was further tested on L2 regularization by varying the regularization parameter lambda. It was observed that the best performance was shown by the model on $\lambda = 0.0001$ and on decreasing the value performance degrades (Fig. 3).

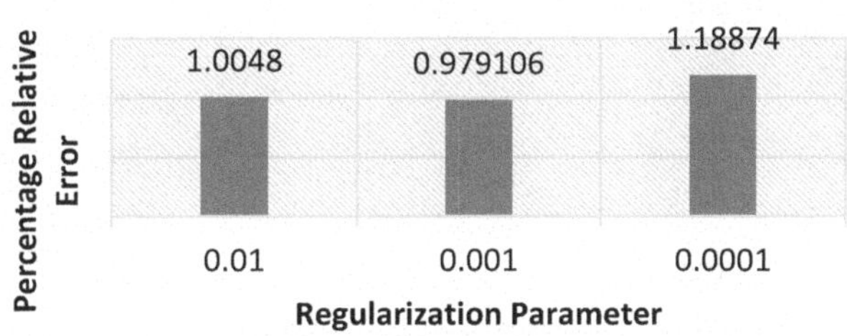

Fig. 3. Variation of error with regularization parameter in L2 regularization

4.2 MNIST Dataset

MNIST Dataset is an image dataset consisting the images of handwritten digits from 0–9. It has 28×28 matrix and 10 classes. That means the total number of features are 784 and labels are of shape 1×10 in one hot form. Dataset is taken from THE MNIST DATABASE of handwritten digits [9].

MNIST Dataset does not need to be preprocessed as the features are nearly on the same scale. The model consists of three hidden layers with 500 units in each of the hidden layers. As MNIST is a computer vision dataset of images of handwritten digits so the possible outcome can be a number from 0–9. Therefore the output class consists of 10 units which output the probability of each number. Relu is applied to all the hidden layers while in the output layer softmax is applied as we want to the probabilities to add up to one. The Gradient descent optimizer is used here to optimize the cost and it is trained for 10 epochs. The accuracy of the model is measured using the inbuilt function of TensorFlow as discussed in Sect. 3 As the dataset is very large the inputs are given in batches (Fig. 4).

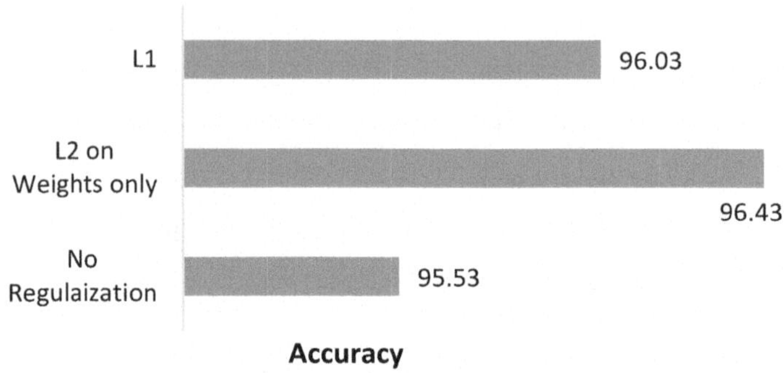

Fig. 4. Accuracy in different regularization techniques

On training the model on MNIST Dataset it was observed that performance of L2 Regularization is better than L1. The performance increased after applying L1 regularization as compared to a model with no regularization (Fig. 5).

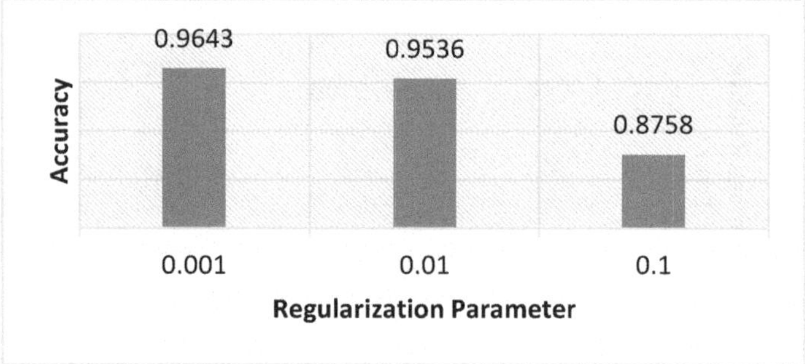

Fig. 5. Variation of accuracy with regularization parameter

On L2 Regularization the effect of regularization parameter λ was investigated and it was observed that it works best when λ is near 10^{-3}.

5 Conclusion

The paper described a detailed overview of a neural network model and its working. The problem of overfitting and its solutions were also discussed and further compared with respect to their performance. In this work, we find that models having less number of features perform comparatively better with L2 Regularization. Regularization parameter in L2 regularization also plays a significant role and yields the better result when its value is kept small. Dropout and DropConnect can be preferred when the numbers of features are high.

References

1. Srivastava, N., Hinton, G., Krizhevsky, A., Sutskever, I., Salakhutdinov, R.: Dropout: a simple way to prevent neural networks from overfitting. J. Mach. Learn. Res. **15**, 1929–1958 (2014)
2. Smirnov, E.A., Timoshenko, D.M., Andrianov, S.N.: Comparison of regularization methods for imagenet classification with deep convolutional neural networks. AASRI Procedia **6**, 89–94 (2014)
3. Lau, K., López, R., Oñate, E.: A neural networks approach to aerofoil noise prediction. In: International Centre Numerical Methods Engineering, vol. CIMNE No-3 (2009)
4. Wan, L., Zeiler, M., Zhang, S., LeCun, Y., Fergus, R.: Regularization of neural networks using dropconnect. In: ICML, no. 1, pp. 109–111 (2013)
5. Ng, A.: Feature selection, L1 vs. L2 regularization, and rotational invariance. In: Twenty-First International Conference Machine Learning - ICML 2004, p. 78 (2004)
6. Golik, P., Doetsch, P., Ney, H.: Cross-entropy vs. squared error training: a theoretical and experimental comparison. In: Interspeech, vol. 13 (2013)
7. Kingma, D., Ba, J.: Adam: A method for stochastic optimization. arXiv preprint arXiv: 1412.6980 (2014)
8. Lopez, R., Brooks, T.F., Pope, D.S., Marcolini, M.A.: Airfoil self-noise data set. UCI Machine Learning Repository (2008)
9. Lecun, Y., Bottou, L., Bengio, Y., Haffner, P.: Gradient-based learning applied to document recognition. In: Proceedings of IEEE, vol. 86, no. 11, pp. 2278–2324 (1998)

Analysis of COCOMO and UCP

Bhawna Sharma(✉) and Rajendra Purohit

Department of CSE, JIET, Jodhpur, India
bvnbhati@gmail.com

Abstract. After an early requirement design, project managers mostly use the requirement specifications to get an estimate of functional size of software which helps in estimating effort required and tentative cost of the software. An accurate estimate is necessary to be able to negotiate price of a software project and to plan and schedule project activities. Function Point sizing method for estimation is used frequently to estimate functional size of software. Another popular method of functional sizing is Use Case Points (UCP). UCP method of estimation although less used than FP based estimation, but is simpler than FP based method. One reason for this is - FP sizing metric often uses COCOMO-II or other effort estimation method to convert size estimate in FPs into effort estimate where as direct conversion formula can be used for converting size in UCPs to effort estimate. This paper compares results of both approaches for two mid-size business applications and tries to understand the correlation between the results of two approaches.

Keywords: Effort estimation · FP (Function Point) · UCP (Use Case Point)
COCOMO (COnstructive COst MOdel)

1 Introduction

Effort estimation is an important part of project management. Planning, budgeting and scheduling of projects highly depend on accuracy of effort estimation. At the same estimating correct and reliable time and cost estimation is also a complex process, which requires experienced project managers [14]. For this reason small projects are generally estimated using expert judgment and analogy based methods. Large projects generally have higher stakes and estimation process is usually either outsourced or there is a team of experts within company which performs estimation based on historic data and other parameters which are specific to company and can affect the estimate. This paper tries to analyze use of FPA and UCP for mid-size projects which are not very much affected by diseconomies of scale, but still require a systematic approach apart from just expert advice [8]. First method uses FPA to calculate size estimate as unadjusted FP count and then uses COCOMO to calculate efforts from unadjusted FP count. Second method calculates UCP based size estimate which is the directly converted to effort estimate using effort per UCP measure. Results are compared to assess the reliability and correlation between the two methods [13].

B. Panda et al. (Eds.): REDSET 2017, CCIS 799, pp. 372–379, 2018.
https://doi.org/10.1007/978-981-10-8527-7_31

2 Related Work

Function Point Analysis (FPA) for estimating functional size of software from user's perspective was developed in 1979 by Allan Albrecht of IBM [1]. In 1984, the International Function Point Users Group (IFPUG) was set up to more formally define the same method and later version was released in 2000 [2, 9].

The Constructive Cost Model (**COCOMO**) is a software cost estimation model developed by Barry Boehm and published in 1981 [3]. 61 projects were surveyed to derive a non-linear parametric model. Later same model was refined for modern programming techniques and named as COCOMO II [4]. COCOMO II was result of study of 163 projects.

Use Case Point (UCP) is another software metric developed by Gustav Karner in 1993 [5].This is influenced from Function Points and was specifically designed to measure functional size of object oriented software which use UML notations for requirements specifications. Although it is not very mature and less used than FPA and COCOMO II, it is still reliable for projects which are not very large in size.

3 Effort Estimation

Estimation is the process of getting an approximate of a value which cannot be correctly determined at the time of estimation due to incompleteness or unavailability of parameters that affect actual value. Software effort estimation is the process of estimating the amount of effort that is required to be implemented while performing all phases of life cycle of a development project. Estimating effort along with other factors requires function size of the project as an essential parameter. An effort estimate of a project helps in knowing cost, number of staff members and schedule of the project.

3.1 Function Point Method

Function Point Counting Procedure begins with identifying elementary processes [10] within the boundary of the software being estimated and then determining the type of function these processes belong to. All functions are categorized as follows.

1 Data Functions
  (i) Internal Logic Files (ILF)
  (ii) External Interface Files (EIF)
2 Transaction Functions
  (i) External Input (EI)
  (ii) External Output (EO)
  (iii) External Inquiry (EQ)

A complexity is assigned to each function and sum of weighted complexity of all function is called unadjusted FP of project. 14 General System Characteristics (GSC) of system are then rated on a scale of 0–5 based on their degree of influence. Sum of these values is used to determine a Value Adjustment Factor (VAF). Product of unadjusted Function Point count and VAF represents adjusted Function Point count (Fig. 1).

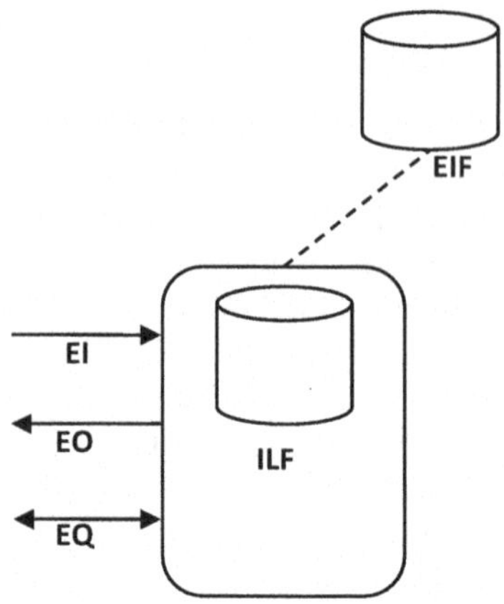

Fig. 1. Components of Function Point analysis (FPA)

3.2 COCOMO II

COCOMO II.2000 is the latest version of COCOMO that is applicable to modern software projects. It defines models for different phases of software. Both the Post-Architecture and Early Design models use the same functional form to estimate the amount of effort and calendar time it will take to develop a software project.

$$\text{Effort in PM} = \text{A} \times \text{Size}^{\text{E}} \times \prod_{i=1}^{n} \text{EM}_i$$

Where
A = 2.94 (for COCOMO II.2000)

$$\text{E} = \text{B} + 0.01 \times \sum_{j=1}^{5} \text{SF}_j$$

B = 0.91 (for COCOMO II.2000)
SF = Scale Factor
Size in KSLOC
EM = Effort Multipliers

The number of effort multipliers depends on the model. The value of n, the number of effort multipliers, EMi, is 16 for the Post-Architecture model effort multipliers, EMi, and 6 for the Early Design model. SFj stands for the exponential scale factors.

The values of A, B, EM1, …, EM16, SF1, …, and SF5 for the COCOMO II.2000 Post-Architecture model are obtained by calibration to the actual parameters and effort values for the 161 projects currently in the COCOMO II database.

We have used Early design Model for our example projects.

3.3 Use Case Point Method

UCP methods uses Use case diagram and use case description of the system to measure project size in UCPs. It is very similar to Function Point estimation. Use case and actors are classified according to their complexity and sum of their weighted complexities represents Unadjusted Use Case Points (UUCP) of project. Few Technical and Environmental factors are rated on a scale of 0–5 to calculate Technical Complexity Factor (TCF) and Environmental Complexity Factor (ECF) of the project. Product of all these represents adjusted Use Case Points (UCP) of project. UCP count provides the effort estimate of the project based on effort required in Person Hour (PH) per UCP.

4 Data Set

In our work we have studied 11 modules of 2 different business systems. First is US-based Medical Billing System (MBS) and another is a Hotel Management System (HMS). The projects have been chosen with the criteria of being not very small and not very large as discussed in Sect. 1. We have gone through complete process of effort estimation using (1) FPA [11] and COCOMO II and (2) UCP [12].

We identified all data and transaction functions, classified them based on their complexities within two systems. After calculating unadjusted FP count of the systems we calculated an SLOC count of FPs. We have assumed Java as programming language of the projects and used 53 SLOC per FP [6]. Using SLOC size estimate we applied COCOMO II.2000 for effort estimation. We defined values for all scaling factors and Effort Multipliers for the two projects and calculated effort estimate in Person Months (PM). The data collected from our case study has been shown in Table 1.

Table 1. FP and COCOMO II data set and effort estimated

Project	Module	ILF	EIF	EI	EO	EQ	Unadjusted FP count	Size in KSLOC	SF	EAF	Effort (PM)
MBS	User registration and login	7	–	9	–	–	16	0.85	12.87	0.95	2.35
MBS	Initial client setup	49	–	26	–	18	93	4.93	12.87	0.95	14.64
MBS	Patient demographic data entry	24	–	20	–	3	47	2.49	12.87	0.95	7.21
MBS	Transaction entry	35	15	10	–	29	89	4.72	12.87	0.95	13.99
MBS	Ins claim generation	14	5	–	14	7	40	2.12	12.87	0.95	6.10
MBS	Electronic payment posting	10	7	12	5	–	34	1.80	12.87	0.95	5.15
MBS	Patient statement generation	10	5	–	15	8	38	2.01	12.87	0.95	5.78
MBS	AR reports generation	–	15	–	–	20	35	1.86	12.87	0.95	5.31
HMS	Room reservations	26	5	21	4	3	59	3.13	8.35	1.00	9.13
HMS	Invoicing and payments	28	15	9	4	9	65	3.45	8.35	1.00	10.05
HMS	Room administration	14	–		–	9	23	1.22	8.35	1.00	3.58

As a supplementary method we also identified all use cases and actors and determined their complexities. We then defined technical and environmental factors of the two projects and calculated UCP count of the system. Assuming Java we used a count of 25 Person Hours per UCP to calculate effort estimate in Person Months (PM). Figures calculated by this process are shown in Table 2.

Table 2. UCP data set and effort estimated

Project	Module	UUCW	UAW	TCF	ECF	UCP	Effort (PM)
MBS	User registration and login	15	3	0.81	1.07	15.60	2.17
MBS	Initial client setup	90	3	0.81	1.07	80.60	11.19
MBS	Patient demographic data entry	55	3	0.81	1.07	50.27	6.98
MBS	Transaction entry	105	3	0.81	1.07	93.60	13.00
MBS	Ins claim generation	45	3	0.81	1.07	41.60	5.78
MBS	Electronic payment posting	40	1	0.81	1.07	35.53	4.94
MBS	Patient statement generation	35	1	0.81	1.07	31.20	4.33
MBS	AR reports generation	40	1	0.81	1.07	35.53	4.94
HMS	Room reservations	45	6	0.94	1.07	51.02	7.09
HMS	Invoicing and payments	60	6	0.94	1.07	66.03	9.17
HMS	Room administration	20	3	0.94	1.07	23.01	3.20

5 Data Analysis

Statistical parameters of the effort estimates from two approaches are shown in Table 3. Comparison and analysis of results of two approaches reveals that Effort estimates based on COCOMO are slightly higher than those results from UCP. Also for larger modules standard deviation is higher. UCP is often criticized for not including diseconomies of scale into the estimation model and it is suggested to include higher number of hours per UCP [7].

Table 3. Statistical properties of effort estimates by COCOMO and UCP

Project	Module	Effort in PM		Statistical properties			
		FP	UCP	Min	Max	Mean	Std Dev
MBS	User registration and login	2.35	2.17	2.17	2.35	2.26	0.13
MBS	Initial client setup	14.64	11.19	11.19	14.64	12.92	2.44
MBS	Patient demographic data entry	7.21	6.98	6.98	7.21	7.09	0.16
MBS	Transaction entry	13.99	13.00	13.00	13.99	13.50	0.70
MBS	Ins claim generation	6.10	5.78	5.78	6.10	5.94	0.22
MBS	Electronic payment posting	5.15	4.94	4.94	5.15	5.04	0.15
MBS	Patient statement generation	5.78	4.33	4.33	5.78	5.06	1.02
MBS	AR reports generation	5.31	4.94	4.94	5.31	5.12	0.26
HMS	Room reservations	9.13	7.09	7.09	9.13	8.11	1.44
HMS	Invoicing and payments	10.05	9.17	9.17	10.05	9.61	0.62
HMS	Room administration	3.58	3.20	3.20	3.58	3.39	0.27

Graphical comparison of the effort estimates of two projects using two approaches have been depicted in Figs. 2 and 3. Except for few modules most of the graphs are closely of same height.

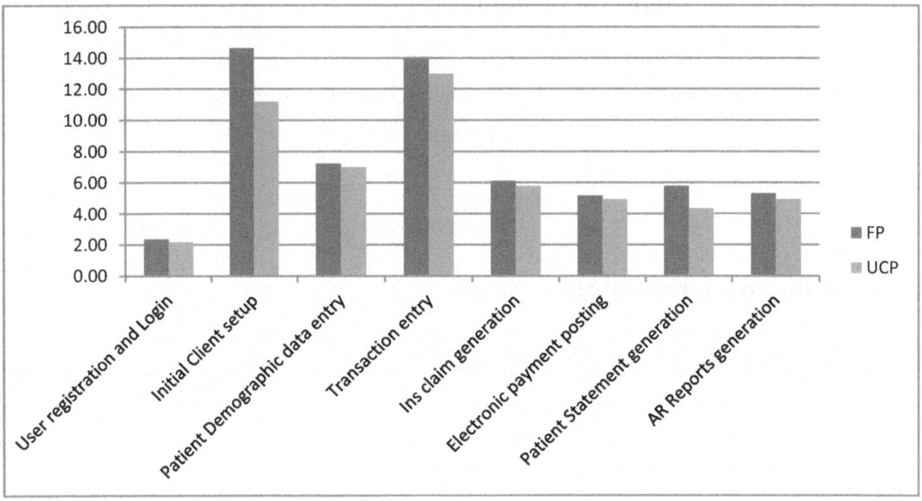

Fig. 2. Graphical comparison for effort estimated (PM) for all modules (MBS)

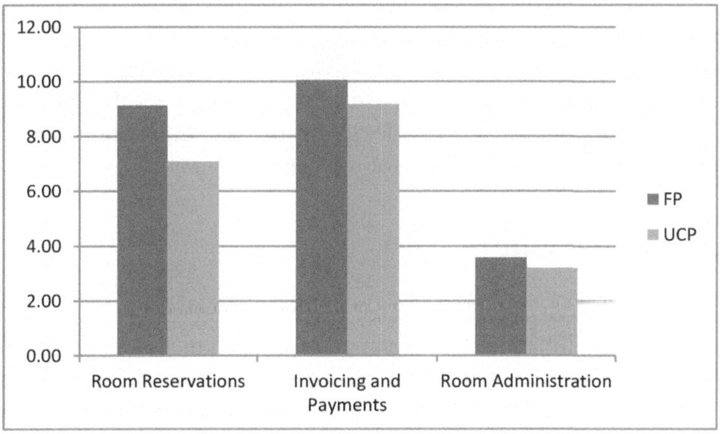

Fig. 3. Graphical comparison for effort estimated (PM) for all modules (HMS)

Tables 4 and 5 give us outcome of correlation analysis of the results of two estimates. Result of this analysis shows strong relationship between the two approaches.

Table 4. Correlation between effort estimation by COCOMO-II and UCP (MBS)

	COCOMO	UCP
COCOMO	1	–
UCP	0.8812	1

Table 5. Correlation between effort estimation by COCOMO-II and UCP (HMS)

	COCOMO	UCP
COCOMO	1	–
UCP	0.8549	1

6 Results and Discussions

Result of above analysis reveals following facts:

- Among two estimation approaches
  - FP followed by COCOMO II and
  - UCP: Second approach is simple, fast and transparent.
- Moreover, strong correlation factor among the results of case study in this paper allows us to conclude that UCP based estimation gives quite close match between effort estimates from COCOMO II based results, for projects which are not very large.
- As the project size grows, overhead factor and diseconomies of scale are higher. UCP needs to be tuned in such cases by increasing effort per UCP.
- Although UCP is criticized for being inconsistent, we can achieve consistency within a company by being more specific for use case complexity levels. Specifically, original UCP does not guide about complexity of use case transactions and companies can define their rules and guidelines for use case transactions.

7 Conclusion and Future Work

In this study, we worked on 11 modules of two projects. We used two different approaches for effort estimation. First approach used two methods and second method (COCOMO-II) was a complex non-linear approach using many parameters to be specified for calculating effort estimate. Second method used a simple linear formula. Results of the two approaches were very close to each other. This leads us to conclusion that - For small to mid-size projects direct linear formulae for converting size to effort estimates provide fairly accurate results. For large project(s) with higher overhead factors COCOMO II is a better option as compared to UCP because it addresses diseconomies of scale within model. In future, same study can be continued using large number of projects. An appropriate size estimate range can be thus defined as a guideline where use of linear method of effort estimation can be used without affecting accuracy of results.

References

1. Albrecht, A.J.: Measuring application development productivity. In: Proceedings of IBM Applications Development Symposium, Monterey, CA, p. 83, 14–17 October 1979
2. Function point counting Practices manual release 4.3.1, January 2010. https://ainfo.cnptia.embrapa.br/digital/bitstream/item/34989/1/0004-3-1-Part-0-2010-01-17.pdf
3. Boehm, B.W.: Software Engineering Economics. Prentice Hall, Upper Saddle River (1981)
4. Boehm, B.W., et al.: Software Cost Estimation with COCOMO II. Prentice Hall PTR, Seitan (2000)
5. Karner, G.: Resource estimation for objectory projects. Objective Systems SF AB (1993)
6. QSM - function point languages table. http://www.qsm.com/resources/function-point-languages-table
7. Laird, L.M., Brennan, M.C.: Software Measurement and Estimation: A Practical Approach. Wiley-IEEE Computer Society Press, Boston (2006)
8. Succi, G., Musilek, P., Sun, N., Pedrycz, W.: On the sensitivity of COCOMO II software cost estimation model. In: IEEE Symposium on Software Metrics (2002)
9. Furey, S.: Why we should use function points. IEEE Softw. **14**, 28–30 (1997)
10. Abran, A., Robillard, P.N.: Function points analysis: an empirical study of its measurement processes. IEEE Trans. Softw. Eng. **22**, 895–910 (1996)
11. Jeng, B., Yeh, D., Wang, D., Chu, S.L., Chen, C.M.: A specific effort estimation method using function point. J. Inf. Sci. Eng. **27**(4), 1363–1376 (2011)
12. Berg, K.V.D., Ton, D., Rogier, O.: Functional size measurement applied to UML-base user requirements. Retrievable from doc.utwente.nl. Accessed 2005
13. Kumari, S., Pushank, S.: Performance analysis of the software cost estimation methods: a review. Int. J. Adv. Res. Comput. Sci. Softw. Eng. **3**(7), 229–238 (2013)
14. Patil, L.V., Waghmode, R.M., Joshi, S.D., Khanna, V.: Generic model of software cost estimation: a hybrid approach. In: 2014 IEEE International Advance Computing Conference (IACC) , pp. 1379–1384 (2014)

Review of Current Software Estimation Techniques

Bhawna Sharma(✉) and Rajendra Purohit

Department of CSE, JIET, Jodhpur, India
bvnbhati@gmail.com

Abstract. Software Effort Estimation is an onerous but still inevitable task project managers have to perform. Project managers often face the dilemma of selection of estimation approach whenever any new project opportunity comes across. Estimation is required for not only setting a price and bidding rounds but also for planning, budgeting, staffing and scheduling of project related tasks. This paper reviews major cost estimation techniques that are relevant in current scenario. The primary conclusion is - all estimation approaches have few advantages and disadvantages and are often complimentary in their characteristics. Observation and Evaluation of several approaches can be insightful and can help in selecting an estimation technique or combination of techniques best suited for a particular project.

Keywords: Software estimation techniques · COCOMO · Linear methods Parametric methods

1 Introduction

Problem of Effort estimation is a topic of research for more than 5 decades. Earliest models were based on regression analysis and parametric methods and have become insufficient to address factors that affect modern software and represent current technology. Few principles still hold true for modern projects but an adaptation or expansion of the model is needed to accommodate wider range of parameters or dependencies. Most common methods in use in industry are SLIM, COCOMO and FP analysis based methods, all of which were introduced in 1970s and 1980s. It is interesting to note introduction of flexibility in traditional models like COCOMO, by using Machine learning methods specifically artificial neural networks (ANN) and Fuzzy logic (FL), both of which are new arenas of research in this field [2].

Next section provides a categorization of Estimation Techniques on the basis of use of the use of a general process or mathematical model- namely non-algorithmic or algorithmic models. There can be other ways of categorizing these techniques like sizing metric used as input or based on top-down or bottom-up approach. Method is open source or proprietary. There can be a completely different class for AI based methods. Regardless of categorization- this work attempts to review all major estimation techniques which are relevant in current scenario. A final section has been introduced to compare and contrast all these methods to the needs of specific projects.

B. Panda et al. (Eds.): REDSET 2017, CCIS 799, pp. 380–399, 2018.
https://doi.org/10.1007/978-981-10-8527-7_32

2 Estimation Techniques

One major type of categorization for the estimation techniques puts those under 2 categories – algorithmic and non-algorithmic [1]. Algorithmic estimation techniques use a systematic approach or method to formally or mathematically calculate some estimation metric. Non-algorithmic techniques use some kind of analogy, judgment or a heuristic approach to make assessment of an estimate. Table 1 compares various characteristics of the two types of models.

Table 1. Algorithmic vs. non-algorithmic models

Non-algorithmic	Algorithmic
High flexibility	Low flexibility
Adaptable to new changes	Model has to be updated by researchers
Learning or expertise based	Model based
Some of project attributes are enough	Many parametric factors required
Unreliable complicated process dependent of estimator's experience	Simple repeatable estimation process
Experts can adjust the method	Model does not allow manual adjustments
Acceptable accuracy of results even in early phase	Inaccurate estimations even at early stages of project

A. *Non-algorithmic techniques*
(1) *Estimation based on analogy*

As the name suggests, these estimation techniques are based on analogy or comparison with past projects. Many companies maintain information pertaining to effort estimation and actual effort spent for their past projects. Extrapolation of this historic data to estimate a proposed project can be done by project managers. This can be considered as methodical form of expert judgment backed by historic data. Experts have to find similarities between finished projects and most similar projects can be used to derive estimation of proposed project. Differences between completed and proposed project also needs to be found and their impact on estimate should be quantified, somehow.

However it is not an easy and direct process and requires experienced personnel to achieve an estimate. There are lots of variables that need to be considered, few directly multipliable, few to be factored and few to be guess differently. Like, number of screens, reports and input/outputs kind of entities can be easily converted, but use of dissimilar components which require updates need to be considered differently. Degree of resemblance or difference between two projects and how much confidence has to be shown on them is not a quantifiable process. Martin et al. [3] proposed – if we compute Euclidean distance in a space of n-dimension, we can find out analogies between components. Here each dimension represents a project feature. Nearest neighbors found out by the method represent most analogous project and analogy with such project gives most effective estimation.

(a) *Case Based Reasoning*

CBR is a comparatively recent trend in machine learning and automated reasoning. Its concept is to solve a problem by looking for the solution of a previously solved problem which is similar to the problem at hand, and thus avoiding working from scratch. Unlike other AI approaches it does not rely on general domain dependent heuristic knowledge but depended on concrete solutions already used for past problems.

Aarmodt and Plaza [4] defined CBR as a cyclic process comprising "the 4 R's" are explained as below:

1 **RETRIEVE** earlier experienced case or cases which are very similar
2 **REUSE** the knowledge gained from the case(s) from step 1, to solve the new problem
3 **REVISE** the solution
4 **RETAIN** the parts of this experience, in the case base for future problems.

(2) *Expert judgment method*

This method conceptually based on utilizing the knowledge and experience of experts to estimate a project. Like all other non-algorithmic methods there is no formal method to be followed. Consultation of a team of experts is taken while estimating the cost of a project. Experts' help in assessing completeness of requirements based on their experience with past projects. They also understand effect of dependencies like use of new technologies, use of commercial off-the shelf (COTS) applications and reusable libraries. Phenomenon of estimation is iterated till a consensus is reached among all major stakeholders of the project. Usually a mix of industry data and history of previous projects is used as an input along with requirements of the project being estimated.

Irrespective of size of the product this method or a variation of it is still a widely used method. Project managers should not solely depend on expert judgments, such judgments should basically compliment other estimation techniques. Some kind of documenting to support the assessment of experts can help in refining the results throughout the lifecycle of the project.

(a) *Work Breakdown Structure*

Work Breakdown Structure is a technique that decomposes the whole project into smaller units of work. These units can be represented as a tree like structure, where root node represents the whole project and leaf nodes represent most refined or decomposed level of work. Each leaf node is a unit of work that can be individually estimated and tracked. Sum of estimation costs for all leaf nodes represents the whole project estimation. As the project progresses any leaf node can be broken down to further refined levels representing sub-tasks under that task. Care must be taken that all terminal or leaf nodes represent an exclusive task and same task is not repeated elsewhere. Different levels of WBS also assist in mapping requirements to different level of project design from system level to modules, sub-modules and individual components of code.

(b) *Buy Vs Make Decision*

Project managers often use COTS (Commercial Off The Shelf components) or reuse modules of previous projects. Sometimes, a component has to be bought or an already available component has to be updated before use. Cost of buying a component or updating an existing component is many times needed to be compared with cost or effort needed to built it from the scratch. A buy vs. Make decision is also part of expert judgment.

(c) *Pricing to Win*

This is a simple expert judgment technique used by many companies for small projects. Only a small set of requirements is available for such project (just to get the contract) and thorough requirements analysis lacks. An initial cost proposal is made for such projects to get the deal from customer. A mutual agreement of refining this proposal to a better bargain can be made after a comprehensive requirement document is ready.

(d) *Delphi or Wideband Delphi Technique*

Delphi is an effort estimation technique which requires consensus of a team. It was developed at the RAND Corporation in the 1940s as a tool for forecasting effort estimate. It can be viewed as a formalization of expert-judgment technique. A team of 3–7 members and moderator conducts a kickoff meeting to create a Work Breakdown Structure (WBS). The team also discusses assumptions and other superficial factors related to the project. Every team member then individually estimates the project. Further meetings discuss individual input and reach a consensus.

In 1970s Boehm et al. developed a variant of Delphi method. They named it as Wideband Delphi Method to correlate with the original method. The Wideband Delphi Technique is more formal and lengthy variation of Delphi Technique. It promotes more communication and interaction among team members. This method takes into consideration the differences between past projects' effort estimates and their actual efforts taken. It also considers various technical factors that can impact effort estimation.

In spite of being detailed this method cannot still quantify the results or cannot document all factors as a single list of parameters like parametric models (Fig. 1).

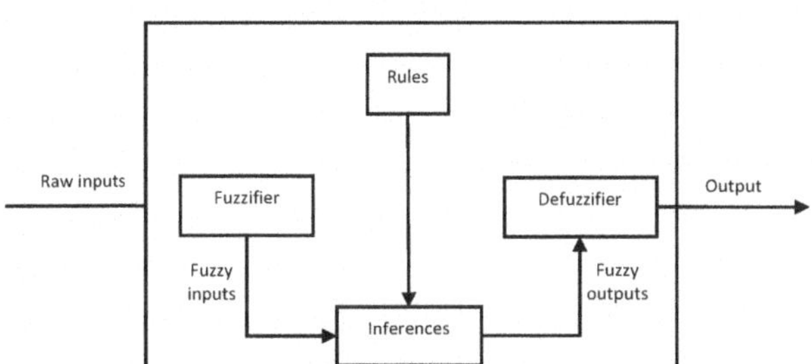

Fig. 1. Components of fuzzy logic system

Planning Poker is a variant of consensus based technique for agile development projects. Each Sprint of the project is represented as a card and deck of cards represents the whole project. Cards are marked with some progression like Fibonacci series or similar to original cards where King or Ave is highest number card when thrown will represent completion of the project.

B. *Soft Computing Techniques*

These are set of methods designed to solve real world problems which are difficult to model, mathematically. These are set of technologies that are combined together to handle ambiguity in real-life situations by means of flexibility in system that processes information. These techniques work to provide an approximate but cost effective solution to problem that may not be formulated very precisely.

(1) *Fuzzy logic based estimation*

Fuzzy Logic is a form of logic different from Boolean-Logic where variables assume truth values of either 0 or 1. In Fuzzy Logic variables may assume truth values as real number ranging between 0 and 1. This logic is frequently applied in artificial intelligence. Humans frequently apply Fuzzy Logic in their day to day life. We do not have exactness on many of our actions, but we instinctively apply quick "fuzzy" estimates based upon previous experience. For example consider throwing a physical object on a target. We assume force needed based on distance and weight of the object.

A Fuzzy system tries to simulate human behavior and reasoning. This is very useful when decision making is tough because input values are either not available or cannot be relied. Fuzzy systems develop a rulebase for whatever input is available. Weightings can also be added to rules to regulate degree of impact of each rule. Components of a Fuzzy system and process of Fuzzy systems is depicted in Fig. 2 below.

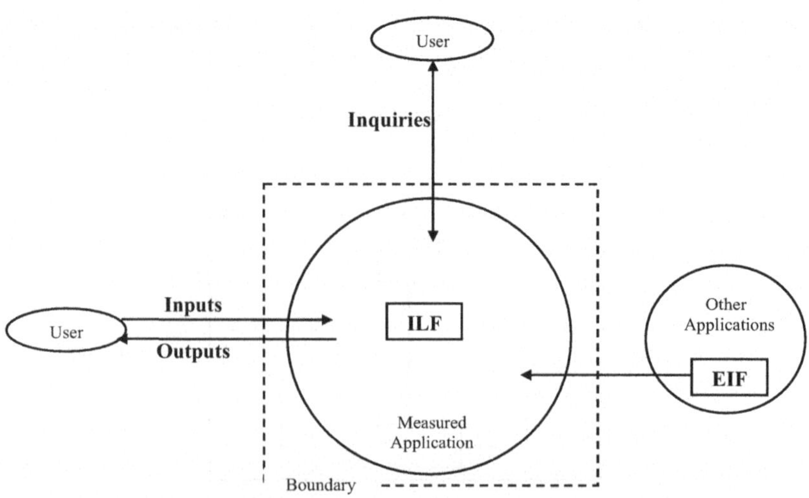

Fig. 2. Components of FPA

Fie and Liu [5] first realized that fuzziness can be applied to several aspects of COCOMO. They observed SLOC based size parameter of COCOMO cannot be determined accurately before starting a project and using a determinate value for it can affect accuracy of estimates. According to them if we involve fuzziness to handle uncertainty of input into ordinary COCOMO we can expect more reasonable output.

(2) *Artificial Neural Networks*

Artificial neural networks (**ANNs**) are systems of similar to biological neural systems that use computations to develop learning capabilities. They are useful is solving problems which are difficult to express in algorithmic way. These systems use a rule-base backed programming approach. An ANN is a collection of neurons interconnected to each other through synapses and can send signals to each other via these synapses. Neurons have state generally represented by a real number. Neurons and synapses also have weights which can vary as learning proceeds. Internal state of a neuron is known as activation level of neuron.

Neurons have a layered organization where each layer is responsible for performing different kinds of transformation on its inputs. Each layer can be viewed as a function and input of first layer and output of last layer is composition of function performed by all layers.

A typical ANN has 3 components –

1 A connection network of layers of neurons
2 Each connection has a weight associated with it which gets updated by learning process and
3 Output activation of each neuron is a function of its weighted input generally called an activation function. Activation functions are mostly sigmoid functions like below

$$f(x) = \frac{1}{1 + e^{-x}}$$

Architecturally, there are 2 types of neural networks:

1 Feed forward networks – these networks do not have any loops or cycles.
2 Feedback networks – these networks can have loops or cycles.

Software metrics researchers mostly use Feed Forward networks with back-propagation. These are also most commonly used in software cost estimation [6].

The training algorithm of back propagation is a 4 step repetitive process

1 Initialize weights
2 Forward propagate to generate output
3 Back propagate errors
4 Update weights and biases

C. *Algorithmic or Parametric techniques*

These techniques follow an objective approach using mathematical equations. The parameters of the equation can be derived using well-defined process described by the method being used. Parameters of the equations are generally software metrics like SLOC, Function points, object points etc. and other parts of the equations are either constants or values derived from factors that can impact effort estimate of the project. Being quantifiable and repeatable these methods are commonly favored by project managers. Generic form of these methods can be given as:

$$\text{Effort} = f(x_1, x_2, \ldots x_n)$$

where, all x_i are cost factors. Different methods can have different number and type of cost factors and estimation function can also vary to a large degree. In this study we have selected some popular algorithmic models.

(1) *Function Point based Analysis (FPA)*

FPA is a common method for Functional Size Measurement of a project; it uses Function Points as software size metric. It measures functionality of the software as viewed by the user. Many algorithmic models, like COCOMO, provide equations for converting the size measure in FPs to effort estimate in person months (PM). Function points were described by Allan Albrecht at IBM in 1979 [7]. FPA technique is an objective process with output that is meaningful to the user.

As of 2013, following ISO standards for FPA were specified.

1 Mark-II: ISO/IEC 20968:2002
2 NESMA: ISO/IEC 24570:2005
3 IFPUG: ISO/IEC 20926:2009
4 FiSMA: ISO/IEC 29881:2010
5 COSMIC: ISO/IEC 19761:2011

IFPUG is most commonly used method now-a-days [8].

Function Point Counting Procedure begins with identifying elementary processes within the boundary of the software being estimated and then determining the type of function these processes belong to.

There are 2 categories of functions Data Functions and Transactional Functions. Data Functions include -Internal Logical File (ILF) and External Interface File (EIF). Transactional Functions include - External Input (EI), External Output (EO), and External Inquiry (EQ).

All inputs that enters from outside boundary whether any data or control information, is considered as External Input. The source of EI can be either user or an external application. Inputs update internal logical files (ILFs) or behavior of the system. Any data coming out of application boundary is External Output. It may be derived from one or more internal logic files and can be passed to user or any external application. An external inquiry is combination of input and output, where input represents some parameters for output selection. Inquiries do not update any Internal Logical Files. Internal Logic files are logically grouped sets of data residing within application's boundary. These are maintained by external inputs. Each external interface file are similar to Internal Logic Files except that they are part of some external application are used for reference purposes only. They are maintained within external applications.

Classification of function is followed by assignment of ranks to the functions. Basis for this ranking is the number of files updated or referenced (FTRs) and the number of data element types (DET's). For Data function instead of FTRs, Record Element Types (RETs) are counted.

Subgroups of data elements, from user's perspective within an ILF or EIF are called Record Element Types (RETs). A data element type (DET) is an individual data/value type that is uniquely identified by user. Each of the following tables assists in the ranking process. After determining complexity of all functions using Tables 2, 3 and 4, function points can be assigned to each function using Table 5.

Table 2. Complexity matrix for external inputs [8]

FTRs	DETs		
	1–4	5–15	>15
0–1	Low	Low	Avg
2	Low	Avg	Hgh
3 or more	Avg	Hgh	Hgh

Table 3. Complexity matrix for external outputs and inquiries [8]

FTRs	DETs		
	1–5	6–19	>19
0–1	Low	Low	Avg
2–3	Low	Avg	Hgh
4 or more	Avg	Hgh	Hgh

Table 4. Complexity matrix for data files [8]

RETs	DETs		
	1–19	20–50	>50
0–1	Low	Low	Avg
2–5	Low	Avg	Hgh
6 or more	Avg	Hgh	Hgh

Table 5. Complexity weights of FPA components [8]

Function type	Complexity		
	Low	Average	High
External input	3	4	6
External output	4	5	7
External inquiry	3	4	6
Internal logical file	7	10	15
External interface file	5	7	10

Next step is to perform rating of 12 general system characteristics (GSC's) on a scale of zero to five. These characteristics represent general functionality of the application and can affect the effort estimate. A brief description of these characteristics in Table 6 has been given, that helps in deciding the degree of influence of the characteristics, from 0 (no influence) to 5 (strong influence).

Table 6. FPA – general system characteristics [8]

General system characteristic		Description
1	Data communications	Communication facilities available to help in exchanging information with the application
2	On-Line data entry	Ratio of information that is entered online
3	On-Line update	Number of ILFs updated by On-Line transaction
4	Performance	Performance in terms of throughput or response time
5	Heavily used configuration	Usage of Hardware on which application resides
6	Transaction rate	Frequency of transaction execution
7	Facilitate change	Level of flexibility or support for change
8	End-user efficiency	Level of end-user efficiency
9	Multiple sites	Number of sites at which application is concurrently used
10	Distributed processing	Level of support for distributed data processing
11	Complex processing	Complexity of processes that provide application functionality
12	Reusability	Possibility of reuse or level of possible use within multiple situations
13	Installation ease	Ease of installation?
14	Operational ease	Ease of effectively operating with application

Much detailed description of these has been included in IFPUG Counting Practices Manual [8]; along with all criteria that can be combined together to evaluate each GSC's rating level.

Value Adjustment Factor (VAF) is calculated based on rating of GSCs using following equation:

$VAF = (TDI * 0.01) + 0.65$

Where, TDI is sum of degrees of influence for all 14 GSCs.

The final Function Point Count is given by following equation.

$FP = UAF * VAF$

Few Parametric models have been proposed on the basis of FPs which is not commonly used in practice.

Matson-Barrett-Mellichamp Model:

Effort $E = 585.7 + 15.12 \times FP$

Albrecht & Gaffney Model:
Effort E = − 12.39 + (0.0545 * FP)
Kermer Model:
Effort E = $60.62 \times 7.728 \times 10^{-8} * FP^3$

(2) *Constructive cost model*

The **Constructive Cost Model** (**COCOMO**) is an algorithmic model for software cost estimation based on a basic regression formula that was built up by Barry W. Boehm. The model uses constant parameters that are derived from survey of 161 projects. It also includes variable parameters that can be calibrated based on characteristic of project being estimated.

COCOMO was first published in 1981 in Boehm's book *Software Engineering Economics* [9]. This is a comprehensive cost model for estimating effort, schedule, and cost of projects. Early studies of this model conducted in early 80 s were based on study of 63 projects with size ranging from 2 K to 100 K SLOC. These projects were written in various languages like assembly and PL/I. All these development projects were developed using waterfall model of software development, most commonly used at that time. This model was called *COCOMO 81* and is of only historic importance in current context.

COCOMO II was developed in 1997 and got published in 2000 in the book *Software Cost Estimation with COCOMO II* [10]. COCOMO II, an updated version of COCOMO 81 - is adapted for estimating software projects of modern era. It has been developed after considering 181 projects. It provides options to calibrate most of the factors common to modern projects and can account for efforts spent in updating reusable code or in using Commercial Off the shelf (COTS) software components.

COCOMO II is actually a hierarchy of three different models.

These models provide increasingly good estimates based on the stage on which development has progressed:

- **The Application Composition Model** is appropriate for projects built with modern tools for building software that are mostly GUI-based.
- **The Early Design Model** is used when basic software architecture has been established but detailed specifications are not yet available.
- **The Post-Architecture Model** is the most refined model of COCOMO-II. It is used when a project's architecture design is finished and construction of software is about to begin.

Most projects typically comprise of new code, reused code that has either been modified or used without modification, and automatically translated code.

COCOMO II uses an aggregate size estimate after creating an equivalent size conversion for reused and automatically translated code. For adjustments - ratio of design, coding and testing for the changed components are taken into account. Ease of understanding the code and the programmer familiarity with the code are also taken into consideration. COCOMO II assumes size estimate in SLOC. A detailed checklist provides guideline for counting SLOC. For Early design estimation it provides a table to convert Unadjusted FP count to SLOC. Effort in PM is calculated using following equation in COCOMO-II.

$$\text{Effort in PM} = A \times \text{Size}^{E} \times \prod_{i=1}^{n} EM_i$$

where

$$E = B + 0.01 \times \sum_{j=1}^{5} SF_j$$

A = 2.94,
B = 0.91,
SF = Scale Factor,
Size in KSLOC,
EM = Effort Multipliers

Number of effort multipliers is different for both models. There are 16 effort multipliers for the Post-Architecture model, and 6 for the Early Design model. SFj stands for the exponential scale factors.

The values of constants A and B, Effort Multipliers (EM_i) and Scaling Factors (SF_j) have been obtained after surveying actual parameters and effort estimates of 161 projects. Tables 7, 8 and 9 represent values of scaling factors and Effort multipliers for Post-architecture Model and Early Design Model. These factors have a major role in affecting time and cost of a project.

Table 7. Interpretation of parameter E in COCOMO equation

Value of E	Effect on economy of scale
<1.0	Economies of scale (mostly represented by very small projects where overheads can be better distributed if size grows)
=1.0	Balance between economies and diseconomies of scale
>1.0	Diseconomies of scale (generally shown by large projects)

We can set each Scale Driver to describe a specific project characteristic. Aggregation of rating (called scaling factor), provided to each Scale Driver, determines the exponent E used in the Effort Equation. These scale factors, affect the relative economies (or diseconomies) of scale that come across software projects of different sizes.

Diseconomy of scale is generally due to two main factors:

1 Interpersonal communications overhead grows with project size due to increase in number of staff members and their varied skill set.
2 System integration overhead grows with project size.

COCOMO II has 17 *Cost drivers* that are basically characteristics of the project which can affect effort required in project completion and so "drives" the cost. Project manager have to assign qualitative ratings to these drivers within range Extra Low to Extra High. An effort multiplier has been assigned by COCOMO II for these ratings as

Table 8. Scale factor values, SFj, for COCOMO II models [10]

Scale factors (*Wi*)	Extra high	Very high	High	Nominal	Low	Very low
PREC	Completely familiar	Very familiar	Quite familiar	Quite unprecedented	Very unprecedented	Never developed before
SFj:	0	1.24	2.48	3.72	4.96	6.2
FLEX	General goals	Some conformity	General conformity	Some relaxation	Occasional relaxation	Rigorous
SFj:	0	1.01	2.03	3.04	4.05	5.07
RESL	Full (100%)	Mostly (90%)	Generally (75%)	Often (60%)	Some (40%)	Little (20%)
SFj:	0	1.41	2.83	4.24	5.65	7.07
TEAM	Seamless interactions	Very cooperative	Quite	Generally cooperative interactions	Difficulty in interactions	Very difficult interactions
SFj:	0	1.1	2.19	3.29	4.38	5.48
PMAT	CMM Level 5	CMM Level 4	CMM Level 3	CMM Level 2	CMM Level 1 (Upper half)	CMM Level 1 (Lower half)
SFj:	0	1.56	3.12	4.68	6.24	7.8

shown in Table 9. Nominal rating value of all cost drivers is 1.00. Values higher than 1.00 represent more effort is required and values below 1.00 show reduction in effort caused by that factor.

Number of months required to complete a software project are predicted using COCOMO II schedule equation, whereas effort equation gives us duration of the project.

$$\mathrm{TDEV} = \left[\mathrm{C} \times (\mathrm{PM})^{(\mathrm{D}+0.2\times(\mathrm{E}-\mathrm{B}))}\right] \times \frac{\mathrm{SCED\%}}{100}$$

Where C = 3.67, D = 0.28, B = 0.91

In Equation components B, C and D can be calibrated. PM is the estimated PM derived from effort equation and does not include the SCED effort multiplier, scaling exponent (Table 10). E is same effort scaling exponent derived from effort equation. SCED% is the factor that decides compression or expansion of schedule from nominal schedule.

(3) *Putnam's SLIM model*

In 1978 Putnam published a paper [11], for his work on collecting effort and size related data for a few project. Based on his observations, he proposed an empirical model for calculating effort and time needed for a project of specific size. It is a proprietary method unlike COCOMO which is open source. Suite of tools developed by him for QSM Inc. has been named as SLIM (Software Lifecycle Management). His work has been considered pioneering in the field for software process modeling [12].

Table 9. Post-architecture model effort multipliers [10]

Post-architecture cost drivers		XH	VH	H	N	L	VL
Product factors	Required Reliability (RELY)	n/a	1.26	1.10	1	0.92	0.82
	Database Size (DATA)	n/a	1.28	1.14	1	0.90	n/a
	Product Complexity (CPLX)	1.74	1.34	1.17	1	0.87	0.73
	Developed for Reusability (RUSE)	1.24	1.15	1.07	1	0.95	n/a
	Documentation Match to Life-Cycle Needs (DOCU)	n/a	1.23	1.11	1	0.91	0.81
Platform factors	Execution Time Constraints (TIME)	1.63	1.29	1.11	1	n/a	n/a
	Main Storage Constraint (STOR)	1.46	1.17	1.05	1	n/a	n/a
	Platform Volatility (PVOL)	n/a	1.30	1.15	1	0.87	n/a
Personnel factors	Analyst Capability (ACAP)	n/a	0.71	0.85	1	1.19	1.42
	Programmer Capability (PCAP)	n/a	0.76	0.88	1	1.15	1.34
	Personnel Continuity (PCON)	n/a	0.81	0.90	1	1.12	1.29
	Applications Experience (APEX)	n/a	0.81	0.88	1	1.10	1.22
	Platform Experience (PLEX)	n/a	0.85	0.91	1	1.09	1.19
	Language and tool Experience (LTEX)	n/a	0.84	0.91	1	1.09	1.20
Project factors	Use of Software Tools (TOOL)	n/a	0.78	0.90	1	1.09	1.17
	Multi-site Development (SITE)	0.80	0.86	0.93	1	1.09	1.22
	Required Development Schedule (SCED)	n/a	1.00	1.00	1	1.14	1.43

While working on projects for the Army Putnam noticed that staffing level during a software development process follows Rayleigh shaped curve.

Putnam gave following relationship between productivity of software staff and effort needed to develop software.

$$\frac{B^{1/3}.\text{Size}}{\text{Productivity}} = \text{Effort}^{1/3}.\text{Time}^{4/3}$$

Table 10. Early design model effort multipliers [10]

Early design cost drivers	Counterpart combined post-architecture cost drivers
Personnel Capability (PERS) and Mapping Example	ACAP, PCAP, PCON
Product Reliability and Complexity (RCPX)	RELY, DATA, CPLX, DOCU
Platform Difficulty (PDIF)	TIME, STOR, PVOL
Personnel Experience (PREX)	APEX, PLEX, LTEX
Facilities (FCIL)	TOOL, SITE
Developed for Reusability (RUSE)	RUSE
Required Development Schedule (SCED)	SCED

Where:
Size = product size in ESLOC (Effective Source Lines of Code).
B = a scaling factor.
Productivity = ability to produce software of a given size at a specific defect rate.
Effort = total effort needed for project in person-years.
Time = time scheduled for the project in years.
So, we can deduce effort equation by rearranging the above.

$$\text{Effort} = \left[\frac{\text{Size}}{\text{Productivity}\ .\text{Time}^{4/3}}\right]^3 .\text{B}$$

According to Putnam's model a small change in project schedule can make substantial changes in effort needed. This model works reasonably well for large products but overestimates the effort for medium or small systems.

One major drawback of the Putnam model is its dependency on accurately estimating the size (in LOC) of the software to be developed. Uncertainty in the software size, that happens quite often while estimating, may result in the inaccurate estimation of cost.

(4) *SEER-SEM*

SEER for Software (SEER-SEM) is a project management software application, based on algorithmic and parametric approach. This estimation method was developed by Galorath Inc. based on Jensen model (first published in 1983) [13, 14]. SEER is a noun, which means "one having the ability to foresee the future". This is a proprietary application that runs on Windows environment and has thousands of licensed users including giant Government and commercial organizations.

SEER for Software (SEER-SEM) is a set of models that work together to estimate of effort, time, staff and defects. SEER-SEM has many parameters in its equations. An appropriate knowledge base can be selected to set initial default values these parameters. Different categories of parameters are as follows:

- Technical and environmental parameters
- Sizing parameters

- Commercial off the shelf (COTS) parameters
- Others such as economic or schedule related factors

It supports many logical and physical sizing methods, which include Function Points, Use Cases, Story points and the Lines of code etc. SEER-SEM requires translation of all these sizing metrics into effective size (S_e) for internal use. For an integrated analysis new, reused, and even COTS code can be represented as S_e. The generic calculation for S_e is:

$$S_e = \text{NewSize} + ((0.4 \times \text{Redesign} + 0.25 \times \text{Reimpl} + 0.35 \times \text{Retest}) \times \text{ExistingSize})$$

SEER-SEM on effort estimation has some limitations also. First, it has lot of input parameters describing various factors affecting the project and this makes estimation a very complex process. The same fact also makes it difficult to discover a nonlinear relationship been parameter input and corresponding outputs.

(5) *Use Case Based Estimation*

Use case modeling is an estimation technique that is frequently used for measuring the functional requirements of a project [15]. Use case model are used to define the functional scope of the system being developed. The 'Use Case Points' method was developed in 1993 by Gustav Karner of Objectory (now Rational Software) [16]. It performs sizing and estimating of object oriented software projects. This method has same philosophy as FPA. Like COCOMO and FPA, UCP method also can be applied is early design phase of the project.

UCP is simple and straight forward method of estimation. It can start just after the use case analysis of a project has been completed. As a first step, actors are classified as simple, average or complex based on details in Table 11. Similarly all use cases are classified based on Table 12. Included and extended use cases are not counted separately in this process. Multiplying number of each type of Actor and Use Case with the weighing factor and summing up the products gives us total unadjusted actor weights (UAW) and unadjusted use case weights (UUCW) respectively. Unadjusted Use Case Point (UUCP) of the system can be estimated now by summing up the two weights.

UUCP = UAW + UUCW

The method also proposes applying Technical and Environmental factors. 13 Technical factors are assigned values ranging from 0 to 5 (no influence to strong influence) and their sum TF is used to calculate Technical Complexity Factor using equation below. These factors have been mention in Table 13.

Table 11. Actor classifications [16]

Actor type	Actor interaction	**Weight**
Simple	Actor uses a well-defined API to interact with the system	1
Average	Actor uses standard communication protocols (e.g. TCP/IP, FTP, HTTP, database) to interact with the system using	2
Complex	Human actor using a GUI application interface	3

Table 12. Use case classification [16]

Use case type	No. of transactions	Weight
Simple	1–3	5
Average	4–7	10
Complex	8+	15

Table 13. Technical factors [16]

Technical factor	Description	Weight
T1	Distributed system	2
T2	Performance	1
T3	End User Efficiency	1
T4	Complex internal Processing	1
T5	Reusability	1
T6	Ease of installation	0.5
T7	Ease of use	0.5
T8	Portability	2
T9	Ease of change	1
T10	Need for Concurrency	1
T11	Special security features	1
T12	Need for direct access to third parties	1
T13	Need for user specific training facility	1

TCF = 0.6 + (TF/100)
Where

$$TF = \sum_{i=1}^{13} W_i \times F_i$$

W = Weight
F = Perceived Complexity Factor
ECF can also be calculated in same way

$$ECF = 1.4 + (-0.03 \times EF)$$

$$EF = \sum_{i=1}^{8} W_i \times F_i$$

W = Weight
F = Perceived Impact
Finally, UCP is calculated using all individual values calculated above.

See Table 14.

Formula for calculating UCP is simple enough as below:

UCP = (UUCW + UAW) × TCF × ECF

Karner proposed using of 20 staff hours per use case point as a productivity factor for a project estimate. Expert experience suggests using some value between 15 to 30 h per use case point. Thus, conversion of use case points to person hours may be an uncertain measure.

Table 14. Environmental factors [16]

Environmental Factor	Description	Weight
E1	Familiarity with UML	1.5
E2	Experience in application development	0.5
E3	Experience in Object Oriented design practices	1
E4	Capability of Lead analyst	0.5
E5	Motivation	1
E6	Stability Requirements	2
E7	Part-time workers	−1
E8	Complexity of Programming language	−1

Critics often point out one major weakness of the Use Case Points method. According to UCP has never been thoroughly calibrated. Applying regression analysis on a statistically sufficient number of projects, and analyzing results is still required to prove usefulness this method. One hindrance in this objective is UCP related work is now copyright of Rational Software (Table 15).

Table 15. Characteristics of estimation techniques

Method	Type	Strength	Weakness
Expert judgment	Non-algorithmic	Adapt to especial projects, Fast prediction, Useful in absence of empirical and quantified data Well suited when the software product is poorly understood	Estimate is highly dependent on Expert's opinion Documenting the factors used by experts is hard and so non-repeatable Not suitable for large projects affected by various factors
Analogy		If past project's data are available result are very reliable	Dependent on availability of past project's data
Fuzzy logic	Machine Learning	Ease of use, no special training or tools required Good for project for which exact mathematical precision of input metrics is not available	Requires lot of data to tune to correct results Crude output needs to be interpreted in right context

(*continued*)

Table 15. (*continued*)

Method	Type	Strength	Weakness
Neural network		Less formal statistical training is required, Complex nonlinear relationships between dependent and independent variables is determined automatically	Training multi-layer neural networks is hard, and needs calibrating lots of parameters
FPA	Algorithmic	Can be applied in any stage of development Language independent functional Sizing	Time consuming method that requires subjective judgment; Depends on other models to convert functional size in FPs to effort estimation in PMs
COCOMO		Open source, objective method that supports modern software development processes and uses any aspects of projects' technical environment to calibrate Different models for different stages of project More predictable and accurate	No support for project sizing depends on other sizing methods and so ignores requirements and all documentation
PUTNAM's SLIM		Simple model based mainly on two variables- size and duration (time)	All other aspects of the SDLC aren't being considered in this method. Extremely sensitive to the technology factors and Sizing input
SEER-SEM		Many sizing methods are available Effort, cost, schedule, staffing, and defects- all are estimated	About 50 input parameters needed so is complex in nature Difficulty in discovering the nonlinear relationship between input and corresponding output parameters
Use case points		Easy to apply after Use Case designs are ready Works well for early design phase	Depends on other models to convert functional size in UCPs to effort estimation in PMs

3 Conclusion

Inaccurate Project estimation is the result of failure of a large percentage of software projects. Use of appropriate software estimation techniques is important in getting a reliable and accurate estimation. Researchers are working hard to improve estimation technique with the same pace as the software development techniques. Keeping abreast with recent estimation techniques is important for project managers. This paper presents an overview of all recent estimation techniques. Soft Computing are still not mature but are being worked by many academics and researchers. The major conclusion of this study is that no single technique is better in all respects and it is often useful to combine more than one technique. Often times these techniques are complementary to each other. For example – FPA and UCP are two functional size measuring methods and need to be combined with other technique COCOMO or SLIM which require size as an input and provide an effort estimation. Analogy based methods are mostly suitable for companies which are established in market and have stored past projects' data in their databases. Learning based methods are suitable for newer companies. Large and small projects also decide suitability of method and Algorithmic methods are more suitable for large projects to be able to address diseconomies of scale. Cost factors also decide whether one should use open source methods like COCOMO-II or hire services of professionals and use SLIM or other proprietary models.

References

1. Abbas, S.A., et al.: Cost estimation: a survey of well-known historic cost estimation techniques. J. Emerg. Trends Comput. Inf. Sci. **3**(2), 612–636 (2012)
2. Idri, A., Zakrani, A., Zahi, A.: Design of radial basis function neural networks for software effort estimation. IJCSI Int. J. Comput. Sci. **7**(4), 11–17 (2010)
3. Shepperd, M., Schofield, C.: Estimating software project effort using analogy. IEEE Trans. Softw. Eng. **23**(12), 736–743 (1997)
4. Aamodt, A., Plaza, E.: Case-based reasoning: foundational issues, methodological variations, and system approaches. AI Commun. **7**, 39–59 (1994)
5. Fei, Z., Liu., X.: f-COCOMO: fuzzy constructive cost model in software engineering. In: IEEE International Conference on Fuzzy Systems, pp. 331–337 (1992)
6. Huang, S.; Chiu, N.: Applying fuzzy neural network to estimate software development effort. Proc. Appl. Intell. J. **30**(2), 73–83 (2009)
7. Albrecht, A.J.: Measuring application development productivity. In: Proceedings of the Joint SHARE, GUIDE, and IBM Application Development Symposium, Monterey, California, 14–17 October, IBM Corporation, pp. 83–92 (1979)
8. Function Point Counting Practices Manual Release 4.3.1, January 2010. https://ainfo.cnptia.embrapa.br/digital/bitstream/item/34989/1/0004-3-1-Part-0-2010-01-17.pdf
9. Boehm, B.: Software Engineering Economics. Prentice-Hall, Englewood Cliffs (1981)
10. Boehm, B.W., et al.: Software cost estimation with COCOMOII. Prentice Hall, Englewood Cliffs (2000)
11. Putnam, L.H.: A general empirical solution to the macro software sizing and estimating problem. IEEE Trans. Softw. Eng. **SE-4**(4), 345–361 (1978)
12. Kemerer, C.F.: An empirical validation of software cost estimation models, May 1987
13. Fischman, L., McRitchie, K., Galorath, D.D.: Inside SEER-SEM. CrossTalk J. Defense Softw. Eng. (2005)
14. Galorath, D., Evans, M.: Software Sizing, Estimation, and Risk Management. Auerbach, Boca Raton (2006)

15. Anda, B., Angelvik, E., Ribu, K.: Improving estimation practices by applying use case models. In: Oivo, M., Komi-Sirviö, S. (eds.) PROFES 2002. LNCS, vol. 2559, pp. 383–397. Springer, Heidelberg (2002). https://doi.org/10.1007/3-540-36209-6_32
16. Karner, G.: Resource estimation for objectory projects. Objective Systems SF AB (1993)
17. Jacobson, I., Booch, G., Rumbaugh, J.: The Objectory Development Process. Addison-Wesley, Boston (1998)

Improved Bee Swarm Optimization Algorithm for Load Scheduling in Cloud Computing Environment

Divya Chaudhary(✉), Bijendra Kumar, Sakshi Sakshi, and Rahul Khanna

Department of Computer Engineering, Netaji Subhas Institute of Technology, Dwarka, New Delhi, India
divyadabas@gmail.com, bizender@gmail.com, sakshi_nsit@yahoo.com, khannar1995@gmail.com

Abstract. The cloud acts as a model that contains an aggregation of resources and data that needs to be shared among users. The scheduling of the load acts as a major challenge to fulfill the requests of the several users. Till now several algorithms have been proposed for fulfilling the purpose of load scheduling in cloud. The latest works are based on swarm-intelligence techniques. However, one such swarm-intelligence technique Bee Swarm Optimization (BSO) has not been exploited for serving this purpose. In this paper, an improvised version of BSO, the Improved Bee Swarm Optimization in Cloud (IBSO-C) has been proposed with the objective of efficient and cost-effective scheduling in cloud. It uses the swarm of particles as bees for scheduling and updated total cost evaluation function. The proposed algorithm is validated and tested by analysis on large set of iterations. The comparison of results with existing techniques has proven, the proposed IBSO-C to be a more cost-effective algorithm.

Keywords: Cloud computing · Load scheduling · Swarm intelligence PSO · BSO

1 Introduction

Cloud computing is a model composed of a pool of configurable, virtual computing resources shared among various tasks that are to be executed for a user. Cloud service providers like Amazon and IBM ensure the reliability and security of the underlying infrastructure. It is a typical example of distributed computing that dynamically allocates as many computing resources to the user tasks as and when they are required. However, this allocation if performed randomly does not lead to optimum utilization of the computing resources, leading to a non-cost-effective process. Thus, the aim of cloud computing in scheduling user applications on a shared set of computing resources must be not only to make this process efficient in terms of both time and cost, but also to ensure an even distribution of the available resources.

Various techniques have been used earlier to achieve this objective. Some of these have been developed specifically to serve this purpose [1, 2], while others have exploited existing optimization methods like heuristics and meta-heuristics for the same. One such

B. Panda et al. (Eds.): REDSET 2017, CCIS 799, pp. 400–413, 2018.
https://doi.org/10.1007/978-981-10-8527-7_33

meta-heuristic that has been extensively employed for the purpose of workflow scheduling in cloud, is the population based optimization technique introduced by Kennedy and Eberhart [3] namely Particle Swarm Optimization (PSO). Besides nature-inspired PSO another meta-heuristic based on the natural foraging behavior of a swarm of bees, Artificial Bee Colony (ABC) exists. It has been experimentally verified, that ABC outperforms other population based algorithms like PSO in optimization problems [4]. Later, another modified and more optimized version of ABC known as the Bee Swarm Optimization (BSO) has been developed.

Although, noteworthy research has been carried out on ABC, the more efficient version of this real world inspired, population based technique (BSO) has not been exploited to its full potential. In this research, we focus on one such unexplored capability of BSO heuristic, which is its use for efficient and cost-effective load scheduling in cloud. Our purpose is to develop and implement an improved bee swarm optimization algorithm for mapping user applications to virtualized resources while minimizing the total cost, which includes costs of transfer and execution. In addition, the algorithm must outperform existing similar approaches that exist so far to fulfil the same purpose. We call our proposed algorithm, IBSO-C (Improved Bee Swarm Optimization in Cloud).

The rest of the paper is organized as follows: Sect. 2 presents related work undertaken prior to the present research. In Sect. 3, we describe our newly proposed IBSO-C algorithm. Section 4 contains an experimental evaluation of the performance of IBSO-C and its comparison with the performance of other heuristic algorithms that have been used earlier for load scheduling in cloud. In Sect. 5, we conclude our research and discuss the possibility of work that could be undertaken in the future.

2 Swarm-Intelligence in Load Scheduling

The swarm refers to a cluster of agents, which may be birds, ants, bees or even termites. Each of these agents behaves independently according to their perception of their neighborhood. The intelligence of a swarm lies in the way the agents behave, their self-organization and their naturally intelligent way of dividing work or solving day-to-day problems like foraging for food. A lot many algorithms have been proposed by researchers on swarm-intelligence, starting with the 90s. These include Particle Swarm Optimization (PSO), based on the swarm behavior of a flock of birds [3]; Ant Colony Optimization (ACO), an algorithm that mimics social behavior of ants while they live in colonies; among others. With the introduction of these algorithms, several new versions have been introduced and described. These have been extensively analyzed and used in many real-world scenarios. A hybrid of PSO, for instance has been introduced by Cui et al, for more compact document clustering than the K-Means algorithm [5].

The first ever survey on the algorithms based on swarm-intelligence of an aggregation of honey bees was presented by Karaboga and Akay [6]. The survey depicted the advances in exploitation of intelligent behavior of honey bees. It described existing algorithms that have been based on the intelligent characteristics of honey bees like communication through dancing, division of labour, nesting, mating and so on. Another algorithm presented in the survey is that proposed by Yang et al [7] called the Virtual bee algorithm, which aims to optimize the solution based on the intensity of interaction among a swarm of bees. Some of the other noteworthy research highlighted in it, include the BeeAdHoc algorithm, defined by Wedde and Farooq [8] and the bees algorithm described by Pham et al. [9], among several others. Following this, an algorithm called the Artificial Bee Colony (ABC), simulating the foraging behaviour of honey bees, has been defined by Karaboga [10]. ABC has been extensively studied, analyzed and applied to solve problems in real-world domain by many researchers, as a result of which several modified hybrid models do exist. I-ABC (improved ABC) and PS-ABC (a hybrid of PSO and ABC algorithms) have been introduced by Li et al. [4] to improve the basic ABC, by jumping in and out of the local optimum as well as speeding up the process of finding optimal parameters. In addition, they have been found to produce low cost, fast and reasonably accurate solutions to complex problems [4]. Another such variant of ABC known as MABC has been developed with the aim of finding solutions to the economic dispatch problem. MABC provides a new method to update solutions in the search space, to reduce premature convergence and obtain stable solutions [12]. Several other more optimized hybrids like best-so-far ABC [11], Gbest-guided ABC (G-ABC) [13] have also been introduced.

Akbari et al. introduced a hybrid of ABC based on the principles of swarm-intelligence, much like PSO. It was called the Bee Swarm optimization (BSO) algorithm [14]. BSO is inspired from foraging behavior of honey bees. In BSO, different patterns are used by the bees to adjust their flying trajectories. When, BSO algorithm was compared with existing bee algorithms on a set of well-known numerical test functions, experimental results have shown that the BSO algorithm is more effective and robust; produces excellent results, and outperforms other algorithms investigated in this consideration [14].

In the proposed IBSO-C algorithm, these advantages of the BSO algorithm have been exploited and a few modifications have been made in basic BSO, for it to serve the purpose of load scheduling in cloud.

3 Proposed Improved Bee Swarm Algorithm in Cloud (IBSO-C)

Bee Swarm Optimization (BSO) is a novel method based on foraging behaviors of honey bee swarms. This approach uses different types of bees to optimize numerical functions. Each type of bee employs a distinct moving pattern. A scout bee, flies randomly over its nearby regions. An onlooker bee selects an experienced employed bee as its interesting elite and moves toward that bee. An employed bee memorizes the information about the best food source found so far by that bee, selects a best experienced employed bee as the elite bee, and adjust its position based on this information [14].

In the present research, we have improvised the existing BSO algorithm, for it to fulfill the purpose of load scheduling in cloud. Improved Bee Swarm Optimization algorithm for Cloud (IBSO-C) also has 3 types of bees - employed(ξ), onlookers(κ) and scouts(ν) and the total number of total bees is n(β). The algorithm is given in Fig. 1.

1. $n(\beta)$, Percentage of type of bees, $Iter_{max}$, dimensions D, Stepsize s, and radius of random walk (τ) are determined.
2. Bees are positioned randomly in search space.
3. Do following until the termination condition is met:
   a. Calculate fitness of bees and sort.
   b. Classify as employed, onlooker or scout on fitness.
   c. For every employed bee
      - Update best position
        If fitness (X(ξ,i)) > fitness(best(ξ.i))
        then,
        best(ξ,i)= X(ξ,i)
      - Update elite position of swarm
        If fitness(best(ξ,i)) > fitness(elite(ξ,i))
        then,
        elite(ξ,i)=best(ξ,i)
      - Update employed bee position using equation (3).
   d. Select elite bee for every onlooker using roulette selection by selection probability:

$$prob_j = \frac{fitness(X(\xi,i))}{\sum_{c=1}^{n(\xi)} fitness(X(\xi,c))} \tag{1}$$

      - Update onlooker position using equation (5).
      - Update scout bee positions using equation (7).
   e. Adjust s and τ.

Fig. 1. IBSO-C algorithm for load scheduling

Firstly, the number of bees n(β), percentage of bees, max number of iterations ($Iter_{max}$), number of dimensions D, stepsize s and radius of random walk for scout bees(τ) are defined. The percentage of onlooker bees is 48% of the swarm, the employed bees is 48% of the swarm, and the scout bees is 4% of the swarm. s is defined to be the number of iteration and τ is defined to be $(X_{max}-X_{min})/s$, where X_{max} and X_{min} are the maximum and minimum values of the search space along any dimension.

Next, the bees are randomly positioned in the search space and their fitness is calculated using a fitness function. Then, the bees are sorted based on this fitness and classified into the mentioned types.

For each employed bee, if fitness at current position is better than that of the best position in its memory, then the best position is updated to the current position. Similarly, if the fitness of the new best position is better than that at the elite position, i.e. the global maximum of the entire swarm, elite position is updated. Using the best and elite positions, the velocity and position of the employed bee is updated as

$$V(\xi, \mathrm{i}) = \omega_b r_b \big(best(\xi, i) - X_{old}(\xi, \mathrm{i}) \big) + \omega_e r_e \big(elite(\xi, i) - X_{old}(\xi, \mathrm{i}) \big) \quad (2)$$

$$X_{new}(\xi, \mathrm{i}) = X_{old}(\xi, \mathrm{i}) + V(\xi, \mathrm{i}) \quad (3)$$

where, X_{new} is the updated position, X_{old} the current position and V is the updated velocity of the bee. Also, r_b and r_e are random variables and parameters ω_b and ω_e respectively control the importance of the best food source found by i^{th} bee and best food source found by elite bee. Each onlooker bee selects one of the employed bees as its own personal elite *e (ξ, i)* using roulette selection. The flowchart for proposed algorithm IBSO-C is provided in Fig. 2.

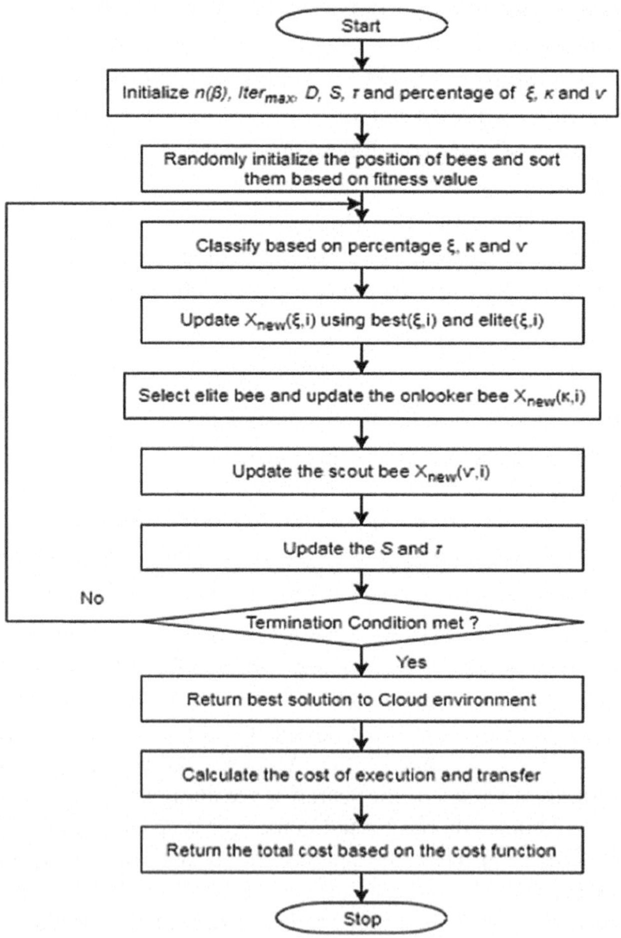

Fig. 2. IBSO-C flowchart for load scheduling in cloud

The probability of selection is given by Eq. (1). Onlooker bee velocity and position are updated using the position of its selected elite as:

$$V(\kappa, \mathrm{i}) = \omega_e r_e \left(e(\xi, i) - X_{old}(\kappa, \mathrm{i}) \right) \quad (4)$$

$$X_{new}(\kappa, \mathrm{i}) = X_{old}(\kappa, \mathrm{i}) + \mathrm{V}(\kappa, \mathrm{i}) \quad (5)$$

ω_e here probabilistically controls the attraction of onlooker bee. The velocity of the Scout bees' is updated by Eq. (6) and position using Eq. (7).

$$V(\nu, \mathrm{i}) = Rw\left(\tau, X_{old}(\nu, \mathrm{i}) \right) \quad (6)$$

$$X_{new}(\nu, \mathrm{i}) = X_{old}(\nu, \mathrm{i}) + V(\nu, \mathrm{i}) \quad (7)$$

It consists of a random walk function *Rw* which is a function of the current position of the bee and random walk radius, τ. Lastly, the values of s and τ are updated. If termination condition is met the best solution is returned, otherwise the process of updating position is repeated for all the bees. The cost is evaluated on the basis of best solution returned. The execution and transfer time of the cloudlets are calculated. The total cost is calculated for parallel computation, so the maximum cost is returned as the solution. This improved cost function with BSO provides far better results than GSA and PSO.

4 Experimental Analysis

In this section, we evaluate the proposed IBSO-C algorithm by comparing it with other heuristic methods that are available for the same purpose of load scheduling in cloud. Such algorithms include, GSA (Gravitational Search Algorithm), an optimization algorithm based on the law of gravity, and PSO (particle swarm optimization).

The CloudSim Simulator is used for designing the algorithm and setting it up for analysis. The Network CloudSim Simulator is simulated on top of CloudSim interface. The proposed and existing algorithms are implemented on the simulator using the JSwarm package. The total cost incurred after load scheduling using IBSO-C, GSA and PSO are presented in a tabulated and graphical manner. 25 particles are distributed to 10, 15 and 20 cloudlets on 8 VMs in the simulator. Every cloudlet contains the fitness value, MIPS, execution and transfer cost handled by the cloudlet and execution cost on the VMs. The total cost is calculated on the basis on an improved cost optimization function.

The tabulated result of the total cost of using PSO, GSA and the proposed IBSO-C algorithm for cloudlets on VMs with respect to number of iterations is provided in Tables 1, 2 and 3. Figures 3, 5 and 7 depicts the graphical analysis of the total cost versus number of iterations for 10, 15 and 20 cloudlets respectively. However, the total cost incurred in the execution of PSO algorithm is much higher than the other two algorithms. Hence, to highlight the advantage of using proposed IBSO-C over GSA on different number of cloudlets, we compare them separately in Figs. 4, 6 and 8.

Table 1. Comparison of algorithms PSO, GSA, L-GSA and IBSO-C on 10 cloudlets

Iterations	PSO	GSA	IBSO-C
10	144670.354	22033.564	20882.071
20	154718.388	22231.076	27653.959
30	146023.003	22646.835	19717.172
40	151117.032	25236.798	25878.788
50	153934.604	21804.132	20882.071
60	146671.563	28238.387	26524.482
70	150630.778	24134.520	21620.188
80	144320.104	27754.698	20996.016
90	150043.444	28324.327	22905.881
100	155538.952	29378.085	25833.865
200	143757.944	22364.729	27136.151
300	155469.762	26501.040	22181.818
400	154534.972	27754.698	19360.000
500	148303.411	22239.871	20996.016
600	143482.749	22364.729	20514.342
700	148181.188	33288.008	20514.342
800	145980.430	26069.204	27830.000
900	145713.846	19760.956	22181.818
1000	150183.341	19879.760	21780.000

Table 2. Comparison of PSO, GSA, L-GSA and proposed IBSO-C algorithm on 15 cloudlets

Iterations	PSO	GSA	IBSO-C
10	251281.517	29867.440	29040.000
20	248417.269	31424.714	28153.998
30	248960.089	30289.439	23684.151
40	247411.824	30289.439	27111.111
50	249097.514	32581.602	28856.305
60	252863.341	25936.255	24134.520
70	233301.076	27111.111	26935.541
80	240275.467	33911.399	32483.221
90	238414.151	27111.111	27842.761
100	246693.713	28961.424	29819.639
200	257046.548	22364.729	29040.000
300	241913.925	26501.040	28343.434
400	250686.566	27754.698	25410.000
500	255247.494	22239.871	26620.000
600	255640.518	22364.729	26454.519
700	240621.622	33288.008	27754.698
800	234732.638	26069.204	26472.488
900	245081.605	19760.956	27878.787
1000	245697.967	19879.760	28472.900

Table 3. Comparison of PSO, GSA, L-GSA and proposed IBSO-C algorithm on 20 cloudlets.

Iterations	PSO	GSA	IBSO-C
10	368649.602	44876.475	38615.232
20	354478.049	41712.666	34358.821
30	345540.580	46517.096	43715.357
40	356553.370	44648.863	41456.147
50	353046.854	50765.556	43901.034
60	355353.891	47062.315	38455.394
70	351187.753	44648.863	43134.495
80	357996.221	36958.024	41714.261
90	371324.589	47707.209	37946.693
100	368448.353	43551.325	38286.853
200	359849.885	48400.000	39170.780
300	347655.150	44876.475	43017.448
400	350306.997	44648.863	41992.032
500	365131.362	39521.912	41517.326
600	366225.261	51872.510	37518.474
700	369217.780	47914.295	42341.146
800	366704.318	42284.396	38720.000
900	362957.682	47195.216	40639.713
1000	363249.969	52452.208	36300.000

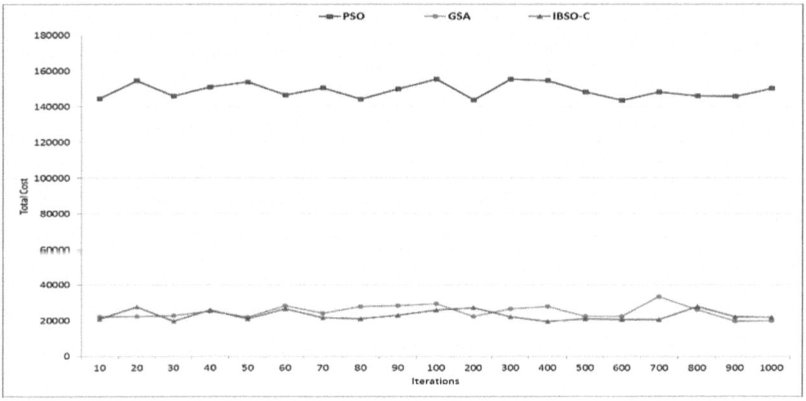

Fig. 3. Comparison of total cost v/s number of iterations for PSO, GSA and proposed IBSO-C

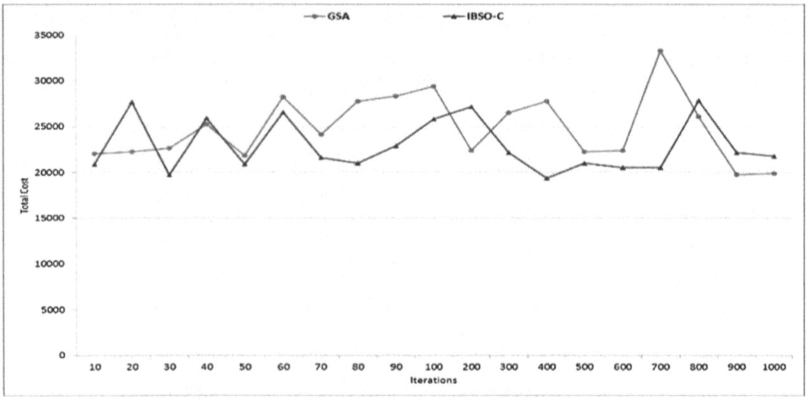

Fig. 4. Comparison of total cost v/s number of iterations for GSA and proposed IBSO-C on 10 cloudlets

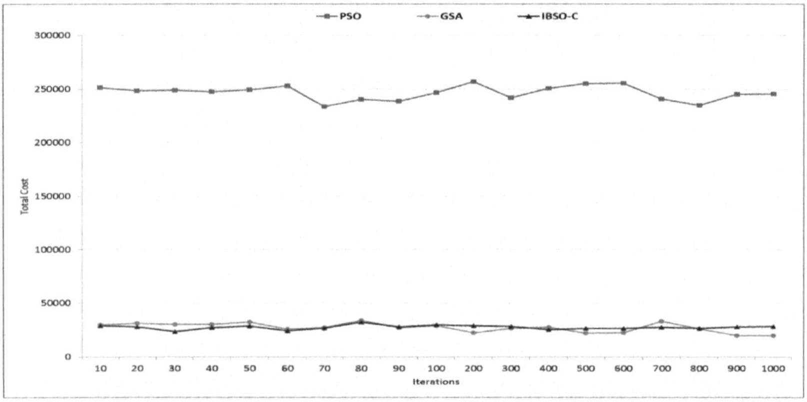

Fig. 5. Comparison of total cost v/s number of iterations for GSA, PSO and proposed IBSO-C on 15 cloudlets

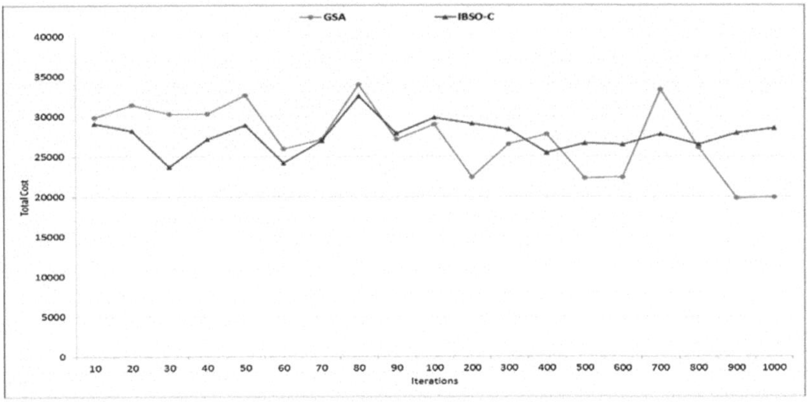

Fig. 6. Comparison of total cost v/s number of iterations for GSA and proposed IBSO-C on 15 cloudlets

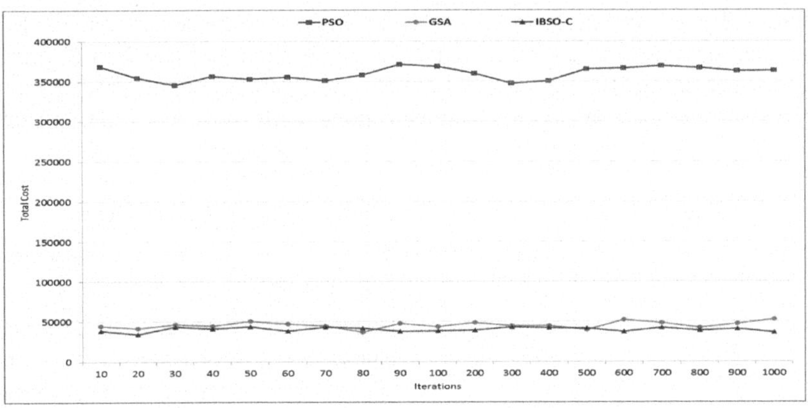

Fig. 7. Comparison of total cost v/s number of iterations for GSA, PSO and proposed IBSO-C on 20 cloudlets

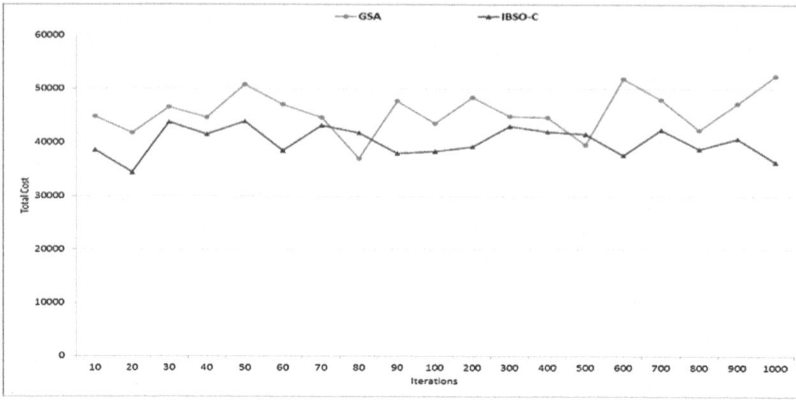

Fig. 8. Comparison of total cost v/s number of iterations for GSA and proposed IBSO-C on 20 cloudlets

Additionally, we also perform the statistical analysis of the performance of IBSO-C and calculate parameters like mean, maximum, minimum and standard deviation for total cost when run on 10, 15 and 20 cloudlets on iterations ranging from 10 to 1000. The statistical analysis values are tabulated along with those for PSO and GSA in Table 4.

Table 4. Statistical analysis of total cost on PSO, GSA and IBSO-C

	Cloudlets	PSO	GSA	IBSO-C
Mean	10	149119.782	24842.390	22915.209
	15	246493.939	27247.733	27605.688
	20	359677.772	45663.909	40147.432
Minimum	10	143482.749	19760.956	19360.000
	15	233301.076	19760.956	23684.151
	20	345540.580	36958.024	34358.821
Maximum	10	155538.952	33288.008	27830.000
	15	257046.548	33911.399	32483.221
	20	371324.589	52452.208	43901.034
Standard deviation	10	4187.166	3618.570	2875.435
	15	6849.873	4359.893	2008.918
	20	7944.934	3956.376	2689.588

Figures 9 and 11 depict that the proposed algorithm IBSO-C is better than the existing approaches PSO and GSA for load scheduling in cloud, based on mean and standard deviation. Since performance of IBSO-C is quite superior to that of PSO and close to that of GSA, the comparison between GSA and IBSO-C is shown more clearly in Figs. 10 and 12.

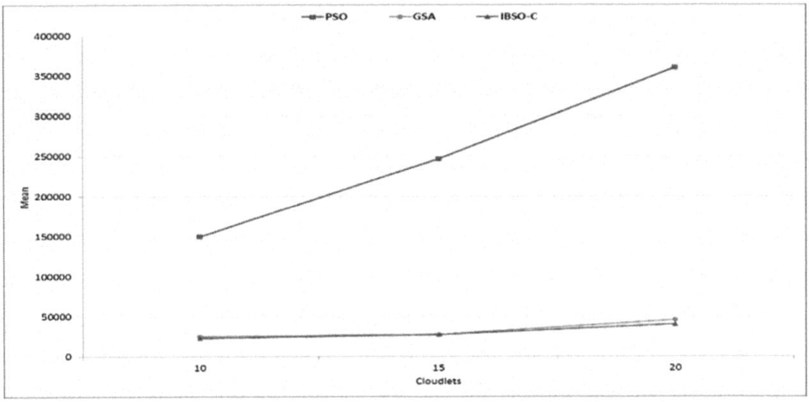

Fig. 9. Comparison of mean v/s cloudlets for GSA, PSO and proposed IBSO-C

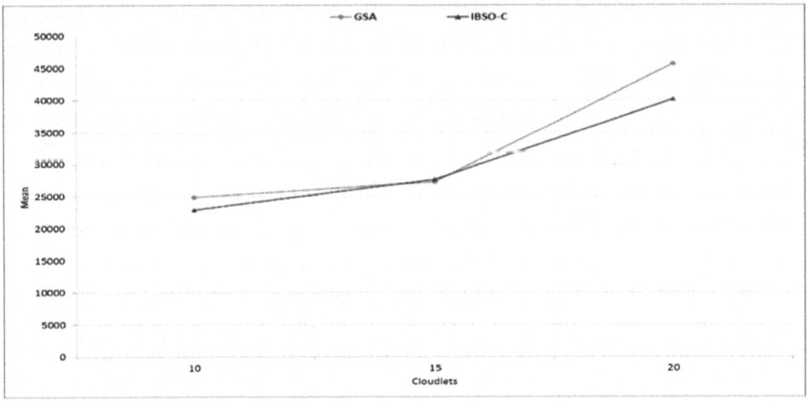

Fig. 10. Comparison of mean v/s cloudlets for GSA and proposed IBSO-C

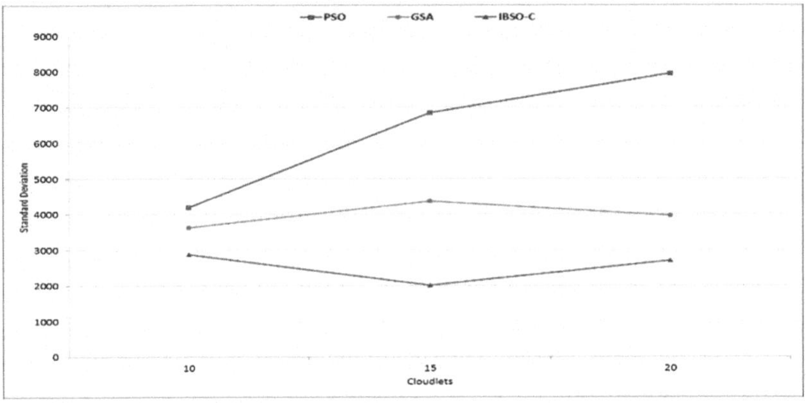

Fig. 11. Comparison of standard deviation v/s cloudlets for GSA, PSO and proposed IBSO-C

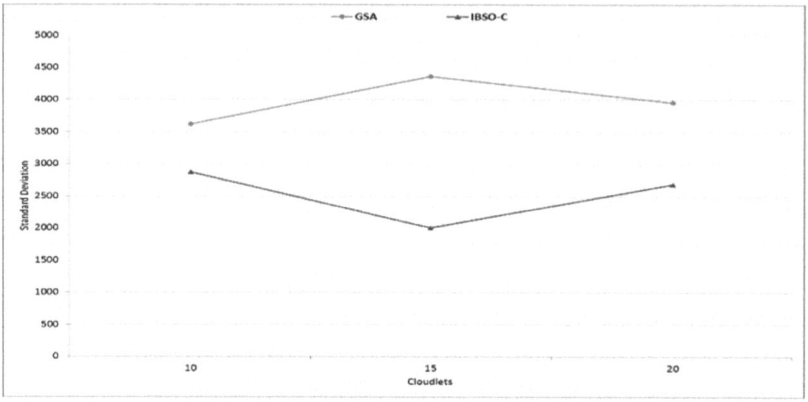

Fig. 12. Comparison of standard deviation v/s cloudlets for GSA and proposed IBSO-C

Thus, the proposed algorithm IBSO-C provides better results than the existing algorithms PSO and GSA for load scheduling in the cloud computing as evident from the results. The IBSO-C is better than the existing approaches of PSO and GSA for load scheduling in cloud, when compared on several parameters like minimum, maximum etc over total cost.

5 Conclusion and Future work

In this paper, a new improved version of Bee Swarm optimization technique based on foraging behavior of bees, the Improved Bee Swarm optimization in cloud algorithm (IBSO-C algorithm) has been presented. It has been proposed for fulfilling the purpose of load scheduling in cloud using swarm-intelligence of honey bees for search space optimization. It has been simulated and analyzed on a number of cloudlets and varying number of iterations. The proposed algorithm IBSO-C gives a better performance by minimizing the total cost than existing load scheduling algorithms in cloud like PSO and GSA when tested experimentally using 10, 15 and 20 cloudlets and a set of 10 to 1000 iterations. It has also been compared to the mentioned algorithms on parameters like mean and standard deviation. The technique can be made more efficient in the future by optimizing the cost function further.

References

1. Wang, S.C., et al.: Towards a load balancing in a three-level cloud computing network. In: 3rd IEEE International Conference Computer Science and Information Technology (ICCSIT), vol. 1 pp. 108–113 (2010)
2. Easwarakumar, D.M.K.: A double min min algorithm for task metascheduler on hypercubic P2P grid systems. Int. J. Comput. Sci. Issues **7**(4), 8–18 (2010)
3. Kennedy, J., Eberhart, R.: Particle swarm optimization. In: IEEE International Conference on Neural Networks, vol. 4, pp. 1942–1948 (1995)

4. Li, G., Niua, P., Xiao, X.: Development and investigation of efficient artificial bee colony for numerical function optimization. Appl. Soft Comput. **12**, 320–332 (2012)
5. Cui, X., Potok, T.E., Palathingal, P.: Document clustering using particle swarm optimization. In: 2005 Proceedings of Swarm Intelligence Symposium, SIS 2005. IEEE (2005)
6. Karaboga, D., Akay, B.: A survey: algorithms simulating bee swarm intelligence. Artif. Intell. Rev. **31**, 61–85 (2009)
7. Yang, X.-S.: Engineering optimizations via nature-inspired virtual bee algorithms. In: Mira, J., Álvarez, J.R. (eds.) IWINAC 2005. LNCS, vol. 3562, pp. 317–323. Springer, Heidelberg (2005). https://doi.org/10.1007/11499305_33
8. Wedde, H.R., Farooq, M.: The wisdom of the hive applied to mobile ad-hoc networks. In: 2005 Proceedings of Swarm Intelligence Symposium, SIS 2005, pp. 341–348. IEEE (2005)
9. Pham, D.T., Ghanbarzadeh, A., Koc, E, Otri, S., Rahim, S., Zaidi, M.: The bees algorithm. Technical report, Manufacturing Engineering Centre, Cardiff University, UK (2005)
10. Karaboga, D.: An idea based on honey bee swarm for numerical optimization. Technical report. Computer Engineering Department, Engineering Faculty, Erciyes University (2005)
11. Banharnsakun, A., Achalakul, T., Sirinaovakul, B.: The best-so-far selection in artificial bee colony algorithm. Appl. Soft Comput. **11**, 2888–2901 (2011)
12. Secui, D.C.: A new modified artificial bee colony algorithm for the economic dispatch problem. Energy Convers. Manag. **89**, 43–62 (2015)
13. Zhu, G., Kwong, S.: Gbest-guided artificial bee colony algorithm for numerical function optimization. Appl. Math. Comput. **217**, 3166–3173 (2010)
14. Akbari, R., Mohammadi, A., Ziarati, K.: A powerful bee swarm optimization algorithm. IEEE (2009)

Simulation and Application Performance Evaluation Using GPU Through CUDA C & Deep Learning in TensorFlow

Ajeet Kumar[1(✉)] and Abhishek Khanna[2]

[1] Birla Institute of Technology and Science, Pilani, India
ajeet108msit@gmail.com
[2] Maharaja Surajmal Institute of Technology, GGSIPU, Delhi, India

Abstract. GPUs have as of late pulled in the consideration of numerous application designers as product information parallel coprocessors. The most current eras of GPU design give less demanding programmability and expanded all-inclusive statement while keeping up the gigantic memory data transfer capacity and computational force of conventional GPUs. This open door ought to divert endeavors in GPU examination to setting up standards and systems that permit proficient mapping of calculation to design equipment. The project, shows the GeForce GTX 560 Ti processors association, highlights, and summed up improvement systems. Method to execution on the platform is by utilizing gigantic multithreading and use vast quantity of centers, cover up global storage inactivity. In order to achieve it, designers confront the test of striking the right harmony between every string's asset utilization and the quantity of all the while dynamic strings. The assets to oversee incorporate the quantity of resistors also the degree of on-chip storage utilized per string, given strings per multiprocessor, also worldwide memory transmission capacity. The researcher likewise get expanded execution on rearranging, gets to off-chip storage and join solicitations for similar else adjoining storage areas therefore, implement established enhancements by diminishing quantity of implemented function. Such methodologies are used over an assortment of utilizations and areas and accomplish between a 10.5X to 14X application speedup. The similar result was achieved with the single core GPU using deep learning technique in TensorFlow framework.

Used Terms: Design · Performance · Languages · TensorFlow

Keywords: GPU parallel processing · Deep learning · Neural nets
TensorFlow

1 Introduction

Because of proceeded with interest for programmability, modern GPUs, for example, the graphics card GTX 560 is planned dynamic designed chip utilizing good portion of cores present on our dynamic chip [16]. As we proceed with expansion of better equipment interfaces, programming them doesn't require particular programming dialects or

B. Panda et al. (Eds.): REDSET 2017, CCIS 799, pp. 414–424, 2018.
https://doi.org/10.1007/978-981-10-8527-7_34

execution through representation APIs, likewise with past GPU eras. This makes a cheap, significantly parallel framework accessible to a more extensive group of use engineers.

The programming model of NVIDIA CUDA [3] is made by creating application program interface specific to given stage. In given paradigm, the framework comprises a server which generally, a conventional Central Processing Unit also, single or multiple register gadgets which generally possess huge information simultaneous active sub processors. Every single CUDA gadget execution capability reinforces the One-Code

Many Source based model [8], generally accessible in simultaneous handling frameworks, when most simultaneous strings depend on the same code, despite the fact that can't be taken after very similar way it gets implemented. Most of the strings have similar worldwide location area.

Compute Unified Device Architecture writing computer programs is finished by laid American National Standards Institute C reached out through watchwords who assign information correspondent capacities, known as pieces, with related information mapping to figure out gadgets capability. Pieces portray the work of a solitary string and commonly are conjured on a great many strings. These strings can, inside engineer characterized groups termed string squares, dispense information merge the research activities by implicit geometry. Compute Unified Device Architecture execution time likewise gives storage capacities to gadget memory administration and information exchanges across the server but also process gadgets. It can be observed clearly Compute Unified Device Architecture in a programming situation empowering programming designers so that they can detach code parts which are main source of information dispensation of implementation by Sub processor particular in abusing huge information dispensation. The outlining feature of Compute Unified Device Architecture code is briefly discussed here [5].

Main forms in programming Compute Unified Device Architecture instruments as well as execution time graphics gtx 560 was made possible pre-release checking. To Compute Unified Device Architecture, the GeForce 560 Ti comprises of 2^4 gushing chips, every 2^3 preparing modules come with, primitive registers, with 2^4 kB integrated in the circuit.

The design permits proficient information dispensing as well as concurrency within tasks which is similar task Capsule [14].

Novel part in the design with respect to few other simultaneous stages was adaptability of task by basic assets, for example, memory module else nearby storage unit, converted into strings. Every SM generally implement varying strings, therefore neighborhood asset is isolated within strings on calculation basis by the software engineer. Such adaptability permits additionally tuning of utilization execution yet changes the suspicions designers can make when performing improvements.

As a community oriented exertion amongst industry and the scholars, an arrangement of finish arithmetic calculations were transferred to be assessed by Compute Unified Device Architecture framework. A few applications inquire about gatherings mentioned within the domain of pharma pictorial data, sub-atomic flow, arithmetic science, neural nets, but also logical perception added to this effort.

The accompanying is the significant standards while determining the program executed by the framework:

1. Support no burden task planning for achieving conceal storage dormancy. While using GeForce GTx 560 Ti there are 128 execution units accessible to utilize, needing many threads to totally possess them. Furthermore, threads can be famished of information because of the delay in reaching the main storage. The common reasoning in Compute Unified Device Architecture which leads to enduring idleness is for producing & keeping up a great many task running. Leading to interesting utilization fast memory so that it can conceal storage lags in processing chip schemes.
2. Optimal utilization of on-chip memory to diminish transfer speed use and repetitive execution. The working memory inside cores comprises fundamentally of storage unit also the embedded code in the device as known as shared storage. The features include high processing power and low response time, constrained limit storage units that apportioned along with other task module is appointed in a similar State Machine according to execution time.
3. Threads inside a thread can interact by means of synchronization, yet can't see work done in main transmission tool be it any modular task. Similar characteristics stays away from requirement to code the equipment assets, empowers implementation of similar Compute Unified Device Architecture code crosswise over processors with a differing quantity of cores, and makes the equipment versatile. In any case, it likewise constrains the sorts of parallelism that can be used inside a single kernel request.

The author initially examines the similar research Sect. 2. Section 3 presents dynamic task division paradigm & running the tool. Section 4 shows the improvement procedure with extensive execution review, utilizing incremental pattern kernels. Section 5 illustrate a few examined applications execution and enhancement data. We finish up with some last articulations and recommendations for further scope of the project.

2 Related Work

Information dialects that were programmed parallelization were viewed as a transitional method between programmed parallelization attempts [7, 28] and unambiguous programmed parallelization version, for example, Open Multi-Processing [15] which help calculating using parallelization. Formula translation 90 [6] had principal broadly that utilized programming language and affected after information parallel languages by presenting cluster of task statements. Like cluster assignments in Formula translation 90 is one of the main execution step of the individual thread's exclusive guideline which is running at the same time on a CPU+GPU in Compute Unified Device Architecture programming framework. Afterward, High-Performance Formula translation 90 [5] was presented as simultaneous code executing block with single program, multiple data. Be that as it may, unpredictability of information transfer and messages improvement procedures, as talked about in the last two parts of [6], were a difficult to-illuminate request. Thus, application designers turned out to be more required in expressly taking care of information dispersion and communication; packet passing libraries, for example, a prototype using versatile parallelization framework [23] turned quite famous. Also, in Compute Unified Device Architecture programming, the designer unequivocally oversees the way data was presented in storage in collaboration with DRAM, Caching information, task manipulation inside task blocks and its different properties.

Eagerness for General-purpose computing on graphics processing units programming is currently driven by the latest enhancements in the programmability of design equipment. Graphics processing unit is used with Stream [9] spilling co-processor. Animating operator [26] is also a good example of model that uses parallelization on data to implement generally valuable estimation on the Graphics processing unit. The C# library developed by Microsoft gives data abstract the capability to make an attempt at data parallel shows. Data parallel cluster estimation is clearly amassed to shader programs by the execution time.

By and large, past Graphics processing unit programming frameworks constrain the size and intricacy of Graphics processing unit code because of their hidden representation application program interface based usage. Compute Unified Device Architecture bolsters parts with much bigger code sizes with another equipment interface and direction storing.

Past Graphics processing unit eras and application program interfaces used with them additionally confined the permitted access designs for memory in GPU, as a rule permitting just consecutive keeps in touch with a direct exhibit. This is because of points of confinement in design application program interfaces and comparing limits in the particular pixel and vertex processors. The GeForce GTx 560 Ti takes into account general tending to of memory through a brought together prototype, which empowers Compute Unified Device Architecture to perform unhindered disperse accumulate operations.

Customary Graphics processing units additionally gave constrained reserve data transfer capacity. Fatahalian et al. examine in [11] that low transmission capacity reserve plans on Graphics processing units limit the sorts of utilizations from profiting from the computational force accessible on these designs. Work talked about in [12] utilizes an investigative store execution forecast model for Graphics processing unit-based calculations. Their outcomes demonstrate that memory streamlining systems intended for Central processing unit-based calculations may not be straightforwardly pertinent to Graphics processing units. With the presentation of sensibly measured low-inactivity, on-chip memory in new eras of Graphics processing units, this issue and its advancements have turned out to be less basic.

3 Architecture Overview

The GeForce GTx 560 Ti GPU is satisfactorily a flowing design of processor focuses capability to make changes into the main storage location. It considers extensive & versatile paradigm compare to past periods of Graphics, which leads to less requesting to architects so that they can realize simultaneously incoming information bits. Here we discuss NVIDIA's Compute Unified Device Architecture (CUDA) and the major small scale architectural segments of the GeForce GTx 560 Ti. A complete portrayal can be found in [3, 14]. It should be seen that this designing, though more revealed than past GPU structures, still has purposes of intrigue that wasn't mapped or straightforwardly revealed.

3.1 Threading Paradigm

ANSI C based Compute Unified Device Architecture framework was connected to a couple of catch phrases and models. The Graphics module work as a sub processor which processes data parallel bit code. The customer supplies a singular source program fusing both host (CPU) and piece (GPU) code. It's detached & totaled as showed up in Fig. 1. Compute Unified Device Architecture framework program includes various stages that are performed on either GPU or CPU. The phases that show for all intents and purposes no information stream are executed (Processor) have, forwarded in American National Standards Institute C & assembled my native IDE as showed up in Fig. 1. Stages that show simultaneously information processing is realized similar to piece limits in the device (GPU) code. A bit limit describes the code to be processed by each of the enormous number of threads to be invoked for a data parallel stage. This bit limits is requested by the Unified Device Architecture framework C framework & processor program compiler. A couple of constraints on bit limits: no iteration be there, constant object is not introduced.

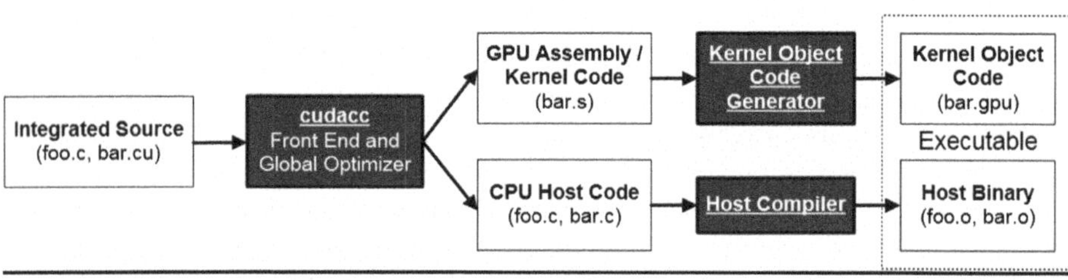


```
> cpu/ngpu
         [,1]     [,2]     [,3]     [,4]     [,5]     [,6]     [,7]     [,8]      [,9]
arr  1.500154 2.000298 2.799169 4.579312 7.200042 6.900684 9.266783 9.792201 10.001151
arr2 1.535290 1.963407 2.841368 4.419769 7.524802 6.606455 8.473858 9.029490  9.804023
arr3 1.560618 1.957248 2.959253 4.480124 7.652461 6.636712 8.510010 9.315964  9.849413
> cpu
       [,1]   [,2]   [,3]   [,4]    [,5]    [,6]    [,7]    [,8]     [,9]
arr   4.877  6.721  9.436 15.419  27.664  56.489 122.164 253.383  503.878
arr2  9.832 12.931 18.861 30.987  55.217 108.696 217.829 455.610  954.755
arr3 19.489 25.912 39.290 63.452 110.073 215.056 433.151 930.730 1908.767
> ngpu
        [,1]   [,2]   [,3]    [,4]    [,5]   [,6]   [,7]   [,8]    [,9]
garr   3.251  3.360  3.371  3.3671  3.8422  8.186 13.183 25.876  50.382
garr2  6.404  6.586  6.638  7.0110  7.3380 16.453 25.706 50.458  97.384
garr3 12.488 13.239 13.277 14.1630 14.3840 32.404 50.899 99.907 193.795
```

Fig. 1. CUDA compilation flow & inputs matrix

Strings implementing code in GTx 560 Ti are dealt with into a three-level hierarchy of management. At the biggest sum, all strings simultaneously implementation block organize outline structure; Every task runs in a similar bit limit. Each framework involves various string pieces. A framework can be at most 216 −1 hinders in both of two estimations, and each section has novel directions.

A programmer in this phase could organize Compute Unified Device Architecture program and obtain social description. PTX are not anonymously implemented, instead set up by implementation constraints.

In outline, there are hard breaking points to the recollections, strings, and aggregate transmission capacity accessible to an application running on the GeForce GTx 560 Ti. Dealing with these cutoff points is basic while upgrading applications, however procedures for keeping away from one breaking point can bring about different breaking points to be hit. They can likewise diminish the quantity of string hinders that can run at the same time. Moreover, dealing with the conduct of strings therefore, those in similar situation contort take after similar command ways and weight contiguous qualities deriving from main storage moreover enhance execution.

4 Optimization and Implementation

The fragment makes use of miniaturized scale benchmark and shows most ideal modifying pool functionalities utilizations are essential to fulfilling profitable implementation resource use & thusly unrivaled on the GTx 560 Ti. There are three fundamental norms to consider while propelling an application for the stage. In any case, the floating-point throughput of an application depends on upon the rate of its rules that are floating point operations. The GPU is prepared for issuing 172.8 billion operations for consistently on the SPs. These fuse interlaced increments incorporate tasks, consider as separate tasks to compute the turnaround time. In case quarter of task's bearing interlink which are intertwined increment incorporates, at that point its execution can be at most 2 * 1/4 FP * 172.8 billion operations for each second = 86.4 GFLOPS. This execution is accomplished when the SPs are totally had, which is achievable in an application that has various strings, does not have various synchronizations, and does not push overall memory transmission limit. In this condition, diminishing the number of rules that don't add to data computation all around brings about piece speedup. Nevertheless, intensifying computational capability can challenge, as a result of discontinuities in the upgrade space [22].

Another, while trying to reach in a situation in the task where it has most erratic behavior, fundamental unease habitually was regulating overall storage idleness. To achieve this we started making good amount of strings so the SPs survives had also various string is marking out for main storage gets to. In effectively communicated, strings requires an high level in granularity compare to ordinary Quadcore implementation so that it can create good amount strings. Required strings related with on upon main storage access ratio and lethargy task done by the core: tools involving little rate in running these task also need less strings for fulfilling SP overall inhabitance. Purpose of control on the integrated chips as well as on pool storage open for every SM forces dynamic amount the strings, occasionally revealing memory inertness. We show one situation where the usage of additional registers in a tried upgrade grants one less string square to be reserved per SM, decreasing execution.

At last, worldwide memory transmission capacity affects the turnaround time of the framework. Expanding strings quantity is of no use in execution while these are circumstance. Lightening weight over worldwide storage transmission capacity for the most part includes utilizing extra integrated chips and main storage reutilizes information, that thusly be restricted in quantity at the same time executing strings. Adjusting the utilization of these assets is regularly non-natural and a few applications will keep running into asset limits other than direction issue on this engineering (Fig. 2).

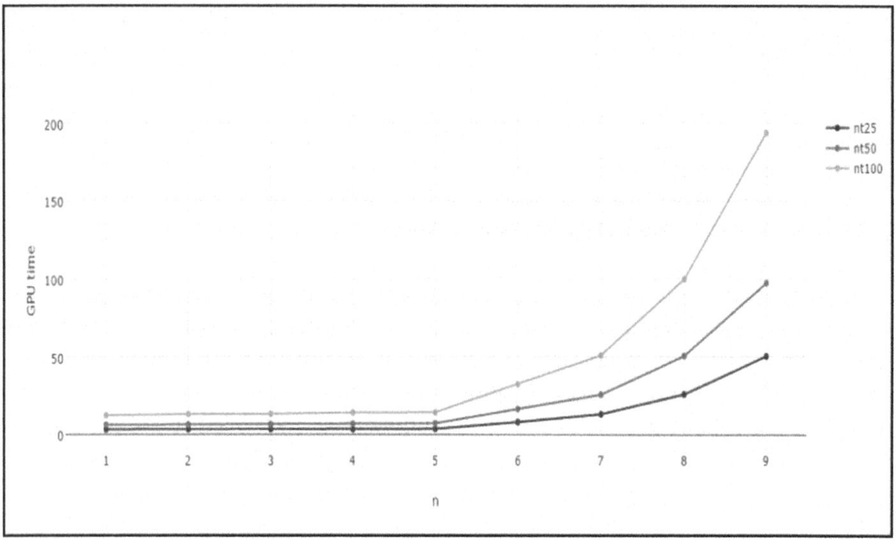

Fig. 2. Performance using GPU hardware

The case we use to delineate these standards is a lattice increase bit. In framework increase, the estimation of a component in the outcome network is figured by processing the dab result of the comparing line of the main grid and section of the second lattice. For this illustration, we accept thickly populated info grids. We break down a few code adaptations and their supported execution while duplicating double grids that has tallness and width of 4096 components. The expressed asset use is for CUDA form 0.8; later forms of CUDA may have diverse uses.

4.1 Existing Workaround

Let's start from straightforward rendition in pattern iteration. Grid iteration kernel makes single task that outcome component to duplicate them, to aggregate a $(2^2 * 2^{10}) * (2^2 * 2^{10})$ strings. Multiple strings made trying to conceal the idleness of comprehensive storage location by location covering runtime. Such strings covers up a grouping which heaps dual esteems in worldwide storage, increases it, but also aggregates esteem. This code utilizes ten registers for each string, enabling the greatest of 768 strings to be planned per SM. For ease, we gather them as three string squares of 256 strings each.

Processing the for this code takes 10.58 Giga floating point operations per second, seems lesser to compare exceptionally enhanced system defined code working on processor using Single instruction, multiple data developments. Taking a gander at the **Parallel Thread Execution in the program**, which leads to approximation that there is only single interlaced image incorporate compare to 2^3 tasks inward circle, in normal theoretical turnaround of 39.8 Giga floating point operations per second. Since the obtained reading show largest outrageous value strings arranged, the congestion seems, from every angle, a main storage information exchange limit. A task's quarter implemented in midst of the circle are troubles from off-chip memory, which would require an information exchange limit of 166 Gigabytes per second (132 SPs * 1/3 headings * 3 B/rule * 2.05 GHz) totally uses the resources therefore a proper planning for updating part this is done for information reusability with decrease main storage get to.

4.2 Use of Local Storage

The figurings of two outcome parts in a similar line or section share a substantial bit of their Information, past program gets to overall storage for every module for each string. An average progression for this sort of get to illustration so that information pooling can be achieved by methods [2]. Nvidia GTx 560 Ti, developers can utilize shared memory to amortize the overall idleness cost when qualities are reused. With the help of less turnaround square sync qualities pooled among tasks: single string gets data fraction & afterward sync with the goal which different strings of similar module uses. At last, lets likewise exploit contiguity in fundamental memory gets to when stacking in values as a square, lessening the cycles expected to get to the information (Fig. 3).

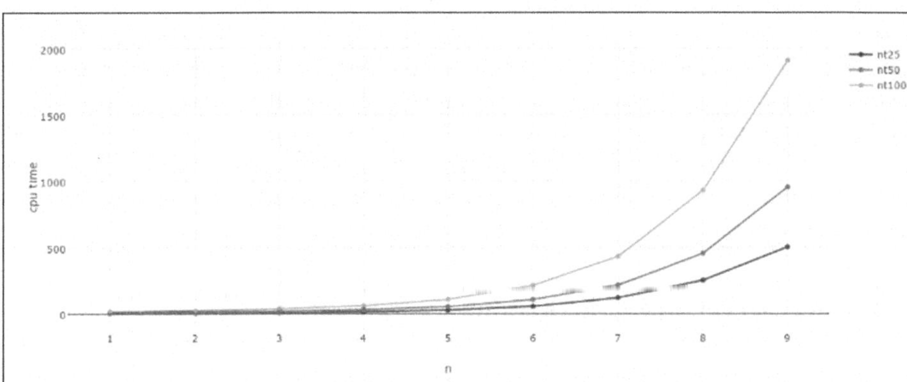

Fig. 3. Performance using CPU hardware alone

Amid implementation tasks run inside double info array which walk crosswise over 2^4 adjacent lines, sections within information grid. Every 2^6 tasks are fixing in particular arrangement of array. This stacks component within facilitate dual info tiles for pool storage, therefore agreeably tasks stack entire array. The heap is sorted out for exploiting main permission to get blend. The tasks at that point sync so that it can build up uniformity, that empowers every task, stack the greater part of its sources of info possessing module comes from the main storage. At long last, tasks compute incomplete speck item to contribute into pool storage inside the circle.

Different tools can be better execution on little array capacity to enable bigger quantity of planned tasks (Fig. 4).

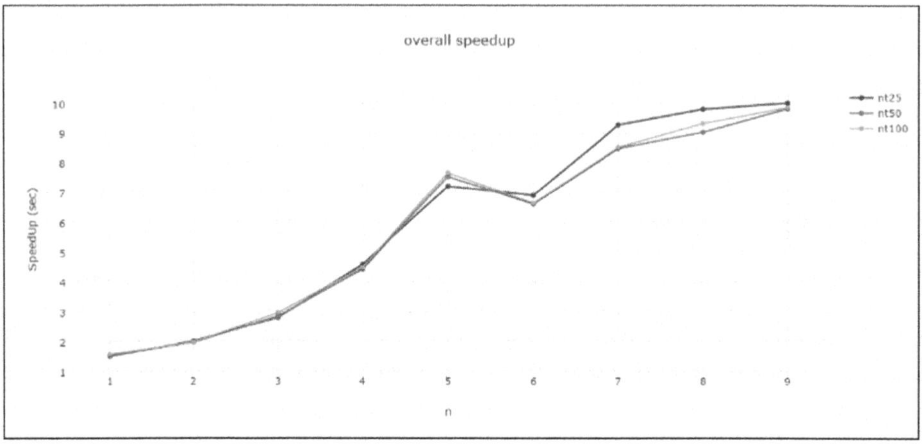

Fig. 4. Speedup performance of matrix multiplication (1-D)

We tried leveraging the power of GPUs to accelerate machine learning and deep learning algorithms using TensorFlow.

Ran a TensorFlow Docker picture on the framework and ran a machine learning model with and without GPUs. We introduced git library utilizing apt get command. [3] Deploy a dynamic, conveyed TensorFlow on DC/OS from the Universe. TensorFlow on DC/OS powerfully devours and discharges resources on the cluster when completed. Ran various TensorFlows on a same cluster with various resource prerequisites. The convolutional network was prepared to be tested, we ran it and measured the execution time. The outcome was much closer to 10 times quicker than CPUs processing time.

5 Future Scope and Conclusion

This research shows an execution examination of Nvidia Graphics 560 GTCxTi configuration through CUDA-C. This GPU is also ready to do great execution on a course of action of different non-outlines applications. This activity gives common benchmarks for streamlining applications for this sort of configuration, to be particular having gainful code, utilizing various strings to cover dormancy, and using block memories to ease load on overall memory exchange speed. We also present an application suite CUDA toolbox, exhibiting the task blocks which shows less overall storage permission of streamlining immense perform between 10.5X to 14X application less overhead than the CPU running time when its not restricted by limited resource allocation.

We experience a couple of critical outline systems. To start with, and preeminent is the principal significance of uncovering adequate measures of fine-grained parallelism to exploit devices like the Tesla-engineering GPU. Following is the significance of blocking calculations, a procedure that actually fits the CUDA string block deliberation and empowers information format and get to designs with huge memory temporal locality. Third, the productivity of information parallel projects where strings of a twist take after a similar execution way, along these lines completely using the GPU's processor centers. At long last, is the advantage of the on-chip, per-square shared memory given by the Tesla framework, which gives rapid, low-idleness scratchpad space that is crucial to the execution of numerous proficient algorithms.

We tried leveraging the power of GPUs to accelerate machine learning and deep learning algorithms using TensorFlow.

Ran a TensorFlow Docker picture on the framework and ran a machine learning model with and without GPUs. We introduced git library utilizing apt get command. [3] Deploy a dynamic, conveyed TensorFlow on DC/OS from the Universe. TensorFlow on DC/OS powerfully devours and discharges resources on the cluster when completed. Ran various TensorFlows on a same cluster with various resource prerequisites. The convolutional network was prepared to be tested, we ran it and measured the execution time. The outcome was much closer to 10 times quicker than CPUs processing time.

References

1. Google TensorFlow Opensource Repository. https://github.com/tensorflow/tensorflow/blob/master/RELEASE.md
2. Buck, I.: Brook Specification v0.2, October 2003
3. CUDA benchmark Suite. http://www.crhc.uiuc.edu/impact/cudabench.html
4. Kennedy, K., Allen, R.: Automatic translation of Fortran programs to vector form. ACM Trans. Prog. Lang. Syst. **9**(4), 491–542 (1987)
5. Atallah, M.J. (ed.): Algorithms and Theory of Computation Handbook. CRC Press LLC, Boco Raton (1998)
6. Kennedy, K., Callahan, D., Carr, S.: Improving register allocation for subscripted variables. ACM SIGPLAN Not. **9**(4), 328–342 (2004)
7. Akeley, K., Glanville, R.S., Kilgard, M.J., Mark, W.R.: Cg: a system for programming graphics hardware in a C-like language. In: ACM SIGGRAPH 2003 Papers, pp. 896–907 (2003)
8. Loveman, D.B.: High performance Fortran. IEEE Parallel Distrib. Technol.: Syst. Technol. **1**(1), 25–42 (1993)
9. Rothberg, E.E., Lam, M.S., Wolf, M.E.: The cache performance and optimizations of blocked algorithms. In: Proceedings of 4th International Conference on Architectural Support for Programming Languages and Operating Systems, pp. 63–74, April 1991
10. Allen, J.R., Kennedy, K.: Optimizing Compilers for Modern Architectures: A Dependence-Based Approach. Morgan Kaufmann Publishers Inc., Burlington (2002)
11. Gray, J., Govindaraju, N.K., Manocha, D., Larsen, S.: A memory model for scientific algorithms on graphics processors. In: Proceedings of 2006 ACM/IEEE Conference on Supercomputing, no. 89 (2006)
12. Sugerman, J., Fatahalian, K., Hanrahan, P.: Understanding the efficiency of GPU algorithms for matrix-matrix multiplication. In: Proceedings of ACM SIGGRAPH/EUROGRAPHICS Conference on Graphics Hardware, pp. 133–137 (2004)

13. Brainerd, W.S., Adams, J.C., Smith, B.T., Martin, J.T., Wagener, J.L.: Fortran 90 Handbook: Complete ANSI/ISO Reference. Intertext Publications Inc./McGraw-Hill Inc., New York (1992)
14. ECE 498AL1: Programming Massively Parallel Processors, Fall 2007. http://courses.ece.uiuc.edu/ece498/al1/
15. The PeakStream Platform: High productivity software development for multi-core processors. Technical report (2006)
16. NVIDIA CUDA. http://developer.nvidia.com/object/cuda.html

Significance of DITMC Technique for Capacity Enhancement in GSM and CDMA Networks

Hemant Purohit[1(✉)], Parneet Kaur[2(✉)], and Kanika Joshi[3(✉)]

[1] Department of ECE, Jodhpur Institute of Engineering & Technology, Jodhpur, Rajasthan, India
hemantpurohit2006@hotmail.com
[2] Department of Electronics and Communication Engineering, MBM Engineering College, Jodhpur, Rajasthan, India
parneetkaur92@outlook.com
[3] BIT Mesra Extension Centre, Jaipur, Rajasthan, India
kanika.karesh@gmail.com

Abstract. By the end of 2020 heavy data traffic flood will dominate the speech traffic and the probability of bandwidth and capacity saturation (in GSM and CDMA networks) seems to be high. During the last decade various traffic models and techniques have been developed in order to optimize bandwidth and capacity of mobile networks. It has been analysed and found that most economic and efficient method to optimize the limited channel capacity and bandwidth in GSM and CDMA networks is to use the silence period during any speech conversation which can be utilized to transmit data as well as other channel allocation. Moreover the simulation studies show that this concept seems to be the most optimized, efficient and economic way to incorporate more users in GSM and CDMA networks. This paper proposes the mathematical model to incorporate DITMC technique for capacity enhancement in GSM and CDMA networks.

Keywords: Blocking probability · Channel utilisation · Congestion Data interleaving · Erlang · Handover

1 Introduction

The Traffic Analysis is the most significant and vital part of Mobile Communication or any other communication network as far as its requirements and capabilities are concerned. During the past decade, a number of traffic models have already been proposed for analyzing the traffic characteristics of a communication network whether it is wireless or wired. As the number of users is exponentially increasing in this century there is indeed a need of a perfect traffic model that can aid in avoiding the expected congestion problem as well as enhancing the capacity of mobile communication networks. The factors to be considered for a reliable traffic model are service, cost and accuracy. The traffic model designed for mobile communication networks must be applicable for both real time (say voice) and non-real time data. The traffic model design must have a 'Goodness-of-fit' i.e. the results obtained from the model must be

B. Panda et al. (Eds.): REDSET 2017, CCIS 799, pp. 425–433, 2018.
https://doi.org/10.1007/978-981-10-8527-7_35

close to the actual data obtained. The traffic model is the requirement for a robust and reliable network leading to better network performance and good QoS (Quality of Service). It should be the best effort in order to maximize the capacity, increase the throughput, minimize the redundancy and latency providing high reliability of services independent of bandwidth available as well as occurrence of failures. There are different traffic models amongst which only few models are generally employed for real life environment. It has been analysed and found that most economic and efficient method to optimize the limited channel capacity and bandwidth in GSM and CDMA networks is to use the silence period during any speech conversation which can be utilized to transmit data as well as other channel allocation. Moreover the simulation studies [3, 7, 8] show that this concept seems to be the most optimized, efficient and economic way to incorporate more users in GSM and CDMA networks.

2 Data Interleaving Technique in Mobile Communication (DITMC)

The Data Interleaving Technique in mobile communication involves utilizing the redundancy in voice bytes transmission having silence period bytes as it is quite often. Whenever the repetition of bytes is more than three, a Battery OFF Code (Data Start Code) is sent so as to indicate the receiver side about the repetition and when the repetition is over a Battery ON Code (Data Stop Code) is sent to indicate the end of interleaving process and the normal bytes transmission continues. This method of data interleaving [3, 7] possesses the essential attributes like speech delay of 2 samples i.e. only 250 μs time, better channel utilization enhancement, no handover, suppression of the transmission of redundant (repetitive) message codes, making channel space available for additional data transmission, detection of much smaller duration speech pauses which are generally more frequent, negligible inbuilt delay in this system and is insignificant for real time applications (Fig. 1).

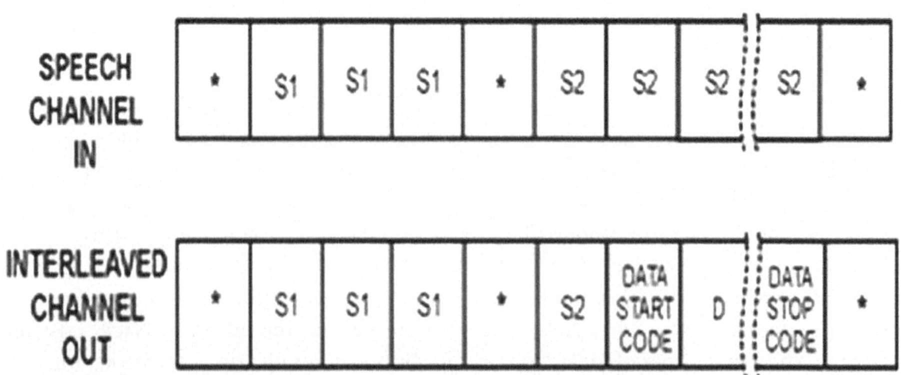

Fig. 1. Philosophy of data interleaving symbols: S1, S2 = repetitive speech bytes, * = speech byte (S), D = data byte (S) [7].

However, the two bytes delay in transmission is neither noticeable by the listener nor effects the operation of the system in any adverse way. Moreover the speech quality maintained by interleaved system is far superior to that of the systems using speech interpolation [6].

3 Traffic and Capacity Analysis in GSM Network

The traffic analysis of GSM Networks [1, 5] is based on the Erlang-B formula for calculation of blocking probability and the expected accuracy. As in mobile networks the users are mobile i.e. moving from one cell to another or within the cell, the complexity of model is always there, so Erlang-B model is used even though it is designed traditionally for fixed networks. The congestion or outage on any piece of the network (network unavailability) can prevent a subscriber from making a call. The following are the various elements for generating congestion due to which the user can be prevented to make a call.

- Congestion on traffic channels (TCH allocation failure).
- Congestion on control channels (SDCCH allocation failure).
- Drop on control channels (Call Establishment Failure).

There are various parameters and definitions used for each cell during a Peak Hour in GSM network which are as follows:

Traffic: It is represented in Erlangs (minutes of calls). Traffic counters are registered in BSC's. The types of traffic used are ***Flow*** and ***Offered.***
TCH: Each call uses a TCH which represents a voice channel. There are eight channels defined (most for traffic channels and some for control channels) for each frequency.
Percentage of TCH utilization: Number of minutes of calls that occurred at the same time over the maximum traffic permitted with a grade of service (GoS) equals to 2%.
Percentage of TCH congestion: It represents the percentage of the number of calls with congestion or no availability of traffic channel, divided by the total number of calls attempted.
Percentage of CCH congestion: It represents the percentage of the number of calls with congestion, or no availability of control channel, divided by the total number of control channels attempted.
Percentage of CCH dropped: It represents the percentage of the number of dropped CCH divided by the total number of established CCH.
Mean Holding Time: It is the mean time that a call is prolonged. The traffic intensity is defined as:

$$A = \frac{\lambda}{\mu} \tag{1}$$

Where λ is the call arrival rate from users
μ is the average call departure rate of users.

The Blocking probability (P_b) is expressed in terms of A (offered traffic in Erlangs) and N (Number of channels) as shown in the Eq. 2. This theory is based upon some assumptions like call service time is assumed to be exponentially distributed, message length is assumed to be exponentially distributed, calls are assumed to be of random arrival, system to be assumed in statistical equilibrium and most importantly the offered traffic is known. As a consequence of these constraints or assumptions, the Erlang-B model [1] is restricted to be used only at the initial stage for designing and architecture.

$$P_b = \frac{\frac{A^N}{N!}}{\sum_{k=0}^{N} \frac{A^k}{k!}} \tag{2}$$

The new arrival traffic is assumed to be Poisson while the handover traffic totally depends upon the total traffic of cell. In case of homogeneous case the flow balance property can be invoked. Consequently in case there is no handover or queuing of newly arrived calls the steady state blocking. P_b and handover failure probabilities P_{hf} are expressed as:

$$P_b = \frac{(A_n + A_h)^c \sum_{k=c}^{c+g} \frac{A_h^{k-c}}{k!}}{\sum_{k=0}^{c-1} \frac{(A_n + A_h)^k}{k!} + (A_n + A_h)^c \sum_{k=c}^{c+g} \frac{A_h^{k-c}}{k!}} \tag{3}$$

$$P_{hf} = \frac{(A_n + A_h)^c \frac{A_h^g}{(c+g)!}}{\sum_{k=0}^{c-1} \frac{(A_n + A_h)^k}{k!} + (A_n + A_h)^c \sum_{k=c}^{c+g} \frac{A_h^{k-c}}{k!}} \tag{4}$$

Where A_h is traffic due to handover calls g is guard channels

λ_h is the handover traffic
P_{hf} is the Handover failure probability
P_b is the Blocked calls probability
N is total number of channels per cell.

4 Traffic and Capacity Analysis in CDMA Network

The traffic analysis of CDMA networks [2, 4] includes the calculation of maximum traffic intensity supported with a specific blocking probability. It can be clearly understood with the ***soft*** capacity and ***hard*** capacity analysis. Traffic Intensity is measured in Erlangs as:

$$\text{Traffic Intensity in Erlangs} = \left[\frac{\text{Call Arrival rate in calls per second}}{\text{Call Departure rate in calls per second}}\right] \tag{5}$$

The capacity of CDMA networks can be ***soft*** as well as ***hard***. If the capacity is limited as a result of hardware then it is known as ***hard*** and is measured by Erlang-B formula. On the contrary side if the traffic intensity is constrained by the interfacing medium (air) then it is known as ***soft*** and is generally not measured by Erlang-B formula. It is a significant parameter to be considered for high bit rate real time applications like video streaming. The capacity of a CDMA network is measured in terms of bit energy to interference density ratio and also maintaining a lower bound on it. It is mathematically expressed in equation as follows [2]:

$$\left(\frac{E_b}{I_O}\right)_i = \frac{E_b}{\frac{\alpha(RE_b)(n_i-1+I_i)}{W}+N_O},\ \mathrm{i}=1,\ldots,\mathrm{M} \tag{6}$$

Where

W is spread signal bandwidth
R is information rate in bits per second
α is voice activity factor
n_i is number of users in cell i

In order to sustain the desired BER (Bit Error Rate) the above mentioned ratio has to be maintained above a specifically set threshold value. Let the threshold be Γ then the upper bound on the number of users in cell is expressed as follows:

$$n_i + I_i \leq \frac{W/R}{\alpha}\left(\frac{1}{\Gamma} - \frac{1}{E_b/N_o}\right) + 1\underline{\underline{\Delta}}c_{eff},\ \mathrm{i}=1,\ldots,\mathrm{M} \tag{7}$$

The capacity co obtained can be equal as well as optimized. In order to have the equal capacity all cells must have the equal number of users. While in case of optimized capacity the following optimization problem must be solved:

$$\max_{\underline{n}} \sum_{i=1}^{M} n_i \tag{8}$$

subject to $n_i + I_i \leq C_{eff}, i = 1,\ldots,M$ is the number of access channels.

5 Proposed Mathematical Model for GSM and CDMA Networks Using DITMC

Traffic intensity is basically a product of average call duration and average number call requests. It is measured in Erlangs which is a dimensionless unit. Mathematically it is expressed as:

$$Ac = \lambda h \tag{9}$$

Where

Ac is the traffic intensity in Erlangs.
λ is the average number of call requests per hour.
h is the average duration of a call measured in hour.

There are two types of Erlang formula i.e. Erlang B and Erlang C. Erlang B is used for wired networks (PSTN) as well as mobile telephone networks. It is used with the assumption that whenever there is a blocking of call faced by the user, the user will not reattempt the call. Further for Erlang B formula the following assumptions are made:

- The calls arrival is random.
- Holding time is exponentially distributed.
- The number of sources is infinite.
- The calls are served in their arrival order.
- All blocked calls will be lost.

Mathematically Erlang B formula for loss probability B_B is stated as:

$$B_B = \frac{(A_N/N!)}{\sum_{i=0}^{N} \frac{A_i}{i!}} \tag{10}$$

Where

N is number of trunks available in the resource group
A is traffic offered to group in Erlangs.

Similarly the Erlang C formula is employed in networks where queuing theory is applicable. It is assumed that there is no rerouting of calls like Erlang B formula case rather the calls are placed in the waiting queue until and unless the resources are available or the queue time expires. The block calls are delayed in this case. Mathematically the relationship between these two blocking probabilities B_B and B_C [7] is as follows:

$$B_c = (\frac{NB_B}{N - A(1 - B_B)}) \tag{11}$$

It is very apparent that whenever the resources are unavailable then for the Erlang C model the blocking rate seems to be higher because of the number of instances in the waiting queue and the resources utilized. Whenever there is no blocking of calls the Erlang B and Erlang C are same. The Enhancement in time utilization in a speech conversation in mobile communication (one side only) can be expressed mathematically as follows [7]:

$$\eta = \frac{T_{ON}}{T_{TOTAL}} \tag{12}$$

Where η is Time Utilization without data interleaving technique

T_{ON} is the ON time of the conversation

$$T_{TOTAL} = T_{ON} + T_{OFF} \tag{13}$$

Where T_{OFF} is the off time observed on channel including silence period.

The Time Utilization with data interleaving technique is mathematically expressed as follows:

$$\eta_{DI} = \frac{T_{eff}}{T_{TOTAL}} \tag{14}$$

T_{eff} is the reduced T_{ON} with data interleaving technique.

So the Enhancement in Time Utilization can be defined as the difference of η and η_{DI}. It is expressed as follows:

$$\phi = \eta - \eta_{DI} \tag{15}$$

This means that if η_{DI} is smaller than η then more enhancement in time utilization can be obtained which will further lead to increased channel utilization enhancement. In GSM networks the enhancement in channel utilization, capacity (number of calls/channels in a cell) can be achieved by the implementation of data interleaving technique. In GSM network the blocking probability with the implementation of data interleaving technique can be mathematically expressed as follows:

$$\hat{P}_b = \frac{(A_{DI} + A_h)^c \sum_{k=c}^{c+g} \frac{A_h^{k-c}}{k!}}{\sum_{k=0}^{c-1} \frac{(A_{DI} + A_h)}{k!} + (A_{DI} + A_h)^c \sum_{k=c}^{c+g} \frac{A_h^{k-c}}{k!}} \tag{16}$$

Where

A_{DI} is the increased traffic due to arrived calls with data interleaving technique
A_h is traffic due to handover calls
g is guard channels
λ_h is the handover traffic
P_{hf} is the Handover failure probability
$\hat{P}_b$ is the Blocked calls probability due to data interleaving technique and N is total number of channels per cell is the number of access channels.

Since the data interleaving technique leads to the enhancement in time utilization of the channels, the more channels can be serviced within the cell at a given time. So it is apparent from the above equation that as the number of calls due to the data interleaving technique increases the blocking probability $\hat{P}_b$ decreases which will further increase the number of channels to be serviced as lesser blocking of calls will be there.

The same concept can also be applied in the case of CDMA networks. In CDMA networks, the capacity of network is defined in terms of the bit energy to interference ratio as the energy is spread and almost the whole allotted spectrum is used. It depends basically on a number of factors. The voice activity factor plays a vital role in deciding this ratio. If this parameter is decreased the bit energy to interference ratio can be increased leading to the increased capacity. As a consequence of the Data Interleaving technique, the voice activity factor α_{di} can certainly be reduced and hence the Capacity of CDMA networks is expressed as follows:

$$\left(\frac{E_b}{I_o}\right)_i^{DI} = \frac{E_b}{\frac{\alpha_{di}(RE_B)(n_i - 1 + I_i)}{W} + N_o} \mathrm{i} = 1, \ldots, M \tag{17}$$

Where

W is spread signal bandwidth
R is information rate in bits per second
α_{di} is voice activity factor due to Data Interleaving technique is number of users in cell i.

6 Experimental Results

The simulation of the proposed mathematical model is yet to be accomplished based on real time data but however the simulation for the justification of DITMC technique has already been performed using Java on 120 speech samples and 125 data samples so as to find out the percentage of interleaving and overhead incurred with the interleaving process. The results show that a considerable amount of time (channel or bandwidth indeed) is wasted during the conversation in silence period as well as in the repetition of speech bytes. The results obtained [7, 8] for the simulation study of DITMC technique forms a strong basis for the proposed model (Table 1).

Table 1. Simulated results of DITMC technique [8]

No. of samples	File type	% Interleaving	% Overhead	Overall channel utilization enhancement
120	.wav	47.32%	0.034%	83.32%
25	.doc/.docx	11.90%	1.25%	47.90%
25	.pdf	1.41%	0.28%	37.41%
25	.ppt	6.22%	1.34%	42.22%
25	.xls	15.43%	2.68%	51.43%
25	.jpg	0.041%	0.015	36.041%

7 Conclusions

It is concluded that with the implementation of Data Interleaving technique in mobile communication both, the capacity and channel utilization enhancement (in GSM and CDMA networks) can be improved and increased. It has been shown mathematically and the 'goodness of fit' of these models can be verified with the simulation study using real time data. It is strongly supported by the simulation study of DITMC technique which shows that the overall channel utilization (with Data Interleaving Technique in Mobile Communication) becomes 83.32% from the original 36% (without using any other channel utilization enhancement technique).

References

1. Opechowski, Z., Correia, L.M.: Analysis of traffic distributions in GSM. In: 13th International Conference on Microwaves, Radar and Wireless Communications, vol. 2, pp. 390–394, 22–24 May 2000
2. Akl, R., Parvez, A.: Impact of interference model on capacity in CDMA cellular networks. In: Proceedings of SCI 04: Communications and Network Systems, Technologies and Applications, vol. 3, pp. 404–408, July 2004
3. Purohit, H., Joshi, K.: Simulation study of DITMC technique for enhancing channel utilization in speech communication of mobile network. In: European Modelling Symposium 2015 Madrid (Spain), Proceedings Published by IEEE Conference Publication Services, pp. 133–136, 6–8 October 2015. ISBN 978-1-5090-0206-1
4. Biebuma, J.J., Omijeh, B.O.: Traffic modelling for capacity analysis of CDMA networks using lognormal approximation method. IOSR J. Electron. Commun. Eng. (IOSR-JECE) **4** (6), 42–50 (2013)
5. Boulmalf, M., et al.: Traffic analysis for GSM networks. In: IEEE/ACS International Conference on Computer Systems and Applications, pp. 498–503, 10–13 May 2009
6. Sharma, K.L.: Study of data interleaving in digital communication network and its application to network management system. Thesis for the Degree of Ph.D. in Electronics and Communication Engineering, Jai Narain Vyas University, Jodhpur (2003)
7. Hemant, P.: Investigation of efficient data interleaving technique in voice and data communication in band limited environment and its implementation in mobile communication for channel utilization enhancement and energy optimization. Thesis for the Degree of Ph.D. in Electronics and Communication Engineering, Jai Narain Vyas University, Jodhpur (2015)
8. Purohit, H., Joshi, K.: Simulation based comparative study on channel utilization enhancement using DITMC technique in speech and data communication of mobile network. In: The 6th International Conference on Information Communication and Management, ICICM 2016, 29–31 October 2016. University of Hertfordshire, U.K. (2016)

Dual Band Micro Strip Patch Antenna for UWB Application

Arun Kumar and Manish Kumar Singh

Department of ECE, JECRC University, Jaipur, India
arun.kumar@jecrcu.edu.in

Abstract. In modern age, life of a human being is closely associated with different kind of technologies to cator the needs of its daily life like, education, health, food production, transportation, communication and many more Technology should be helpful to ease the daily life of a common man. The problems must be addressed in real time system so that relevant remedies can be obtained in time. In today's digital world wireless technology with high data rate services are the necessity of time to provide the solution in real time systems. Ever increasing to demand for higher data rates require appropriate radiation systems with large bandwidth and stable gain. Microstrip antennas with unidirectional radiation patterns and stable gain are the most useful for this purpose. In the present work, an UWB (Ultra Wide Band) antenna is implemented by using a micro strip patch antenna for application in next generation wireless communication and Internet of Things. A micro strip patch antenna ground plane defect is used to breed multiband applications. The performance of gain, directivity, and bandwidth is enhanced and also reduces the geometry, shape and size of an UWB antenna. Output result reveals efficient performance with respect to wideband operation.

Keywords: UWB · Micro strip · Return loss · VSWR

1 Introduction

UWB antennas find its most of the applications, namely missile, mobile, satellite, aircraft in the UWB range of frequency for 3 GHz to 10 GHz [1–6]. A printed circuit technology with minute substrate area is applied to implement a micro strip patch antenna. Various parameters like voltage standing wave ratio (VSWR), antenna design, transmission lines decrease the efficiency of the system. The maximum power can be achieved by matching the antenna load with impedance characteristics [7–12]. The parameters like gain, directionality, and bandwidth can be ameliorated by utilizing several techniques mentioned in [13–15]. Micro strip antennas are utilized for the multiband applications. Design techniques like fractal geometry are as well being employed for designing of UWB antenna, but it sticks in the losses and reduces the coupling between the elements [16–20]. In this work micro strip patch antenna with inset feed as an elementary element is designed for better performance with respect to gain, return loss, VSWR. This structure

B. Panda et al. (Eds.): REDSET 2017, CCIS 799, pp. 434–441, 2018.
https://doi.org/10.1007/978-981-10-8527-7_36

can be used for low power short range transmission of information. In future, Reconfigurability may be realized by using several approaches. In [21–23] kotch fractal antenna is used with an array size of 2 × 2 array to increase the bandwidth, gain and size of antenna is also reduced. In [24–26] novel dual band multi patch antenna is designed for the wireless application. The proposed work shows an increment of bandwidth, gain, efficiency and better returns loss.

2 Mathematical Modeling

For the greater frequencies, the most of the fringing field lines quintessence in the substrate. The ε_{tf} is given by [27–29].

$$\varepsilon_{tf} = \frac{\varepsilon_t + 1}{2} + \frac{\varepsilon_t - 1}{2}\left[1 + 12\frac{ha}{Wa}\right]^{-\frac{1}{2}} \quad (1)$$

The L or W of ground plane is given as:
$W_g = 6h + W$ (1)
$L_g = 6h + L$(2)

2.1 Antenna Design

The UWB antenna is implemented by considering the ideal standards of the numerous overhead said constraints. In this work, the ideal parameter was nominated and other limitations were improved by setting it. Parametric study and simulation were obtained by using CST-MWS. The structure and geometry of suggested antenna are given in Figs. 1 and 2. FR-4 1.6 mm thickness substrate through (tan δ) of 0.025, dielectric constant of 4.3 is considered for the purported purpose. The rectangular patch with

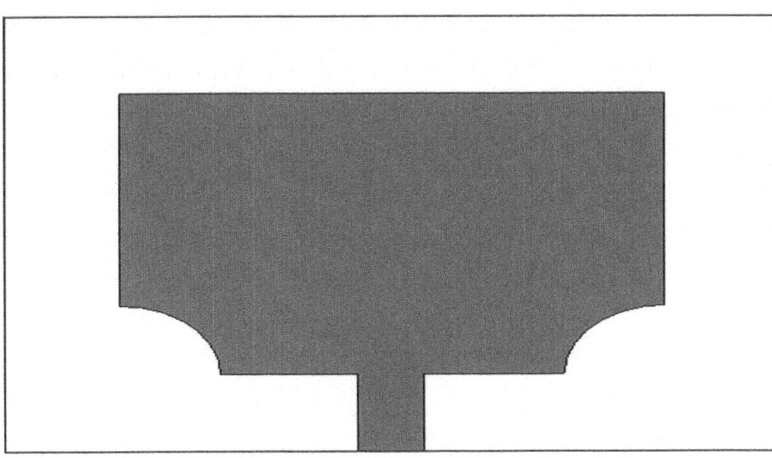

Fig. 1. Upper view

$W_p \times L_p$ dimension. It contains of two flat, curved or circular junctions at the fading edge with radius r of the lap. The present study suggests a novel micro strip patch UWB antenna through the fractional ground plane to upsurge the bandwidth of the recommended aerial an appropriate for UWB solicitations. The spectrum of the antenna is affected due to the increase in radio wave due to the curved junctions which unswervingly disturbs the bandwidth of the transmitting aerial. The work also suggests that bandwidth of an antenna can be extended by confiscating the ground plane underneath the radiating area.

Fig. 2. Bottommost view

3 Results and Discussion

Using the above equation, the micro strip patch antenna is implemented with the resonant frequency of 4 GHz. The others parameters of the proposed work is given in Table 1.

Table 1. Parameters used in simulation.

S. No.	Basic component	Variable	Dimension (mm)
1.	Patch	L	17.40
		W (Width)	02.75
		M (Thickness)	00.035
2.	Ground plane	L_g (Length of ground)	03.55
		m_t (Thickness of material in patch)	0.035
3.	Substrate	W_s	32.42
		L_s	27.00
		H	01.60

The S parameter of proposed structure is given in Fig. 3. Return loss is given as −26 dB at 4.7 GHz and −46.174 dB at 9.7 GHz.

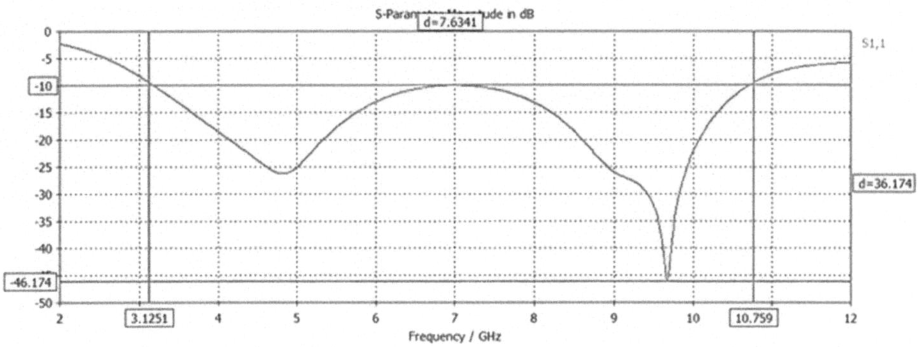

Fig. 3. Return loss

The VSWR is shown in Fig. 4. VSWR of an antenna should be in the range of 1 and 2. The VSWR is 1.5.

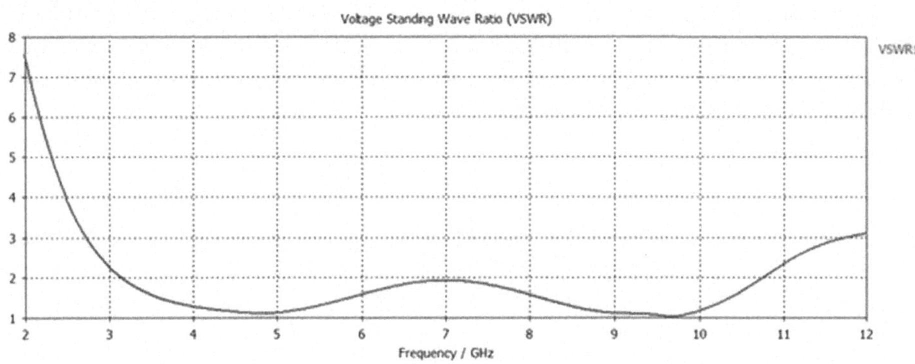

Fig. 4. VSWR graph

Figure 5 shows the radiation of an antenna at 4.8 GHz with center lobe of 2.4 dB, side lobe level is given as −0.9 dB, which means smallest power, is propagated at undesired path and angular width is 106.4 degrees to the main lobe directions of 173.0 degrees. The figure shows that the desired propagation is obtained and interference is also shortened by cutting the side lobe of an antenna.

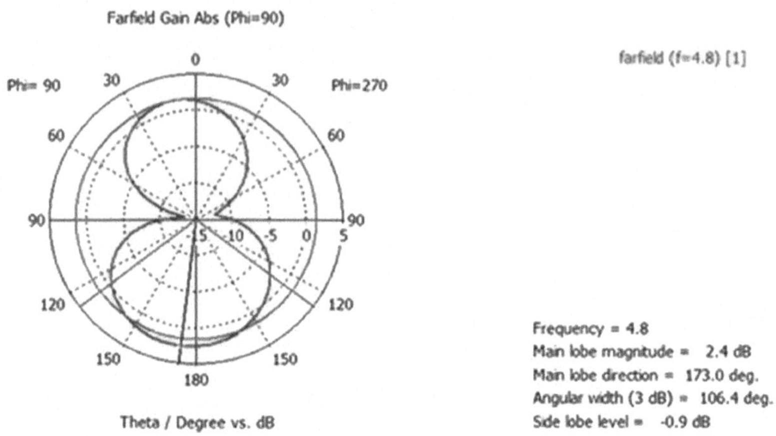

Fig. 5. Polar plot at 4.8 GHz

Figure 6 shows the radiation of an antenna at 9.7 GHz with center lobe of -0.6 dB, side lobe level is given as −5.6 dB and angular width is 60 degree with main lobe direction of 52 degree. The pattern shows that the desired propagation is smooth with good return loss.

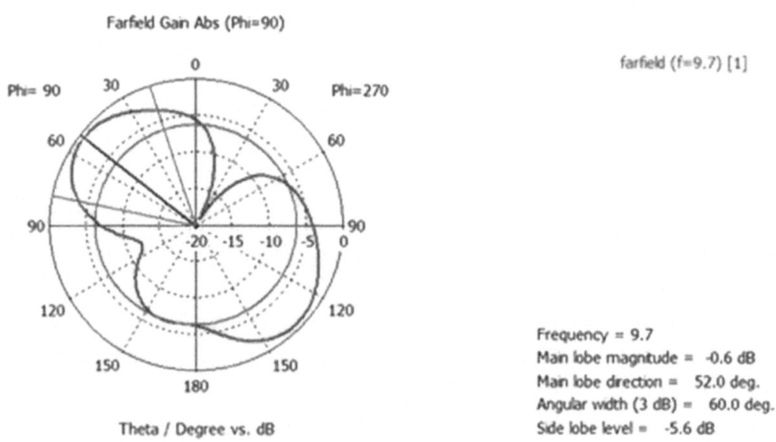

Fig. 6. Polar plot at 9.7 GHz

Figure 7 shows the three dimensional radiation patterns at 4.8 GHz. The gain of an antenna is given as 2.42 dB.

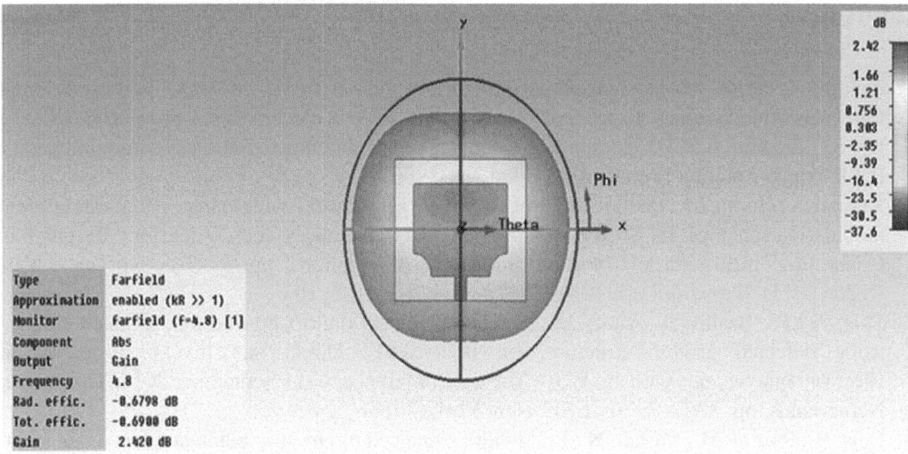

Fig. 7. 3D radiation pattern at 4.8 GHz

Figure 8 gives the radiation pattern at 9.7 GHz. The gain is given as 5.48 dB.

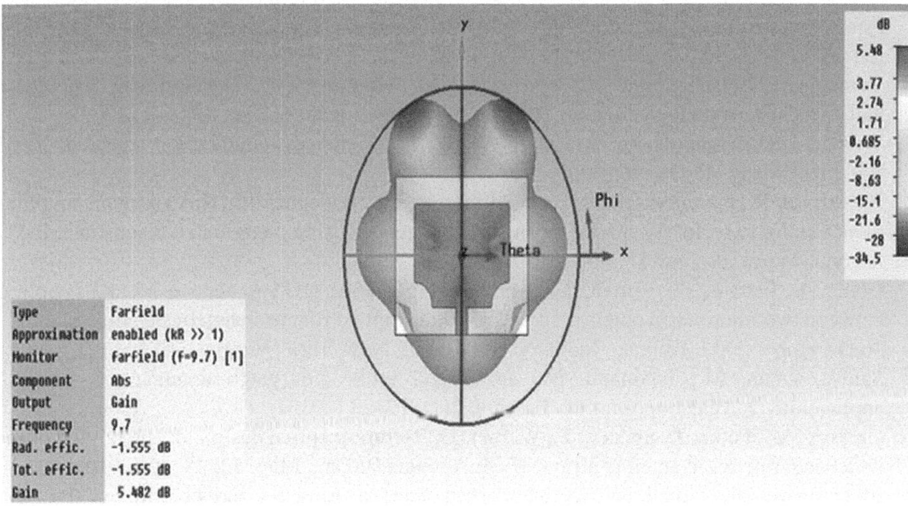

Fig. 8. 3D radiation pattern at 9.7 GHz

4 Conclusion

In this work paper, micro strip patch antenna is designed for UWB application which will play an important role. It is found that the proposed technique reduces the size of an antenna and bandwidth is also increased. The dispersal of surface current is speckled nearby the slot at higher resonant frequency of 4.8 GHz and 9.7 GHz. It usually finds its application in WI-FY, WLAN, X-ray, radar etc.

References

1. Kumar, A., Gupta, M.: Design and performance evaluation of MB-MIMO-UWB for different transmission techniques. Proc. Natl. Acad. Sci. India Sect. A: Phys. Sci. pp. 1–10 (2017)
2. Ko, S.C.K., Murch, R.D.: Compact integrated diversity antenna for wireless communications. IEEE Trans. Antenna Propag. **49**(4), 954–960 (2001)
3. Kumar, A., Gupta, M.: Design and evaluation of BER for ultra-wide-band system for different modulation schemes. In: Shetty, N.R., Prasad, N.H., Nalini, N. (eds.) Emerging Research in Computing, Information, Communication and Applications, pp. 97–108. Springer, New Delhi (2015). https://doi.org/10.1007/978-81-322-2550-8_10
4. Shah, S.I.H., Bashir, S., Altaf, A., Shah, S.: Compact multiband micro-strip patch antenna using defected ground structure. In: IEEE 2014 Direct and Inverse Problems of Electromagnetic and Acoustic Wave Theory Conference, 6–11 September 2014, The Hague, Netherlands, pp. 2367–2370. IEEE, New York (2014)
5. Bala, B., Rahim, M., Murad, N.: Bandwidth enhanced micro-strip patch antenna using metamaterials. In: IEEE 2012 Applied Electromagnetics Conference, 12–13 December 2012, Melaka, Malaysia, pp. 280–282. IEEE, New York (2012)
6. Anguera, J., Ortigosa, E., Puente, C., Borja, C., Soler, J.: Broadside triple-frequency microstrip patch radiator combining a dual-band modified Sierpinski fractal and a mono-band antenna. IEEE Trans. Antenna Propag. **54**(4), 3367–3373 (2006)
7. Biswas, S., Kumar, C.: Control of higher harmonics and their radiation in micros-trip antennas using compact defected ground structures. IEEE Trans. Antenna Propag. **61**, 3349–3354 (2013)
8. Vemagiri, J., Balachandran, M., Agarwaland, M., Varahramy, K.: Development of compact half-Sierpinski fractal antenna for RFID applications. Electron. Lett. **43**, 1–2 (2007)
9. Werner, D.H., Ganguly, S.: An overview of fractal antennas engineering research. IEEE Antenna Propag. **45**, 38–56 (2003)
10. Hafezifard, R., Naser-Moghadasi, M., Mohassel, J.R., Sadeghzadeh, R.A.: Mutual coupling reduction for two closely spaced meander line antennas using meta-material substrate. IEEE Antenna Wirel. Propag. **15**, 40–43 (2016)
11. Guha, D., Biswas, S., Kumar, C.: Annular ring shaped DGS to reduce mutual coupling between two micro-strip patches. In: IEEE 2009 Applied Electromagnetics Conference, 14–16 December 2009, Kolkata, India, pp. 1–3. IEEE, New York (2009)
12. Samsuzzaman, M., Islamand, M.: Dual-band multi slot patch antenna for wireless applications. J. Telecommun. Inf. Technol. **2**(1), 19–23 (2013)
13. Gregory, M., Petko, J., Spence, T., Werner, D.: Nature-inspired design techniques for ultra-wideband a-periodic antenna arrays. IEEE Antenna Propag. Mag. **52**, 28–45 (2010)
14. Elhefnaway, M., Ismail, W.: A micro-strip antenna array for indoor wireless dynamic environments. IEEE Trans. Antennas Propag. **57**(12), 3998–4002 (2009)
15. Beenish, Saraswat, T., Tripathy, M.R., Mahendru, G.: Design of a high gain 16 element array of micro- strip patch antennas for millimeter wave applications. In: 2nd International Conference on Contemporary Computing and Information (IC3I), vol. 36, no. 6, pp. 182–184 (2016)
16. Ahmed, M., Das, D.K., Rahman, A.: Study of a conformal UWB antenna designed on various non-planar surfaces. In: Annual IEEE India Conference (INDICON), vol. 26, no. 4, pp. 136–146 (2013)
17. Vidhate, G.R., Kakade, A.B.: Comparative design and analysis of both conventional and metamaterial loaded microstrip patch antenna. In: Annual IEEE India Conference (INDICON), vol. 56, no. 9, pp. 1–7 (2014)

18. Ather, S.N., Verma, R.K., Singhal, P.K.: Band with enhancement for truncated rectangular micro-strip antenna using stacked patches and defected ground structure. In: 5th International Conference on Computational Intelligence and Communication Networks, vol. 23, no. 7, pp. 55–60 (2013)
19. Margaret, D.H., Anith, S., Duraisamy, M., Muneeswaran, K.P.K.: Cross slot antenna with open ended truncated patch feed for ultra wide band applications. In: Annual IEEE India Conference (INDICON), vol. 53, no. 9, pp. 1–7 (2009)
20. Inclain-Sanchez, L., Vazquez-Roy, J.L., Raso-Iglesias, E.: Gain enhancement of a multilayer microstrip patch antenna by means of truncated planar perodic structure, vol. 48, no. 10, pp. 316–330 (2015)
21. Duy, T.N., Van, Y.V.: Combining two methods to enhance band-notch characteristic of ultra wide band antenna. In: The International Conference on Advanced Technologies for Communications, vol. 45, no. 9, pp. 206–209 (2009)
22. Prabu, R.T., Benisha, M., Bai, V.T., Yokesh, V.: Millimeter wave for 5G mobile communication application. In: IEEE International Conference on Advances in Electrical, Electronics, Information, Communication and Bio-Informatics (AEEICB 2016), vol. 62, no. 6, pp. 587–592 (2016)
23. Islam, M.N., Subramanian, S., Partyka, A., Sampath, A.: Coverage and capacity of 28 GHz band in indoor stadiums. In: IEEE Wireless Conference and Networking Conference, vol. 78, no. 7, pp. 643–648 (2016)
24. Roy, P., Vishwakarma, R.K., Jain, A., Singh, R.: Multiband millimeter wave antenna array for 5G communication. In: International Conference on Emerging Trends in Electrical, Electronics and Sustainable Energy Systems, vol. 67, no. 8, pp. 102–105 (2016)
25. Kim, Y., Lee, H.Y., Hwang, P., Patro, R.K., Lee, J., Roh, W., Cheun, K.: Feasibility of mobile cellular communications at millimeter wave frequency. IEEE J. Sel. Top. Sig. Process. **10**(3), 589–599 (2016)
26. Chen, Z.N., Qing, X., Yeap, S.B., Xu, J.: Design and measurement of substrate-integrated planar millimeter wave antenna arrays at 60–325 GHz. IEEE Radio Wirel. Symp. (RWS) **34**(6), 532–569 (2014)
27. Han, W., Yang, F., Ouyang, J., Yang, P.: Low-cost wideb and high gain slotted cavity antenna using high-order modes for millimeter-wave application. IEEE Trans. Antennas Propag. **63**(11), 4624–4631 (2015)
28. Zheng, L., Tse, N.C.: Diversity and multiplexing: a fundamental tradeoff in multiple-antenna channels. IEEE Trans. Inf. Theory **49**(6), 1073–1096 (2003)
29. Fallahi, R., Kalteh, A.A., Golparvar, M.: A novel UWB elliptical slot antenna with band notched characteristics. Prog. Electromagn. Res. **82**(8), 127–136 (2008)

Smartphone with Solar Charging Mechanism to Issue Alert During Rainfall Disaster

Neeraj Kumar(✉), Alka Agrawal, and Raees Ahmad Khan

DIT, SIST, BBAU, Lucknow, India
req.mrt@gmail.com, alka_csjmu@yahoo.co.in, khanraees@yahoo.com

Abstract. Rainfall-induced disaster is long duration disasters that have a probability of power failure that makes disaster worst due to lack of communication. Flash Flood, long duration flood, and landslides are few examples of them. In this case, Communication between victims is a challenging job. This paper presents an idea to overcome these kinds of situations. Different tools have been developed Alert about disaster including in flood disaster but during the flood, power failure makes these impossible to work for a long duration while flood is long duration disaster. This paper introducing an Alert Network designed by different technologies including WSN, MANET, and IoT. This architecture will be able to communicate in absence of any fixed infrastructure as well as it will be able to communicate through the social media if available. For supporting the architecture, the use of the screen with a solar cell as well as OLED with a screen to enhance the battery life of a Smartphone is discussed.

Keywords: Disaster management · Ad-hoc networks
Disaster management network · Disaster monitoring system · Alert system

1 Introduction

Rainfall-induced disasters are classified into two categories; including flood and landslide. Flood comes due to lack of handling of water while landslide happened due to random strike or storage of this water on angular land. Losses by these disasters can be minimized or stopped through proper alert and monitoring with safety measures. In case of a landslide, no progress is still observed to detect or manage. However, the Indian govt. has successfully controlled the occurrences of flood due to overflowing rivers in last few decades, unfortunately, rainfall triggered flood still a challenge for the researchers as well as managers.

Table 1 throws light on few of the most dangerous rainfall-induced disasters of the last few decades in India along with their cause and effects. A common factor to make these disasters worst are the absence of communication or alert system. This paper introduces a mechanism used to issue an alert during the mitigation phase of disaster management. Rest of the paper is organized as: the second section discusses the technology to help the victims and rescue team. These technologies include information systems for post-disaster hazards and help to inform to flood victims. In the third part, list of different possible technologies is included that is helpful for communication,

B. Panda et al. (Eds.): REDSET 2017, CCIS 799, pp. 442–449, 2018.
https://doi.org/10.1007/978-981-10-8527-7_37

victims and rescuer team with possible limitations and drawbacks. The fourth section includes our novel architecture of alert network to overcome the drawbacks of existing technologies with the knowledge of devices to design the networks.

Table 1. Rainfall-induced disasters in India with cause/effects.

Disaster, Year	Cause/effects
Kurseong [12], Tindharia, Darjeeling, 1998	250 houses damaged, NH-55 damaged, 10 people died
Darjeeling Sadar [12], 2000	11 people died
Maharashtra flood [19], 2005	1094 death, 167 injuries, 54 missing
Surat flood [6], 2006	150 died directly, 100 died due to leptospirosis and 3000000 directly affected
Kosi flood [19], Bihar, 2008	557 deaths, 3329423 affected, 222754 houses damaged
Nigiri's Landslides [7], 2009	1150 landslides in Nilgiri district. This is dangerous in terms of lives
U.K. floods, [18], 2013	A cloudburst caused flash floods of 14-17 June, killed 580. And lost 5474 missing people, assumed to be dead
Malin landslide [14] 30/7/2014	134 people killed in Ambegaon, Pune. 160 to 200 people were believed to have been buried in 44 houses
J & K Floods, [17], 2014	Heavy rain and flash floods, over 278 killed, rendered hundreds of thousands homeless
Assam Flood [5], 2016	1725730 peoples affected in 23 districts

2 Related Work

Currently, several Alert systems are using different technologies to intimate and alert in these disasters. Related work throws a light on these technologies discussed below:

Geo-based tools are very important for disaster management out of which Geo-Conference described by Siegel et al. [8] to provide geographic data, ArcPAD [9] of ESRI for mobile devices to capture, analyze and display geographic information, are important to use. In this row, Capata et al. [3] developed an application for rescue teams using MANET devices. Fazardo's application [1] MyDisasterDroid to find Geographic location via SMS or app installation is also a good application.

Points to point networks and MANET, both are very useful to start communication in absence of infrastructure. Point to Point Network (P2P) based system P2Pnet [10] and RISED [11] are used to set up communication in few minutes by minimum network designers. The Idea of local cloud system [13] given by Amro et al. to share information through P2P fashion using MANET to connect online world have importance to make communication for long distance.

CSN project [15] uses Smartphones to transmit alert during any disaster through a local network designed within the group. This project is successfully running to handle flood like situations and might be beneficial to Indian scenario if the power failure is not a problem. Unfortunately for Indian scenario, it is not fully applicable due to a power failure in raining season. Table 2 presents a summary of tools used for flood disaster management.

Table 2. Summary of tools useful in disaster management

Tools	Manufacturer	Application
Emergency [20]	American RedCross society	Provides information about most of the disaster in America
Flood [21]	American RedCross society	Provides information and prepare possible victims of the flood to survive in a disaster.
Disaster alert [22]	Pacific disaster center	Provides a list of users with an interactive map of disaster all around the globe and share it through social media
Flood watch [23]	D5G technology llc.	On the basis of data from U.S. geological survey and national weather service, it provides the position of flow in its river
Emergency radio [24]	EdgeRift, Inc.	US-based Police scanner for emergencies
FEMA [25]	FEMA	Provides weather alert based on data taken by US National weather service
Flood petrol [26]	Ateneo Java Wireless Competency Center	Philippines based app to help during flood through monitoring and mapping
Water4 thai [27]	Piesoft Company Limited	Provides information on flood and rainfall based on reliable sources
ubAlert [28]	Bump Networks Inc.	Provides information about disaster in social media

2.1 Apps Helpful in Disaster Management

Various tools and applications are available to help in a disaster, out of which few are enlisted in Table 2.

2.2 Problem Scenario

GIS or other technologies can only help when devices used in the network has the power [2] to keep safe its long lifetime in the long-term disasters. Rainfall-induced disasters are long-term disasters due to its duration from days to weeks and sometimes months also. In this case, if devices are communicating each other then not a problem, even within a network. For a flood or in rainfall-induced disasters, the problem starts with the failure to sensing about rainfall triggered disaster or failure of intimation to the possible victims of the disaster. A big problem occurs on communication failure during the disaster as per situation occurred in Uttarakhand flood [18] and J & K flood [17]. So, in this case, there will be three scenarios to develop a model of Alert network. These are:

Scenario 1: There is no sensing mechanism to sense the symptoms of disaster through environmental change.

Scenario 2: Sensing mechanism available but due to low battery or failure of charging mechanism or power failure it doesn't have the capability to intimate central monitoring station about the symptoms of disaster. While it is understood that rainy season always suffered by a power cut in India, So power failure for any kind of power operated device is always a problem.

3 Solution to Problem Scenario

In any disaster, when devices network is communicating with each other, then no problem. The problem starts with the network failure due to any reason. The researchers are considering network failure due to fewer lifetimes of nodes caused by a power failure in problem scenario 2. To overcome the problem, there is a need to develop an architecture which is able to communicate within problem scenario. To design this desired architecture, researchers here investigated different technologies and found out the features of MANET and WSN which make them useful to work in this problem scenario. The architecture of the network is discussed as:

3.1 Architecture

The architecture of Alert network is assumed as a hybrid Adhoc network as shown in Fig. 1. Without the help of any fixed infrastructure, the Alert mechanism will be able to communicate across the obstacle. The only requirement of this network is lifetime or a charging mechanism to its battery. To get prior information about the disaster, this architecture uses WSN while post information transmission is made possible through MANET. It may use the partially wired network as per the need. Protocols used by all three networks are compatible with each other including Zigbee and Bluetooth. To overcome the problem of a power failure there is a need for charging mechanism. To overcome the problem researcher has used for solar charging mechanism. Following section briefly discusses solar charging concept for a solar cell. Component of the alert network are considered as Wireless Sensor Network (WSN), Mobile Adhoc network (MANET), and Partially Wired Network discussed below:

WSN has two types of interconnected sensing devices called motes and sensor. These motes are equipped with a power source, transceiver unit, a processing unit, and a sensing unit. Motes are powerful devices than the sensors. *MANET* is assumed to be made up of Smartphone and laptop devices able to communicate each other in absence of fixed infrastructure. *Partially Wired Network* has the devices to facilitate the WSN and MANET such as WLAN and Arduino kit. In Fig. 1, SM indicated to Smartphone devices interconnected with laptop shown, to form MANET while sensor devices to form WSN. In an emergency they may be facilitated by the partially wired network it may be a Wi-fi or other devices. MANET, WSN, and partially wired network collectively form an alert network.

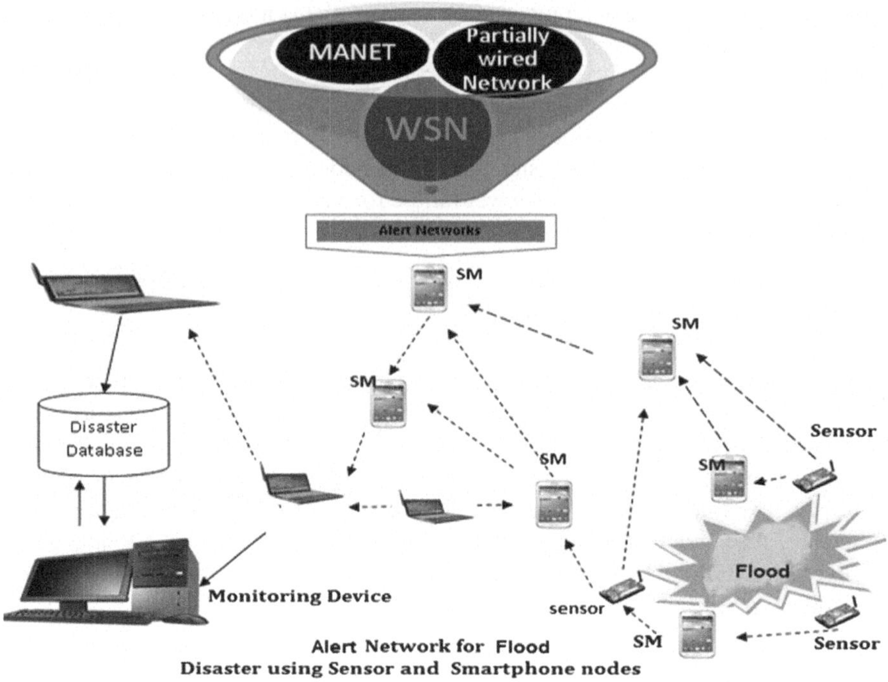

Fig. 1. Alert network for flood disaster

In the Fig. 1, Idea is to design an Alert network with the help of MANET, WSN and Partially Wired Networks that having the Smartphone devices, WSN Motes and Sensing devices to be connected with base Station and Monitoring Station.

3.2 Device Design for MANET to Be Used in Disaster Management

Our idea is to develop architecture of network discussed in Fig. 1. The architecture should be facilitated with a small architecture of solar cell to provide power backup to the network in typical disaster situation. This idea will work in situation where power will be unavailable and nobody is able to provide battery backup to the communication system. In our idea we are going to suggest the grid of solar cell behind the screen of Smartphone as per Fig. 2, discussed by Neil [10]. This screen made up of the elements listed below:

- PV element
- OLED
- Substrate
- Wasted illumination
- Useful illumination
- Optical filter and display glass

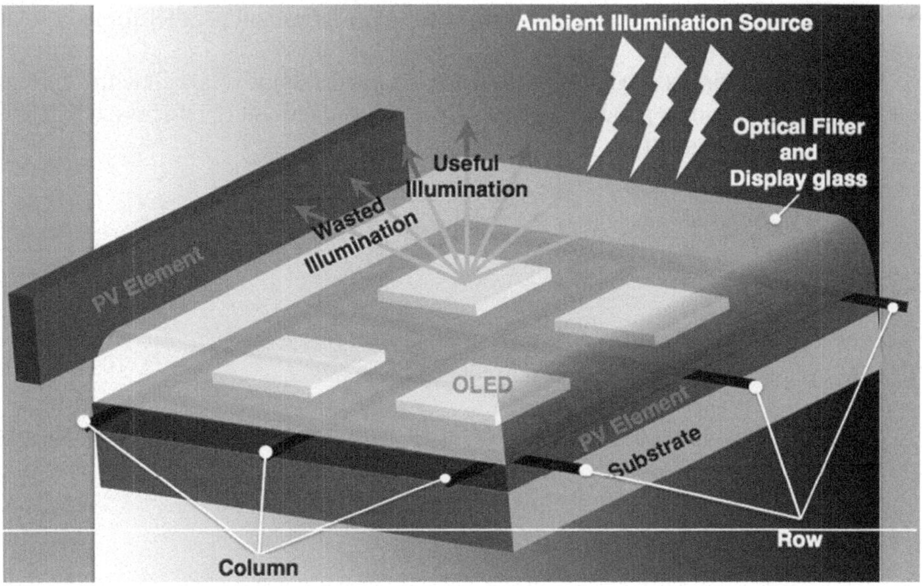

Fig. 2. A thin-film system harvests energy from wasted light in an OLED display taken from Neil [10].

3.3 Solar Charging Mechanism

Characteristics of a solar cell basically based on three parameters including temperature, current and voltage. IC LM317 is used to design a solar charger for wireless machine

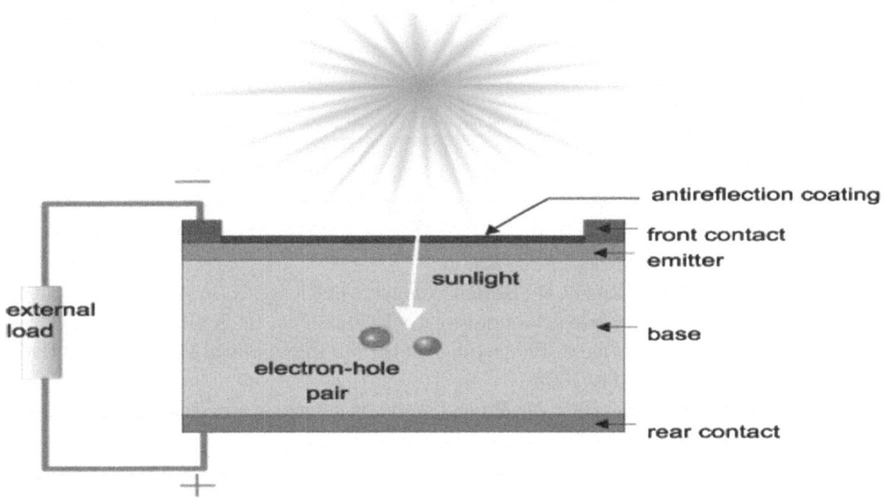

Fig. 3. Solar charging concept for wireless devices [4]

as the cover of device [4]. Few solar cells lined up in series and parallel forms a solar panel as shown in Fig. 3.

Apart from the discussion by Neha [4], Here assumed a single solar cell with a current source, two diodes, and a parallel register. Solar induced current (I_s) discussed by Gow and Manning [16] is given as

$$I_s = \frac{Ir}{Ir0} X\, I_{s0} \tag{1}$$

where,

$I_r =$ Irradiance (light intensity) in W/m^2 falling on the cell.
$I_{s0} =$ Measured solar-generated current for the Irradiance I_{r0}

Gow and Manning [16] simulated different parameters of the solar cell and its combination.

4 Conclusion and Future Work

At the end of the discussion, it is simple to say, that, in all around the globe, there is a lot of communication mechanism and application has been designed to help in disaster situations. These applications are helpful to victims as well as rescuers but can work only when the mobile phone is charged. Unfortunately, flood or rainfall-induced disaster is generally not possible to maintain backup for a long time. So, the mobile phone or Smartphone can be designed with the solar cell to provide back up. The same can be used in the alert network designed by the authors.

Performance study of parameters after merging a solar charging mechanism with the screen is a big task in case of Smartphone. So, to design this architecture, the study of Smartphone's performance is quite important and this will be the future work under this row.

References

1. Fajardo, J.T.B., Oppus, C.M.: A mobile disaster management system using the android technology. Int. J. Commun. **3**(3) (2009)
2. Tomaszewski, B.: Geographic Information Systems (GIS) for Disaster Management. CRC Press, Taylor & Francis Group, Boco Raton
3. Capata, A., Marrella, A., Russo, R., Bortenschlager, M., Rieser, H.: A geo-based application for the management of mobile actors during crisis situations. In: A Geo-based Application for Mobile Actors Management, Proceedings of the 5th International ISCRAM Conference, Washington, DC, USA, May 2008
4. Kondekar, N., Gupta, A.K., Bhat, N.: Project report on solar charger circuit using IC LM 317. Centre for Nano Science and Engineering IISC
5. Hazarika, N.: Flood report. Assam state Disaster management authority, Govt. of Assam, 30 July 2016

6. Mavalankar, D., Shrivastava, A.K.: Lesson from massive floods of 2006 in Surat city: a framework for application of MS/OR techniques to improve dam management to preven flood. In: Research and Publication, Third National Conference on Management Science and Prectices, IIM Ahmedabad, India (2008)
7. Ganapathy, G.P., Hada, C.L.: Landslide hazard mitigation in the Nilgiris district, India-environmental and societal issues. Int. J. Environ. Sci. Dev. **3**(5), 497–500 (2012)
8. Siegel, C., Fortin, D., Pellerin, E.: Bringing geospatial expertise to emergency operations management with geoconferencing. In: Proceedings of the 98th Conference of the Canadian Institute of Geomatics, Ottawa, Canada (2005)
9. ESRI: ArcGIS 9, ArcPad Reference Guide, USA (2005)
10. Savage, N.: Solar cells in Smartphone screens: Researchers advance thin film energy harvesters", IEEE Spectrum, 18 January 2012. https://spectrum.ieee.org/consumer-electronics/portable-devices/solar-cells-in-smartphone-screens
11. Jang, H.-C., Lien, Y.-N., Tsai, T.-C.: Rescue information system for earthquake disasters based on MANET emergency communication platform. In: Proceedings of International Workshop on Advanced Topics in Mobile Computing for Emergency Management: Communication and Computing Platforms (MCEM 2009), Leipzig, Germany, June 2009
12. Nad, C.: Landslide hazard management of Darjeeling hill- acritical need for inhabited. Int. J. Humanit. Soc. Sci. Invent. **4**(3), 48–60 (2015)
13. Al-Akkad, A., Raffelsberger, C., Boden, A., Ramirez, L., Zimmermann, A.: Tweeting 'when online is off'? opportunistically creating mobile Ad-hoc networks in response to disrupted infrastructure. In: Proceedings of the 11th International ISCRAM Conference, University Park, Pennsylvania, USA, May 2014, pp. 662–672 (2014)
14. Shaikh, A.F., Gunjal, P.K., Chaple, N.V.: Report on landslide in Malin village in Pune. Int. J. Eng. Sci. Technol. **4**(4), 111–113 (2015)
15. Faulkner, M., Clayton, R., Heaton, T., Chandy, K.M., Kohler, M., Bunn, J., Guy, R., Liu, A., Olson, M., Cheng, M., Krause, A.: The caltech CSN project collects sensor data from thousands of personal devices for realtime response to dangerous earthquakes. CSN project (2014)
16. Gow, J.A., Manning, C.D.: Development of a photovoltaic array model for use in power-electronics simulation studies. IEEE Proc. Electr. Power App. **146**(2), 193–200 (1999)
17. Sphere India: J&K floods: Flood affected districts, Jammu & Kashmir, India (28 September 2014), pp. 1–17, 29th September 2014
18. NIDM: Proceedings of the National Workshop on Uttarakhand Disaster 2013: Lessons Learnt, National workshop on Uttarakhand Disaster 2013: Lessons Learnt, p. 3, 19 Aug 2013
19. Disaster management in India: GoI-UNDP Disaster Risk Reduction Programme (2009–2012)
20. Emergency - American Red Cross. https://play.google.com/store/apps/details?id=com.cube.arc.hzd&hl=en
21. Flood - American Red Cross. https://play.google.com/store/apps/details?id=com.cube.arc.ffa&hl=en
22. Disaster Alert. https://itunes.apple.com/in/app/disaster-alert-pacific-disaster/id381289235?mt=8
23. Flood Watch. https://itunes.apple.com/fm/app/floodwatch/id386505889?mt=8
24. Emergency radio. https://itunes.apple.com/en/app/emergency-radio-free-police/id312951771?mt=8
25. FEMA app. https://play.google.com/store/apps/details?id=gov.fema.mobile.android&hl=en
26. Flood petrol. https://play.google.com/store/apps/details?id=xtend.noah
27. Water for Thai. https://itunes.apple.com/us/app/water4thai/id548984244?mt=8
28. ubAlert. https://itunes.apple.com/in/app/ubalert-disaster-alert-network/id455647397?mt=8

Check for updates

Performance Analysis of OSPF Routing Protocol Under Single and Multiple Link Failure

Himanshi Saini(✉) and Amit Kumar Garg

ECE Department, D.C.R.U.S.T, Murthal, Sonepat 131027, Haryana, India
himanshi.4887@gmail.com

Abstract. This study aims at highlighting OSPF (Open Shortest Path First) routing technique and its performance under different network failures. A single failure in high-speed networks even for fraction of second can disrupt millions of users. Therefore it is imperative to analyze performance of routing protocol under network failure. In this paper, OSPF routing technique is examined under single and multiple link failures. Investigations are performed on basis of average E2E (end to end) delay, throughput and jitter. In this investigation, convergence time for link failures is calculated. It is observed that network has least average E2E delay when working path does not experience any failure. Under single link failure, average E2E delay is least when failed link is nearest to the source node. Under double link failure, average E2E delay is maximum when failed links are farthest apart. Convergence time for multiple link failure is more than single link failure. It is observed that convergence is least for failed link immediately connected to the source node. As observed from plots, network achieves high throughput when working path does not experience any failure and throughput reduces for multiple link failures. Average jitter is maximum for the network without failure and its value reduces for multiple link failures. The investigations in this paper provide insight into the performance of OSPF routing technique. Analysis performed and values of performance metrics obtained for various link failures provide knowledge of critical links and backup routes with respect to application specific QoS (Quality of Service) requirements.

Keywords: Routing · E2E delay · Throughput · Jitter · Convergence

1 Introduction

Maintaining the connection availability is a factor of great concern in high-capacity future optical networks as failure of optical connection in high speed network will interrupt a vast amount of services running on-line [1]. It is imperative to implement routing technique supporting resilience in high-speed networks. Resilience can be implemented through dynamic routing techniques. Dynamic routing schemes can adapt to changes in network state. Less administrative overhead is required in dynamic routing protocols as compared to static routing [2].

OSPF is one of the most commonly used Interior Gateway Protocols in high speed networks. OSPF is a link state protocol. Its operation is based on creating, maintaining,

B. Panda et al. (Eds.): REDSET 2017, CCIS 799, pp. 450–458, 2018.
https://doi.org/10.1007/978-981-10-8527-7_38

and distributing link-state information. This information is database containing description of collection of nodes, operational interfaces, interconnection, and the cost to use the interfaces [3]. Nodes exchange link state information with neighboring nodes. Each node implements Dijkstra's shortest path algorithm to compute the best route to each node in the network.

Shortest Path Calculation by Dijkstra's Algorithm [4]

1. set source node distance to itself as 0
2. set distance from the source of all other nodes to infinite initially
3. set predecessor of source to NIL
4. while Q is not empty where Q is queue of all nodes each holding a key value corresponding to its distance from source node
   a. Extract node with minimum key value, Nmin
   b. For all the neighboring nodes (Nadj) of Nmin which are not visited earlier
      if **d[Nadj] > d[Nmin] + w(Nmin, Nadj)**,
      where d[Nadj] is distance of Nadj from source
      d [Nmin] is distance of Nmin from source
      w (Nmin, Nadj)is cost of link Nmin, Nadj
   c. Calculate updated distance from source node
      d [Nadj] = d[Nmin] + w(Nmin, Nadj)
   d. Update the key values in Q
   e. Set predecessor of Nadj to Nmin
   f. Nmin is removed from queue
5. Repeat from 4

Each node in network is responsible for creating and updating its local view of network topology with help of LSAs (link- state advertisements) and passes this information to all other nodes. Bandwidth is adapted as cost value for links. Cost of a definite link is static because the bandwidth is fixed [5].

In the presented work, a network of 14 nodes NSFNET (National Science Foundation Network) is simulated using NS2 (Network Simulator 2). The analysis in this paper provides insight into OSPF routing technique and its performance analysis by measuring average E2E delay, throughput, convergence and jitter. This analysis is performed without failure and with single as well as multiple link failures. The novelty of this work lies in the implementation of all possible link failures on working path and mathematical analysis of each failure case. Section 2 covers some of the related works. Simulation model along with simulation parameters of the network are covered in Sect. 3. Simulation results are presented in Sect. 4. Section 5 concludes the paper along with the future scope.

2 Related Work

OSPF routing has been used in various spheres of communication. Various studies have been done to trace the impact of OSPF parameters like hello interval and dead interval on overall network performance. Investigations have been carried out to analyze the performance of OSPF routing in survivable networks.

Goyal et al. [6] investigated the optimal value for the HelloInterval. The investigations resulted in fast failure detection in the network and optimization of false alarm occurrence. Impact of network congestion and topology on the optimal HelloInterval value is examined. Siddiqi and Nandy [7] developed an algorithm based on network congestion to dynamically tune OSPF failure threshold. They have reduced convergence time in response to network failure. In order to maintain stable routing, failure threshold is increased during network congestion and decreased during light load on network. Absar et al. [8] implemented OSPF on six different network scenarios to calculate shortest path from source to destination. It is observed that performance of balance area OSPF is better to find the shortest path for traffic sent after a link fails. George and Shyamala Devi [9] proposed LSA (link state advertisement) and SPF (shortest path first) throttling method to provide dynamic mechanism to slow down link-state advertisement updates in OSPFv3 during times of network instability. It allows faster convergence by providing LSA rate limiting in milliseconds. Nagendra and Sathyanarayana [10] evaluated the performance analysis of OSPF protocol based on metrics such as convergence time and CPU power utilization in order to reduce convergence time and CPU power utilization. Zhao et al. [11] investigated OSPF convergence behavior in presence of multiple failures. Dynamics of convergence process is generated through interactions between process of failure detection and routing. It is demonstrated that convergence time increases for multiple failures. Duta et al. [12] analyzed the impact of failures on convergence. They have determined components consideration in order to reduce the convergence time in a network topology based on OSPF. Zhao et al. [13] demonstrated OSPF convergence behaviors in presence of correlated failures, where the reactive protocol dynamics could be enlarged. It is shown that the interactions between failure detection and routing calculation scheduling could lead to complicated protocol response to correlated failures. Hosny et al. [14] Incorporated specific parameter for OBS (optical burst switching) in OSPF protocol. They have changed the scaling factor to calculate cost of links in accordance with OBS.

3 Simulation and Modeling

Simulation is performed on NS-2 (Network Simulator 2). NS-2 is an event-driven simulation tool which is useful for studying vigorous nature of communication networks [15]. Figure 1 shows NSFNET with 14 nodes and 21 links simulated in NS2. Packets are seen traversing the working path 1-2-5-13. OSPF routing technique is simulated and analyzed on the network under test. Investigations are performed for single and multiple link failures. The link-state routing protocol available in the standard distribution of NS-2 does not support explicit signaling [16]. To support explicit signaling, OSPF patch [17] is integrated with NS2.

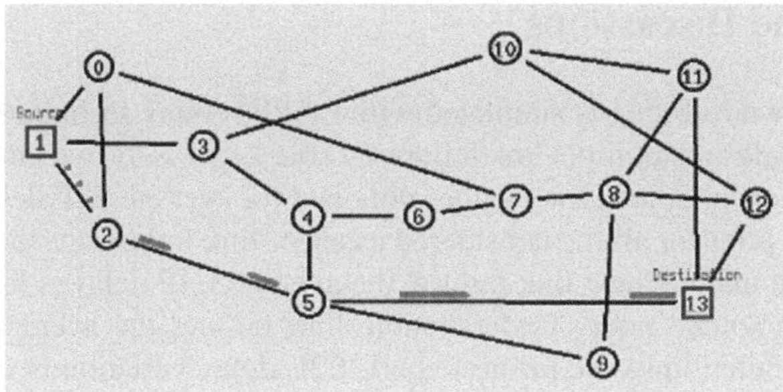

Fig. 1. Schematic for network under test

The parameters shown in Table 1 have been used for simulation of all considered failure scenarios.

Table 1. Simulation parameters

Parameter	Value
Link bandwidth	10 Gb
Link delay	5 ms
Link queue limit	10
Source, destination node	1, 13
Traffic	UDP (User Datagram Protocol)
Routing	OSPF
Application	CBR (Constant Bit Rate)
	Packet size: 500 Bytes
	Transmission rate: 600 Kbps
Queuing mechanism	DropTail
OSPF helloInterval	1 s
OSPF routerDeadInterval	4 s

Link failure scenarios are analyzed with help of mathematical model of average E2E delay, average throughput, instantaneous throughput, convergence and average jitter. E2E delay is combination of delay due to transmission, propagation, processing and queuing. Average delay is delay incurred due to all the packets. Average throughput is total number of bytes received at the destination averaged over simulation time [18]. Instantaneous throughput is bytes received at each time instant. Jitter is variation in packet delay. Average jitter is jitter due to all the packets. Convergence time is combination of failure detection time, event propagation time, event processing time, SPF (Shortest Path First) calculation time, updating forward structures time. It is calculated by summating delay due to all the OSPF packets transmitted to find alternate route once the failure occurs and adding router dead interval to delay obtained.

4 Results and Discussions

The network shown in Fig. 1 is simulated with OSPF routing technique. This analysis is made under single and multiple link failures. Table 2 shows the backup path traversed by packets under each failure case. Values obtained for average E2E delay, throughput, convergence and jitter for all the considered cases of link failure are shown in Table 3. It is observed that under single link failure, the average E2E delay is least when failed link is nearest to source node. Under double link failure, the average E2E delay is maximum when failed links are farthest apart. E2E delay variation is shown in Fig. 2. Convergence time for multiple link failure is more than single link failure. It is observed that convergence is least for failed link immediately connected to source node. Convergence for failure scenario cases is shown in Fig. 3. Average throughput is calculated by adding bytes received over simulation time, so it is maximum for 5-13 link restoration path. During router dead interval, packets keep on traversing 1-2 and 2-5 links which increases average throughput for 5-13 failure restoration path. Instantaneous throughput coplot for no link and all link failure is shown in Fig. 4. It is observed that all links failure on working path reduces throughput to great extent as compared to case with no link failure. Instantaneous throughput co-plot for all cases of single link failure is shown in Fig. 5 and coplot for all scenarios of double link failure is shown in Fig. 6. Average jitter is maximum for network without failure and its value reduces for multiple link failures.

Table 2. Backup routes

Failure scenario	Failed link/links	Backup route
1	1-2	1-0-2-5-13
2	2-5	1-3-4-5-13
3	5-13	1-3-10-11-13
4	1-2 and 2-5	1-3-4-5-13
5	2-5 and 5-13	1-3-10-11-13
6	1-2 and 5-13	1-3-10-11-13
7	1-2, 2-5 and 5-13	1-3-10-11-13

Table 3. Parameter values for single and multiple link failure cases

Failure scenario	Average E2E delay (ms)	Average throughput (Mbps)	Average jitter (ms)	Convergence (Seconds)
1	7.97	1.37	2.54	5.11
2	9.66	1.49	0.82	6.14
3	10.89	1.74	1.12	6.14
4	10.61	1.33	0.56	6.52
5	9.82	1.55	0.87	6.52
6	10.89	1.38	0.76	6.52
7	10.68	1.37	0.59	6.82
Without failure	7.72	1.62	4.29	–

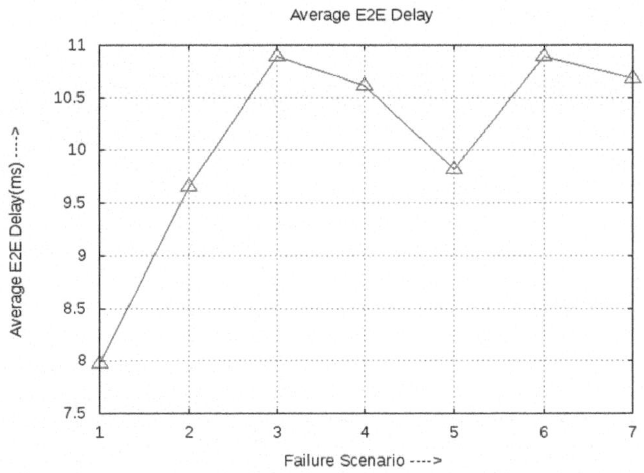

Fig. 2. Average E2E delay plot for various link failure cases

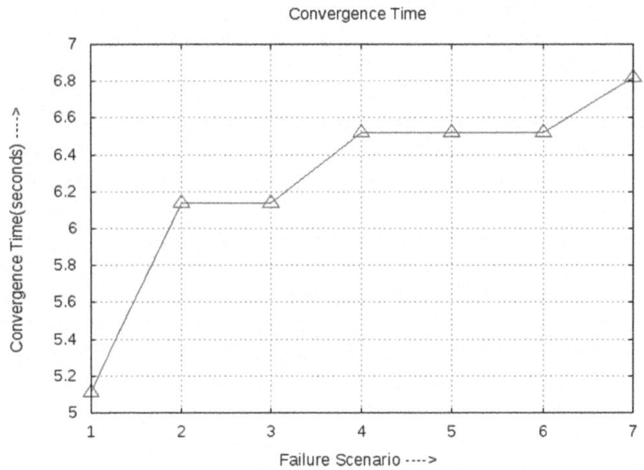

Fig. 3. Convergence plot for various link failure cases

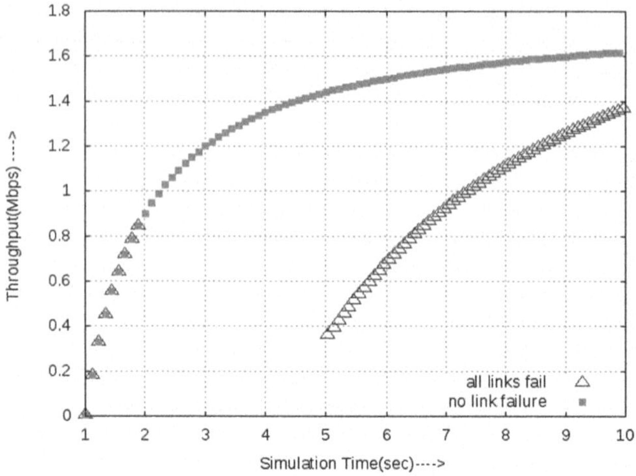

Fig. 4. Instantaneous throughput versus simulation time co plot for no link failure and all links failure (scenario 7)

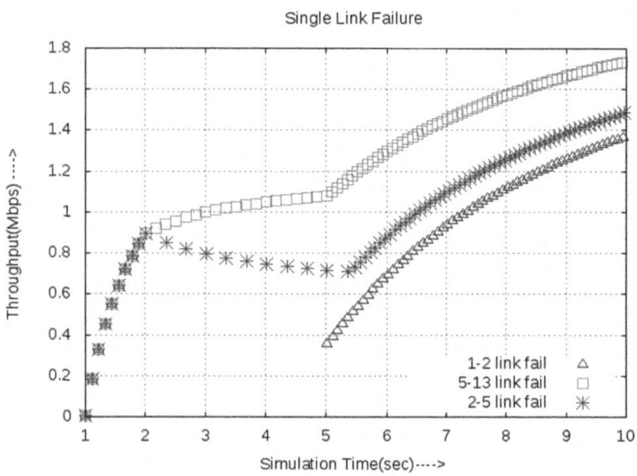

Fig. 5. Instantaneous throughput versus simulation time co plot for single link failure (scenario 1, 2 and 3)

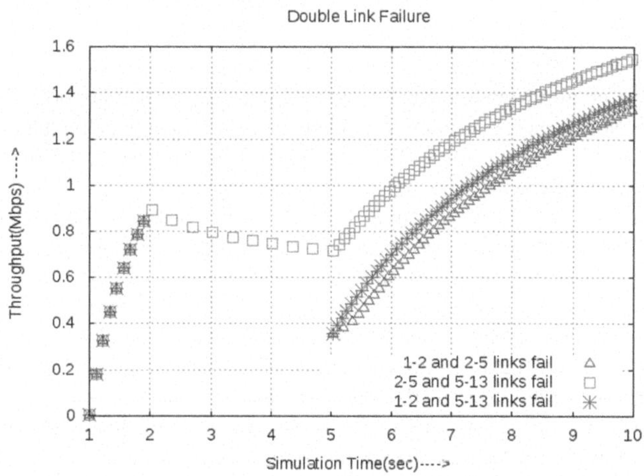

Fig. 6. Instantaneous throughput versus simulation time co plot for double link failure (scenario 4, 5 and 6)

5 Conclusion and Future Scope

QoS requirements of high-speed networks have made it imperative to design network infrastructure supporting resilience. Routing protocols have to be cautiously selected foreseeing the routine failure types. In this paper, the performance of OSPF routing technique for high-speed network has been investigated. QoS requirements are tested through mathematical modeling of average E2E delay, average throughput, instantaneous throughput, convergence and average jitter. A network of 14 nodes, NSFNET is simulated without failure and with multiple link failure. Simulation, network modeling and mathematical analysis are performed using NS2 version 2.35. Average E2E delay, average and instantaneous throughput, jitter and convergence are calculated for the network configured with OSPF routing under cases of link failure/failures on working path. It is observed that, under single link failure, the average E2E delay is least when failed link is nearest to the source node. Under double link failure, the average E2E delay is maximum when failed links are farthest apart. Convergence time for multiple link failure is more than single link failure. Network achieves high throughput when working path does not experience any failure and throughput reduces for multiple link failures. Average jitter is maximum for the network without failure and its value reduces for multiple link failures. The investigations in this paper provide insight into OSPF routing implementation for various link failure possibilities. The presented investigations can be extended to development of an automated system to select routing protocol foreseeing the common network failures.

References

1. Wosinska, L., et al.: Network Resilience in Future Optical Networks. In: Tomkos, I., Spyropoulou, M., Ennser, K., Köhn, M., Mikac, B. (eds.) Towards Digital Optical Networks. LNCS, vol. 5412, pp. 253–284. Springer, Heidelberg (2009). https://doi.org/10.1007/978-3-642-01524-3_10
2. Dey, G.K., Ahmed, M.M., Ahmmed, K.T.: Performance analysis and redistribution among RIPv2, EIGRP & OSPF routing protocol. In: 1st International Conference on Computer and Information Engineering, pp. 21–24 (2015)
3. Bhosale, S., Joshi, R.: Conformance testing of OSPF protocol. In: IET International Conference on Wireless, Mobile and Multimedia Networks, pp. 42–47 (2008)
4. Snoeren, A.C.: Lecture 12: Link-State Routing, CSE 123: Computer Networks. UCSDCSE. https://cseweb.ucsd.edu/classes/fa10/cse123/lectures/123-fa10-l12.pdf
5. Liu, P., Sun, R., Yan, Z.: Dynamic OSPF protocol. In: 4th IEEE International Conference on Broadband Network and Multimedia Technology, pp. 51–55 (2011)
6. Goyal, M., Ramakrishnan, K.K., Feng, W.-C.: Achieving faster failure detection in OSPF networks. In: Proceedings of the IEEE International Conference on Communications (ICC 2003), Alaska (2003)
7. Siddiqi, A., Nandy, B.: Improving network convergence time and network stability of an OSPF-Routed IP network. In: Boutaba, R., Almeroth, K., Puigjaner, R., Shen, S., Black, James P. (eds.) NETWORKING 2005. LNCS, vol. 3462, pp. 469–485. Springer, Heidelberg (2005). https://doi.org/10.1007/11422778_38
8. Absar, N., Wahab, M.A., Sikder, M.K.U.: Performance measurement of open shortest path first (OSPF) protocol in IP networks. Int. J. Eng. Res. **6**(2), 110–115 (2017)
9. George, D., Shyamala Devi, B.R.: The performance analysis of OSPF in IPV6 secured network. Int. J. Inf. Futur. Res. (IJIFR) **4**(8), 7129–7140 (2017)
10. Nagendra, M., Sathyanarayana, R.V.S.: Performance optimization of OSPF protocol in IPv6 networks. Int. J. Innov. Res. Comput. Commun. Eng. **4**(10), 18096–18102 (2016)
11. Zhao, D., Hu, X., Wu, C.: A study on the impact of multiple failures on OSPF convergence. Int. J. Hybrid Inf. Technol. **6**(3), 65–74 (2013)
12. Duta, C.-L., Gheorghe, L., Tapus, N.: Analyze OSPF convergence time in the presence of single and multiple failures. In: EMERGING 2015: The Seventh International Conference on Emerging Networks and Systems Intelligence, pp. 72–78 (2015)
13. Zhao, D., Wu, C., Hu, X., Wang, X., Zhao, B.: Characterization of OSPF convergence with correlated failures. In: 12th IEEE International Conference on Trust, Security and Privacy in Computing and Communications, pp. 1351–1356 (2013)
14. Hosny, W., Mahmoud, M., Aly, M.H., El-Badawy, E.S.A.: New optical parameters dependent metric for OSPF protocol for OBS networks. In: IFIP International Conference on Wireless and Optical Communications Networks, pp. 393–396 (2009)
15. Issariyakul, T., Hossain, E.: Introduction to Network Simulator NS2. Springer Science + Business Media, New York (2009). https://doi.org/10.1007/978-1-4614-1406-3
16. Balandin, S., Heiner, A.P.: OSPF protocol and statistical tools for network simulations in NS-2. In: 24th International Conference Information Technology Interfaces, pp. 465–470 (2002)
17. OSPF patch for ns2. https://sourceforge.net/projects/ospf4ns/. Accessed 08 May 2017
18. Nayak, A.K., Rai, S.C., Mall, R.: Computer Network Simulation using NS2. CRC Press/Taylor & Francis Group, Boca Raton (2016)

Application of ICT by Small and Medium Enterprises in Ogun State Nigeria

Oyediran Oyebiyi[1], Sanjay Misra[1](✉), Rytis Maskeliūnas[2], and Robertas Damaševičius[2]

[1] Department of Electrical and Information Engineering, Covenant University, Ota, Nigeria
sanjay.misra@covenantuniversity.edu.ng
[2] Kaunas University of Technology, Kaunas, Lithuania

Abstract. Small and medium enterprises (SMEs) have emerged as promising opportunities to eliminate and reduce unemployment globally. Increasing levels of technological advancement has revolutionized the dynamics of the business terrain. However, SMEs in developing countries are yet to fully explore the benefits of Information and Communications Technology (ICT). Survey data was collected from 75 SME ICT users in Abeokuta and Otta through a structured questionnaire using stratified random sampling technique. Results of regression analysis revealed that demographic variable (Staff Strength) significantly influences ICT application among SMEs while SME service delivery had no influence. Also, analysis of variance on the categories of SMEs was not a determinant factor on the use of ICT. The outcome of this study has implications for owners of SMEs, stakeholders, government and academic researchers in developing countries as it can provide patterns to help bridge the existing digital divide especially among Nigerian SMEs.

Keywords: Information and Communication Technology (ICT) Small and Medium Enterprises (SMEs) · Factors · Category

1 Introduction

Small and medium enterprises play very essential roles across different sectors in any nation. The experience of developed countries as regards SMEs buttresses the fact that their roles cannot be overemphasized especially among developing economies [1]. Different regions of the world define SMEs differently. In Nigeria, SMIEIS and CBN [2] define the cottage industry as one having an entire capital employed that is not greater than N1.5 M without adding the cost of a fixed asset such as land and working capital. Total workforce is put at a maximum of ten; small-scale industry as one having funds above N1.5 without exceeding N50 M, these total fund excludes the fees for land and operational funds. Workforce is between ten to hundred. The medium-scale industry is categorized as one having about N50 M as capital but not exceeding N200 M. This fees are exclusive of land and operational capital. Workforce is between 100 to 300 workers. This study however adopts the SMEDAN [3] definition of small-scale industries. Therefore, SMEs in this study refers to organizations having a

B. Panda et al. (Eds.): REDSET 2017, CCIS 799, pp. 459–471, 2018.
https://doi.org/10.1007/978-981-10-8527-7_39

total number of 10 to 100 employees and a capital asset exceeding N1.5million without surpassing N50 million with fees for land and building non-inclusive.

1.1 Problem Statement

Despite the notable developments witnessed in western countries like USA, Britain and Germany, SMEs in developing countries like Nigeria still continue to perform poorly [4]. Their performance and effectiveness as an instrument of economic growth and development in Nigeria has long been under scrutiny. The reason is not far-fetched considering the fact that SMEs are still beleaguered with several main but otherwise surmountable challenges. Accordingly, a recent study [5] asserted that problems and challenges of SMEs in Nigeria are consequently tied to certain economic variables that generally characterize the nation's economy.

The success level of SMEs in Nigeria still leaves much to be desired [6]. As unemployment assumes a frightening dimension, efforts undertaken by the Nigerian government to encourage technology use across different industries have not yielded desired dividends; many SMEs have failed to reap the benefits evenly.

The significant influence of business type on the spread of high-tech innovation among SMEs remains uncertain which represents a gap in useful information. In similar vein, though studies like [2, 7] abound. Such researches were carried out on single SME sectors within a given state. Hence, these studies did not effectively address peculiar factors affecting sectors of trading, agro-allied, telecommunications, pharmaceuticals, manufacturing, textile, building & construction, transport, tourism as well as events and entertainment. Also, the nature of ICT used by specific SME sectors and their specific applications were not determined.

Furthermore, it is still quite unclear whether the factors that affect SMEs in Nigeria cuts across different SME sectors or are restricted to particular sectors. Likewise, research in the area of ICT utilization among developing countries is still under researched and Nigerian SMEs are no exception.

The major aim of this study is to investigate factors that promote and inhibit ICT use among SMEs in Ogun state. The specific objectives of the study are to:

- Identify the type of ICTs used by the selected SMEs s in Ogun State.
- Identify the transactions/activities ICTs are used for in the SMEs.
- Identify elements that promote and inhibit use of ICT among the SMEs in Ogun State.

A dearth of literature on the level of ICT utilization exist amongst Nigerian SMEs. Consequently, this study enhances existing body of literature and makes particular contribution on the types of ICT commonly used by the SMEs.

This study also highlights the inadequacies of previous research in recognizing stakeholders stimulating effective utilization of ICT amongst Nigerian SMEs. The research highlights factors promoting ICT adoption as well as inherent advantages of ICT with respect to the organizations and their performance. Though some literatures have studied both the gains and consequences of ICT adoption, only a handful have reflected on SMEs' specific utilization of ICT. This research enhances available knowledge by corroborating the findings on factors hindering SMEs'growth in Nigeria, and also highlights chief motivating factors promoting ICT use.

Although research on SMEs in developing countries, Nigeria inclusive abound, several of these studies have been primarily conducted on specific sectors of the economy. There is a dearth of research on the application of ICT among SMEs across different sectors in specific regions within Nigeria. This study is an attempt to bridge the gap. For SMEs in Nigeria, an awareness of the type of ICT to deploy might result in superior service delivery and increased returns while also motivating more SMEs to deploy ICT in their operations. Therefore, this study makes a significant contribution to both practitioners and researchers.

The paper is organized as follows. The next section highlights the role of ICT among SMEs, perceived benefits of ICT and the factors promoting and inhibiting ICT use among SMEs. Section 3 describes the methodology based on Sects. 2, 3 and 4 discusses findings from the study while Sect. 5 provides a recommendation to the issues raised as well as a conclusion

2 Role of ICT Among SMEs

In order to guide the study, relevant bodies of literature were reviewed. The term ICT has become a part of daily language use synonymous with mobile phones, PDAs, handheld devices etc. often times, and ICT is used as an extended synonym for information technology. In the real sense, ICT is the convergence of telecommunication equipment's and devices through a link system for the sole aim of sharing resources.

[8] view ICT as a form of tool that offers a reasonable gain, while also adding business value in organizations. In today's fast paced and highly dynamic business environment, change is inevitable. ICT is increasingly becoming a catalyst of such revolutions within organizations [9]. It has metamorphosed from a luxury to a necessity and accordingly, the need to persist and succeed in the ever-changing business terrain has made commercial outfits even in remote areas of Nigeria to begin to imbibe ICT.

On a grander scale, the study in [10] observed that the influences of ICT on business development have become pervasive such that it is becoming increasingly tough for establishments to compete effectively in the world market without proper ICT infrastructure. Though ICT is vital to SMEs, a balanced understanding of appropriate forms of ICT needed by SMEs is equally necessary as different SMEs do not have to embrace ICT to equal grades of intricacies. For instance, the chief ICT tool that many SMEs take on are simple communication structures followed by a PC with basic software. With the Internet, SMEs leverage on advanced communication systems such as e-mail and online transaction. This may prove adequate for some, especially those in service industries such as tourism.

However, more importantly, like any organization, SME decides which type of ICT product to accept by carefully reviewing tangible benefits obtainable, employee ICT capacity and the available funds.

In today's technology driven age, ICT is crucial in making one or more deliberate choices. Though evidences of SMEs use of ICT for tactical goals is related, the study in

[11] opined that SMEs have the opportunity to gain modest benefit from advances in ICT through novelty, marketing, and improved customer responsiveness.

2.1 Benefits of ICT to SMEs in Nigeria

The benefits of ICT span across different sectors of a nation's economy and all other fields of human activities. ICT plays a major role in the way organization products are produced, promoted and provided [12].

SMEs represent a key supporter in Nigeria's march towards economic independence thus the effective utilization of ICT is of uttermost importance in making informed choices. Also, several significant benefits to SMEs include better productivity, improved internal business operations, global connection, improving inventory management systems amongst other benefits.

2.2 Factors Affecting ICT Use Among Nigerian SMEs

According to [13], generally, ICT usage in a developing economy like Nigeria is plagued with many problems, and regardless of the enhanced infusion progress rate of modern technologies, the diffusion ratio in Nigeria remains low.

Accordingly, Roy et al. [14] categorized these challenges to include internal and external barriers. The internal obstacles include; proprietor/manager features, cost and returns on investment, low ICT literacy, lack of finance and many more while the external blockades are more of socio- cultural, political, and regulatory issues.

Furthermore, several studies [15–22] conducted within developing countries abound and they have identified one or more contributing factors in developing economies such as Nigeria. Similarly, the electricity constraint in Nigeria is described as a prominent reason affecting the implementation of ICT among Nigerian organizations. Many studies confirm the poor state of infrastructure as another major reason for the slow uptake of ICT among businesses. The lack of these vital infrastructures ranges from inadequacies in their provision on the part of the government to poor service delivery on the part of service providers. The study in [23] observed that inadequate availability of a proper communication backbone and high speed Wide Area Networks for interconnectivity is responsible for low levels of ICT use among SMEs. Likewise, the study in [24] identified ICT implementation fee as a likely factor constraining many Nigerian SMEs from using ICT.

3 Methodology

The study adopted a stratified random sampling research design, which involves collection of data from SMEs in pharmaceutical, manufacturing, textile, telecommunication, agro-allied, tourism, printing, building & construction, events & entertainment and trading based on sectoral distribution. The dispersed nature of the subjects and the unavailability of ample data on registered SMEs in the state justify selecting a few respondents from whom generalization about the population could be made.

Ease of access to the SMEs was negotiated through their professional associations. SMEs in Nigeria belong to various associations like: Nigerian Association of Small-Scale Industrialists (NASSI), Small and Medium Enterprises Development Agency of Nigeria (SMEDAN), Chamber of Commerce and Industries.

To select a sample for the study, the researcher visited the various offices of the different SME associations. However, no comprehensive list of firms operating within the state could be provided while some associations out rightly refused to divulge any information. The Ogun state chamber of commerce however proved helpful as it had a list of 113 registered firms across the different sectors within the state. The researcher also independently discovered that some unregistered SMES had incorporated the use of basic ICT's like the mobile phone and the computer system in their business activities. Conversely, this development made the researcher to purposively select 75 SMEs who use other forms of ICT, which specifically include (the internet, intranet, e-mail, web portal, video conference). Nonetheless, the unevenness in the population made the researcher to randomly select variable sampling elements to ensure proportional representation of the different SME sectors.

3.1 Data Presentation

This section presents the demographic characteristics of SMEs and the research questions used in the study.

Demographic Characteristics of SME ICT Users

The demographic characteristics of the SMEs were obtained using a number of measures that include nature of organization, organization type, age of organization, staff strength of organization, (Table 1) owner ICT literacy and number of years of ICT usage.

Research Question 1a: What are the types of ICTs used by SMEs in Ogun State?

Results revealed that majority of the organizations used mobile telephone 32 (86.5%) in their businesses, 31 (83.7%) reported that they used computer, 29 (78.4%) used internet while 27 (72.9%) used the electronic mail. However, very few of the sampled organizations made use of video conference and credit card system as portrayed by 9 (24.3%) and 15 (40.5%) respectively, the reason for the low volume can be attributed to the nature of their businesses as shown in Table 2.

Research Question 1b: What Services do SMEs use ICT to deliver?

Table 3 revealed the services SMEs use ICT to deliver.

Table 3 shows that the sampled organizations primarily use ICT to keep up with competitors on a daily basis as indicated by 44 (58.6%). Thirty seven 37 (49.3%) admitted using ICT for online transaction daily while 35 (46.6%) said they used ICT to communicate with members of staff daily. Also from the table, results showed that 32 (42.6%) used ICT to communicate with customers and suppliers on a monthly basis and 9 (24.3%) used ICT to communicate with customers and suppliers on a weekly basis. Likewise, 29 (38.6%) said they used ICT to provide company information online annually.

Table 1. Demographic characteristic of the SMEs

	ICT users	
Organization nature	*Frequency*	*Percent*
Private Limited Company	8	10.6
Public Limited Company	20	26.6
Partnership	11	14.6
Sole proprietor	29	38.6
Family Owned Business	7	9.3
Others		
Organization type	*Frequency*	*Percent*
Manufacturing	15	20
Textile	9	12
Telecommunication	7	9.3
Tourism	7	9.3
Building & Construction	11	14.6
Printing	13	17.3
Pharmaceutical	4	5.3
Events & Entertainment	3	4
Trading	4	5.3
Agro - Allied	2	2.6
Age of organization	*Frequency*	*Percent*
0–5 years	26	34.6
>5 years	49	65.3
Staff strength	*Frequency*	*Percent*
0–9	45	60
10–49	9	12
50–100	11	14.6
101–250	8	10.6
>250	2	2.6
Owner ICT literacy	*Frequency*	*Percent*
Yes	57	76
No	18	24
Years of ICT use	*Frequency*	*Percent*
1–3 years	15	20
4–6 years	25	33.3
7–10 years	14	18.6
>10 years	11	14.6
No response	10	13.3

Research Question 2: What factors promote or inhibit use of ICT among the SMEs in Ogun state?

The distribution of factors that promote ICT use among SME ICT users is presented in Table 4.

Table 2. Distribution of types of ICT used by SMEs

Sectors	Video conference		Internet		E-mail		Credit card system		Web portal		Computer		Intranet		Telephony (mobile)		(Radio/Tv)	
	Freq	%	Freq	%	Freq	%	Freq	%	Freq	%	Freq	%	Freq	%	Freq	%	Freq	%
Pharmaceutical	1	20	3	60	3	60	2	40	3	60	4	80	4	80	4	80	3	60
Manufacturing	5	71.4	7	100	6	85.7	5	71.4	5	71.4	6	85.7	3	42.8	7	100	5	71.4
Textile	0	0	2	66.7	3	100	1	33.3	1	33.3	3	100	3	50	3	100	3	100
Telecom-munications	0	0	2	100	1	50	0	0	0	0	1	50	1	100	1	50	0	0
Agro-allied	0	0	2	66.7	2	66.7	2	66.7	3	100	2	66.7	3	66.7	3	100	2	66.7
Tourism	0	0	2	100	2	100	0	0	1	50	1	50	1	50	2	100	0	0
Printing	1	25	2	50	2	50	1	25	2	50	4	100	2	66.7	3	75	2	50
Building & Construction	0	0	3	100	3	100	0	0	2	66.7	3	100	1	50	3	100	1	33.3
Events & Entertainment	0	0	3	100	2	66.7	2	66.7	3	100	3	100	2	66.7	3	100	1	33.3
Trading	2	40	3	60	3	60	2	40	2	40	4	80	5	83.3	3	60	1	60
Total	9	24.3	29	78.4	27	72.9	15	40.5	22	59.5	31	83.7	25	67.6	32	86.5	18	48.7

Table 3. Distribution of services SMEs use ICT to deliver and frequency of use

ICT services	Daily		Weekly		Monthly		Yearly		No response	
	Freq	%	Freq	%	Freq	%	Freq	%	Freq	%
Online transaction	37	49.3	15	20	13	17.3	8	10.6	2	2.6
Communicating with the members of staff	35	46.6	25	33.3	10	13.3	5	6.6	5	6.6
Keep up with competitors	44	58.6	10	13.3	8	10.6	5	6.6	8	10.6
Providing company information online	25	33.3	6	8	8	10.6	29	38.6	7	9.3
Communicating with customers and suppliers	9	12	18	24	32	42.6	11	14.6	5	6.6
Obtaining information about new market value	9	12	6	8	29	38.6	20	26.6	11	14.6

Table 4. Distribution of internal factors promoting ICT use among SMEs

Possible factors	Disagree		Agree		No response	
Internal	Freq	%	Freq	%	Freq	%
Owner's high level awareness of ICT	47	62.6	20	26.6	8	10.8
Large size of the organization	38	50.6	32	42.6	5	6.6
Use of ICT by customers and suppliers	20	26.6	52	69.3	3	4
Perceived benefits of ICT	25	33.3	37	49.3	13	17.3
ICT Infrastructure	20	26.6	53	70.6	2	2.6
Adequate ICT literate staff	45	22.6	51	68	7	9.3
Owners decision to use ICT	29	38.6	35	46.6	11	14.6
High cost of ICT infrastructure	24	32	47	62.6	4	5.3
Nature of your organization's business	20	26.6	57	76	8	10.8
Low ICT maintenance costs	8	10.6	47	62.6	10	13.3

Among the internal factors promoting ICT use, 57 (76%) agreed that the nature of business of their organization was a major reason for their use of ICT. The table further shows 53 (70.6%) agreed that adequate ICT literate staff in the different organizations was also a major reason for use of ICT followed by use of ICT by customers and suppliers with 52 (69.3%) and adequate ICT literate staff with 51 (68%) respectively.

Table 5 presents the distribution of external factors promoting ICT use

The table shows that 55 (73.3%) agreed that preference of customers and suppliers of the SMEs was a major factor promoting use of ICT. The table further shows that 44 (58.6%) agreed that popularity of online marketing and sales was also responsible for their usage of ICT in their businesses while 31 (41.3%) attributed their use of ICT to reliable Internet service. Nineteen (25.3%) indicated adequate legal framework for businesses using ICT as a factor promoting their use of ICT.

Table 5. Distribution of external factors promoting ICT use among SMEs

Factors	Disagree		Agree		No response	
External	Freq	%	Freq	%	Freq	%
Consistent government policies	39	52	20	41.3	16	21.3
Adequate legal framework for businesses using ICT	51	68	19	25.3	5	6.6
Customers and suppliers preference	19	25.3	55	73.3	1	1.3
Reliable internet service	48	64	31	41.3	7	9.3
Popularity of online marketing and sales	26	34.6	44	58.6	5	6.6

Hypothesis 1: There is no significant relationship between SMEs' demographic profiles and the use of ICT.

Table 6 presents the significant relationship between SMEs' demographic profiles and the use of ICT.

Table 6. Showing regression analysis of SME demographic profile on use of ICT

	B	Std. Error	Beta	T	Sig
(Constant)	19.751	5.769		3.423	.002
Nature of organization?	.741	.698	.181	1.062	.297
Type of organization?	−.663	.334	−.336	−1.927	0.063
For how long has your company been in operation?	.863	2.411	.059	.358	.723
What is the staff Strength of this company?	1.820	.812	.403	2.242	.033
Is the owner of this company ICT literate?	.768	2.476	.054	.310	.758
Since when has your organization adopted ICT for its operations?	−.965	1.846	−.086	−.523	.605
a. Dependent Variable: USEFICT					

Table 6 revealed that strength of staff of a company among other SMEs' demographic profiles was significant ($p < 0.05$), other variables such as nature of organization, type of organization, how long the organization had been in existence, ICT literacy of SME owner and period of adoption of ICT are not significant ($p > 0.05$). This implies that SMEs who have higher staff tend to use ICT.

Hypothesis 2: Use of ICT will not have a significant influence on SME service delivery

Table 7 presents the influence of ICT use on SME service delivery.

Table 7. Showing the influence of ICT use on SME service delivery

Model	Unstandardized coefficients		Standardized coefficients	T	Sig
Service Delivery	**B**	**Std. Error**	**Beta**	−0.772	0.450
	−0.229	0.296	−0.179		

Results from Table 7 shows that use of ICT does not have a significant influence on SME service delivery. The result revealed that the null hypothesis is accepted and the alternative hypothesis is rejected ($t = -0.772$; $p > 0.05$). This implies that there is no significant influence of ICT use on SME service delivery.

4 Discussion of Findings

The studies revealed that majority of the SMEs are still at the early stage of ICT use. They predominantly use basic ICT equipment like mobile telephones and computers. This explains why Irefin et al. [2] noted that the most rudimentary ICT tool for SMEs include basic communication competences through fixed or mobile phones. Subsequently, the SMEs may then use a personal computer with basic software for office related activities. Quite remarkably, result also revealed that, few of the companies have begun to use some advance communication equipment like the electronic mall, internet browsing, web portal and intranet. These suggests that ICT use by SMEs vary from elementary devices such as radio and telephone lines to more cutting-edge technology such as emails, e-transacts and information processing systems.

However, availability does not imply use. Further enquiry into the services delivered by the SMEs using available ICTs revealed they are channeled towards keeping up with competitors and providing online transaction services while also using it to communicate with members of staff of the organization thereby suggesting that the technologies are predominantly used as a marketing and communication tool. This form of ICT use is considered beneficial on the long run. The capacity of organizations to interconnect successfully with consumers and suppliers can position a company to attain greater levels of business advantage.

In understanding the reasons why organizations tend to use ICT, results revealed that the nature of business, adequate ICT staff, available ICT infrastructure and use of

ICT by customers and suppliers significantly stimulate a company's use of ICT. Little wonder Mpofu et al. [25] noted that organizational readiness is usually echoed in the size, type, nature of business as well as ICT proficiency and the apparent benefits upheld by the management and employees.

From the study, result revealed that SMEs now boast of having adequate ICT infrastructures for promoting their various businesses as opposed to findings from previous studies. This can be attributed to the presence of numerous ISPs and mobile operators within the country. Also, ICT is changing the way we live, work and study. Findings from the study revealed that SMEs are being driven to integrate ICT into their business operations by external influence of customers and suppliers. This discovery agrees with [26], which identified use of ICT by SMEs in Southeast England as reason for improvement of customer service, keeping up with competitors and enhancing supplier relations.

Likewise, factors inhibiting use of ICT were also considered. The study revealed that high ICT maintenance cost was a chief factor inhibiting ICT use. Accordingly, [23] noted that high cost associated with execution makes organizations to often for-go the utilization of ICT. The researcher therefore suggests more effort on the part of the government, ICT providers and regulatory authorities to make ICT readily available for business owners.

Among other factors inhibiting use of ICT discussed in this study, little returns on investment were discovered to be a second leading reason as stated by more than two-third of the organizations. This could be an extension of [26] who affirmed that besides cost, the sole biggest restraint on ICT venture was the uncertainty over envisaged benefits. This finding do not however downplay the effect of external factors like power failure and customer willingness to engage in online transactions in Nigeria due to various security concerns and restrictions in the global market.

In this study, certain demographic characteristics of SMEs were considered to determine their influence on SMEs who use ICT. SMEs in Nigeria are firmly tied to proprietorship pattern, which often centers around an individual or a household. Among SMEs who use ICT, findings on the nature of SMEs from this study reveals no significant influence on ICT use. The study in [27] affirmed that Nigerian SMEs are principally in possession of a sole administrator or group. In such arrangements, capital for running the business is raised among friends, relatives and acquaintances. A major implication of such organization type however is that it limits the capacity for expansion while also mostly restricting the business within the confines of the local environment in which it operates consequently leaving very little capital left for ICT consideration or uptake. This observation is in agreement with [28] who also noted that the manager/proprietor's vision in sole proprietorship business is often within a small operational jurisdiction of the business in a community. In such arrangements, there is usually little or no knowledge of the wider or distant markets. Similarly, [28] opined that business mortality amongst SMEs remains high possibly due to an inherent shared suspicion and the desire for total dominance of the sole proprietor. This attitude militates against growth and extension. Similarly, [29] opined that businesses lack continuity due to poor futuristic planning such as death of the owner. This occurrence may signal doom of such establishments.

SMEs deliver various forms of services. The outcome of this study shows an opposing view to widely acclaimed influence of ICT use on performance as there was no significant influence of ICT use on Service delivery among SMEs. The reason for such among Nigerian SMEs may not be far-fetched. [30] rightly suggested that wider benefits are achieved when technological investment is pooled with human and organizational changes. These key factors are still lacking among SMEs in Nigeria. Most of the SMEs are owned by proprietors who often times are resistant to change, aim at maximizing profit as well as reducing all other forms of cost including staff development.

5 Recommendations and Conclusion

The challenges among SMEs in Nigeria in relation to ICT though huge is not insurmountable. As such, satisfactory levels can be achieved through a multi-faceted approach by concerned stakeholders

Thus for SMEs in Ogun State to stay relevant and succed, a new form of knowledge is required to help develop a strategic vision. In light of the above, the following recommendations are made:

- The ICT industry must intermittently develop ways of making SMEs owners/managers realize the supplementary value and latent benefits inherent in the use of appropriate ICT while also developing products and services targeted at addressing specific business needs. This is achievable through interactive seminar sessions from where feedback links can be established to fix problematic areas..
- This study also recommends that Government has a role to play in providing enabling infrastructure to prospective entrepreneurs for them to thrive particularly in early years of startup.

Findings from this study give better insight into some of the issues concerning the use of ICT among SMEs in Ogun state. SMEs within the state are still at the early stages of ICT use. Although SME owners are often times aware of ICT functions, awareness of strategic benefits of ICT can be further improved upon. The findings from this study approve that most of the SMEs are unable to integrate ICT into their businesses. However, it is believed that an external motivator can effectively tilt the scale towards more pronounced use of ICT especially among SMEs in Ogun state. The researcher opines that an innovative brand leader can sufficiently influence many SMEs by developing tailor made ICT solutions and services that showcases short and long term benefits of ICT.

Acknowledgement. We acknowledge the support and sponsorship provided by Covenant University through the Centre for Research, Innovation and Discovery (CUCRID).

References

1. Chidiebere, O.N., Iloanya, K., Udunze, U.: Youth unemployment and entrepreneurship development: challenges and prospects in Nigeria. Kuwait Chapter Arab. J. Bus. Manag. Rev. **4**(4), 20–35 (2014)
2. Irefin, I.A., Abdul-Azeez, I.A., Tijani, A.A.: An investigative study of the factors affecting the adoption if information and communication technology in small and medium scale enterprises in Nigeria. Aust. J. Bus. Manag. Res. **2**(2), 1–9 (2012)
3. Small and Medium Enterprises Agency of Nigeria (SMEDAN): SME Success Digest. vol. 3, no. 1 (2005)
4. Ihua, U.B.: SMEs key failure-factors: a comparison between the United Kingdom and Nigeria. J. Soc. Sci. **18**(3), 199–207 (2009)
5. Fatai, A.: Small and medium enterprises in Nigeria: the problems and prospects. (Doctoral thesis). University of Ibadan, Nigeria, vol. 2 (2013)
6. Osagie, C.: Embrace entrepreneurship, SMEDAN urges youths. This Day **15**(5483), 36 (2010)
7. Bankole, B.R.: Adoption and use of E-business by SMEs in Ibadan. (Master project), Africa Regional Centre for Information Science, University of Ibadan, Nigeria (2010)
8. Apulu, I., Latham, A.: Knowledge management: facilitator for SMEs competitiveness in Nigeria. In: UKAIS 2009 Conference. St Anne's College, Oxford, United Kingdom (2009)
9. Bekaroo, G., Bokhoree, C., Pattinson, C.: Impacts of ICT on the natural ecosystem: a grassroot analysis for promoting socio-environmental sustainability. Renew. Sustain. Energy Rev. **57**, 1580–1595 (2016)
10. Ali, V., Cullen, R., Toland, J.: ICTs and tourism in small island developing states: the case of the Maldives. J. Glob. Inf. Technol. Manag. **18**(4), 250–270 (2015)
11. Basu, R., Bhola, P., Ghosh, I., Dan, P.K.: Critical linkages between quality management practices and performance from Indian IT enabled service SMEs. Total Qual. Manag. Bus. Excell. pp. 1–39 (2016). http://www.tandfonline.com/doi/abs/10.1080/14783363.2016.1252259?journalCode=ctqm20
12. Taddeo, R., Simboli, A., Ioppolo, G., Morgante, A.: Industrial symbiosis, networking and innovation: the potential role of innovation poles. Sustainability **9**(2), 169 (2017)
13. Omorogbe, C.A.M.: Digital divide as it affects the development of e-commerce in Nigeria: a qualitative research study. Doctoral dissertation, Capella University (2012)
14. Roy, A., Sekhar, C., Vyas, V.: Barriers to internationalization: a study of small and medium enterprises in India. J. Int. Entrep. **14**(4), 513–538 (2016)
15. Heart, T., Kalderon, E.: Older adults: are they ready to adopt health-related ICT? Int. J. Med. Inform. **82**(11), e209–e231 (2013)
16. Moghaddam, B.K., Khatoon-Abadi, A.: Factors affecting ICT adoption among rural users: a case study of ICT center in Iran. Telecommun. Policy **37**(11), 1083–1094 (2013)
17. Neirotti, P., De Marco, A., Cagliano, A.C., Mangano, G., Scorrano, F.: Current trends in smart city initiatives: some stylised facts. Cities **38**, 25–36 (2014)
18. Law, R., Buhalis, D., Cobanoglu, C.: Progress on information and communication technologies in hospitality and tourism. Int. J. Contemp. Hosp. Manag. **26**(5), 727–750 (2014)
19. Albion, P.R., Tondeur, J., Forkosh-Baruch, A., Peeraer, J.: Teachers' professional development for ICT integration: towards a reciprocal relationship between research and practice. Educ. Inf. Technol. **20**(4), 655–673 (2015)

20. Ahmad, S.Z., Abu Bakar, A.R., Faziharudean, T.M., Mohamad Zaki, K.A.: An empirical study of factors affecting e-commerce adoption among small-and medium-sized enterprises in a developing country: evidence from Malaysia. Inf. Technol. Dev. **21**(4), 555–572 (2015)
21. Awiagah, R., Kang, J., Lim, J.I.: Factors affecting e-commerce adoption among SMEs in Ghana. Inf. Dev. **32**(4), 815–836 (2016)
22. Wyche, S., Steinfield, C.: Why don't farmers use cell phones to access market prices? Technology affordances and barriers to market information services adoption in rural Kenya. Inf. Technol. Dev. **22**(2), 320–333 (2016)
23. Apulu, I., Latham, A., Moreton, R.: Factors affecting the effective utilisation and adoption of sophisticated ICT solutions: case studies of SMEs in Lagos, Nigeria. J. Syst. Inf. Technol. **13** (2), 125–143 (2011)
24. Hassan, H., Ogundipe, A.A.: ICT adoption by micro and small scale enterprises in Nigeria: a case study of the federal capital territory, Abuja (2017)
25. Mpofu, C.K., Milne, D., Watkins-Mathys, L.: ICT adoption and development of E-business among SMEs in Malaysia. Int. J. Bus. Manag. **4**(2), 112–125 (2009)
26. Harindranath, G., Dyerson, R., Barnes, D.: ICT adoption and use in UK SMEs: a failure initiatives? Electron. J. Inf. Syst. Eval. **11**(2), 91–96 (2008)
27. Obasan, K.A., Shobayo, P.B., Amaghionyeodiwe, A.L.: Ownership structure and the performance of small and medium enterprises in Nigeria. J. Small Bus. Entrep. Dev. **4**(1), 11–21 (2016)
28. Ogunsiji, A.S., Kayode, L.W.: Entrepreneurial orientation as a panacea for the ebbing productivity in Nigerian small and medium enterprises: a theoretical perspective. Int. Bus. Res. **3**(4), 192–199 (2010)
29. Atsu, D.W.: Culture and management transition planning in Nigerian family businesses: mixed methods study. Doctoral dissertation, University of Phoenix (2016)
30. Mouelhi, R.: Impact of the adoption of information and communication technologies on firm efficiency in the Tunisian manufacturing sector. In: ERF 15th Annual Conference, Cairo, Egypt (2008)

Social and Web Analytics

Leveraging Movie Recommendation Using Fuzzy Emotion Features

Mala Saraswat(✉) and Shampa Chakraverty

Division of Computer Engineering, NSIT, University of Delhi, New Delhi, India
malasaraswat@gmail.com, apmahs.nsit@gmail.com

Abstract. User generated data like reviews encapsulate bursts of emotions that are generated after reading a book or watching a movie. These emotions garnered from reviews can be used in recommending items from entertainment domain with similar emotions. Till now much work has been done using emotions as discrete features in recommender system. In this paper, we delve deeper to use fuzziness in the emotion categories. The use of emotional features such as *love, joy, surprise, anger, sadness and fear* has been shown to be effective in identifying items with similar features for recommendations. However, there is a certain degree of vagueness and blurring boundaries between the lexicons of these categorical emotion features that has hitherto been largely ignored. In this paper, we tackle the problem of inherent vagueness in emotional features by proposing a framework for movie recommendation using fuzzy emotion features by taking each emotion category as a linguistic variable. We develop a Mamdani Model to extract fuzzy classification rules for recommending movies from emotions extracted from their corresponding reviews. Results show that Guassian fuzzy model with 5 linguistic variables yield 68.43% F-measure which is 10.5% improvement over the SVM based crisp model for recommending movies.

Keywords: Recommender system · Emotions · Reviews · Linguistic variable
Movies · Fuzzy rule based system

1 Introduction

A recommender system acts as a decision aid that offers personalized suggestions to users for different items. Emotions have also been demonstrated to be significant contextual factors in a variety of personalized and adaptive systems, that led to enhance the performance of applications such as modeling user behavior [1], searching results [2], and recommender systems [3]. Extracting, modeling and adopting emotions poses challenging problems in distinct areas that intersect with Psychology and Social Sciences such as Artificial Intelligence and Robotics [4], Human Computer Interaction [5], Opinion Mining and Sentiment Analysis [6], and Information Access and Retrieval [7].

With the increasing prevalence of e-commerce and social media sites, users are fascinated to naturally write reviews describing their evaluation of items. A user feels a whole range of emotions while reading a book, watching a movie or listening to music.

B. Panda et al. (Eds.): REDSET 2017, CCIS 799, pp. 475–483, 2018.
https://doi.org/10.1007/978-981-10-8527-7_40

Researchers in their work have mined the abundant emotional composition from user reviews [8].

Prior works using emotions in recommender systems have focused on different models of emotions that can be categorized according to the emotional theories they adopt. They include:

(a) Categorical emotion theory – which characterizes emotions as discrete units.
(b) Emotional dimension theory – which conceive emotions as points in a continuous space
(c) Appraisal theory – which represents emotions as outcomes of events and situations.

In recent years several authors have suggested that the term *emotion* and specific emotion words such as *anger, fear, sadness* etc. designate fuzzy sets. For example, Rusell [9] asserted that "*each emotion word, can be considered a label for a fuzzy set, defined as a class without sharp boundaries in which there is gradual but specifiable transition from membership to non-membership*". Such an observation for emotion bearing words is consistent with the view that fuzziness is characteristic of natural language categories [10]. It may therefore be fruitful to view emotion labelling process as a mapping function. Each emotion state would have associated with it a value specifying with it a grade of membership in each fuzzy set that corresponds to an emotion label. Zadeh [11] proposed fuzzy logic as extension of classical set theory to model real world problems in a realistic manner. Unlike classical mathematics that takes a deterministic world view, fuzzy logic enables us to reason about the rules and parameters that govern a system while considering the inherent inaccuracies and uncertainties that are typical of a practical world.

In the work [12], the authors, build the emotion profile of tweets using a lexicon for each of the six primary emotions: *love, fear, anger, joy, surprise and sadness* [13]. Each of these six primary emotions was used to form a lexicon. Secondary and tertiary emotions may be formed by combining two or more emotions. For example, the primary emotions *anger* combines with another primary emotion *surprise* to form *outrage* [10]. As such, these emotions may not be exactly indicative of a single unique emotion. Similarly, the keywords *amazingly, amazing* overlap in both lexicon of *happy and surprise*. Likewise, *shock, hurt, horror, furious* overlap in lexicon of *anger and fear*. The terms *agony, hurt, anguish* overlap in basic emotion lexicon of *sad and anger* [12]. Thus there is overlapping in the lexicon of the emotion which leads to fuzziness in the emotion set. In this work, we develop a fuzzy framework based on the Mamdani model [14] for recommending movies using emotions extracted from reviews of the movies. We used the R package *frbs* [15] for our experiments to evaluate the performance of the proposed approach.

The remainder of the paper is organized as follows. Section 2 provides an overview of existing work using emotions in the domain of recommender system. We explain our proposed fuzzy-driven approach in Sect. 3. Section 4 comprises of the experiments and the results using Movielens dataset. This is followed by the conclusion and future work in Sect. 5.

2 Prior Work

In this section we discuss the previous work in recommender system that uses emotions features. Recently, emotions have been exploited for recommending items [3, 8, 16] using various techniques. Emotions influence interactions, behaviors and thinking [17] and thus act as an important factor towards decision making. The use of emotions in recommender system is mainly concerned with discerning and modelling the user's mood. In their work Winoto and Ya Tang [3] carried out a study on how the user's mood influences the ratings given to movies. Such biased ratings, compromise the accuracy of recommender systems that use collaborative-filtering (CF). The author proposes a mood-aware CF by incorporating users' moods in a traditional CF based recommendation approach.

In a work by Kaminskas and Ricci, they present a music recommender system based on places of interest [16]. The link between music and places of interest is provided by means of social tags that represent the user's emotional state when listening to music and visiting places. The authors use the Geneva Emotional Music Scale (GEMS) model to attach emotional tags to music and places. In another work, Fernández-Tobías et al. uses item annotations in social tagging systems to extract their emotional information. It then transforms the tags into emotion item profiles [18]. Authors in [8], exploit emotions extracted from user generated content like reviews in entertainment domains to provide Cross Domain Recommendations.

This work is different from the previous works using emotions for recommender system due to the inclusion of degree of vagueness as an attribute. In this work, we consider each emotion category as a linguistic variable [19]. The values of this linguistic variable are the lexicon of that emotion category. The lexicon of each emotion category associated strength of membership for each keyword [12].

3 Proposed Approach

This section discusses our fuzzy driven approach for review based emotion profiling of movies and users for a movie recommendation system. The proposed recommender system comprises three modules namely *Data processing, Emotion extraction, Model building*.

3.1 Data Processing

Users express and share their opinions and experiences by writing reviews about an item on social and ecommerce sites. This module extracts all reviews about a movie and concatenates it to build an emotion laden textual corpus of that movie. This module also extracts user-item ratings matrices for all movies from Movielens dataset [20].

The users write reviews in very informal style. Because of this preprocessing of the review corpus is performed to wipe off the irrelevant content and filter the relevant content. The preprocessing of the review corpus involves the following steps:-

(i) Tokenization: All constituent words of the review corpus are extracted into tokens.
(ii) Stop word removal: Some of the very common words which form a token like 'a', 'an' 'the', 'is', 'at', 'which' etc. which are irrelevant for emotion analysis are removed from the corpus.
(iii) Conversion to Lowercase: The whole review corpus is changed to lowercase so as to maintain coherence among all the tokens.
(iv) Stemming: In this step tokens map to their root word. For example, the words 'shock', 'shockingly', 'shocked' all map to root word 'shock'.
(v) Word compression: While writing reviews users have tendency to elongate expressive words like writing 'coooool' instead of 'cool' or ''happy' to 'happppy''. This step identifies and compresses such elongated words.

3.2 Emotion Extraction from Reviews

Emotion Lexicon

In [12], the authors chose Parrott's list of emotions which is a mixed, hierarchical model for emotion classification. We need to build lexicon for these six distinct, innate emotions: *love, joy, surprise, anger, sadness and fear.* Firstly, primary emotion keywords in Parrott's list for each of the six parent emotions were added to their respective lexicons. Secondary emotions are derived from primary emotions which then activate a combination of tertiary emotions. The reviews form an unstructured text that conveys a mix of distinct emotions of various hues. Since Parrot's list contain a very limited set of emotion bearing words. We augment the respective emotion lexicon by adding wordnet synonyms to all these keywords in the respective emotion category at each of the three level i.e. primary, secondary and tertiary. Primary emotions keywords have a weight of 3, secondary emotion keywords a weight of 2 and tertiary emotion keywords with the least weight of 1. The weight of a keyword *kw* corresponding to an emotion e_k is represented using $e_k(kw)$. The complete augmented emotion lexicon in contains a total of 1166 keywords.

Generating Movie Emotion Profile

In this subsection we detect the preponderance of various emotions carried by reviews of a movie. For this we utilized the compiled emotion lexicon set for each of the given emotion as is done in [13]. Let e_k represent the emotion strength of category k, where $k \in \{1 \ldots 6\}$ represent the six basic emotions. For generating movie emotion profile, the emotion strengths of all six emotions are initialized to zero. Then one by one token is read from the review. Now the given token ω, is matched with the lexicon of each of the six emotion categories. The value of emotion strength for emotion e_k is incremented by the token's corresponding emotion weight $e_k(kw)$ if ω is found in lexicon of e_k. This process is repeated till all tokens of the review are read. The final emotion profile of the movie is generated:-

$$E(l) = \{e_{love}, e_{joy}, e_{surprise}, e_{anger}, e_{sad}, e_{fear}\}$$

The six emotions extracted from review of a movie have some numerical value. We first normalize it to range [0, 1]. The probability of normalized emotion strength of a movie is given by:

$$e'_k(l) = \frac{\left(e_k(l)\right)}{\sum_{k=1}^{6}\left(e_k(l)\right)} \quad (1)$$

The final normalized emotion profile of the movie l is denoted as:-

$$E'(l) = \left\{e'_{love}, e'_{joy}, e'_{surprise}, e'_{anger}, e'_{sad}, e'_{fear}\right\}$$

Generating User Emotion Profile

Users rate an item after assessing the emotion profile of the item. Hence, we compute the emotion profile of an active user by weighing each item that the user has rated with its rating and aggregating these values for all the items rated by the user.

Let us consider a user i who is active in the movie domain. Let $r\ (i,\ l)$ denote the rating given by user i to movie l. The emotion strength of user i, $e_k(i)$ for emotion k by user i is given by:

$$e_k(i) = \frac{\sum_l e'_k(l) \times r(i,l)\}}{\sum_l r(i,l)} \quad (2)$$

We normalize the emotion strength of user i to be within the range [0, 1]. The probability of normalized emotion strength of the user is given by:

$$e'_k(i) = \frac{\left(e_k(i)\right)}{\sum_{k=1}^{6}\left(e_k(i)\right)} \quad (3)$$

The final normalized emotion profile of the user i is denoted as:-

$$E'(i) = \left\{e'_{love}, e'_{joy}, e'_{surprise}, e'_{anger}, e'_{sad}, e'_{fear}\right\}$$

3.3 Model Building

Since our emotion lexicon set contains overlapping words we use fuzzy set theory proposed by Zadeh [19]. The fuzzy set theory enhances the classical set theory to model sets whose elements have various degrees of membership of a function. The lexicon of each emotion contains words that conceptualize from human language. Since human language is inherently vague, we conjecture to use fuzzy set theory for emotion analysis.

We employ the Mamdani model [14] that is built out of linguistic variable for creating fuzzy rule based object from the training data. We chose the Wang and Mendel learning method [21] to construct fuzzy rule based systems for classification from the emotion based user profile. This method uses space partitioning to divide equally the input and output spaces of the given emotion category into fuzzy regions. These fuzzy regions refer to intervals for the linguistic terms like “small”, “medium” and “large”.

Let X is a set, then a fuzzy subset A of X is defined by a membership function μ_a where $\mu_a(x)$ gives membership degree of x in A. In our case the emotion profile $E'(j)$ of a user is the set and the fuzzy subset include emotion categories like *joy, anger, surprise* where $\mu_a(x)$ is the emotion strength $e'_k(j)$ of each emotion in user emotion profile. A choice of an appropriate membership function is dictated by the nature of input and the complexity of the problem at hand. In our proposed fuzzy rule based movie recommender system, we elucidate that the Gaussian membership function is well suited to the very smooth transitions in concepts that emanate from human language. We performed experiment using different membership functions to analyze and verify our results in the next section.

The Gaussian membership function is defined as $f(x;\sigma;c) = \frac{e^{-(x-c)^2}}{2\sigma^2}$, where c and σ are parameters of the Gaussian distribution. In the Movielens dataset, user gives ratings from 1 to 5. We grouped user ratings into two classes: *like* and *dislike*. We labelled the movies with ratings 4 or 5 as *like* and with ratings 1 or 2 as *dislike*. We did not considered the movies with rating 3 as it indicated a fuzzy opinion. Since we are performing binary classification, we use a class label, $y \in \{1, 2\}$ where ‘1’ indicates ‘dislike’ and ‘2’ indicate ‘like’.

4 Experiments and Results

We used the R package *‘frbs’* V3.1-0 [15] available in CRAN repository to implement Wang and Mendel’s technique for generating fuzzy rules [21]. For our experiments, we used the Movielens dataset [20] to extract the ratings of movies of the user. Then using emotion profile of movie and rating we generated emotion profile of user as discussed in Sect. 3.2. We divided the randomized dataset into training and testing datasets in the ratio of 80:20.

We use Zadeh implication with ‘MIN’ function as T-norm and ‘MAX’ function as S-norm for fuzzy rule generation. Zadeh implication generated forty two fuzzy rules for classifying each movie as *liked* or *disliked* based on its emotion content. Two of the rules generated based on three linguistic variable i.e. “small”, “medium” and “large” are shown below.

Rule1: IF love is small and joy is small and surprise is small and anger is small and sad is large and fear is small THEN class is 1

Rule2: IF love is medium and joy is medium and surprise is small and anger is small and sad is small and fear is small THEN class is 2

The graph for membership functions is shown in Fig. 1. We evaluated our model using the classification metrics *accuracy, precision, recall* and *F-score*.

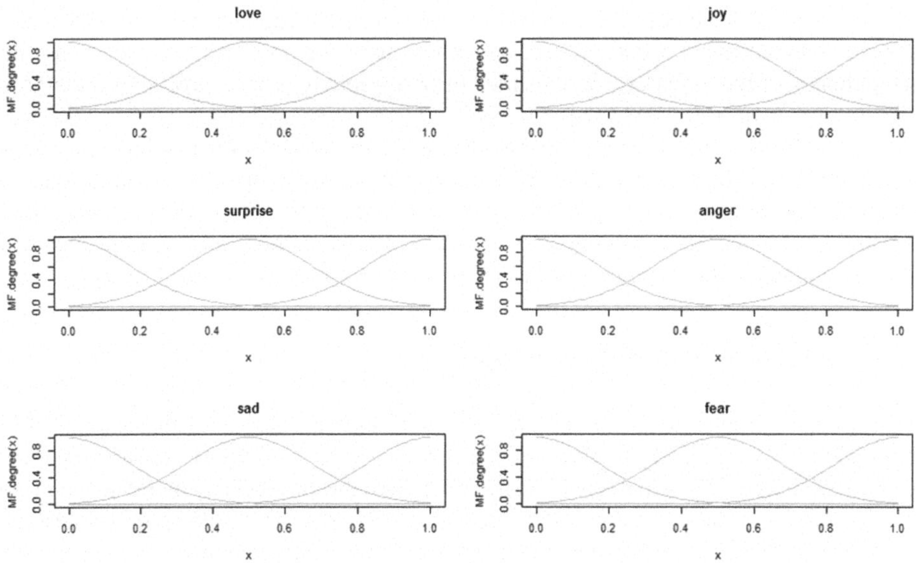

Fig. 1. Membership function for six emotion features for number of Linguistic Variable = 3

We conducted the experiments over different membership functions namely Gaussian, trapezoid and triangular for analysing their effect on the generated model. We analyse the effect of parameters such as type of membership function and number of linguistic variables (3, 5 and 7) and compare the proposed model with crisp features on Support Vector Machine (SVM) based classifier (*Polynomial Kernel and C = 1*) available in the R package *'kernlab'* [22].

Table 1 shows the comparison of the accuracy, precision, recall and F- measure of our experimental analysis of our fuzzy rule based movie recommender system. We observe that our proposed fuzzy model with Gaussian membership function with number of linguistic variables = 5 performs best with an F- measure of 68.43%.

Table 1. Impact of fuzzy emotion features on movie recommender system

Model	MF	A	P	R	F1
SVM (CrispFeatures)	NA	51.02	84.42	50.28	67.72
Fuzzy Model #Linguistic Variable = 3	Gaussian	48.95	99.98	48.96	65.73
	Trapezoid	49.49	99.96	49.49	66.21
	Triangle	49.92	98.80	49.07	65.57
Fuzzy Model #Linguistic Variable = 5	**Gaussian**	**51.04**	**99.99**	**52.01**	**68.43**
	Trapezoid	49.75	99.89	49.01	65.76
	Triangle	49.27	62.66	49.03	55.02
Fuzzy Model #Linguistic Variable = 7	Gaussian	48.97	99.96	48.98	65.75
	Trapezoid	49.75	99.89	49.01	65.76
	Triangle	49.01	99.93	49.02	65.77

Legends: MF-Membership Function; A-Accuracy; P-Precision; R-Recall; F1-F- measure

The crisp model using SVM shows comparable performance with the Gaussian-fuzzy model in terms of accuracy, precision and F-measure. However, it is worth noting that inclusion of fuzzy features has resulted in 18% improvement in precision and 10.5% in F-measure, over the SVM-crisp model.

The results clearly show that performance of a fuzzy model varies with the membership function and granularity of linguistic values. Gaussian distribution is a more suitable representation when size of linguistic variables = 5. It can be seen with 5 as the number of linguistic values, the proposed model retains the vagueness and overlap between different classes without being too specific or generic about the value of features.

5 Conclusions and Future Scope

In this paper, we reflected upon the aspect of the inherent vagueness that is present in emotional or psychological features such as *anger and fear* or *happy* and *surprise* etc.

We used each emotion category as a linguistic variable to precisely model the overlap and uncertainty in the user emotion profile. We proposed a fuzzy rule based framework based on Mamdani's model using Wang and Mendel learning technique to generate the fuzzy IF-Then rules from the training data. This fuzzy rule based system is used for recommending movies to users with the similar emotion profiles extracted from movie reviews. The experimental results indicate that fuzzy logic is a promising avenue to reflect the vagueness in emotions that are embedded in reviews for movies.

In this work, we restricted our experiments to recommendations in movie domain only. We will extend to other entertainment domains like books, TV shows, music etc. We will also use it for cross domain recommender systems using different domains, for solving the cold start problem.

References

1. Hastings, J., Ceusters, W., Smith, B., Mulligan, K.: The emotion ontology: enabling interdisciplinary research in the affective sciences. In: Beigl, M., Christiansen, H., Roth-Berghofer, T.R., Kofod-Petersen, A., Coventry, K.R., Schmidtke, H.R. (eds.) CONTEXT 2011. LNCS (LNAI), vol. 6967, pp. 119–123. Springer, Heidelberg (2011). https://doi.org/10.1007/978-3-642-24279-3_14
2. Meyers, O.C.: A mood-based music classification and exploration system. MSc thesis, School of Architecture and Planning, MIT (2007)
3. Winoto, P., Tang, T.Y.: The role of user mood in movie recommendations. Expert Syst. Appl. **37**(8), 6086–6092 (2010)
4. Breazeal, C.: Emotion and sociable humanoid robots. Int. J. Hum Comput Stud. **59**, 119–155 (2003)
5. Cassell, J.: Nudge wink: elements of face-to-face conversation for embodied conversational agents. In: Embodied Conversational Agents, pp. 1–27 (2003)
6. Carrillo de Albornoz, J., Plaza, L., Gervás, P.: A hybrid approach to emotional sentence polarity and intensity classification. In: 14th International Conference on Computational Natural Language Learning, pp. 153–161 (2010)

7. Shi, Y., Larson, M., Hanjalic, A.: Mining mood-specific movie similarity with matrix factorization for context-aware recommendation. In: Workshop on Context-Aware Movie Recommendation, pp. 34–40 (2010)
8. Chakraverty, S., Saraswat, M.: Review based emotion profiles for cross domain recommendation. Multimedia Tools Appl. **76**, 1–24 (2017)
9. Russel, J.A.: A circumplex model of affect. J. Pers. Soc. Psychol. **39**, 1161–1178 (1980). https://doi.org/10.1037/h0077714
10. Labov, W.: The boundaries of words and their meanings, pp. 340–373 (1973)
11. Zadeh, L.A.: Fuzzy sets. Inf. Control **8**(3), 338–353 (1965)
12. Chakraverty, S., Sharma, S., Bhalla, I.: Emotion–location mapping and analysis using Twitter. J. Inf. Knowl. Manag. **14**(03), 1550022 (2015)
13. http://www.theemotionmachine.com/classification-of-emotions/. Accessed Oct 2016
14. Mamdani, E.H.: Application of fuzzy algorithms for control of simple dynamic plant. In: Proceedings of the Institution of Electrical Engineers, vol. 121, no. 12, pp. 1585–1588. IET, December 1974
15. Riza, L.S., Bergmeir, C.N., Herrera, F., Bentez Snchez, J.M.: frbs: fuzzy rule-based systems for classification and regression in R. American Statistical Association (2015)
16. Kaminskas, M., Ricci, F.: Location-adapted music recommendation using tags. In: Konstan, J.A., Conejo, R., Marzo, J.L., Oliver, N. (eds.) International Conference on User Modeling, Adaptation, and Personalization. UMAP 2011. LNCS, vol. 6787, pp. 183–194. Springer, Heidelberg (2011). https://doi.org/10.1007/978-3-642-22362-4_16
17. TenHouten, W.D.: Emotion and Reason: Mind, Brain, and the Social Domains of Work and Love, pp. 12–13. Routledge (2014)
18. Fernández-Tobías, I., Cantador, I., Plaza, L: An emotion dimensional model based on social tags: crossing folksonomies and enhancing recommendations. In: Huemer, C., Lops, P. (eds.) E-Commerce and Web Technologies. EC-Web 2013. LNBIP, vol 152, pp. 88–100. Springer, Heidelberg (2013). https://doi.org/10.1007/978-3-642-39878-0_9
19. Zadeh, L.A.: The concept of a linguistic variable and its application to approximate reasoning—I. Inf. Sci. **8**(3), 199–249 (1975)
20. Harper, F.M., Konstan, J.A.: The MovieLens datasets: history and context. ACM Trans. Interact. Intell. Syst. (TiiS) **5**(4), 19 (2015). https://doi.org/10.1145/2827872
21. Wang, L.-X., Mendel, J.M.: Generating fuzzy rules by learning from examples. IEEE Trans. Syst. Man. Cybern. **22**(6), 1414–1427 (1992)
22. Zeileis, A., Hornik, K., Smola, A., Karatzoglou, A.: kernlab- an S4 package for kernel methods in R. J. Stat. Softw. **11**(9), 1–20 (2004)

Analyzation and Detection of Cyberbullying: A Twitter Based Indian Case Study

Aastha Sahni[1(✉)] and Naveen Raja[2]

[1] Department of Information Technology,
Indira Gandhi Delhi Technical University for Women (IGDTUW), Delhi, India
aasthasahni9@gmail.com

[2] National e-Governance Division (NeGD), Department of Electronics and Information Technology (DeitY), Ministry of Electronics and Information Technology (MeitY), Delhi, India
naveen.talent08@gmail.com

Abstract. Social networking sites like Facebook and Twitter specially involves large population connected worldwide. Though these social networks aim to bring people from around the world together yet it has its own cons associated with it. With the increase in these Social Networks there is an exponential increase in cybercrimes on these sites. Cyberbullying or Trolling is one such crime where victim is bullied with abuses, personal remarks, false claims and sarcasm on social networking sites and sometimes is traumatized to great extent. There have been many cyberbullying detection methods and systems already developed to cater to the problem but major concern lies on the fact that nearly 80%–90% users on such sites are Indians owing to one of most populous countries in the world, they use Hinglish (Hindi written in English) to communicate mostly on social networking sites majorly Facebook and Twitter. Our research aims at analyzing Cyberbullying content based on Hinglish tweets on one such social network that is Twitter. We analyzed tweets based on textual analysis and performed classification also. Through this we concluded our findings and future scope of work for detection of Cyberbullying on more complex data.

Keywords: Cyberbullying · Hinglish · Trolling · Twitter · Social media Cyberbullying detection · Textual analysis

1 Introduction

Social media platforms like Facebook, Twitter and Instagram etc. have become very popular and they draw millions of users who are engaged in sharing and posting information of their interest. This information involves users expressing their opinions on latest news happenings around the world. Often users of conflicting views and opinions are found to express themselves freely over social media. However, it is observed that malicious users repeatedly post content targeted to malign or harass or abuse or threaten other users (victims). This phenomenon is referred commonly as trolling or cyberbullying in research community. As a consequence, it becomes very difficult for the victims to continue to use the services of these social media platforms. Their state of mind gets

B. Panda et al. (Eds.): REDSET 2017, CCIS 799, pp. 484–497, 2018.
https://doi.org/10.1007/978-981-10-8527-7_41

affected adversely and in extreme cases the victims get traumatized to such an extent that they resort to extreme measures. Malicious users misuse the freedom of expression and the ease of content publishing offered by these social media platforms to launch these cyberbullying attacks. They are often emboldened with the notion that their activities on social media cannot be tracked and their identities in the real world cannot be identified. There are large instances of cyberbullying being widely reported. There are no appropriate automated intelligence methods to tackle the situation specifically when a large amount of users of such social media platforms are Indians who use mostly hinglish (writing Hindi content in English) language to communicate with each other.

Our work aims to fill the gap by analyzing content involved in cyberbullying on social media networks with an eventual aim of proposing how automated methods for detection of cyberbullying can be developed since it takes into account complex data (Hindi text in English) which involves huge data analysis and evaluation. For our analysis, we have used Twitter as the social media platform to analyze content related to cyberbullying. As a case study, we analyzed in detail one of the famous twitter trolling case of Bollywood singer Sona Mohapatra when she tweeted her opinion on actor Salman Khan's "raped comment" during shooting of movie Sultan. We performed data analysis and classification of tweets content. As a result of our work we have proposed an algorithm for detecting cyberbullying on the basis of textual analysis.

2 Motivation

In recent years, cyberbullying has grown into a major problem with the growth of online communication and social media. Cyberbullying has been recognized recently as a serious national health issue among online social network users since it creates mental imbalance, depression and its emotional and psychological effects are destructive [2]. According to Centers for Disease Control and Prevention (CDC) suicide is the third leading cause among death of young people with approximately 4,400 deaths per year with more than 14 percent of high school students have considered suicide and nearly 7 percent have attempted it as a result of cyberbullying[1].

Twitter is a popular social media site where users can post and share thoughts, ideas, and opinions in 140 character tweets. Many businesses and celebrities utilize this social media platform to contact consumers and fans. This type of cyberbullying tends to be overlooked because of the preconceived notion to pretend that celebrities are not 'real' people. Many celebrities receive death threats on a daily basis on Twitter, which can be problematic for some who cannot cope with that much hate. The number of cases involving celebrities in cyberbullying has been increasing leading to personal and professional devastation. This has sometimes forced them to leave Twitter after suffering abuse at the hands of trolls.

Twitter has faced many challenges in past years, including dipping user growth and increasing financial losses. However, the hate speech, abusive or offensive content, bullying and mob mentality that run rampant on the platform are problems Twitter has

---

[1] The Top Six Unforgettable Cyberbullying Cases Ever https://nobullying.com/six-unforgettable-cyber-bullyingcases/.

battled for roughly a decade. From an internal memo obtained from TheVerge.com former CEO Dick Costolo confessed that twitter actually sucks when dealing with trolls faced by people every day and has lost many of the core users due to it[2].

Cyberbullying has become one of the major reasons for many twitter users which includes many known public figures to quit the social media platform due to unstoppable hate, abusive tweets and tweets containing personal remark against users. It prohibits one from expressing his/her views or opinions freely. Indian government is also now taking initiatives in this area in order to protect women and child abuse/ harassment on online social media especially on Twitter. Union Minister for Women and Child Development Maneka Gandhi has also started a major anti-trolling initiative on twitter to address the issue of cyberbullying named #IamTrolledHelp[3]. Where victims are asked to use this hashtag so that government is notified or alarmed about their problem on Twitter and Facebook. So government agencies are also recognizing these issues and it has also become quite a challenge for them to come up with accurate systems to detect such incidents of cyberbullying on Social Media. Our work can eventually contribute in this area and help government in its initiative.

3 Related Work

Cyberbullying has been part of various research works which even involved case studies concerning related incidents on social media sites specially twitter, thereby characterizing its effects, behavior and detection.

3.1 Cyberbullying and Detection Techniques

Galán-GarcÍa et al. [1] worked on a school based case study where attacker were students of that school only and assumed that every attacker's profile was fake and followed by the real profile of the user behind the fake one order to reach the real culprit behind fake profile by using authorship analysis techniques. This assumption was based on the fact that these kinds of users wanted to stay updated on the activity that surrounds the fake profile. Besides, each individual writes in a characteristic way. Studying different features of the written text was possible to determine the authorship of, for example, e-mails. In this case, despite users behind fake profiles tried to write in a different way to avoid detection, Twitter provided other characteristics that, in conjunction with the text analysis was used to link a trolling account to a real user's profile. Al-garadi et al. [2] proposed a set of unique features derived from Twitter; network, activity, user, and tweet content, based on these features developed a supervised machine learning solution for detecting cyberbullying in the Twitter. An evaluation demonstrated that the developed detection model based on proposed features, achieved results with an area under the receiver-operating characteristic curve of 0.943 and an f-measure of 0.936. These results

[2] http://www.theverge.com/2015/2/4/7982099/twitter-ceo-sent-memo-taking-personal-responsibility-for-the.

[3] https://yourstory.com/2016/07/maneka-gandhi-iamtrolledhelp/.

indicated that the proposed model based on these features provides a feasible solution to detecting cyberbullying in online communication environments.

Dredge et al. [3] investigated whether self-presentation behaviors in Facebook can lead to cyberbullying by recording content of 147 adolescent Facebook profile pages and used them for predicting cyberbullying victimization and also found that series of Facebook features and experiences of traditional cyberbullying were quite related and one of the key factors for predicting of cyberbullying victimization. Alim [4] studies 7,315 tweets associated with cyberbullying, performed sentimental analysis of positive and negative tweets showed users sentiments towards cyberbullying, manually analyzed 400 tweets for content analysis. Results showed 33% of tweets contained advice and support for cyberbullying victims. Van Hee et al. [5] constructed a Dutch dataset of social media messages containing cyberbullying and proposed and evaluated a methodology for adequate annotation for data, the ultimate goal of automatic cyber-bullying detection was to reduce manual monitoring efforts on social media. They did a thorough qualitative analysis of the classification results to gain insight into the linguistic realization of cyberbullying and more specifically a series of fine-grained categories related to cyberbullying.

Mangaonkar et al. [6] worked on the fact that it is critically important to efficiently detect cyberbullying behavior by analyzing tweets. Their research focused on improving cyberbully detection tasks using principles of collaborative computing, where preliminary results indicated an improvement in time and accuracy of the detection mechanism over the stand alone paradigm.

Van Royen et al. [7] emphasized that automatic cyberbully detection has potential for signaling harmful messages but desirability of such automatic systems seems a challenge. Of the 179 experts contacted, 50 28% responded. Most of these experts favored automatic monitoring, but mentioned clearly the conditions under which such systems should be implemented, including effective follow-up strategies, protecting the adolescents' privacy and security.

Dinakar et al. [8] worked on binary classifiers which out-performed multiclass classifiers for detecting textual cyber-bullying and came up with the conclusion that textual cyber-bullying can be tackled by building individual topic-sensitive classifiers. Worked on classifying textual cyberbullying on YouTube comments by using binary as well as multiclass classifiers. Problem Decomposition stated in paper is "A comment involving a combination of negativity or profanity and topics that are personal and sensitive are those can are most hurtful, forming candidates for cyberbullying". Tweet labels were on the basis of sexuality, race and intelligence and then further classifying comments on each type of label as positive or negative based on sensitivity in content.

Calvin et al. [9] studied hashtags associated with public mentions of bullying on twitter from January 1, 2012 to December 31, 2012. Identification of differences in the daily usage of hashtags used with bullying keywords were recorded. The differences showed that bullying has both an immediate, large scale influence as well as a more every day presence on twitter. Reynolds et al. [10] worked on formspring.me website to detect posts on cyberbullying by downloading a list of bad words from a website and each word was given severity level to form a feature set and classifying using weka tools.

Silva et al. [11] proposed an automated model for cyber-bullying detection based on research findings from psychology community and measuring the degree of cyberbullying on Facebook and developing an app based on the proposed model to notify parents about it. The model was more focused on cyberbullying from adolescent's point of view. Dalal et al. [12] worked on comments in Hindi that can be detected as insult to other person. Data collection was done from different Hindi forums, some of the English dataset was converted into Hindi by using google translator and a dictionary containing abuses in Hindi was created as part of data set. Classification was done using supervised machine learning approach. The size of data set was small but overall aim of research was to detect such insults that get difficult to identify.

Joshi et al. [13] implemented classifier system for sarcasm detection on the basis of incongruity in the text. The research was based on approach that incongruity is the basis for sarcasm. Data was collected from twitter as well as discussion forum and features selected on basis of implicit congruity, explicit incongruity, lexical and pragmatic. This research outperformed two of the past works but did not considered Hindi words in English that is Hinglish. It totally worked on English content. Xiang et al. [14] focused on detection of offensive content in tweets, worked using sentimental analysis and bootstrapping algorithm in NLP for feature extraction. Four classifiers were used for classification J48 decision tree learning, SVM, LR (logistic regression) and RF (random forest).

Hosseinmardi et al. [15] studied on analyzing user behavior, negative data content and likes on the content on site Ask.fm to understand cyberbullying behavior on social networks. Royen et al. [7] worked on monitoring of cyber-bullying on social networks, took suggestions from experts and people about various look up strategies to be taken while monitoring cyberbullying online keeping in my privacy and security of users online. Kansara and Shekokar [16] proposed a framework for cyberbullying detection on social network based on content and images posted online. Hosseinmardi et al. [17] worked on images posted on Instagram and how images are used for cyberbullying, designed a labelling for images in terms of cyberbullying and used labelled data for further training classifier to detect events of cyberbullying.

Nandhini and Sheeba [18] proposed a cyberbullying detection techniques on social newtorks using fuzzy logic and genetic algorithms. Wang et al. [19] worked on automatic predicting crime events using twitter posts. They designed a model via linear modelling which predicted future hit and run cases, the model outperformed a baseline model designed for same prediction.

Dadvar et al. [20] proposed three models for bully detection based on an expert system, a supervised machine learning and a hybrid of both using data from YoutTube. They assigned a score to each bully content highlighting its severity and finally showed that expert system outperformed machine learning model and hybrid one gave even better performance. Vanhove et al. [21] worked on multimedia data analysis in order to design an architecture which is pluggable with reusable components to detect inappropriate content based on text, image, audio and video on social networks.

Nalini and Sheela [22] proposed an effective approach of classifying tweets based on text classifiers based on weighting scheme of feature selection. Ghasem et al. [23] designed a framework for detection of cyberstalking which contained five modules namely detection module, attacker identification module, personalization module, aggregator module and evidence collection module.

Kovacevic and Nikolic [24] worked on detection of cyberbullying using text mining techniques with software. Nahar et al. [25] proposed a detection graph model for detecting victims and predators involved in act of cyberbullying and rank the most influential users (victim or attacker). The model proposed proved highly accurate. Lau et al. [26] contributed in the development of a supervised cybercriminal network mining method proposed under a probabilistic generative model enhanced by Gibbs sampling method. It proved to be a successful method for mining cybercrimes from social media networks. Simanjuntak et al. [27] Created a text classification system which classified text in documents using different classification techniques. SVM outperformed all other methods of classification with 100% accuracy. Chandramouli [28] explored various methods and technological challenges involved in social media security and privacy and concluded their research with fact that mitigating social media crimes and vulnerabilities includes all kinds of support from government to people then only the problem can be tackled since it involves people from all over the world with distinct age groups, educational- cultural background and languages.

3.2 Summary

From the study of above research works it is clearly seen that a lot of work has been done in area of cyberbullying but all of them deal with different scenarios and considerations. The fact that all these above works take either English or Hindi content into consideration whereas our research deals with tweets containing both Hinglish and English content based on the case study taken into account, which is quite challenging to deal with and is something different from all the works mentioned above. Our work is the seed to new kind of data analysis and results.

4 Methodology

4.1 Data Collection

We collected data using twitter search API and python py-query module. Following are the data collection results (Table 1):

Table 1. Shows data collection details

Date	20-06-2016 to 01-08-2016
Tweets collected	10,239
Re-tweet range	1294
Number of tweets manually annotated	1000

4.2 Assumptions

- Only textual content of a tweet is taken into consideration for identifying cyberbullying.
- Certain factors are taken into account while considering a tweet valid in context to cyberbully. Cyberbullying can occur in many ways, including:
  (1) Abusive texts containing Hindi and English abuses
  (2) Hurtful texts kind of insulting the user to whom tweet is directed.
  (3) Humiliating others online-sarcastic tweets leading to indirect insult or hurt
  (4) Warning
  (5) Personal remarks
  (6) Making false claims.

4.3 Work Flow Analysis

The following flowchart shows the proposed approach:

The block diagram in Fig. 1 describes the work flow approach. The next step after data collection is data cleaning where stop-words and other unnecessary content is removed from the tweets using **RE** and **NLTK** python module. After cleaning the tweets manual annotations and sentiment analysis is performed on 1000 tweets. Manually annotated tweets will be further used to design a training set and test set for the classifier which will eventually classify the tweets and additionally results from manually annotated tweets will be compared with result of sentiment analysis so as to see how tweet sentiment corresponds to manual annotations. Sentiment Analysis is performed using text-blob library in python. Sentiment Analysis is used to analyze what the user emotion behind a tweet is the user tweeting the tweet shows positive or negative sentiment which is described by the words contained in the tweets. The polarity value (-1 to1) which we get after performing this step helps to analyze does the sentiment (positive or negative) of tweets.

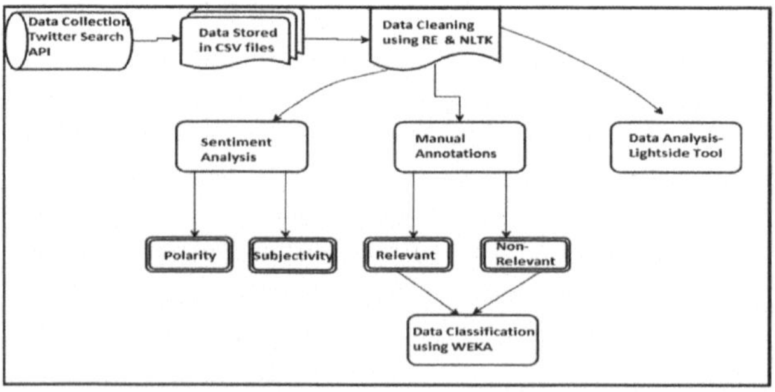

Fig. 1. Proposed workflow

For analyzing the textual features of tweets in more details we used **Lightside Reseacher's Workbench** from CMU (**Carnegie Mellon University**) for extracting feature tables on the basis of Unigrams, Bigrams and Trigrams respectively. We generated a feature table for each of the n-grams mentioned above with count of occurrence of each n-gram in the table. In order to understand true nature of the text in tweets it is important to understand the analysis and nature of unigrams, bigrams and trigrams which altogether defines the nature of the tweet whether it is cyberbullied or not.

Very often abuses in text clearly reflects the obscenity in text but bigrams and trigrams add more meaning to our analysis and approach most importantly when a group of words define the nature of sentence. While dealing with tweets containing sarcasm, it is more of human identified approach and seeks more understanding of how words and phrases which are used in indirect way to target others. After completing the analysis approach the next step is classification for which WEKA tool is used.

4.4 Proposed Algorithm

Detecting cyberbullying from tweets containing both hinglish and English content becomes highly complex since there is no hinglish dictionary of words which could be used in detection of such content from text. This is something very new from data analysis and mining point of view. It requires data collection and analysis in massive amount, our research is a seed towards this direction. As a result of our analysis we propose an algorithm. Before proposing the algorithm for cyberbullying detection, we have kept following facts as assumptions,

- The attacker (user who is tweeting trying to bully victim (another user)) is either only the follower of victim and victim is not following the attacker.
- The attacker is not following the user (victim) but is able to tweet on victim's public twitter profile (if not private)

Following terms are defined, to be used in proposed algorithm

(1) **Set_of_tweets** = Tweets collected
(2) **clean_tweet** = Tweets after stop word removal
(3) **Key_words** = Unigrams, Bigrams, Trigrams containing abuses (English, Hindi,) and personal remarks (Hinglish, English)

The proposed algorithm is as follows:

Algorithm 1. Detection of Cyberbullied Tweets

1. **For** each tweet in Set_of_tweets **do**
2. Count $\leftarrow$ 0
3. input $\leftarrow$ clean_tweet
4. all_tokens $\leftarrow$ word_tokenise(input)
5. **If** token in all_tokens contains key_words **then**
6. Count $\leftarrow$ Count + 1
7. **If** Count $\geq$ 1 **then**
8. Tweet is Cyberbullied
9. **Else**
10. Tweet is not Cyberbullied
11. **End For**

5 Results

This section describes the results of our analysis and classification performed. The manually annotated data of 1000 tweets was categorized into three main categories abusive, personal remarks and sarcasm. Table 2 shows some of the manually annotated tweets with their respective category.

Table 2. Manually annotated tweets with features

Tweet	Class	Features (category)
@sonamohapatra enjoy as much as u can…these 4 days of fame and attention that ur getting due to Salman Khan….enjoy	Yes	Sarcasm, personal remark
Standing up to misogyny Always brings slander in his patriarchal society. More courage to you, so that you can fight bold. @sonamohapatra	No	Support
@sonamohapatra @RamSampathLive another flop show by c grade artist couple… #ramsampath & sona mohapatra #attention seekers #sour losers	Yes	Personal remark, sarcasm
@sonamohapatra tera career na bana hai na kabhi bnega kitni b footage lene ki koshish karle smji bhag ab yaha se!	Yes	Personal remark

The Table 3 shows polarity and subjectivity calculated using Text-blob for performing sentiment analysis on manually annotated tweets. Polarity of some of the results are 0 due to use of pure hinglish language in tweets whose sentiment could not be decided hence neutral since Text-blob dictionary contains only English words.

Table 3. Result showing polarity and subjectivity of tweets

Tweet	Polarity	Subjectivity
love wannabe celebs like poke nose matter call big bro pm help	0.25	0.35
isky songs horror movies super hit rahein gy koi pata ni gaa rhi hy k daraa rhi hy	0.33	0.66
whole day salman related tweets seems like life going end name obsessed much	−0.025	0.5

The Fig. 2 shows how manually annotated classes of tweets marked as 0 (No) and 1 (yes) corresponded with the polarity of tweets calculated using text-blob. Y-axis shows the result of manual annotation and X-axis shows the polarity sentiment of the tweets calculated. Since values 0 and 1 are taken for marking classes for tweets relevant or not the scatter plot graph mostly scatters along 0 and 1 only. The result of sentiment analysis from Fig. 2 is quite interesting as since tweets classified as cyberbullied showed a uniform distribution around −1 to 1 range and additionally some tweets showed 0 polarity which means neutral sentiment since mostly tweets collected are in hinglish or contains both hinglish and English. As a result text-blob dictionary does not contains hinglish words and could not decide the polarity of such tweets. This concludes how complex it is to decide sentiment of tweets containing hinglish content.

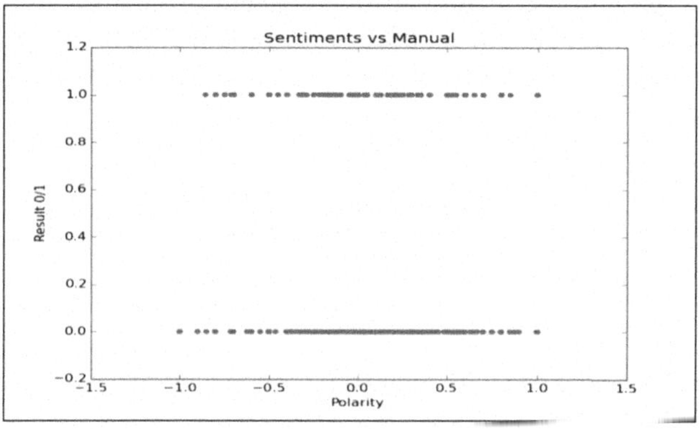

Fig. 2. Scatter plot – polarity vs manually annotated results (0/1)

Textual analysis with the help of Light side tool provided with results as follows Uni-grams contains more abuses related words, Bi-grams contains more of personal remarks whereas tri-grams contains purely personal remarks. Table 4 shows count of major textual features with respective to occurrence in terms of unigrams, bigrams and trigrams (Fig. 3).

Table 4. Features in terms of unigrams, bigrams and trigrams

Features	Unigrams	Bigrams	Trigrams
Abuses (English, Hindi, Slang)	139	40	12
Personal remarks (Hindi, English)	353	253	16

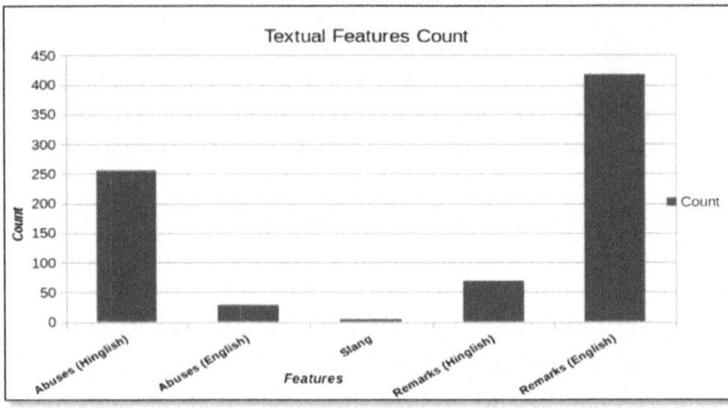

Fig. 3. Textual features count

As an extension to our analysis we performed classification using WEKA tool based on manually annotated data. We took three major classifiers into account namely Naive Bayes, Random Forest and J48. All three of them performed equally on test data and provided equivalent results as shown in Table 5 with fine accuracy and Kappa statistics. The result of classification are relevant with respect to data collected, if any other data is tested under the trained data then results may vary (accuracy may decrease) since data collected under current case study may not contain all hinglish related cyberbully content, therefore we decided to propose an algorithm which aims at analyzing all possible bully content and thereafter detecting cyberbullied tweets based on algorithm.

Table 5. Classifier performance results

Classifiers	Accuracy	Kappa statistic
Naive bayes	99.375	0.9858
Random forest	99.375	0.9858
J48	99.375	0.9858

From our research we came up with interesting text analysis:

- Indian population writes a word in hinglish in several ways like one of the words "Haan" which means "Yes" in English language is written in 4 to 5 ways by indians like "haan", "han", "h", "ha". Some use a mix of hinglish and English text for communicating on social media (Twitter, Facebook, WhatsApp etc.), here Twitter is the social media used.
- People sometimes use sarcasm to attack other people on social media, which involves whole text in a tweet to understand its nature since sarcasm is something which cannot be defined in a direct sentence and one or more words and is most complex to detect from machine learning point of view.
- For detecting Cyberbullying on more hinglish data a dictionary of all hinglish words needs to be made which requires data analysis on large basis which will take a longer time for collection, analysis and detection.

6 Conclusion

With the increase in number of cybercrimes, these is a dire need to prevent them online. Focusing on cyberbullying which is growing on a high rate from innocent locals to celebrities it requires action to be taken towards this area to prevent further such victims. As part of our research we analyzed one such case with all text analysis related to it and following results can be concluded for future work where intelligent system can be built to detect the same:

- Perform transliteration and further translation of content for such hinglish data
- Building intelligent systems for classifying such content from normal data.
- Restrict posting of such content on social media
- Placing punishment charges on users repeatedly using such content.

References

1. Galán-GarcÍa, P., De La Puerta, J.G., Gómez, C.L., Santos, I., Bringas, P.G.: Supervised machine learning for the detection of troll profiles in twitter social network: application to a real case of cyberbullying. Log. J. IGPL. **24**(1), 42–53 (2016)
2. Al-garadi, M.A., Varathan, K.D., Ravana, S.D.: Cyber-crime detection in online communications: the experimental case of cyberbullying detection in the Twitter network. Comput. Hum. Behav. **63**, 433–443 (2016)
3. Dredge, R., Gleeson, J., de la Piedad Garcia, X.: Presentation on Facebook and risk of cyberbullying victimization. Comput. Hum. Behav. **40**, 16–22 (2014)
4. Alim, S.: Analysis of tweets related to cyberbullying: exploring information diffusion and advice available for cyberbullying victims. Int. J. Cyber Behav. Psychol. Learn. (IJCBPL) **5**(4), 31–52 (2015)
5. Van Hee, C., Lefever, E., Verhoeven, B., Mennes, J., Desmet, B., De Pauw, G., Hoste, V.: Automatic detection and prevention of cyberbullying. In: International Conference on Human and Social Analytics (HUSO 2015), pp. 13–18. IARIA (2015)
6. Mangaonkar, A., Hayrapetian, A., Raje, R.: Collaborative detection of cyberbullying behavior in Twitter data. In: 2015 IEEE International Conference on Electro/Information Technology (EIT), pp. 611–616. IEEE, May 2015
7. Van Royen, K., Poels, K., Daelemans, W., Vandebosch, H.: Automatic monitoring of cyberbullying on social networking sites: from technological feasibility to desirability. Telemat. Inf. **32**(1), 89–97 (2015)
8. Dinakar, K., Reichart, R., Lieberman, H.: Modeling the detection of textual cyberbullying. Soc. Mob. Web **11**, 02 (2011)
9. Calvin, A.J., Bellmore, A., Xu, J.M., Zhu, X.: # bully: uses of hashtags in posts about bullying on Twitter. J. Sch. Violence **14**(1), 133–153 (2015)
10. Reynolds, K., Kontostathis, A., Edwards, L.: Using machine learning to detect cyberbullying. In: 2011 10th International Conference on Machine Learning and Applications and Workshops (ICMLA), vol. 2, pp. 241–0244. IEEE, December 2011
11. Silva, Y.N., Rich, C., Hall, D.: BullyBlocker: towards the identification of cyberbullying in social networking sites. In: The 2016 IEEE/ACM International Conference on Advances in Social Networks Analysis and Mining (ASONAM), San Francisco, CA, USA (2016)
12. Dalal, C., Tandon, S., Mukerjee, A.: Insult detection in Hindi (2014)

13. Joshi, A., Sharma, V., Bhattacharyya, P.: Harnessing context incongruity for sarcasm detection. In: Proceedings of the 53rd Annual Meeting of the Association for Computational Linguistics and the 7th International Joint Conference on Natural Language Processing, vol. 2, pp. 757–762 (2015)
14. Xiang, G., Fan, B., Wang, L., Hong, J., Rose, C.: Detecting offensive tweets via topical feature discovery over a large scale Twitter corpus. In: Proceedings of the 21st ACM International Conference on Information and Knowledge Management, pp. 1980–1984. ACM, October 2012
15. Hosseinmardi, H., Ghasemianlangroodi, A., Han, R., Lv, Q., Mishra, S.: Towards understanding cyberbullying behavior in a semi-anonymous social network. In: 2014 IEEE/ACM International Conference on Advances in Social Networks Analysis and Mining (ASONAM), pp. 244–252. IEEE, August 2014
16. Kansara, K.B., Shekokar, N.M.: A framework for cyberbullying detection in social network. Int. J. Curr. Eng. Technol. **5**, 494–498 (2015)
17. Hosseinmardi, H., Mattson, S.A., Rafiq, R.I., Han, R., Lv, Q., Mishra, S.: Detection of cyberbullying incidents on the instagram social network. arXiv preprint arXiv:1503.03909 (2015)
18. Nandhini, B.S., Sheeba, J.I.: Online social network bullying detection using intelligence techniques. Procedia Comput. Sci. **45**, 485–492 (2015)
19. Wang, X., Gerber, M.S., Brown, D.E.: Automatic crime prediction using events extracted from twitter posts. In: Yang, S.J., Greenberg, A.M., Endsley, M. (eds.) Social Computing, Behavioral - Cultural Modeling and Prediction. SBP 2012. LNCS, vol 7227, pp. 231–238. Springer, Heidelberg, April 2012. https://doi.org/10.1007/978-3-642-29047-3_28
20. Dadvar, M., Trieschnigg, D., de Jong, F.: Experts and machines against bullies: a hybrid approach to detect cyberbullies. In: Sokolova, M., van Beek, P. (eds.) AI 2014. LNCS (LNAI), vol. 8436, pp. 275–281. Springer, Cham (2014). https://doi.org/10.1007/978-3-319-06483-3_25
21. Vanhove, T., Leroux, P., Wauters, T., De Turck, F.: Towards the design of a platform for abuse detection in OSNs using multimedial data analysis. In: 2013 IFIP/IEEE International Symposium on Integrated Network Management (IM 2013), pp. 1195–1198. IEEE, May 2013
22. Nalini, K., Sheela, L.J.: Classification of tweets using text classifier to detect cyber bullying. In: Satapathy, S., Govardhan, A., Raju, K., Mandal, J. (eds.) Emerging ICT for Bridging the Future - Proceedings of the 49th Annual Convention of the Computer Society of India CSI Volume 2. AISC, vol 338. Springer, Cham (2015). https://doi.org/10.1007/978-3-319-13731-5_69
23. Ghasem, Z., Frommholz, I., Maple, C.: A machine learning framework to detect and document text-based cyberstalking. In: LWA, pp. 348–355 (2015)
24. Kovacevic, A., Nikolic, D.: Automatic detection of cyberbullying to make Internet a safer environment. In: Handbook of Research on Digital Crime, Cyberspace Security, and Information Assurance, p. 277 (2014)
25. Nahar, V., Unankard, S., Li, X., Pang, C.: Sentiment analysis for effective detection of cyber bullying. In: Sheng, Q.Z., Wang, G., Jensen, C.S., Xu, G. (eds.) APWeb 2012. LNCS, vol. 7235, pp. 767–774. Springer, Heidelberg (2012). https://doi.org/10.1007/978-3-642-29253-8_75
26. Lau, R.Y., Xia, Y., Ye, Y.: A probabilistic generative model for mining cybercriminal networks from online social media. IEEE Comput. Intell. Mag. **9**(1), 31–43 (2014)

27. Simanjuntak, D.A., Ipung, H.P., Nugroho, A.S.: Text classification techniques used to facilitate cyber terrorism investigation. In: 2010 Second International Conference on Advances in Computing, Control and Telecommunication Technologies (ACT), pp. 198–200. IEEE, December 2010
28. Chandramouli, R.: Emerging social media threats: technology and policy perspectives. In: 2011 Second Worldwide Cybersecurity Summit (WCS), pp. 1–4. IEEE, June 2011

Characterizing and Detecting Social Outrage on Twitter: Patel Reservation in Gujarat

Sulbha Singh[1(✉)] and Rajeev Pal[2]

[1] Department of Information Technology, Indira Gandhi Delhi Technical University for Women, Delhi, India
singhsulbha@gmail.com
[2] Capita plc, London, UK
rajeevpal1980@gmail.com

Abstract. Social Media is a platform to share ideas, opinions and discussions. This provides scope to study social behavior and perform analysis around events discussed over it. The idea behind this study is to analyze the social characteristics during unrest in society. The analysis further can be used to identify the trend of social behavior and utilize for decision making and anticipatory governance. For this paper recent social outrage in Indian context related to caste based reservation has been studied using social media platform Twitter. A number of analytical methodologies have been used to understand the variations in opinions over social media during unrest. This paper researches the potential of tension during social outrage and the factors affecting it. Sentiment analysis and different machine learning methods used to detect level of tension and compared the results against manual annotation. To improve the performance of classification results, a rule based algorithm has been developed to detect tension during social outrage.

Keywords: Caste reservation · Lexical analysis · Machine learning Opinion mining · Outrage detection · Sentiment analysis · Social media Social outrage · Structural analysis

1 Introduction

Social outrage is form of growing dissent among people in the society which typically gets manifested through public expressions of anger in form of non-cooperation, strikes, agitation etc. With the advent of social media, these outrage events have found a new platform of expression. Social media is often found to be used as weapon to spread dissent and creating havoc among civilized society. Popular social media platforms like Facebook, Twitter, WhatsApp etc. which were designed to connect people are now being used as a medium for spreading information and distortion of information within and between online and offline 'communities'. Since it would have an adverse effect on the socio- economic fabric of a nation; governments are concerned about the widespread misuse of social media. We often find governments completely shut down the use of Internet (and social media) in the outbreak of these social unrest events in order to prevent escalation.

B. Panda et al. (Eds.): REDSET 2017, CCIS 799, pp. 498–515, 2018.
https://doi.org/10.1007/978-981-10-8527-7_42

In a decade or so, we came across through many public dissent events (positive/negative) across the world where social media viz. Facebook, Twitter etc. have been used as platform to spread either awareness or creating havoc. In India where Anna Hazare Movement[1], can be considered as positive dissent, a few viz. JNU agitation[2], Gujarat's Patel dissent[3] have divided people over social media. Various opinions shared across social platform in different pretexts raised concerns over miscommunication among civil society, thereby, causing agitations and loss of society/nation image. Study over such events will help us in identifying the nature of thought participation and respective trend.

In this paper, we have analyzed one popular social outrage event that happened in India's state of Gujarat recently in which Patel community was agitating for reservations. The first impression of the agitation on social media was captured in the month of August, 2015. During this protest, it was widely reported that people used Twitter for posting tweets in support or against the cause event. We studied this form of spreading information how social outrage events that occur offline have the potential to affect the social order using online social media platforms. We can measure and characterize this interaction via a series of metrics. These metrics can then be used for opinion mining and help the law enforcing agencies and government in characterizing content and users on social media related to social unrest event. We performed this characterization by analyzing human behavior and studying opinions of users over social media. We focus our characterization study on a popular micro blogging service, Twitter, which is used extensively to spread news. Twitter allows registered users to post and read short text messages (tweets) of at most 140 characters, which may contain URLs to detailed content. A user can also spread the content in their social network by re tweeting or commenting on another user's tweet. Users make use of hashtags, symbol #, before a relevant keyword or phrase in their tweet to categorize those tweets. A lot of research is performed on opinion analysis of social media in past years due to increasingly use of social media platforms. Using these platforms people can post their opinions as frequently as they want. These contents (tweets) can be programmatically access using application programming interfaces (APIs).

The requirement for opinion mining is to first characterize the entity, its attributes, sentiment towards the entity and the time at which the opinion expressed towards the entity. In this requirement, the major challenge is to classify the sentiment towards the entity on the basis of pre-defined classes, viz. positive, negative, and neutral. In this paper, we classify the sentiment using range of pre-defined classes. Machine learning approaches are also used to detect the level of tension and compare the performance result against the human coded sample data. The result was not satisfactory therefore to improve the performance of classification for detecting social outrage during an event;

[1] http://www.annahazare.org/anticorruption-movement.html.

[2] http://indianexpress.com/article/india/india-news-india/jnu-agitation-questioned-by-police-for-talking-to-students-under-scanner-five-journalists-speak-out.

[3] http://www.financialexpress.com/industry/at-mega-patel-mega-rally-for-obc-quota-demand-hardik-patel-warns-bjp-govt-of-consequences/125651/.

we developed a rule based algorithm. Finally, we concluded the study with suggestions, future scope of this research and benefits and limitations of the results.

2 Related Work

The impact of social outrage has been studied by various individuals and analyzed and detected the social behavior for specific events. Poell et al. [1] examined G20 summit of 2010 in Toronto, Canada and analyzed how the social media is used by the protesters of that summit as a platform of alternative journalism. The network that coordinated the protest encouraged the participants to propagate this news of protest over twitter, you tube and flickr. They analyzed a set of 11,556 tweets, 222 videos, and 3,338 photos. It was also observed that only Twitter provides platform where large scale people can participate and associate themselves with event. Eltantawy et al. [2] showed how to select and work on features of specific case viz. Egyptian Revolution, to understand its impact and produce qualitative result. By examining the common and unique features of Egyptian Revolution, their study shows how it transformed into anti government protest leading to resignation of President Hosni Mubarak. Bajpai et al. [3] proposed a framework for analyzing Twitter data related to Thailand protest with arguable reasons. They utilized distributed database postGRES to collect and correlate twitter data for categorical analysis viz. Structural analysis and Content analysis based on keywords. Compton et al. [5] developed system with help of studying Latin American unrest by collecting small data set of tweets available publicly and predicts by integrating similar tweets into detailed and easily understandable format with which end user can gather information about forthcoming/occurring events. Panagiotopoulos et al. [6] shows power of social media communication with study of London riots and its positive affect in controlling and restoring the system during emergency or protest. The study collects official tweets posted during event period of 5 days in month of August, 2011 where Government authorities utilized the platform for blocking the rumors, sharing help line information for civilians and issuing instructions against offenders.

Aday et al. [10] prepared a report and analyzed the role of social media in the Arab Spring protests of 2011–12. Researchers also analyzed only some attributes of twitter related to the event. Bruns et al. [4] performed comparative study of more than 40 different cases and draws communicative metrics on the distinct discussion observed on twitter. The metrics showed various factors influencing the events based on original tweets, re-tweets, replies and posted links. Recuero et al. [7] studied a number of hash tags which were used by protesters during the Brazilian protest in June 2013. They examined around 46,090 hash tags from 2,321,249 collected tweets. Content analysis was performed for examination of hash tag functions. Researcher of this study also analyzed how the protesters used tags to show their opinions. For this purpose they used 500 most retweeted tweets. Compton et al. [8] proposed a method for geo-locating the locations of active twitter user without using the location information shared by users. They used for geo-location only the twitter data which is publicly available. They proposed a distributed algorithm for solving the geo-tagging problem. Using their algorithm they can geo-tag 80% of public tweets.

A lot of research is performed on detecting and predicting social unrest. Burnapa et al. [9] collected and analyzed data from the Twitter streaming API. They combined text mining and computational conversation analysis to detect tension during an event related to racial abuse and compares the results to machine learning and sentiment analysis. Their work investigated the possibility of forecasting spikes at the time of event created tension. Xu et al. [11] worked on detecting rising social unrest events by analyzing a large micro blogging streams over tumbler. They proposed an early detection system which is based on classification of text. This system was used to identify post related to social unrest event and based on their topics, times and locations. This method detects only relevant posts from a large volume of data directly. Kallus [12] worked on the prediction of occurrence of events, their time frame and the geographic locations where they can occur based on data taken from open web sources and include 7 languages. Their research focused on 2013 Egypt coup d'état which validated and quantified the fact that social media can predict event occurrence beforehand. Korolov et al. [17] also worked on social unrest prediction on twitter. Lerman et al. [13] studied how the information spread across the network. For analysis, they have used data from two popular social news sites. Digg and Twitter platform were used for the collection of data and analyzed how the news stories spread on these platforms.

Hua et al. [18] proposed a ranking algorithm for social unrest analysis. They have given the rank to the top most keyword of the event. They used Google Translate to convert the tweets in English because the tweets were in Spanish. In future we may also prepare a dictionary which contains Hindi and Hinglish words also include regional words that could be converted in English. Taboada et al. [20] proposed a lexicon based approach for sentiment analysis. They also described how to create dictionary using Semantic Orientation CALculator (SO-CAL). Researchers of [21] mainly focus on prediction of personality viz. anti-social psychoanalysis, which helps in predicting social behavior of twitter user. Barbosa et al. [22] proposed a approach of sentiment analysis classification. Baccianella et al. [23] described the working of SentiWordNet 3.0, a lexical analyzer which is publically available for research studies. Chen et al. [24] proposed a new approach for event detection of heterogeneous network. Ma et al. [25] proposed an automatic detection model for identifying rumors on microblogging sites. Their approach is based on capturing temporal characteristics of context features and detecting rumors before it broadcast. Krishna Kumar et al. [26] proposed the use of cognitive psychology for evaluating the spreading of misinformation in online social media. They proposed an algorithm for detecting spreading of misinformation on twitter online social media platform. Xu et al. [27] developed an algorithm for conveying a clear information about an emergency event and to help governments or a social groups to handle these events positively and efficiently. Aggarwal et al. [28] studied the event detection problem using both the supervised and unsupervised learning and presented the results which explain the network structure for content based methods. Pak et al. [29] were used twitter microblogging social media platform for sentiment analysis. They performed data collection automatically and linguistic analysis over the collected corpus. Finally build a sentiment classifier to classify the corpus in positive, negative and neutral sentiment. In this research study we aim to first analyze the event using qualitative analysis method and develop a rule based algorithm to detect tension during social outrage.

3 Methodology

Figure 1 describes the overall method from data collection to analysis and result. The below sections explain the method in detail.

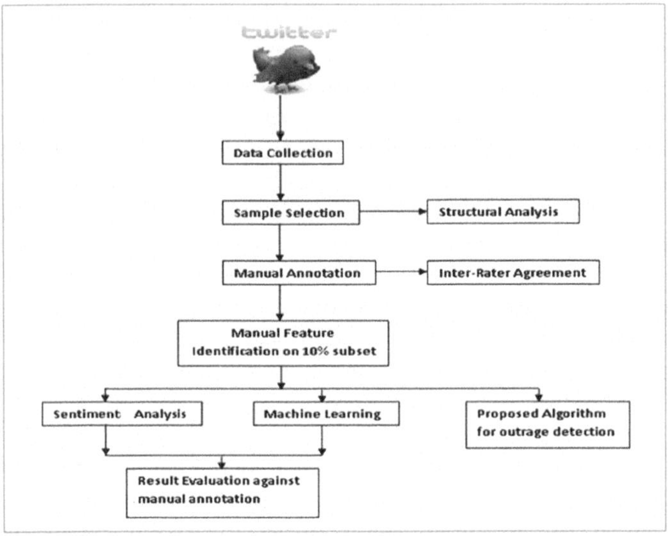

Fig. 1. Methodology

3.1 Data Collection

For this study, the source data obtained from micro blogging site twitter. Twitter provides application programming interfaces for tweet collection such as (1) search API, for past tweets retrieval based on user-specified criteria, (2) streaming API, for collection of live tweets based on user-defined criteria as per availability. The tweets have been collected by using Twitter's search API and python script "py query" module. Collected data have been analyzed through ".csv" file format.

The research study of past events such as London rights [6] and Arab Springs [10], shows that tweets surrounding periodic events expected to cause tension in form of outrage and for its political benefits. Therefore, tweets with respect to particular event have used as dataset for study. So, decided to collect the tweets which are posted exactly around a particular event (Kranti rally) of the selected case (Patidar agitation event). "Kranti rally" was part of "Patidar Agitation Event", which held on 25 August, 2015. This rally was led by a 22 year old boy named "Hardik Patel". During this protest, Hardik Patel and some supporters of patel reservation were demanding Gujarat CM to come and meet them to consider their memorandum related to the patel reservation. But CM has rejected their request that led to protester to go for hunger strike. As protest started catching attention of common people, people at social media invoked participation in their own way of protest by posting tweets in favor or against on twitter using the name of Hardik Patel and associated hashtags. Here, we have analyzed some of these tweets and observed that some of them are in support of this protest while some are not. Therefore, we predicted that there could be chances of provoking tension because of this event.

Data was collected from twitter using search API for one month period of event and post two months of event to analyze, how the tension started from offline to online. The analysis may help us in predicting the possibility of increasing tension levels during similar social outrage events. For analysis, 10,203 tweets have been collected using the keyword ‘Hardik Patel’. We could have included other key-word like ‘patidarana-matandolan’ or ‘charchaonreservation’, etc. to extend the data set. The tweets collected were posted during event and include the keyword ‘hardik patel’ with hashtags such as #hardik patel or #hardikpatel. The collected tweets were stored in ‘.csv’ file format for further study.

3.2 Sample Selection

Sample data set of collected tweets was extracted for further analysis. For structural analysis, we selected 6,436 tweets which were posted during the event from 25 August 2015 to 31 August 2015. The tweets posted from 1 August 2015 to 24 August 2015 are not part of structural analysis because of limited count of tweets i.e. only 84 tweet. Also, tweets posted after the event were not selected because associated events started during this period such as filing of sedition charges against protesters and thereby, tweet contents too changed. For categorization of tweets, 1004 tweets have been selected that were posted on 25 August 2015, the day when the event happened. For machine learning classification, this is relatively a small data set but for the validation of results, it is required to select a small data set that was coded by human coders. Figure 2 illustrated the count of tweets posted before, during and after event.

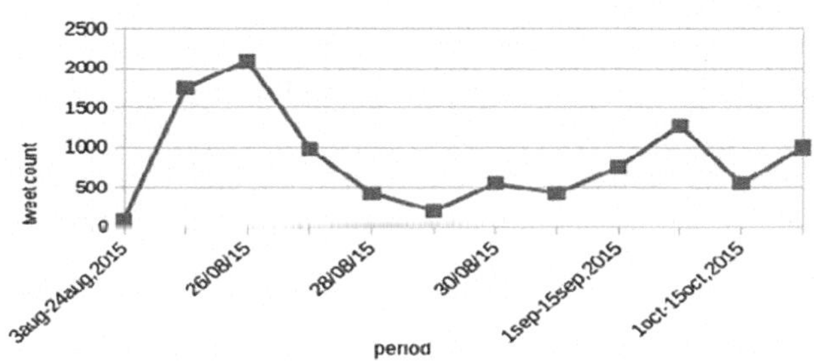

Fig. 2. Tweet volume from 3rd August, 2015 to 31st October, 2015

3.3 Annotation

The sample data set were manually annotated to provide “ground truth” for the data. It should be noted that different human coders themselves have different assessment of sentiment. Therefore human coders should be expertise in the subject for better assessment of sentiment. As it is evident in research study [9], the human coders were specialist police officers and data set were manually annotated by them. For this study, the sample data set were manually classified in four different class viz. irrelevant, informational (simply providing/sharing information about event), opinion (sharing their opinion/ideas/thoughts with respect to event) and aggression (sharing ideas/thoughts in provoked form). Opinion may or may not be the reason of outrage. Similar to Opinion, but Aggression is in definite form in support of or against of event. We have given a range of numbers between 0 to 3 to these classes for evaluation viz. 0 is for irrelevant, 1 is for informational, 2 is for opinion and 3 is for aggression.

Irrelevant class contains the tweets which maybe (1) not related to the event i.e. not contain search keyword #Hardik Patel (2) related to the event i.e. contain keyword #Hardik Patel, but not related to this event (3) tweets were not written in English (4) tweets contain only images. In informational class, users were simply passing information about the protest. Opinion class contains the tweets (1) General opinion of users which may be in support of or not in support of event (2) Asking questions in form of opinion (3) making fun of Hardik Patel by non-supporters. Aggression class contains aggressive, abusive words and expletives e.g. idiot…

3.4 Inter Rater Agreement

We have used Cohen's Kappa coefficient [14] for Inter rater agreement or inter rater reliability which calculates the degree of agreement among two independent raters. The responses from two raters were measured on a nominal scale and the classification categories should be mutually exclusive. Measure 0 is used for no agreement and measure 1 is for perfect agreement. The level of agreement was around 0.57 for sentiment analysis which is not a satisfactory agreement. The reason may be flexibility between the levels of classes.

4 Analysis and Results

For analysis, we used qualitative case study method as described by researchers of [2, 19] which is useful for developing a deep understanding about a particular case, its features, and its impact. To decide how much and how long this case should be studied is based on judgment and based on a set of criteria described in below sections.

4.1 Structural Analysis

As study of G20 protest [1] & twitter framework [3], we have observed that structural analysis of data set would be more beneficial. For this study, we have concentrated only on the qualitative text content and time frame of tweets. We have also used other tweet attributes for identifying views of user.

Figure 3 shows the count of tweets that were posted per day of the protest. Researchers believed if the percentage of tweets posted per day are increasing; the event will become big and tensed. Percentage of tweets that were posted per day in this case are respectively 27%, 32%, 15%, 7%, 3%, 8%, 6%. As per results as shown below, it is clearly showing that the maximum number of posts were posted on second day of the event and as time progressed number of tweets declined. Therefore the

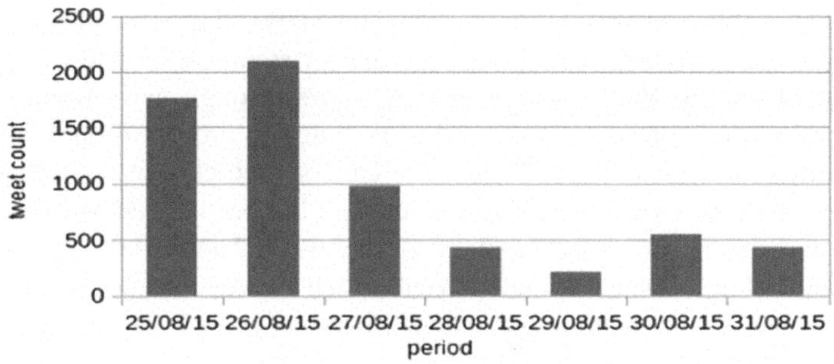

Fig. 3. Tweets count per day

researchers believed that this protest will not make this event big. If people support this kind of event, number of tweets will definitely increase per day of the event.

According to Poell et al. [1] the most retweeted posts can be considered as the most relevant posts. In this case, approximately 38% tweets are retweeted from sample data set. But only 1% tweets came under top ten retweeted messages. It means number of retweeted posts is very less. Therefore we cannot consider retweeted tweets relevant. Figure 4 illustrated the top ten retweeted messages of the data set. The range of top ten retweeted posts is from 58 to 214. It is clearly shown from the Fig. 4; only five tweets were retweeted more than 100 times. Researchers can consider these top 10 tweets relevant but it is not beneficial for the study in this case.

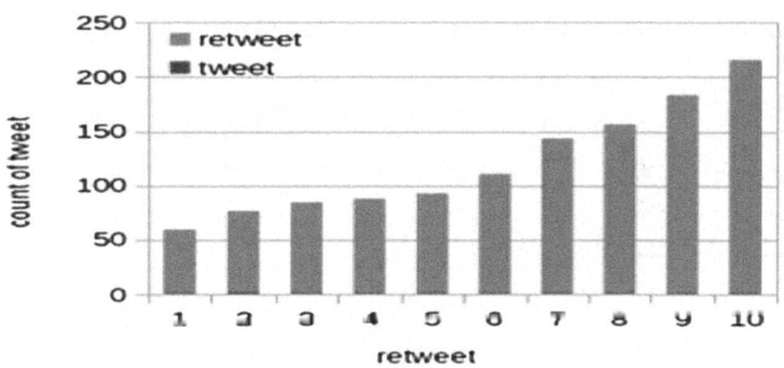

Fig. 4. Count of top 10 re-tweeted posts

In the next stage of the structural analysis, number of users has been identified on the basis of their account names contributed before, during and after the protest. Here, the question arises that whether a small number of users or large number of crowd is responsible for that kind of protest over online social media platforms. For answering such question, Pareto principle is used. According to Poell et al. [1] Pareto principle says 80% of effects are result of 20% of causes. In this case if number of top active users is more then there will be chances of large crowd participation in this protest. Tables 1, 2 and 3 represents the top active user accounts and their tweet count which are posted before, during and after event respectively. Number of tweets posted by top active users before event in Table 1 is very low viz. 3, 2. This shows that most of the people who contributed to event are not aware before starting of event on 25 August, 2015. Once event happened (Kranti Rally) and people got news through news forums and other platforms they started spreading news and contributed to protest through online social media platforms. It is clear from Table 1 we cannot predict about this kind of event before it happened. As shown in Tables 1, 2 and 3, it has been concluded that the protest was the result of large crowd participation for the event. There was no common active user identified before, during and after event which proves that it is not created by a group. It is clearly shown that the percentage of tweets posted before, during and after event by top most active users are respectively 0.17%, 4% and 5.3% i.e. small number of users were actively participated in the event. Therefore it was clear that the small number of users or a group of user were not contributed this social outrage protest. Therefore it is not required to verify the user identities participated in the event.

Table 1. Top active users before event

User_handle	Tweet count
Narayansharma	3
Aloksrii	2
sudhirs30223957	2
vishvagujrat	2
whyarif	2

Table 2. Top active users during event

User_handle	Tweet count
drgarekar	47
hindustanse	34
deshkijantaa	30
dravarma	24
satismohite	23
naina0806	22
nitin_nitingarg	21
bimal_pr	21
socialmediatbn	20
channelrt	19

Table 3. Top active users after event

User_handle	Tweet count
divya_bhaskar	65
stvenglish	56
oneindia	36
5n0q3n	31
novocaln	31
hindustance	27
indiatvnews	26
ashishaminngs	25
jagopatidar	24
oneindiagujrat	24

4.2 Content Analysis

We considered the research study of Bajpai et al. [3] and categorized the content of the tweets on the basis of some extracted features from the tweets.

Feature Extraction: This is the first step of manual categorization of content. Manually extracting some features from content on the basis of subject and nature (sentiment) of content. We have manually inspected 1,004 tweets which were posted on 25

August, 2015 of sample data to identify the features on the basis of that we have to classify the tweets in different categories. Table 4 shows tweet level features which we extracted through manual inspection.

Table 4. Tweet level features

Feature	Description	Example
Informational	Post which provides/sharing information about protest	ETV Gujrati showing damage done to vehicles post rally #hardik patel
Opinion	Posts which contains views/thoughts/opinion of users	Dear people of Gujarat, india can hardly ill-afford another kejriwal. Please stop supporting #hardik patel before its too late
Question	Posts which ask questions about protest	Dear #hardik patel you want fight for reservation. Cool but why challenging and disrespecting SC?
Expletives	Posts contains expletives	Hardik patel......!..............get well soon! #hardik patel
Aggression	Posts contains aggressive and anger words	Ashamed of u as being patidar u ruined all your brothers effort bcz of your stupid decisions and ego #hardik patel
Fun	Posts contains fun/parody	Parthiv patel wants reservation in cricket #hardik patel
No. of hashtags	No. of hashtags in a post	No. of "#hardik patel" in a post
Abusive	Posts contains abusive words	Hard dick patel is a soft dick rascal #hardik patel
Hyperlinks	Does the post contain hyperlinks?	Get Hardik Patel updates here http://www.jagopatidar.com

Feature Identification and Manual Classification: For classification, it is required to identify only those features on the basis of that we can classify the content in distinct classes. We have decided to take only some of the features and combined some features in one class for low noise and better categorization. Manual classification of the tweets has been categorized in four class's viz. Irrelevant, Informational, Opinion and Aggression. We have decided to give a range of number to these classes for comparison with other classifiers. 0 is for irrelevant, 1 is for informational, 2 is for opinion and 3 is for aggression. Opinion class contains the features of opinion, question and making fun. Similarly, aggression class contains the features of aggression, abusive and expletives.

Our sample data set for categorization displayed only 62.35% of tweets being relevant to event. Approximately 30% of tweets were in Hindi, Gujarati, Hinglish language and tweets containing images considered irrelevant for the analysis and hence not included for research study. We believe that if the percentage of relevance is low, chances of noise will also become low. In addition, among relevant tweets, only 8% tweets contained links and all the classified classes contains hyperlinks. Therefore we have not taken the hyperlinks for classification. Among relevant tweets, only 9% tweets are comes under informational class and 4% tweets are under aggression class. Opinion class contains 49% tweets. Aggression class contains only 4% tweets it means a chance of high tension because of this event is very low. Figure 5 shows the count of tweets of different classes as defined above. We again categorize the opinion class and aggression class into two sub-categories viz. supporting the event and non-supporting the event. It is clearly shown in the Fig. 6 that supporting sub-class contains only 35 tweets whereas non-supporting sub-class contains 505 tweets i.e. only 6.5% were supporters of this event whereas 93.5% were non-supporters. It is clearly shown from Fig. 6 percentage of supporters of this event is very low.

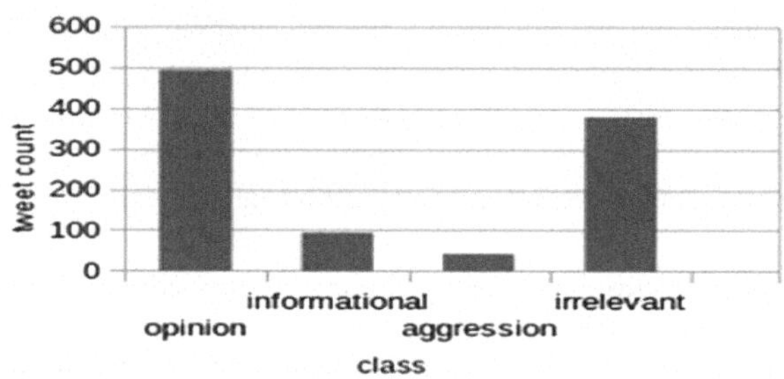

Fig. 5. Tweet classification

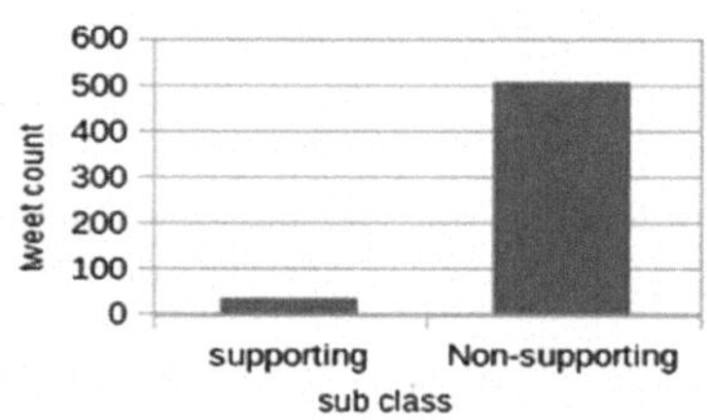

Fig. 6. Tweet sub-classification

From this analysis, it is clear most of the users related to this protest are non-supporters. Also, a very small amount of tweets were showing aggression, means there is no chance of creating tension in response to this protest. Similarly supporters of the protest are also very low. Therefore there is no chance of making this event big.

4.3 Sentiment Analysis

While analyzing the sentiment of tweets it is necessary to consider the performance of other commonly used sentiment classifier. For comparison with the manual classification, we used TextBlob[4] classifier, a sentiment analysis tool i.e. a TextBlob library

---

[4] http://textblob.readthedocs.io/en/dev/quickstart.html#sentiment-analysis.

has been used by the TextBlob classifier. In order to compare the varied results and obtain common NLP tasks, with help of simple API, TextBlob have been used [15]. The sentiment analyzer function calculates the polarity on the basis of given string and result float value between [−1.0, 1.0]. To enhance the efficiency, settings and threshold values for classification have been modified. Generally, the polarity value 0.1 or greater than 0.1 is considered as positive and the polarity value lower than 0.1 is considered as negative. For this study, the positive or negative sentiments indicating aggression have been valued between ±0.5 to 1. For Opinion, the sentiments have been valued between ±0.2 to 0.4 and for Information, the sentiments have been valued as ±0.1 and 0 has been considered as irrelevant.

Data which is obtained from twitter is not used in its original form for extracting features automatically. Thus to make this data used for mining we have to pre-process this data by removal of stop words (English) and removal of symbols such as @, # and punctuation marks programmatically using "NLTK" (Natural language Toolkit)[5] and "re" module of python.

Result Evaluation Against Manual Annotation: Classification results are provided by using standard text classification measures viz. positive predicted value also called precision (i.e. for a particular class say, c, how frequently tweets are classified as c when they should not be), recall also called as sensitivity (i.e. for a particular class say, c, how frequently tweets are not classified as c when they should be). Therefore, precision and recall are measure of relevance. The accuracy of test is measured using F-score. It requires both precision and recall of the class, c, to compute the score. F-score can be defined as weighted average of the precision and recall. And the accuracy, the total number of tweets which are correctly classified normalized by the total no. of tweets. The value of the result for all the measures described above are between 0 (worst) and 1 (best).

Formula for calculating the results of above mentioned measures for each class which we classified are as follows (where TP = true positive, FP = false positive, TN = true negative, FN = false negative):

- $\text{Precision} = \text{TP}/(\text{TP} + \text{FP})$
- $\text{Recall} = \text{TP}/(\text{TP} + \text{FN})$
- $\text{F-score} = 2 * ((\text{precision} * \text{recall})/(\text{precision} + \text{recall}))$
- $\text{Accuracy} = (\text{TP} + \text{TN})/(\text{TP} + \text{FP} + \text{TN} + \text{FN})$

Figure 7 contains tables showing comparative performance results of classification measures of TextBlob sentiment analysis for all classes. It is clearly shown from the Fig. 7, the precision and recall of "irrelevant" class are 0.54 and 0.88 respectively i.e. count of false positive tweets are more. F-score is satisfactory and accuracy is 0.68. The precision and recall of "informational" class are 0.30 and 0.34 respectively i.e. count of false positive and false negative tweets are more. F-score is not satisfactory. The reason may be there is no "clear" feature for the informational class and accuracy is 0.86 which is good for classifying "informational" tweets. The precision and recall of "opinion" class are 0.83 and 0.38 respectively i.e. count of only false negative tweets

[5] http://www.nltk.org/book/ch03.html.

"irrelevant"			
	Human coder		
		yes	no
machine	yes	328	279
	no	46	351

Precision – 0.54
Recall – 0.88
F-score – 0.66
Accuracy – 0.68

"informational"			
	Human coder		
		Yes	no
machine	yes	32	75
	no	61	836

Precision – 0.30
Recall – 0.34
F-score – 0.32
Accuracy – 0.86

"opinion"			
	Human coder		
		yes	no
machine	yes	186	39
	no	307	472

Precision – 0.83
Recall – 0.38
F-score – 0.52
Accuracy – 0.66

"aggression"			
	Human coder		
		yes	no
machine	yes	31	31
	no	10	932

Precision – 0.50
Recall – 0.76
F-score – 0.60
Accuracy – 0.96

Fig. 7. TextBlob performance result against manual annotation

are more. F-score is satisfactory and accuracy is 0.66. The precision and recall of "aggression" class are 0.50 and 0.76. F-score is satisfactory and accuracy is 0.96 which is very good score for classifying "aggression" that would be contribute to detecting outrage. The tweets manually classified as aggression are mostly accurate with outcome of sentiment analysis.

The result shows a good performance considering ordinal scale. Because of a lot of dissimilarity between positive and negative as compare to opinion and aggression, it is difficult to classify on the basis of nominal scale.

4.4 Machine Learning

After implementation of sentiment analysis, machine learning methods were used to classify the sample data set. As research study of [9], shows that Naïve Bays (NB) and support Vector Machine (SVM) methods of machine learning are performed best on the twitter data. Naïve Bays and SVM which are based on probabilistic approach have performed best on short text messages. The probabilistic methods have been used the N-gram approaches using as a feature, combination of one, two and three word. The NB classifier supports multiple n-gram features; therefore it is good for machine learning algorithm for twitter data. The NB classifier considers presence of n-gram and also the frequency of n-gram.

The WEKA[6] machine learning tool is used for the implementation of machine learning algorithms. Random Forest is also implemented using WEKA for better prediction. It is believed by the researchers that random forest is good for predicting high dimensional data [16].

6 http://www.cs.waikato.ac.nz/ml/weka/.

Result Evaluation against Manual Annotation: The macroaveraged performance result of the Naïve Bays, SVM and Random Forest classifiers are presented in Fig. 8. All the three machine learning classifiers performed same.

Irrelevant	Precision	Recall	F-score
Naïve Bays	0.92	0.22	0.36
SVM	0.92	0.22	0.36
Random Forest	0.92	0.22	0.36

Informational	Precision	Recall	F-score
Naïve Bays	0.00	0.00	0.00
SVM	0.00	0.00	0.00
Random Forest	0.00	0.00	0.00

Opinion	Precision	Recall	F-score
Naïve Bays	0.57	0.98	0.72
SVM	0.57	0.98	0.72
Random Forest	0.57	0.98	0.72

Aggression	Precision	Recall	F-score
Naïve Bays	0.00	0.00	0.00
SVM	0.00	0.00	0.00
Random Forest	0.00	0.00	0.00

Fig. 8. Macroaveraged performance results for three machine learning methods

As Fig. 8 shows the Naïve Bays classifier not classifies any tweets as 'Informational' and 'Aggression'. The SVM and Random Forest also failed to classify any tweet as 'Informational' and 'Aggression'. Only 9% and 4% tweets belongs to 'Informational' and 'Aggression' class respectively as a fraction of entire sample dataset. It is clearly showing that small fraction of entire data set have a great impact on performance of machine learning classifiers which used supervised learning methods. Therefore, it is not possible for a classifier (supervised) to classify a new tweet as 'Informational' or 'Aggression' using such a small fraction of entire data set. Therefore overall accuracy of classifiers is 61%. In future we may increase the number of informational and aggression level tweets to check whether it increases the performance or not. The machine learning classifiers performed best for 'Irrelevant' class. Precision (P = 0.92) shows less false positive rate for irrelevant class. Also recall is fewer (R = 0.98) for 'Opinion' class which indicate that we can select more tweets for opinion class which we not selected. Because of this combination of results we suggested a rule based algorithm for 'outrage detection' which may implement in future for better performance results.

4.5 Proposed Algorithm for Outrage Detection

Algorithm started first with handling the noise in the data set, i.e. the data set also contains the irrelevant tweets means the tweet may contains the 'relevant term' 'hardik patel' but not related to the context. Therefore for identifying the relevant tweets, we included some additional terms related to context called as 'related term'. The next task was to classify the tweets in categories viz. informational, opinion or aggression. For this classification we used some additional identified features. Presence of hyperlink in tweets was not considered for classification because hyperlinks may present in all classes as observed during manual classification. Tweets which contain words which show anger, aggression, abuse or expletives were classified in class 'aggression'. If tweets contain words which gives information about protest like 'rally', 'strike', 'ultimatum', etc. were classified in class 'informational'. Tweets which not contained 'aggression' and 'informational' feature but contained the 'related term' were classified in 'opinion' class.

A rule based algorithm was defined based on the above manually identified features for detecting outrage for an event which is described in Algorithm 1. This algorithm is defined for a particular event viz. 'patidar agitation event' but in future this can be used for other outrage related event or political event by changing the 'relevant term' and 'related term'. 'Relevant', 'Related', 'Informational' and 'Aggression' terms were constructed using a 'bag of words' identified during manual classification. Terms which are used in the algorithm are described below:

- T = Sample_tweets
- Relevant Term (R) = {hardik, hardik patel, hardikpatel}
- Related Term (RE) = {patel, patidar, reservation, support, guj, aap, aam aadmi party, arvind, kejri, cast, politic, quota, backward, wrong, community, obc, andolan, revolution, justice, bjp, minority, demand, destabili}
- Informational Term (I) = {rally, protest, ultimatum, memo, police, damage, clash, speech, anandiben, strike, crowd, ahemdabad, charge, cm, gmdc, announce, kranti, fast, violent, deadline, thrown}
- Aggression Term (A) = {a bag of aggressive, anger, abusive words and expletives}

Algorithm for Detection of Social Outrage

For each tweet t in sample_tweets (T)

1. Count no. of times R in tweet t
2. **If** R > 1, tweet (t) is considered relevant and go to step 4
3. **If** R = 1,

   then

   check **If** tweet (t) contains RE

   (i) check **If** RE >= 1, tweet (t) is considered relevant and go to step 4.

   (ii) check **If** RE < 1, tweet (t) is considered irrelevant

   End

4. (i) check **If** tweet (t) contains A >= 1, tweet (t) is considered aggression

   End

   (ii) **Else If** tweet (t) contains I >= 1, tweet (t) is considered informational

   End

   (iii) **Else** tweet (t) is considered opinion

   End

5 Conclusion

The paper shows that there was certain level of tension while analyzing tweets data set but since it was more toward non-support of protest, the aggression level can be considered as low. The result was based on various level of study of tweets by categorizing it in Informational (passing information about event), Opinion (sharing thoughts either in support or non-support of protest) and Aggression (actively posting tweets provoking social media crowd to react over it). As Twitter is not so common in Indian context of social media utilization, the data set can be considered as representation of large crowd with respect to user involvement. It is easily understandable the scope of analysis for future events can be broadened with more and more users have accessibility to network, smart-phones and active participation over social sites. The analysis can be further enhanced with use of automated tools, thereafter, mapped with intelligent App to gather and analyze tweets related to such events in real time with input of some key values. The analyzed data after further examination can be used as recommendation for anticipatory governance to take appropriate action before event took outrageous or social disruption form.

Due to restrictions of 140 characters, people tend to use more of texting acronyms like ROFL, LOL, LMAO or partially masked word. Moreover in Indian context, it becomes further more difficult to analyze the tweets because of regional language support over smart phones/Apps. Hence, we decided not to classify as referring them as irrelevant tweets, but these factors can be useful if we are able to analyze them over tools.

The focus of this study was around an event in identifying the social behavior and its social trend by analyzing the difference in action between aggression, opinion and informational. This was achieved by study the factors associated with event such as event pick (cast reservation), primary participants (Hardik Patel) and terms used with regards to event either in support or non-support including abusive and expletive terms. These factors have been used in studying the sentiment analysis to identify the trend either in positive and negative direction of trend. More and more dataset used and use of intelligent tools can further improve the result and can be helpful in future events for anticipatory governance. The machine learning classifiers performance result demonstrate a low degree of accuracy indicating the requirement of improved classification techniques in future research studies of outrage detection.

References

1. Poell, T., Borra, E.: Twitter, YouTube and Flickr as platforms of alternative journalism: the social media account of the 2010 Toronto G20 protests. SAGE J. (2011). https://doi.org/10.1177/1464884911431533. sagepub.co.uk/journalsPermissions.nav
2. Eltantawy, N., Wiest, J.B.: Social media in the Egyptian revolution: reconsidering resource mobilization theory. Int. J. Commun. **5**, 1207–1224 (2011). 1932–8036/2011FEA1207
3. Bajpai, K., Jaiswal, A.: A framework for analyzing collective action events on Twitter. In: 8th International ISCRAM Conference, Lisbon, Portugal, May 2011

4. Bruns, A., Stieglitz, S.: Quantitative approaches to comparing communication patterns on Twitter. J. Technol. Hum. Serv. **30**(3–4) (2012). https://doi.org/10.1080/15228835.2012.744249. Methods for Analyzing Social Media
5. Compton, R., Lee, C., Lu, T.-C., De Silva, L., Macy, M.: Detecting future social unrest in unprocessed Twitter data: "Emerging phenomena and big data". In: IEEE International Conference on Intelligence and Security Informatics (ISI) (2013). https://doi.org/10.1109/isi.2013.6578786
6. Panagiotopoulosa, P., Bigdelib, A.Z., Samsa, S.: Citizen–government collaboration on social media: the case of Twitter in the 2011 riots in England. Gov. Inf. Q. J. **31**, July 2014. https://doi.org/10.1016/j.giq.2013.10.014. ISSN 0740-624X
7. Recuero, R., Zago, G., Bastos, M.T., Araújo, R.: Hashtags functions in the protests across Brazil. SAGE J., May 2015. https://doi.org/10.1177/2158244015586000
8. Compton, R., Jurgens, D., Allen, D.: Geotagging one hundred million Twitter accounts with total variation minimization. In: IEEE International Conference (2014). https://doi.org/10.1109/bigdata.2014.7004256
9. Burnapa, P., Ranaa, O.F., Avisa, N., Williams, M., Housley, W., Edwards, A., Morgan, J., Sloan, L.: Detecting tension in online communities with computational Twitter analysis. Technol. Forecast. Soc. Change J. **95**, 96–108 (2013). https://doi.org/10.1016/j.techfore.2013.04.013
10. Aday, S., Farrell, H., Lynch, M., Sides, J., Freelon, D.: New Media and Conflict After the Arab Spring. United States Institute of Peace (2012)
11. Xu, J., Lu, T.-C., Compton, R., Allen, D.: Civil unrest prediction: a Tumblr-based exploration. In: International Social Computing, Behavioral Modeling and Prediction (SBP) Conference (2014)
12. Kallus, N.: Predicting crowd behavior with big public data. In: International World Wide Web Conference Committee (IW3C2), WWW 2014 Companion, Seoul, Korea, 7–11 April 2014. ACM (2014). 978-1-4503-2745-9/14/04
13. Lerman, K., Ghosh, R.: Information contagion: an empirical study of the spread of news on Digg and Twitter social networks. In: Fourth International AAAI Conference on Weblogs and Social Media, March 2010
14. McHugh, M.L.: Interrater reliability: the kappa statistic. US National Library of Medicine National Institute of Health, October 2012
15. Ezpeleta, E., Zurutuza, U., Gomez Hidalgo, J.M.: Does sentiment analysis help in Bayesian spam filtering? In: International Conference on Hybrid Artificial Intelligent Systems, April 2016. https://doi.org/10.1007/978-3-319-32034-2_7
16. Lakshmi Devasena, C.: Comparative analysis of random forest, REP tree and J48 classifiers for credit risk prediction. In: IJCA Proceedings on International Conference on Communication, Computing and Information Technology (2015)
17. Korolov, R., Lu, D., Wang, J., Zhou, G., Bonial, C., Voss, C., Kaplan, L., Wallace, W., Han, J., Ji, H.: On predicting social unrest using social media. In: IEEE/ACM International Conference on Advances in Social Networks Analysis and Mining (ASONAM) (2016)
18. Hua, T., Lu, C.-T., Ramakrishnan, N., Chen, F., Arredondo, J., Mares, D., Summers, K.: Analyzing civil unrest through social media. IEEE J. Mag. **46**(12) (2013). https://doi.org/10.1109/mc.2013.442
19. Rathi, D., Given. L.: Research 2.0: framework for qualitative and quantitative research in Web 2.0 environments. In: 43rd International Conference on System Sciences (2010)
20. Taboada, M., Brooke, J., Tofiloski, M., Voll, K., Stede, M.: Lexicon-based methods for sentiment analysis. Comput. Linguist. **37**, 267–307 (2011)

21. Sumner, C., Byers, A., Boochever, R., Park, G.J.: Predicting dark triad personality traits from Twitter usage and a linguistic analysis of Tweets. In: Proceedings of the 2012 11th International Conference on Machine Learning and Applications, ICMLA 2012, vol. 02. IEEE Computer Society, Washington, D.C. (2012). https://doi.org/10.1109/icmla.2012.218
22. Barbosa, L., Feng, J.: Robust sentiment detection on Twitter from biased and noisy data. In: 23rd International Conference on Computational Linguistics. Association for Computational Linguistics (2010)
23. Baccianella, S., Esuli, A., Sebastiani, F.: SentiWordNet 3.0: an enhanced lexical resource for sentiment analysis and opinion mining. In: Proceedings of the Seventh Conference on International Language Resources and Evaluation (LREC 2010), May 2010
24. Chen, F., Neill, D.B.: Non-parametric scan statistics for event detection and forecasting in heterogeneous social media graphs. In: Proceedings of the 20th ACM SIGKDD International Conference on Knowledge Discovery and Data Mining, August 2014. https://doi.org/10.1145/2623330.2623619
25. Ma, J., Gao, W., Wei, Z., Lu, Y., Wong, K.-F.: Detect rumors using time series of social context information on microblogging websites. In: Proceedings of the 24th ACM International on Conference on Information and Knowledge Management (2015). https://doi.org/10.1145/2806416.2806607
26. Krishna Kumar, K.P., Geethakumari, G.: Detecting misinformation in online social networks using cognitive psychology. Hum. Centric Comput. Inf. Sci. (2014). https://doi.org/10.1186/s13673-014-0014-x
27. Xu, Z., Liu, Y., Xuan, J., Chen, H., Mei, L.: Crowd-sourcing based social media data analysis of urban emergency events. Multimedia Tools Appl. **76**(9), 11567–11584 (2017). https://doi.org/10.1007/s11042-015-2731-1
28. Aggarwal, C.C., Subbian, K.: Event detection in social streams. In: Proceedings of the 2012 SIAM International Conference on Data Mining (2012). https://doi.org/10.1137/1.9781611972825.54
29. Pak, A., Paroubek, P.: Twitter as a corpus for sentiment analysis and opinion mining. In: Proceedings of the Seventh Conference on International Language Resources and Evaluation (LREC 2010), May 2010

Optimizing Accuracy of Sentiment Analysis Using Deep Learning Based Classification Technique

Jaspreet Singh[1(✉)], Gurvinder Singh[2], Rajinder Singh[3], and Prithvipal Singh[1]

[1] Guru Nanak Dev University, Amritsar, Punjab, India
profjaspreetbatth@gmail.com,
prithvipalsingh89@gmail.com

[2] Faculty of Engineering, Guru Nanak Dev University, Amritsar, Punjab, India
gurvinder4371@gmail.com

[3] Department of Computer Science, Guru Nanak Dev University, Amritsar, Punjab, India
tovirk@yahoo.com

Abstract. The sentiment or opinion of a person expressed with words and phrases reflect the thoughts of polarities ranging from positive to neutral as well as negative. The emotions hidden in expressions indicate positivity or negativity in the opinion such as words DISTRESS ejaculates more negativity than the word SAD does. Sentiment analysis is the study of concepts of polarities hidden in natural languages. The use of natural language processing is to elucidate information hidden inside the text referred to as sentiment analysis. Sentiment analysis is widely applied to reviews of social media for a variety of applications covering the domains of business, health and government performance evaluations. This type of evaluation extracts the attitude of an author with respect to the context of the topic that to what extent whether the hidden information is related to joy/sadness, amaze/anger, positive and negative emotions. This paper will introduce the proposed technique with Convolution Neural Network used for text classification. The performance of proposed classifier is validated against the performance of Naïve Bayes, J48, BFTree, OneR, LDA and SVM. Examination of efficacies is done on three manually annotated datasets, one dataset is taken from IMDB movie portal and two datasets are infatuated from Amazon product reviews. The accuracies of these seven machine learning techniques are compared and the proposed technique is noticed more precise in generating the accuracy of 85.2% in precision, 82.9% in F-measure and 85.46% of correctly classified sentiment.

Keywords: Sentiment prediction · Opinion classification · Movie reviews Product services · Convolution Neural Network

1 Introduction to Sentiment Analysis

In the rapidly growing electronic media based society, opinions are the key influencers of our attitude online. The organizations nowadays are keen to evaluate their customers or public opinions about their products and services. The significant expansion of social

B. Panda et al. (Eds.): REDSET 2017, CCIS 799, pp. 516–532, 2018.
https://doi.org/10.1007/978-981-10-8527-7_43

networking sites made consumers to discuss their experiences about products and services. The companies are largely dependent upon social data on blogs, forums, comments, tweets, movie reviews and product reviews for their decision making and amelioration of quality of their products [12, 20]. The wakefulness of applications of sentiment analysis has taken place all around the compass covering areas like social events, election scenarios, healthcare, consumer products and services [15]. The maturity of use of the internet by business organizations has felt that opinionated web text has reshaped business and largely changed our socio-political systems [16, 17]. Automated sentiment analysis systems are required because the analytical capability of an average human reader can never compete with the huge amount of opinionated web text on each portal of the web.

1.1 Levels of Sentiments

There was little research in NLP or linguistics in the last decade of the 20th century as there was a scarcity of opinion text available in digital form. The exponential growth of web text necessitates researchers to define different levels of granularities. Sentiment analysis classifies the web text in three levels to consider namely document level, sentence level, and the entity or aspect level. At document level, the main task is to evaluate and conglomerate the sentiments dispersed in the document into a single resulting sentiment. Sentence level sentiment analysis relate to the subject of a sentence with factual information to determine its polarity. However, entity-level sentiment analysis discovers real opinions by focusing on targets of entities. The summary of levels of sentiments with its four parameters is given below in Table 1.

Table 1. Levels of sentiment along with their attributes

Level	Delimiter	Depth of granularity	Multiplicity of sentiments	Interpretation of sentiments
1. Document [4]	'\n'	Opinion at paragraph level	One to Many	Single document's overall sentiment
2. Sentence [5]	'.'	Topic polarity	Many to Many	Subjectivity
3. Entity or aspect level [7, 17]	'Space'	Words as entities	One to One	Two-tuple like <Sentiment, target>

1.2 Features Used

Term Presence (TP). Term presence is the traditional feature vector of text indicating the presence of individual terms in text. It makes $M^{p}_{n\times 1}$ column matrix with n distinct terms from text. Presence of term is indicated with binary 1 and absence with value 0 in this column matrix.

Term Frequency (TF). Term frequency is real valued column matrix $M^F_{n\times 1}$ shown in Eq. (1) contains entries corresponding to the frequency of particular term present in the text. Here one thing common with $M^P_{n\times 1}$ that 0 in $M^F_{n\times 1}$ represents the absence of term.

$$[M^F_{i\times 1}] = k \mid \text{i}^{\text{th}}\text{term occurs k times in the text.} \tag{1}$$

Term Frequency-Inverse Document Frequency (TF-IDF). In the above definition of term frequency, column matrix $M^F_{n\times 1}$ is a single vector for one document. In other words, if the whole text corpus is taken to be in a single document then this column matrix will be huge one. However taking whole dataset in a single file is a bad choice of preprocessing. So if the text from corpus is shifted to different documents or files, the preprocessing would be done in a better way. Following the same lines, term frequency can be redefined as the following Eq. (2):

$$\begin{aligned} TF(t,d) = n_k \mid d \in D(\text{Set of Documents}), \\ t \in d(\text{term present in document d with } n_k \text{ occurrences} \end{aligned} \tag{2}$$

Inverse document frequency defines the weighting term for a document. The value of IDF is a logarithmic measure describes the importance of a term or 'word' for a document given in Eq. (3).

$$IDF = \log\left(\frac{|D|}{1 + |d \in D : t \in d|}\right) \tag{3}$$

TFIDF is calculated as a product of TF and IDF in the Eq. (4) below:

$$TFIDF(t,d,D) = n_k \times \log\left(\frac{|D|}{1 + |d \in D : t \in d|}\right) \tag{4}$$

where $|D|$ is the total number of documents, $|d \in D : t \in d|$ represents number of documents in which term 't' appears and n_k is the number of times the term 't' appears in document 'd'. Addition of 1 in the denominator in logarithmic term is taken (to avoid zero in the denominator) for those cases where there is no document containing the target term.

N-Grams (Beyond unigram features). In language processing n-grams represents the sequences of n-words taken from text to exploit semantic parsing of a language. When n = 1, n-grams are termed as unigrams which reflects the similar process as tokenization of text. So unigrams are the word tokens without white spaces, punctuation marks and carriage return characters. Taking n = 2 generates bigrams, n = 3 trigrams and so on. Also described in Markov model which is similar to n-grams, it is used to predict next word from previous n–1 words. The probabilistic measure for predicting next word is given as:

$$P(x_i | x_{i-(n-1)}, \ldots\ldots\ldots\ldots, x_{i-1}) \tag{5}$$

with this P-value range (0,1), n-gram model predicts x_i based on previous $x_{i-(n-1)}, \ldots\ldots\ldots\ldots, x_{i-1}$ terms.

Parts of Speech (POS). POS feature refers to identification of words as nouns, verbs, adjectives and adverbs. Tagging words with these POS is known as POS-tagging in computational linguistics [18]. The Penn-Treebank project provides the way of classifying words into their POS tags for lexical categorization. Following is alphabetically listed 36 POS tags given by Penn-Treebank project with their respective examples in Table 2:

Table 2. Alphabetical list of POS-tags used in Penn-Treebank's project

S.No.	POS Tag	Description	Example
1	CC	Coordinating conjunction	and, but, for, or, so
2	CD	Cardinal number	1, 2, two, three
3	DT	Determiner	a, the, every
4	EX	Existential there	there is
5	FW	Foreign word	obrigada
6	IN	Preposition or subordinating conjunction	in, of, like
7	JJ	Adjective	green, sweet, large
8	JJR	Adjective comparative	greener, larger
9	JJS	Adjective superlative	greenest, largest
10	LS	List item marker	(1), (2), (3)
11	MD	Modal	can, may, must, will
12	NN	Noun singular or mass	book, table
13	NNS	Noun plural	books, tables
14	NNP	Proper noun singular	Joe, John, Adam
15	NNPS	Proper noun plural	Vikings, Adams
16	PDT	Pre determiner	both the boys
17	POS	Possessive ending	friend's
18	PRP	Personal pronoun	I, He, You
19	PRP$	Possessive pronoun	My, His, Her
20	RB	Adverb	however, usually
21	RBR	Adverb comparative	better
22	RBS	Adverb superlative	Best
23	RP	Particle	give up
24	SYM	Symbol	$, %
25	TO	To	to go, to him
26	UH	Interjection	huhh..
27	VB	Verb base form	Take
28	VBD	Verb past tense	took
29	VBG	Verb gerund or present participle	taking
30	VBN	Verb past participle	taken
31	VBP	Verb non 3rd person singular present	Take
32	VBZ	Verb 3rd person singular present	takes
33	WDT	Wh determiner	Which
34	WP	Wh pronoun	Who, What
35	WP$	Possessive Wh pronoun	Whose
36	WRB	Wh adverb	Where, When

Consider an example of tagging text with POS-tagging in Python3 as: Text is "We follow the teachings of Guru Nanak Dev Ji", and tagged text is [(We, PRP), (follow, VBP), (the, DT), (Teachings, NNS), (of, IN), (Guru, NNP), (Nanak, NNP), (Dev, NNP), (Ji, NNP)].

2 Machine Learning Techniques for Sentiment Analysis

The interest of researchers in the field of sentiment analysis is growing from last few years. This is due to the fact that social networking sites provide data freely. People put up their views and emotions [13] online publically about different products and services they experienced. The organizations hire researchers to analyze their hidden facts about their products, where elucidating the true sentiments out of web text is their main concern. Automatic and spontaneous determination of sentiments from raw web text is the agenda of most multinational corporate [21]. Automatized sentiment analysis is done through machine learning techniques as discussed below.

The polarity of emotions depends upon the mindset of an author of text whether positive or negative [16, 20]. Sentiment analysis considers emotion extraction from the text as a primary task in the text classification. Naïve Bayes classifier provides a way to express positive, negative and neutral feelings hidden in web text. The very first step involved in this classification is the preprocessing of web text. Text from movie reviews is unstructured one. Preprocessing involves ingesting of unstructured text into an ARFF file as a dataset for refinement of unstructured web text. Secondly, Naïve Bayes classification allows the calculation of probabilities [14] as according to the relation in Eq. (6) and probability in Eq. (7):

$$\mathrm{P(y\ /\ x1,\ x2,\ x3,\ \ldots\ldots,xn)} = \mathrm{P(y)} \times \prod\nolimits_{i=1}^{n} \frac{P\left(\frac{xi}{y}\right)}{P(x1, x2, x3, \ldots.., xn)} \tag{6}$$

For Example: Consider a Movie Review for movie "Exposed"

[1]"The film starts effectively as a detective story with Keanu trying to find a killer. As we follow the developing story there are some odd events making the viewers wonder is this is Science fiction or not."

Worth = {{"watch", "effective start"}, {"watch", "a detective story"}, {"watch", "odd events"}, {"watch", "Science fiction"}, {"watch", "wonder viewers"}}
Prob(Watch) = #("effective", "Science", "wonder", "detective") / #(positive terms)
Prob(worth) = #("Watch") / #(Total Positive terms)

[1] http://www.imdb.com/title/tt4019560/reviews?ref_=tt_ov_rt.

$$Prob(Worth\,watching) = \frac{\mathrm{Prob(Worth)} \times \mathrm{Prob}\left(\frac{\mathrm{Watch}}{\mathrm{Worth}}\right)}{\mathrm{Prob(Worth)}} \tag{7}$$

A tree based algorithm known as J48 Algorithm, describes the hierarchical way of how feature- text behaves at various instances. The main concern is to generate rules for predictions of target variables. Collected instances from text features to their corresponding class represented with leaf nodes labeled. Every time when near attribute to the labeled one is found, it is being made attached to the higher levels in the tree of same class. The respective classes of text corresponding to positive, negative or neutral gradually generated in different branches of the tree.

$$\text{Entropy (Term)} = -\sum\nolimits_{j=1}^{n} \frac{|Term\,j|}{|Term|} \log_2 \frac{|Term\,j|}{|Term|} \tag{8}$$

J48 classifies test on the basis of entropy of terms given in Eq. (8). Terms can be uni-grams, bi-grams or tri-grams. Here in this example, terms "wonder viewers", "Effective start", and "detective story" express positive opinion about the movie, whereas terms like "Fiction" and "Odd events" introduces negative sentiments. The Fig. 1 below represents the working model of J48 algorithm for extracting sentiment from text. The entropies of terms favoring the target opinion evaluate sentiment of worth watching.

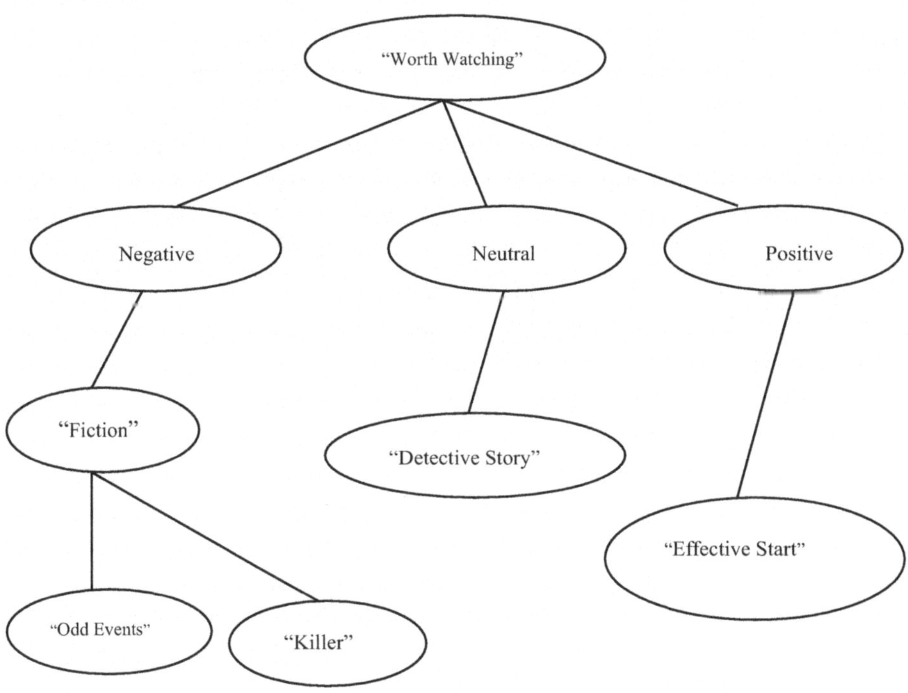

Fig. 1. J48 Tree for terms of above movie review example

Another hierarchical based BFTREE algorithm digs the document for best supporting positive and negative terms. The classification by BFTREE falls under the category of heuristic algorithms which probe all collected items and classify them into their respective classes. The classification tree built from movie review data evaluates sentiments at document level where each document is tagged positive negative or neutral. The first step of algorithm proceeds with the elimination of best node from list of open nodes and sets its status closed. If the selected term represents the goal state then its sentiment score is compared with corresponding term stored in test case of training set.

Another algorithm used for sentiment prediction is OneR algorithm, generates one rule for classification of text. The criterion of consideration of one rule with smallest error is repetitive evaluation of occurrences of terms. The most frequent terms which are housed in a particular target term is classified with the class of that target. The brief footprints of steps of OneR algorithm for estimation of smallest total error in sentiment classification are given below:

```
Step1: Generate features of selected term from training
dataset.
Step2: Repeat step3 to step7 until total error is reduced
to a minimum threshold.
Step3: Count Feature terms and generate frequency table.
Step4: Find most frequent terms.
Step5: Make a rule of assignment of most frequent term to
selected term's class.
Step6: Find errors occurred in other frequent terms.
Step7: Take estimation of smallest total error.
```

Support Vector Machines (SVM) is another classifier used for text classification. SVM considers distance of word vectors from hyper-plane of decision boundary. Generally this distance parameter is taken from Eulerian, Manhattan and Lagrangian distances of vectors. The word vectors which are falling away from certain minimum range of threshold should be ignored [19, 22]. Only those which fall within the radius of decision boundary are taken to support the given class. If a data point (x_k, y_k) with weight 'w' falls on the right side of decision plane, the minimum Lagrangian distance (L) and small slack S_k to be qualified in the Eq. (9) as:

$$\min L = \frac{1}{2}w'w - \sum \lambda_k(y_k(w'x_k + b) + S_k - 1) + \alpha \sum S_k \tag{9}$$

Where S_k being a small distance of data point (xk, yk) to be misclassified on the wrong side of decision plane, $(y_k(w'x_k + b) \geq S_k - 1)$ and λ_k is learning rate of training data.

Another method used for text sentiment classification is Latent Dirichlet Allocation (LDA). The proposal of probabilistic measure for classification using LDA was introduced by David Blei, Andrew Ng and Michael Jordan in early 2003. LDA represents text into concepts taken from mixture of randomly generated words from corpus. It was assumed that web text consists of k-independent concepts. Each concept gives presence of word 'w' into topic 'θ' and therefore a tuple (θ, w) in LDA's mathematical modeling. The probability distribution for Dirichlet parameters 'α' and 'β' of topic 'θ', 'z' as a set of topics and 'W' as set of words is given in Eqs. (10) and (11) below:

$$P(\theta, z, W/\alpha, \beta) = P(\theta/\alpha). \prod_{n=1}^{N} P\left(\frac{z_n}{\alpha}\right).P(w_n/z_n, \beta) \tag{10}$$

Moreover this probability distribution considers only topic pairs and provides the chance of occurrence of each word within its associated topics:

$$P(w_{mn}, z_{mn}) = \int P(\theta_k).\left(\prod_{n=1}^{N} P(z_n/\theta).P(w_n/z_n)d\theta\right) \tag{11}$$

3 Related Work

Kiritchenko and Mohammad [1] explored sentiment composition lexicons for phrases of opposite polarity. They have taken manually annotated dataset using twitter API to collect 11 million tweets containing emotions. They have analyzed opposing polarity phrases and executed both supervised and unsupervised machine learning techniques. The features used in supervised sentiment classification were constituent words, parts of speech, sentiment scores, emotions, and embedding vectors. The supervised classifier has achieved accuracy of 82.6% for bigram and 80.9% for trigrams in sentiment composition.

Dashtipour et al. [2] compared the accuracies of different machine learning techniques for multilingual sentiment analysis. They have examined number of sentiment lexicons for improving the performance of sentiment classification. The study includes SenticNet, SentiWordNet, General Inquirer and SEL lexicons, where General Inquirer is a German lexicon built using Google translator and SEL is a Spanish Language Lexicon. They have used an English language dataset to evaluate the performance of SVM (Support Vector Machines), MNB (Multinomial Naïve Bayes) and Maximum Entropy classifiers proposed by Joachims [3] and reported 86.35% of accuracy in sentiment classification.

Mohammad [4] have developed automatic classifier for 2012 presidential election tweets of US. They have delivered a query questionnaire containing ten questions to be unfolded from electoral tweets. They introduced eight features for representing emotional state in tweets. Features include word n-grams, punctuation marks, elongated words, emoticons, emotion lexicons, negation feature, position feature and combined feature. The automatic system has obtained the accuracy of 56.84% which is noticeably above the accuracy of major in baseline.

Mohammad et al. [5] proposed a stance detection system that has outperformed from all 19 teams participated in Sem-Eval 2016 competition. The proposed system obtained the accuracy of 70.3% of correctness in sentiment classification. They have introduced linear kernel SVM classifier with various sentiment features like word n-grams and word embedding.

Turney and Mohammad [6] introduced three techniques for sentiment extraction from web text. Two of techniques namely balAPinc and ConVecs used context matrices for evaluation of sentiment scores and has achieved the accuracies of 68.7% and 70.2% respectively, whereas third one named SimDiff used SVM classifer and has got accuracy of 74.5% correctness in sentiment extraction.

Poria et al. [7] have explored the concept level sentiment analysis that amalgamates linguistics, computations and machine learning techniques for improving accuracy in sentiment detection. They have trained SVM and ELM (Extreme Learning Machine) classifier over training set of movie review dataset. ELM classifier leads SVM in terms of accuracy of sentiment classification. ELM has obtained the accuracy of 67.35% while SVM procured 65.67% only.

Mohammad et al. in Sem-Eval-2016 Task-6 [8] have proposed an automatic system for detection of stance in tweets. 19 teams submitted the task on supervised stance detection. The best results obtained by team named MITRE with overall average F-measure as 67.82%. They have trained recurrent neural network classifier to predict task relevant hashtags on unlabeled twitter corpus.

Kiritchenko et al. in Sem-Eval-2016 Task-7 [9] have presented his work on automatic sentiment score determination model. They have taken words and phrases from English twitter and Arabic twitter corpus. Accuracies of sentiment score determination is expressed using Kendall's rank correlation coefficient K. Team ECNU has outperformed with K = 0.704 for General English sentiment modifier and K = 0.523 for English twitter mixed polarity, while in Arabic Twitter test set, team iLab-Edinburgh leads with K = 0.536.

Salameh et al. [10] presented sentiment lexicons for Arabic social media using distant supervision techniques on Arabic tweets, and translating English sentiment lexicon into Arabic using Google translator. They have obtained best accuracy of 66.6% using both Dialectal hashtag Lexicon and translated NRC Emotion Lexicon.

Noman et al. in [23] compared the accuracies of six different classifiers including LDA and SVM. They have classified mental levels of person using infrared spectroscopy signals. Artificial Neural Network classifier outperformed over LDA and SVM in their experimental observation.

In [24], Poria et al. 2017 performed personality detection from text by using text classification. They have proposed a Convolution Neural Networks (CNN) based model utilizing SVM in classification tasks.

3.1 Classifier Performance Benchmarks

The summary of benchmarks related to machine learning techniques in terms of accuracy of classification is listed in the Table 3. SVM and Naive Bayes are proving better in terms of benchmarks than other machine learning techniques.

Table 3. Benchmarks of classifier's accuracies

Author(s) and year of publication	Classifiers & features used	Description	Accuracy of classification (in %age)
Sventlana Kiritchenko and Saif M. Mohammad (2016a)	SVM with RBF kernel, POS, sentiment score, emoticons, embedding vectors [1]	The proposed technique has exploited real valued score of sentiment and analyzed data from social network sites.	82.60 for bigrams 80.90 for trigrams
Dashtipour et al. (2016) Joachims, T. (2002)	SVM, MNB, Maximum entropy [2, 3]	The devised methodology has improved the accuracy of sentiment classification using multilingual text.	86.35
Mohammad, S. M., et al. (2015)	Automatic SVM Elongated words, emoticons, negation feature, position feature. [4]	The authors have tracked presidential elections of USA during 2012 from electoral Tweets and automatized the process of emotion extraction.	56.84
Sobhani, P., et al. (2016)	Linear kernel SVM, n-grams and word embeddings [5]	Coined a system for stance detection and sentiment extraction	70.30
P.D. Turney & Saif. M. Mohammad (2014)	Lexicon based entailment, SVM [6]	Designed three algorithms viz. balAPinc, ConVecs & SimDiffs and validated the results on three different datasets	68.70 for balAPinc 70.20 for ConVecs 74.50 for SimDiffs
Poria, S., et al. (2014)	Maximum Entropy, Naive Bayes and SVM, ELM [7]	Analyzed sentiment at concept/Topic level from movie review corpus.	67.35 for ELM and 65.67 for SVM
Mohammad, S. M., et al. Sem-Eval (2016) Task 6	SVM, unigrams, n-grams, hashtags, combined features. [8]	An investigation of Tweets for stance detection. (MITRE team has attained maximum accuracy)	F_{avg} = 67.82
Mohammad, S.M., et al. Sem-Eval (2016) Task 7	Supervised Learning, Random Forest, PMI, Gaussian regression, NRC emoticons, SentiWordNet [9, 14]	Authors have designed a model for sentiment's score calculation and validated their model on three datasets viz. General English Corpus, Twitter English and Twitter Arabic corpus.	Kendall's Rank Coeff. (K) K = 0.704 for Gen. English 0.523 for English Twitter, & 0.536 for Arabic Twitter
Salameh, M., et al. (2015)	Linear Kernel SVM, n-grams, all caps, hashtags, punctuation marks [10]	Sentiment lexicons for Arabic Social media using distant supervision techniques on Arabic tweets.	66.6
Socher, R. (2016).	SVM, Naive Bayes [11]	Deep Learning for Sentiment Analysis	85.40
Tan, S. & Zhang, J. (2008)	Naive Bayes, SVM and k-NN [25]	A text classification system for sentiment detection of Chinese Documents	82

4 Datasets Taken

Three Datasets are manually annotated, two of which are taken from www.amazon.in. First dataset consists of product reviews of Woodland's wallet and are taken from 12th October 2016 to 15th April 2017 for training set and from 16th April 2017 to 15th June 2017 for testing the product reviews with their sentiments prediction using four machine learning algorithms. Second dataset consists of 7465 Digital Camera reviews of Sony and are taken from 01st October 2016 to 10th April 2017 for training set and 1000 reviews are from 11th April 2017 to 15th June 2017 for test dataset. Third dataset consists of movie reviews taken from www.imdb.com. It contains 2421 reviews for training set and 500 reviews for test set.

5 Proposed Work

The proposed approach for sentiment analysis is inspired from recurrent neural networks and introduced word embeddings to represent word vectors from corpus words. The training sets of above three datasets are labeled with positive negative and neutral tags manually. Three persons from linguistics and two from sciences are asked to label the sentences followed by the pre-processing of web text through Python's NLTK toolkit.

5.1 Text Pre-processing

Text from web pages contains many unwanted tags and symbols, nltk's word_tokenize function make tokens of whole text with delimiter as white space, comma, question mark, carriage return, new line character, period character and exclamation sign [13]. The bs4 library of Python3 is used for cleaning of data, which removes unwanted symbols and html tags, followed by parts of speech tagging with Stanford's POS Tagger. The tagged token are then stemmed with Porter's Stemmer and lemmatization removes slang or foreign words from these tokens. The tagged and refined tokens are then undergo stopword filtering with nltk filter function and produces processed text ready to be inputted to the input layer of proposed framework. Figure 2 below shows the steps of pre-processing of raw web text.

5.2 Architecture of Proposed System

The proposed deep learning model using convolution neural network is developed to investigate the sentiment of text. The three corpora are broken into three sets, one for training, one for development and one for testing the neural classifier. The training set is labeled by human resources while development and testing sets are kept unlabeled. The word embeddings of these sets are implemented in Python3 using Glove and word2vec modules. Five different features of text are extracted using conventional nltk functions. Features include TP, TF, tfidf, n-gram and POS tags. The Convolution Neural Network (CNN) is trained with the pre-processed training set. The input of

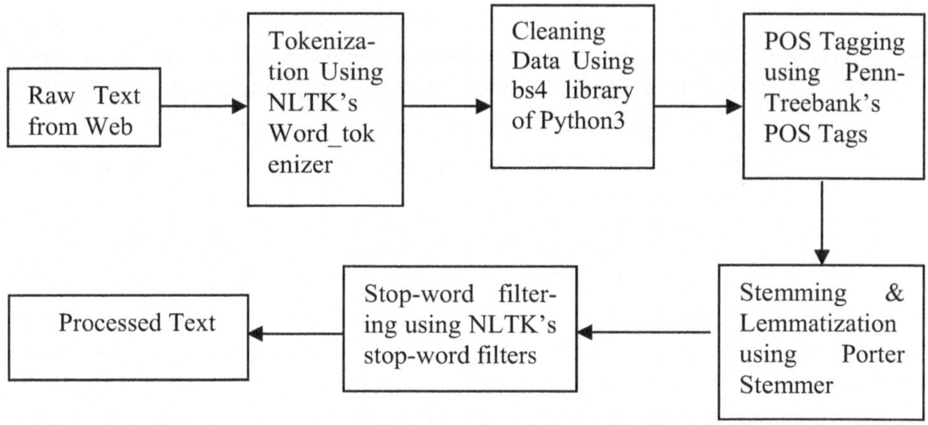

Fig. 2. Pre-processing framework of proposed architecture

proposed CNN based model is processed document D with word sequence w_1, w_2, ... w_n. The output of this model gives sentiment class of document.

Taking $CL(w_i)$ as left context and $CR(w_i)$ as right context of word (w_i). Equations (12) and (13) provide the matrices of left and right context matrix of word w_i are evaluated as:

$$CL(w_i) = f\left(W^{(l)}CL(w_{i-1}) + W^{(sl)}e(w_{i-1})\right) \quad (12)$$

$$CR(w_i) = f\left(W^{(r)}CR(w_{i+1}) + W^{(sr)}e(w_{i+1})\right) \quad (13)$$

Where $W^{(l)}$ and $W^{(r)}$ are the matrices providing the map of one hidden layer to the next hidden layer in convolution neural networks respectively. $e(w_i$-1) and $e(w_i + 1)$ are embedding vectors of the words on the left and right side of the context word (w_i) respectively. The matrices used for semantic computation of target word in reference to left and right contexts are $W^{(sl)}$ and $W^{(sr)}$ respectively. CNN scans the word window from left to right computing all $CL(w_l)$'s and from right to left generating all $CR(w_i)$'s of context word (w_i). Equation (14) gives the word window of the context word (w_i) is represented with embedding vector (xi) as:

$$x_i = [CL(w_i) : e(w_i) : CR(w_i)] \quad (14)$$

The activation function in the Eq. (15) below is used by CNN consumes this embedding vector (x_i) with linear transformation of context matrix $W^{(2)}$ computes the result for next hidden layer as:

$$y_i^{(2)} = \tanh\left(W^{(2)}x_i + b^{(2)}\right) \quad (15)$$

$y_i^{(2)}$ is evaluated for each word in the input text thereby generating semantic vector representation of words. The next layer takes maximum value from the whole set of word vectors $y_i^{(2)}$'s depicted in Eq. (16) below and known as max pooling layer:

$$y^{(3)} = \max_{1 \leq i \leq n} y_i^{(2)} \tag{16}$$

At the end, the output layer of CNN evaluates latent semantic representation of word vectors using linear combination of previous layer word vectors and matrix maps as shown in Eq. (17) below:

$$y^{(4)} = W^{(4)} y^{(3)} + b^{(4)} \tag{17}$$

In the last stage Eq. (18) gives the softmax probabilities are used for validation of class of text.

$$P_i = \frac{\exp(y_i^{(4)})}{\sum_{k=1}^{n} \exp(y_k^{(4)})} \tag{18}$$

The proposed architecture takes the value of k = 5. This softmax probability for a class k is evaluated using Eq. (18) and corresponding word window is classified in its respective class. The architecture of proposed method is shown below in Fig. 3.

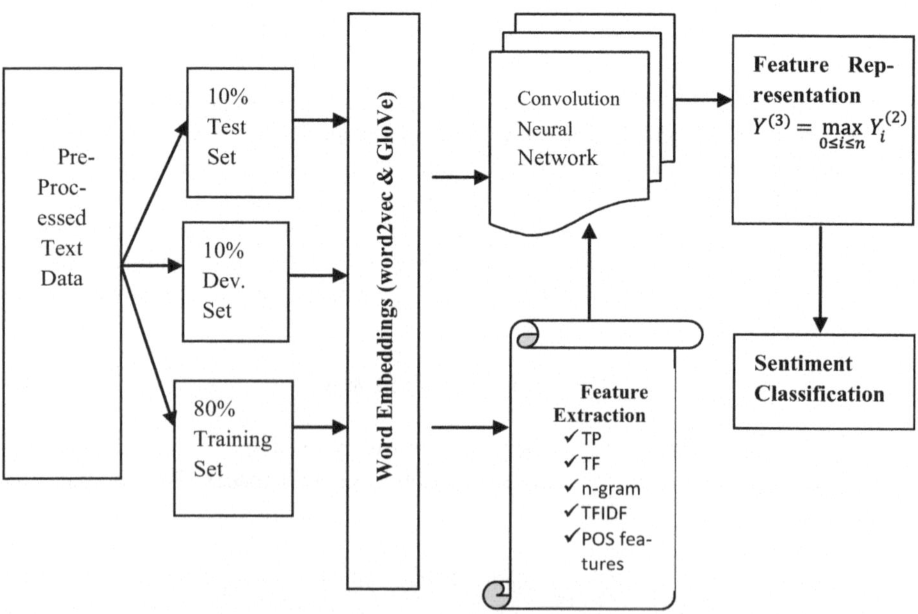

Fig. 3. Proposed system's Architecture with CNN

6 Results and Discussions

Software tools used for classification purpose are WEKA and Python3.5, WEKA is a freeware product of University of Wekaito, New Zealand and Python3.5 is a stable version of Python. The standard libraries of Python3 used for the experimentation are numpy, scipy, bs4, matplotlib, sklearn and nltk. Proposed classifier is accurate in correctly classifying the user's test instances and also outperformed in precision and F-measure. Naive Bayes is proved to be fastest among all the classifiers considered in this paper as shown below in Table 4. Accuracy in True Positive rate is more in case of SVM algorithm while J48 has shown lesser False Positive rate among others in the experiments.

Table 4. Performance evaluation of classifiers

Classifiers	Time taken (sec)	Correctly classified instances	Incorrectly classified Instances	Accuracy TP rate	Accuracy FP rate	Precision	F-measure
Naïve Bayes	7.79	75.24	14.61	0.456	0.134	0.731	0.712
J-48	49.73	69.73	11.33	0.671	0.003	0.777	0.617
BFTree	21.12	70.07	9.03	0.792	0.025	0.783	0.721
OneR	24.45	72.34	8.66	0.690	0.061	0.613	0.672
LDA	19.52	78.12	12.18	0.645	0.054	0.565	0.512
SVM	11.37	80.15	8.76	0.809	0.018	0.802	0.818
Proposed (with CNN)	10.43	85.46	6.84	0.799	0.019	0.852	0.829

6.1 Comparison of Results Classification Approaches

The proposed method with CNN classifier outperformed over other classifiers in correct classification of text. The performance comparison of seven classifiers is the average of 10 epochs of experimentation. Naïve Bayes, LDA and SVM classifiers have performed almost equally well. OneR seems to be the better algorithm than J48 and BFTree algorithms for accurately classifying the sentiments from the text. The performance comparison in the bar graph below in Fig. 4 is average of all three datasets.

6.2 Test Accuracies of Different Classification Algorithms for Three Datasets

After training these seven classification algorithms on trainings sets of respective three datasets, accuracy of classification is tested for test sets with 5 features (TP, TF, n-gram, tfidf and POS) and 2 features (bigrams and POS). These features are extracted using feature-extractor of text in sklearn library of Python3. The common behavior of all classifiers is observed and it was found that accuracies in classification of all the techniques are better for 5 features of text as compared to 2 features of text as shown in Table 5. This proves that higher number of features raise the learning capability of machine learning algorithms.

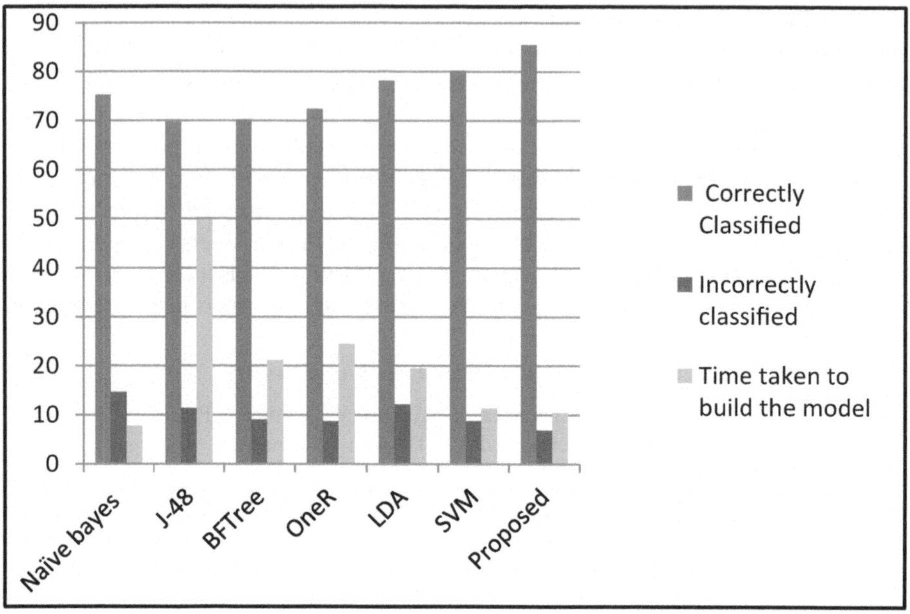

Fig. 4. Comparison of classification results of classifiers

Table 5. Test accuracies of classification algorithms for three datasets (where DS1: Woodland's Wallet product reviews dataset, DS2: Sony Digital Camera Product Reviews dataset and DS3: IMDB Movie Reviews dataset

Classification algorithm	Data Set	Test accuracy with 5 features of text (in %)	Test accuracy with 2 features of text (in %)
Naïve Bayes	DS1	78.19	66.81
	DS2	73.12	61.29
	DS3	74.41	65.84
J-48	DS1	71.79	55.45
	DS2	63.72	53.44
	DS3	72.71	54.85
BFTree	DS1	77.13	60.32
	DS2	65.36	45.15
	DS3	68.54	40.56
OneR	DS1	71.38	54.45
	DS2	73.31	43.78
	DS3	72.34	48.51
LDA	DS1	81.23	59.34
	DS2	77.54	62.43
	DS3	76.44	66.76
SVM	DS1	88.78	71.23
	DS2	71.87	70.12
	DS3	81.98	69.56
Proposed	DS1	90.75	75.34
	DS2	82.58	78.43
	DS3	84.64	71.76

7 Conclusion and Future Scope

This paper involves seven sentiment classification techniques based on machine learning and made an attempt using experimentation on three manually annotated datasets. The examination of reactions of these techniques in terms of accuracies in Table 4 shows that proposed technique with CNN is more precise in classifying the correct sentiments of web text. On the other hand, Naïve Bayes, LDA and SVM are also significant in sentiment classification. Table 5 reveals that the learning ability of all algorithms grows with the rise in number of features of featured web text. Proposed algorithm seems better in test accuracies when more number of features is considered. These techniques are facing challenges while in preprocessing of featured text to extract features like hashtags, foreign words, local slangs and elongated words etc. The future work in the extension of this study has scope in melioration of preprocessing in these techniques for enhancing the accuracy of sentiment classification.

References

1. Kiritchenko, S., Mohammad, S.M.: Sentiment composition of words with opposing polarities. In: Proceedings of the 2016 Conference of the North American Chapter of the Association for Computational Linguistics: Human Language Technologies (2016). https://doi.org/10.18653/v1/n16-1128
2. Dashtipour, K., Poria, S., Hussain, A., Cambria, E., Hawalah, A.Y., Gelbukh, A., Zhou, Q.: Multilingual sentiment analysis: state of the art and independent comparison of techniques. Cogn. Comput. **8**(4), 757–771 (2016). https://doi.org/10.1007/s12559-016-9415-7
3. Joachims, T.: Text classification. In: Joachims, L. (ed.) Learning to Classify Text Using Support Vector Machines. Springer, Boston (2002). https://doi.org/10.1007/978-1-4615-0907-3_2
4. Mohammad, S.M., Zhu, X., Kiritchenko, S., Martin, J.: Sentiment, emotion, purpose, and style in electoral Tweets. Inf. Process. Manag. **51**(4), 480–499 (2015). https://doi.org/10.1016/j.ipm.2014.09.003
5. Sobhani, P., Mohammad, S., Kiritchenko, S.: Detecting stance in Tweets and analyzing its interaction with sentiment. In: Proceedings of the Fifth Joint Conference on Lexical and Computational Semantics (2016). https://doi.org/10.18653/v1/s16-2021
6. Turney, P.D., Mohammad, S.M.: Experiments with three approaches to recognizing lexical entailment. Nat. Lang. Eng. **21**(03), 437–476 (2014). https://doi.org/10.1017/s1351324913000387
7. Poria, S., Cambria, E., Winterstein, G., Huang, G.: Sentic patterns: dependency-based rules for concept-level sentiment analysis. Knowl. Based Syst. **69**, 45–63 (2014). https://doi.org/10.1016/j.knosys.2014.05.005
8. Mohammad, S., Kiritchenko, S., Sobhani, P., Zhu, X., Cherry, C.: SemEval-2016 task 6: detecting stance in Tweets. In: Proceedings of the 10th International Workshop on Semantic Evaluation (SemEval-2016). https://doi.org/10.18653/v1/s16-1003
9. Kiritchenko, S., Mohammad, S., Salameh, M.: SemEval-2016 task 7: determining sentiment intensity of English and Arabic phrases. In: Proceedings of the 10th International Workshop on Semantic Evaluation (SemEval-2016) (2016). https://doi.org/10.18653/v1/s16-1004

10. Salameh, M., Mohammad, S., Kiritchenko, S.: Sentiment after translation: a case-study on Arabic social media posts. In: Proceedings of the 2015 Conference of the North American Chapter of the Association for Computational Linguistics: Human Language Technologies (2015). https://doi.org/10.3115/v1/n15-1078
11. Socher, R.: Deep learning for sentiment analysis - invited talk. In: Proceedings of the 7th Workshop on Computational Approaches to Subjectivity, Sentiment and Social Media Analysis (2016). https://doi.org/10.18653/v1/w16-0408
12. Bermingham, A., Conway, M., McInerney, L., O'Hare, N., Smeaton, A.F.: Combining social network analysis and sentiment analysis to explore the potential for online radicalisation. In: 2009 International Conference on Advances in Social Network Analysis and Mining (2009). https://doi.org/10.1109/asonam.2009.31
13. Cambria, E., White, B.: Jumping NLP curves: a review of natural language processing research [review article]. IEEE Comput. Intell. Mag. **9**(2), 48–57 (2014). https://doi.org/10.1109/mci.2014.2307227
14. Cernian, A., Sgarciu, V., Martin, B.: Sentiment analysis from product reviews using SentiWordNet as lexical resource. In: 2015 7th International Conference on Electronics, Computers and Artificial Intelligence (ECAI) (2015). https://doi.org/10.1109/ecai.2015.7301224
15. Chetty, G., Wagner, M., Goecke, R.: A multilevel fusion approach for audiovisual emotion recognition. A Pattern Anal. Approach 437–460 (2015). https://doi.org/10.1002/9781118910566.ch17
16. Parvathy, G., Bindhu, J.S.: A probabilistic generative model for mining cybercriminal network from online social media: a review. Int. J. Comput. Appl. **134**(14), 1–4 (2016). https://doi.org/10.5120/ijca2016908121
17. Hammer, H.L., Solberg, P.E., Øvrelid, L.: Sentiment classification of online political discussions: a comparison of a word-based and dependency-based method. In: Proceedings of the 5th Workshop on Computational Approaches to Subjectivity, Sentiment and Social Media Analysis (2014). https://doi.org/10.3115/v1/w14-2616
18. Wanton, T. M., et al. OPINION POLARITY DETECTION - using word sense disambiguation to determine the polarity of opinions. In: Proceedings of the 2nd International Conference on Agents and Artificial Intelligence (2010). https://doi.org/10.5220/0002703504830486
19. Pang, B., Lee, L., Vaithyanathan, S.: Thumbs up? In: Proceedings of the ACL-02 Conference on Empirical Methods in Natural Language Processing - EMNLP 2002 (2002). https://doi.org/10.3115/1118693.1118704
20. Poria, S., Cambria, E., Gelbukh, A., Bisio, F., Hussain, A.: Sentiment data flow analysis by means of dynamic linguistic patterns. IEEE Comput. Intell. Mag. **10**(4), 26–36 (2015). https://doi.org/10.1109/mci.2015.2471215
21. Xia, Y., Cambria, E., Hussain, A., Zhao, H.: Word polarity disambiguation using Bayesian model and opinion-level features. Cogn Comput **7**(3), 369–380 (2014). https://doi.org/10.1007/s12559-014-9298-4
22. Zadeh, L.: Toward human-level machine intelligence. In: 2006 18th IEEE International Conference on Tools with Artificial Intelligence (ICTAI 2006) (2006). https://doi.org/10.1109/ictai.2006.114
23. Noman, N., et. al.: Analysis of different classification techniques for two class functional near infrared spectroscopy based based-computer interaction. Computat. Intell. Neurosci. (2016). https://doi.org/10.1155/2016/5480760
24. Poria, S., et al.: Deep learning based document modeling for personality detection from text. IEEE Intell. Syst. **32**, 74–79 (2017). https://doi.org/10.1109/MIS.2017.23
25. Tan, S., Zhang, J.: An empirical study of sentiment analysis for Chinese documents. Expert Syst. Appl. **34**(4), 2622–2629 (2008). https://doi.org/10.1016/j.eswa.2007.05.028

Intuitionistic Fuzzy Shortest Path in a Multigraph

Siddhartha Sankar Biswas[1(✉)], Bashir Alam[2], and M. N. Doja[1,2]

[1] Jamia Hamdard, New Delhi, India
ssbiswas1984@gmail.com
[2] Jamia Millia Islamia, New Delhi, India

Abstract. Mutigraphs are a generalized model of graphs. Multigraphs may have multiple edges between a pair of its vertices. The existing algorithms to find the fuzzy shortest path or intuitionistic fuzzy shortest paths in graphs is not applicable to multigraphs. Our work here is on the theory of multigraphs. In this paper we develop a method to search for an intuitionistic fuzzy shortest path in a directed multigraph and then develop, as a special case, a fuzzy shortest path in a multigraph. We re-construct classical Dijkstra's rule that is applicable to graphs with crisp weights which can then be extendable to IFN multigraphs. It's claimed that the tactic might play a significant role in several application areas of technology, specifically in those networks that may not be shaped into graphs but however into multigraphs.

Keywords: IFS · IFN · IF-min-cost arch-set · IF min path estimation
IF relaxation

1 Introduction

Multigraphs [13, 24–26, 29, 38–42] are generalization of graph-theory, in which more than one edge might connect any two nodes. Few of the directed multigraphs, connecting-arcs cost don't seem to be perpetually crisp though it may be intuitionistic fuzzy (or fuzzy). Throughout our work here, we've got worked with multigraphs which does not have any loops.

Sathi [34] developed an interesting method to find in IFSP in a graph. Here we solve this problem to find intuitionistic fuzzy shortest path in a multigraph where the arc-weights are intuitionistic fuzzy numbers (IFNs), and then we reduce the method to the case of finding FSP in a multigraph. We follow the concept of classical Dijkstra's algorithm for graphs and extend this concept to multigraphs where the weights of the arcs are IFNs. Earlier in [39] we made a generalization of Dijkstra's Algorithm for a directed multigraph, all data being crisp neither fuzzy nor intuitionistic fuzzy. Then in [40] we proposed a fuzzy shortest path in a directed multigraph. In [41] we introduced a new mathematical modeling in the theory of multigraphs by incorporating variable costs with respect to real time information. Then we considered an intuitionistic fuzzy 'real time' multigraph in [42–45] where we presented a theoretical mathematical modeling only.

B. Panda et al. (Eds.): REDSET 2017, CCIS 799, pp. 533–540, 2018.
https://doi.org/10.1007/978-981-10-8527-7_44

2 IF-Shortest-Path in Multigraph

Heuristic methodology to determine the IFSPP for graph using the IFHG operator, with proposal of Dijkstra's algorithmic rule was first used by Sathi [34]. The present work here is mainly motivated by the problem posed in [34] by Sathi, but in a multigraph. In [28], Karunambigai, Rangasamy, Palaniappan conferred a model supporting dynamic programm to search out the min weighted path in IF graph. Gani in [4] additionally developed a way on looking out IFSP in an exceedingly network. But the work in this paper is on a multigraph, and not developed as a generalization of any previous work. The technique used here solves SPP for multigraphs where we tend to additionally use Dijkstra's algorithmic-rule but with easy soft-computations [6].

2.1 IF-Min-Weight -Arc-Set of a Directed Multigraph

Assume a IFweighted directed-multigraph B with n range of connects from u to v in B, considering that n may be a non-negative integer. Set Wuv, whose components are the connections between u and v.

$$\therefore \quad Wuv = \{(uv1, w1uv), (uv2, w2uv), (uv3, w3uv), \ldots.., (uvn, wnuv)\}$$

If many range of IF weights are same then it will randomly select at the corresponding place in which wuv equals IF-min value of the multiset, i.e. Wuv = {w1uv, w2uv, w3uv, ……., wnuv}. Clearly, wuv = w1uv.

2.2 d[v] in Directed Multigraph

Let s is that the commencement vertex and u be live tracked vertex. Also consider that weight cost of curve between r and t is not always similar. We understand IF most limited way gauge i.e. d[r], amid coordinated multigraph as beneath (see Fig. 1):

(estimate IF min path for t) =
(estimate IF min path for r) ⊕ (IF-Min calculated for every IF weigh).

$$\text{or,} \quad d[r] = d[t] \oplus w_{(r\,t)}\,.$$

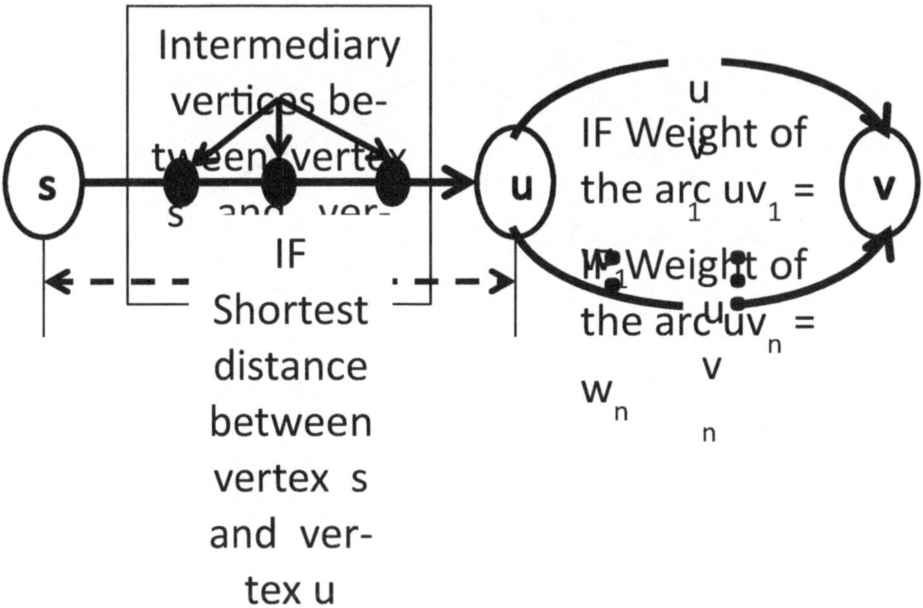

Fig. 1. Estimation procedure for d[v]

2.3 IFSP Algorithm

Here we propose the main algorithmic rule IFSP in which we try to extracts u using ranking in IF concept and re-update J.

```
IFSP (D, d)
IF-INIT-SINGULAR-COMMENCEMENT (D, d)
W ← IFMWA (J)
D ← Ø
J ← V[D]
   WHILE  J ≠ Ø
         DO  u ← EXTRACT-IFMIN (J)
              D ← D ∪ {u}
              In  each vertex  v  element of  Adj[u]
                 Execute  IF-RLX (u, v, W)
```

Example. Multigraph G with IF price (as shown in Fig. 2). we would like to resolve the singular-commencement IFSP with the vertex A because the commencement vertex and therefore the vertex D as the last vertex.

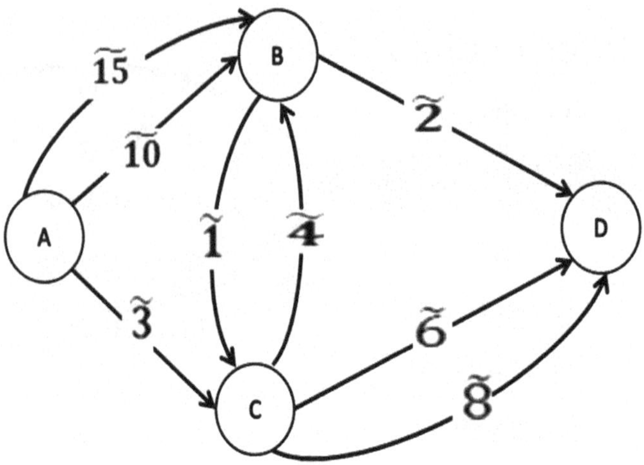

Fig. 2. Multigraph G.

Let us see how the IFSPA algorithm computes here.

$$
\begin{aligned}
W_{AB} &= \left\{\left(AB, \widetilde{15}\right), \left(AB, \widetilde{10}\right)\right\} \Rightarrow w_{AB} = \widetilde{10}. \\
W_{AC} &= \left\{\left(AC, \widetilde{03}\right)\right\} \Rightarrow w_{AC} = \widetilde{03}. \\
W_{BC} &= \left\{\left(BC, \widetilde{01}\right)\right\} \Rightarrow w_{BC} = \widetilde{01}. \\
W_{CB} &= \left\{\left(CB, \widetilde{04}\right)\right\} \Rightarrow w_{CB} = \widetilde{04}. \\
W_{BD} &= \left\{\left(BD, \widetilde{02}\right)\right\} \Rightarrow w_{BD} = \widetilde{02}. \\
W_{CD} &= \left\{\left(CD, \widetilde{06}\right), \left(CD, \widetilde{08}\right)\right\} \Rightarrow w_{CD} = \widetilde{06}.
\end{aligned}
$$

Therefore, in step-2, IF MWA(G) returns W as below:

$$W_{AB} = \{(AB, \widetilde{10}), (AC, \widetilde{03}), (BC, \widetilde{01}), (CB, \widetilde{04}), (BD, \widetilde{02}), (CD, \widetilde{06})\}.$$

Initially by Step-3 and 4,

$$Q = \{A, B, C, D\} \quad \text{and} \quad S = \Phi.$$

Step-6 to 9 yield (by step-5 i.e. satisfying the WHILE condition)

$Q \neq \Phi$ is TRUE

$$\begin{cases} u = A \\ S = S \cup \{A\} = \{A\} \text{ i.e. } S : A \\ Q = \{B, C, D\} \end{cases}$$

$Q \neq \Phi$ is TRUE

$$\begin{cases} u = C \\ S = S \cup \{C\} = \{A, C\} \text{ i.e. } S{:}A \rightarrow C \\ Q = \{B, D\} \end{cases}$$

$Q \neq \Phi$ is TRUE

$$\begin{cases} u = B \\ S = S \cup \{B\} = \{A, C, B\} \text{ i.e. } S \ : \ A \rightarrow C \rightarrow B \\ Q = \{D\} \end{cases}$$

$Q \neq \Phi$ is TRUE

$$\begin{cases} u = D \\ S = S \cup \{D\} = \{A, C, B, D\} \text{ i.e. } S \ : \ A \rightarrow C \rightarrow B \rightarrow D \\ Q = \{\} \end{cases}$$

Since the condition '$Q \neq \Phi$' is now FALSE, the IFSPA algorithm terminates yielding the following results:

IFSP from the commencement vertex A is: A to C to B to D.

And the d–values of d[A] is 0, d[C] is IFN3, d[B] is IFN7, d[D] is IFN9.

3 FSP in a Multigraph

The idea of fuzzy sets could be an explicit instance of the thought of intuitionistic fluffy sets. In the event that the hesitation half is nil for all portions in AN IFS, it mechanically lessens to a set of fuzzy numbers. Subsequently, the IF methodologies and calculations created in Sect. 3 above lessens to the fuzzy techniques as an extraordinary case that are offered underneath.

By fuzzy-relaxation, we tend to mean here the relaxation strategy for a arc-segment whose weight could be a fuzzy weight. As just if there should arise an occurrence of intuitionistic fuzzy cases, we keep an eye on first instate the chart together with its starting vertex and fuzzy most limited way gauge for each vertices of the graph G.

FISS (G, s)
vertex v element of V[G]
d.[v] is infinity
v.π is NIL
d.[s] equals 0

F-RLX (u, v, W)
When d[v] greater than d[u] XOR w
In that case d[v] equals d[u] XOR w_{uv}
With v.π ← u

Now, we present FSPA.

FSPA (G, s)
FISS (G, s)
W equals FMWA (G)
S tends to ∅
Q tends to V[G]
When Q ≠ ∅
Execute u thends EXTRACT-FUZZY-MIN (Q)
S ← S ∪ {u}
In each vertex v ∈ Adj[u]
execute F-RELAX

4 Conclusion

Multigraphs may be considered as is a generalized version of graph-theory. There are a few genuine issues of network, transportation, correspondence, circuit frameworks, and so on, In a few of those coordinated multigraphs, arc price aren't invariably fresh yet intuitionistic fuzzy (or fuzzy). Amid this paper we have built up a system to search out IF most brief way from a commencement to a goal of a coordinated multigraph, with an exceptional where technique diminishes to the strategy of finding fuzzy most brief way in an exceedingly coordinated multigraph. There are some great strategies (viz. [34]) created by different creators to explain IFSPP in graphs, yet in this work we have understood IFSPP in multigraphs.

References

1. Abbasbandy, S.: Ranking of fuzzy numbers, some recent and new formulas. In: IFSA-EUSFLAT, pp. 642– 646 (2009)
2. Allahviranloo, T., Abbasbandy, S., Saneifard, R.: A method for ranking of fuzzy numbers using new weighted distance. Math. Comput. Appl. **16**(2), 359–369 (2011)
3. Varghese, A., Sunny, K.: Centroid of an intuitionistic fuzzy number. Notes Intuitionistic Fuzzy Sets **18**(1), 19–24 (2012)
4. Gani, A.N.: On searching intuitionistic fuzzy shortest path in a network. Appl. Math. Sci. **4**(69), 3447–3454 (2010)
5. Atanassov, K.: Intuitionistic fuzzy sets. Fuzzy Sets Syst. **20**, 87–96 (1986)
6. Atanassov, K.: Intuitionistic Fuzzy Sets: Theory and Applications. Springer, Heidelberg (1999)
7. Atanassov, K.: On Intuitionistic Fuzzy Sets Theory. Springer, Berlin (2012)
8. Atanassov, K.: More on intuitionistic fuzzy sets. Fuzzy Sets Syst. **33**, 37–46 (1989)
9. Atanassov, K.: Index matrix representation of the intuitionistic fuzzy graphs. In: Fifth Scientific Session of the Mathematical Foundations of Artificial Intelligence Seminar, Sofia, 5 October 1994, pp. 36–41. Preprint MRL-MFAIS-10-94 (1994)
10. Atanassov, K.: On index matrix interpretations of intuitionistic fuzzy graphs. Notes Intuitionistic Fuzzy Sets **8**(4), 73–78 (2002)
11. Atanassov, K.: Temporal intuitionistic fuzzy graphs. Notes Intuitionistic Fuzzy Sets **4**(4), 59–61 (1998)
12. Atanassov, K., Papadopoulos, B., Syropoulos, A.: An application of the theory of intuitionistic fuzzy multigraphs. Mathw. Soft Comput. **11**(1), 45–49 (2004)
13. Balakrishnan, V.K.: Graph Theory. McGraw-Hill, New York (1997)
14. Bollobas, B.: Modern Graph Theory. Springer, New York (2002)
15. Li, D.F.: A ratio ranking method of triangular intuitionistic fuzzy numbers and its application to MADM problem. Comput. Math Appl. **60**, 1557–1570 (2010)
16. Dat, L.Q., Yu, V.F., Chou, S.-Y.: An improved ranking method for fuzzy numbers using left and right indices. In: 2nd International Conference on Computer Design and Engineering, IPCSIT, vol. 49, pp. 89–94 (2012). https://doi.org/10.7763/ipcsit.2012.v49.17
17. Li, D.F., Nan, J.X., Zhang, M.J.: A ranking method of triangular intuitionistic fuzzy numbers and application to decision making. Int. J. Comput. Intell. Syst. **3**(5), 522–530 (2010). https://doi.org/10.1080/18756891.2010.9727719
18. Diestel, R.: Graph Theory. Springer, New York (2000)
19. Dubois, D., Prade, H.: Fuzzy Sets and Systems. Academic Press, New York (1980)
20. Farhadinia, B.: Ranking fuzzy numbers based on lexicoograhical ordering. World Academy of Science, Engineering and Technology, pp. 1029–1032 (2009)
21. Harary, F.: Graph Theory, Addison Wesley Publishing Company (1995)
22. Mitchell, H.B.: Ranking intuitionistic fuzzy numbers. Int. J. Uncertain. Fuzziness Knowl. Based Syst. **12**(3), 377–386 (2004)
23. Jenson, P., Barnes, J.: Network Flow Programming. Wiley, New York (1980)
24. Ivančo, J.: Decompositions of multigraphs into parts with the same size. Discuss. Math. Graph Theory **30**(2), 335–347 (2010)
25. Ivančo, J., Meszka, M., Skupień, Z.: Decompositions of multigraphs into parts with two edges. Discuss. Math. Graph Theory **22**(1), 113–121 (2002)
26. Bryś, K., Kouider, M., Lonc, Z., Maheo, M.: Decomposition of multigraphs. Discuss. Math. Graph Theory **18**(2), 225–232 (1998)
27. Klein, Cerry M.: Fuzzy shortest paths. Fuzzy Sets Syst. **39**, 27–41 (1991)

28. Karunambigai, M.G., Rangasamy, P., Atanassov, K., Palaniappan, N.: an intuitionistic fuzzy graph method for finding the shortest paths in networks. Adv. Soft Comput. **42**, 3–10 (2007)
29. Meszka, M., Skupien, Z.: Decomposition of a complete multigraph into almost arbitrary paths. Discuss. Math. Graph Theory **32**(2), 357–372 (2012)
30. Okada, S., Soper, T.: A shortest path problem on a network with fuzzy arc lengths. Fuzzy Sets Syst. **109**, 129–140 (2000)
31. Parandin, N., Araghi, M.A.F.: Ranking of fuzzy numbers by distance method. J. Appl. Math. **5**(19), 47–55 (2008). Islamic Azad University of Lahijan
32. Biswas, Ranjit: Fuzzy numbers redefined. Information **15**(4), 1369–1380 (2012)
33. Rao, P.P.B., Shankar, N.R.: Ranking fuzzy numbers with a distance method using circumcenter of centroids and an index of modality. Adv. Fuzzy Syst. **2011**, 1–7 Article ID 178308, https://doi.org/10.1155/2011/178308
34. Mukherjee, Sathi: Dijkstra's algorithm for solving the shortest path problem on networks under intuitionistic fuzzy environment. J. Math. Model. Algorithms **11**(4), 345–359 (2012)
35. Saneifard, R., Ezzati, R.: A new approach for ranking fuzzy numbers with continuous weighted quasi-arithmatic means. Math. Sci. **4**(2), 143–158 (2010)
36. Shannon, A., Atanassov, K.: A first step to a theory of the intuitionistic fuzzy graphs. In: Lakov, D. (ed.) Proceedings of the First Workshop on Fuzzy Based Expert Systems, Sofia, 28–30 September, pp. 59-61 (1994)
37. Shannon, A., Atanassov, K.: On intuitionistic fuzzy multigraphs and their index matrix interpretations. In: Proceedings of 2004 Second International IEEE Conference Intelligent Systems, vol. 2, pp. 440–443 (2004)
38. Biswas, S.S., Alam, B., Doja, M.N.: A theoretical characterization of the data structure 'multigraphs'. J. Contemporary Appl. Math. **2**(2), 88–106 (2012)
39. Biswas, S.S., Alam, B., Doja, M.N.: Generalization of dijkstra's algorithm for extraction of shortest paths in directed multigraphs. J. Comput. Sci. **9**(3), 377–382 (2013). https://doi.org/10.3844/jcssp.2013.377.382, ISSN 1549–3636
40. Biswas, S.S., Alam, B., Doja, M.N.: Fuzzy shortest path in a directed multigraph. Eur. J. Sci. Res. **101**(3), 333–339 (2013). ISSN 1450-216X/1450-202X
41. Biswas, S.S., Alam, B., Doja, M.N.: Real time multigraphs for communication networks: an intuitionistic fuzzy mathematical model. J. Comput. Sci. **9**(7), 847–855 (2013). https://doi.org/10.3844/jcssp.2013.847.855, ISSN 1549-3636
42. Biswas, S.S., Alam, B., Doja, M.N.: Intuitionistic fuzzy real time multigraphs for communication networks: a theoretical model. In: Proceedings of DCS©2013, Singapore (2013)
43. Sujatha, L., Elizabeth, S.: Fuzzy shortest path problem based on similarity degree. Appl. Math. Sci. **5**(66), 3263–3276 (2011)
44. Yao, J.-S., Lin, F.-T.: Fuzzy shortest-path network problems with uncertain edge weights. J. Inf. Sci. Eng. **19**, 329–351 (2003)
45. Yu, Jing-Rung, Wei, Tzu-Hao: Solving the fuzzy shortest path problem by using a linear multiple objective programming. J. Chin. Inst. Industrial Eng. **24**(5), 360–365 (2007)
46. Skupien, Zdzislaw: On distance edge coloring of a cyclic multigraph. Discuss. Math. Graph Theory **19**, 251–252 (1999)
47. Zadeh, L.A.: Fuzzy sets. Inf. Control **8**, 338–353 (1965)

A Rough Set Based Approach for Web User Profiling

Geeta Rani[1(✉)] and Shampa Chakraverty[2]

[1] GD Goenka University, Gurugram, India
geetachhikara@gmail.com
[2] NSIT, Dwarka, Delhi, India

Abstract. E-governance plays a pivotal role in the domain of online services by ensuring round the clock accessibility of a wide spectrum of services. However, the huge amount of uploaded information and a vacillating user base makes it rather difficult to access the desired information from the portal. This requires a system which intelligently presents a personalized user interface. A challenging requirement in designing such a system is classifying the diversified users on the basis of their web experience. Traditional web usage mining techniques have been used to cluster similar users primarily on the basis of their page access patterns. In this paper, we veer our attention towards the level of user experience by introducing three parameters namely, page switching behavior, page probing behavior and session count which predominantly decide the level of experience acquired by e-governance users. We make an innovative use of Rough Set Theory to derive a rule-based classification system using three reduct optimization algorithms namely, Johnson Algorithm, Genetic Algorithm and Basic Minimal classification method. In order to test our system, we classified the user base that is publically available in the CTI dataset into two categories. The Basic Minimal method reports the highest accuracy of 74.90% with five fold cross validation.

Keywords: Web-users · Classification · Switching behavior
Page probing behavior · Session count · Rough Set Theory · E-governance

1 Introduction

E-Governance (e-gov) is a transparent and agile system for information dissemination [1]. It has contributed in no small measure towards the development of an intelligence driven e-society with round the clock accessibility of an array of e-gov services [2]. A major problem in this scenario is the vast and vacillating user-base that renders a static user interface fairly ineffective. We must therefore progress towards adaptable and personalized man-machine interfaces that can flexibly meet the needs of users with varying levels of familiarity with a web portal. This requirement motivates us to classify web users using more refined browsing experience oriented features and more practical classification techniques that recognize the approximations inherent in the real world. Towards this end, we propose a new Rough Set Theory (RST) driven classification of e-gov users using features that reflect their experience gathered over due course of interaction with a given portal. The remaining paper is organized as follows. Section 2 gives a view on the background of rough set theory and E-Governance. Section 3 details

B. Panda et al. (Eds.): REDSET 2017, CCIS 799, pp. 541–553, 2018.
https://doi.org/10.1007/978-981-10-8527-7_45

the technical aspects of our proposed system, the RST based model. Section 4 demonstrates our experimental results. We present a comparative analysis of our work with existing work in Sect. 5. We draw conclusions and give directions for future work in Sect. 6.

2 Background

A voluminous body of research works in the area of Web User Profiling, WUP offer a variety of techniques such as K-Means clustering, KNN clustering, Naïve Bayesian classifier as reviewed in [3, 4]. These techniques divide a large user base into categories based on the similarity in their behavioral attributes. Web users are thus categorized into disjoint sets on the basis of their feature values. However, in a real world scenario, it is quite possible that novice and experienced users exhibit similar online characteristics. For example, a young enthusiast who is in an exploratory mode as a new user may switch between pages very fast to get an overall taste of a website, thus giving the impression of being an experienced user. Likewise, a novice user may hit a page of interest accidentally and then remain engaged with it for a long time, just as expected from an experienced user. In another scenario, an experienced user who has undergone a number of sessions may still find it difficult to switch rapidly between pages or remain engaged with a given page due to his personal proclivity. This may give an expression of being a novice. Thus, we find the existence of a "boundary region" where apparently equivalent classes of people with same or similar attributes can end up under different categories of experience. RST is an effective approximate computation paradigm to deal with such boundary situations. RST is a relatively new paradigm in approximate computing that creates lower and upper approximations of crisp sets. It is a supervised, rule-based classification methodology which generates a set of sure rules and possible rules by extracting optimal reducts from a decision labeled database of objects and their attributes. Techniques such as biclustering and fuzzy logic can not identify users in the boundary region of a decision [5]. A biclustering technique identifies user-attribute biclusters which may overlap. However, it cannot map these clusters into predefined decision classes. Fuzzy logic effectively deals with vagueness and imprecision in data with the help of linguistic sets and membership functions. However, after inferencing and defuzzification, it is difficult to isolate the set of objects lying in the boundary region of each decision class. Rough set theory works on an information system. An information system is a tabular representation of input data of a particular domain such as users' web behavior, medical history of patients and learning behavior of students. Rows of an information system are known as objects or entities. Columns represent attributes corresponding to all objects. Attributes further lie under two categories namely condition attributes and decision attributes. Table 1 shows a sample Web Profiling Information System, WPIS for four users. Rows of the table are labeled as User Ids, UIds. For example 10, 7,138 and 540 denote the four UIds, Columns are labeled as Navigation Pattern (NP), Access Frequency (AFS), Page Probing Behavior (PPB) and Switching Behavior (SB) NP, AFS, PPB and SB represent the condition variables. The last column marked as Session Count (SC) is the decision variable. RST uses the concept of indescernibility. Equivalence relation determines indescernibility in a dataset. Let a non empty finite set, U called universe holds binary relation I such that xIy where x, y U. The relation, I is equivalence if it has following three characteristics.

$$\text{reflexive} : xIx\forall x \in U \tag{1}$$

$$\text{symmetric} : xIy \rightarrow yIx\forall\, x, y \in U \tag{2}$$

$$\text{transitive} : xIy \rightarrow yIz \rightarrow xIz\forall x, y, z \in U \tag{3}$$

As an example, Let us consider Table 1 in which UId 7 and 540 are indiscernible to each other on the basis of their SB. Both the UIds show same values of SB. Another set of UIds 7 and 138 are indiscernible to each other based on their PPB.

In Table 1, there are two indiscernible sets: {SB) = {{7,540},{10,138}} and {PPB} = {7,138}.

RST applies two basic operations lower approximation I_{lower}, and upper approximation I_{upper} as approximations on the input data as given below.

$$I_{lower}(X) = \{x\varepsilon U : I(x) \subseteq X\} \tag{4}$$

$$I_{upper}(X) = \{x \in U : I(x) \cap (X) \neq \infty\} \tag{5}$$

The lower approximation ensures the presence of an object only in one category but the objects in the upper approximation lie in at least two categories. Using I_{lower} and I_{upper} we can find the boundary region of a dataset as given below.

$$I_{boundary}(X) = \left\{\left\{I_{upper}(X)\right\} - \left\{I_{lower}(X)\right\}\right\} \tag{6}$$

The elements that lie in boundary region show different values of decision variables for the same values of condition variables. Therefore, it is difficult to decide a category for such elements.

Reducts: All attributes do not actually participate in categorizing elements of a dataset. So there is a need to identify a set of attributes that give useful information for categorizing elements available in an information system. RST extracts non redundant and minimal sets of attributes that preserve indiscernibility and consequently preserve the set approximation. Such sets of attributes are known as reducts. The system uses reducts for categorization. Web portals generate a huge database of users' online history. With such a rich repertoire of web experiences, one can conveniently utilize a Rule Based classifier that can mine the existing database to extract classification rules. A rule can be seen as an antecedent or a set of conditions implying a consequent:

$$Rule: ANTECEDENT \rightarrow CONSEQUENT$$

One or more features of the historical web data reflect various decision classes or concepts. For example, the number of hits gathered on a particular page may indicate its popularity. Let us label them as Decision Attributes. These attributes map to the consequent of the rules. Other features such as the navigation sequence traversed by users represent conditional attributes. A Boolean combination of these condition-attributes maps to the antecedent of the rules. A decision rule is a if-then rule in which if part comprises of a set of attributes in a reduct and the else part comprises of decision classes [6].

The use of approximations arises from the fact that real world concepts such as popularity of web page, do not exactly match with the attributes of the objects that follow these concepts. It is here that fuzzy and approximate analysis finds practical use in solving real world problems. As an example in web usage, behavioral attributes such as a given user profile (such as access frequency, age, navigation pattern) do not always map to a specific concept such as popularity of a web page. In this work, we tap the field of Rough Set Theory (RST), an approximate supervised learning method, to mine sure and possible rules for classifying web users.

A Rough set based approach reports a success in classifying web users under uncertain boundaries based on similarity in their behavioral attributes [7–9]. Pawlak proposed the concept of RST [5]. RST is an equivalence relation based classification technique. It works well when the dataset is imprecise such as traced in web logs.

Publicly available RST tools such as ROSETTA [10] and ROSE2 [11] apply different kinds of analytical or meta-heuristic driven optimization algorithms such as Lattice Search algorithm. Johnson's algorithm and Genetic algorithm for removing redundant attributes. They identify a set of essential attributes i.e. reducts. Johnson algorithm is based on heuristic search. It identifies the reducts based on frequency of occurrence of attributes in the discernibility matrix [12]. Genetic algorithm calculates the fitness function for each attribute. It keeps those attributes in a reduct which have higher value of fitness function [13]. The lattice search algorithm considers all attributes as a distinct lattice point. It selects one of the attributes as a centre of the cluster and identifies its distance from other attributes. It finds the reducts based on distance of attributes with each other as well as with the cluster centre [14, 15].

The process of attribute selection may yield several reducts, each capable of discerning objects to varying degrees. A high degree of discernability yields too many sure rules which do not have adequate support. As a result, the classifier may be unable to find a rule that classifies a new object. On the other hand reducts with few attributes give a lower degree of discernability, generating too many possible rules. Under this scenario, a new object will be classified under some possible rule, but the classification accuracy could be low. Thus, proper selection of reducts from a huge dataset is important in order to lower the computation complexity of classification while ensuring acceptable accuracy of classification.

3 RST Based WPR Model

This work makes an effective use of RST for categorizing web users based on their browsing experience using a combination of sure and possible rules. Figure 1 shows the overall framework for rough set based classification of web users.

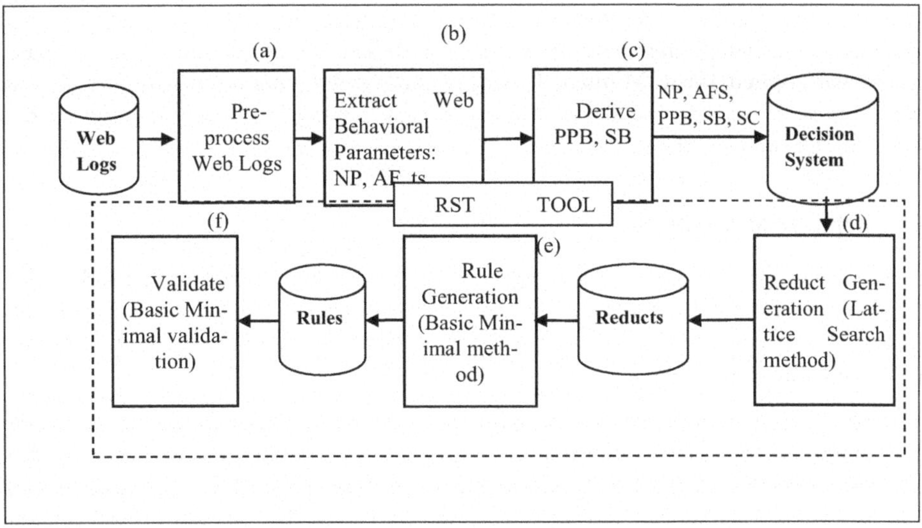

Fig. 1. Overall scheme of rough set based web user profiling.

The RST based approach involves a set of activities for categorizing users under rules based on lower and upper approximations. The system begins its task with preprocessing of web logs. This step removes irrelevant data such as failed HTTP requests, requests from robots and special symbols that are recorded in web logs. It assigns a unique Id to each user, using the IP address of the system she is logged in to. It ignores the possibility that multiple users can log in from the same IP address at different instants of time (Fig. 1(a)). After preprocessing, the system extracts behavioral attributes such as: SC, NP, AFS and Time duration spent on a page, ts (Fig. 1(b)). The system derives SB from the NP of a user. It finds PPB from the AF data (Fig. 1(c)). These behavioral parameters are detailed in the next section.

The various browsing features of users are recorded into a Web WPIS. The NP, AF, PPB and SB are stored as condition variables and SC is used as a decision variable to indicate the level of engagement of users with the website - Naïve or Experienced. The WPIS is input to a rough set tool suite. Our scheme is generic and one can use any publicly available RST software system or an in-house developed tool suite. For the sake of illustration, we used the software system ROSE 2. ROSE – Rough Set Data Explorer, is a software tool suite created at the Laboratory of Intelligent Decision Support Systems of the Institute of Computing Science in Poznan-Poland, that implements the basics of RST [16].

We chose the Lattice Search method to identify the reducts (Fig. 1(d)). The information system that we develop comprises of independent discrete values of attributes. Lattice search algorithm is a suitable method for identifying reducts from such an information system because it considers all independent behavioral attributes as different lattice points. It selects those non-redundant behavioral attributes in reducts which are significant for decision making. We applied the Basic Minimal Covering method [17] to generate rules for classification (Fig. 1(e)). This method is popularly known as

Learning from Example Modules (LEM 2). It produces single decision rule for each attribute rather than giving all minimal rules for each attribute. For validating user categories, we applied Basic Minimal Covering method for validation which makes an effective use of rules and reducts for classifying web users into two categories: Naïve and Experienced (Fig. 1(f)).

3.1 Behavioral Attributes

There is an e-gov portal, P which is defined as a collection of N interlinked web pages, Wi. There is a unique identity *i.e.* PId for each web page. An e-gov user is uniquely identified with a unique UId_i logs in a web portal. Her browsing behavior can be defined using following attributes.

(i) Navigation Pattern: A user accesses a sequence of pages following a specific pattern. A sequence of PIds that she visits during a complete session forms her NP. For example, if a user UId2 visits a sequence of three pages, PId = 2, 5 and 6 during a session, then her NP becomes {2, 5, 6}. A NP provides some information about the browsing experience of users. We derive further information from it by analyzing the user's style of switching between pages, as explained in the next feature, Switching Behavior.

(ii) Access Frequency Sequence: The number of times a user visits a page during a session is the access frequency for that page. The AFS is the sequence of access frequencies corresponding to the NP of a user. For example a user, UId2 five times visits a page with PId 2, twice a PId 5 and six times a PId 6, then her AFS turns out to be {5, 2, 6} corresponding to her NP{2, 5, 6} during a session. We use AF of a user to derive her PPB.

(iii) Switching Behavior: A user makes switches among different pages of a website during her browsing session. The number of switches from one page to another during a complete session represents her SB. Given a user (UId2) who follows a NP = {2, 5, 6} during a session, her SB becomes 3 as she switches among three pages during her complete session. We assume that a naïve user makes a minimum number of switches among pages of a website because she is unaware about the depth of information authored on different pages of a website. On the other hand, an experienced user switches frequently among most of the pages so as to satisfy her quench for information.

(iv) Page Probing Behavior: This is a series of time duration, ts in minutes that a user spends on each page of her navigation sequence during a given session. For example given a user (UId2) spends three minutes on PId 2, two minutes on PId 5 and one minute on PId 6 then PPB for a NP{2, 5, 6} will be PPB{3, 2, 1}.

(v) Session Count: A session represents the time interval between the time instant when a user logs in and the time instant when she logs out subsequently. The number of times a user visits a website during different sessions represents her SC. This count increments every time a user logs in. The SC indicates the browsing experience of a user. A naïve user turns into experienced users as her SC on a given web portal gradually increases.

(vi) Decision Threshold, ω: This is minimum number of sessions that a user needs to visit to become familiar with a website. The average number of sessions on a website by all users decides the threshold. The value of threshold is website specific. It depends upon the popularity of a website.

3.2 Pre-set Classes for Web Users

Browsing experience of a user is the conceptual characteristic. It changes gradually with increase in familiarity of a user to a website. We represent the browsing experience of a user in terms of the following two classes.

(i) Naive User Class: A beginner is less familiar to a website therefore she makes a minimum number of switches among different web pages. She gradually learns, as her SC increases. Here, we assume that a user whose SC is below a threshold ω has rarely visited a website therefore she will be categorized to naïve user class. We assign a Class_Id of 1 to users of this class.

(ii) Experienced User Class: A continuous interaction of a user extends her familiarity to a website. Her greater interest towards accessing the relevant information makes her a frequent visitor to a website. She delves into the deeper levels of information as her SC increases. We assume that a user whose SC exceeds a decision threshold, ω has visited a website for a significant number of times, therefore she will be categorized to an experienced user class. We assigned a Class-Id of 2 to users of this class.

4 Experimental Results

This system implemented by conducting a set of experiments for categorizing users into two categories: Naïve and Experienced user classes based on their browsing experience. We compare our approach with prior RST based approaches for WUP.

4.1 Dataset

We evaluated our approach on the Computer science, Telecommunication and Information Systems (CTI) dataset which is online available in the CTI web server of De Paul University at [18]. Web access data was collected over a period of two weeks during April 2002. It contains web logs of 5446 users who navigated through 683 pages in a total 20950 sessions. CTI dataset contains multiple sessions of a user. This gave us an opportunity to label users into Naive and Experienced user classes. In CTI logs, there are 3.84 average numbers of sessions for each user. Therefore we set the value of the decision threshold, ω as 4. We split preprocessed CTI dataset into training and testing sets. The training set and testing set consists of 16406 and 4101 sessions respectively.

4.2 Evaluation Metrics

This system uses accuracy and Coverage as a parameter to evaluate the performance of decision rules. The RST based approach uses the following evaluation metrics as given in [19]. The universe, U is collection of all users. Their WPIS is a compilation of all users in U as rows with their attributes: {NP, AFS, PPB, SB}. The parameter SC gives a basis for generating the decision variable, as explained in Sect. 3.1. $[\mathbf{x_A}]$ is the number of users that satisfy formula x in condition A of rule r. For example PPB and NP are two condition attributes which categorize users in the naïve category by following a particular rule from the rule base. This reports that $|[\mathbf{x_A}]| = 2$.

(i) Accuracy of a Decision Rule: This is the ratio of the number of attributes from universe that follow a formula x in condition A to that of total number of attributes that follow a formula x in A.

$$Accuracy(A, r, U_i) = \frac{|U_i \cap [x_A]|}{|[x_A]|} \tag{7}$$

(ii) Coverage of a Decision Rule: This is the ratio of the number of attributes from universe that follow a formula x in condition A to that of total number of attributes in universe that belongs to x_A.

$$Coverage(A, r, U_i) = \frac{|U_i \cap [x_A]|}{|U_i|} \tag{8}$$

4.3 Steps for Classification

We begin our experiment with enrichment of WPIS that is fed to the Rose 2: A RST based tool suit.

(i) Preparing Information System: This model uses the behavioral attributes NP, AFS SB, PPB as condition variables and SC as the decision variable. We extracted 52 condition variables and one decision variable from the CTI logs. We use 'A' with column number of a condition attribute that acts as a marker in our WPIS. For example condition variables: A1 to A17 represent a NP. A18 to A34 denote the AFS, A35 to A51denote the PPB, A52 represents the SB of a user during a session. The last column D1 denotes the decision variable, SC. A user gets a class label based on her SC recorded in the WPIS. Her class is labeled as *Naïve* if she has visited a very few sessions which are below the decision threshold, ω (for CTI dataset we set ω = 4). Her class label becomes *Experienced,* if she records number of sessions atleast equal to the decision threshold, ω.

Table 1 shows a sample of sub part of WPIS comprising of the browsing behavioral attributes of 4 users. Here, we do not present all the missing values in the sample WPIS.

For example a user (UId_1) visits only five pages during a session, therefore it shows actual values only for 16 condition variables, leaving 36 missing values.

Table 1. A sample WPIS for four users.

UId	NP					AFS					PPB					SB	SC
(1)	(2)	(3)	(4)	(5)	(6)	(7)	(8)	(9)	(10)	(11)	(12)	(13)	(14)	(15)	(16)	(17)	(18)
10	9	83	11	10	57	1	4	9	2	3	8	10	15	10	2	3	1
7	48	9	9	52	?	2	8	9	9	1	4	4	3	6	?	4	1
138	13	10	55	?	?	1	3	5	?	?	4	4	3	?	?	3	1
540	52	55	46	48	?	7	4	4	8	?	1	1	3	1	?	4	1

The first column in Table 1 shows UId of users. Column 2 to 6 shows their NP. The next five columns from 7 to 11 present their AFS. Column numbers 12 till 16 represent the PPB. 17th column shows the SB and the last column denotes the SC of users. It must be noted that different users have variable lengths of NP and AFS and PPB. Therefore, the initial WPIS may contain missing values. We represent such missing values with the symbol "?". We apply the *Concept-wise Closest Fit* pre-processing method for enrichment of missing values in the information system. This substitutes a missing attribute value by the known value in another case that matches the affected object the closest in terms of the remaining attributes within the same concept.

(ii) Identifying Reducts: We apply Lattice Search method for identifying reducts from the WPIS that we enriched. From a set of 52 condition variables, this method identifies a sub-set of non redundant condition variables which actually contributes in categorizing users. We observed that the SB and the PPB have been identified as the core attributes. These two attributes equally contributes in classifying users. Lattice Search method yielded 20 reducts from the CTI dataset. As a demonstration we present a sample of 5 reducts in Table 2. Its column 1 denotes the reduct number. Column 2 shows the condition variables in a reduct.

Table 2. Five sample reducts given by lattice search method on CTI dataset.

Reduct no.	Attributes in a reduct
1.	{4, 6, 33, 38, 39, 41, 44, 46, 49, 51, 52}
2.	{3, 6, 9, 28, 38, 44, 46, 49, 51}
3.	{4, 6, 33, 38, 39, 41, 44, 46, 48, 51, 52}
4.	{3, 6, 9, 28, 38, 44, 46, 48, 51, 52}
5.	{4, 6, 33, 38, 39, 40, 43, 44, 46, 49, 51, 52}

(iii) Identifying Rules: We applied Basic Minimal Covering method for identifying sure and possible rules for classification of CTI dataset. We obtained 309 rules from this dataset. We present 5-sure rules in Table 3 as an example. Its first column represents the rule number and second column shows the rule. The third column highlights the accuracy% and the last column shows coverage% of a rule.

Table 3. Five sample rules identified by Basic Minimal Covering method on CTI dataset.

Rule no.	Rule	Accuracy %	Coverage %
1.	(A11 = 9) & (A19 = 9) & (A43 = 9) & (A51 = 9) → (D1 = 1)	100	5.92
2.	(A4 = 9) & (A43 = 9) & (A51 = 9) → (D1 = 1)	100	3.82
3.	(A46 = 10) & (A53 = 56) & (A54 = 53) → (D1 = 1)	100	4.84
4.	(A28 = 52) & (A39 = 52) & (A47 = 57) & (A52 = 9) → (D1 = 2)	100	0.40
5.	(A26 = 10) & (A34 = 55) & (A47 = 9) & (D7 = 49) → (D1 = 1)	100	0.38

(iv) Approximations: We identified the number of users either in lower approximation or in upper approximation by using Basic minimal algorithm. This algorithm categorized 20950 total number of sessions under lower and upper approximations of *Naïve* and *Experienced* user class. Table 4 demonstrates the number of sessions categorized under two approximations. This algorithm classified 9898 sessions into *Naïve* user class and 10609 sessions into the *Experienced* user class. We obtained 9567 and 10330 sessions under the lower approximation of *Naive* and *Experienced* user classes respectively. There are 10177 and 10940 sessions in upper approximations of *Naïve* and *Experienced* user classes respectively. A significant number of sessions in the upper approximations indicate that a large number of users are turning from naïve to an experienced. They are continuously learning about a website.

Table 4. Number of users under lower and upper approximations given by Basic Minimal Covering method on CTI dataset.

Approximation	User class	
	Naïve	Experienced
Lower approximation	9898	10609
Upper approximation	10177	10940

(v) **Confusion Matrix:** At the next step, we applied Basic Minimal method for classifying users into *Naïve* and *Experienced* user classes. We obtain the confusion matrix as shown in Table 5. Column 1 represents the Class type, column 2 shows the number of users predicted in *Naïve* user class, column 3 shows the number of users classified to *Experienced* user class. Its last column denotes the number of users that remained unclassified.

Table 5. Confusion matrix given by Basic Minimal Covering method on CTI dataset.

Actual	Predicted	
	Naive	Experienced
Naive	5277	4621
Experienced	527	10082

(vi) **Validation:** We applied K-fold cross validation using the Basic Minimal method for validating the classification quality. We noticed a best average accuracy of 74.90% for a five-fold cross validation at 21% majority threshold and 60% similarity. Table 6 shows the values of average accuracy for the CTI dataset. The first column in Table 6 contains the value of number of folds (K), that we apply for validation. In our experiments we used the following k-fold cross validations: (i) one-fold (ii) three-fold and (iii) five-fold. The next column includes the values of majority thresholds. We considered two different values for the majority threshold that are: 21% and 50%. The third column contains the values of the minimum similarity. We considered three different values of the minimum similarity: (i) 50% (ii) 60% and (iii) 70%. The fourth column contains the value of average accuracy. The last column includes the time taken for executing the Basic Minimal Method on CTI dataset at different K-fold cross validations.

Table 6. Average accuracy and execution time using K-fold cross validation for Basic Minimal method on CTI dataset.

K	Majority threshold (%)	Minimum similarity (%)	Average accuracy (%)	Execution time (in seconds)
1	21	60	61.59	3790
3	21	50	74.39	10711
5	50	70	74.78	19549
3	21	60	74.32	10680
5	21	60	74.90	19973

The experimental results in Table 6, shows that the average accuracy improves with increase in the minimum similarity. It also increases with increase in the number of cross fold, K-fold. We observe that the execution time increases with increase in value of K-fold.

5 Comparative Analysis

Comparison with Existing RST based WUP: In [20] the authors propose a RST based approach for categorizing students into “crammers”, “studious” and “workers” classes by analyzing their browsing behavior on a university website. The authors use the following features: number of sessions, types of documents downloaded and the time and day of visiting a website. These features provide elementary information about the learning style of users. On the other hand, we extract features in the form of page probing behavior and switching behavior that describe web users’ browsing characteristics more meaningfully.

The work in [8] applies RST based clustering for identifying user groups based on their navigation sequence on a website. This system categorizes those users together who access similar page categories during a session. As users interests are continuously evolving therefore there is need to extract more information about their browsing behavior so that we can personalize the website according to their interests. Our approach extract more features such as their NP, SB, AF and PPB which can provide information about their learning style as well as her experience on a website. A user profile comprising these features can be utilized to suggest more relevant paths to a user.

6 Conclusion

We observe the following from the experimental results that we obtain by using algorithms available in Rose 2 tool-kit.

(i) SB and PPB are the core condition variables that are actively involved in classification of CTI dataset.
(ii) Lattice search algorithm identifies 20 reducts from the set of 54 condition variables which represent the behavior of 5446 users over 20940 sessions.
(iii) The Basic Minimal method identifies 309 rules for categorizing users under Naïve and Experienced user classes. A large number of sessions in upper approximations i.e. 10177 in Naïve and 10940 sessions in Experienced user class proves that browsing experience of users in CTI logs is gradually evolving. They are turning from naïve to experienced users as their session progresses.
(iv) Basic Minimal method reported a best average accuracy of 74.90% on five fold cross validation at 21% majority threshold and 60% minimum similarity.

References

1. E-Governance: Initiatives in India, pp 26–58. http://arc.gov.in/11threp/arcthreport_ch4.pdf. Accessed 20 July 2015
2. Chitra, V., Davamani, A.S.: A survey on preprocessing methods for web usage data. Int. J. Comput. Sci. Inf. Secur. (IJCSIS) **7**(3), 78–83 (2010)

3. Lei, M., Fan, L.: A web personalization system based on users' interested domains. In: IEEE 7th International Conference on Cognitive Informatics, ICCI 2008, 14–16 August 2008, pp. 153–159 (2008)
4. Khadangi, E., Bagheri, A.: Comparing MLP, SVM and KNN for predicting trust between users in Facebook. In: 3th International Conference in Computer and Knowledge Engineering (ICCKE), pp. 466–470 (2013)
5. Pawlak, Z.: Rough sets. Int. J. Comput. Inf. Sci. **2**, 341–356 (1982)
6. Wang, S.: Algorithms for solving the reducts problem in rough sets. Master's projects. San Jose State University, SJSU Scholar Works (2012)
7. Lingras, P., Peters, G.: Applying Rough Set Concepts to Clustering, Rough Sets: Selected Methods and Applications in Management and Engineering. Advanced Information and Knowledge Processing, pp. 23–37. Springer-Verlag London Limited, London (2012). https://doi.org/10.1007/978-1-4471-2760-4
8. Hannah Inbarni, H., Thangavel, K.: Rough set based user profiling for web personalization. Int. J. Recent Trends Eng. **2**(1), 103–107 (2009)
9. Bal, M.: Rough sets theory as symbolic data mining method: an application on complete decision table. Inf. Sci. Lett. Int. J. Inf. Sci. Lett. **2**, 35–47 (2013)
10. Rosetta: A Rough Set Tool. http://www.lcb.uu.se/tools/rosetta/. Accessed 20 July 2014
11. Rose 2.2: A Rough Set Tool. http://idss.cs.put.poznan.pl/site/rose.html. Accessed 20 June 2014
12. Khashashneh, A.E.A., et al.: Evaluation of discernibility matrix based reduct computation techniques. In: 5th International Conference in Computer Science and Information Technology (CSIT), 27–28 March 2013, pp. 76–81 (2013)
13. Elshazly, H.I., et al.: Rough sets and genetic algorithms: a hybrid approach to breast cancer classification. In: World Congress in Information and Communication Technologies (WICT), 30 October–2 November 2012, pp. 260–265 (2012)
14. Lattice Search. http://www.mpri.lsu.edu/textbook/Chapter5-a.htm. Accessed 12 Nov 2015
15. Shao, X., et al.: A Dynamic Lattice Searching Method for Fast Optimization of Lennard Jones Clusters, pp. 1693–1698. Published Online in Wiley Interscience (2004). www.interscience.wiley.com
16. Predki, B., Słowiński, R., Stefanowski, J., Susmaga, R., Wilk, S.: ROSE - software implementation of the rough set theory. In: Polkowski, L., Skowron, A. (eds.) RSCTC 1998. LNCS (LNAI), vol. 1424, pp. 605–608. Springer, Heidelberg (1998). https://doi.org/10.1007/3-540-69115-4_85
17. Inuiguchi, M., et al.: LEM2-based rule induction via clustering decision classes. In: IEEE International Conference in Systems, Man and Cybernetics, 10–12 October 2005, vol. 3, pp. 2781–2786 (2005)
18. Preprocessed DePaul CTI Web Usage Data. http://facweb.cs.depaul.edu/mobasher/classes/ect584/resource.html. Accessed 20 Oct 2013
19. Performance Evaluation. http://www.seas.gwu.edu/~bell.csci243.lectures/performance.pdf. Accessed 10 July 2014
20. Joshi, M., Vaidya, R., Lingras, P.: Automatic determination of learning styles In: 2nd International Conference on Education and Management Technology IPEDR, vol. 13, pp. 1–7. IACSIT Press, Singapore (2011)

Analysis and Detection of Fruit Defect Using Neural Network

Tanya Makkar, Seema Verma(✉), Yogesh(✉), and Ashwani Kumar Dubey(✉)

Amity University, Noida, Uttar Pradesh, India
munishmakkar65@yahoo.com,
{sverma9,akdubey}@amity.edu, eceyogesh@gmail.com

Abstract. Fruit quality detection is important to maintain the quality of fruits. Generally, fruit inspection is done manually which is ineffectual for farmers in the agriculture industry. This paper proposes an approach to identify fruit defects in the agricultural industry for reducing the production cost and time. Since different fruit images may have similar or identical color and shape values. Therefore, we used a method to increase the accuracy level of fruit quality detection by using color, shape and size-based method with Artificial Neural Network (ANN). ANN is a special kind of tool that is used to estimate the cost and various artificial intelligence field like - voice recognition, image recognition, robotics and much more. The fruit quality inspection acquires images as external input and then the captured image is used for detecting defects by applying segmentation algorithm. The output of the processed image is then used as input to ANN. The network uses backpropagation algorithm, was tested with training dataset and hence predicted defects with good efficiency and in much shorter time than the human inspectors. On comparing predicted and training dataset together, the feasibility of an approach reveals the efficient defect detection and classification in the agricultural industry.

Keywords: Image recognition · Preprocessing · Segmentation
Artificial Neural Network · Feature extraction

1 Introduction

Many hundreds of fruits are sold every day. But what if, few are defective out of it? As fruits are generally high in fiber, water, and vitamins. Regular consumption of fruits is generally associated with reduced risks of several diseases. A lot of time is wasted while monitoring the quality of crops. Therefore, an effectual and enhanced method should be there to fulfill the demand of the agricultural industry [1, 2]. In this paper, a commercial and secure process is used to analyze the fruit or vegetable quality which is based on color, shape or size. Being sensitive and delicate material, fruits should be tested through non-destructive techniques. The most important physical properties are fruit size while color resembles visual properties. To export a good quality of fruits, it is important to discover its infection in it. The common methodologies for diseases inspection and identification of fruit depending on the visual monitoring which further

B. Panda et al. (Eds.): REDSET 2017, CCIS 799, pp. 554–567, 2018.
https://doi.org/10.1007/978-981-10-8527-7_46

leads to ineffective for the horticulture industry. Hence, an automatic identification system should be present to analyze the fruit diseases at right time. Nowadays, Artificial Neural Network (ANN) are applicable in many scientific fields like-artificial intelligence, medicine, neuroscience and much more [3]. An Artificial Neural Network is a model composed of a group of interconnected computing elements or neurons. Typically, a neuron computes a sum of its inputs which may be the output of other neuron or might be an external input to the method and then pass this sum to nonlinear functions. Each neuron has only one output but this output is further multiplied by weights function if it is to be used as input to another neuron. ANN is used to detect shape, size, and color of fruit image and hence suited best for pattern classification and recognition [4]. In this paper, a commercial and secure process is used to analyze the fruit or vegetable quality which is based on color, shape or size. Being sensitive and delicate material, fruits should be tested through non-destructive techniques. The most important physical properties are fruit size while color resembles visual properties. In our proposed work, an input and target dataset have been created in order to predict the efficiency of ANN. Now, a neural network has the ability to optimize the relationship between the input and the output through training, testing, and processing in order to get reliable solutions. [5]. As neural network made up of three layers-input, hidden and output layers. These layers are interconnected by node or neuron. Also, these connections are unidirectional, which mean signals or information being processed can only pass through the network in a single direction. Now, feedforward network commonly uses backpropagation algorithm applied on the weights and bias value for each neuron in the network. Backpropagation comes in action after finding an error when actual output is different from target output, the error is propagated backward direction from output layer to input layer through the hidden layer. Self-Organizing Map (SOM) has been used in this approach. SOM has a special feature to organize their neuron structure automatically based on topographical structure. Thus, topological structure helps to maintain input data in order to reduce the dimension making them useful for visualizing problem [6].

2 Previous Work

An independent grading of fruit has been implemented using soft computing technique. It has been proposed that this technique not only improve the quality of the fruit at the consumer but will also reduce the cost of industry. The above implementation is done using different methods like- Neural Network, Fuzzy logic, Neuro-fuzzy and Support Vector Machine (SVM) [7]. A study has been done where soft computing models have shown an extraordinary performance. In this approach, the designed algorithm is applied to ten different types of fruits along with AI and soft computing techniques. Then, highest accuracy rate has been calculated separately for each of the fruit with different classifier used and also concluded that non-destructive methods give promising results [8]. Furthermore, three color camera system has been used for identification of detection of a defect in apple for image processing. Different types of image processing techniques have been included in this approach like- segmentation, denoising and much more. Then, the region of interest (ROI) has been defined for further analysis [9]. Then, the detection has also analyzed on the basis of distinctive color and texture technique by feature extraction and other various image processing technique which has been further utilized to it. To conduct the approach efficiently, a comparison has been depicted between the performance of state of art method which includes two situations- fruit and vegetable classification and fruit disease classification [10]. Not only by the artificial neural network, other methods are also used for classification like- SVM (Support Vector Machine), Fuzzy logic. Then, general grading has been done by sorting fruits and vegetables into different grades according to size, shape, color, and volume. Furthermore, different general grades have been categorized in this approach into different classes. These classes describe the level of error tolerance with varying quality over general appearance. After categorizing, classification has been done using mutual grading and machine vision system grading which include a conveyer belt and a color image obtained by CCD camera with a lightning system for image capturing [11]. As ANN is considered to be one of the successful approaches which is used for pattern recognition and in other fields too. Likewise, ANN is also capable in medical imaging technique which has been done to detect breast cancer. A literature review has been presented in which a discussion is carried out regarding state of art of neural network in medical imaging and medicine. Also, it addresses a hybrid neural network algorithm for breast cancer detection [12]. Also, segmentation of an image has also done using ANN found on textual aspects towards the background of a picture. A basic approach has been discussed here which includes thresholding of image on the basis of gray level values which have been calculated and then pixel has been recollected to check the thresholding value and at last, the conclusion raised that segmented image was the result [13, 14]. A brief review has done by studying the pre-existing segmentation methods. Out of which, on implementing these various methods, k-means work well when clusters are not well separated from each other. Also, with the k-means algorithm, one may get some faulty segmented pixels while the use of neural network may increase the performance but some error might remain [15]. In the ANN construction, the allocation weights over processing units produce the number of free variables, the simplified presentation of the network. The present segment consists of a detection of contaminated fruits. A predictable approach has been presented with an adaptive method collected of the subdivision approaches that are used to improve the descriptions and the pre-segmented images are utilized for traits withdrawal. The feature withdrawal method is used for mining the unhealthy part of the image sample to examine the infected part of input. At previous, organization of fruit infection remains completed [16].

3 Methodology

The proposed system is designed to overcome the problems of manual inspection in horticulture. The system consists of several steps of image processing like- image acquisition, preprocessing, segmentation, feature extraction, and testing and training the sample from ANN. Features like the color of fruit, shape of fruit and size of fruit are extracted. The whole process is elaborated in flow chart Fig. 1.

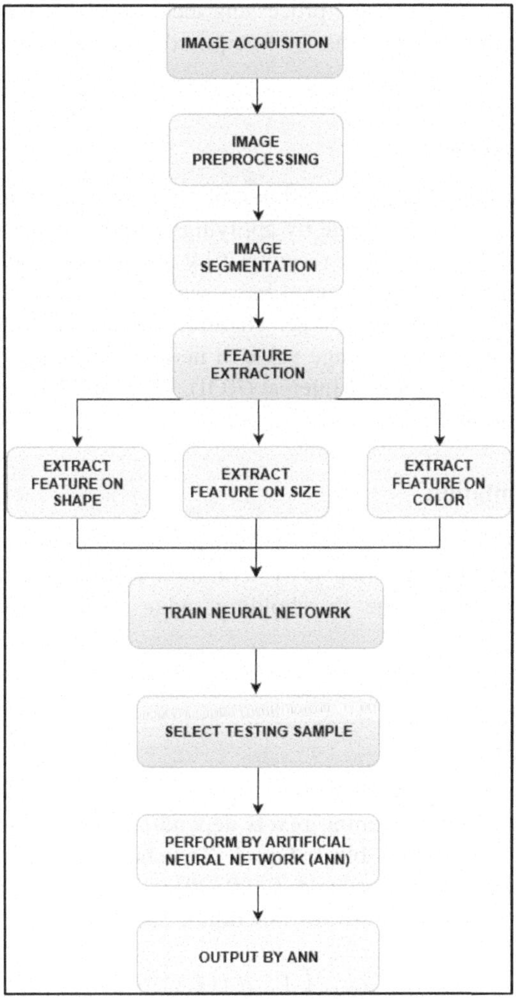

Fig. 1. The methodology of the input image

3.1 Image Acquisition

The first stage of any vision system involve is the image acquisition. Image acquisition means to capture an unprocessed image from hardware in order to pass it to other operation of a proposed approach. Various types of cameras can be used for this step such as digital camera, CCD (Charged Coupled Device) etc. The image is loaded into the system and specified functions read the image from its particular path. The image will be stored in a matrix form of rows and columns such that it stores an image as in form of M-by-N array when an image is grayscale in nature otherwise store M-by-N-by-3-array form when an image is RGB in nature. Then, the database is created and thereafter various image processing techniques are applied to improve the quality of an image. If the image has not acquired properly, the target could not be achieved [17].

3.2 Image Preprocessing

Pre-processing of an image means that different types of operations are performed on the image so as to improve the image by applying specific operation like- rotating the image clockwise and anticlockwise, resizing it by any value, flipping dimensions etc. Now, in an image, the neighboring pixel have same or similar pixel brightness value subjected to one object in the real image. Therefore, if any of pixel is picked from an image, it usually restores as an average value of neighboring pixels. Gray scaling of an image can be done to get Region of Interest (ROI). Filter and histogram processing can be applied to improve the quality of an image [18].

3.3 Image Segmentation

Image segmentation means portioning an image into groups of pixels which are homogeneous regions implementing it by 'common feature' Fig. 4. It can be classifying into categories like-image thresholding, edge detection, mask segmentation fragments etc. [19].

4 Thresholding

It is a simplest segmentation method. It is a process of dividing the image into background and foreground by portioning pixels depending upon intensity. The results of thresholding are either white or black Fig. 4. Thresholding can be determined algebraically using an appropriate threshold T [20–22].

Where g (x, y) is threshold form of function x and y

$$g(x,y) = \begin{cases} 1 & if f(x,y) > T, \\ 0 & if f(x,y) \leq T \end{cases} \tag{1}$$

5 Edge Detection

The process of edge detection significantly reduces the amount of data Fig. 3. The point at which pixel brightness changes distinctly are arranged into of arched line segments and termed as edges. Algebraically [23],

$$f(\mathrm{x}) = \frac{I_r - I_l}{2}\left(\mathrm{erf}\left(\frac{x}{\sqrt{2}\sigma}\right) + 1\right) + I_r \quad (2)$$

At the left-hand side of edge, the intensity is $\mathrm{I_l} = \lim_{x \to -\infty} f(x)$ and the right-hand side of the edge, intensity is $\mathrm{I_r} = \lim_{x \to \infty} f(x)$.

6 Feature Extraction

It is a method of extracting properties of segmented image on the basis of size, color, shape and reduces resources to describe large dataset before classification of image. Geometric feature has been extracted like- Area, perimeter, major axis length, minor axis length, centroid and eccentricity. It plays an important role in the field classifying image.

7 Artificial Neural Network

It is a group of interconnected computing elements or neurons. Generally, a neuron computer sum of its inputs and pass its sum through a nonlinear function. Each neuron has only one output which is further multiplied by a weighted factor that to be used as input to another neuron. This network is based on the concept of biological neuron system and has proved to be robust in dealing with the complex data and kind of problem that require the involvement of a large amount of data. ANN has a great potential in solving complex relationship between input and output or to find a pattern in data. it consists of three layers [24] as shown in Fig. 2:

1. **Input Layer**
   The layer which receives inputs from outside world through input nodes and just passes it to the hidden layer, which helps network to recognize the pattern and learn from it. No computation is done in this layer.
2. **Hidden Layer**
   The layer which exists between input and output layer and helps to transfer information from input to output nodes. Every type of computation done here.
3. **Output Layer**
   The layer which is responsible for computation and transferring output to the outside world with the help of output nodes. The concept of the neural network is totally based on human biological nervous system and have proved robust in dealing with complex data. Neural Network has a great potential in solving complex relationship between input and output or to find the pattern in data.

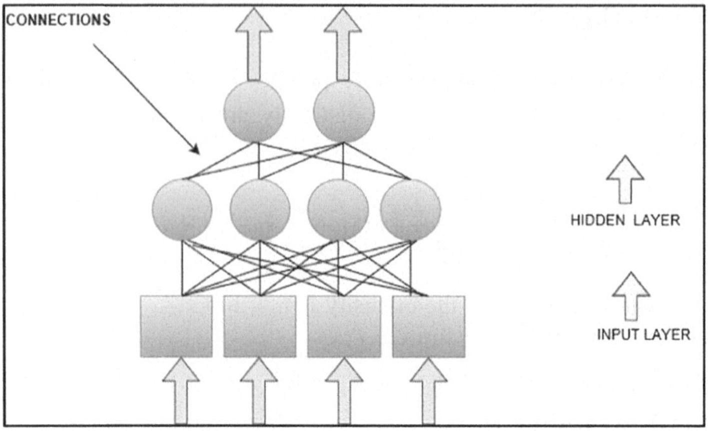

Fig. 2. The architecture of Artificial Neural Network (ANN)

A SOM (Self Organising Map) has been used in this approach which maintain the topology of input image while reducing the dimension, and making them useful for manual inspection (Fig. 5). A SOM is called "Self Organising Map" because they can adjust their neuron structure based on the topological structure of the inputs, which can be used best for image segmentation techniques like edge detection. Once the image has captured and loaded into the system, feature extraction is performed. Then the result of segmentation is a set of partitioned pixels collectively cover the entire image. The network is trained with training algorithm known as backpropagation algorithm. Now, for training the network, there is predefined function named sum squared error performance which is used to analyze the performance of network Fig. 6(a). After training the network, it is simulated. Thereafter, based epochs and learning rate and validate checks of performance has been depicted in Fig. 6(b). Followed by this check, the network resulted a predicted output set Table 1 and training set Table 2. The resulted dataset has been further compared Fig. 7 and recognized the pattern efficiently Fig. 8.

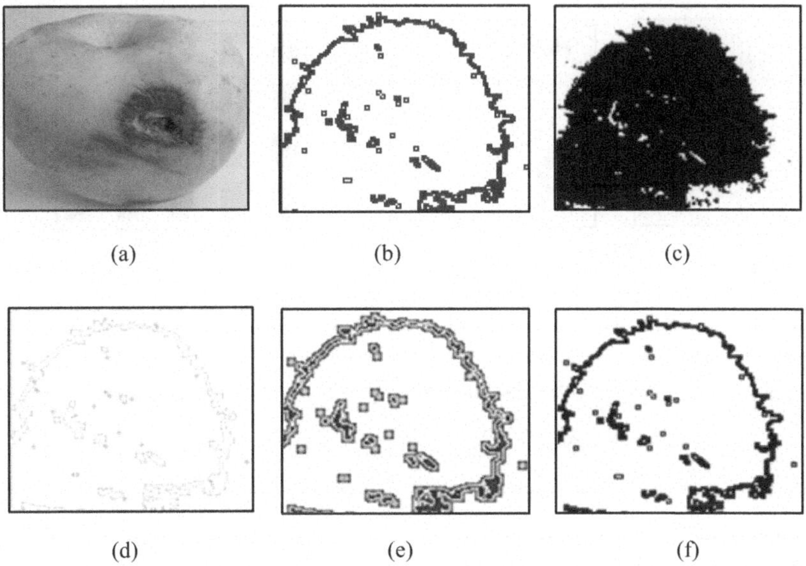

Fig. 3. Different pre-processing stages: (a) original image (b) histogram equalizer (c) Otsu Binarize method (d) mask segmentation fragments (e) unsharp masking filter (f) edge detection

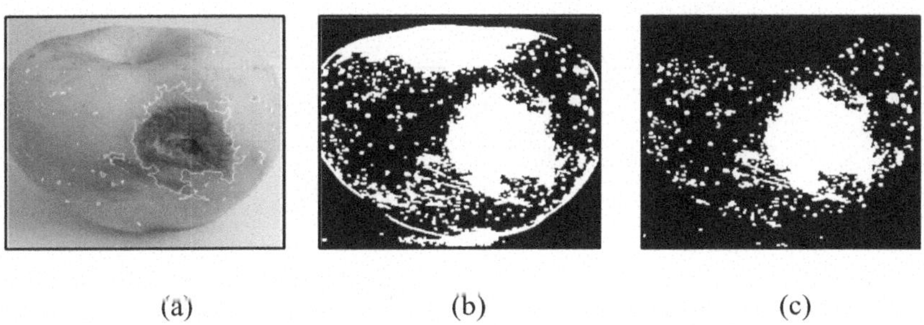

Fig. 4. Cluster of different segmented images: (a) binary image with filled holes (b) cleared border image (c) dilated image

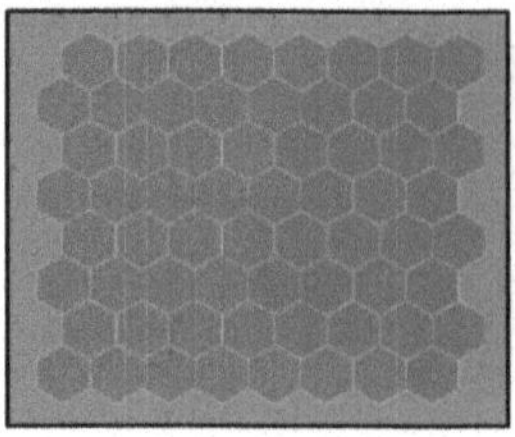

(a)

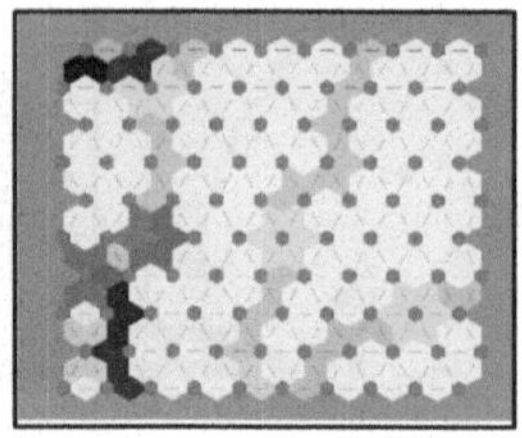

(b)

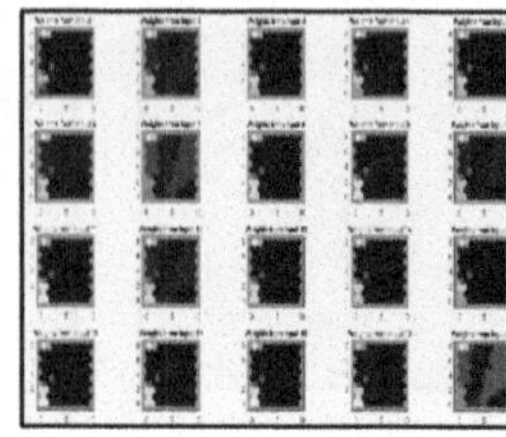

(c)

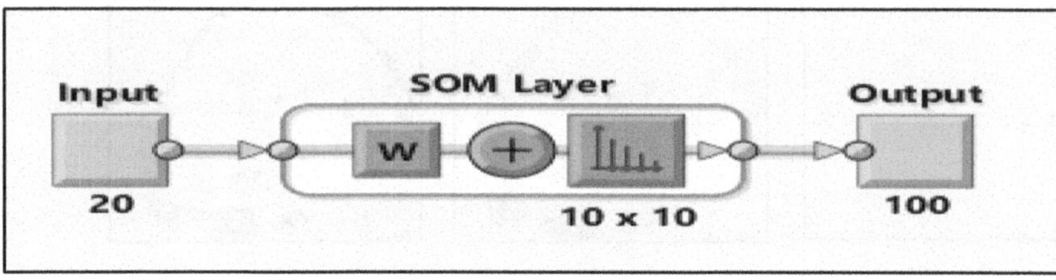

(d)

Fig. 5. Topological view of defected sample: (a) SOM topology (b) SOM neighbor weight distances (c) SOM input planes (d) SOM architecture

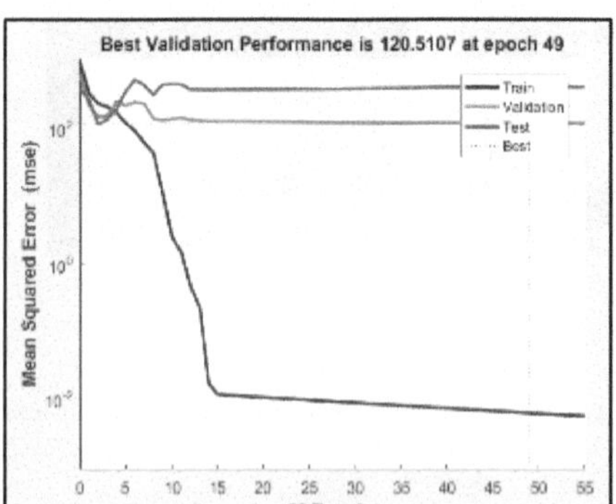

(a)

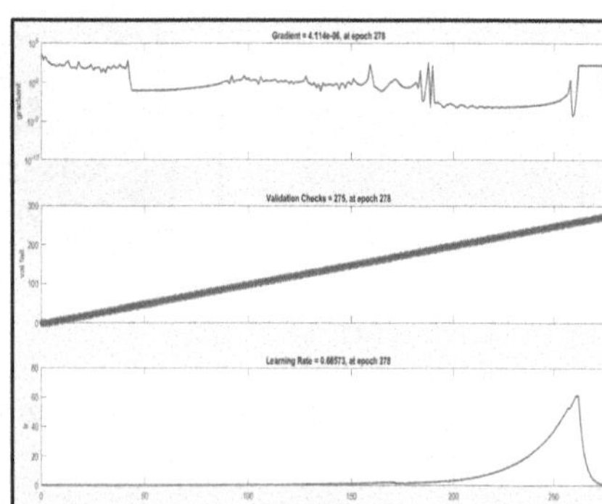

(b)

Fig. 6. (a) Best validation performance (b) Training state using minimum gradient method

Table 1. Prediction set for neural network

	In 1	In 2	In 3	In 4	In 5	In 6	In 7	Pred. Out 1
►1	1.0000000	61.0000000	228.0000000	1.1547005	1.1547005	0.0000000	1.1283792	1.000000
2	15.0000000	147.8000000	161.8666667	7.6381030	3.5686045	0.8841459	4.3701937	1.000000
3	1.0000000	145.0000000	166.0000000	1.1547005	1.1547005	0.0000000	1.1283792	1.000000
4	2. 0000000	146.5000000	180.5000000	3.0550505	1.1547005	0.9258201	1.5957691	1.000000
5	1. 0000000	147.0000000	166.0000000	1.1547005	1.1547005	0.0000000	1.1283792	1.000000
6	7.0000000	149.7142857	149.5714286	5.2603086	3.0996879	0.8079437	2.9854107	1.000000
7	65.0000000	153.7538462	180.9692308	16.5275176	10.6308758	0.7656791	9.0972837	1.000000
8	2.0000000	149.5000000	147.0000000	2.3094011	1.1547005	0.8660254	1.5957691	1.000000
9	1.0000000	151.0000000	145.0000000	1.1547005	1.1547005	0.0000000	1.1283792	1.000000
10	1.0000000	152.3333333	156.4166667	7.5381728	3.4574165	0.8886147	3.9088201	1.000000
11	1.0000000	152.0000000	141.0000000	1.1547005	1.1547005	0.0000000	1.1283792	1.000000
12	13.0000000	155.9230769	140.2307692	8.3025560	3.7440960	0.8925457	4.0584289	1.000000
13	3.0000000	155.0000000	150.0000000	4.7609523	1.1547005	0.9701425	1.9544100	1.000000
14	2.0000000	155.5000000	164.0000000	2.3094011	1.1547005	0.8660254	1.5957691	1.000000
15	2.0000000	155.5000000	190.0000000	2.3094011	1.1547005	0.8660254	1.5957691	1.000000
16	1.0000000	156.0000000	146.0000000	1.1547005	1.1547005	0.0000000	1.1283792	1.000000
17	1.0000000	156.0000000	157.0000000	1.1547005	1.1547005	0.0000000	1.1283792	1.000000
18	1.0000000	157.0000000	144.0000000	1.1547005	1.1547005	0.0000000	1.1283792	1.000000
19	1.0000000	158.0000000	137.0000000	1.1547005	1.1547005	0.0000000	1.1283792	1.000000
*20	120.0000000	174.3750000	187.3916667	39.8897284	5.9865230	0.9886743	12.3607745	1

Table 2. Training set for neural network

	In 1	In 2	In 3	In 4	In 5	In 6	In 7	Out 1	Pred. Out 1
► 1	1.0000000	61.0000000	228.0000000	1.1547005	1.1547005	0.0000000	1.1283792	0.0000000	0.997509
2	15.0000000	147.8000000	161.8666667	7.6381030	3.5686045	0.8841459	4.3701937	20.0470000	0.998072
3	1.0000000	145.0000000	166.0000000	1.1547005	1.1547005	0.0000000	1.1283792	0.0000000	0.997509
4	2.0000000	146.5000000	180.5000000	3.0550505	1.1547005	0.9258201	1.5957691	2.8120000	0.998048
5	1.0000000	147.0000000	166.0000000	1.1547005	1.1547005	0.0000000	1.1283792	0.0000000	0.997509
6	7.0000000	149.7142857	149.5714286	5.2603086	3.0996879	0.8079437	2.9854107	11.9920000	0.998068
7	65.0000000	153.7538462	180.9692308	16.5275176	10.6308758	0.7656791	9.0972837	77.4350000	0.998067
8	2.0000000	149.5000000	147.0000000	2.3094011	1.1547005	0.8660254	1.5957691	1.9600000	0.998042
9	1.0000000	151.0000000	145.0000000	1.1547005	1.1547005	0.0000000	1.1283792	0.0000000	0.997509
10	12.0000000	152.3333333	156.4166667	7.5381728	3.4574165	0.8886147	3.9088201	17.4340000	0.998072
11	1.0000000	152.0000000	141.0000000	1.1547005	1.1547005	0.0000000	1.1283792	0.0000000	0.997509
12	13.0000000	155.9230769	140.2307692	8.3025560	3.7440960	0.8925457	4.0684289	20.8080000	0.998073
13	3.0000000	155.0000000	150.0000000	4.7609523	1.1547005	0.9701425	1.9544100	5.6240000	0.998073
14	2.0000000	155.5000000	164.0000000	2.3094011	1.1547005	0.8660254	1.5957691	1.9600000	0.998042
15	2.0000000	155.5000000	190.0000000	2.3094011	1.1547005	0.8660254	1.5957691	1.9600000	0.998042
16	1.0000000	156.0000000	146.0000000	1.1547005	1.1547005	0.0000000	1.1283792	0.0000000	0.997509
17	1.0000000	156.0000000	157.0000000	1.1547005	1.1547005	0.0000000	1.1283792	0.0000000	0.997509
18	1.0000000	157.0000000	144.0000000	1.1547005	1.1547005	0.0000000	1.1283792	0.0000000	0.997509
19	1.0000000	158.0000000	137.0000000	1.1547005	1.1547005	0.0000000	1.1283792	0.0000000	0.997509
* 20	120.0000000	174.3750000	187.3916667	39.8897284	5.9865230	0.9886743	12.3607745	108.1500000	0.9980747

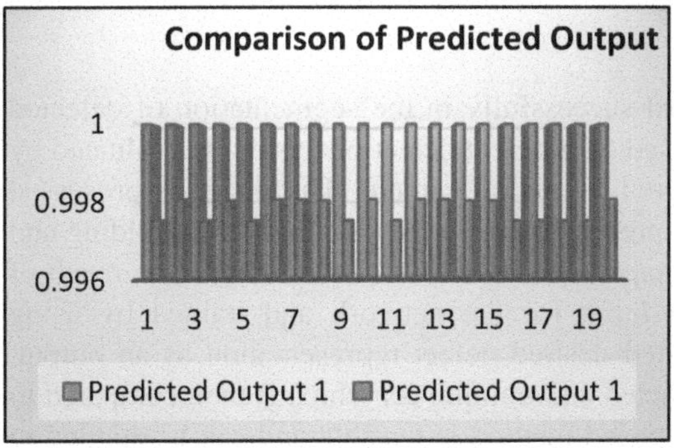

Fig. 7. Comparing the predicted and training dataset

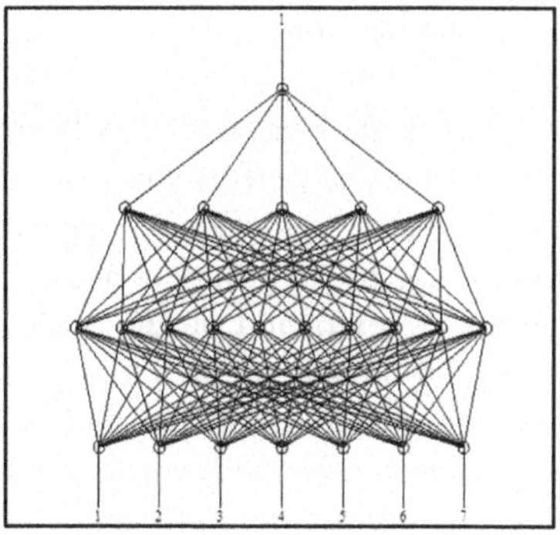

Fig. 8. Neural network structure of defected region

8 Results

See (Table 3).

Table 3. Predicted set of neural networks where predicted output 1 is of defected image and predicted ouput2 is of prediction accuracy of neural network for detected the defected part

S. No	Predicted output 1 (predicted set)	Predicted output 1 (training set)
1	1	0.9975091
2	1	0.9980724
3	1	0.9975091
4	1	0.9980476
5	1	0.9975091
6	1	0.9980679
7	1	0.9980667
8	1	0.9980422
9	1	0.9975091
10	1	0.9980724
11	1	0.9975091
12	1	0.9980725
13	1	0.9980728
14	1	0.9980422
15	1	0.9980422
16	1	0.9975091
17	1	0.9975091
18	1	0.9975091
19	1	0.9975091
20	1	0.9980747

9 Conclusion

Artificial Neural network has been used successfully in the segmentation of defected fruit region. The performance of proposed fruit defect detection system is evaluated by using defected apple fruit image captured by digital camera. The image is processed using image processing technique like- preprocessing, edge detection, thresholding and features are extracted on the basis of shape, size and color of the image. The result of segmented image is then used as an input for the network and trained by using backpropagation algorithm and generated desired defect representation as an output. The experimental result shown by predicted and training set which is then compared to detect the prediction and hence the proposed method is feasible and can be applied in horticulture.

References

1. Yogesh, Dubey, A.K.: Fruit defect detection based on speeded up robust feature technique. In: 2016 5th International Conference on Reliability, Infocom Technologies and Optimization (Trends and Future Directions) (ICRITO), Noida, pp. 590–594 (2016)
2. Kaur, M., Sharma, R.: Quality detection of fruits by using ANN technique. IOSR J. Electron. Commun. Eng. **10**, 35–41 (2015)
3. Samajpati, B.J., Degadwala, S.D.: A survey on apple fruit diseases detection and classification. Int. J. Comput. Appl. (0975–8887) **130**(13) (2015)
4. Rogers, R.D., Riess, A.G.: Detection and classification of CCD defects with an artificial neural network. Publ. Astron. Soc. Pac. **106**(699), 532 (1994)
5. Jiang, J., Trundle, P., Ren, J.: Medical image analysis with artificial neural networks. Comput. Med. Imaging Gr. **34**(8), 617–631 (2010)
6. Banumathi, P., Nasira, G.M.: Fabric inspection system using artificial neural networks. Int. J. Comput. Eng. Sci. **2**, 20–27 (2012)
7. Singh, S.P., et al.: Classification ofapples using neural networks (2015)
8. Gill, J., Sandhu, P.S., Singh, T.: A review of automatic fruit classification using soft computing techniques. Int. J. Comput. Sci. Electron. Eng. **2**(2), 3–16 (2014)
9. Xiao-bo, Z., Jie-wen, Z., Yanxiao, L., Holmes, M.: In-line detection of apple defects using three color cameras system. Comput. Electron. Agric. **70**(1), 129–134 (2010)
10. Dubey, S.R., Jalal, A.S.: Application of image processing in fruit and vegetable analysis: a review. J. Intell. Syst. **24**(4), 405–424 (2015)
11. Banot, S., Mahajan, P.M.: A fruit detecting and grading system based on image processing-review. Int. J. Innov. Res. Electr. Electron. Instrum. Control Eng. **4**(1), 47–53 (2016)
12. Mehdy, M.M., et al.: Artificial neural networks in image processing for early detection of breast cancer. Comput. Math. Methods Med. **2017** (2017)
13. Satyawana, S.: A review paper on image segmentation and object recognition procedures. Sci. Eng. Technol. 67 (2016)
14. Zhao, W., Zhang, J., Li, P., Li, Y.: Study of image segmentation algorithm based on textural features and neural network. In: International Conference on Intelligent Computing and Cognitive Informatics (ICICCI), pp. 300–303 (2010)
15. Chandhok, C.: A novel approach to image segmentation using artificial neural networks and K-means clustering. Int. J. Eng. Res. Appl. (IJERA) ISSN **2**(3), 274–279 (2012)

16. Pushpa, B.R., Meghana, T.K., Tripulla, K.H.: Detection and classification of fungal disease in fruits using image processing. Int. J. Appl. Eng. Res. (IJAER) **10**(55) (2015)
17. Raut, S., Fulsunge, A.: Review on fruit disease detection using image processing techniques
18. Sonka, M., Hlavac, V., Boyle, R.: Image pre-processing. In: Sonka, M., Hlavac, V., Boyle, R. (eds.) Image Processing Analysis and Machine Vision, pp. 56–111. Springer, New York (1993). https://doi.org/10.1007/978-1-4899-3216-7
19. Jeon, B., Yung, Y., Hong, K.: Image segmentation by unsupervised sparse clustering. Pattern Recognit. Lett. **27**, 1650–1664 (2006). science direct
20. Bhosale, P., Gokhale, A.: Segmentation of color images based on different. Int. J. Electron. Comput. Sci. Eng. **2**, 640–644 (2013)
21. Mohamed Razali, M.R., Ahmad, N.S., Zaki, Z.M., Ismail, W.: Region of adaptive threshold segmentation between mean, median and otsu threshold for dental age assessment. In: 2014 International Conference on Computer, Communications, and Control Technology (I4CT), Langkawi, pp. 353–356 (2014)
22. Morse, B.S.: 1998–2000 Last modified on Wednesday, 12 January 2000 at 10:00 AM. Brigham Young University
23. Lindeberg, T.: Edge detection and ridge detection with automatic scale selection. Int. J. Comput. Vis. **30**(2), 117–154 (1998)
24. Nataraj, K., Patnekar, N.: Neural networks for image analysis and processing in measurements, instrumentation and related industrial applications. Neural Netw. Instrum. Meas. Relat. Ind. Appl. **185**, 145 (2003)

Sentiment Analysis of Indians on GST

Amogh Madan, Ridhima Arora(✉), and Nihar Ranjan Roy(✉)

GD Goenka University, Gurugram, Haryana, India
amoghmadaan@gmail.com, ridhima02050@gmail.com,
niharranjanroy@gdgoenka.ac.in

Abstract. Twitter has become one of the most popular communication medium among internet users. Millions of users share their opinions on it, therefore making it a rich source of data for opinion mining and sentiment analysis. Taking our context as Goods and Services Tax, which has been one of the most debated topic in media not only in India but also outside India. In this paper, we collected the data from the twitter and tried to infer about the way Indians have understood Goods and Services Tax. We have discussed the methodology to prepare a corpus from Twitter for sentiment analysis and opinion mining. The analysis of the collected corpus is done using a 'lexicon-based approach'. Using this approach, we can determine the opinion in three major categories; positive, negative and neutral sentiments of the document.

Keywords: GST India · Sentiment analysis · Twitter

1 Introduction

Goods & Services Tax (GST) Law was introduced in India on July 1st 2017 [1]. It is a comprehensive, multi-stage, destination based tax that will be levied on every value addition. It was made applicable throughout India; GST replaced multiple cascading taxes levied by the central and state governments. There are various advantages of GST, as claimed by one of the leading website dealing in Taxation [2];

- It will remove cascading taxes.
- There will be higher threshold for registration
- It offers composition scheme for small businesses
- Simpler procedure for GST through online portal
- Lesser compliances
- Defined treatment for e-commerce
- It will increase efficiency of logistics industry
- It will regulate the unorganized sector

While it is claimed that all the indirect taxes are merged in to a single taxation system called GST Tax but GST itself has multiple variations; CGST, IGST, SGST and UGST (Fig. 1). Since GST replaces indirect taxes collected by central government (service tax, excise duty, custom duty) as well as state government (like VAT and luxury taxes), these governments depends on GST for tax revenue.

B. Panda et al. (Eds.): REDSET 2017, CCIS 799, pp. 568–575, 2018.
https://doi.org/10.1007/978-981-10-8527-7_47

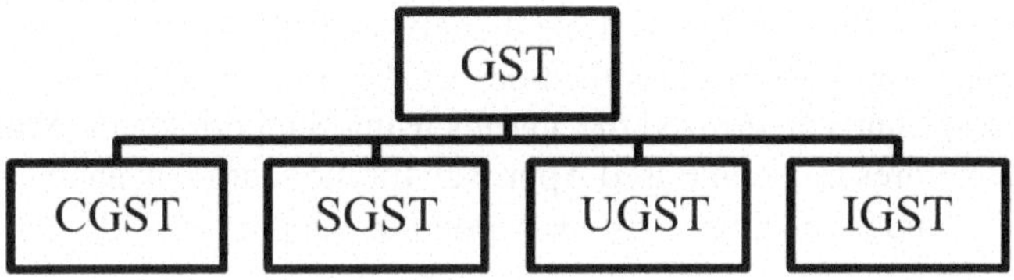

Fig. 1. Types of GST

If interstate transactions are involved, GST considers share for center (CGST) as well as state/union territory (CGST/UTGST). Integrated Goods and Service Tax is collected by central government and is applicable on interstate transactions (two states). The central government thereafter distributes part of it with involved states. It eliminates the trouble of dealing with every state, states have to deal only with the central govt.

Social Media has become a platform for people to post their thoughts and their feelings, views & opinions about current topics. Internet based applications like Twitter [3, 4], Facebook, Quora, Reddit, [5] etc. all come under social media. With the help of these platforms it has become easier for people to share their opinion on any topic as per their interests. Twitter is a micro- blogging website where people tweet about recent topics of their interests using text, images, animations and videos, making it a rich source for text mining. So, in this paper we are using Twitter as a data source for understanding the attitude and opinion of people towards GST.

There are various tools available for statistical programming, we chose R because of the various packages available for text mining and sentiment analysis. Sentiment analysis is the field of study where we study the complete text and try to classify the text into different categories of feelings; here we are working on Positive, Negative and Neutral. We chose the lexicon based approach because it is a simple, viable and practical approach to Sentiment Analysis of Twitter data without the need of any training set [6]. The use of dictionary is taken as a major player as it has a set of words which are already marked as positive, negative or neutral. This helps in classifying the text using the defined dictionaries, which then identifies the feelings of a person into desired categories related to the topic [7].

2 Related Work

Numerous research papers and studies in the last few years have been done in the field of sentimental analysis. These studies are used to develop various techniques for detecting and identifying the sentiment of a given text, there are three main approaches named Machine Learning Approach, Lexicon Based Approach and Hybrid Approach [5]. The Machine Learning Approach uses the well-known ML algorithms like Naive Bayes Classifier, SVM etc. The Lexicon Based Method is based on opinion lexicons which are made up of pre-compiled terms, opinions and phrases. The Hybrid Approach incorporates the characteristics of both Machine Learning Approach and Lexicon Based Approach. Giachanou et al., 2016 has also done 50 papers on the similar topic to highlight the importance of sentiment analysis [8]. Riberio et al., 2016 has presented his work with the help of twenty-four sentiment analysis methods applied on eighteen data sets for the binary and tertiary classifications of the sentiments. Then, Sudhir Kumar Sharma et al., 2017 had categorized the Tweets using Support Vector Machines [9].

This paper explores Lexicon Based Approach for the sentiment analysis and opinion mining for better understanding of the view point of people for GST.

3 Research Methodology

This section represents research methodology followed, and the tools and libraries used to analyze the opinion of citizens of India on GST. The use of Open-source packages and libraries is extensive in this paper.

3.1 System Architecture

This section defines the basic approach about the analysis done in this paper with the help of flow charts. Figure 2 shows the work flow i.e. first of all the tweets are extracted from the twitter website using twitter API, followed by pre-processing and application of Lexical base approach on this data. Figure 3 shows the division of work i.e. categorization of the opinions in three categories namely; Positive, Neutral and Negative.

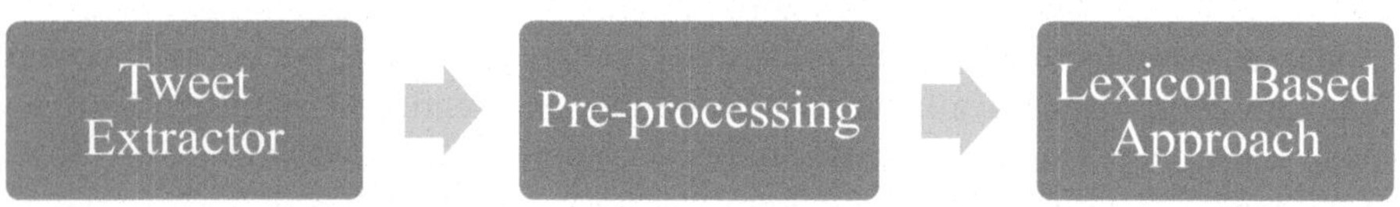

Fig. 2. Work flow description

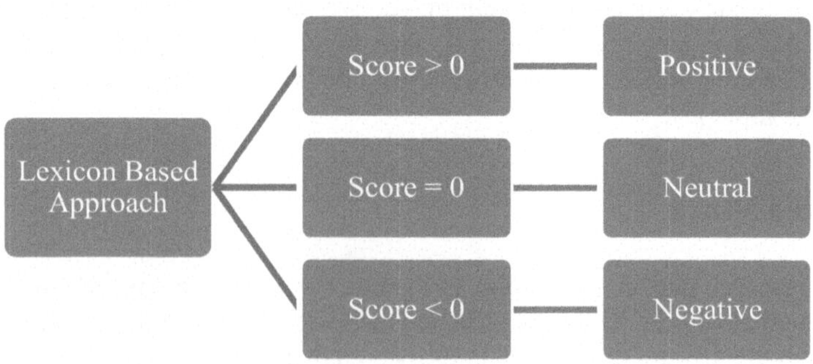

Fig. 3. Division of work

4 Data Extraction

The data was collected for the month of July, 2017. In this section we discuss the process and R API/functions used for data extraction and pre-processing of data.

4.1 Data Extraction

Twitter offers number of APIs which are used for extracting data with the help of code on any event by providing the required information or specific keywords. People Tweet using some specific hashtags related to the topic of discussion. The hashtag used related to GST was #GST. The total number of Tweets collected was 10,000. Data set contains seven columns namely Tweet ID, Username, Date Time, Location, Text, Re-Tweeted and Favorited. We used the following packages to pull data from twitter [10]: -

1. TwitteR - It provides an interface to the Twitter Web API. It provides a function searchTwitter() which will issue a search of twitter based on the supplied searched string.
2. RCurl – It provides function to allow one to make a general HTTP request and provides functions to fetch URLs in GET and POST form and then process the result returned by the web location you are trying to retrieve the data from.
3. ROAuth – Provides interface to the OAuth 1.0 specifications which allows the users to authenticate themselves via OAuth to the server of their choice for data extraction.

4.2 Pre-processing

Data pre-processing is one of the most important part of text analysis. Especially when the data is collected social platforms it might contain many words or symbols which might not be of our use. So it is very important to cautiously remove these symbols, urls and words. We perform word tokenization process to classify the text into units which are easy to understand by the machine. We also convert all the extracted text into lower case. The packages and functions used are: -

1. Plyr
   It helps in breaking down the bigger problem into smaller chunks which are easy to handle and then convert them back into a bigger set.
2. Stringr
   It is an easy way to use wrappers around the 'stringi' package. It is actually used to deal with the 'NA' and the zero length values. It also has options for patter matching and handling locale text. It also helps in adding, removing or manipulating white-spaces.
3. Gsub()
   This function replaces all matches of a string, and returns the processed string. Unmatched words are returned as it is.

5 Result and Analysis

In this section we describe the Lexical based approach and its choice, followed by the algorithm used and plotting and analysis of the result;

5.1 Lexicon Based Approach (LBA)

The reason we opted for LBA is because LBA methods for sentiment analysis are robust and give good cross-domain performance [7].

Semantic orientation (SO) is defined as a measure of subjectivity and opinion in text. It usually captures an evaluative factor (positive, negative or neutral) and potency or strength (degree to which the word, phrase, sentence, or document in question is positive, negative or neutral) [7].

The lexicon-based approach involves calculating orientation of the view presented in the document from the semantic orientation of words or phrases present in that document [11]. This approach is based on the dictionary of words which can be created manually [12, 13], or automatically, using these seed words to expand the list of words. Much of the research carried using lexicon-based approach uses adjectives as indicators of the semantic orientation of text [14].

Lexicon-based approach uses unsupervised learning as an approach for classifying the text. The existing text can be used to classify the words in to a positive, neutral or negative sentiment [9, 15]. Which makes it a preferable approach for saving time as the training and testing has already been done on the classifier which classifies the content in to different sentiments of suitable interests.

5.2 Algorithm

```
1. start
2. extract tweets
3. store in csv format
4. read column with text
5. call the lexicon dictionaries
6. pre-process the data
7. compare the text for getting a score
8. if (score == 0)
       neutral++
     else if (score > 0)
       positive ++
     else
       negative++
9. end
```

5.3 Graphical Representation of the Results and Analysis

ggplot2 [16, 17] is a data visualization package for the statistical R programming. It has many advance features in comparison to its base graphics package. It helps in creating multi-layered graphics in a hassle-free way.

In Fig. 4 we present the output of the three categories followed by word cloud for reach category positive, neutral and negative in Figs. 5, 6 and 7 respectively.

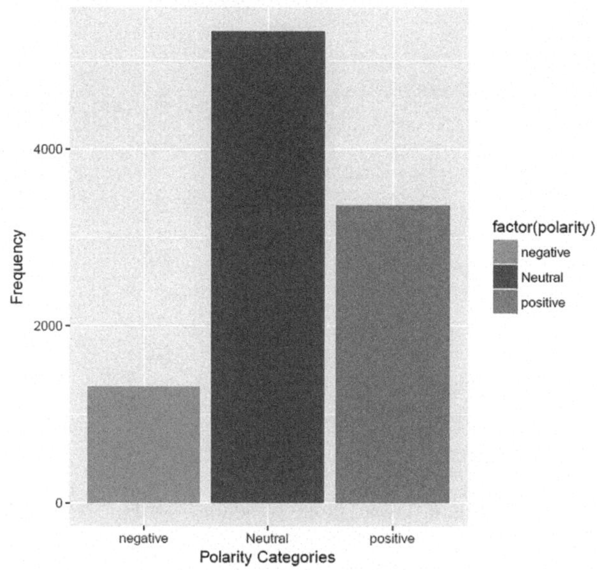

Fig. 4. Output graph

Fig. 5. Word cloud of positive words

After doing the analysis it can be seen that out of the 10000 tweets that were extracted, 5334 tweets were neutral, 3359 were positive and 1307 were negative. According to the analysis done we can concluded that maximum people are neutral about GST because either they are unaware about the consequences or they are considering it as another tax which will replace the existing taxes without any change.

Fig. 6. Word cloud of neutral words

Fig. 7. Word cloud of negative words

6 Conclusion

In this paper we have used the lexical based sentiment analysis to estimate the mood of the Indians on GST. We have used the data from the social network called twitter. After preprocessing it we used the adjective based dictionary to categories the sentiments in three categories; Positive, negative and neutral. Our results show that among 10000 thousand data sets 33% are positive and 13% are negative. 54% are neutral, by neutral we mean that they don't oppose the move of its implementation and in future if more light is thrown they may further add to the positive section. Increasing its % share. Thus we may conclude that Indians have positive opinion about GST.

References

1. Government of India: GST Portal, Govt. of India (2017). https://www.gst.gov.in/about/gst/history
2. ClearTax, Defmacro Software Pvt. Ltd., 4 August 2017. https://cleartax.in/s/benefits-gst
3. Agarwal, A., Xie, B., Vovsha, I., Rambow, O., Passonneau, R.: Sentiment analysis of Twitter data. In: Proceedings of the Workshop on Languages in Social Media, pp. 30–38 (2011)
4. Liu, B.: Sentiment analysis and opinion mining. Synth. Lect. Hum. Lang. Technol. **5**(1), 1–167 (2012)
5. Russell, M.: Mining the Social Web: Data Mining Facebook, Twitter, LinkedIn, Google+, GitHub, and More, 2nd edn. O'Reilly Media, Sebastopol (2013)
6. Kumar, A., Sebastian, T.M.: Sentiment analysis: a perspective on its past, present and future. Int. J. Intell. Syst. Appl. (IJISA) **4**(10), 1–14 (2012)
7. Taboada, M., Julian, B., Milan, T., Kimberly, V., Stede, M.: Lexicon-based methods for sentiment analysis. Comput. Linguist. **37**(2), 267–307 (2011)
8. Giachanou, A., Crestani, F.: Like it or not: a survey of Twitter sentiment analysis methods. ACM Comput. Surv. **49**(2), 28:1–28:41 (2016)
9. Sharma, S.K., Hoque, X.: Sentiment predictions using support vector machines for odd-even formula in Delhi. Int. J. Intell. Syst. Appl. (IJISA) **9**(7), 61–69 (2017)
10. Twitter Documentation, August 2017. https://dev.twitter.com/overview/documentation
11. Turney, P.D.: Thumbs up or thumbs down? Semantic orientation applied to unsupervised classification of reviews. In: Proceedings of the 40th Annual Meeting on Association for Computational Linguistics, Philadelphia, Pennsylvania (2002)
12. Stone, P.J., Hunt, E.B.: A computer approach to content analysis: studies using the general inquirer system. In: Spring Joint Computer Conference, Detroit, Michigan, 21–23 May 1963
13. Tong, R.: An operational system for detecting and tracking opinions in on-line discussions. In: Working Notes of the SIGIR Workshop on Operational Text Classification, pp. 1–6 (2001)
14. Pedrycz, W., Chen, S.-M.: Sentiment Analysis and Ontology Engineering: An Environment of Computational Intelligence. Springer Nature, Cham (2016). https://doi.org/10.1007/978-3-319-30319-2
15. Ciubotariu, C.C., Hrisca, M.V., Gliga, M., Darabana, D., Trandabat, D., Iftene, A.: Minions at SemEval-2016 Task 4: or how to build a sentiment analyzer using off-the-shelf. In: Proceedings of SemEval, pp. 247–50 (2016)
16. Chang, W.: R Graphics Cookbook: Practical Recipes for Visualizing Data. O'Reilly Media, Sebastopol (2013)
17. Teutonico, D.: Ggplot2 Essentials. Packt Publishing, Birmingham (2015)

Security in Data Science Analytics

Virtual Consciousness from 3D to 4D Password: A Next Generation Security System Inspiration

Saurabh Allawadhi[(✉)], Nitin Kumar, and Sanjib Kumar Sahu

USICT, Guru Gobind Singh Indraprastha University, New Delhi, India
saurabhallawadhi029@gmail.com,
nitinrajput053@gmail.com, sahu_sanjib@rediffmail.com

Abstract. We have many authentication schemes presently, but they all have a few disadvantages. So recently, the 3D password paradigm was introduced. The 3D password is multi-factor authentication system as it uses various authentication techniques such as graphical password, textual password etc. Most important part of 3D password is inclusion of 3D virtual environment. However the 3D Password is still in its initial stages. Designing various kinds of 3D virtual environments, interpreting user feedback and deciding on password spaces, and experiences from such environments will bring about upgrading and enhancing the client experience of the 3D Password. Moreover, gathering attackers from various foundations to break the system is one of the future works that will lead to system improvement and demonstrate the complexity of breaking a 3D password. This paper introduces a study of the 3D password and reinforce it by including a Fourth dimension, that deals with time recording and gesture recognition, and that would help strengthen the authentication paradigm. Henceforth we endeavor to propose a 4D Password as a one-up technique to the 3D Password.

Keywords: Authentication · 3D environment · Biometric · Security Privacy

1 Introduction

Computing Scheme is the essential security service provided to systems and to authenticate these systems that are build using complex algorithms. In order to provide users a environment that is both secured and friendly so that they can access their information securely, computing mechanisms are made using 3D and 4D passwords. Every computing method have their pros but with certain loopholes. Nevertheless these schemes are considered to be secured and safe. These mechanisms in micro terms consists of textual passwords graphical password, Biometric authentication, etc. But in macro terms these are classified into four major types such as:

- **Profiency based:** This means what you knowledge you have. This includes Textual password.

B. Panda et al. (Eds.): REDSET 2017, CCIS 799, pp. 579–586, 2018.
https://doi.org/10.1007/978-981-10-8527-7_48

- **Sign based:** This means what symbols you have. This includes ATM cards, debit card, credit card etc.
- **Biometrics:** This means how an individual can be identified using physical or behavioral traits. This includes Thumb prints, eye scanners etc.
- **Recall Based:** This means what you able to remember and recognize. This includes graphical features, face remembering, names etc.

Since many years this subject was always been a point of discussion among researchers. Due to advancement in technology, security features to protect an organization data is getting better day by day but Hackers also uses smart techniques to break these security protocols and steal the private information of users. So we need a Silver Bullet to protect systems that can be 4D-password. We are provided with many password types such as textual passwords of short size, biometric scanning, tokens or cards (such as an ATM card like OTPs) etc. But there are many loopholes in current systems. The most common method is to use alphanumeric usernames and passwords as they are easy to remember by the users as they are no able to remember complex passwords and usernames. Studies have shown that users tend to pick short passwords or usernames that are easy to remember. Unfortunately, these passwords can also be easily guessed or broken or hacked. On the other hand, passwords that are hard to guess are tend to be forgotten by users also. Since user knowledge base is limited so it uses limited passwords or uses same passwords for multiple accounts. Graphical passwords can also be used as they are easier to remember than textual passwords. But this technique is not fruitfull as remembering pictures can be a tedious task as multiple images confuses the user. To address these problems Biometrics schemes are utilized as it is unique for every individual. Biometric act as a natural or universal signature of an individual and also Tokens or cards makes data secured.

As the technology has changed many fast processors and tools are available on internet it has become very easy. The 3D passwords scheme has been introduced as a one up solution to these schemes.

2 The 3D Password Scheme

2.1 Architectural Study

This section tells how different schemes can be utilized to create 3D passwords. 3D Password is multi-component computing scheme.in which biometrics or images or numbers can used to create a unique password. Selection of the method or type of scheme depends on various factors like who is going to use, need of the security etc. and this is the duty of the coder to select the best algorithm to create a one. Figure 1 shows the state diagram of 3D Password Creation.

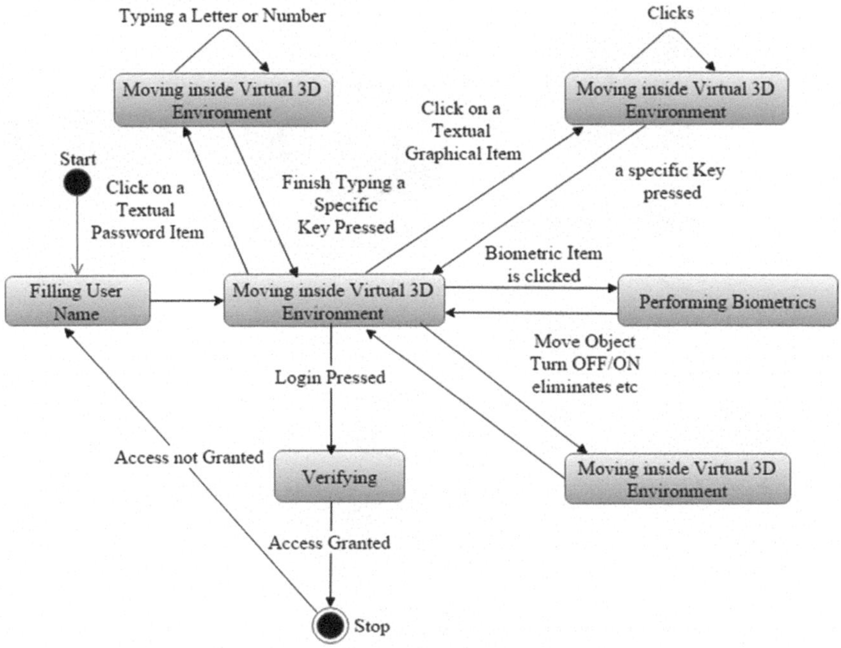

Fig. 1. State diagram of creating 3D password

2.2 Working of 3D Password

In 3D password user have to be first validated using simple textual password. Once verification is successful then user moves into 3D virtual environment, then further a virtual keyboard on the computer screen appears for the user. Using the keyboard on the screen user enters the password that is already been saved in the database in simple text format in encrypted coordinates in X, Y, Z. After successful matching, user automatically enter into an environment in which there is an art gallery in which he/she has to select multiple points in that gallery or he/she performs a unique action just like button on/off or action on an object like closing of door.

The continuous selection of either multiple points or action on object is stored in text report or file using encryption algorithm. Once all this is saved completely, system generates a particular unique password set for that user. In order to select the points we have used a simple algorithm i.e. convex hull algorithm from analysis and design algorithm. Now user when to access his account he has to select the object that he selected when creating the password or perform the same action on the specific object. When user enters his action it is then verified using the data already stored in encrypted format.

If there is successful match then there is access granted for user otherwise access denies and then user enters again password. 3D password working algorithm is shown in Fig. 2. This will give the flowchart for 3D password creation & authentication process.

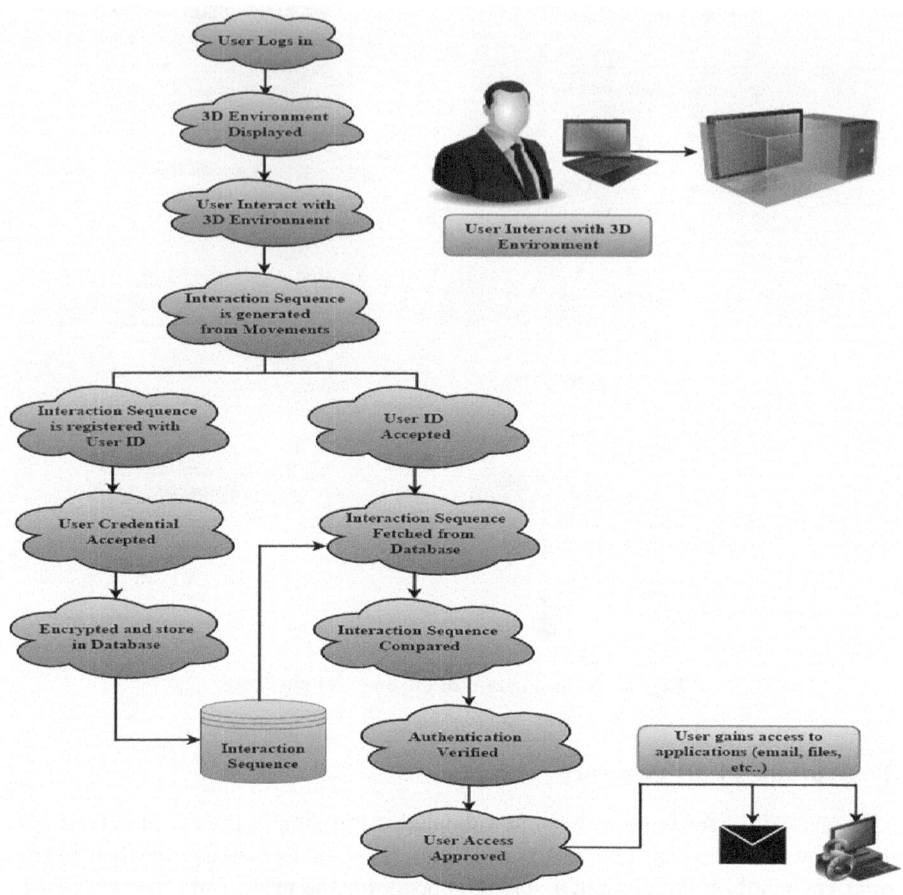

Fig. 2. Working of 3D password

3 Introducing 4D Password

As the 3D Password authentication scheme suffers from several weaknesses such as timing attack shoulder surfing attack, brute force attack etc., there is the chance of hacking the 3D password. The 4-D Password scheme is an attempt to create the existing scheme even more secure, robust and powerful. Adding another feature to the current scheme i.e. 3D passwords, will both increase efficiency and stability and this makes the data of the user to be more protective from the attacker. This extra feature, is to refer as the 'FOURTH DIMENSION'. A webcam is to use in order to capture the user movement coordinates that are called hand gestures and stored in encrypted format in the database. Physical presence of the user is now unavoidable in the process of login. Hence, the final password of the user would be:

User View:

3D Password + Movement Coordinates <Hand Gestures>

Now in for the system a mapping function is to be chosen as F(a) in which movement coordinates of the user is put as input string B. The output of this function is what the user gets a unique password. F(B) output as final encrypted values for the user, F(A) is the mapping function we used and input string is B that user enters using webcam. What is necessary for the user is the final encrypted values all the other things are hidden. What is required from the user is the hand movements by webcam that is to stored as a binary string. The system conjoins this encrypted coordinates to the available 3D password in order to create a 4D password for the user hence, the final password for the user by the system:

4D password = 3D Password + F(B).

The addition of function F(B) at the end would actually increase the complexity of the password. The attacker will now have to guess the string "B" as well as try to decipher function F(x), further to the complex techniques required to decipher a user's 3-D password itself.

3.1 Signup Process

Consider a Thermo-Nuclear Power Plant in which every scientist and engineer has their account in which he can access their place of entry, place of research and personal details related to their job. This environment employs the 4-D password scheme. As a new user, an engineer or scientist sign up as follows:

- Initially the applicant (scientist or engineer) login into system to register himself and submit details as in the form of name, photograph.
- After registration is done, it redirects to the domain to capture the 3D password.
- On entering to this domain, user select certain objects or perform certain action on the object.
- By performing that actions the user it is directed to screen where user is made to give movement gestures in front of webcam or camera.
- All these actions are saved, a particular username and 4D passwords IDs are given to the scientist or engineer.
- Sign up process is complete.

3.2 Login

Applicant enters the username and performs the specific motion of gesture in order to login into the system. Now when applicant logs in, he will have to enter the username, and afterward perform the gesture. After the user submit details a verification and validation is done. Now, there is access granted if there is successful match otherwise access denied (Fig. 3).

Fig. 3. Gesture recognition [9]

3.3 Significance

The main crux of the system is to get the registration form with details such as name, photograph, biometrics and hand gestures filled by applicant online and get these details of scientists or engineer whose testament is verified for its geniuses by 4D password system with respect to already existing information in the database. The addition of a further gesture will create an unlimited host of password combinations. Also it will make sure that there is someone attempting to login, and not some automated program or a software, or bot. 4D passwords are time bound means user enters the details in specific stipulated time period. If there is attack on the system this time is a boom to avoid attack as the if the user is taking much lesser time than the stipulated time then it might be a hacker or if the user is taking more time then it might be a certain other user trying to login into system.

4 Analysis of Security

4.1 Shoulder Surfing Attack

In this type of attack, the hacker uses a spy camera to know the 3D password. This is attack is best suited for attackers it sees all the actions performed by the user. The user never able to find how its information is hacked. Even if the attacker know the gesture for 4D password he must match physique of the user as by the physique movement coordinates are calculated.

4.2 Timing Attacks

In this type time is the major factor. 4D password is time bound means user signs in its account in stipulated time period. It is totally dependent on how much clock time a user takes to sign up in account using its username and gesture. Now here two cases arises

(a) If time is more than the stipulated time then there is condition that some other user is trying to enter or attacker is not able to recognize the passwords.
(b) If time is much lesser than the stipulated time then there is condition of hacking only this condition is more severe than the former.

As 4D password scheme are more secure, this type of attacks are not easily possible.

4.3 Keylogger

In this type of attack, a software program or hardware is used to record keystrokes on keyboard generally known as spyware and convert it to a text file. In this procedure hacker finds the possibilities of passwords by going through the file so it is time consuming too. But 4D password not only has textual password but series of various password schemes, so this type of attack is not affective.

4.4 Brute Force Attack

In this type attacker makes the complete same environment that he wants ro hack. But now he has to go through the various possibilities This attack is also effected by the cost that is needed to create a prototype of the system. 4D password require biometrics and gestures which costly to maintain.

5 Application Area

5.1 Thermo-Nuclear Power Plants

4D password are more effective than 3D passwords as they use gestures (hand gestures). It is a comprehensive approach so that we can decide which person is given restricted permission to enter certain areas of the nuclear plants. Initially the applicant (scientist or engineer) login into system to register himself and submit details as in the form of name, photograph, biometrics and hand gestures. These are stored in the database and verification process is done by the head of the plant being admin, Ministry executive being Ministry Admin and police and then specific IDs cards are issued to applicant.

5.2 Military Areas

3D passwords if effective technique to remove weaknesses of graphical & textual passwords. This system adopts fingerprints as biometrics which are specific to every person. Initially a soldier reports to his senior and submit all his details as in form of name and fingerprints. These are stored in the database and verification is done by the

Admin being head of the cantonment and Ministry person being ministry admin and then specific ID cards are issued to the soldier so there records can be maintained.

6 Future Scope

There is always a chance of threat in 3D password as it is more prone to hacking. Also, 3D suffers from weakness like timing attacks, brute force attack etc. Therefore another level of security is added in 3D password to transform it to 4D password. 4D password consist of three parts that is all existing schemes of 3D password like text or graphic codes, a virtual 3D environment and a gesture recognition system. This schemes is completely user friendly i.e. user can easily select what type of authentic scheme like biometric or gestures along with 3D password it want to use for its organization. It is also a very successful in preventing attacks against hackers. The 3D layer all alone is still not easy to hack but the addition of gestures makes it more powerful since gestures are based on an individual person and his personality i.e. they are unique and cannot be replicated by attacker. Also 4D Password scheme ensures that the user is always physically present to access the system and hacker is not hacking the system remotely. We need to create algorithms to implement such schemes and make them available to user.

Our future work is to work upon various gesture recognition mechanisms to capture motion fast and correctly. Next, work upon the algorithms that help in capture the motion and convert them to geometric coordinates. Also, hand movements can be combined with palm sensors in order to extra layer of security of biometrics. This makes the 4D dimension is of vital importance.

References

1. Gadicha, A.B., Gadicha, V.B.: Virtual realization using 3D password. Int. J. Electron. Comput. Sci. Eng. **1**, 216–223 (2016). ISSN 2277-1956
2. Sindhuja, V., Shiyamala devi, S., Vinitha, S.: A review of 3D protected password. Int. J. Innov. Res. Comput. Commun. Eng. pp. 3995–4001 (2016). ISSN 2320-9801
3. Shelke, P.M., Shelke, F.M., Pund, B.G.: Advance authentication technique: 3D password. Int. J. Recent Innov. Trends Comput. Commun. 632–635 (2016). ISSN 2321-8169
4. Kolhe, V., Gunjal, V., Kalasakar, S., Rathod, P.: Secure authentication with 3D password. Int. J. Eng. Sci. Innov. Technol. **2**, 99–105 (2013). ISSN 2319-5967
5. Raval, D., Shukla, A.: Security using 3D password. Int. J. Comput. Appl. **120**, 36–38 (2015)
6. Bilapatte, M.S., Bhattacharjee, S.: 3D password: a novel approach for more secure authentication. Int. J. Comput. Sci. Eng. Technol. 150–156 (2014). ISSN 2229-3345
7. Kelkar, A., Mukadam, K.: 3D password modern approach to security. Int. J. Comput. Eng. Appl. **9**, 31–38 (2015). ISSN 2321-3469
8. Khurana, S., Patel, M., Singh, P.K.: Study of 3D and 4D password security. Int. J. Res. Comput. Sci. 49–56 (2016)
9. https://static1.gamespot.com/uploads/original/1179/11799911/2963346-kinect.jpg

Efficient and Secure Nearest Neighbor Search Over Encrypted Data in Cloud Environment

Kaur Upinder(✉) and R. Suri Pushpa

Department of Computer Science and Applications, KUK, Kurukshetra, India
drupinder2016@gmail.com

Abstract. Nearest neighbor search is the most general search queries on large data sets, location base services, spatial databases, graph applications, etc. With the growth of cloud computing, the trend of outsourcing the sensitive data demands the fast and secure nearest neighbor solutions over the existing solutions. In our paper, propose a new secure and efficient nearest neighbor search for encrypted data with mOPE (mutable order preserving encryption). In our proposed model use the probabilistic data structure skip graph for the efficient indexing. Then encrypt the indexes using mOPE for efficient nearest neighbor search. With the thorough analysis of our scheme achieve a perfect balance between security and nearest neighbor search query compared to another scheme.

Keywords: Nearest neighbor search · Cloud computing · Skip graph

1 Introduction

The nearest neighbor problem aims at finding the most similar point to a query point from the database. It is used in different applications like location-based services, data mining, multimedia databases, spatial data, etc. Several amounts of research have focused on efficiently nearest neighbor queries with minimum computational overhead. The large data set is managed locally with various known spatial indexes for approx. nearest neighbor queries. But with the emergence of cloud computing, data owner outsourced their data into the cloud to remove the burden of a massive amount of data management in a cost effective manner. Cloud computing is a new paradigm that helps the user the metered services "pay as per use." The result of the cloud environment is losing in controlling over the remote placement of data and became the security concern for data owner. Therefore the past research for nearest neighbor search is not efficient enough. Many researchers have proposed various methods to address these problems of security and privacy of nearest neighbor query. The general approach adopts by data owner is to encrypt the outsourced data.

Many research schemes have been proposed to enable functionality over the encrypted data over cloud environment, but these are not compatible with advance queries like nearest neighbor search. The authors [1–5] proposed some nearest neighbor search queries on encrypted data, but they still face some limitations. Some have proposed kNN queries are failing to support high dimensional data or building efficient kNN algorithm. The challenge here is to calculate the distance from the query point to

B. Panda et al. (Eds.): REDSET 2017, CCIS 799, pp. 587–598, 2018.
https://doi.org/10.1007/978-981-10-8527-7_49

the data point in encrypted data and compare the distance with the other data points to finally retrieve the minimum distance to the query point.

In this paper, our primary focus on the problem of nearest neighbor search in encrypted data in the cloud environment. There are existed cryptographic primitives themselves do not preserve the distance between the data after encryption. The Oder preserving encryption allows performing various database functions over encrypted data. Here, using the more efficient mOPE combined with our secure index skip graph for a more efficient solution for nearest neighbor search in encrypted data in a cloud environment.

2 Related Work

The existing traditional searchable encryption schemes [5–10], cannot be directly processed as plain text. Various researchers proposed efficient schemes to support executing the query on encrypted data. Wong et al. [11] proposed ASPE (Asymmetric Scalar Product Preserving Encryption), for nearest neighbor search on encrypted data, but only limited to the linear search. Similarly, Hu et al. [12] proposed scheme with tree structure and ASPE, for faster and better search efficiency. Also, Yao et al. presented another solution with Voronoi Diagrams to retrieve the exact nearest neighbor solution. Some new scheme for secure nearest neighbor search proposed by [13, 14], they consider search between two parties and manages their database, but not efficient for large data sets. Some proposed only query privacy not covered data privacy [15].

3 Problem Statement

3.1 System Model

In our scheme, consider a cloud server, data owner and a user as shown in Fig. 1. The data owner outsourced its data to the cloud server. The user wants to execute the query from the outsourced data, and mainly focus on the nearest neighbor search inherently

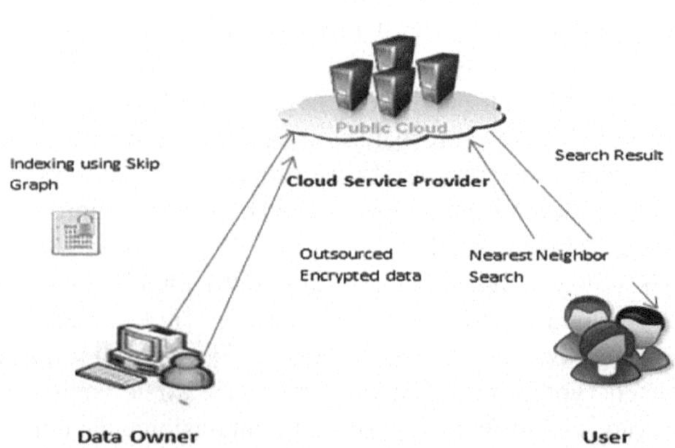

Fig. 1. System architecture

multidimensional view. As we know the cloud server is honest-but-curious to the data owner and user, which may result in the leakage of the user query. For this, it is required to encrypt the outsourced data as well as the query submitted to the cloud server.

Our proposed model consists of three parties in the cloud environment.

Data Owner: A data owner is one who manages a database D with d dimensional points outsourced the database to a cloud server and in encrypted form e(D) and no local backup is there.

Cloud Service Provider: It provides the cloud storage and computing services to store the encrypted database e(D) and on that run queries for the user.

User: A user who requests the query Q from the database and result in the formation of the data point in the database.

Based on the above model, define our nearest neighbor search. To achieve the fast and efficient query result, built a secure index using the skip graph. Then indexed all the data records and each data record is a point of data space. For the privacy of the query, encrypt the contents of the query by a secure cryptography scheme E. To search the encrypted data from the cloud server we submit both the encrypted index data and the query e(D) and cloud server returns the nearest point to the q as (q1,.....qd).

3.2 Security Model

The cloud service providers are honest as well as curious to know the additional information stored and processed by a user. This assumes that the cloud service provider provides data storage and return correct answer to the user. A user has authenticated the user as there is mutual trust between the data owner and a user. The secret key is reasonable means of authentication and establishes a secure channel between the data owner and user.

4 Methodology

In this section, provide our methodology. For efficient and secure nearest neighbor search, make a choice for the better data structure for secure indexes, than search algorithm designed and then compare the encrypted query and secure indexes with high efficiency. To manage the data in the cloud, the data owner built the secure index and outsourced the encrypted data to the cloud server. The cloud service provider performs the required nearest neighbor search on the secure index e(q) of the user. As the data and query, both are in encrypted form, and the cloud service provider cannot be able to learn anything about the data searched. And the user gets the nearest neighbor search to the point q as in result.

4.1 Secure Skip Graph Indexing

In this paper used a hybrid approach, secure k-D tree [16] on the d dimensional data and organize nodes according to the membership key in skip graph (SG). For secure indexing, encryption the data content, to make it safe form the cloud environment. To efficiently search the encrypted data on the cloud, adopt the mOPE (mutable order-preserving encoding), which enables us to compare the search query point with the encrypted data. So construct the index then encrypt it before outsourced it to the cloud.

SG Index Construction

In this, use the hybrid approach as shown in Figs. 2 and 3; firstly partitioned the set of data points by secure k-D tree space decomposition method. Then further split the set of points into equal cardinality using horizontal and vertical splits. Each splitting nodes organized in their region without overlapping. After that, arrange the data points into a skip graph using the region codes as the membership keys. For retrieving the data point, use the standard routing in skip graph structure i.e. starting from the highest level node and routes the query to the neighboring data nodes. As the query reaches the destination data query point, the progressively lower level is used. It is highly efficient for the fast nearest neighbor query.

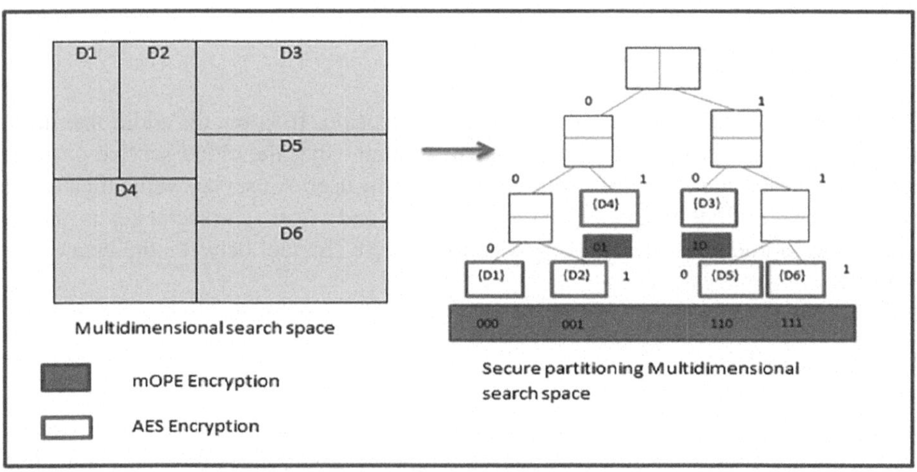

Fig. 2. Partition the multidimensional search space by secure k-D tree

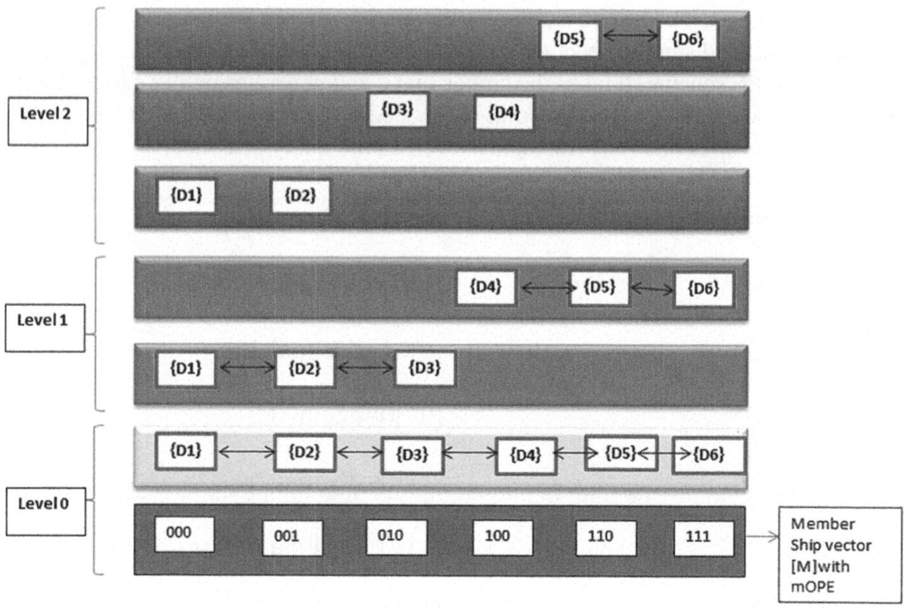

Fig. 3. Indexing encrypted data nodes in skip graph.

SG Index Encryption

The SG index structure is then encrypted using the mOPE (mutable Order-Preserving Encryption scheme) as shown in Fig. 3, and the actual data is encrypted with a secure symmetric encryption method, AES. In this, use mOPE to encrypt the SG index into secure indexes. So each node in the graph contains cipher-text C for indexed data point based on the order of its plain text. The cloud server does not know the actual plaintext data. The SG index is encrypted into cipher-text C and preserves the order of plaintext by using mOPE encoding.

5 Proposed Secure Nearest Neighbor Scheme

Our proposed scheme includes the encryption of the data, secures indexing of data and encrypts the user query. In this section presents the detailed working of our proposed scheme. It consists of the following algorithms.

Generate key (GK): GK(1^k) → (SK_d, SK_{OPE})

In this step, the data owner generates a secret key (SK_d), which is used to encrypt the both data D and Query q. SK_{OPE} is a secret key generates while index construction.

Built Secure Index: SGIndex (SK_{OPE} , D, m) → c, Order(c) → E

In the first step from the given data set, the data owner uses the SG index to build the securely encrypted index. It takes the input as secret key SK_{OPE}, Data set D and the membership vector m, and output the cipher-text c. It is used to generate encrypted data using the secret key. The secure SG index and encrypted text both stored on the cloud server. In the second step, we encode the encrypted data using membership key in skip graph with mOPE scheme. It takes the cipher-text c and generates output e using mOPE scheme. As shown in Fig. 4 the data point is encoded by construction the mOPE scheme, and cloud server does not know the data as well as the query searched.

Membership key	mOPE Encoding
000[D1]	[]000=decimal 0
001[D2]	[0]01=decimal 1
010[D3]	[01]0=decimal 2
100[D4]	[1]00=decimal 4
110[D5]	[11]0=decimal 6
111[D6]	[11]1=decimal 7

Fig. 4. mOPE table

Encryption: Enc(SK_d, D) → e(D), Enc(SK_d, q) → e(q)

The data owner encrypts all the data points in database D{d1, d2,……..dn) using secret key (SK_d), data stored on cloud server in encrypted form e(D) {[d1], [d2], [dn]}. AES is the encryption algorithm used in our scheme. After this, the data owner outsourced the encrypted database e(D), Secure SG Index c, and mOPE encoding E to the cloud server. The registered users can access the data from the cloud server with their generated secret key.

Secure Nearest Neighbor Search: NNSearch(e(q), c(q)) → eq

This step is performed on the cloud server in encrypted data. When the user generates query q, it runs on data stored on the cloud server, and the cloud serves to search the secure SG Index c. After receiving user query q, the cloud server encodes c(q) using the encoding scheme and denotes it as e(q). Now the cloud server traverses the indexed data source while traversing the SG index have to compute the secure distance of data point from the query point and then select the minimum distance among all the data point according to the query point. After that, return the corresponding nearest neighbor data query point in encrypted form e(q). The detailed algorithm given in Fig. 5.

```
SECURENN Algo {NNSearch(e(q), c(q))→eq}
Input: the encrypted query and secure SGIndex
Output: DecryptedRange of NN queries.
  1. For i←1 to n do
  2. If c(q)I is in the mOPE table then
     Compute its mOPE encoding E(q)I
  3. For j←1 to w
  4.         "Get the encryption key"
                 Get e(q) and c(q)
  5. Select the region R from where the nearest neighbor located
  6. While(e(q) not empty) do
  7.     E(d)← (secDis(E(q), c(q))
  8. End while
  9. Minum←Secmin (E(d1),E(d2),...........(E(dw))
  10. Get the secure minimum distance as minum==E(dj)
  11. Get the result query as Res
  12. Resi(e(qj), E(dj)
  13. NN←DecKey (dq,Resi)
  14. secDis(E(qi),,di)→(E|qi-di|^2)
  15. {
  16. set Q1 and P1;
  17. Q1={E(q),sk}
  18. P1= E(|q-dj|^2)
  19. Return P2
  20. }
  21. Secmin(E(d1,...........(E(dn))→[dmin]
  22. {
  23. P1 has (E[d1],. . . , E[dn]); P2 has sk
  24. P1:
        a. [d'i]←[di], for 1 ≤i ≤n
        b. num←n
  25: P1 and P2, for i = 1 to ⌈log2 n⌉:
     (a). for 1 ≤j ≤ num2 :
        if i = 1 then
              [d'2j-1]←SMIN([d'2j-1], [d'2j])
              [d'2j]←0
        else
                 [d'2i(j-1)+1]←SMIN([d'2i(j-1)+1], [d'2ij-1])
                 [d'2ij-1]←0
     (b). num← [num/2]
     P1:
     (a.) [dmin]←[d'1]
}
```

Fig. 5. Algorithm for secure nearest neighbor search

Decryption: DecKey(e_q, SK_d) → dq

To check the output, the user needs to decrypt the query result using secret key (SK_d). Once the user decrypts the output received, the corresponding nearest neighbor query point retrieved.

6 Security Analysis

6.1 Data Privacy

In our scheme, the database is encrypted using the secret key before outsourced it to the cloud server. So without the secret decryption key, the data cannot be decoded into plaintext. It also analyze that the cloud service provider cannot analyses the information from the encrypted data. But in case, if the attacker gets the access to the encrypted text, plain text cannot be decrypted the secret key. Because indexing is done in encrypted, it becomes difficult for the attacker or the cloud service provider to deduce the plaintext from the ciphertext. So we analyze that the cloud service provider can access the encrypted index but nothing more than that.

6.2 Query Privacy

The encoding scheme is used to encode the encrypted query with the secure index, the cloud service provider allowed to search the secure index for the required encrypted query search. But as the query and database both are encrypted, the cloud server can learn e(q) and the encrypted index c. The cloud server can generate the query result in an encrypted form. Hence, our scheme doesn't provide and information access to the cloud service provider or attacker.

7 Experimental Evaluation

In this proposed scheme, developed a Java based code and tested under simulated environment. AES scheme is used for encryption. For the experiment, use two data sets, a synthetic data set uniformly distributed and a real graph data set from road networks from the central USA. Then performed test over above datasets with different scale and selected 30 random nearest neighbor queries, and evaluated. Here, used the three metrics for evaluation of proposed scheme over the existing nearest neighbor scheme i.e. (1) data processing time (2) query response time and communication cost at the user end.

7.1 Data Processing Time

It consists of two phase at the data owner end in the first phase, create the index and in the second phase, encrypt the data for secure indexing. We observe that the data processing time increases with the increase in data size as shown in Fig. 6. We also observe that the both the scheme linearly increases with the increase in data. The time consumed in the second phase is less as compared to the first phase because of the encryption time as shown in Fig. 7. However, this is the only one-time index building cost for efficient, optimized query processing time.

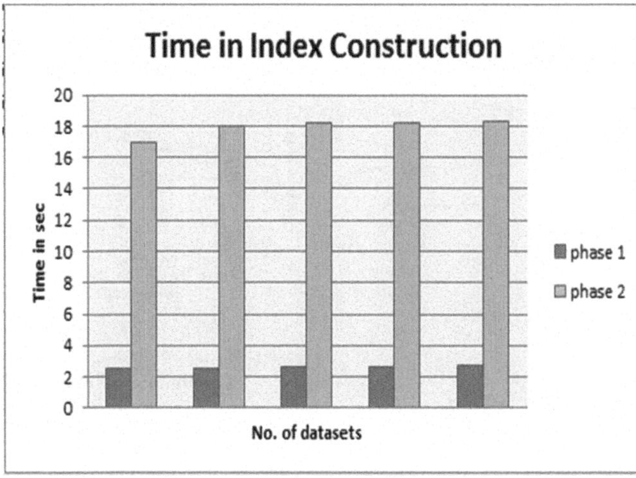

Fig. 6. Time for index construction by data owner.

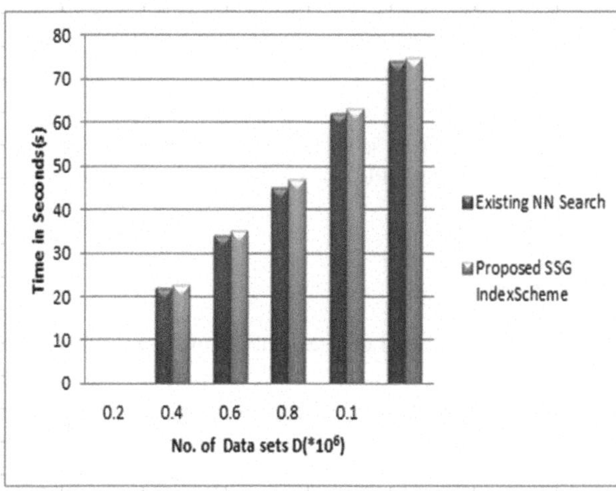

Fig. 7. Data processing times is taken by data owner

7.2 Query Response Time

Our performance metrics indicate the time required to execute the query on the above datasets. It includes the computation time at the user end, proxy server, and the cloud server. Since all the values here are treated in the same way, they are encrypted. Our query response time is slightly better than the existing scheme as shown in Fig. 8. It concludes the query processing time according to the CPU response time into end user, server communication time on real datasets. We achieve the lower end user CPU time, fewer servers CPU and better performance on interactive communication time between the user and cloud server as consuming in existing schemes.

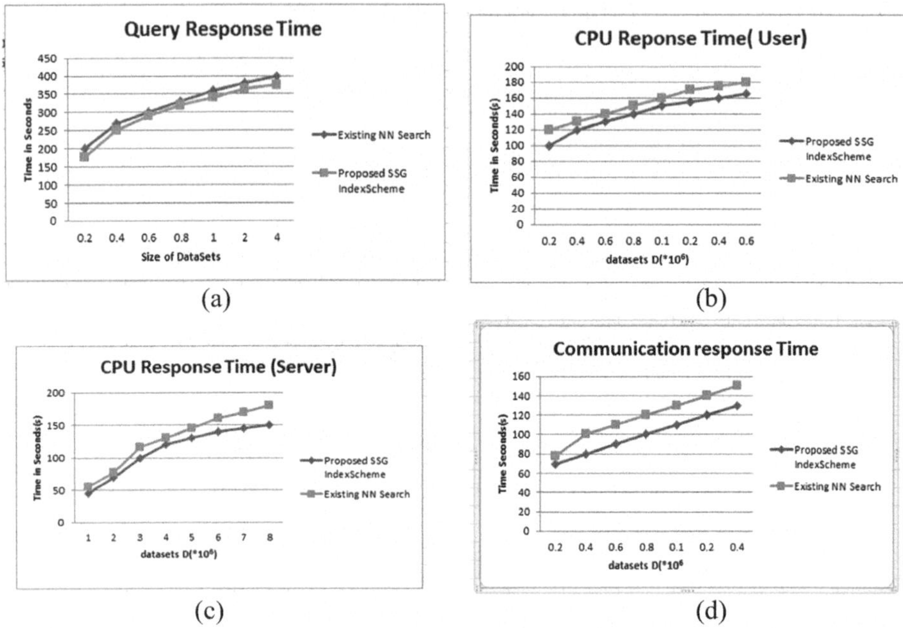

Fig. 8. (a) Query response time in proposed scheme. (b) Query response time in the user CPU. (c) Query response time by the server CPU. (d) Communication cost between the user and the cloud server.

7.3 Communication Cost

The amount of data communicated between the cloud server and the end user. Our scheme achieves the negligible amount of communication cost as compared to the other schemes as shown in Fig. 9. It is because of the indexing structures used and the better data partition scheme. Also, our scheme provides better interaction between user and cloud server, and better result due to mutable order-preserving encryption.

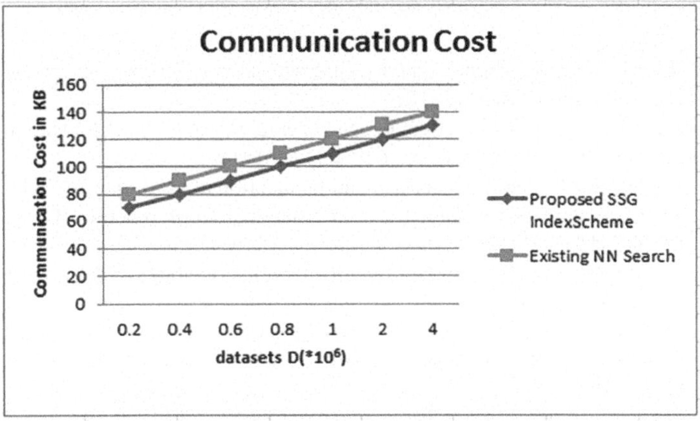

Fig. 9. Communication cost for user

8 Conclusion

In this paper proposed a new and efficient scheme for the secure nearest neighbor search in the encrypted data. In this outsourced the data and secure index to the cloud service provider in the encrypted form. Due to the encrypted data, the computation of the query becomes complex difficult. So required to use the better encoding scheme OPE, we use mutable order preserving scheme. It protects both the secure index and the query. It provides the protection of privacy of data content on the cloud server. From the extensive experiment evaluation; found our scheme is more efficient and scalable as compared to the existing schemes. In future, extend our work to support other environments and similarity queries.

References

1. Yang, Z., Ren, K., Cao, N., Wang, C., Lou, W.: Privacy-preserving query over encrypted graph structured data in cloud computing. In: 2011 31st International Conference on Distributed Computing (ICDCS), pp. 393–402. IEEE (2011)
2. Cheng, K., Wang, H., Wang, L.: Secure k-NN query on encrypted cloud data with multiple keys. IEEE Trans. Big Data, 1–14 (2015)
3. Gao, Y., Miao, M., Wang, J.: Secure approximate nearest neighbor search over encrypted data. In: 9th International Conference on Broadband and Wireless Computing, Communication and Applications, pp. 578–583 (2014)
4. Choi, S., Ghinita, G., Lim, H.-S., Bertino, E.: Secure KNN query processing in untrusted cloud environments. IEEE J. Trans. Knowl. Data Eng., 1–14 (2013)
5. Ghinita, G., Kalnis, P., Khoshgozaran, A., Shahabi, C., Tan, K.: Private queries in LBS: anonymizers are not necessary. In: SIGMOD (2008)
6. Papamanthou, C., Kamara, S.: Parallel and dynamic searchable symmetric encryption. In: Proceeding of FC (2013)

7. Li, F., Yao, B., Xiao, X.: Secure nearest neighbor revisited. In: Proceeding of IEEE ICDE (2013)
8. Wang, B., Li, M., Hou, Y.: Practical and secure nearest neighbor search on encrypted large scale data. In: IEEE INFOCOM (2016)
9. Yi, X., Bertino, E., Paulet, R.: Practical K-nearest neighbor queries with location privacy. In: Proceeding of the 30th IEEE ICDE, pp. 640–651 (2014)
10. Chen, Q., Hu, H., Xu, J.: Privacy preserving authentication of range queries in location-based services. In: Proceeding of the 29th IEEE International Conference on Data Engineering (ICDE), pp. 1312–1315 (2013)
11. Wong, W., et al.: Secure kNN computation on encrypted databases. In: Proceeding of ACM SIGMOD, pp. 139–152 (2009)
12. Xu, J., Ren, C., Hu, H., Choi, B.: Processing private queries over untrusted data cloud through privacy homomorphism. In: Proceeding of IEEE ICDE, pp. 601–612 (2011)
13. Samanthula, B., Elmehdwi, Y., Jiang, W.: Secure K-NN query over encrypted data in outsourced environments. In: Proceeding of ICDE (2014)
14. Atallah, M.J., Qi, Y.: Efficiently privacy preserving k-nearest neighbor search. In: Proceeding of IEEE ICDCS, pp. 311–319 (2008)
15. Kushilevitz, E., Ostrovsky, R.: Replication: single database, computationally-private information reterival. In: Proceeding of IEEE FOCS (1997)
16. Peng, Y., Li, H., Cui, J., Zhu, Y., Peng, C.: An efficient range query model over encrypted outsourced data using secure k-d tree. In: Proceeding of International Conference on Networking and Network Applications, pp. 250–253 (2015)

RREQ Flood Attack and Its Mitigation in Ad Hoc Network

Shweta Rani, Bhawna Narwal(✉), and Amar K. Mohapatra

Indira Gandhi Delhi Technical University for Women, New Delhi, India
shwetarg.it@gmail.com, bhawnanarwal@gmail.com, mohapatra.amar@gmail.com

Abstract. RREQ Flood Attack is one of the prominent attack in Wireless Adhoc Network. In the flood attack, a malicious node fills up all the routing tables with its own packets and hence communication between source and destination becomes paralyzed. To secure against flooding attack, a mitigation scheme is proposed which uses Time to Live value to mark and remove the malicious node that floods the network. In the proposed scheme, RREQ limit is set which is dynamically checked after certain period so that the flood attack does not occur. The Simulation of the proposed scheme is done by Qualnet and the result shows that the scheme prevents the flooding attack, reduces the end-to-end delay and increases the throughput.

Keywords: AODV flood attack · Qualnet · Route request (RREQ) Route reply (RREP) · Time to Live

1 Introduction

Wireless devices such as Mobile phones, Computer, Tablets, Laptops, Printer are making our day to day life activities such as E-Commerce, E-printing, E-Learning etc. easier [14]. High usage of digital formatted data started with rapid growth of Infrastructure based network as well as infrastructure less network [15]. Infrastructure less network allows communication between nodes without the help of routers and called Ad Hoc network [3]. The wireless Ad Hoc network is a decentralized network, which creates routes on demand and mobility is achieved throughout the network. This network is useful when there is no current infrastructure and there is a requirement to communicate for business meetings. Hence it becomes easy to share reports, ideas or diagrams among each other on demand basis. Thus, without the help of routers switches or cables can communicate. Nowadays, many applications can run through mobile networks such as banking activities, social networking etc. Moreover, there is a limitation of available re-sources like frequency, bandwidth, response time or pressure etc. Many attacks are possible on Ad Hoc networks as it enables to join the network anywhere and everywhere. A single attacking node can grab a large area of network thus secure and reliability of the communication is required.

There are many routing techniques related to Ad Hoc network [13]. Proactive routing is to maintain a fresh list of neighbor nodes after a fixed time interval. The route is selected based on the minimum distance between two routes. No additional delay

B. Panda et al. (Eds.): REDSET 2017, CCIS 799, pp. 599–607, 2018.
https://doi.org/10.1007/978-981-10-8527-7_50

occurs in Proactive routing protocol. Reactive routing protocol maintains the fresh route for each coming request and does not require information of all the neighboring routes. Route is selected by sending the RREQ packet to each node, which in return sends RREP. Thus, this packet contains information about the source address, destination address as well as one hop distance node. All these parameters help in finding the shortest path.

AODV protocol is an on demand distance vector routing protocol [13]. That uses the bi-directional links to communicate with each other. AODV protocol works in two phases. In route discovery phase (first phase), node sends the Route Request RREQ packet to each node to find the path to communicate. Path is said to be discovered if node is itself a destination or node has a successful entry in its routing table [13]. Each node maintains the precursor list which contains list of all the neighbors that are one hop away from the node that is used in case of link breakage. Sequence number tells about the newness and freshness of routes. Out of all routes the minimized route is the best route to be selected. But the drawback of this route is, if one link breaks than it is unable to make alternative path to communicate. Route discovery part [12] is when a node sends RREQ packet to a node for communication to a destination and it immediately set up a reverse path for particular node in routing table. Using that reverse path RREP packet is sent where sequence number is observed to check the updated value of sequence number. In route maintenance phase, protocol is used to check links which gives feedback about the links of the route and the routes are modified in case of any link breakage.

RREQ flood attack fills the routing table of neighbor with RREQ packets by which communication between the two nodes gets choked. As routing table is filled by flooding packets and only very less number of data packets are able to reach the destination as attacker takes advantage of the principle of this system like resource sharing, openness and so on. Hence it is required to detect and mitigate the attack. Mobility in nodes makes the situation worse as it changes the network topology frequently which makes it difficult to address the attack. This attack consumes the network bandwidth a lot as the network gets saturated due to bombarding of a large number of packets. Unnecessary packets lead to wastage of bandwidth and energy of network which leads to congestion in network, called as flooding attack. Attacker selects IP address which is not the part of network to congest larger area. A malicious node is called an attacking node which sabotages the whole network.

The rest of the paper is organized as follows in Sect. 2, related work is described. Section 3 illustrates the proposed mitigation algorithm. In Sect. 4 simulation scenario and parameters used are described. In Sect. 4 the performance of attacking and mitigation is described and Sect. 5 concludes the paper.

2 Related Work

Li and Li [7] proposed a method of attack and analyzed the results of UDP over TCP. In this paper, the authors showed how attack intensity relates to attack timings. Buffer size relates more with attack timing hence it controls the flood traffic. It also shows that UDP type attack is stronger than the TCP attack. However, in this paper no method is specified for mitigation of attack. Balakrishnan et al. [1] proposed an algorithm to identify and eliminate the nodes that are flooding the network. In this work, shared resource technique is used based on shares, firstly nodes compare the shares and then only communicates with each other. Moreover, trace back of nodes is not possible as no source or destination address is used in this technique. Venkataraman [10] focused on trust evaluation and establishment in Ad Hoc networks. The author proposed trust function to mitigate the flooding attack. This approach is based on the friendship between the nodes. It makes node co-operative in nature and prevents flooding attacks. The unnecessary traffic is reduced and hence the node can process the legitimate traffic. Yi [11] proposed new neighbor suppression and path cut-off technique. In this paper priority is decreased per rate of incoming queries. Low priority queries are discarded side by side when node identifies that sender is originating data flooding, it cuts off path and send error message. Moreover, flooding packet still exists in the network. Pires [8] presented the technique of evaluating the flood attack in WSN network. In this paper the author compared the expected and the actual signal strengths of the received signal. By using the signal strength, it becomes easy to find out the malicious one if it consumes high power. Kum et al. [6] presented the technique that effectively identifies the broadcast storm problem suitable for WMNs by using the count value check to restrict the propagation of RREQs packets destined towards gateways to limit the retransmission of RREQ packets.

3 Proposed Approach for Mitigation of Flood Attack

Flood attack is a breach in the security of MANET. RREQ flood attack leads to filled up the routing tables with the entries of RREQ packet so that no further communication is possible [2]. In this paper, a Time to Live (ttl) based technique is proposed to counter the flooding attack. The proposed approach can efficiently identify and isolate the malicious node that floods the network.

Firstly, the destination IP address is selected which is out of range of network. An Event is created which will repeat itself in duration of 100 ms. Following parameters are important to perform attack:

- RREQ: Message Field Modifications for attack [5].
- The Event: New event case is generated, which is initialized in INIT function.
- Hop count: Increase the hop count value.
- The Destination IP Address: Replace with another IP address outside the range.

In the proposed approach we use Ad Hoc on Demand Distance Vector (AODV) as routing protocol. This protocol notifies the mobile node about the link breakage that invalidates the lost link. In the literature, the RREQ value was limited but no reset option was considered hence the attacker can perform flooding very easily [4, 9]. Some of the authors suggested in the literature hop count as a metric to counter the flood attack but it may be possible that the attacker may be placed in the same network and can perform attack from all directions. In the proposed approach, the focus was to reset the time period. After fixed interval of time, all counter and timing needs to reset. To minimize the attack, it is important to repeatedly check the time period. In earlier work, only hop-count was considered but it may be possible that many more attackers sit on that same network and can attack from all direction. Hence malicious node can send large number of packets so that routing table can be filled [1]. This results in paralyzing the legal legitimate communication.

In the proposed approach, ttl value and RREQ accept-limit for the source address is considered as the parameter to identify malicious nodes. At an interval of every four second, counter is reset and current time is updated. If, the Counter reaches to twenty, then the source node is considered as legal node. We have included the delay of four seconds between current node and last node. The proposed algorithm is presented in Fig. 1.

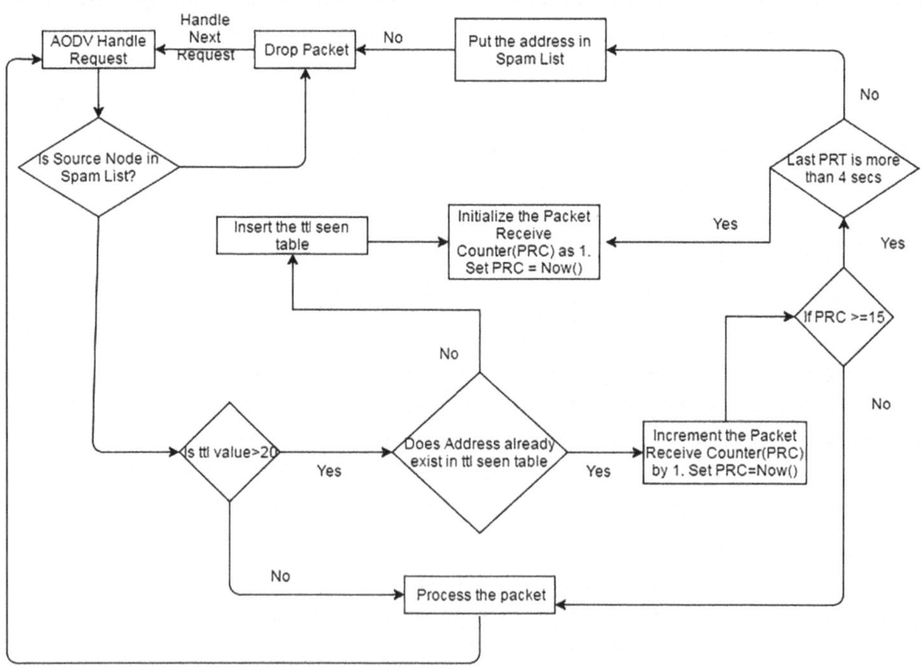

Fig. 1. AODV mitigation flowchart

The complete algorithm is shown in Table 1 depicting the mitigation of flood attack.

Table 1. Algorithm for flood attack mitigation.

```
If a node receives RREQ flooding packet from node[i]
  if node[i] is in "isInSpam"
 Drop packet;
 else if (ttl <20)
   Process as normal packet;
 else if(SameAddress(ttlSeenAddress, SrcAddress)
         PacketReceiveCounter++;
if (PRC <=15)
    process normally;
   else if (packetRecieveTimer, PRT< 4 seconds)
   put in SpamTable;
  else
       reinitialise PRC=1;
    PRT=now ();
else
          put in ttlSeenTable;
```

If the node is found to be a malicious node then that node is deleted from the ttlSeenTable and is inserted into spam table. This condition is put in aodvhandlerequest and if node is present in aodvSpamTable then drop all the packets.

4 Simulation Environment

In this section, the performance of attack and mitigation with AODV is compared using Qualnet simulator through packet level simulation [13]. We have considered an area of 1500 m × 1500 m. The performance was evaluated by increasing the no of nodes (Table 2).

Table 2. Simulation parameters.

Parameters	Value
Simulation time	30 s
Area	1500 × 1500
Number of channels	1
Mobility	1 m/s
Traffic type	CBR
Mobility model	Random waypoint
No. of nodes	10, 20, 30, 50, 60, 80, 90, 100
Protocol	AODV

The above mentioned parameters in Table 1 were used to simulate the proposed approach. Figure 2 shows the scenario in which 50 nodes are taken with mobility of 1 m/s.

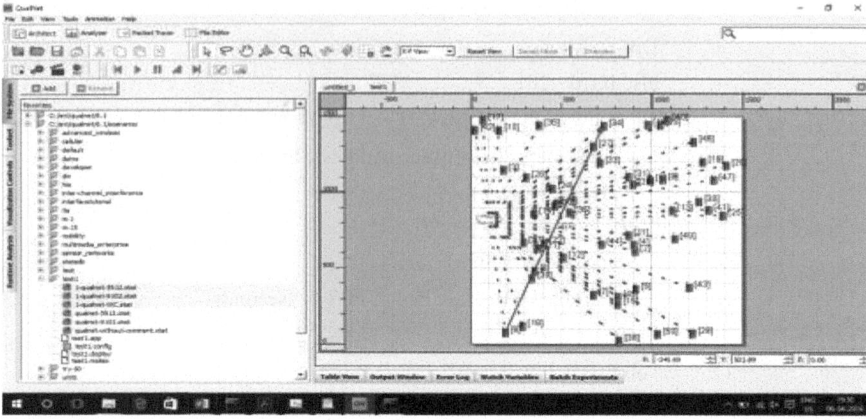

Fig. 2. Simulation scenario

4.1 Performance Parameters

The performance of the proposed scheme is measured in terms of throughput, end-to-end delay, total unicast messages [4, 9, 10, 13].

4.1.1 Throughput

Throughput or network throughput is the average rate of successful message delivery over a communication channel. Throughput is measured in bits per second [10].

Throughput = [(Total Bytes Sent * 8)/(Time Last Packet Sent − Time First Packet Sent)] where 'time' is in seconds. [9].

Figure 3 Shows the total throughput of the proposed algorithm.

The simulation results show that, if a node is introduced which causes flood attack in the network then throughput is 34.97%, however, the proposed mitigation increases the throughput to 46.95%.

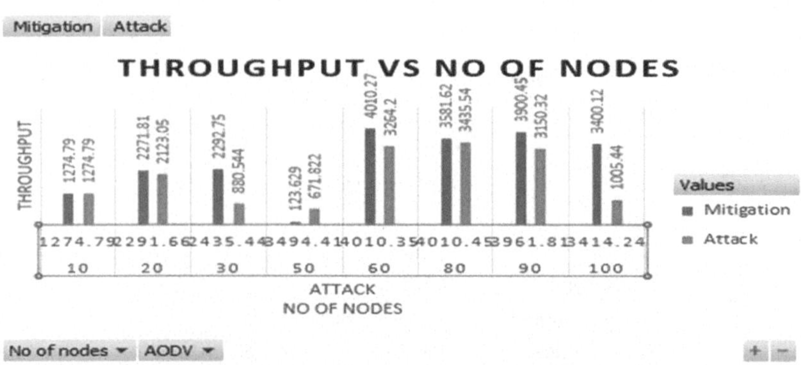

Fig. 3. Simulation results: total throughput

4.1.2 End-to-End Delay

End-to-End Delay refers to the time taken for a packet to be transmitted across a network from source to destination [4]. Figure 4 shows the introduction of the malicious nodes which floods the packets increased the delay to 202.24% whereas after the proposed mitigation AODV protocol decreased the delay to 53.97%.

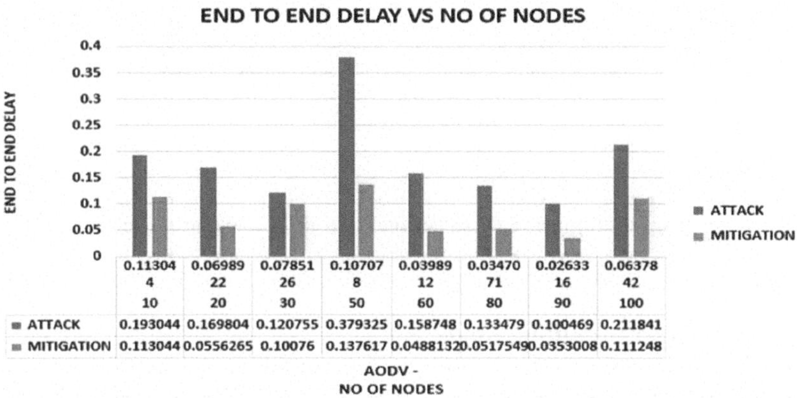

Fig. 4. Simulation results: average end-to-end delay

4.1.3 Total Unicast Mesages

Total unicast messages are the total no of received messages. Figure 5 Shows that, if an attack node is introduced in the network, the total no-of received messages are decreased to 42.13%. In contrary, if the proposed mitigation AODV protocol was used then received number of messages increased to 84.60%.

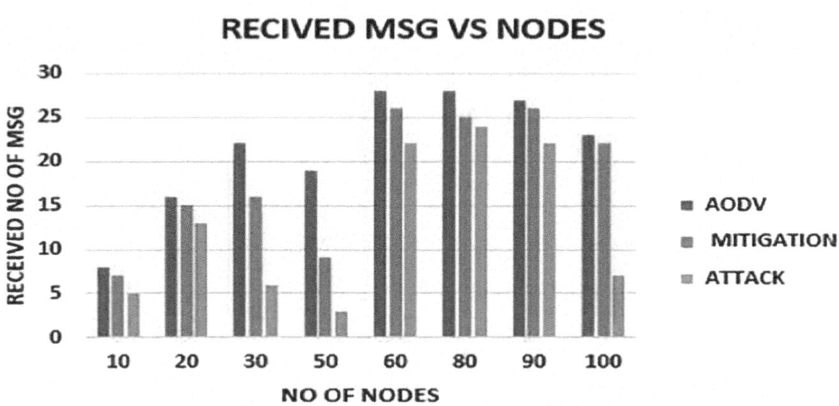

Fig. 5. Simulation results: total receive number of messages

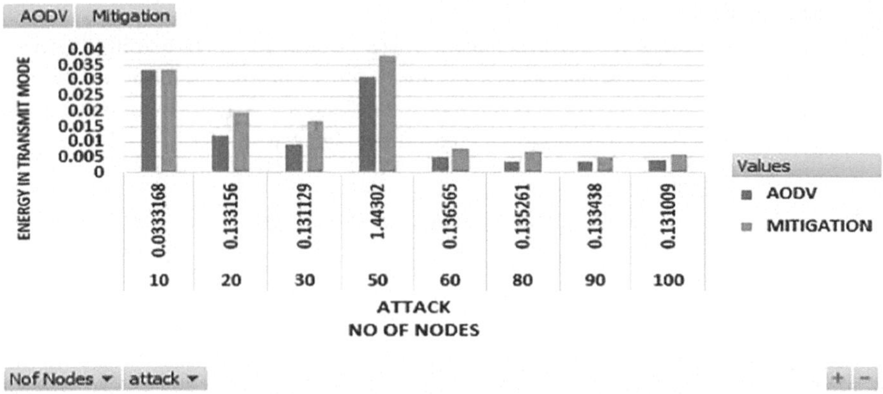

Fig. 6. Simulation results: total energy in transmit mode

4.1.4 Energy in Transmitting Mode

Figure 6 Shows, if a flood attack node is introduced in the network then energy consumption in transceiver mode increased to 2520.25%. When proposed mitigation AODV protocol was used in the same network, then energy consumption decreased to 81.40%.

4.1.5 Energy in Receiving Mode

Figure 7 shows, if a flood attack node was introduced, then energy in receiving mode increased upto 1920.65%. When the proposed mitigation AODV protocol was used in the same network then the energy consumption decreased upto 71.34%.

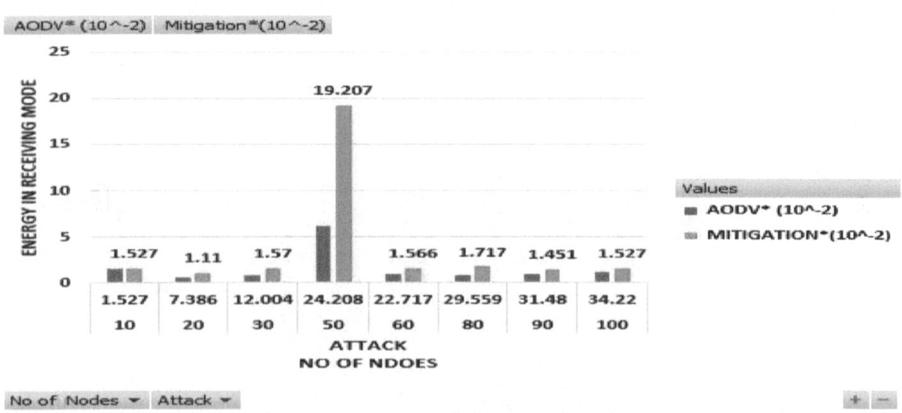

Fig. 7. Simulation results: total energy in receiving mode

5 Conclusion

In this paper, the proposed AODV uses ttl value to limit the scope of rebroadcast of route request packets during route discovery. Simulation results showed proposed mitigation scheme can reduce end-to-end delay through RREQ packets and can enhance overall throughput compared to attacking scenario. In future work the proposed approach can be applied in sensor network to make them more secure.

References

1. Balakrishnan, V., Varadhrajan, V., Tupakula, U.: Mitigating flooding attacks in mobile ad-hoc networks supporting anonymous communications. In: Wireless Broadband and Ultra Wideband Communications, vol. 2, p. 29 (2007)
2. Bandyopadhyay, A., Vuppala, S., Choudhury, P.: A simulation analysis of flooding attack in MANET using NS-3. In: Wireless Communication, Vehicular Technology, Information Theory and Aerospace & Electronic Systems Technology (Wireless VITAE), pp. 1–5 (2011)
3. Chauhan, N., Yadav, S.: Flooding attacks prevention in MANET. Int. J. Comput. Technol. Electron. Eng. **1**(3), 68–72 (2011)
4. Choudhury, P., Nandi, S., Paul, A., Debnath, N.: Mitigating route request flooding attack in MANET using node reputation. In: IEEE 10th International Conference on Industrial Informatics, vol. 10, pp. 1010–1015 (2012)
5. Guo, Y., Perreau, S.: Trace flooding attack in mobile ad hoc networks. In: International Conference on Intelligent Sensors, Sensors Networks and Information, vol. 3, pp. 329–334 (2007)
6. Kum, D., Le, A., Cho, Y., Toh, C., Lee, I.: An efficient on-demand routing approach with directional flooding for wireless mesh networks. J. Commun. Netw. **2**(1), 67–73 (2010)
7. Li, M., Li, J.: Simulation study of flood attacking of DDOS. In: International Conference on Internet Computing in Science and Engineering, pp. 286–293 (2008)
8. Pires, W., Figueiredo, T., Wong, H., Loureiro, A.: Malicious node detection in wireless sensor networks. In: Proceedings of the 18th International Parallel and Distributed Processing Symposium, vol. 18, p. 24 (2004)
9. Song, J., Hong, F., Zhang, Y.: Effective filtering scheme against RREQ flooding attack in mobile ad hoc networks. In: Proceedings of the 7th International Conference on Parallel and Distributed Computing, Applications and Technologies, vol. 7, pp. 497–502 (2006)
10. Venkatraman, R., Pushpalatha, M., RamaRao, T.: Performance analysis of flooding attack, prevention algorithm in MANETs. Int. J. Comput. Electr. Autom. Control Inf. Eng. **3**(8), 2056–2059 (2009)
11. Yi, P., Dai, Z., Zhong, Y., Zhang, Z.: Resisting flooding attacks in ad hoc networks. In: Proceedings of the International Conference on Information Technology: Coding and Computing (ITCC 2005), vol. 2, pp. 657–662 (2005)
12. RFC 3561 of AODV protocol
13. www.Qualnet/6.1/documentation
14. Grover, N., Mohapatra, A.K.: Digital image authentication model based on edge adaptive steganography. In: Proceedings of the 2013 2nd International Conference on Advanced Computing, Networking and Security, pp. 238–242. IEEE Computer Society, December 2013
15. Khandelwal, A., Mohapatra, A.K.: An insight into the security issues and their solutions for android phones. In: 2015 2nd International Conference on Computing for Sustainable Global Development (INDIACom) (2015)

A Study on Integrating Crypto-Stego Techniques to Minimize the Distortion

Neha Sharma(✉) and Usha Batra

G D Goenka University, Gurugram 122003, Haryana, India
nehasharma0110@gmail.com, usha.batra@gdgoenka.ac.in

Abstract. Now a days on-line services has end up as a big part of our lives that performs communication electronically. This e-communication requires confidentiality and information integrity to protect from unauthorized users. Security can be provided by using two widespread techniques i.e., cryptography and steganography. However, no single technique in itself is well acquainted to cater to our needs in implementing a secure, and robust system. Steganography helps in hiding the data behind the cover image. But once known secret message can be captured very easily. Moreover, by embedding the data into the image medium, we increase the risk of distortion. If the distorted image is sent over the communication channel, the intruder can easily guess that some secret data has been sent and that secret data can be easily recovered. As we know, cryptography ciphers the text so that the secret data sent over the communication link cannot be understood. But if both the security mechanisms can be integrated we can come up with a system which is more secure and robust. This paper presents the study of hybrid crypto-stego techniques so as to reduce distortion by maintaining the imperceptibility, robustness and providing high security for the e-communication between two authorized parties.

Keywords: Cryptography · Steganography · Encryption · Decryption

1 Introduction

E-activities such as communication, business, and online transactions have tremendously increased. Internet has become powerful mechanism to perform these activities. Users ting their sharing their personal matters on social networking sites. While performing online transactions like purchasing items online, funds transfer etc., security and privacy has become a foremost concern. On the other hand, intruders have become so active and they are able to obtain secret information, due to the availability of sophisticated hacking tools. Therefore, in order to provide security to confidential information over the network, the two traditional techniques can be taken into consideration like cryptography and steganography. Cryptography [1] is the secure transmission of confidential data over the internet by using some encryption algorithms to protect against adversaries. Steganography [2] technique is used to send the secret message by hiding information in digital media files. Such highly secure data transfer is either known by the sender or the receiver. Researchers either use cryptography or steganography to

B. Panda et al. (Eds.): REDSET 2017, CCIS 799, pp. 608–615, 2018.
https://doi.org/10.1007/978-981-10-8527-7_51

provide security. Both the techniques have their own advantages. In cryptography, it is always known to the unauthorized party that the message has been sent over the communication link and the intruder tries to break that encryption in order to read the secret message or for any malicious use. Whereas in steganography the unauthorized party does not have any idea about the communication. The image with the secret message embedded in it, is sent to the intended recipient. The receiver extracts the message with the extraction process. A steganographic process in combination with cryptography is illustrated in Fig. 1.

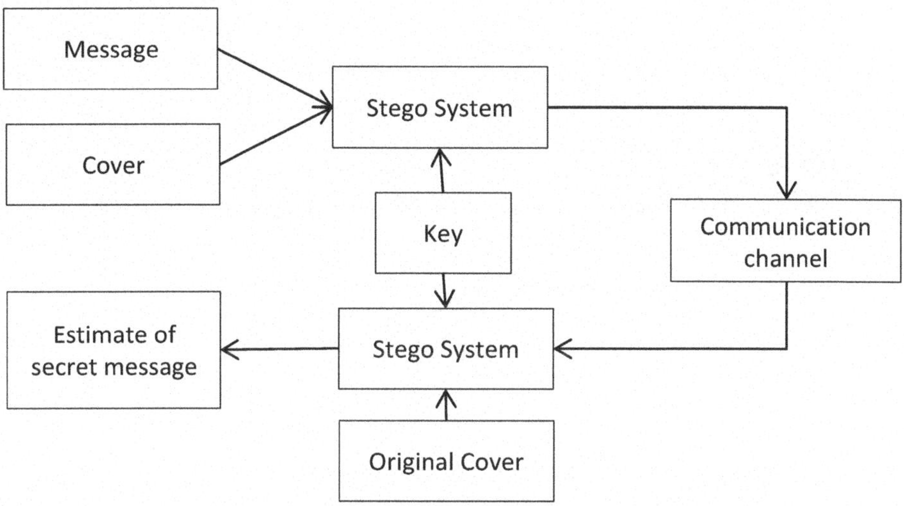

Fig. 1. Model of steganography process with cryptography [3].

Through Fig. 1, we can see that the secret message can be embedded to the cover object through a stego-key. Another key, can be used to encrypt the secret the message before embedding. Then this stego image is sent over the communication channel to the intended recipient. The receiver decodes the stego object through the stego-key and then decrypts the encoded message through either private key or public key.

This paper briefly outlines the related definitions and terminologies. Then moving towards Sect. 3, which contains the literature review and finally comes the conclusion in Sect. 4.

2 Definitions and Terminologies

2.1 Cryptography

The principle of cryptography technique is to modify the data content, make it resemble like an arbitrary code to accomplish the motivation behind securing the data content. Cryptography is derived from Greek word "krypto" meaning "hidden" and "graphene" meaning "writing" [6, 7]. Cryptography serves the purpose of secrecy, integrity, authentication, non-denial, accessibility and availability. The various cryptographic techniques are illustrated in Fig. 2.

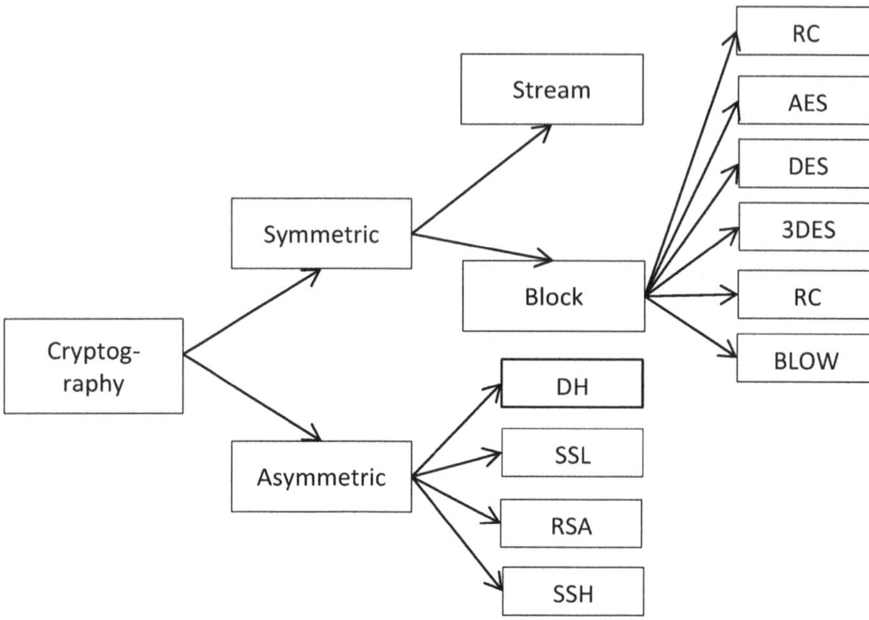

Fig. 2. Cryptographic techniques.

Cryptographic techniques are categorized as symmetric key cryptography and asymmetric key cryptography. The former technique makes use of one single key to encrypt and decrypt the data content and the later one focuses on two different keys. One key is used for encryption and the other for decryption. Algorithms such as DH, RSA, etc. all fall under the asymmetric cryptography. Symmetric key cryptographic technique is further categorized as block and stream ciphers. The algorithms such as RC, DES, AES, BlowFish, etc. are all the examples of block cipher.

2.2 Steganography

Steganography is a method or an art and science through which communication is done invisibly. It is accomplished by hiding information in some cover medium, thus hiding the existence of the information.

Steganography is derived from Greek word "stegos" meaning "cover" and "grafia" meaning "writing" [4] defining it as "covered writing". Steganography consists of 3 basic components as shown in Fig. 2. The cover object in the image is selected medium (audio, video, text, or image) to hide the message to be transmitted. Stego-key is used to hide into cover object and recover the original message from the cover object. Figure 3 represents the different steganographic components. The cover object in steganographic process is used to hide the information inside it, i.e. data is embedded inside the cover object. It may be a text, image, audio or video. Stego-key is used for embedding and recovering the data from cover object. Once the data is being embedded into the cover object, this results into the stego-object, which sent over the network for communication. This stego-object is then received by the intended recipient and with the help of stego-key, the user is able to recover the original data content.

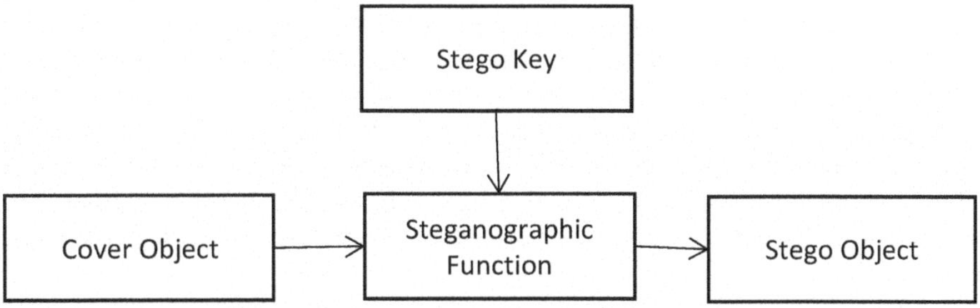

Fig. 3. Steganography components [5]

2.3 Combination of Cryptography and Steganography

Both the techniques have their own susceptibilities so integrating them may overcome several issues that these techniques may be facing individually and using it as this option can be a better idea (Fig. 4).

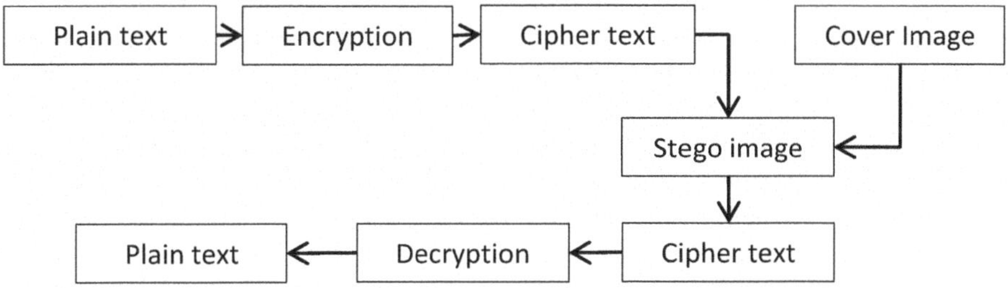

Fig. 4. Combination of cryptography and steganography [6]

The secret message that is sent by the sender takes the form of plain text. This plain text is then transformed to the cipher text using some encrypting algorithm. This cipher text is then used as an input to the steganography systems i.e. the cipher text is then used to embed into the cover image resulting in the stego-image. Now, the generated stego-image is transferred to the receiver over a communication link without revealing that the secret information has been transmitted. This is known as a direct approach [7] where cryptography and steganography both are combined; one is used for encrypting the secret message and the other, to conceal its existence.

3 Literature Review

This section briefly discusses some algorithms are used to minimize the distortion in order to enhance the security of secret message transmitted over a communication channel. Distortion Techniques hides the data content through signal distortion and then check for the difference value between original cover image and stego image to recover the hidden original data content. In-depth knowledge of decoding the original cover is required for using distortion techniques [8]. For example, Adam hides some data into cover object to get steganographic object; He hides the data in such a way that it corresponds to the secret message. Bobby measures the deviances from the original cover image and recreate the changes applied by Adam with respect to the secret message. Such systems are not useful in many applications as the receiver doesn't have that access. If for example, Richard also has access to them, so he can easily detect the entire communication.

The authors in [9], have used different error correcting codes in steganographic process. An ideal code is one that uses most of the data payload capacity or we can call it maximum embeddable (MLE). The method proposed by the author uses matrix encoding procedures that necessitates the sender and receiver to agree in advance on a parity check matrix. The authors have processed the cover medium in order to extract a sequence of symbols, which has to be updated into stego data so as to embed the message and any kind of modifications on stego data are transmitted on to the cover-medium to obtain the stego-object. In addition to this the authors have also discussed the relationships between steganographic algorithms and error correcting codes.

The authors in [10], have proposed image restoration technique for steganography. The cover image used is first blurred before hiding the secret message using special point spread function and then they had generated the key randomly. The information embedding is done through sequential LSB technique. The first row of the cover image is used to encrypt the number of rows and columns of the secret message to be embedded. Before inserting the original message the image is blurred using specific point spread function (PSF). A secured channel is used to send the secret key values. Two keys are used to recover the secret message from the cover image and randomly a third key is generated depending on the content & message. Table 1 represents the research articles for distortion techniques based on steganographic methods.

After taking into consideration algorithms used to minimize the distortion, now we highlight various research articles that combines the cryptography and steganographic techniques in order to enhance the robustness, payload capacity and imperceptibility.

The author in [11] has proposed a new technique for image steganography that is based on Discrete Wavelet Transformations and Huffman encoding in such a way and has obtained desired privacy, high capacity and good invisibility by achieving 54 db PSNR value. In [3], the author has proposed a technique by integrating hash LSB technique with RSA algorithm to be more secure and efficient. In order to provide strong authentication the authors in [5] have combined cryptography and steganography techniques, there by selecting a hashing algorithm. This procedure has improved the security and ensured a protected communication channel. In order to improve the security, visual cryptography and steganography were used together by [12]. The authors here are

Table 1. Distortion techniques based steganographic methods listed in chronological order.

Reference no.	Year of publication	Techniques used	Benefits	Additional constraints
[9]	2010	Error correction codes in steganography	Enhanced efficiency for embedding data	Performance evaluation is made through various parameters like, average distortion, embedding rate & expected number of changes in cover object.
[10]	2010	Image distortion through sequential LSB embedding	Improved security & robustness than simple LSB	The value '7.3064e-008' of random key is used for a.png image file of size 24 KB

Table 2. Research articles related to combination of cryptography and steganography techniques to minimize distortion.

Reference no.	Year of publication	Method used	Benefits	Other parammeters	Source
[11]	2011	Haar wavelet transform, Huffman encoding, DWT	High capacity, good invisibility	54.93 db PSNR, 507856 BITS CAPACITY	IJCSS
[3]	2013	RSA, LSB, H-LSB	More secure and more efficient	51.1655 db PSNR, 0.4972 MSE for LSB with RSA; 73.544 db PSNR, 0.0029 MSE for H-LSB with RSA	IJARCSSE
[5]	2015	MD5, SHA	Secure and efficient	—	IEEE
[12]	2016	AES, IWT, RBF, LSB	High security and high image quality	59.511 PSNR, 0.0727 MSE	IEEE
[13]	2016	RSA, LSB	High security, identity authentication	56.513 PSNR	IEEE

concerned in identifying the best locations in the cover image to embed the secret data and thus, they have used neural networks for both improving the image quality and finding the suitable location to hide the secret data. The authors in [13] has combined LSB technique with RSA algorithm to obtain high security and identity authentication by achieving a high PSNR value of 56.5 db. The Table 2 lists the research articles related to the integration of cryptographic and steganographic techniques to minimize the distortion and enhance the security.

4 Review Analysis

Cryptography and steganography are the terms that are interlinked to each other in terms of security, privacy, integrity, etc. But the techniques differ from each other on the basis of their working. Cryptography is responsible for protecting data in terms of security whereas steganography is responsible for concealing its existence. Steganography transmits the data in any of the cover medium like text, audio, video, image etc. but cryptography mainly uses text for transmitting the data over the communication link. Security services offered by steganography are authentication, confidentiality and identification whereas cryptography offers confidentiality, identification, integrity, non-repudiation and authentication. Steganography can be broken only if the attackers gets to know that it has been used but in case of cryptography the attacker already knows about its existence and keeps on trying to break the encryption. The resultant file of cryptography is termed as cipher text and in case of steganography it is the stego-file.

Both the techniques have their own shortcomings; combining the techniques lead to more secrecy, privacy etc. According to Sect. 3 as discussed above the researchers have combined the advantages of both the techniques in order to achieve better results in terms of payload capacity, robustness, and imperceptibility as compared to the results that were achieved earlier while using the techniques in person. This hybrid approach will help in securing the confidential information communication with better results across different parameters like PSNR (Peak signal to noise ratio) value which should be the highest as possible. As can be seen from the Table 2 the researchers are able to achieve the higher PSNR value i.e., 73.544 db. The other parameter used in review is MSE (Mean square error) value which should be the lowest as possible. The minimum value of MSE that has been achieved is 0.0029. By achieving these values the security mechanisms are enhanced for better practical usage.

5 Conclusion

Providing security for transactions over internet has end up as an essential problem. As we have seen from the above research articles that embedding data in the cover image leads to the distortion. More the distortion less the privacy of the data. The present security mechanisms systems are ought to be made more robust. This is also obtrusive that, no single approach can offer complete protection mechanisms in the direction of developing threats. So, the integration of two techniques provide much better results like low distortion, maximum capacity thereby enhancing the security.

References

1. Wajgade, V.M., Kumar, S.: Stegocrypto – a review of steganography techniques using cryptography. Int. J. Comput. Sci. Eng. Technol. **4**, 423–426 (2013). ISSN 2229-3345
2. Johnson, N.F., Jajodia, S.: Exploring steganography seeing the unseen. Computer **31**, 26–34 (1998). IEEE
3. Kumar, A., et al.: A secure image steganography based on RSA algorithm and hash–LSB technique. IJARCSSE **3**(7), 363–371 (2013)
4. Cole, E., Krutz, R.D. (eds.): Hiding in Plain Sight, Steganography and the Art of Covert Communication. Wiley Publishing, Inc., Hoboken (2003)
5. Madhuravani, B., et al.: Strong authentication using dynamic hashing and steganography. In: ICCCA. IEEE (2015)
6. Budi, P., Gernowo, R., Si, M., Noranita, B., Si, S., Kom, M.: The combination of bit matching-based steganography and DES cryptography for data security (2013)
7. Joseph Raphael, A., Sundaram, V.: A survey on cryptography and steganography. Int. J. Comput. Technol. Appl. **2**(3) (2011). ISSN 2229-6093
8. Johnson, N.F., Katzenbeisser, S.: A survey of steganographic techniques. Information hiding techniques for steganography and digital watermarking, pp 43–78 (2000)
9. Medeni, M.B.O., Souidi, E.M.: Steganography and error correcting codes. Int. J. Comput. Sci. Inf. Secur. **8**(8), 147–149 (2010)
10. Gaikwad, D.P., Wagh, S.J.: Colour image restoration for an effective steganography. i-Manag. J. Softw. Eng. **4**(3), 65–71 (2010)
11. Nag, A., et al.: A novel technique for image steganography based on DWT and Huffman encoding. IJCSS **4**(6), 561–570
12. Seethalakshmi, K.S., et al.: Security enhancement in image steganography using neural networks and visual cryptography. IEEE (2016)
13. Zhou, X., et al.: An improved method for LSB based color image steganography combined with cryptography. IEEE (2016)

Performance Analysis of Cloud Data Verification Using MD5 and ECDSA Method

G. L. Prakash(✉), Manish Prateek, and Inder Singh

School of Computer Science Engineering, University of Petroleum and Energy Studies, Dehradun, India
prakashgl@ddn.upes.ac.in

Abstract. Cloud computing enable the users to outsource and access data economically using storage as a service. In this storage model, the data owner doesnot have any control of the data once its stores on cloud server. Therefore, privacy and security of the data is a challenging issue in cloud computing. To provide the integrity of the outsourced data, we have proposed a lightweight data auditing technique such as MD5 and ECDSA signature method using third party auditor. The result analysis of the proposed method shows that, ECDSA has better security performance than the computation as compared to MD5 method for larger data size. The selection of the signature method depends on the priority of the data size and frequency of accessing.

Keywords: Storage service · Verification · Security
Third party auditor · Public auditing

1 Introduction

Cloud computing is one of the on-demand high quality service delivery models with a lower cost. Amazon Web Service (AWS) is one of the well known cloud service provider, who provides various services such as; Amazon Elastic Compute Cloud (EC2) an IaaS service, Amazon Elastic Beanstalk provides a PaaS service for hosting applications, Amazon Elastic Block Storage (EBS), Amazon Simple Storage Service (S3) for storage, AWS Identity and Access Management (IAM) service for securely control access to AWS.

Although. Cloud computing provides various services with minimal overheads, which has many challenges on the performance of the system. Security of the data at rest is one of the big challenge in cloud computing. The security of the data is provides in three ways such as confidentiality, integrity and availability. Data integrity is the one of the most important parameter for data security in cloud storage. The integrity of the cloud data cannot be guaranteed due to the following reasons;

B. Panda et al. (Eds.): REDSET 2017, CCIS 799, pp. 616–628, 2018.
https://doi.org/10.1007/978-981-10-8527-7_52

- Due to loses the control of the outsourced data the traditional data integrity checking methods can not be applied directly.
- Due to hardware failure and software failure, the cloud service provider may hide the data corruption for his storage service reputation point of view.
- To save the data maintenance cost, the cloud service provider can delete the rarely accessed data from the storage or can change to offline method of storage.

For these reasons, the cloud data users has to find the better remote data integrity verification methods to verify the outsourced data without retrieving the entire data from the storage server. There are many existing protocols are proposed by different researcher's to verify the remote data integrity. Each method of data verifications has follows the various requirements such as, stateless verification, dynamic operations and batch auditing, etc.

In all these techniques, the verification process consumes more computation and communication resources due to the complex operations at resource constrained end devices. In this paper, we proposed a simple and light weight computational data verification techniques using Message Digest 5 (MD5) and Elliptic Curve Digital Signature Algorithm (ECDSA) algorithms.

The contribution of our proposed method of data verifications as follows.

- Due to the lightweight operations in data verification process which provides better performance than the existing methods.
- We are introduced the smaller metastable size for remote data verification without retrieving the entire data from the server, which reduces the storage cost.
- In the proposed method, the data is highly secure from the untrusted entities such as CSP and TTP because they cannot derive the data blocks from the metadata information.

The rest of this paper is organized as fallows; In Sect. 2, we present the related work to the proposed method, Sects. 3 and 4 defines the statement of the problem and defines the role of each entity in the proposed system respectively. Section 5 discus the MD5 and ECDSA digital signature method and Sect. 6 present analysis of our proposed method and finally concluded in the Sect. 7.

2 Related Work

Without knowledge of data owner private parameter's, data integrity auditing using a third party auditor (TPA) different public data verification schemes [1–6] are presented in the following section.

In [1] Liu et al., proposed a techniques to check integrity of outsourced data and to recover corrupted data using a TPA (Third Party Auditing) for public auditing. The TPA checks data integrity on behalf of owner of data. Due to uploading files in an encrypted format, TPA converts this data into safe place. Provided with a semi- trusted proxy to recover a data against corruption, user can recover failed data using proxy server. There are some disadvantages in this method such as; it does not support dynamic auditing, data is not stored in encrypted format, there is heavy storage on the server, the performance evaluation of that RDC is expensive for both clients and servers.

In [2] Zhu et al. proposed a cooperative Provable data possession (cPDP) for integrity checking of outsourced cloud data on distributed cloud storage. In this method of data auditing for smaller block sizes of data which takes more number of bilinear operations. Due to this complex operations to verify the remote data which take more computation and communication cost. Secondly, to maintain the metadata of the outsourced data on cloud storage server the index size of the metadata table is also grows linearly due to more number of block data blocks signature. Finally the signature generation includes complex computation operations like exponentiation and multiplication operations which increases the signature generation cost of the data blocks.

In [3] Wang et al., proposed to perform the remote data integrity checking, it incur considerable overhead since the verifier will check the certificate when it checks the remote data integrity. In the Identity based Public key cryptography method a key is provided to the client so that he can access his data in the cloud and the Provable data possession model, the verifier can check the remote data integrity without retrieving or downloading the whole data. Public-key cryptography may be vulnerable to impersonation, even if user's private key is not available.

Yu et al. [4] introduced a identity-based Remote data integrity checking (RDIC) for storing owner's data on untrusted cloud server. This method of auditing utilizes the key-homomorphic cryptographic primitive operation to verifies the outsourced data blocks. The drawback of this method has more computational overhead at the resource constrained verifier device compared to the public verifier end.

Verification of outsourced data on cloud storage Zhang et al. [7] proposed public verification protocol using message authentication code tags of the data blocks. This method is suffers from the detection of malicious auditor so that which can missuses the outsourced user data on a untrusted storage server.

In [6] Wang et al. proposed a workload distribution scheme such as Online/Offline Provable Data Possession data auditing on cloud server. In his method the light weights file processing computations are assigned to the offline mode and heavy weight computation to the online mode. The main drawback of this method is the segregation of light and heavy workload has a challenging task.

There are various cryptographic techniques are proposed for data auditing methods using message authentication [8], homomorphic linear authenticators [9] and Boneh-Lynn-Shacham (BLS) based homomorphic methods [10]. Heterogeneous data also exists and this data runs only on IP networks which contains several types of message. Hence, the data also has different provisioning requirements that must be harmonized to provide rational knowledge to the cloud client.

3 Statement of the Problem

Consider a cloud storage system consists of three computing entities such as; data owner, public verifier and cloud service provider. The detailed functions of the system model as follows (Fig. 1);

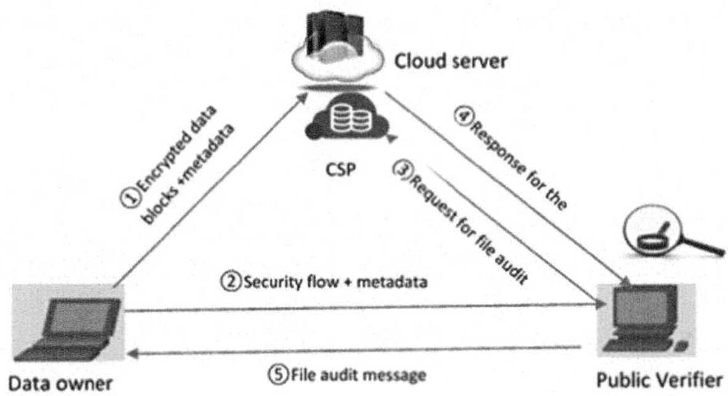

Fig. 1. System model

1. The data owner splits the file (F) into n blocks of size s i.e. $Fi = \{m_{ij}\}$ where i = 1 to n and j = 1 to s. Each block is encrypted using Advanced Encryption Standard algorithm with a specific key rotated bitwise split file number of times and uploads each block to the CSP. The user shall also send the metadata to the CSP.
2. User then uploads the private key as well as the meta information of the uploaded file to the public verifier.
3. The public verifier sends the data audit request message to the CSP regarding a specific file using its ID.
4. The CSP sends the file tag for the requested file ID. Once the tag is verified, the public verifier shall query file blocks to the CSP. The CSP shall send the digital signatures of the requested blocks. Once the tag and all the signatures are verified, the public verifier shall confirm the validity of the file in CSP.
5. When the file data blocks are verified by public verifier then sends the status of the auditing to the data owner.

Objectives: The following objectives are considered in our proposed security system.

- Improving security of existing cloud architecture
- Choice of hashing function for ensuring the file integrity
- File content protection using encryption
- Use TTP for detection frauds by CSP.

Metadata Representation: The metadata table consists of six fields such as; $OWNER\_ID$: which is a unique identifier to identifies the owner of the file. Filename: which is the name of the file stored on cloud server. fileID: an unique identifier to identifies the file, tag: it is signature of the entire file. blockID: which is the different data blocks metadata, which contains the signature of the contents and block identifier, signType: which holds the type of the algorithm used to generate the signature. The structure of metadata as shown in the Fig. 2.

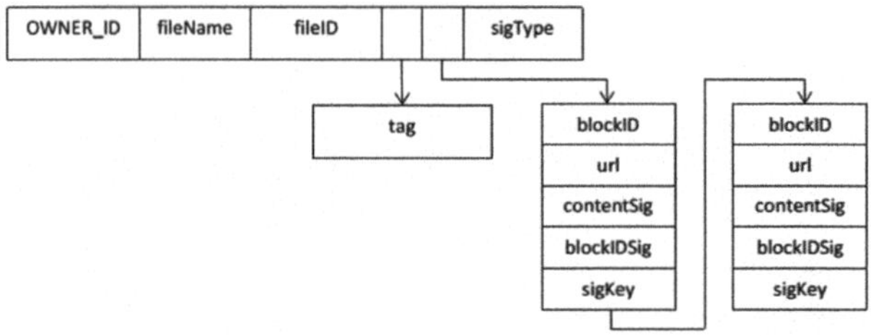

Fig. 2. Metadata representation

4 Proposed Method

In the proposed method there are three functional modules are designed in the system model such as; Data owner model, Trusted Third Party (TTP) and Cloud service provider (CSP). The role of each module explained in the following section.

4.1 User Role

The user has four operation's to outsource and manage his data on cloud server in a cost effective manner. The operations are; *Upload*: Used to upload file to CSP, *Download*: Allows download of specific file, *FetchAvailableFileList*: Fetches all the files that are stored in the CSP. *Delete*: Allows to delete a specific file in CSP and TTP.

4.2 Cloud Service Provider

The Cloud Service Provider has the following opreations to maintain the user data on shared server. *handleUpload*: Allows to handle the incoming file upload from the user. *handleAudit*: Handles the audit request from the TTP. *handleDelete*: Deletes a specific file information as well as remove the corresponding file blocks from the storage. *handleListing*: Responds back with all the files that are stored in the CSP.

4.3 Truster Third Party Aduritor (TTP)

Available Operations: *handleNewFile*: Allows the user to store the metadata of a new file, *audit*: Allows auditing for a specific file stored in the CSP, *delete*: Removes the stored meta entry for the specified filename.

5 MD5 and ECDSA Algorithms

5.1 MD5 Algorithm

MD5 [11–13] is one of the message authentication protocol to verifies the outsourced file content. Which maps the variable length of data block to a fixed length (128 bit) of hash value. The MD5 hash value has some properties such as; i). Change in a single bit in data block changes the hash by almost 50% and ii). It is computationally impossible to derive the data block from the hash. The detailed algorithm as follows

Algorithm 1. Signature generation using MD5

1 Split data block into multiple of 512 bits block and insert the length of the file at the end,

2 if the file is not multiple of 512 bits then additional bits are added to the end.

// **for** each data block of the file **do**

3 Split the each block (m) into 16 words of 32 bits size i.e. $m_0, m_1, ..m_{15}$.

4 Initializes the MD5 four buffers A, B, C, and D each of 32 bits long and K. where $K[i] := floor(232 \times abs(sin(i+1)))$, i= 0 to 63, $s[]$ specifies the per-round shift values

5 // calculate the hash value for each data block

for i from 0 to 63 **do**

if $(i \leq 15)$ then, $F := (B\&C)|((B)\&D)$, $g := i$

else if $(i \leq 31)$ then, $F := (D\&B)|((D)\&C)$, $g := (5 \times i + 1)$ mod 16

else if $i \leq 47$ then, $F := B \oplus C \oplus D$, $g := (3 \times i + 5)$ mod 16

else if $(i \leq 63)$ then, $F := C \oplus (B|(D))$, $g := (7 \times i)$ mod 16

endif

//update the four buffers

$t := D$, $D := C$, $C := B$, $B := B + leftrotate((A + F + K[i] + M[g]),, s[i])A := t$

end for

//Add this chunk's hash to result so far

6 Return the 128 bits hash value i.e. $A + B + C + D$

end for

5.2 ECDSA Algorithm

The ECDSA [14,15] is designed based on the points on the elliptic curve and bilinear pairing. It consists of two stages for data identification such as data block signing and data block verification [16]. The signing stage generates $signature_1$ and $signature_2$ using one of the point on the elliptic curve as follows.

$P(x1, y1) = k \times p1()$ and $signature_1 = x1 \bmod n$

Where P is the new point on the elliptic curve generated using one of the point $p1$, and k the random integer number.

$Signature - 2 = (h(m) + d \times Signature_1)k^{-1} \bmod n$

Where $h(m)$ is the hash value of the data block and d is the data owner's private key.

In the verification stage, the Third party auditor verifies the outsourced data block on cloud server as follows.

$Q(x2, y2) = (h(m)(signature_2)^{-1} \bmod n) \times p1() + ((signature_2)^{-1} signature_1 \bmod n) \times p2()$

$Signature_3 = x2 \bmod n$

Where $p2 = d \times p1()$ is the other point on the curve The third party auditor compares the $signature_1$ and $signature_3$, if both are same then it declared the data block m is a valid, otherwise it declares as invalid block [17,18]. The over view of the ECDSA block diagram as shown in the Fig. 3.

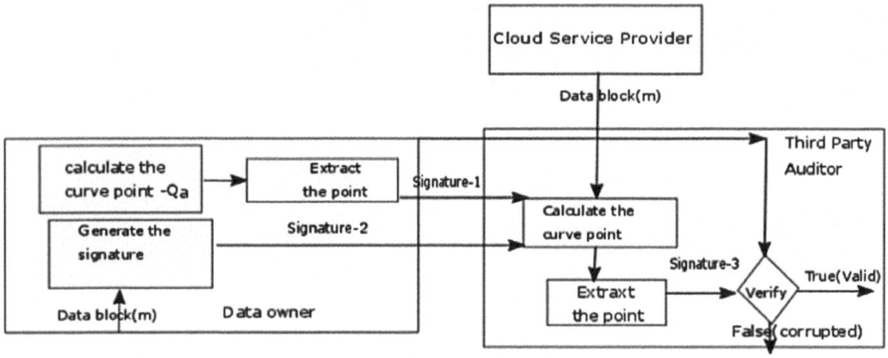

Fig. 3. ECDSA signature calculation

6 Performance Analysis

6.1 Simulation Setup

To evaluate the performance of our proposed data auditing method the following simulation setup are considered. All the algorithms are implemented using Python programming language with built functions in Python library [19]. The simulation results tested on Amazon Web Service [20] virtual machines (VM). One VM run as a cloud server and one VM run as a third party auditor with Ubuntu operating system, t2.small vCPU and 2 GB EBS storage configuration. The data owner runs on a Laptop with 64 bit Windows 10 operating system, i3 Intel processor and 4 GB physical memory configuration.

Algorithm 2. Signature generation using ECDSA

The TTP and the user has to agree upon the curve parameters ($CURVE$, G, n).

- $CURVE$ - the elliptic curve field and equation used.
- G - elliptic curve base point, a generator of the elliptic curve with large prime order n
- n- integer order of G, means that n x $G = O$
- User creates a key pair, consisting of a private key integer da, randomly selected in the interval $[1, n-1]$; and a public key curve point $p_2 = da$ x p_1.

Signature generation algorithm (User):

1 Calculate $e = HASH(m)$, where HASH is a cryptographic hash function, such as SHA-2.
2 Let z be the Ln leftmost bits of e, where Ln is the bit length of the group order n.
3 Select a cryptographically secure random integer k from $[1, n-1]$.
4 Calculate the curve point $P(x_1, y_1) = k$ x $P1$
5 Calculate $Signature_1 = x_1 \bmod n$. If $r = 0$, go back to step 3.
6 Calculate $Signature_2 = k^{-1}(z + Signature_1 \times da) \bmod n$, If $s = 0$, go back to step 3.
7 The signature is the pair $(Signature_1, Signature_2)$.

Signature verification algorithm (TTP):

For TTP to authenticate User's file signature, TTP must have a copy of the public-key curve point p2

TTP verify p2 is a valid curve point n x $p2 = O$

After that, TTP follows these steps:

1 Verify that $Signature_1$ and $Signature_2$ are integers $[1, n-1]$. If not, the signature is invalid.
2 Calculate $e = HASH(m)$ where HASH is the same function used in the signature generation.
3 Let z be the Ln leftmost bits of e.
4 Calculate $w = (Signature_2)^{-1} \bmod n$.
5 Calculate $u_1 = z \times w \bmod n$ and $u_2 = Signature_1 \times w \bmod n$.
6 Calculate the curve point $Q(x_2, y_2) = u1$ x $p_1 + u_2$ x p_2
7 The signature is valid if $Signature_1 == x_1 \pmod n$, invalid otherwise.

6.2 Result Analysis

Consider for a given file of 10 MB data file with different block size, the performance of the proposed system analysed based on the signature generation time, valid block verification time, and the invalid block detection cost using MD5 and ECDSA signature generation algorithms.

Signature generation time: In Fig. 4. Explains the signature generation cost for different data block sizes using ECDSA and MD5 algorithms. The X-axis

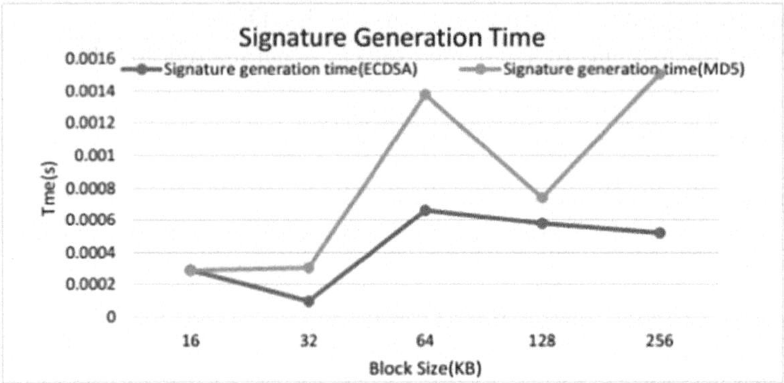

Fig. 4. Signature generation cost for different blocks

represents the different data block sizes in terms of Kilo Bytes and Y-axis represents the signature generation cost in seconds(s). The graph shows that for smaller data block size both the method has linear cost of signature generation, but for larger data blocks MD5 takes more time compared to the ECDSA algorithm due to the more complex computations operations are defined in the MD5 algorithm. The different file data blocks of 10 MB file signature generation computation cost as shown in the Table 1 (Fig. 5).

Table 1. Signature generation cost for different blocks

Blocks size (in KB)	Signature generation time (ECDSA) in seconds	Signature generation time (MDS) in seconds
16	0.000291	0.000289
32	0.0001	0.000306
64	0.000663	0.00138
128	0.000581	0.000741
256	0.000522	0.00151

Block verification time: The verification of the variable sized outsourced data block verification cost with different number of auditing data blocks as shown in the Fig. 6.

In Fig. 6 X-axis represents the different number of auditing data blocks with different sizes and Y- axis represents the data blocks auditing cost. The result shows that, the data auditing cost of ECDSA algorithm takes more time than the MD5 algorithm. Which means that, ECDSA has more secured compared to the MD5 algorithm. The simulation result for 5 sets of the data as shown in the Table 2.

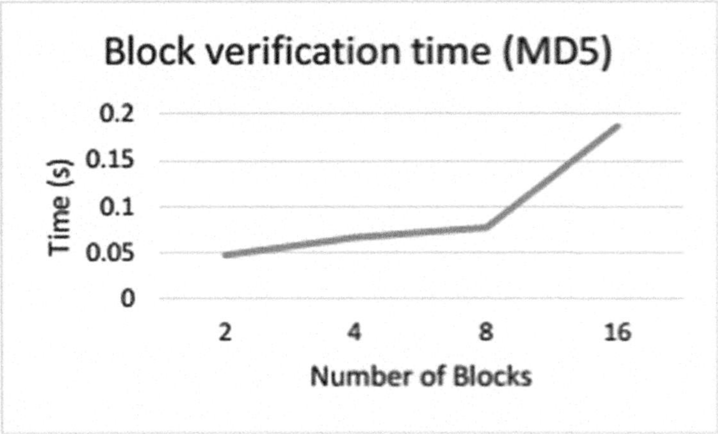

Fig. 5. Data block verification cost using MD5

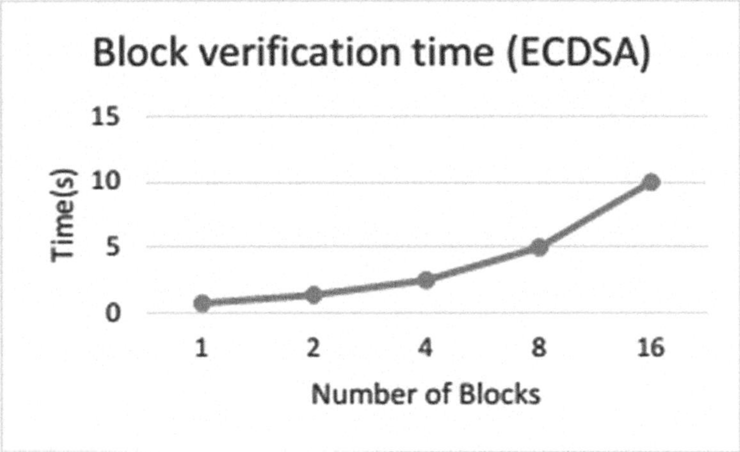

Fig. 6. Data block verification cost using ECDSA

Table 2. Data block verification cost

Block size	Number of blocks	Block verification time (ECDSA) in seconds	Block verification time (MD5) in seconds
16 KB	1	0.709039	0.041719
32 KB	2	1.323842	0.046722
64 KB	4	2.479758	0.065753
128 KB	8	4.972582	0.076521
256 KB	16	9.992979	0.187577

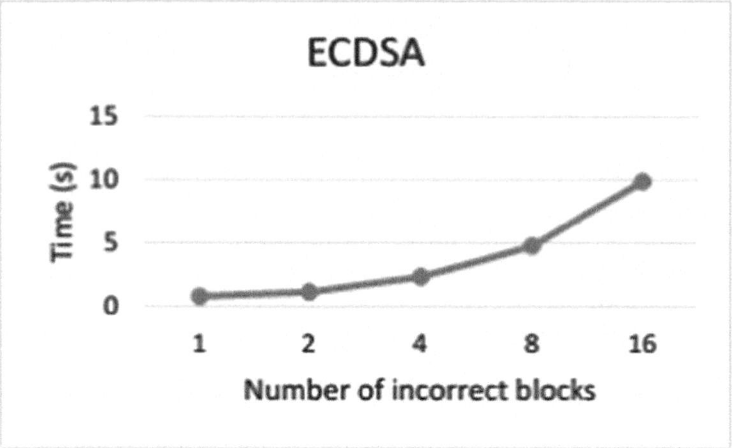

Fig. 7. Incorrect verification blocks time using ECDSA

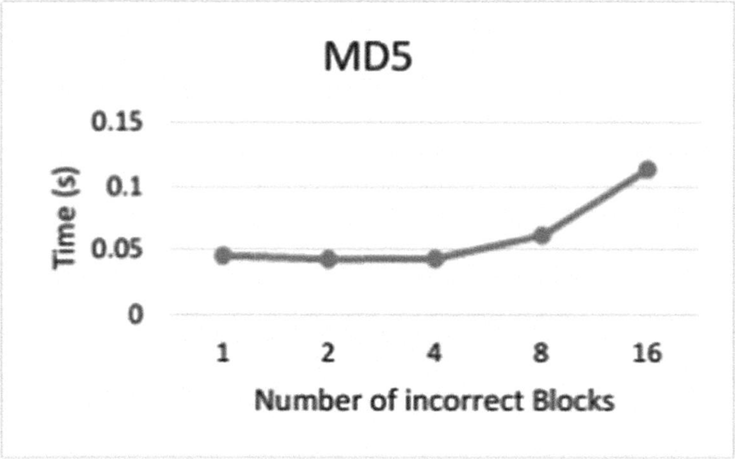

Fig. 8. Incorrect verification blocks time using MD5

Corrupted data block verification: The performance analysis of the ECDSA and MD5 for corrupted data block verification as shown in the Figs. 7 and 8. compared to MD5 algorithm ECDSA has higher cost for more blocks because it contails a complex bilinear operations but it has better security performance than the MD5 (Table 3).

Table 3. Incorrect verification blocks time comparisons

Number of incorrect Blocks	ECDSA	MD5
1	0.892414	0.045784
2	1.250494	0.043072
4	2.418545	0.043461
8	4.842195	0.061608
16	9.915086	0.11287

7 Conclusions

The outsourced data verification is an important solution to solve the problem of verifiable cloud data. We propose a MD5 and ECDSA signatures methods for remote data integrity checking. Besides the data integrity checking, the proposed methods supports the cipher text database to provide the confidentiality of the data. We analyze the performance of MD5 and ECDSA methods of data verification in terms of data auditing computation and storage overheads. The performance analysis shows that, ECDSA has better performance than the MD5 method for larger data file size.

References

1. Liu, J., Huang, K., Rong, H., Wang, H., Xian, M.: Privacy-preserving public auditing for regenerating-code-based cloud storage. IEEE Trans. Inf. Forensics Secur. **10**(7), 1513–1528 (2015)
2. Zhu, Y., Hu, H., Ahn, G.J., Yu, M.: Cooperative provable data possession for integrity verification in multicloud storage. IEEE Trans. Parallen Distrib. Syst. **23**(12), 2231–2244 (2012)
3. Wang, H., He, D., Tang, S.: Identity-based distributed provable data possession in multi-cloud storage. IEEE Trans. Inf. Forensics Secur. **11**(6), 1165–1176 (2016)
4. Yu, Y., Au, M., Ateniese, G., Huang, X., Susilo, W., Dai, Y., Min, G.: Identity-based remote data integrity checking with perfect data privacy preserving for cloud storage. IEEE Trans. Inf. Forensics Secur. **12**(4), 767–778 (2017)
5. Yang, L., Xia, L.: An efficient and secure public batch auditing protocol for dynamic cloud storage data. In: IEEE International Computer Symposium, pp. 671–675 (2016)
6. Wang, Y., Wu, Q., Qin, B., Shi, W., Deng, R.H., Hu, J.: Identitybased data outsourcing with comprehensive auditing in clouds. IEEE Trans. Inf. Forensics Secur. **12**(4), 940–952 (2017)
7. Zhang, Y., Xu, C., Liang, X., Li, H., Mu, Y., Zhang, X.: Efficient public verification of data integrity for cloud storage systems from indistinguishability obfuscation. IEEE Trans. Inf. Forensics Secur. **12**(3), 676–688 (2017)
8. Bellare, M., Canetti, R., Krawczyk, H.: Keying hash functions for message authentication. In: International Cryptology Conference on Advances in Cryptology (CRYPTO 1996), pp. 1–15 (1996)

9. Wang, B., Li, B., Li, H.: Oruta: privacy-preserving public auditing for shared data in the cloud. IEEE Tran. Cloud Comput. **2**, 43–56 (2014)
10. Yang, K., Jia, X.: An efficient and secure dynamic auditing protocol for data storage in cloud computing. IEEE Trans. Parallel Distrib. Syst. **24**(9), 1717–1726 (2013)
11. Chauhan, M.M.: An implemented of hybrid cryptography using elliptic curve cryptosystem (ECC) and MD5. In: IEEE International Conference on Inventive Computation Technologies (ICICT), vol. 3, pp. 1–6 (2016)
12. Indrayani, R., Nugroho, H.A., Hidayat, R., Pratama, I.: Increasing the security of MP3 steganography using AES encryption and MD5 hash function. In: IEEE 2nd International Conference on Science and Technology-Computer (ICST), pp. 129–132 (2016)
13. Zhong, L., Wan, W., Kong, D.: Javaweb login authentication based on improved MD5 algorithm. In: IEEE International Conference on Audio, Language and Image Processing (ICALIP), vol. 3, pp. 131–135 (2016)
14. van Rijswijk-Deij, R., Jonker, M., Sperotto, A.: On the adoption of the elliptic curve digital signature algorithm (ECDSA) in DNSSEC. In: IEEE 12th International Conference on Network and Service Management (CNSM), pp. 258–262 (2016)
15. Li, H., Zhang, R., Yi, J., Lv, H.: A novel algorithm for scalar multiplication in ECDSA. In: IEEE International Conference on Computational and Information Sciences, pp. 943–946 (2013)
16. van Rijswijk-Deij, R., Hageman, K., Sperotto, A., Pras, A.: The performance impact of elliptic curve cryptography on DNSSEC validation. IEEEACM Trans. Netw. **25**(2), 738–750 (2017)
17. Kneevi, M., Nikov, V., Rombouts, P.: Low-latency ECDSA signature verificationa road toward safer traffic. IEEE Trans. Very Large Scale Integr. VLSI Syst. **24**(11), 3257–3267 (2016)
18. Yalin, T.: Compact ECDSA engine for IoT applications. IEEE Electron. Lett. **52**(15), 1310–1312 (2016)
19. Redondo, J.M., Ortin, F.: A comprehensive evaluation of common python implementations. IEEE Softw. **32**(4), 76–84 (2015)
20. Sun, D., Fu, M., Zhu, L., Li, G., Lu, Q.: Nonintrusive anomaly detection with streaming performance metrics and logs for DevOps in public clouds: a case study in AWS. IEEE Trans. Emerg. Topics Comput. **4**(2), 278–289 (2016)

Research Trends in Malware Detection on Android Devices

Leesha Aneja(✉) and Sakshi Babbar

GD Goenka University, Gurugram, India
{leesha.aneja,sakshi.babbar}@gdgoenka.ac.in

Abstract. Mobile phones have become the necessity of modern human life to store our valuable information such as passwords, reminders, messages, photos, videos and social contacts. The advent in mobile technology has made human life easier and more efficient. However, at the same time, our excessive dependency on mobile devices has drawn attention of malware authors and cyber criminals leading to large number of cyber-attacks. Amongst all, the major concern of security threat is on Android smartphones. The key reason for it is that it does not restrict users to download applications from unsafe sites. So, it is important to develop robust and efficient Android Malware detection system in order to protect our sensitive data from cyber-attacks on Android platform. In this work, we discuss different types of Android Malwares and provide critical review on their detection approaches that exist in literature. We also highlight promising new directions of research in the domain of Malware detection on Android devices.

Keywords: Security · Android Forensic · Malware
Intrusion detection techniques

1 Introduction

The recent development in the manufacturing and research of Small Scale Digital Devices (SSDD) has led to the world of ubiquitous computing. As, mobile phones are a piece of SSDD and they are pervasive to the point that they administer us from multiple points of view, for example, business, online trade, SMS, MMS, video calls, photography, electronic mail etc. They store and oversee individual data by means of Personal Information Management (PIM) applications (e.g., contacts, timetable, and so on). The increasing demand of this technology is also increasing the market of Malwares and Cyber Crimes. These crimes require proper investigation to attribute evidence to specific suspects. Digital Forensics (DF) came into existence because of the need for investigation of these cyber-crimes. There are various disciplines of Digital Forensics as shown in Fig. 1. Depending upon attributes of processing and the type of gadgets used, the main categories include Memory Forensics, Computer Forensics, Network Forensics, Multimedia Forensics, Mobile Device Forensics (MDF) and Android Forensic (AF). Mobile device forensics is considered to be one of the prominent disciplines of digital forensics and digital forensics includes obtaining information from the device under forensically sound conditions which is also called as digital evidence.

B. Panda et al. (Eds.): REDSET 2017, CCIS 799, pp. 629–642, 2018.
https://doi.org/10.1007/978-981-10-8527-7_53

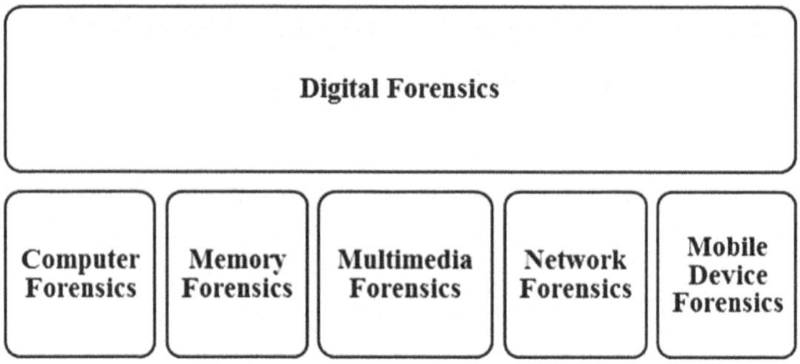

Fig. 1. Classification of digital forensics

As the mobile technology has acquired incredible development. This development has pulled in the normal users as well as the malware designers and the hackers prompting an expanded number of digital crimes and malware threats. In the couple of years, the rate of stolen telephones have additionally expanded. As these telephones contained delicate individual data, it is dangerous in the event if they are lost or stolen. Logical examination of these devices by application developers and the client themselves can make them more aware on how and which data to store or not to store on these devices.

The significant use of mobile devices carry along a high organizational risk. Over the previous years and even in the current months it has been seen that prominent organizations have been hacked and information has been leaked. Some driving industry masters say every organization is defenseless against hack strikes and, many of them do not know when they have been hacked. The recent attack that occurred was "WannaCry" Ransomware which really highlighted this issue.

There are mainly three Security Concerns of any organization or an individual entity such as *Breaches of Confidentiality, Data Devastation and Data Control.* Breaches of Confidentiality is the one in which each business will relate to the need to keep certain basic data private from contender eyes. Data Devastation includes demolition of information that can extremely disable the victim concerned and Data Control is a more severe threat than a system break-in which may be easily detectable through tokens left by hackers. Any organization is considering only network security to protect its data, then it is ignoring the vulnerabilities of mobile devices which act as connecting devices to the network.

Securing computers in an organization system should be a need for organizations of different kinds and sizes however securing cell phones can't be disregarded. As companies move towards greater mobility with their representatives signing in remotely and finishing a number of business related assignments on cell phones - the need to safeguard these mobile mechanisms becomes particularly acute.

This paper will help new researchers to understand the security concerns of mobile devices (basically Android) and how malwares are taking advantage of its vulnerabilities. The paper provides a brief introduction to various categories of malware and covers most of techniques of intrusion detection used to unleash malwares in an elaborated manner.

1.1 Contributions of the Paper

The main contributions of the paper are highlighted as follows:

1. This paper aims to help new researchers to comprehend the security models of iOS and Android and to recognize the reason of expanding malwares in Android devices in contrast with iOS.
2. To give a brief overview of the various categories of malwares and its vulnerabilities.
3. To discuss Intrusion detection system (IDS) in mobile devices.
4. To signify the utilization of machine learning algorithms in different IDS techniques (Static, Dynamic and Hybrid) that are capable of detecting the malwares effectively.

The further organization of the paper proceeds as follows. Section 2 provides security concerns of Android over iOS. Section 3 describes architecture and design details of the Android. Section 4 discusses the different types of Android Malware. Section 5 gives an insight of intrusion detection system and its techniques. Finally, Sect. 6 presents the conclusion.

2 Security Concerns of Android over iOS

Nowadays, with the digitization of trivial daily-life tasks people have become highly dependent on the mobile phones. Major players in the mobile market are – Apple's iOS and Google's Android which bring new security techniques with a host of additional features. iOS malware rate in comparison to Android Malware is not too acute. Classes for interfacing with the camera, GPS and different assets on the gadgets are given by the Apple, and limitations are put on applications from accessing to a large number of the components straightforwardly.

The purpose behind Apple signing the application is to ensure the applications have not been modified from their unique binary. The Apple additionally tests the integrity of an application keeping in mind the end goal to check whether there was unsigned code infused into the application that is accessing the resources which it is not permitted to.

Another security concept is the encrypted key chain which gives central authority the capacity and recovery of network passwords and other credentials. The Apple's security structure encourages low level functionality for reading and writing the data to and from the keychain and performing encryption and decryption. The information inside the key-chain is consistently zoned with the goal that the application cannot get to the encrypted information stored by various applications. Apple's Common Crypto architecture gives cryptographic APIs to the engineers who might want to make utilization of encryption in their applications. However, iOS is not 100% resistant. Late cases, for example, the iOS-based malware, XCodeGhost have demonstrated that iOS is powerless against malevolent assaults too.

Like Apple, Google gives a concentrated market to versatile applications called Google Play Store. However, that is counterbalanced by the Android's capacity to introduce applications from outsider sources. Some are outstanding and legitimate, for example, Amazon. So, Android has also become the prime target for cybercrimes by means of malware and viruses. Approximately 85.1% market share of android system gives us the view of its comparatively higher user base. The key reason for it is it does not restrict its users to install the applications from unsafe sites apart from the official store. Irrespective of the updates over the past few years, security remains the ultimate battleground in the field of Android mobile phones. The designers can produce a self-signing authentication without outside help or consent (and this is the fundamental difference with Apple's iOS). The central authority does not necessarily sign the applications like iOS applications do. Basically, in Android operating system, central authority verification is not considered mandatory and hence it is more prone to malware attacks.

3 Android Security Model and Architecture

The fundamental building blocks of Android gadgets are Android hardware, Android operating system, and Android application runtime. The Android runs on a wide range of various hardware configurations. These incorporate cell phones, tablets, set-up boxes. All the assets of the Android, for example, camera work, GPS-information, Bluetooth capacities, communication capacities, network connections, are altogether accessed through the OS.

The Android programs are written in Java programming and are run on Dalvik virtual machine. These programs are compiled and form Byte code and then are further translated into Dalvik Bytecode (.dex file). There are two types of applications in Android: Pre-introduced applications and Client introduced applications. Pre-introduced applications incorporate applications, for example, telephone, email, date-book, program and contacts. Pre-introduced applications can likewise be produced by OEM (Original Equipment Manufacturer) device. The client introduced applications are the outsider applications made by different engineers or developers.

The Android allots every client application an ID and runs it as a different client in a different procedure. The application signing empowers the clients to remarkably recognize the creator or author of the application and gives them the right to edit or update their application without coping with complicated interfaces and permissions. When the designer makes the application, he needs to sign it. In the event that there is an endeavor to introduce an unsigned application, the Google Play store will dismiss it. This makes the common trust between the Google and the designer. The application can particularly be distinguished and its engineer and designers can be held responsible for the conduct of their applications. The application signing ensures that one application cannot get to some other application with the exception of through well-defined Inter Process Communication.

The applications do not have to be signed necessarily by the central authority like iOS applications. The central authority verification is currently not mandatory for Android operating system [44]. Thus, it is leading to intrusion of more and more malwares everyday as depicted in Fig. 2.

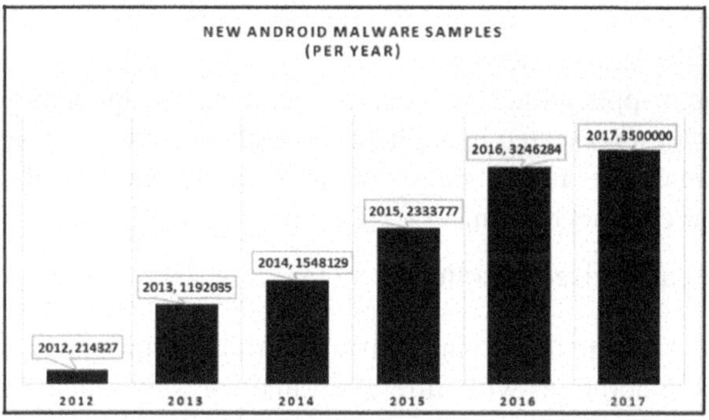

Fig. 2. Android malware rate [4]

The Android security model depends on its working framework, and is authorized by making application designers announce consent in the "Android Manifest.xml" document in their application. The client is asked before establishment whether he might want to concede the consent asked for by the applications, and has no power over micromanaging which authorization can be permitted and which can't subsequent to as per the designer each one of those authorizations would be required to guarantee the best possible usefulness of the application. Regularly we see consents, which are point less being asked for by applications, the clients must be careful about this, however tragically the main decision of such applications is to introduce the client to such applications [44]. There are four layers in the android stack model, (a) Android application layer, (b) Application structure, (c) Android runtime and (d) the Linux part. Since Android is an open source OS, it permits security scientists to concentrate on communications at the bit level and acquire valuable data. Android applications are produced utilizing Java programming alongside the instruments and API's given by the Android Software Development Kit (SDK) [25].

4 Android Malware Categories

Malware is a term used for "malicious software" which is any kind of bad software installed without adequate consent of user for various unethical reasons, vandalism, crimes, spying or just for pranks. The malware working can be explained in three phases wherein the first phase involves infecting the host, second phase includes accomplishing the goal and in the third phase, the malware is spread to other systems.

Main drivers for Android malicious portable applications:

1. Android working framework permits clients to present any versatile application from the outside market, that may try no endeavors to check the wellbeing of the product in application that they disseminate.
2. Simple and adaptable to port a windows-based botnet existing customer applications to android based cell phones.

3. Application designers can transfer their applications with no mediation, check of reliability and declaration power.
4. Various portable applications have been changed in the application market and the malware have been presented in applications and spread through informal archives. The complex malwares in application distinguish the nearness of a refined domain, and adjust their conduct design.

The malwares are categorized as follows:

Virus Malware – The one that connects itself to running programs and spreads itself through clients' collaborations with different frameworks/systems. They are infectious and destructive software that are known to spread when the file is shared between computers or devices. Its primary motto is to replicate itself onto other host to spread further and not to cause damage. It can be carried in form of mails, attachments, downloads and target the existing programs on that computer.

Worm Malware – The type of malware that proliferates itself from one contaminated host to different hosts by means of endeavours in the OS interfaces normally the framework call interface or system call interface. Unlike Viruses which do not cause damage, the worms destroy files saved on the devices and cause harm to network. The files can be data files or operating system files on drive. They do not replicate and are network aware.

Trojan Malware – This masquerades as non-malware and acts noxiously once introduced (opening secondary passages, meddling with framework conduct, and so forth). It is a non self –replicating program which conceals itself in a benign application and steal personal or financial information. The "Trojan Horse" was derived from History when Greeks captured the City of Troy by gifting Trojans with a big wooden Horse wherein they used to hide their soldiers and attacked the city from inside.

Adware Malware – This powers the client to manage undesirable commercials. It is a software which supply advertisements in order to provide monetary benefits to its author. The advertisements have the tendency to examine the most frequently used sites by the user and presents those kind of advertisements to him. It may or may not have malicious code but it can harm the performance of a computer.

Spyware Malware – It subtly watches and gives an account of clients PC utilization and individual data open in that without user's permission. Like Viruses, spyware does not have tendency to replicate and cause infections. Once installed, it works on victim's device and sits silently to avoid detection. Key logger is one of the common spyware used by organizations intentionally to track its employees. Its basic functioning include capturing keystrokes, emails, user ids, passwords, documents, chats which can be read by malicious hacker.

Rootkit Malware – These are malicious programs designed in order to gain root or administrative access of a computer. Once the attackers gets the admin privilege, it can exploits user's system in the way he wants. It conceals its reality from different applications and clients.

Zombie Malware – It has similar working as that of spyware. But it does not gather data from the devices but simply sits and follow commands given by the hacker.

Botnet Malware – A group of compromised computers which when connected to Internet, can attack other Networks. It utilizes a client's PC as an individual from a system of tainted PCs controlled by a focal malicious organization.
Ransomware Malware – Ransom ware comes packaged with installation files masquerading as official software updates, installing which downloads malware code which encrypts all the important files on the system and ask ransom from the user for the same in form of bit coins typically.

5 Intrusion Detection System (IDS)

An intrusion can be defined as any kind of entry to anyone's area without permission. But in computer science, any activity which leads to compromise of privacy, security and integrity of a network or system is termed as Intrusion. To monitor the working of an application, network or system with the intend of finding any malicious activities performed by cyber criminals or attackers, an Intrusion Detection System is used. This intrusion detection concept originated in 1980's due to sudden threats to security architecture. As discussed in the Introduction section, there are various categories of attacks and to detect these attacks different types of Intrusion detection Techniques are being used. So, IDS takes this task of monitoring information about different types of intrusions, trics to handle them and generates a report for security analysts or users [11]. Its working can be related to an Alarm system of the house whose functioning is to detect whether the lock has been broken when someone tries to intrude into the house and

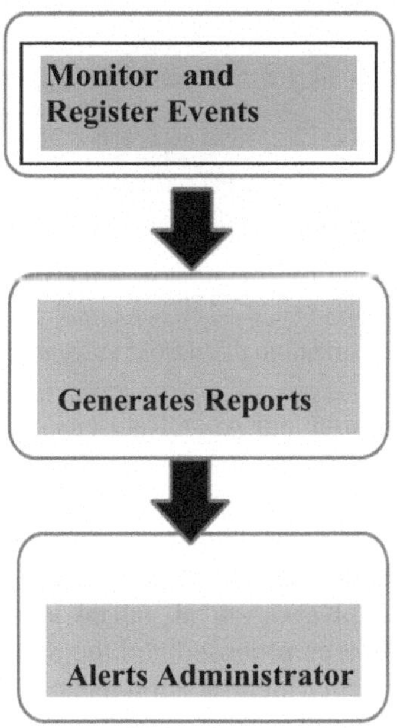

Fig. 3. Key functionalities of an IDS

quickly warns the owner by raising an alarm. Key functionalities of an IDS are showcased in Fig. 3. The functions of Intrusion Detection System (IDS) can be many and basically includes Observing and monitoring the user, system or a network, Identifying patterns of attacks, generating reports on intrusion, keeping a track of users' policy violations and registering events related to suspicious activities.

This is done through system file comparisons against malware signatures, scanning processes that detect signs of harmful patterns, monitoring user behavior to detect malicious intent and monitoring system settings and configurations. Upon detecting any violation in security, it sends an alert to the administrator.

5.1 IDS Techniques

In view of the components used to characterize an application, the intrusion detection techniques can be categorized as Static, Dynamic and Hybrid as shown in Fig. 4. Static analysis involves analysis of code without running an application. Features for Static Analysis include, (a) Permissions, (b) API calls that can be obtained from the Android-Manifest.xml document. Dynamic investigation analyze features that are extracted from the application while running, which includes (a) Battery utilization, (b) Network traffic, (c) IP address, and so forth. The third techniques is known as crossover/hybrid investigation which consolidates the components from static and dynamic analysis techniques [3]. The categorization of these static, dynamic and hybrid features is shown in Fig. 4.

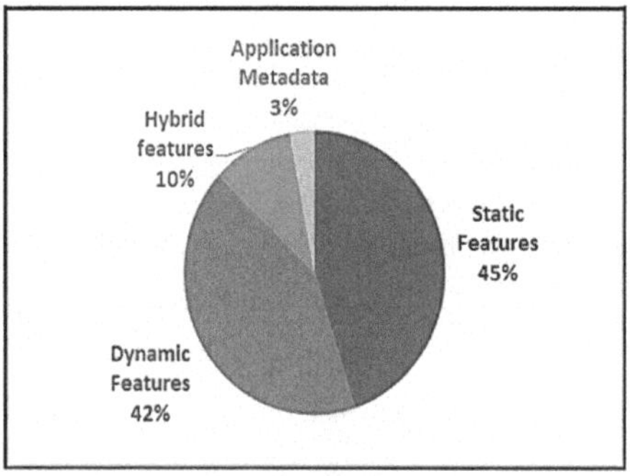

Fig. 4. Categorization of android malware features [9]

In April 2016, Balaji Baskaran and Anca Ralescus compressed late improvements in android malware discovery utilizing machine learning algorithms. Detection procedures and frameworks that utilize static, dynamic and cross breed/hybrid methodologies are examined and highlighted. It can incredibly help in the improvement of better android malware discovery techniques, by knowing how the known malware act and influence android gadgets [3]. Kavesh et al. talked about various android malware discovery strategies that have been proposed and the patterns are seen in the research adapted towards discovering better identification techniques. It can mainly help in the improvement of better android malware recognition techniques, by knowing how the known malware carry on and influence android devices [33].

5.1.1 Static Analysis

In static investigation, the components are extracted from the application record without executing the application. This philosophy is asset and time productive as the application is not executed. But, this examination experiences code confusion procedures the Malware creators utilize to sidestep from static discovery strategies. One of extremely mainstream avoidance procedure is the Update Attack: an application is introduced on the cell phone and when the application gets an upgrade, the malignant substance is downloaded and introduced as a component. This cannot be identified by static investigation strategies which will filter just the considerate application. The most routinely used static components are the Permission besides, API calls. Since these are isolated from the application AndroidManifest.xml and effect the malware area rate to a high degree, extensive research has been made with these as components furthermore combined with various components expelled from meta-data open in Google Play-Store, for instance, version name, version no., author's name, last updated time, etc.

In Static examination, the system gives a comprehension of the code structure, and can guarantee that the code holds fast to industry benchmarks. Modernized devices can help programming experts and organizers in completing static examination. The way toward investigating at code alone (by looking printout, for instance), without the help of robotized instruments, is now and again called program comprehension or system appreciation.

In [15], a versatile recognition framework is outlined utilizing Multi-feature community decision framework (MCDF). The different elements of a malignant record like consent based components and API call based elements are considered keeping in mind the end goal to give better discovery via preparing a group of classifiers and joining their choices utilizing community approach in view of probability hypothesis to take a shot at the best arrangement of elements that can be removed effectively at run time. The essential good position of static examination is the way that it can reveal errors that don't show themselves until a supplant happens weeks, months or years after release. Taking all things into account, static examination is only an underlying stage in a thorough programming quality-control organization. After the usage of static examination, dynamic examination is performed with a true objective to uncover inconspicuous defects. Dynamic examination incorporates the testing and assessment of a venture in perspective of execution. Other static features besides permissions and Java code, some researchers analyze several other static features that are as follows:

(a) *Intent Filter* – One of the components depicted in the manifest document or file. It is a unique data around an operation, with which we deduce aim of the applications. For instance, pick a contact, take a photograph, dial a number, and so on. In view of goal filters, Android takes proper activities. Specialists have been utilizing goal channels for malware recognition, since attackers order malware to send private information to them that requires the nearness of intentions in the intent filter portion of AndroidMan-ifest.xml file.

In DroidMat [32], different components from an Android file including intent filters are extracted and are broken down. The creators used a few machine learning calculations, for example, k-implies, k-closest neighbors and guileless bayes to create malware identification framework. To start with, the DroidMat extracts the information (e.g. asked for authorizations, Intent message passing, and so forth) from every application's manifest document, and considers components (Activity, Service, Receiver) as an entry point penetrating down for checking API Calls identified with consents. Next, it applies K-implies calculation that upgrades the malware demonstrating ability. The number of clusters are chosen by Singular Value Decomposition (SVD) technique on the low rank estimate. At last, it utilizes kNN algorithm to order the application as kind or vindictive. Assessment of DroidMat displayed a change over comparable frameworks in that time. A framework (named A3) was distributed that considers few components incorporating purpose channels in Android establishment record [30]. It then builds a call diagram that speaks to stream of the Java code execution. It then uses A* calculation to decide the most brief way that along these lines demonstrates the conduct of the malware.

DREBIN [20] presents a wide static investigation and utilizes features from the Manifest file including intent filters using Support Vector Machine(SVM) as a machine learning algorithm. The consequences of the examination appeared that DREBIN distinguished 94% of malware with low false alarm.

Feng et al. exhibited Apposcopy, another semantics-based approach which consolidates (i) a high level language for determining signatures that depict semantic characteristics of malware signature. The signature uses a blend of static flow investigation and another type of program representation called Inter-Component Call Graph to proficiently identify Android applications that have certain control and information stream properties.

(b) *Network Address*: Specialists search for system address or IP address of the C&C server in code of Android installation files. The system address was fused as one of the static components in their frameworks [20, 30].
(c) *Strings*: It is communicated that one of the comprehensively used systems as a piece of good malware revelation is analysing strings available in the file [29].
(d) *Hardware Components*: DREBIN [20] utilized Hardware components for static analysis. The AndroidManifest.xml document includes permissions for Camera, GPS which can be used by malware to report the area of the victim to the attacker.

5.1.2 Dynamic Analysis

Dynamic investigation is the process of analyzing the code of an application at the time of its running. This procedure is hard to actualize when contrasted with static examination, because of the overhead of executing the application [2, 5].

Taindroid is another dynamic examination framework which catches the system information for breaking down applications. In another examination by the creators of Maline have proposed a malware recognition instrument, in view of following framework calls and order them in view of machine learning calculations. System calls and network traffic are being frequently used for dynamic analysis. System calls such as read, write and open are used to provide services and resources to applications. Monitoring network traffic of mobile devices is another way of detecting the malware as applications send and receive data through networks and the same can be used for leaking data to attackers maliciously.

Shabtai et al. discussed a behavior based anomaly detection system for detecting meaningful deviations in a mobile applications network behavior by detecting mobile malware with self-updating capabilities. The detection of such can be performed based on applications' network traffic patterns only [19].

5.1.3 Hybrid Analysis

The Hybrid analysis is a combination of Static and Dynamic analysis which involves analysing the application and obtaining information while the application is running, respectively. Though it increases the accuracy level of the detection rate, but it makes the system cumbersome and the analysis process time consuming [3].

MARVIN was developed in 2015 which laboured on the desktop finding out strategies used for classification of Apps Centred on distinctive features which can be gathered through static and dynamic analysis, network degree behavior and meta-data like author fingerprints and app lifetime [12]. Centred on this rich and comprehensive set of elements, it assigns malice rankings to unknown apps in a range from 0(benign) to 10(malicious). This cellular app is valuable for newbie and authorities considering the fact that they are able to publish apps through net interfaces or a dedicated mobile.

Malik and Khatter in June 2016 explored the behavior of 10 general android malware families focused on approach name pattern of those families. In this paper, authors extracted system call hint of 345 malicious applications from 10 android malware families named FakeInstaller, Opfake, Plankton, DroidKungfu, base-bridge, iconosys, kmin, adrd and gappusin making use of strace android tool and when compared it with procedure name sample of 300 benign apps to justify behavior of malicious application. It was once observed that malicious apps invoke process calls extra most of the time than benign functions. This analysis can be used in designing intrusion detection procedure for an android mobile gadget with more accuracy [7].

Also, a novel hybrid approach was proposed where execution knowledge of sample malware and benign apps utilizing a net_ link technological know-how to generate patterns of system calls concerning file and network access. They constructed up malicious sample set and a traditional sample set for detecting an unknown application, they used a dynamic system to accumulate its process calling information. Then examine with both malicious and natural patterns to judge. This technique is found on difference between malware and benign apps in runtime system calls. It applies a dynamic procedure to acquire the runtime procedure calling data of mobile apps and makes use of a static approach to investigate the collected data for malware detection at a strong detection server [5].

In 2015, AndroInspector was developed which derives, extracts and analyse primary features of android app making use of static analysis and subsequently classifies the app utilizing machine learning strategies and dynamic evaluation [9]. Static evaluation is in charge for classifying the app as both malware or benign whereas dynamic analysis identifies malicious moves carried out via app throughout execution. The system of classification includes of extracting 24 features, assigning weights to points and ultimately using assortment of function weight as a characteristic set. The mixture of characteristic set and random forest classifier model to classify given pattern as either benign or malware. Setting up a classifier model which considers info from both static and dynamic analysis even as classifying an android application.

In [2], namely two noteworthy strategies anomaly based and signature based methods are discussed. Also distinctive portable malware recognition frameworks are talked about here. Signature based Techniques can be upgraded utilizing DNA coordinating methods connected as a part of other domains. Also, permission system can be used and a mixture strategy can be created for enhanced performance as far as accuracy, precision etc.

Taken a shot at the machine learning strategies utilized for grouping of Apps in view of various components which are gathered through static and element examination, organize level conduct and meta-data like creator fingerprints and application lifetime. Based on this rich and thorough arrangement of features, MARVIN allocates malignance scores applications in a range from 0(benign) to 10(malicious). This Portable application is valuable for tenderfoot and specialists since they can submit applications through web interfaces or a committed mobile [12].

6 Conclusion and Future Scope

This paper has discussed the different Android malware analysis and detection techniques and has also explained the Android malware's ability to evade the detection process. This study is different from the previous research as it emphasizes on Android malware attacks, and more general Android security rather than studying mobile security in general. As Android has become the prime target for cybercrimes by means of malware and viruses. Approximately 85.1% market share of android system gives us the view of its comparatively higher user base. Like Apple, Google gives a concentrated market to versatile applications called Google Play Store. However, that is counterbalanced by the Android's capacity to introduce applications from outsider sources. Some are outstanding and legitimate, for example, Amazon. Therefore, it has led to rise of malwares which assault the Android devices in various forms, for example, exchanging messages without the user's permission and removing them, sending users' confidential data to some other server, gaining root privileges, downloading malicious software, masquerading as a system app and many more. So there is an incredible need to shield user's information from these malware.

The steadily expanding malware dangers have constrained the Android anti-malware industry to build up the answers for alleviating malignant application risk on Android cell phones and other Android gadgets. Three fundamental methodologies identified for this reason and discussed in this paper are: Static approach, Dynamic approach and Hybrid approach. Antivirus programs utilize one of these ways to shield the frameworks from malware assaults. However, the overall risk situation of android users is difficult to assess. Thus, it has become important to build up a security suite and an efficient intrusion detection system using a novel algorithm/technique to handle invasion in Android device applications. Thus, the efficient IDS framework for cell phones can become one of the important junctures for future research. Also, a novel classifier model which considers information from both static analysis and dynamic analysis while classifying an Android application can be developed.

References

1. Varol, N., Aydogan, A.F., Varol, A.: Cyber attacks targetting android cell-phones. IEEE (2017)
2. Malhotra, A., Bajaj, K.: A survey on various malware detection techniques on mobile platform. Int. J. Comput. Appl. **139**(5) (2016). ISSN 0975-8887
3. Baskaran, B., Ralescu, A.: A study of android malware detection techniques and machine learning. In: MAICS 2016 (2016)
4. Kapratwar, A.: Static and dynamic analysis for android malware detection. San Jose State University (2016)
5. Tong, F., Yan, Z.: A hybrid approach of mobile malware detection in android. J. Parallel Distrib. Comput. **103**, 22–31 (2016)
6. Roy, N.R., Khanna, A.K., Aneja, L.: Android phone forensic: tools and techniques. In: IEEE Conference, Galgotias University, Greater Noida (2016)
7. Malik, S., Khatter, K.: System call analysis of android malware families. Indian J. Sci. Technol. (IJST) **9**(21) (2016)
8. Rana, S., Aneja, L.: Static and dynamic analysis of android malware. In: International Conference, REDSET 2016 (2016)
9. Feizollah, A., Anuar, N.B., Salleh, R., Wahab, A.W.A.: A review on feature selection in mobile malware detection. Digit. Investig. **13**, 22–37 (2015)
10. Babu Rajesh, V., Reddy, P., Himanshu, P., Patil, M.U.: Androinspector: a system for comprehensive analysis of android applications. Int. J. Netw. Secur. Appl. (IJNSA) **7**(5) (2015)
11. Vijayarani, S., Sylviaa, M.: Intrusion detection system – a study. Int. J. Secur. Priv. Trust Manag. (IJSPTM) **4**(1) (2015)
12. Lindorfer, M., Neugschwandtner, M., Platzer, C.: MARVIN: efficient and comprehensive mobile app classification through static and dynamic analysis. In: IEEE 39th Annual International Computers, Software and Applications Conference (2015)
13. Kaushik, P., Jain, A.: Malware detection techniques in android. Int. J. Comput. Appl. **122**(17) (2015). ISSN 0975-8887
14. Mahesh, P., Jayawant, A., Kale, G.: Smartphone security: review of attacks, detection and prevention. Int. J. Adv. Res. Comput. Sci. Softw. Eng. **5**(3) (2015)
15. Sheen, S., Anitha, R., Natarajan, V.: Android based malware detection using a multifeature collaborative decision fusion approach. Neurocomputing **151**, 905–912 (2015)
16. Malik, S., Khatter, K.: AndroData: a tool for static and dynamic feature extraction of android app. Int. J. Appl. Eng. Res. **10**, 98–102 (2015)
17. Walnycky, D., Baggili, I., Marrington, A., Moore, J.: Network and device forensic analysis of android social-messaging applications. Digit. Investig. **14**, S77–S84 (2015)
18. The volatility framework: volatile memory artifact, Systems, Volatile. http://secxplrd.blogspot.in/2011/10/volatility-framework-volatile-memory.html. Accessed 9 Oct 2015
19. Shabtai, A., Tenenboim-Chekina, L., Mimran, D., Rokach, L., Shapira, B., Elovici, Y.: Mobile malware detection through analysis of deviations in application network behaviour. Digit. Investig. **43**, 1–8 (2014)
20. Arp, D., Spreitzenbarth, M., Hubner, M., Gascon, H., Rieck, K.: Drebin: effective and explainable detection of android malware in your pocket. In: Network and Distributed System Security (NDSS) Symposium (2014)
21. Quick, D., Choo, K.-K.R.: Impacts of increasing volume of digital forensic data: a survey and future research challenges. Digit. Investig. **11**, 273–294 (2014)

22. Uppal, H.A.M., Javed, M., Arshad, M.J.: An overview of intrusion detection system (IDS) along with its commonly used techniques and classifications. Int. J. Comput. Sci. Telecommun. **5**(2) (2014)
23. Ayers, R., Brothers, S., Jansen, W.: Guidelines on mobile device forensics. NIST Special Publication 800-101r1, May 2014. http://dx.doi.org/10.6028/NIST.SP.800-101r1
24. Dhaya, R., Poongodi, M.: Detecting software vulnerabilities in android using static analysis. IEEE (2014)
25. Raveendranath, R., Rajamani, V., Babu, A.J., Datta, S.K.: Android malware attacks and countermeasures: current and future directions. IEEE (2014)
26. Dua, L., Bansal, D.: Review on mobile threats and detection techniques. Int. J. Distrib. Parallel Syst. (IJDPS)
27. Kaart, M., Laraghy, S.: Android forensics: interpretation of timestamps. Digit. Investig. **11**, 234–248 (2014)
28. Chakraborty, N.: Intrusion detection system and intrusion prevention system: a comparative study. Int. J. Comput. Bus. Res. (IJCBR) **4**(2) (2013)
29. Sanz, B., Santos, I., Laorden, C., Ugarte-Pedrero, X., Bringas, P., Álvarez, G.: PUMA: permission usage to detect malware in android. In: Herrero, Á., et al. (eds.) International Joint Conference CISIS'12-ICEUTE'12-SOCO'12 Special Sessions. AISC, vol. 189, pp. 289–298. Springer, Heidelberg (2013). https://doi.org/10.1007/978-3-642-33018-6_30
30. Zhang, Y., Yang, M., Xu, B., Yang, Z., Gu, G., Ning, P., et al.: Vetting undesirable behaviors in android apps with permission use analysis. In: ACM SIGSAC Conference on Computer & Communications Security, p. 611e22 (2013)
31. Demme, J., Maycock, M., Schmitz, J., Tang, A.: On the feasibility of online malware detection with performance counters. In: ISCA 2013 (2013)
32. Wu, K.-P.: DroidMat: android malware detection through manifest and API calls tracing. In: Information Security (Asia JCIS), pp. 62–69 (2012)
33. Shaerpour, K., Dehghantanha, A., Mahmod, R.: Trends in android malware detection. J. Digit. Forensics Secur. Law **8**(3)
34. Casey, E.: Digital Evidence and Computer Crime: Forensic Science, Computers, and the Internet. Elsevier Academic Press, Amsterdam (2011)
35. Oh, J., Lee, S., Lee, S.: Advanced evidence collection and analysis of web browser activity. Digit. Investig. **8**, S62–S70 (2011). https://doi.org/10.1016/j.diin.2011.05.008. ISSN 1742-2876
36. Thing, V.L., Ng, K.-Y., Chang, E.-C.: Live memory forensics of mobile phones. Digit. Investig. **7**(Suppl.), S74–S82 (2010). https://doi.org/10.1016/j.diin.2010.05.010. ISSN 1742-2876
37. Enck, W., Ongtang, M., Drew, P.: Understanding android security. IEEE Secur. Priv. **7**(1), 50–57 (2009)
38. Mislan, R.P., Wedge, T.: Designing laboratories for small scale digital device forensics. In: ADFSL Conference on Digital Forensics, Security and Law (2008)
39. Aron, L., Hanacek, P.: Overview of security on mobile devices. IEEE (2015)
40. Zhou, Y., Jiang, X.: Dissecting android malware: characterization and evolution. In: IEEE Symposium on Security and Privacy (2012)
41. https://www.google.co.in/search?noj=1&biw=1517&bih=681&tbm=isch&sa=1&q=android+malware+statistics+2017&oq=android+malware+statis-tics+2017&gs_l=img.3..0i24k1.9898.12225.0.12716.5.5.0.0.0.0.430.831.0j1j1j0j1.3.0....0...1.1.64.img..2.3.827...0i30k1j0i5i30k1.Hfr7MeKT9cs#imgrc=Q56MG4_VzRqMSM

An Insightful View on Security and Performance of NoSQL Databases

Upaang Saxena[1(✉)] and Shelly Sachdeva[2(✉)]

[1] Minjar Cloud Services Private Limited, Bangalore, India
upaang.saxena@minjar.com

[2] Jaypee Institute of Information Technology, Noida, India
shelly.sachdeva@jiit.ac.in

Abstract. The recent advancement in cloud computing and distributed web applications has created the need to store large amount of data in distributed databases that provide high availability and scalability. Due to this problem, in recent years, a non-relational database is needed to scale the growing need of industry and at the same time, must be highly efficient. This gave rise to NoSQL databases which are highly scalable and can store large amount of data. NoSQL databases are- 'Not Only SQL' databases and supports almost all the SQL features in addition to several other features. NoSQL is completely schema less and can store any kind of data. A large amount of data is stored in these databases every day, including sensitive data. Security of this sensitive data is an area of concern. Research looked into the security aspect of the top three open source NoSQL databases which are Mongo DB, Cassandra, and Redis. In this research, surprisingly, it has been found that data file encryption is missing in all three databases. Cassandra and Mongo DB are safe from Injection attacks, but there are many other ways to get into these databases and access the data at backend. Researchers provided useful methods to enhance the security for these databases and also evaluated the performance, after improvement in security.

Keywords: NoSQL · Security in NoSQL · Cassandra · Mongo DB · Redis Big data

1 Introduction

With growing demand and data, the way the data is stored has changed a lot. Earlier, relational database were enough to store the data and a single schema was enough to store the data, but now, we need a distributed environment and one database is not enough to store all the data. We have moved from one database approach to distributed databases approach, where part of data is stored in multiple databases. We are in Big Data age and we need our databases to store these large data and scale accordingly. In traditional databases, all the information is arranged in forms of fields, records and files. For example, a telephone book is a file and it contains list of records. Each record has multiple fields associated and all the fields have certain values which are the properties of the record. But, as the demand to store the fields increases, this traditional approach

B. Panda et al. (Eds.): REDSET 2017, CCIS 799, pp. 643–653, 2018.
https://doi.org/10.1007/978-981-10-8527-7_54

of storing data failed to fulfill the requirements of users and there came the concept of Big Data.

Due to these problems, a new kind of databases came into existence which has the functionality of these traditional relational databases, and also they can be scaled to Big Data. They do not follow any fixed schema. These databases are called as 'NoSQL' databases [14].

Figure 1 illustrates the problems faced by relational database users in storing the data in SQL like databases. This describes about the reason why people are moving to Big Data, and the reason why SQL users are shifting to use NoSQL databases like Cassandra, Mongo DB, etc.

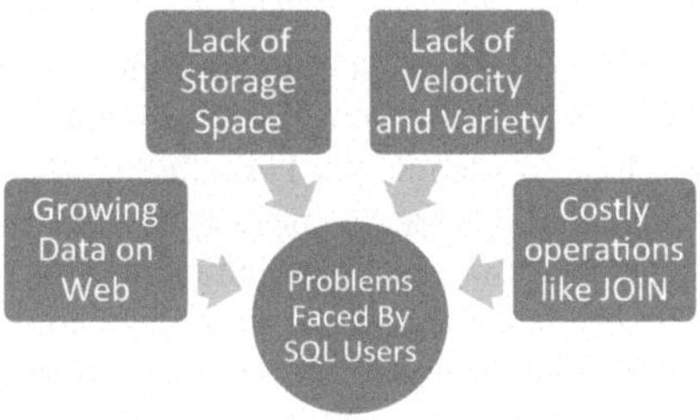

Fig. 1. Problems faced by SQL users

The NoSQL databases are widely used in distributed environment and companies like Facebook, Twitter, Amazon and Google (which store 100–1000 million records), started using and developing these NoSQL databases [16]. Nowadays, we have almost 225 NoSQL databases and all are for different purpose and are widely used [1]. The open source NoSQL databases are more popular. In this research, we are focussing on top three open source NoSQL databases, which are Cassandra, MongoDB and Redis.

As the data grows, security of the data is the main concern. The research aims for identifying the security loopholes in these three NoSQL databases and help the readers selecting the best suitable database which will keep their data more secure. The researchers have conducted their research based on the following factors: Encryption of Data files, Authentication/Encryption for Server/Client, Inter cluster Encryption, Script Injection, and Denial of Service attacks. The researchers also analysed the security vulnerabilities of each database and have proposed various best practices to be followed to secure their data in these databases. Further, a comparative study is made between three databases after fixing the security loopholes, on the basis of their Read and Write Operations.

2 Background Study

As the data is growing, we are shifting to an era of schema-less data storage systems, like NoSQL, NewSQL, etc. These data storage systems can contain any structure of data and store Big data, without any storage space constraint. These databases can be used in places where there is a need of scaling out, whenever needed. There are some websites and analyst who have made their studies in these NoSQL databases and have given complete comparison and analysis of them. According to a website – www.nosql-database.org [2] there exist almost 225 NoSQL databases, till date. Various organizations have analyzed these NoSQL databases and have ranked these databases, based on their popularity. A website 'www.bigdataanalyticsnews.com' [3] has ranked the top 12 open source databases in February, 2014; a website 'www.nosql.findthebest.com' [4] has ranked the top 16 databases in year 2013. In particular, this research focused on the top three open source NoSQL databases ranked by these websites. The NoSQL databases studied and analyzed in this research are Mongo DB, Cassandra, and Redis, respectively.

Mongo DB is an open-source document database, and one of the leading NoSQL database. Mongo DB is written in C++. Mongo stores documents on the basis on the basic of named keys, i.e. in JSON or BSON format [5]. This gives the dynamicity needed for the documents and we can modify or remove the documents very easily. As every value is attached by a key, indexing is also possible and it helps in giving faster search results in Mongo DB. Secondary Indexing is also possible in case of Mongo DB. It's completely flexible and due to its schema less nature, its more dynamic and its performance does not depends on number and size of the document.

Apache Cassandra is an open source distributed database management system designed to handle large amounts of data across many commodity servers, providing high availability with no single point of failure [6]. Cassandra is a write friendly database and handles million write request per minute normally. Cassandra does not support Joins and Sub-queries. Rather, Cassandra emphasizes de normalization through features like collections. Apache Cassandra was born at Facebook and is built on Amazon's Dynamo and Google's Big Table. Redis is also an open source NoSQL database but it is key-value store rather than document database. Redis is a data-structure server as it contains strings, hashes, lists, sets and sorted sets. Redis stores the complete dataset in-memory, which ensures that Redis is extremely fast and efficient. It uses the disk only for persistence. Redis supports master-slave replication. Data from any Redis server can replicate to any number of slaves [7]. A slave may be a master to another slave. This allows Redis to implement a single-rooted replication tree. All the Redis operations are atomic, which ensures that if two clients concurrently access Redis server will get the updated value.

Comparison on the Basis of Security

The data at rest is unencrypted. The latest Cassandra (Enterprise 3.2) provides an optional feature for Transparent Data Encryption to protect data that is flushed out from the memory (memtable) and written to disk. To some extent, this feature can be enabled to protect sensitive data. By default, neither the client- node communication, nor the inter-node communication is encrypted. SSL can be turned on by editing the corresponding settings under client encryption options in the "cassandra.yaml" file after generating valid server certificates. The administrative user or authentication is not enabled by default in Cassandra. It has very weak password storage.

Two broad classes of approaches to encrypt data at rest with MongoDB are Application Level Encryption and Storage Encryption [13]. TLS/SSL (Transport Layer Security/Secure Sockets Layer) used to encrypt all of MongoDB's network traffic. In MongoDB, authorization and authentication are disabled by default. MongoDB provisions authorization on a per-database level by using a role-based approach. Basic MongoDB does provide support for authentication on a per-database level. Users exist in the context of a single logical database.

Redis does not support data encryption and all data is stored as plain text. The RDB [19] persistence performs point-in-time snapshots of the dataset at specified intervals. Communication between Redis client and server is not encrypted. While Redis does not try to implement access control, it provides a tiny layer of authentication that is optionally turned on editing the "redis.conf" file. When the authorization layer is enabled, Redis will refuse any query by unauthenticated clients. A client can authenticate itself by sending the AUTH command followed by the password [8].

MongoDB supports access rights for users and roles. For Cassandra, access rights can be established per object. Redis supports uncomplicated password based access control.

3 Current Research

3.1 Security Vulnerabilities of the Top 3 Open Source NoSQL Databases

We have analysed these databases on various grounds and have created a combined study for all three of them under following categories.

Table 1 gives us the top level view about the various security categories which we have analysed and made a combined study for these three NoSQL databases: MongoDB, Cassandra and Redis.

A. **Data at rest:** MongoDB Enterprise 3.2 introduces a encryption option, which encrypts all the data stored in MongoDB and it ensures that only the intended user with right key can decode it. AES256-CBC(256-bit Advanced Encryption Standard in Cipher Block Chaining mode) via OpenSSL is provided in MongoDB. AES-256 uses a symmetric key; i.e. the same key to encrypt and decrypt text. Cassandra 3.2 provides an optional feature for Transparent Data Encryption (TDE) to protect data that is flushed out from the memory (*memtable*) and written to disk. But, as the encryption certificate is stored locally, a secured file system is necessary before TDE is turned on. Also, the commit log file, which stores all the events data of Cassandra, is not encrypted. Where as in Redis, data is not encrypted at database level. Anyone who has access to the server can access the whole data at the server. Redis was originally designed to be accessed by a group of trusted clients, inside a trusted environment [7].
B. **Data at Motion:** MongoDB supports TLS/SSL (Transport Layer Security/Secure Sockets Layer) to encrypt all of MongoDB's data in motion in network. All the network data is ensured to be delivered to the intended client and TLS/SSL ensures that the communication is secure and only intended client can read it. In Cassandra, the client-node communication is not encrypted by default. Cassandra utilizes Apache Thrift framework to communicate with the client. Now, current version of Cassandra has SSL, but it's not enabled by default. In Redis, transport layer is not encrypted and is a major pitfall for the Redis users. Data is not encrypted even while

sending data from one server to another and from one application to another. Redis makes connections over TCP, and offers no transport layer security.

C. **Authentication:** Mongo DB does not provide any authentication by default. Although, Basic MongoDB does provide support for authentication on per-level Users exists in the context of a single logical database [12]. In Cassandra, by default, the settings are ***AllowAllAuthenticator***, which means essentially there is no authentication. Redis, by default also listens on all available IP addresses on port 6379, with no authentication required at all.

D. **Authorization:** Authorization check in MongoDB is disabled by default. Though, it provides some provisions for it by making users authorized per-database level by using a role based approach [12]. Cassandra by defaults allows all the clients without requiring any credentials. But, as Cassandra is a schema-less database, the data models are not properly provided like a traditional RDBMS. But, Cassandra do provides some Authorizers for controlling the access to the privileged users. According to official document of Apache, if *CassandraAuthorizer* is selected, then the privileged administrators can be granted any of the privileges like ALTER, AUTHORIZE, CREATE, DROP, MODIFY, SELECT, on any resources (ALL KEYSPACES, KEYSPACE, TABLE) to a selected user, by executing CQL (Cassandra Query Language) statements. [6] Redis has a weak password storage method. The major threat for Redis is brute force attack [8], as the password for redis is set in clear text and the number of password attempt is not rate limited or restricted in any way.

E. **Injection Attacks:** Mongo DB uses JavaScript extensively at server side for its performance enhancement and because of this; it is always open to these attacks. Its internal operator "$where", designed to be used as a filter like the "where" clause in SQL, can also takes sophisticated JavaScript functions to filter data [9]. The CQL functions under Thrift and in a level of RPC so it will not be attacked by the SQL injection. Although the study of Aniello et al. [10] suggested that Cassandra possesses little vulnerability, those were not the CQL's. The redis is somewhat safe from the injection attacks. It doesn't allow 'string escaping' and it also not supports multiple commands at a time.

F. **Public Port Access:** Mongo DB runs on port 27017 by default and this is publicly accessible. Cassandra runs on port 8888 by default [12]. If the hacker knows the port of Cassandra server and makes enough connection, it can freeze the Cassandra server and can make it stop. As Cassandra uses Thrift Protocol, the Cassandra makes one thread for a single client, and as it does not have the time-out feature for the inactive clients, the thread pool of Cassandra can soon be occupied and it can crash. Redis is always listening to Port 6379 by default. According to a study, many of the servers are facing the internet and can be easily accessed by the attackers. Once, someone checked out for the open servers and found 48 open servers on Internet/24 and this is a big security threat [9].

G. **IP Binding:** In MongoDB, all the data is stored on a public IP and is publically accessible [15]. Cassandra is by default open to public. If not kept under a VPC or NAT, anyone can access the data inside Cassandra with no checks. Redis is also open to public by default and anyone who checks for its port number: 6379 will able to see the Redis server data easily.

Table 1. Security vulnerabilities in NoSQL databases

Category	MongoDB	Cassandra	Redis
Data at rest	To encrypt data at rest, approaches are application level encryption and storage encryption	Partially present; but optional data encryption is available	Does not support data encryption and all data is stored as plain text
Data at motion	TLS/SSL used to encrypt all of MongoDB's network traffic	By default, neither client-node, nor inter-node communication is encrypted	Communication between Redis client and server is not encrypted
Authentication	Not present as default	Partially present, but weak	Do not support by default
Authorization	Not present by default, but authorization is available on a per-database level by using a role-based approach	Not present as default setting	Not present
Injection attack	Possible, using JavaScript	Possible using CQL	Not possible
Public port access	Runs on port 27017 by default and this is publicly accessible	Runs on port 8888 by default, and can be excessed with this port	Redis is always listening to Port 6379 by default
IP binding	By default it is publicly accessible	Cassandra is by default open to public	By default open to public

These are the major security loopholes in these databases. We can easily infer that with more data and more advancement, the databases are at major threat and we need to follow certain best practice to tune the security of these databases.

3.2 Improvement of these Security Loopholes

We have also found remediation of these security loopholes and have ensured that following steps will help people make their datastores safe and reliable.

A. **Data at Rest:** In MongoDB, Application Level Encryption provides encryption on a per-field or per-document basis within the application layer [13]. At database level also, various security measures are required, such as segregation of data to different nodes of MongoDB. For Redis, we need some encryption algorithm to encrypt data before writing the data to database at application layer itself. Strong file system security is also recommended for more protection. As Cassandra already has Transparent Data Encryption (TDE) present in current versions of Cassandra, but the encryption certificate is stored locally only. So, a secured file system, like a key based mechanism should be preferred to protect our data before TDE. Also, the commit log files are needed to be encrypted and the key must not be stored locally. In Redis, the only way to secure the data is to encrypt it using a Key based algorithm and sending the encrypted key along with the data in network.

B. **Data at Motion:** In Mongo DB, we have to make sure that the SSL encryption is on and all the communications are happening through it. A .pem file containing a public key certificate and its associated private key is a must before SSL communication [13]. Use MongoDB generated SSL certificate, as it will ensure that server is validated. In Cassandra SSL can be turned on by editing the corresponding settings under *client_encryption_options* in the *cassandra.yaml* file after generating valid server certificates. Inter-node SS communication can also be configured by editing the corresponding settings under *server_encryption_options* in the *cassandra.yaml* file [6] In Redis, SSH tunneling is recommended to be used to ensure that data is secure at the time of transfer. SSH tunnel encrypts the data before sending to the transport layer and decrypts it back to the original data at other server [11].

C. **Authentication:** Authentication in MongoDB and Cassandra can be enabled by enabling passwords in two layers for the users. This 2-layered protection will check the password, as well as the keys at 2 levels and will help enhancing the security [13]. MongoDB provisions authorization on a per- level by using a role-based approach [12]. Though, Enterprise Cassandra can further provide *Kerberos authentication,* which requires setting up separate Kerberos servers and installing Kerberos client software on all joining Cassandra hosts [6]. Redis can have authentication using password, which is stored in the *redis.conf* file. It is also a good practice to restrict access to your redis.conf file, because in some cases it can contain sensitive data.

D. **Authorization:** As granular access control does not exist in Mongo DB, alternate means are used to protect data [12]. A database must be protected and must not be visible to the user with the help of Front end web services which contains all the business logic including the access control rules for the application. Apart from this, Mongo DB must not be allowed to be accessed as a root and permissions to access the DB must be minimised [15]. Cassandra, by defaults allows everyone to access the data. It is recommended to change this default configuration and by allowing very few users to access the Cassandra server. Even, different users must be given different permissions and roles and should be controlled at the server level itself. Permissions and users must be created using GRANT statement. For example;
GRANT permission ON resource TO user;
To protect Redis, we need to select a very strong password, as it does not protect us from repeated password try. So, the password must be as random as possible, and at the same time it should be long enough. We can use command *pwgen -sy 32* **1** for generating a very strong password [8].

E. **Injection Attack:** As MongoDB is vulnerable to Injection attacks, one must only be allowed to access the server if the input is completely valid and is thoroughly checked. Various checks must be deployed to check the validity of the input [13]. Developers must also work on consistency of the application, as it will provide a fundamental structure for taking inputs and allowing the users to access the application. As Cassandra uses Thrift protocol, Injection attacks are not possible in Cassandra. Still, it is recommended to 'pre-encode' the data and make it safe. No column-family or key should have the same name as in UI. And also, validation of input can also help in protection from Injection attacks. Whereas Redis protocol has no concept of string escaping, so it is not vulnerable to injection attacks using a normal client library.

F. **Public Port Access:** As Mongo DB runs on a public port by default, one should always ensure to run it at some other port. Disable the HTTP status interface, as MongoDB by default provides a http interface running by default on port 28017 which provides the "home" status page. Use the "*nohttpinterface*" configuration setting to disable the http interface. The default connection configuration for Cassandra also must change. Connection and access to the Redis server should only be allowed through a set of IP's and at a certain port, and that too using key transfer or authentication. Redis must only be accessed through a NAT or VPC, and that to only to some specific IPs.

G. **IP Binding:** For protecting the IP binding in all these databases, firewalls must be used. This will restrict which entities are allowed to use your DB and connect to the server. Best practice is to only allow your application servers access to the database. If, your application is hosted on Cloud platforms like AWS and Azure, one can make use of Security groups to bind the access to public IP's and ports. If any other service providers are used, we should protect it using 'ip_tables'. These IP tables will store only those IP's, which are allowed to access the servers and can access the data from the database.

3.3 Performance Evaluation of these NoSQL Databases

Machine Specifications

1. Processor: 4x Intel(R) Core(TM) i5-3230 M CPU @ 2.60 GHz
2. Memory: 8 GB RAM
3. Operating System: Ubuntu 16.04
   a. Kernel-Version: Linux 3.8.0-33-generic (x86_64)

Firstly, researchers evaluated these NoSQL databases- MongoDB, Cassandra and Redis, *without improving their security* on the basis of Read and Write Operations.

Dataset Specifications

Researchers have considered small size data set and have performed the study with 10, 100, 1000, 10000, and 50000 records. The data set contains information of all the users of an application, which is taken from [17, 18]. It stores all the user attributes along with their preferences. Query execution time is calculated using *trace* in CQL, adding "*.explain (executionStats)*" to query in MongoDB and using log commands in Redis.

The observation shows that the Redis performed the best, if no security measure is applied. If the default configurations of these NoSQL databases are not modified, the Redis is better of these three databases (Table 2).

Table 2. NoSQL database IOPS operation time (in ms)

Number of records	Mongo DB read	Mongo DB write	Cassandra read	Cassandra write	Redis read	Redis write
10	4	6	2.1	.2	2	3
100	9	29	65	1.4	12	7
1000	78	125	93	33.8	33	27
10000	799	1061	504	56.4	221	208
50000	3998	6884	1734	122.5	914	921

Mongo DB is not magically faster. MongoDB resembles the traditional SQL databases in term of storing data. So, if you store the same data, organized in basically the same fashion, and access it exactly the same way, then it's crazy to expect your results to be wildly different. But, still it is widely used as a document-storage database and gives good results.

People are seeing real world Mongo DB performance largely because Mongo DB allows you to query on data in a more structured way, which is more sensible to your workload.

Cassandra can be monitored very easily using Datastax OpsCentre. All the latencies and operation counts can be monitored using the graphical tool in OpsCentre and its values can be obtained from there.

When the durability of data is not needed, the in-memory nature of Redis allows it to perform extremely well compared to database systems that write every change to disk before considering a transaction committed. There is no notable speed difference between write and read operations. Redis operates as a single process and single-threaded (Table 3).

Table 3. NoSQL database IOPS operation time (in ms) after fixes

Number of records	Mongo DB write	Mongo DB read	Cassandra write	Cassandra read	Redis write	Redis read
10	8	5	.2	2.3	.5	2
100	34	11	1.5	71	8	13
1000	153	93	36.4	106	44	39
10000	1394	980	58.7	566	270	251
50000	8713	5218	133.5	1910	993	958

Researchers enhanced the security of these NoSQL databases, and the table clearly shows that for writing big data to Database to make it persistent and at the same time, by not compromising on security of the data, Cassandra is the best NoSQL database among these three. But, Redis read operation performance is clearly outstanding and it clearly the best NoSQL database for an application with more read operations (Fig. 2).

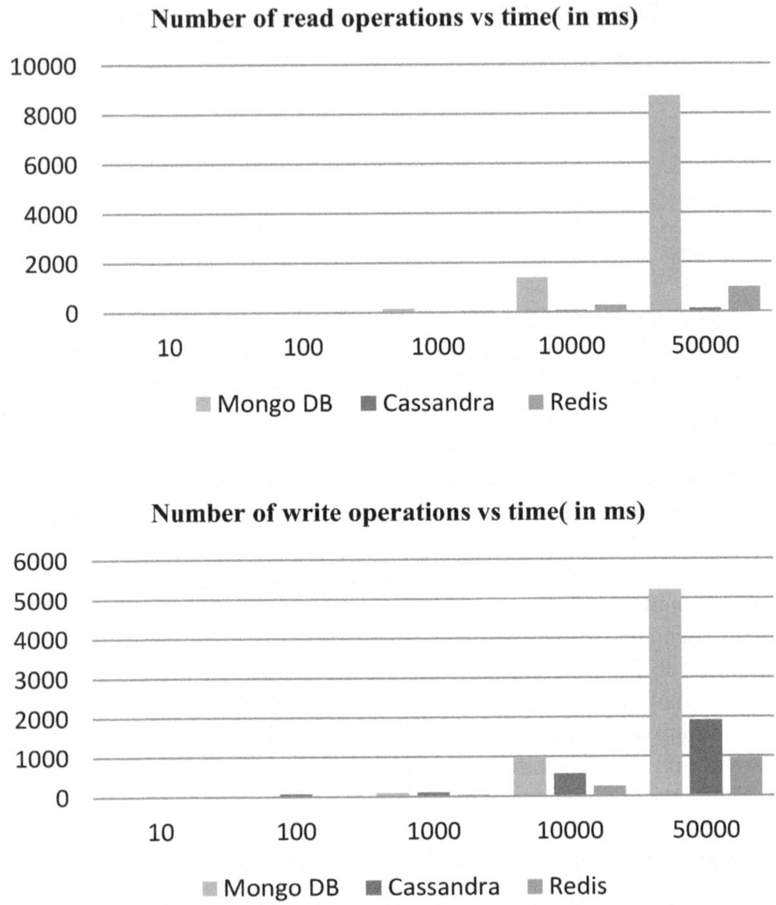

Fig. 2. Read and write operation graph (number of operations VS time in milliseconds)

4 Conclusion

The authors have suggested that the big data as key-value pair, is best stored in Redis, as it is both fast in read operations as well as write operations, and at the same time, it is secure enough if handled carefully and the above mentioned steps are followed. Mongo DB, on the other hand do ensures basic security best practices but the performance dipped after solving the remaining security issues and thus, the use of Mongo DB in applications should be specific, and proper care must be taken to store the document in Mongo DB. We can also look for CouchBase DB and Rethink DB, as alternatives to store the documents other than Mongo DB. Cassandra is still a very good option for a write oriented NoSQL database, as suggested by the performance results, even after security measures were enforced.

References

1. All NoSQL Databases. www.nosql-database.org/
2. Benchmarking Top 10 NoSQL Databases, 13 April 2015. www.endpoint.com
3. Best Free and Open Source NoSQL Database. www.bigdataanalyticsnews.com
4. Best NoSQL Databases. www.nosql.findthebest.com
5. MongoDB Official Documentation. www.mongodb.org/about/introduction/
6. Apache: Apache Cassandra 2.0 Official Documentation, 24 September 2015
7. Redis Labs: Redis Official Documentation. www.redis.io/documentation
8. Redis Security. http://redis.io/topics/security
9. Noiumkar, P., Chomsiri, T.: A comparison the level of security in top 5 open source NoSQL database, July 2014
10. Aniello, L., Bonomi, S., Breno, M., Baldoni, R.: Assessing data availability of Cassandra in the presence of non-accurate membership. In: Proceedings of the 2nd International Workshop on Dependability Issues in Cloud Computing, (DISCCO 2013) (2013). http://www.dis.uniroma1.it/~midlab/articoli/discco2013.pdf
11. Stunnel. www.stunnel.org
12. Mongo DB Authetication. https://docs.mongodb.org/manual/core/authentication-mechanisms/#authentication-mechanism-default
13. MongoDB Security Guide Release 3.2.1. MongoDB, Inc. 09 February 2016, ©MongoDB, Inc. (2008–2015)
14. Stonebraker, M.: SQL databases v. NoSQL databases. Commun. ACM **53**(4), 10–11 (2010). https://doi.org/10.1145/1721654.1721659
15. Aggarwal, P., Rani, R.: Security issues and user authentication in MongoDB. In: Elsevier Second International Conference on Emerging Research in Computing, Information, Communication and Applications, NMIT Bangalore, 1–2 August 2014 (2014)
16. Perdue, T.: NoSQL: an overview of NoSQL databases (2014). http://newtech.about.com/od/databasemanagement/a/Nosql.htm
17. Abramova, V., Bernardino, J.: NoSQL databases: MongoDB vs Cassandra. In: C3S2E 2013 Proceedings of the International C* Conference on Computer Science and Software Engineering, Portugal, 10–12 July 2013 (2013)
18. MongoDB 3.2 vs Couchbase Server 4.5: Comparing NoSQL Databases with YCSB Standard Benchmark, June 2016
19. ObjectRocket™ for Redis | Cover. https://objectrocket.com/files/objectrocket-forredis-white-paper.pdf

Author Index

The manufacturer's authorised representative in the EU is Springer Nature Customer Service Centre GmbH, Europaplatz 3, 69115 Heidelberg, Germany. If you have any concerns regarding our products, please contact ProductSafety@springernature.com

Printed and bound by CPI Group (UK) Ltd, Croydon, CR0 4YY
22/09/2026
02220983-0012